HYPNOSIS

Questions & Answers

A NORTON PROFESSIONAL BOOK

HYPNOSIS
Questions & Answers

Bernie Zilbergeld, Ph.D.

M. Gerald Edelstien, M.D.

Daniel L. Araoz, Ed.D.

editors

W · W · NORTON & COMPANY · *NEW YORK* · *LONDON*

Published simultaneously in Canada by Penguin Books Canada Ltd,
2801 John Street, Markham, Ontario L3R 1B4

Printed in the United States of America.

Library of Congress Cataloging-in-Publication Data

Main entry under title:

Hypnosis questions and answers.

   Includes bibliographies and index.
   1. Hypnotism — Therapeutic use. I. Zilbergeld,
Bernie. II. Edelstien, M. Gerald, 1928–
III. Araoz, Daniel L., 1930–   . [DNLM: 1. Hypnosis —
methods. WM 415 Q54]
RC495.Q47 1986   615.8′512   85-25838

ISBN   0-393-70018-6

W. W. Norton & Company, Inc., 500 Fifth Avenue, New York, N.Y. 10110

W. W. Norton & Company LTD., 37 Great Russell Street, London WC1B 3NU

  2   3   4   5   6   7   8   9   0

Contents

Contributors

Brian M. Alman, Ph.D.
Private Practice
San Diego, CA

Daniel L. Araoz, Ed.D.
Department of Counseling,
Long Island University
Greenvale, NY

Elgan L. Baker, Ph.D.
Department of Psychiatry,
School of Medicine,
Indiana University
Indianapolis, IN

Joseph Barber, Ph.D.
Department of Psychiatry,
University of California,
Los Angeles

Theodore X. Barber, Ph.D.
Cushing Hospital
Framingham, MA

Franz Baumann, M.D.
Private Practice
San Francisco, CA

Kenneth S. Bowers, Ph.D.
Department of Psychology,
University of Waterloo
Waterloo, Ontario, Canada

Bennett G. Braun, M.D.
Associated Mental Health Services
Chicago, IL

Jill Bond Caire, Ph.D.
Mental Research Institute
Pacific Medical Center
San Francisco, CA

Peter A. Carich, Ph.D.
Private Practice
Granite City, IL

Bryan D. Carter, Ph.D.
Bingham Child Guidance Clinic,
University of Louisville
School of Medicine

John F. Chaves, Ph.D.
Department of Psychiatry,
St. Louis University
Medical Center
St. Louis, MO

David B. Cheek, M.D.
Private Practice
San Francisco

Sheldon Cohen, M.D.
Private Practice
Atlanta, GA

Michael J. Diamond, Ph.D.
Department of Psychiatry,
University of California
Los Angeles, CA

M. Gerald Edelstien, M.D.
Department of Psychiatry,
Kaiser Permanente Medical Group
Fremont, CA

Marlene R. Eisen, Ph.D.
Private Practice
Evanston, IL

Gary R. Elkins, Ph.D.
Scott and White Clinic
Temple, TX

Carol Rinkleib Ellison, Ph.D.
Private Practice
Piedmont, CA

Frederick J. Evans, Ph.D.
Carrier Foundation
Belle Mead, NJ

Dabney M. Ewin, M.D.
Private Practice
New Orleans, LA

Judith Janaro Fabian, Ph.D.
Department of Psychiatry,
Kaiser Permanente Medical Group

William Fezler, Ph.D.
Private Practice
Los Angeles, NY

Michael Finegold, M.D.
Private Practice
San Francisco, CA

David C. Frauman,
St. Vincent Stress Center
Indianapolis, IN

Harold P. Golan, D.M.D.
Private Practice
Boston, MA

George Goldberg, D.D.S.
Private Practice
Jackson Heights, NY

William L. Golden, Ph.D.
Private Practice
New York, NY

Sol S. Gould, Ph.D.
New Mexico Pain Clinic
Albuquerque, NM

Eric Greenleaf, Ph.D.
Private Practice
Berkeley, CA

Brian Grodner, Ph.D.
Milton Erickson Institute
Albuquerque, NM

D. Corydon Hammond, Ph.D.
Sex and Marital Therapy Clinic,
University of Utah Medical School
Salt Lake City, UT

John W. Hedenberg, Ph.D.
Private Practice
Los Angeles, CA

Jean Holroyd, Ph.D.
Neuropsychiatric Institute, UCLA
Los Angeles, CA

Seymour Holzman, Ph.D.
Private Practice
New York, NY

Richard Horevitz, Ph.D.
Associated Mental Health Services
Chicago, IL

Ronna Jevne, Ph.D.
Cross Cancer Institute
Edmonton, Canada

Daniel P. Kohen, M.D.
Minneapolis Children's
Medical Center
Minneapolis, MN

Errol R. Korn, M.D.
Private Practice
Chula Vista, CA

Louise Labelle, B.A.
Psychology Department,
Concordia University
Montreal, Quebec, Canada

Stephen R. Lankton, M.S.W.
Private Practice
Gulf Breeze, FL

Jean-Roche Laurence, Ph.D.
Concordia University
Montreal, Quebec, Canada

Billie S. Lazar, Ph.D.
Department of Psychology
University of Illinois
Chicago, IL

Arnold A. Lazarus, Ph.D.
Graduate School of
Professional Psychology
Rutgers University
Piscataway, NJ

Marc Lehrer, Ph.D.
Private Practice
San Francisco, CA

Alexander A. Levitan, M.D.
University of Minnesota
Minneapolis, MN

Brian J. Lewis, Ph.D.
Private Practice
Sarasota, FL

David Lipschutz, Ph.D.
Psychology Department,
York College, CUNY
New York, NY

Daniel Lutzker, Ph.D.
Milton H. Erickson Institute
of New York
New York, NY

Steven J. Lynn, Ph.D.
Psychology Department
Ohio University
Athens, OH

Herbert Mann, M.D.
Private Practice
San Jose, CA

Gerald I. Manus, Ph.D.
Department of Psychiatry,
Kaiser Permanente Medical Group
Fremont, CA

Clorinda G. Margolis, Ph.D.
Department of Psychiatry
Thomas Jefferson University
Philadelphia, PA

George Matheson, Ph.D.
Private Practice
Toronto, Ontario, Canada

Elizabeth McMahon, Ph.D.
Department of Psychiatry,
Kaiser Permanente Medical Group
Fremont, CA

Joan M. Murray-Jobsis, Ph.D.
Private Practice
Chapel Hill, NC

Charles B. Mutter, M.D.
Private Practice
Miami, FL

Robert Nadon, M.A.
Concordia University
Montreal, Quebec, Canada

Esther Negley-Parker,
R.N., B.S.N., M.S.
Brandywine School of Nursing
Coatesville, PA

Anthony B. Newey, Ph.D.
Private Practice
Walnut Creek, CA

Martin T. Orne, M.D., Ph.D.
Department of Psychiatry,
University of Pennsylvania
Philadelphia, PA

Campbell Perry, Ph.D.
Department of Psychiatry,
Concordia University
Montreal, Quebec, Canada

George J. Pratt, Ph.D.
Psychology and Consulting Associates
La Jolla, CA

Helmut Relinger, Ph.D.
Private Practice
Berkeley, CA

Ernest L. Rossi, Ph.D.
Private Practice
Los Angeles, CA

Shirley Sanders, Ph.D.
Psychiatry Department,
University of North Carolina
Chapel Hill, NC

Donald W. Schafer, M.D.
Department of Psychiatry,
University of California, Irvine
Irvine, CA

Jerome M. Shneck, M.D.
Private Practice
New York, NY

Robert Sigman, Ed.D.
Private Practice
New York, NY

Alexander H. Smith, Ed.D.
Private Practice
New York, NY

David Spiegel, M.D.
Department of Psychiatry,
Stanford University
School of Medicine
Stanford, CA

Andrew E. St. Amand, M.D.
Lahey Clinic Medical Center
Burlington, MA

Jeff Stone, D.M.D.
Private Practice
San Francisco, CA

Peter Tilton, M.D.
Santa Barbara Holistic
Medical Center
Santa Barbara, CA

John G. Watkins, Ph.D.
Psychology Department,
University of Montana
Missoula, MT

Helen H. Watkins, Ph.D.
Psychology Department,
University of Montana
Missoula, MT

Andre M. Weitzenhoffer, Ph.D.
Private Practice
Nathrop, CO

William C. Wester, II, Ed.D.
Behavioral Science Center, Inc.
Cincinnati, OH

Erika Wick, Ph.D.
St. John's University
Jamaica, NY

Ian Wickram, Ph.D.
Department of Psychiatry,
Eastern Virginia Medical School
Norfolk, VA

Elliot N. Wineburg, M.D.
Associated Biofeedback
Medical Group
New York, NY

Gerald D. Winter, Ed.D.
Psychology Department,
St. John's University
Jamaica, NY

Michael D. Yapko, Ph.D.
Milton H. Erickson Institute
of San Diego
San Diego, CA

Jeffrey K. Zeig, Ph.D.
Milton H. Erickson Foundation, Inc.
Phoenix, AZ

Bernie Zilbergeld, Ph.D.
Private Practice
Oakland, CA

Introduction

It seems appropriate to say at the outset why we put this book together. The reason is simple: Health professionals who use hypnosis, especially those without a lot of experience with this ancient art, need all the help they can get. This work is intended to be a friendly reference, one to be turned to both for advice and reassurance.

Advice is being sought eagerly at courses, lectures, and in a great variety of books now on the market. Reassurance is more difficult to find. The experts seem infallible and that is intimidating, not reassuring at all. As yet, most practitioners do not have a large number of colleagues to whom they can turn for support, nor is there the reassurance of knowing that they are following well established and honored tradition. Indeed, most of the current hypnotherapists have dared to leave behind some of the traditions they were originally taught in order to explore new and more efficient methods of helping their patients.

Hypnosis seems to carry more fear and confusion than perhaps any other therapeutic approach. Regarding confusion, we hear very basic questions — e.g., "What is hypnosis?"; "What is trance?"; and "How does hypnosis differ from relaxation?" — from people who've been using the method for years, as well as from beginners. Regarding fear, the results of a number of informal surveys we have conducted indicate that a majority of people who take hypnosis courses and workshops do not use the method in their work or at least not very much or for very long.

The reasons they give are instructive: not being able to get the results their teachers get; not understanding exactly what hypnosis is or what they are supposed to be doing; concerns about suggesting certain responses such as relaxation or amnesia and not getting them; and concerns about when to use hypnosis or a particular induction or suggestion. One of the major concerns is a fear of failure or of causing harm, a fear that is out of all proportion since little harm is likely to occur, and since hypnosis has no more failures than other therapeutic methods they use. These are all people who very much want to use hypnosis and believe it is a powerful tool, but doubt their own abilities to use it well.

One of the great problems with hypnosis, especially for beginners but also for experienced practitioners, is that it is shrouded in mythology. Since its inception, hypnosis has been closely connected to the unconventional, the mysterious, and the occult. Mesmer, regarded as the father of modern hypnosis, apparently cured many people, but his theory of animal magnetism was unacceptable even by the standards of the late 1700s. It was because of his theory, not his results, that both he and hypnosis lost favor. Since that time, hypnosis has always attracted occultists, astrologers, psychic healers, and others whose beliefs are far beyond the range of what is acceptable to science and even the lay public. In our own time, past-lives regression and psychic surgery are two activities often associated with hypnosis, to the embarrassment of most practitioners.

Entertainers and magicians calling themselves hypnotists appear in night clubs and in the media, doing to subjects what no self-respecting clinician would attempt. The clinician may believe, however, that he could not accomplish the same feats even if he tried, thus reducing his own sense of confidence, while patients and prospective patients become fearful that they might be subjected to the same indignities that befall the subject on the stage. We hope that we can help dispel these apprehensions.

The myths about hypnosis are spread by many others as well, partly because the language of hypnosis readily lends itself to misconception. Hypnosis comes from the Greek work for sleep, and terms such as "you are getting sleepy" and "you will wake up" are frequently used by hypnotists, even though hypnosis has almost nothing to do with sleep. The commonly used term trance has several meanings, one of which is a zombie-like state. This allows a connotation of being controlled by the hypnotist and a connection with things like brainwashing, which generates many bad movie plots and greater confusion.

Hypnotherapists have contributed to the confusion and concern about their method. In their publications and demonstrations, they present the most dramatic manifestations of hypnosis, often seeming to rival stage hypnotists in their attempt to produce the miraculous and please the audience. What goes on in their offices with patients is usually very different, but few observers are in a position to know this. It is not unusual for beginners in hypnosis to be overwhelmed by demonstrations and to feel that they will never be able to accomplish what they have just seen.

This is especially true for the work of Milton Erickson, the man responsible for a lot of the renewed interest in hypnosis. Erickson was widely considered to be a master therapist and a masterful hypnotist. Most people who saw his demonstrations or read about his cases consider him the best. For some, this has led to constructive attempts to understand and follow his work. But for many others, the response has been a deep sense of professional inadequacy. As one psychiatrist said, "I tried some of his stuff, gave it my best shot, and failed almost totally. I haven't used hypnosis since then. No way I'm going to use a method that makes me feel so inferior every time." We get asked a lot of questions about Erickson, some of which are addressed in this book, and it is clear that not only is his work widely misunderstood but also that it is, in the kind of paradox he would have easily grasped and probably hated, causing many professionals *not* to use hypnosis. This response has been abetted by the tendency of some of his followers to deify him and to measure the work of others on how closely it follows Erickson's.

Because of all the above issues, it is a problem to distinguish the flowers from the weeds. Although the number of books and articles on hypnosis is steadily increasing, it is still not easy for the average physician, therapist, dentist, or other professional to find out what experienced and successful practitioners think about various issues and do in their work with patients and clients. Our book gives them the opportunity to find out.

We sent out questionnaires to over 600 health professionals who had taken a hypnosis course in the last three years, asking what questions they had about hypnosis and its clinical use. We also asked our colleagues and considered questions that had been raised in our courses and talks. The questions we received, many more than we could answer in one book, seemed to fall naturally into a number of categories and these groupings make up the sections of the book (although we admit there is a fair degree of overlap in the sections and that it would be just as easy to group the questions in other ways). We hope they answer many of the issues raised in the preceding pages.

Some readers may be surprised by some of the questions, because not only do we have the expected ones such as, "How can hypnosis be used with this and that problem?" and "How can I get the kinds of results Erickson did?" but we also got large numbers of questions regarding, "What is this thing called hypnosis?" "What is its relationship to things like relaxation, sleep, and meditation?" Further, many people wanted to know about phenomena such as fire-walking, past-lives regression, and stage hypnosis. We took all these questions seriously. Most health professionals do not want to use hypnosis as an entertainment, but nonetheless some of their patients bring up questions about stage hypnosis or past-lives regression. We believe our answers to these and similar questions will help clinicians feel better prepared to deal with these issues when they arise.

To answer the questions, we contacted practitioners known to us personally or by reputation. In each case, they are people with years of experience whose expertise is acknowledged by others in the field. Many of the best–known professionals in hypnosis accepted our invitation to contribute and readers may recognize their names. Some of our respondents are not as well-known, usually because they devote themselves solely to clinical work rather than writing, but readers are assured that they are all experienced and highly qualified.

We do not view this book as providing right answers, but instead as something clinicians can turn to when they have questions or want to learn how a recognized authority handles a particular issue. There are, in fact, no right answers, no one-and-only best way. Even though the best-known hypnotherapist in the world treats a certain problem a certain way, this is no reason to think that his or her way is the only or even the best way. That way may well be worth considering and trying out, but what works for one problem, client, or professional may not work as well for another; it may not even work as well for the same professional at another time. In accord with this idea, our respondents represent a variety of positions and practices: physicians, psychologists, dentists, and others; those who might be called traditionalists, and others who are Ericksonians or devotees of what some have called the new hypnosis; behaviorists, analysts, and others in between; and those who specialize in brief treatment and others who usually do long-term work.

Along these lines, it is important for readers to keep in mind that hypnosis is an art, not a science. As such, it is subject to different interpretations and uses. We do not agree with all that is said by our contributors, they almost certainly don't always agree among themselves, and in some cases the three of us have three different opinions about an issue or technique. While some may lament the lack of consensus, it cannot be otherwise at the current stage of development of hypnosis and of the healing arts generally. Rather than lament what we don't have, we choose to celebrate the increasing acceptance of hypnosis and the rapid accumulation of knowledge about how best to use it. We hope the reader will come to see hypnosis as we see it: as neither magical nor miraculous, but a useful tool in a wide variety of situations.

Edited books are frequently criticized for being uneven and ours will be no exception. Although many of the contributions have gone through numerous revisions and heavy editing, we believe the distinctive taste of the authors comes through and we wouldn't have it any other way. Some authors used references and some didn't; some gave detailed case examples and a few didn't; some gave very brief answers and some went on at length; and of course they all have different writing styles. As with authors, so with readers, each of whom brings to the book a unique constellation of personality, training, experience, and current practice, meaning different readers will respond better to and find more in certain answers than in others. And so it should be.

Putting together a book is hard work and we will not put our credibility to the test by saying how much fun it was. It was a lot of things, but fun wasn't one of them. Nonetheless, we are pleased with the results. Even though the three of us have used hypnosis for a combined total of over sixty years, we all learned from many of the responses. And even though we are reasonably secure about our work and results, we were reassured to find that none of our contributors has any secret techniques.

The responses allowed us to learn what a lot of men and women whose work we respect actually think and do, in plain English and without the stilted language that abounds in most books and journals. It was like having some great conversations with masters of the art of hypnosis. We hope that other readers will feel the same way. If our work allows some practitioners to feel more confident and knowledgeable in their use of hypnosis and does something to reduce the mumbo-jumbo that surrounds the topic, we will be satisfied.

HYPNOSIS

Questions & Answers

SECTION I *What Is Hypnosis?*

A source of great embarrassment to those who do hypnosis and a source of great confusion to the public is the lack of agreement as to exactly what hypnosis is. Despite the fact that hypnosis has been used for centuries, there is very little understanding about what the phenomenon consists of and how it works, though there is little disagreement that it does work.

It is quite common for health professionals and laypeople alike to ask how hypnosis differs from sleep, meditation, relaxation, and other activities (and indeed this question is the first one addressed in this section). It is not surprising that such questions are widely asked because confusion is rampant. This is compounded by the fact that although hypnosis has nothing in common with sleep, hypnotherapists use many terms having to do with falling asleep and waking up.

There are those who claim hypnosis is not much more than relaxation and those who say it is an altered state of consciousness. But here again things are far from clear. If it's just relaxation, why don't we call it relaxation? If it's an altered state, what exactly is altered?

It would be of immense help if we could point to some physiological correlates of hypnosis, but so far a lot of research has come up empty. There are no known physiological correlates of hypnosis to differentiate it from relaxation or meditation or a number of other things. It would also help if there were some sure way of telling if someone was or was not hypnotized, but such a way does not exist. People told to simulate hypnosis can fool the

3

most experienced clinician. Even Milton Erickson, with decades of experience using hypnosis with patients and research subjects, was unable to pick out the simulators in Martin Orne's laboratory.

In many respects, hypnosis is a great deal like psychotherapy, another activity for which there is no agreed upon definition. The questions asked about hypnosis have parallels in those asked about therapy, e.g., "How is it different from just talking to a friend or just sitting by yourself, figuring out what's wrong, and then determining how best to fix it?"

Although we can't say for sure what hypnosis is, we can do better on the other side and say what it isn't. A number of the answers in this book make mention of the harm done by erroneous ideas about hypnosis, especially the confusion between what is called stage hypnosis and what is done in therapists', doctors', and dentists' offices. People viewing "stage hypnosis" often become convinced that no sane person would undergo such a procedure and are then reluctant when their doctor suggests hypnosis for them. Interestingly, we have found that many hypnotherapists have no good idea of how "stage hypnotists" accomplish their feats. Because an understanding of this phenomenon is often crucial to dealing with patients who have seen stage hypnosis, we include a paper on this topic.

We can also say some things about what hypnosis does not or cannot do. Hypnosis does not alter physiology so that people can walk safely across hot coals. The conclusion of the paper in this section on that topic is that anyone can accomplish this seemingly impossible feat, with or without hypnosis. And despite recent publicity to the contrary, there is no evidence that hypnosis can regress people to previous lives, a concept that assumes a worldview totally at odds with what most scientists accept. The paper on that subject is in the section on validity.

The Relationship
Between Hypnosis and Other
Activities Such as Sleep

Question:

> How does hypnosis differ from sleep, meditation, acupuncture,
> the relaxed imagery athletes use, and neurolinguistic program-
> ming?

Discussion by WILLIAM C. WESTER, II, Ed.D

I define hypnosis to my patients as "an altered or changed state of awareness,
concentration, or perception." I avoid using words like "trance," and quickly
indicate to patients that they are in complete control at all times and will
not lose consciousness during the session. I even go so far as to tell them that
if at any time during the session they feel at all uncomfortable, they should
open their eyes and terminate the procedure. However, I also tell them that
I have never had a patient terminate the procedure in my many years of
clinical practice, since this is a very pleasant, comfortable and relaxed state.

I also explain that almost everyone has experienced one form or another
of hypnosis at some time in his or her life: "Think of those times when you
were driving on an expressway and caught yourself briefly unaware of what
you were doing, or when you or your children were so engrossed in a TV
program that you were unaware that someone else had entered the room.
There is nothing to fear, because hypnosis is a safe procedure when used professionally. The relaxation you will experience will be pleasant and refreshing." Thus begins my preparation for hypnosis. Using this definition of hypnosis, we can begin to differentiate hypnosis from similar states.

Hypnosis is not sleep. Sleep is defined as "the natural periodic suspension
of consciousness during which the powers of the body are restored." Of all
of the different states, sleep is at the most distant end of the continuum, since

the individual is not conscious and aware, at that moment, of what is happening or taking place. Myths, such as the belief that hypnosis is identical with sleep, can be clarified by reassuring patients that they will not fall asleep and will remain in control of themselves at all times. The stage one sleep EEG pattern is similar to that of the normal waking state except for the presence of rapid eye movements (REM's). The EEG record of the hypnotic state is consistently similar to that of the waking state.

Meditation is defined as "the process of focusing one's thoughts, or engaging in contemplation or reflection." In one form or another, we all have meditated at some time. Some of us just sit and think while others can really experience daydreaming. Meditation can be incidental or structured. There is a fine line between states such as meditation and hypnosis; however, I like to point out that the more formalized states of meditation are structured and planned with a specific purpose in mind. I once had a professor who drew a picture of a funnel on the board, indicating that hypnosis would be at the top of the funnel, namely a broader and more aware state, and formal meditation would be at the tip of the funnel, indicating a very focused state, as one might experience chanting a mantra.

The ancients employed magical rites and incantations to induce meditation by chanting, breathing exercises and dancing. It is obvious that the cadence and intonations of prayer in a relaxing environment, along with assumed postures, eye fixation, and rhythmic chanting, are hypnagogic. The self-contemplation and self-absorption characterizing prayer and meditation are practically identical with modern-day autohypnosis. Meditation, as a modality for changing behavior, has certainly withstood the test of time. The modern form of meditation is referred to as transcendental meditation. Although the rituals for the older and more modern forms of meditation differ, they are fundamentally the same and are based on similar principles of conditioning.

Acupuncture is defined as "an original Chinese practice of puncturing the body (as with needles) to cure disease or relieve pain." Acupuncture utilizes the specific perception of the individual, as well as the direct physiology of the body, making it quite different from hypnosis. Puncturing the body is not a hypnotic induction procedure or technique, but experts in the field of hypnosis generally agree that acupuncture includes hypnotic elements. Li and others (1975) analyzed the difference in the effects of hypnosis, placebo-acupuncture (needles inserted in the "wrong" places), and acupuncture in the pain produced by electrical stimulation in 14 subjects. As the stimulus intensity was increased, the levels necessary to produce a minimum sensation, the first perceptible pain, and the maximum tolerable pain were successively noted. With hypnotic suggestion of analgesia, the intensity of stimulation needed to produce all of these effects was increased. Neither acupuncture nor placebo-acupuncture produced any raising of the threshold.

Saletu et al. (1975) compared hypnosis and acupuncture with each other and with analgesic drugs. Pain, induced by electrical stimulation on the wrist, was evaluated by subjective and physiological measures. It was significantly reduced by both hypnosis and analgesics, but acupuncture was only effective when the needles were applied to the specific loci and electrically stimulated. EEG changes in hypnosis varied with the wording of suggestions but were characterized in general by an increase in fast waves. Acupuncture produced just the opposite EEG changes. These two studies suggest that hypnosis and acupuncture are likely to be two different phenomena in spite of their superficial similarities or the presence of implied suggestion in the acupuncture procedure.

Relaxation is defined as "the act or fact of relaxing or of being relaxed." Imagery is "the product of image makers or mental images; the products of imagination." An image is defined as "a reproduction or imitation of the form of a person or thing."

Relaxation and imagery are part of a wide range of hypnotic procedures, but are not necessary to produce a hypnotic state. Recently I have found that many patients have experienced some form of relaxation procedure through a self-help course, reading, or stress management programs. I typically begin my first induction procedure with a relaxation exercise since this is an easy, nonthreatening process to follow. It can also help patients move to a self-hypnotic model.

Relaxation and imagery both involve a degree of concentration and help to reduce anxiety that might otherwise interfere with one's performance. It is difficult to be anxious and relaxed at the same time. If athletes can learn to relax while concentrating and focusing their attention, their performance improves. Imagery has also been extremely helpful to athletes as a means for them to rehearse and/or model behavior prior to an actual performance.

J. H. Schultz drew attention to the relationship of self-hypnotic methods to physical exercise in his first book on autogenic training in 1932. Great improvement of sportsmen's performance was mentioned in the first English edition of Schultz's book (Schultz & Luthe, 1959), with training and performance becoming less strenuous and exhausting after varied periods of autogenic training.

Jencks and Krenz (1984) have carefully evaluated the clinical application of hypnosis in sports, emphasizing that the terms "hypnosis" and "altered states of consciousness" can be used interchangeably. These professionals assist athletes to recognize the self-induced hypnotic states they have been using without awareness. The essential difference is that relaxation is only bodily relaxation and hypnosis is an altered state whereby the subconscious is more available to suggestion.

Neurolinguistic programming is a trademark term derived from the early work of Richard Bandler and John Grinder. Neurolinguistic programming is an interesting communication process utilizing verbal and nonverbal feedback to assist individuals in arriving at solutions to their problems. There is a great emphasis on the sensory experience, in terms of cues and feedback. The use of metaphors and storytelling is very similar to Milton Erickson's indirect hypnosis. It is interesting to note that modern-day hypnosis is moving in this direction. Experts in hypnosis are moving away from traditional induction methods and direct suggestion to a greater use of such communication processes as subtle inductions, indirect suggestions, imagery, and metaphors. This intricate approach of communicating with the subconscious mind opens fresh and exciting avenues to assist patients in discovering new ways to change their behavior, whether physical, emotional, or mental. At the present time, therefore, NLP can be considered a subset of hypnosis utilizing a special communication style.

It is important to remember that any technique is only as effective as the therapist using that skill. Someone who has had extensive training in acupuncture, relaxation training, hypnosis, or neurolinguistic programming may be effective in bringing about a favorable change in the patient's condition or behavior. If the therapist has the skill and specialized training offered in his profession and can establish good rapport with this client, the therapist will probably be effective.

Professionals with advanced training in hypnosis have a bias and generally feel their treatment approach is more effective because under hypnosis the therapist has the added advantage of communicating with the patient's subconscious mind. The subconscious is a "helper" and can learn how to assist the troubled patient.

References

Jencks, B., & Krenz, E. (1984). Clinical application of hypnosis in sports. In W. C. Wester & A. H. Smith (Eds.), *Clinical hypnosis: A multidisciplinary approach*. Philadelphia: Lippincott.

Li, C. L., Ahlberg, D., Lansdell, H., Gravitz, M. A., Chen, T. C., Ting, C. Y., Bak, A. F., & Blessing, D. (1975). Acupuncture and hypnosis: Effects on induced pain. *Experimental Neurology, 49*, 272–280.

Saletu, B., Saletu, M., Brown, M., Stern, J., Sletten, I., & Ulett, G. (1975). Hypno-analgesia and acupuncture analgesia: A neuro-physiological reality. *Neuropsychobiology, I* (4), 218–242.

Schultz, J. H. & Luthe, W. (1959). *Autogenic training: A psychophysiologic approach in psychotherapy*. New York: Grune & Stratton.

Q&A 2 Physiological Correlates and Effects of Hypnosis

Question:

> What are the physiological correlates and effects of hypnosis and what brain waves dominate during trance?

Discussion by ESTHER NEGLEY-PARKER, R.N., B.S.N., M.S.

The physiological correlates of hypnosis have been studied in detail by investigators such as T. X. Barber (1981), Edmonston (1979), and Bowers (1976). However, clinicians are interested less in experimental details than in the physiological correlates that indicate that the patient is hypnotized, the physiological changes that result from suggestion, and the physiological manifestations of possible danger.

There is the possibility that differences between brain waves of the hypnotized and "awake" subject are too subtle to be picked up by the relatively crude measurements of the electroencephalogram, but the available evidence indicates that brain waves are practically the same in hypnosis or out of it. We do know, however, that alpha waves, which predominate when relaxation occurs, are facilitated by the closing of the eyes, and this justifies the old custom of asking patients to close their eyes during hypnosis.

A number of investigators have sought physiological correlates other than brain wave changes for the hypnotic state, but by and large they have come up empty. There are no differences in blood pressure, pulse rate, or respiratory rate between hypnotized subjects and those who are relaxed but not hypnotized (Bowers, 1976). The basal metabolic rate does not change in hypnosis, and blood levels of glucose, calcium, and phosphorous remain at normal levels. There are conflicting reports on temperature changes. One physiological difference that has been found in *deep* hypnosis is the development of circumoral pallor.

9

Without denying the possibility that physiological correlates of hypnosis may be discovered in the future, for now the conclusion closest to the data is that, physiologically speaking, there is nothing specific found in the hypnotic state.

On the other hand, Edmonston (1979) has demonstrated that hypnosis correlates with relaxation, and relaxation per se can produce certain physiological changes. Relaxation activates the parasympathetic nervous system, that division of the autonomic nervous system which regulates bodily functions when no danger threatens and which brings the body back to optimal functioning after emergencies. It may be more exact to say that relaxation gives the parasympathetic a chance to take over. In this sense, hypnosis is a mental activity enhancing the general physical health of the individual, since the parasympathetic facilitates the normal function of all bodily systems.

Since hypnosis facilitates relaxation, and this means that the parasympathetic is taking over, the repeated experience of hypnosis brings with it healthier and more normal bodily functioning. It must be clearly emphasized that for these benefits to occur perseverance and methodical practice of hypnosis are essential. One of these benefits, as studied by Benson (1975) and others, is a normalization of blood pressure. (However, it is common to observe a speeding up of the heartbeat during the first moments of hypnosis.)

Pragmatically, the depth of relaxation can be used as an indication of the "depth" of hypnosis. With patients who find it difficult to relax it is useful either to try a paradoxical technique or to refine the imagery employed. The paradoxical technique consists of suggesting that the patient become as tense as possible by straining all the major muscles in the legs, arms, back, abdomen and head. Once this is achieved, the patient is asked to hold the tension for a few seconds and then to let go of it. The sensations of letting go of the tension are labeled relaxation. This exercise is repeated three or four times and the last time the clinician may say, "Now, allow that 'let go' sensation to stay in your body while you take a very deep breath. Allow yourself to feel the 'let go' sensation all over, very deeply. Let your internal organs benefit from it, too: your heart, your stomach, your liver, etc."

The reason for using a paradoxical method is to aid in the activation of the parasympathetic nervous system, which normally is engaged after bodily tension has peaked.

If the patient has not relaxed yet, refined imagery may be used. To refine one's relaxation imagery the patient has to be asked how his/her tension was represented mentally. Assuming that the patient imagines her tension as outstretched rubber bands, ready to break, refining the imagery employed means using the patient's images paradoxically. This is done by suggesting a vivid mental picture of those rubber bands, noticing their tension, testing them with one's finger, etc. Then the counter-images are built up: The rubber bands become soft, untense and flaccid; they look relaxed, smooth, pliable and supple. The patient is to visualize them very clearly now, etc.

Another way of refining the imagery is by asking the patient to calmly check what mental pictures come to mind when thinking of tension and stress. Then counter-images are employed. For instance, if a patient reports that the thought of stress brings images of a dreary day, nasty and cold, all in grey, the clinician then suggests counter-images of sunshine, flowers of many colors, comfortable temperature, and the like.

When the signs of relaxation are discernible — diaphragmatic breathing, slowing down of eye movement, simplified speech, and a general state of physical passivity — the therapist can assume hypnosis is starting to take place. The alteration of consciousness that is occurring is manifest by a reality orientation that is weaker than at other times, and the mental focus is on inner experiencing or internal mental processes. This altered state may also be achieved by methods other than hypnosis, such as meditation.

Because of the energy conservation that occurs when the parasympathetic function is activated by relaxation, the client is able to become more introspective in an experiential way (a receptive mental mode), rather than in an intellectual, analytical manner. This is the explanation for the common phenomena of imagery, inner awareness, and retrieval of long past memories witnessed in hypnosis.

When we consider the ways in which hypnotic suggestions can effect physiological changes, we are faced with a vast array of possibilities. A few of the more dramatic changes include: control of bleeding during dental procedures; less severe response to thermal burns and more rapid healing from them; clearing of skin rashes and disappearance of warts; and rapid relief of asthmatic attacks. We cannot discuss all these here, but we can look at one way in which hypnotic work can affect respiratory functions, and consider other aspects of the "healing mind" elicited through hypnotic intervention.

Oriental disciplines such as Zen and yoga put great emphasis on correct breathing. The deep hypnotic state produces a decrease in breathing rate, but only when the suggestions used are of relaxation rather than of emotional states. Studies have reported decrease in oxygen consumption during hypnosis (Bowers, 1976; T. X. Barber, 1981). In practice, when the clinician notices the patient breathing rhythmically in a diaphragmatic way, he/she may safely assume that the patient is in hypnosis.

The following case exemplifies a situation where breathing was intimately connected with tension, but in which the therapeutic intervention had to proceed through a preliminary stage. The patient was a successful, married, 41-year-old businessman who traveled across the country twice a month. He had frequent attacks of hyperventilation. During the previous three years, he had uncontrollable hyperventilation for about 15 minutes several times each week. He had first gone for psychoanalytic therapy on a three times a week basis but without improvement in his condition. This lasted one year, after which he sought medical assistance, but the medication did not help his pathology. My therapy was as follows: He was taught to relax by focusing not on his breathing but on his muscular sensations. Only when he learned to perceive a difference in his muscle tone in specific muscle groups, such as legs, chest, shoulders and arms, was his attention brought back to his breathing. The muscle relaxation was accomplished through his own imagery. An excerpt of the preliminary stage of treatment follows to illustrate how his "relaxed scene" was used.

THERAPIST: Now that you are feeling the difference, let that nice feeling increase or stay the same. What happens?
PATIENT: Nice. Very relaxed.
THERAPIST: Notice what mental pictures come to mind. Any good memories?
PATIENT: The Appalachian Mountains.
THERAPIST: Make that picture sharper. What season is it?
PATIENT: Fall.
THERAPIST: Enjoy the colors, admire the beauty. Stay with it and let your whole body react to that grandeur. Are you with it?
PATIENT: (Nods yes and sighs with a smile, still in hypnosis.)
THERAPIST: Notice the temperature, a nice, cool breeze perhaps, the chill in the air. Invigorating. Yes?
PATIENT: Great.
THERAPIST: Listen to the nature sounds. Enjoy. Admire, relax, rejoice. Inner peace and quiet.

This type of mental activity was practiced repeatedly and an audiotape of it was given him to continue the exercise at home. Then, while still imagining himself in the Appalachian Mountains, he was asked to think of a situation that produced the tension leading to hyperventilation. As soon as the tension started, he was instructed to quickly change the mental picture to that of his "relaxed scene." This was practiced several times until the thought of tension elicited the relaxed scene. Once more, home practice was prescribed until he was able to control his breathing, no matter how tense a situation he brought to mind. After five sessions he was seen once more for follow-up six weeks later. Hyperventilation had recurred only twice, was very brief and mild, and the patient had controlled it quickly. Compared to the severe attacks three to four times a week before hypnosis, the patient assessed the treatment as "miraculously successful."

This case points to the beneficial effects of hypnosis in correcting a pathological respiratory function which had not responded to other treatments. The physiological correlates of hypnosis in this case are evident. Because of this treatment the patient gained greater control of autonomic nervous system functioning for his well-being.

The many beneficial effects connected with the activation of the parasympathetic nervous system through hypnosis lead to the controversial, yet increasingly respectable, issue of the healing mind. It is controversial because established medicine has been indifferent, indeed rather antagonistic, to the concept of self-healing. On the other hand, the evidence regarding the mind's crucial role in healing cannot be ignored without denying a massive accumulation of data, as presented in writings by Pelletier (1979), Jaffe (1980), Hall (1984) or T. X. Barber (1981), just to mention some of the scientifically sophisticated authors.

The human body has powerful healing forces or energies which are affected by "thoughts." Studies have shown that negative mental images regarding one's health produce measurable results significantly different from those obtained through positive mental imagery (see Barber, 1981, and Hall, 1984). Thus, patients who were encouraged to think of their disease as an inner weakness, rather than a powerful destructive force, and of the medical treatment as strong and effective, giving new energy to their immune system to make the self-healing process more effective, showed the following results. They recovered more quickly postoperatively than those who did not receive these suggestions, responded better to medication than the control group, and remained in good health after illness longer than the other patients. Many such controlled studies have been conducted, leading one to believe that the placebo effect is partly a spontaneous positive self-hypnotic process, elicited by the suggested belief in the efficacy of the treatment. The body responds to the "thoughts" we harbor in our minds. The management of pain through hypnosis and other psychological means seems to occur by a similar nonconscious but nevertheless effective mental activity.

Other experiments, reviewed by Barber (1981), have shown the beneficial effects of hypnosis in specific functions of such systems as the respiratory, cardiovascular, genitourinary, gastrointestinal, endocrinological and metabolic. Especially dramatic results have been obtained in dermatological conditions and central nervous system functions. At this time it is impossible to establish a clear causal relationship between hypnosis and the positive outcomes reported because it is still unknown *how* "thoughts" affect the neurological pathways through which different body systems are influenced. However, that "thoughts" *do* affect the body seems evident.

The clinician is advised to keep in mind the powerful effects of suggestions on bodily functions. In using words, he/she may take advantage of their positive effects — or he/she may inadvertently foster negative self-hypnosis.

A case referred by an internist illustrates this point. The patient was a

24-year-old graduate student who had difficulty urinating for six years. He also had symptoms of hypochondriasis. Believing that his retention of urine could produce "internal damage and infections" [sic], he had visited the internist, complaining of headaches "produced by this problem," insomnia and dizziness, especially while driving after being unable to urinate. The case was complicated, but the relevant highlights are that the patient's father, a gambler and an alcoholic, for many years had embarrassed him in different ways. One expression used referred to the patient dying young and not being able "to piss his life away" like the father did, supposedly a source of pride for the latter. The son, through some non-intellectual understanding, had "translated" these statements somatically, developing hypochondria and urinary pathology.

Hypnotherapy consisted of 1) making him conscious of his father's damaging statements, as the patient had translated them somatically; 2) obliterating those negative messages; and 3) simultaneously substituting constructive and ego-syntonic messages and images which, through repetition, became operative. The main point is that this patient's health forces had been affected negatively by his father's remarks and were reactivated, as it were, by hypnotherapy.

A very brief explanation of the three treatment stages just mentioned is in order. In the first stage, he became conscious of those statements by age regression, reliving his reactions to his father's words. He noticed that he had felt "like a burning" in the area of the bladder when his father said those things. He also became aware of his inability to imagine himself older, connected with his fear/belief that he would die young. The second and third stages were reconstructive, focusing especially on his health forces, stronger than his father messages, able to destroy their ill effects and to free his urinary processes to act in a normal, healthy manner. It is logical to assume that hypnosis played an important part in his recovery since the treatments used in the previous six years had failed and when this new clinical variable was introduced there was a dramatic change in physiological functioning.

Finally, we should look at the physiological "dangers" of hypnosis. The late Dr. August (1963) stated, in his comments towards the end of the classic movie of a Caesarean delivery with hypnosis as sole anesthesia, that the real dangers of hypnosis lie in the untrained and unexperienced clinician, not in the procedure itself. Consequently, the following list may be seen as a matter of simple common sense and is not intended to be exhaustive. Before the use of hypnosis it is always imperative to have a medical history in order to avoid unnecessary waste of time. For instance, with a person who has respiratory problems such as emphysema or asthma, the clinician should not use induction procedures involving breathing. If the patient wears hard contact lenses, he cannot be expected to keep his eyes closed for any length of time. When there is already low blood pressure, excessive relaxation might produce lightheadedness and even fainting. To avoid this, hypnosis may be presented as a very active mental experience in which one's mind is dynamically engaged.

During hypnosis the patient may experience discomfort or other symptoms. The general rule (assuming his medical history points to no reason for abandoning this procedure) is to work on the problem, rather than discontinuing hypnosis. This is done by asking the patient to go with the pain or headache or dizziness, to stay with it and to notice *any* change. Is it staying the same? Is it becoming worse? Is it moving to another area? If the symptom is becoming more acute, the clinician should suggest that the patient allow it to peak and subside. It is possible that a person without a previous adverse history may have a heart attack or a stroke in the midst of hypnosis, but the probability is minimal, and it is humanly impossible to be absolutely risk-free.

Coe and Ryken (1979) reviewed the physiological dangers of hypnosis and concluded that, with the necessary precautions referred to here and in other parts of this book, clinical hypnosis is a safe medical procedure. To avoid posthypnotic symptoms such as numbness, dizziness or a slight ache, two points should be considered. First, and generally, the clinician should always give posthypnotic suggestions of well-being and of feeling alert, energetic and vital after the trance. I add, "By the time your eyes open all the ordinary sensations will be back in every part of your body." The second point is more specific. If a patient, after the first hypnotic experience, reports any symptom, the clinician should inquire what might have precipitated the symptom during hypnosis. Frequently patients know, and that information should be used to change or omit whatever might have been related to the posthypnotic symptom.

As a general rule, the clinician should not panic when symptoms occur during or after hypnosis. If the patient has been carefully screened for the procedure, the symptoms are mild and manageable.

References

August, R. V. (1963). *Hypnosis as sole anesthesia for caesarian section*. Upjohn Professional Film Library. Kalamazoo, MI: Upjohn Laboratories.

Barber, T. X. (1981). Medicine, suggestive therapy and healing. In R. J. Kastenbaum, T. X. Barber, S. C. Wilson, B. L. Ryder, & L. B. Hathaway (Eds.). *Old, sick and helpless: Where therapy begins*. Cambridge, MA: Ballinger.

Benson, H. (1975). *The relaxation response*. New York: Morrow.

Bowers, K. S. (1976). *Hypnosis for the seriously curious*. Monterey, CA: Brooks/Cole.

Coe, W. C. & Ryken, K. (1979). Hypnosis and risk to human subjects. *American Psychologist*, 34(8), 673–681.

Edmonston, W. E. (1979). The effects of neutral hypnosis on conditioned responses: Implications for hypnosis as relaxation. In E. Fromm & R. E. Shor (Eds.). *Hypnosis: Developments in Research and new perspectives* (2nd ed.). New York: Aldine.

Hall, H. R. (1984). Imagery and cancer. In A. A. Sheikh (Ed.). *Imagination and healing.* Farmingdale, NY: Baywood.

Jaffe, D. T. (1980). *Healing from within.* New York: Pantheon.

Pelletier, K. (1979). *Mind as healer, mind as slayer.* New York: Delta.

$\underset{A}{\overset{Q}{\varepsilon}}3$ Hypnosis and Ultradian Rhythms

Question:

> What is the connection between hypnosis and ultradian rhythms? What might be the significance of these rhythms in the therapeutic use of hypnosis?

Discussion by ERNEST L. ROSSI, Ph.D.

The connection between hypnosis and ultradian (ul-tray-dee-ann) rhythms involves a new field of scientific investigation concerning mind/body regulation. The discovery of this connection (Rossi, 1982) was made when I noticed that many of the "readiness for trance indicators" used by Milton H. Erickson were identical with the rest-phase behaviors of the 90- to 120-minute psychophysiological rhythms of normal everyday life.

For some time we have known that during sleep we have dreams every hour and a half, whether or not we remember them. It has recently been shown that these rhythms continue even while we are awake. In daily life we usually need to take a break every hour and a half or so, due to our natural ultradian rhythm of activity and rest. If we chronically deny ourselves these needed rest breaks, we run the risk of upsetting the delicate rhythms of mind/body regulation so that we become prone to an amazingly broad range of stress-related disorders. Overeating, sexual dysfunctions, psychosomatic pain, mood disorders, depressions, and psychological problems of all varieties are in part related to a dissynchrony of ultradian rhythms. Hypnosis is useful in treating these disorders because it provides a natural way of normalizing ultradian rhythms.

17

Ultradian Trance Induction

Most experienced hypnotherapists intuitively recognize when hypnotic induction is appropriate. Typically patients enter the therapy hour with a busy thrust of telling their story of "what's going on." After pouring out their problems there comes a moment of pause when they may turn either inward in self-reflection or outward to the therapist in an appeal for an answer. This is the creative moment for an ultradian trance induction.

Each patient manifests his own individual pattern of ultradian trance readiness behaviors. In general there is a spontaneous quieting and slowing down of all body movements. The head, hands, and feet seem fixed in a natural form of catalepsy and sometimes the fingers seem to be frozen in mid-gesture. The eyelids may close momentarily or droop and blink a few times. There may be a reddening of the sclera of the eyes. Sometimes a "softening" of the eyes is evident due to dilation of the pupils and/or the welling up of a slight tear film. There may be a reddening or blanching of the nose, cheeks, or neck. The facial features may become less animated as the jaw relaxes and the lips part slightly. Most importantly, there is a quiet sigh, or one or two deeper breaths, as the patient spontaneously slips into an altered state of mind/body rhythms. This natural altered state results from a generalized shift toward parasympathetic and right-hemispheric dominance (Rossi, in press).

When such behavioral patterns are evident the patient will readily enter therapeutic trance with permissive remarks from the hypnotherapist, such as the following:

> That's right, just let yourself take a break for a few moments.
>
> Let yourself enjoy the comfort that comes all by itself while you rest. (Pause)
>
> And if your unconscious is willing to let that comfort deepen so that it can work on [whatever problem] while you rest quietly in trance, you'll find those eyes closing all by themselves. (Pause)

When patients are obviously entering the natural rest phase of their ultradian rhythms, they usually accept this type of induction with relief and gratitude. At such times it is much easier to enter trance than to stay normally awake! If patients do not close their eyes after a moment or two, the author will typically turn the above situation into a therapeutic double bind by continuing with the following remarks:

> But if your unconscious needs to bring up another issue *before* you

enter trance, you'll find yourself talking about that first.

If another issue is discussed, it serves to reinforce the patient's trance readiness when therapeutic trance is next offered. This approach to hypnotherapy thus utilizes the patient's natural ultradian rhythms to turn inward, as well as the patient's own motivation and expectancy for problem-solving. In the simplest model of using the creative unconscious (Nugent, Carden, & Montgomery, 1984), the therapist need do little else. The patient is then awakened from trance with whichever of the following therapeutically double-binding implied directives seems appropriate:

> When your unconscious knows it has resolved [whatever problem], you will find yourself moving those fingers and hands, stretching a bit, and opening your eyes as you come fully awake, alert, and refreshed.

> When your unconscious knows that it has dealt with [whatever problem] to the optimum degree possible at this time, and can continue working with it successfully, you'll find yourself with an urge to move and stretch and come fully awake and refreshed.

In the more complex model of hypnotherapy (Erickson & Rossi, 1979), the therapist will "awaken" the patient one or more times during the trance period to get feedback about what is being experienced and what further hypnotherapeutic suggestions are needed in the "trance." Whenever the patient's conscious mind seems "stuck" and needs an answer, trance can be re-induced by a significant look from the therapist and a remark such as, "Let yourself explore what your unconscious has to give you about that." Soon, whenever the therapist asks what the patient's "unconscious" feels about any issue, it becomes a conditioned situation for a permissive reinduction of therapeutic trance.

Posthypnotic suggestions are usually most effective when they are associated with the "inevitabilities" of the patient's life. What could be more inevitable than the fact that patients will experience natural shifts in their ultradian rhythms every one and a half to two hours throughout the day and night? Patients can be taught to use their ultradian rest periods as a natural form of self-hypnosis to reinforce the gains made during the therapy hour. When hypnosis and posthypnotic suggestion are associated with ultradian rhythms in this way, a very effective form of state-dependent learning and conditioning is developed. Indeed, the author has stressed that the fundamental nature of therapeutic trance can be most usefully conceptualized as a special form of state-dependent memory and learning (Erickson, Rossi, & Rossi, 1976).

The Common Everyday Trance and Hypnosis

Ultradian rhythms are the biological basis of the "common everyday trance," during which we find ourselves daydreaming or just taking a break:

> The housewife staring vacantly over a cup of coffee, the student with a faraway look in his eyes during the middle of a lecture, and the driver who automatically reaches his destination with no memory of the details of his route, are all examples of the common everyday trance. (Rossi, 1982, p. 22)

These normal periods of turning inward can be used as a natural form of self-hypnosis. I explain this process to my patients somewhat as follows:

> You can use a natural form of self-hypnosis by simply letting yourself really enjoy taking a break whenever you need to throughout the day. You simply close your eyes and tune into the parts of your body that are most comfortable. When you locate the comfort you can simply enjoy it and allow it to deepen and spread throughout your body all by itself. Comfort is more than just a word or a lazy state. Really going deeply into comfort means you have turned on your parasympathetic system — your natural relaxation response. This is the easiest way to maximize the healing benefits of the rest phase of your body's natural ultradian rhythms.
>
> As you explore your inner comfort you can *wonder* how your creative unconscious is going to deal with whatever symptom, problem or issue that you want it to deal with. Your unconscious is the inner regulator of all your biological and mental processes. If you have problems it is probably because some unfortunate programming from the past has interfered with the natural processes of regulation within your unconscious. By accepting and letting yourself enjoy the normal periods of ultradian rest as they occur throughout the day, you are allowing your body/mind's natural self-regulation to heal and resolve your problems.
>
> Your attitude toward your symptom and yourself is very important during this form of healing hypnosis. *Your symptom or problem is actually your friend!* Your symptom is a signal that a creative change is needed in your life. During your periods of comfort in ultradian self-hypnosis, you will often receive quiet insights about your life, what you really want, and how to get it. A new thoughtfulness, joy, greater awareness, and maturity can result from the regular practice of ultradian self-hypnosis."

Most stress-related psychosomatic and mood disorders can be ameloriated with this permissive form of self-hypnosis.

References

Erickson, M., Rossi, E., & Rossi, S. (1976). *Hypnotic realities*. New York: Irvington.

Erickson, M., & Rossi, E. (1979). *Hypnotherapy: An exploratory casebook*. New York: Irvington.

Nugent, W., Carden, N., & Montgomery, D. (1984). Utilizing the creative unconscious in the treatment of hypodermic phobias and sleep disturbances. *American Journal of Clinical Hypnosis, 26*(3), 201–205.

Rossi, E. (1982). Hypnosis and ultradian cycles: A new state(s) theory of hypnosis? *American Journal of Clinical Hypnosis, 25*(1), 21–32.

Rossi, E. (in press). Altered states of consciousness in everyday life: The ultradian rhythms. In B. Wolman (Ed.). *Handbook of altered states of consciousness*. New York: Van Nostrand.

4 Realities of Stage Hypnosis

Question:

> Patients and friends have regaled me with stories of stage hypnotists who, as far as I can tell, are producing far greater effects than I am. Are those guys really doing hypnosis? Do they have secrets worth knowing, and if so, how do I learn them?

Discussion by THEODORE X. BARBER, Ph.D.

I think we need to distinguish between two types of hypnosis. Hypnosis as used by doctors, dentists, and therapists is a healing art employed, usually with other interventions, to help people change and feel better. The client or patient is the whole focus of the intervention. Stage hypnosis is an entertainment whose only purpose is pleasing the audience, with the subject (the one who is supposedly hypnotized) being used as a prop of the performer. Stage hypnosis is close to magic, which may be considered legitimate deceit. The following two quotes from *A Complete Course in Stage Hypnotism* make the distinction clear:

> To the serious minded student of hypnotism, who wishes to produce a hypnotic show for entertainment purposes, it is recommended that he forget all about trying to be a legitimate hypnotist. . . . Modern show business demands rapid and sensational routine, comedy relief, and of course, audience participation . . . experience has shown down through the years that the hypnotic show must be faked, at least partially so, to hold audience interest and be successful as an entertainment. (Nelson, 1965, p. 3)

> The successful hypnotic entertainer of today is actually not in-

terested whether or not the subjects are really hypnotized—his basic function is to *entertain*. He is interested in his ability to *con* his subjects into a pseudo performance that appears as hypnotism —to get laughs and entertain his audience. . . . [The subjects] enjoy their part and react as they are *told* to do. Hypnotism, as done today for entertainment, is as simple as all this. (Nelson, 1965, pp. 29–30)

Stage hypnotists can produce fascinating phenomena because their work is largely the result of very careful selection of subjects, fakery, and the expectancies of both subjects on stage and the audience. If you want to use hypnosis for entertainment, then certainly you can learn a lot from experienced stage hypnotists. Unfortunately, there is not much to be learned from them that will help in treating patients.

The most important task of a stage hypnotist is to very carefully pick his subjects (Meeker & Barber, 1971). He uses only selected individuals who are ready to think and imagine with suggestions and to comply with requests and commands. The procedure he employs to select responsive subjects is clear-cut. He gives several test suggestions to individuals who volunteer to come up to the stage. Although there are many test suggestions, they typically include limb rigidity or hand clasp. For instance, the hypnotist asks his volunteers to clasp their hands together tightly and then suggests repeatedly that the hands are rigid, solid, stuck together, and cannot be pulled apart. He selects only those volunteers who respond to the suggestion—that is, who struggle to pull their hands apart but do not do so until he states, "Now you can relax the hands and you can unclasp them."

Since many of the volunteers pass the first test, the stage hypnotist usually has too many subjects. Consequently, he goes on to give a second test suggestion and, if necessary, a third. He may suggest that the subjects cannot open their mouths, cannot move a leg, or cannot open their eyes. Volunteers who fail one or more of the tests are sent back to the audience and only those remain on stage who have passed all of the test suggestions. *The Encyclopedia of Stage Hypnotism* (McGill, 1947, pp. 181–182 and p. 252) places heavy emphasis on this aspect, stating that the stage hypnotist should diplomatically get rid of uncooperative subjects by whispering to them to leave the stage quietly. *The Encyclopedia* also emphasizes that the removal of "poor" subjects is the first thing the stage hypnotist must learn in order to carry out a successful show.

Sometimes the stage hypnotist selects subjects by using typical hypnotic induction methods, but these relaxation, drowsiness, and sleep suggestions are used in the same way as other test suggestions. That is, if the subject does not pass—does not appear relaxed and sleepy—he is sent back to the audience and not used in the rest of the demonstration. Although the stage hypnotist does not need to give suggestions of relaxation and deep sleep, he usually does so for at least three reasons: a) It is expected by the subjects; b) it impresses the audience; and c) it formally defines the situation as hypnosis with the strong implication that the situation is both unusual and important.

Once the performer has his carefully selected subjects, he can give them direct requests or commands — for example, "Sing like Frank Sinatra" or "You are Frank Sinatra" — and the subjects will almost certainly comply. Some of the reasons for the compliance include the following: a) The subjects have been carefully selected for readiness to respond to suggestions and commands. Individuals who have negative attitudes, motivations, and expectancies toward the stage situation and who are unwilling to think and imagine with the themes of the suggestions either do not volunteer for the stage performance or are excluded during the process of subject selection. b) The stage performer has been advertised as a highly effective hypnotist and has high prestige and strong expectations working for him. c) The stage performer will carefully observe his selected subjects and ask the one who appears to be the most highly motivated and the most extroverted to sing like Frank Sinatra. d) Since the subject is facing an eager and expectant audience and is surrounded by other eager subjects, he would have to be highly negativistic to surmount the pressure and say, "I am not Frank Sinatra" or "I will not sing." Nelson (1965, p. 30) emphasizes that a subject finds it difficult to refuse a request or command because to do so would make him stand out among the other subjects as a "hold out." Also, Nelson notes that the subject "gets into the act," "falls into the fun idea," acts the part of a hypnotized subject, realizes that he has "a perfect shield to hide behind" — namely, "hypnosis" — if he engages in odd or silly behavior, is reinforced by the reactions and applause of the audience, and begins competing with the other subjects for the best performance.

The stage hypnotist utilizes a series of social-psychological variables that are present in the stage situation. *The Encyclopedia of Stage Hypnotism* describes some of these variables as: The subject is clearly in a submissive role while the stage hypnotist has the role of leader or stage director; the attention and expectancy of the audience are centered upon the subject; the subject feels tense and expectant while he is on the stage; and there is a helpful stage "atmosphere" which derives from the lights, music, curtains, and other stage props (McGill, 1947, p. 257). *The Encyclopedia* also points out that some of the subjects tend to simulate, but the simulation is not "voluntary deception"; on the contrary, it derives from a strong desire to cooperate and to "help out the show."

The audience does not hear everything the stage performer says to his subjects. Since the audience is some distance away, the performer can prevent it from hearing such statements as "Sing like Frank Sinatra" simply by whispering or by turning away his microphone. However, the audience is allowed to hear the next statement, which might be: "You are Frank Sinatra." In other words, the stage hypnotist can mislead the audience into believing that the subject is deluded (thinks he is Frank Sinatra), when actually the subject is only responding to a direct request to imitate the singer.

If the subject refuses to comply with a suggestion, the stage performer is not especially bothered. Typically, he will simply ask the subject to leave the stage and will then work with a more compliant subject. But he can also use another tactic. He can whisper to the subject, so the audience does not hear, "Please sit down and then close your eyes." It is likely the subject will comply with this polite request and, when he is sitting down and closing his eyes, the stage hypnotist can make hand motions over him and intone aloud so that the audience hears, "You are going into a deep hypnotic trance." Thus the performer turns the situation to his advantage, leading the audience to believe that he placed the subject in a "trance" in a very quick and amazing way.

Schneck (1958) discusses another technique of stage hypnosis, "the failure to challenge technique." The hypnotist suggests to the subject that he cannot take his clasped hands apart or he cannot bend his outstretched arm, but he does *not* challenge the subject to try to unclasp his hands or to try to bend his arm. Members of the audience, however, assume that the suggestions were effective even though they were not tested. Schneck comments:

> The point to be noted is the play on the suggestibility of the audience rather than the examination of the subject response. The implication was to the effect that when the subject retained, even for a few seconds, the arm in an outstretched position, it followed that he would in fact be unable to bend it. This was clearly a non sequitur. No verbal or other response at this point was requested of the subject. (p. 175)

Another way of making the show exciting and impressive is having subjects demonstrate "amazing feats" that are actually rather easy to perform. For instance, the hypnotist can suspend one of the subjects between two chairs, one chair beneath the subject's head and neck and the other beneath the ankles. As the subject remains suspended between the two chairs, the hypnotist can ask the orchestra to play a crescendo or he can impress the audience by stating that the subject is able to perform the human plank feat because he is in "a cataleptic third stage of somnambulistic trance." Of course, trained stage hypnotists know, but very few members of the audience know, that practically anyone at any time can easily remain suspended between two chairs. It does not require any special effort and practically no one falls. After two or three minutes, the neck muscles begin to tire and most normal individuals, as well as "hypnotized" individuals, wish to discontinue the "human plank feat" (Barber, 1969; Collins, 1961).

After the audience is impressed by this feat, the hypnotist can demonstrate another one that appears even more amazing. He places a male subject between two chairs, one chair beneath the subject's *head and shoulders* and the other beneath the *calves of his legs*. The subject is told to keep his body rigid. The hypnotist then asks an attractive woman to stand on the chest of the suspended subject. The audience is impressed, especially when the hypnotist says that the subject is able to support the weight of the woman on his body because he is in a "profound, somnambulistic, hypnotic trance." Of course, the stage hypnotist knows, but very few members of the audience know, that when a normal man is suspended between two chairs, he can support at least 300 pounds without much discomfort.

The performance can be made even more dramatic by placing a felt pad and then a large stone on the chest of the suspended subject and then breaking the stone by striking a blow with a large sledgehammer. Although this stunt appears spectacular, McGill (1947, p. 219) notes that since the rock is made of sandstone, it breaks easily. The subject experiences only a slight jar because the force of the blow is absorbed by the felt pad over the subject's chest and by the rock itself.

Other stage demonstrations — for instance, tests of "anesthesia" — are also not what they appear to be. After the hypnotist has asked one of his selected subjects to place his hand straight out, he may state repeatedly that the hand is dull, numb, and insensitive. Whether or not the subject experiences the insensitivity is unimportant to the demonstration that follows. The stage hypnotist takes a match or cigarette lighter and places the flame close to or upon the subject's outstretched palm and then moves the flame slowly across the palm. Although the demonstration looks impressive, the stage performer knows that when a flame is held close to or placed directly on the subject's palm, no burning results *as long as the flame is moved along slowly*. The subject feels heat, but it is not too uncomfortable. Any normal person can tolerate the heat, and no burning results (Meeker & Barber, 1971).

Next, the hypnotist may take a sterilized pin and quickly push it through the loose skin in the middle of the subject's arm. Stage hypnotists do this quickly, without informing the subject, and usually when the subject's eyes are closed (McGill, 1947). Although the fingertips and most part of the hand are quite sensitive to pinprick, the fleshy part of the arm is not. The subject may feel a tiny prick on the arm, which he can easily tolerate; if he is distracted, he may not notice it at all. To make this demonstration dramatic, the hypnotist uses a fine needle with a large head.

Because the whole point of stage hypnotism is to entertain the audience, it is not especially important whether the subjects experience what is suggested to them. As Nelson (1965, pp. 29–31) notes, it is not even important that the subjects be "hypnotized." As long as the stage hypnotist excludes uncooperative volunteers and carefully selects subjects who are ready to respond to his suggestions and carry out his requests, he can put on a successful entertainment by resorting to various techniques such as private whispers and by capitalizing on the gullibility of the audience, as well as its ignorance of the capacities of the human body.

When well done, stage hypnosis is great fun and wonderful amusement. The only problem is that people in the audience forget or don't know that what they see on the stage has no connection whatsoever with the hypnosis that their doctor or therapist may recommend to them. Because of stage performances, hypnosis gets associated in many people's minds with trickery, silliness, and impossible feats, thus reducing its credibility as a healing art.

References

Barber, T. X. (1969). *Hypnosis: A scientific approach*. New York: Van Nostrand.
Collins, J. K. (1961). Muscular endurance in normal and hypnotic states: A study of suggested catalepsy. Honors thesis, Department of Psychology, University of Sidney.
McGill, O. (1947). *The encyclopedia of stage hypnotism*. Colon, MI: Abbot's Magic Novelty Co.
Meeker, W. B., & Barber, T. X. (1971). Toward an explanation of stage hypnosis. *Journal of Abnormal Psychology, 77*, 61–70.
Nelson, R. A. (1965). *A complete course in stage hypnotism*. Columbus, OH: Nelson Enterprises.
Schneck, J. M. (1958). Relationship between hypnotist-audience and hypnotist-subject interaction. *Journal of Clinical and Experimental Hypnosis, 6*, 171–181.

Hypnosis and Fire-walking

Question:

I've heard that hypnosis can alter physiology so that a person can walk unharmed over extremely hot coals (fire-walking). Is this really possible, and if so, how is it accomplished?

Discussion by BERNIE ZILBERGELD, Ph.D.

The ancient practice of fire-walking is enjoying a rennaisance. A flyer I received this year advertises "A Firewalk with John Grinder," co-founder of Neuro-Linguistic Programming. It promises that in an evening with John, you will "learn to develop a state of excellence so powerful" that "you can alter your physiology so as to walk safely." A new quasi-therapy group in Southern California, which seems something like Est, uses fire-walking as its central focus. It claims that the ability to walk unharmed over hot coals allows the walkers to experience very powerfully their strength and to realize that many things, including those that frightened them in the past, are within their grasp. Sure enough, it does have a dramatic effect on some people, at least immediately after the event. A television report on the phenomenon included interviews with several people shortly after their walks, and almost all said the same thing: "If I can do something that's impossible, I can do almost anything at all."

Sometimes fire-walking is associated with hypnosis, sometimes not. Grinder's flyer does not mention hypnosis but talks instead of "a state of excellence" and the learning of techniques. But whether or not the word hypnosis is used, the implication is that some extraordinary technique is involved.

Perhaps the most important thing to keep in mind about fire-walking is that most people, especially in western cultures, assume it's impossible. It seems inconceivable that someone could walk unharmed over hot coals, stones, or logs without suffering grievous harm. Given this assumption, it follows that some magical ingredient — hypnosis, a suspension of the laws of nature, or trickery (maybe the coals really aren't as hot as they look) — must be at work.

The assumption of something being impossible without hypnosis is not restricted to fire-walking. Most people are quite ignorant of the capacities of the human body and therefore easily fooled into thinking that such and such a phenomenon is possible only in some altered state or with the benefit of some secret technique. Stage hypnotists capitalize on this ignorance in many ways, e.g., in the human plank tricks. The stage performer gives the audience to understand that his subject can lay rigid between two chairs with another person standing on his chest *only* because he is hypnotized. The fact is that almost any healthy man can do the same without hypnosis or anything else.

The same is true of fire-walking. It does not require hypnosis, it does not require special states of mind, and it does not depend on the intervention of the Almighty. The only thing required is to walk steadily and without hesitation. This does not mean fire-walking is without danger. Although accounts of people getting burned in the endeavor are rare, it can happen and I did talk to a woman who had a few small blisters on her feet as a result of her experience. Here as perhaps nowhere else, one who hesitates is lost. You must have enough confidence or whatever else you need to make sure you keep moving. Also, the material walked on must have certain characteristics, the most important of which are that it must not exceed 800° Centigrade and it must not be too long. Most fire-walks are very short, with pits ranging from six to 18 feet long, which means that only about three to eight steps are actually taken. Another requirement is that fire-walking be done socially rather than individually. Group pressure will help keep you moving. And if you should hesitate, someone in the group can come to your rescue.

No one seems quite sure why fire-walking is possible without harm. Various theories have been put forth, including the notion that perspiration on the feet acts as a buffer between the hot material and the feet (Coe, 1978). Whatever the mechanism, there is no doubt that almost anyone who is willing and able to walk firmly and without hesitation can do it safely without any tricks or techniques or states of mind. After conducting a number of experiments using both professional fire-walkers and amateurs, Price (1939) concluded:

> Any person with the requisite determination, confidence, and steadiness, can walk unharmed over a fire as hot as 800 degrees Centigrade. The experiments proved once and for all that no occult or psychic power, or a specially induced mental state, is necessary in a fire-walker. (p. 262)

So yes, it is possible for most people to walk across very hot coals or logs without getting burned (Coe, 1957, 1978; Mishlove, 1975; McElroy, 1978; Price, 1939; Rosner, 1966). But no alteration of physiology is required; such a feat is within our natural abilities. And hypnosis has nothing to do with the matter.

References

Coe, M. R. (1957). Fire-walking and related behaviors. *Psychological Record, 7*, 101–110.
Coe, M. R. (1978). Safely across the fiery pit. *Fate, 31*, 84–86.
McElroy, J. H. (1978). Fire-walking. *Folklore, 89*, 113–115.
Mishlove, J. (1975). *The roots of consciousness*. New York: Random House.
Price, H. (1939). *Fifty years of psychical research*. London: Longmans, Green & Co.
Rosner, V. (1966). Fire-walking the tribal way. *Anthropos, 61*, 177–190.

SECTION II *Validity of Hypnosis*

The validity of hypnosis and the phenomena associated with it have been under serious attack at least since the days of Mesmer. The hypnotic state itself, although it did not acquire that name until much later, was believed to be a tool of the gods by the ancient Egyptians, and a tool of the Devil during the Middle Ages. It has been viewed as an indication of disease (hysteria), and as a method that can be used to combat disease. It has been viewed as a physiological response and as a purely psychological response.

There are those who say there is no such thing as hypnosis and those who say that everything is hypnosis. As one observes inductions becoming increasingly informal and suggestions becoming increasingly permissive and indirect, and as one observes how mere words and gestures can influence "non-hypnotized" subjects, it becomes easier to believe that both sides are correct.

But is there a real, observable, reproducible state of hypnosis? The paper by Dr. Weitzenhoffer offers some fascinating information on this question.

If we assume that hypnosis is an actual phenomenon, can the information obtained from hypnotized subjects be considered accurate? The result of the subject trying to please the hypnotherapist? The product of vivid imagination? Or merely an answer that the hypnotist already suggested? The discussions by Relinger, Orne, and Diamond are pertinent in coming to some conclusion about these possibilities. The paper by Perry and his colleagues offers a scholarly view of the validity of past-lives regression and reincarnation, topics that have been pushed to the forefront by some hypnotherapists, much to the embarrassment of many others.

And what about the changes and improvement obtained through hypnosis? Are these of significant benefit, or are patient and therapist merely deluding one another into believing that something worthwhile has occurred, when, in reality, any apparent improvement is only temporary? Lipschutz addresses this issue directly.

This section has much to offer the skeptic and the believer, and perhaps both can read it and learn something new.

Scientific Support for
Hypnosis and Its Effects

Question:

> Since learning hypnosis I've encountered a number of colleagues
> who say there is no scientific support for the notion of hypnosis
> and its effects. Are they right?

Discussion by ANDRE M. WEITZENHOFFER, Ph.D.

My answer to this question has to be both a qualified "yes" and "no." For
one thing, the term "hypnosis" has been used in a ubiquitous manner in recent times: 1) It denotes a state of being. 2) It is a class of behavioral phenomena. 3) It is the study and use of this state and these phenomena. As
will become clear, one cannot give the same answers in regard to all three
meanings.

We should also keep in mind that what constitutes adequate scientific support is not as well agreed upon as one might think or hope. As a study, hypnotism is basically a study of human behavior, and whether or not the study
of human behavior constitutes a science or can even be one has been a subject of debate. It certainly is amenable to some of the more basic aspects
of the scientific method and to this extent it is meaningful to ask questions
regarding the adequacy of scientific support in its context. At the same time,
it must be realized that the answers may vary depending on how strict a
position one takes with regard to what constitutes adequate scientific proof
or evidence. For instance, shall we accept or reject self-reports as data? Shall
we accept qualitative or only quantitative data? In the latter case, what
kinds? Shall we accept or reject data based on a sample of one? And on and
on it goes. The questions here are many and a detailed discussion of them
lies beyond the scope of this paper. In many cases, there are no final set

answers and for this reason other answers depending on them often have to be qualified.

It was de Puységur who in 1782 first observed fortuitously the occurrence of overt, behavioral sleep symptoms in certain individuals under conditions not usually associated with their appearance. This event turned out to be replicable and observable by others. De Puységur first named the condition "magnetic somnambulism" and later renamed it "artificial somnambulism." The name "hypnotism" for this condition was introduced by Braid in 1841. Both investigators reasonably inferred from the only data they had that they were dealing with a sleep-like condition (Braid, 1843).

Roughly a hundred years were to pass before scientific methodology could evolve the necessary physiological instruments and provide new data showing that individuals said to be hypnotized are, physiologically speaking, actually awake. If "hypnosis," as this inferred condition eventually came to be known, is not sleep, then what is it? More to the point, is there any scientific support for even saying that certain persons are hypnotized or in a state of hypnosis? Etymologically, certainly not, and should it turn out that one can still say they are not in their usual, normal state of wakefulness, then we certainly do need to use other terms than these. But what about this matter of another state of wakefulness? To answer this question we need to look at another aspect of the subject matter, keeping in mind that current physiological data do not support this notion either.

Had the whole matter regarding hypnotic behavior been merely one of individuals falling asleep, it is doubtful this would have attracted as widespread and as lasting an interest as it did, no matter how strange or unusual the circumstances surrounding it may have seemed. But there were other phenomena of much greater interest seemingly associated with the sleep in question. Some of these were shown to be artifacts, first by Braid and later by other investigators. However, others withstood testing. One which did was a dominant feature of hypnotic behavior, and remains so to this day. This was that this behavior came about in the context of a two-person interaction in which one person, the "hypnotist," was viewed as eliciting much, if not all, of the behavior in or from the other person, or "subject," largely through verbal communications. What was remarkable about this interaction was that within its context the subject appeared to develop an unusually high degree of selective responsiveness, compliance, and psychic malleability to the instructions, requests, commands, and other communications coming from the hypnotist. This feature seemed in turn to be associated, at least in part, with a bypassing of the subject's normal, waking, volitional apparatus. From this feature the notion of "suggestibility" eventually evolved.

By the end of the 19th century, and actually quite a bit earlier, suggestibility had become the accepted medium through which all hypnotic phenomena, including hypnosis, were said to be produced. The work of one man, Bernheim, was primarily responsible for this development and for setting down the foundation of much of 20th century hypnotism. Bernheim (1886) originally spoke more in terms of "suggestion" than of suggestibility. Suggestion, he stated, is the basis of all hypnotic phenomena, including hypnosis. A suggestion, he further stated, is any idea that gives rise to an "immediate" response by the subject (that is, a response not mediated by the higher, volitional cortical processes). He even posited a cortical reflex process, "ideodynamic action," as the physiological mechanism behind it. This mechanism could manifest itself at the sensory, motoric and affective levels. For reasons one can only guess at, modern workers in this area have chosen to speak of only one of its components, "ideomotor action," in this connection.

Bernheim was also the first to point out that suggestions affect a large segment of the population and that a person does not have to be hypnotized to be suggestible. He showed how one can quantify suggestibility and provided the model for later scales of suggestibility, of "hypnotic depth," of "hypnotic susceptibility," and of "hypnotizability." According to Bernheim, some presumably nonhypnotized individuals can be as suggestible as the most suggestible, presumably hypnotized subjects, but it is generally the case that a hypnotized subject will show an appreciably enhanced suggestibility as compared to his nonhypnotic ("waking") suggestibility. Bernheim was so impressed by this enhancement that he eventually came to view "hypersuggestibility" as the dominant characteristic of hypnosis and went on to define hypnosis as being simply a state of hypersuggestibility.

Bernheim considered the suggestibility of presumably hypnotized subjects as reflecting that hypnosis has depth or degree and he took this suggestibility as a direct measure of it. However, he never stated how he had arrived at this conclusion. Possibly he did so because he viewed hypnosis as a suggestibility state and because presumably hypnotized subjects show variable suggestibility. If so, then clearly he was actually making an assumption regarding the above connection between suggestibility and hypnosis. If he had other reasons, his failure to record them leaves us in the position of having to guess, and we are no better off.

Furthermore, Bernheim never explicitly stated how he determined a subject was hypnotized in the first place. Inasmuch as he had made the point that some nonhypnotized persons can be as suggestible as the best hypnotized subjects, it should be clear that he could not have used the mere presence of suggestibility, no matter how great, as evidence of hypnosis. True, he did view hypnosis as a state of hypersuggestibility and could have chosen, therefore, to use a demonstrated increase in suggestibility as an index of the presence of hypnosis. There are no indications that he ever took the necessary steps to make this demonstration. Other criteria were used in his day, but inasmuch as he considered they were suggested artifacts he could not have used them. In the absence of data to the contrary, we can then again only take the position that we are most likely dealing here with a second assumption on Bernheim's part.

As a matter of fact, nowhere in his writings does one find references to any actual demonstrations on an individual basis that presumably hypnotized subjects are more suggestible than when they are not hypnotized. Here, then, is a third apparent assumption on his part. Bernheim's writings suggest he was a keen observer and adept at utilizing naturally occurring situational controls. One suspects he probably relied on general impressions he validly formed of how the "hypnotic" suggestibility of his subjects compared to their normal suggestibility as he worked with them over long periods of time and did come to some sensible conclusions on this basis. But this is only guesswork and in the end we are faced with the fact that the connections Bernheim made between hypnosis and suggestibility, if we accept them, must be viewed to be in the nature of two assumptions and to rest upon a third one.

The significance of these remarks is simply that failure to recognize the existence of these assumptions has led the majority of students and users of hypnotism who have followed since Bernheim to proceed as if they were facts; as a result, much of what has been attributed to hypnosis since his time can, at best, only be attributed to suggestibility (Weitzenhoffer, 1953). It should be added that the hypersuggestibility assumption ceased to be one in 1960 when by means of test-retest techniques it was finally established that, in fact, following the use of an induction of hypnosis procedure, many subjects show an increase in suggestibility as defined by appropriate scales (Weitzenhoffer & Sjoberg, 1961). Unfortunately, most investigators and users of hypnotism have continued to ignore the above issues and have continued to proceed as if it were an established fact that evidence of suggestibility following an induction of hypnosis procedure is sufficient to speak of hypnosis and hypnotic suggestibility when it is not.

The above discussion actually assumes that we are scientifically entitled to talk about suggestibility. This still remains to be seen. The nonvolitional character of the response to a suggestion is, of course, what makes it stand out among communications. But what evidence do we have that there is such a class of communications? In the majority of instances, the ultimate test lies in what the subject can report regarding how he experienced his behavior. From a strict behavioristic standpoint, the evidence from these cases is thus very poor. On the other hand, one can certainly argue that since self-reports are themselves overt responses they are legitimate objects of study and legitimate data and, in fact, cannot legitimately be disregarded. Additionally, with a small number of subjects, certain effects have been observed in relation to communications intended to serve as suggestions ("intended suggestions") which give support to the suggestion concept. These effects have consisted of responses which can reasonably be said, independently of any self-reports, not to have belonged to the subject's normal volitional repertoire. At least for this group the reality of suggestions seems fairly well established. In the light of this, it is most likely that at least some, if not all, self-reports of nonvolitional responses are veridical, too.

In further support of Bernheim's hypersuggestibility hypothesis, in recent times it has been found, too, in these self-report situations, that a traditional induction of hypnosis procedure is associated with an increase in the number of individuals who report nonvolitional experiences (Weitzenhoffer, 1974). On the whole, then, the concept of suggestion can be said to be scientifically supported. At the same time, it can be seen that it is not possible to decide that a communication is a suggestion except *a posteriori*, i.e., only after a response has been obtained that permits one to state it evoked a nonvolitional act. It is a major weakness of much of the work upon which modern hypnotism is founded that it is generally assumed *a priori* that a communication used as an intended suggestion has effectively functioned as one ("effective suggestion") when, obviously, the evidence for this is lacking. Thus, when one hears or reads that someone gave or received a suggestion in the technical sense we are using this term, it may well be that all that happened was that a communication was made which was acted upon at a purely voluntary level for one reason or another. It is, therefore, quite understandable that some investigators have been able to marshall evidence in support of the notion that all suggestion effects are a matter of role playing, and that other investigators have been able to secure data showing that, with appropriate motivation, subjects will perform so much like presumably hypnotized subjects as to be indistinguishable from them. In any case, it should be clear that one cannot disprove the reality of hypnotic effects through the existence of like effects occurring under different circumstances.

It remains for us to look at one last aspect of hypnotic behavior. One symptom left unmentioned that both de Puységur and Braid relied on in deciding they were dealing with a form of sleep was the presence of a spontaneously appearing ("posthypnotic") amnesia for transpired events which followed the subject's "waking" from his presumed sleep. Braid considered this one symptom so important that for the 20 years he devoted to hypnotism he declined to speak of hypnosis as having been present unless this amnesia was also present, even though other remarkable effects might have occurred. When Bernheim made suggestion the nuclear element, surprisingly, he also clearly indicated his belief that there was a class of subjects who developed a spontaneous amnesia unrelated to any explicit or implicit suggestions. Generally, these were also the subjects who showed the greatest suggestibility. Although he felt a need to place these subjects on the same continuum of hypnotic depth as those who did not, he also felt they should be distinguished from the latter by specifying they had attained a special "somnambulistic" phase or degree of hypnosis.

Bernheim did not recognize that he had never actually demonstrated an identity or even a one-to-one correspondence between hypnotic depth and suggestibility. If he had, he might have stated the matter somewhat differently and more accurately. In any case, it has frequently been argued since Bernheim's time that the amnesia in question is not particularly significant because it most likely was the result of suggestions implicit in the very notion of sleep traditionally associated with the induction procedure. To this day this remains a pure conjecture. At best, it is an unverifiable hypothesis. This argument, therefore, has very little scientific weight. The fact is that a very small number of individuals do develop a spontaneous amnesia, as contrasted to those who only do so more or less well in response to suggestions of posthypnotic amnesia or do not develop it at all. Another fact is that these individuals usually show by far the highest degrees of suggestibility. Because it has been the practice for many years now to suggest posthypnotic amnesia prior to dehypnotizing subjects, the existence of this group has been masked. It is a group that needs specific attention if for no other reason than it appears to present suggestibility with an added dimension.

Besides spontaneous amnesia and hypersuggestibility, a number of other "signs" of hypnosis can be found listed in the literature. Although many investigators have attested to their existence and for this reason alone one is tempted to give them weight, it should be recognized that few of these signs have been satisfactorily studied and their exact place and significance in the scheme of things are generally unclear. Two signs which bear further mention are that subjects who are in a state of high suggestibility are characteristically prone to be literal and that they are likely to use a different form of logic than the one they otherwise use when normally suggestible.

Even if hypersuggestibility were the only occurrence we had to work with, we would still be in a position to refer to a change in state in connection with its production. The concept of "state" has been widely used in many scientific areas with benefits. The manner in which a state is defined or specified is partly a function of the domain of application. One particular use of the concept which appears to be especially well suited for our topic is its use in relation to systems that can be said to possess a set of inputs and a set of associated outputs. Such systems can be described as also having internal states specific to each paired set of inputs and outputs. Although in many cases one can do so, it is not required that one be able to point to actual and specific internal changes in the system to make valid use of the state concept. Among other things, the state concept provides a useful shorthand for describing the behavior of systems. On the other hand, states are not meant to be used as explanations or causes.

Going into more detail in this regard lies beyond the scope of this paper. It is sufficient to say it is scientifically valid to view the controlled appearance and disappearance of this constellation of four suggestion effects — hypersuggestibility, spontaneous amnesia, literalness, and a different logic — as associated with a change from a normal state of wakefulness to one and possibly two other states (of wakefulness). "Suggestion states" would seem to be the logical and appropriate designation for them. This does leave us without an easy way of denoting the process of bringing these states about or of stating that an individual is in such a state. For lack of something better at this time and with the understanding that it is etymologically incorrect, we can probably continue to use "hypnosis" as second-best here. We can then understand that "to hypnotize" is to create a situation conducive to the development of a suggestion state, and that a "hypnotized" person is one in such a state.

Although it appears then that one can speak of suggestibility phenomena and of suggestion states (hypnosis) with some degree of scientific confidence, confusion over what is fact and what is merely assumption has led to some highly equivocal results over the years. Additionally, the increasing tendency in recent years for workers in the field to accept minimal evidence of suggestibility, such as muscular relaxation alone, or eye closure alone, as evidence of hypnosis being present, the tendency to extend unwarrantedly the concept of hypnosis to all kinds of presumed altered states of consciousness (daydreaming, drug states, states of concentrated attention, etc.), and the increasing use of so-called indirect methods of suggestion and induction, which frequently leave subjects and observers in a state of uncertainty as to what has actually been said and done — all have led to an increasing confounding of what might be veridical suggestion effects, if not hypnosis, with responses of a possibly totally different nature (Weitzenhoffer, 1980). Consequently, a great deal of what has passed for hypnotic and suggested behavior in recent times is questionably so. Hence, my initial qualified "yes" and "no."

References

Bernheim, H. (1886). *De la Suggestion et de ses Applications a la Therapeutique*. Paris: O. Doin.

Braid, J. (1843). *Neurypnology: On the rationale of nervous sleep considered in relation to animal magnetism*. London: John Churchill.

Weitzenhoffer, A. M. (1953). *Hypnotism: An objective study in suggestibility*. New York: Wiley.

Weitzenhoffer, A. M. (1974). When is an instruction an "instruction"? *International Journal of Clinical and Experimental Hypnosis, 22,* 258–269.

Weitzenhoffer, A. M. (1980). Hypnotic susceptibility revisited. *American Journal of Clinical Hypnosis, 22,* 130–146.

Weitzenhoffer, A. M. & Sjoberg, B. M., Jr. (1961). Suggestibility with and without "induction of hypnosis." *Journal of Nervous and Mental Diseases, 132,* 204–220.

$\underset{A}{Q_{\&}}7$ Fabrication in Hypnosis

Question:

Can a subject fabricate in hypnosis? One of my specialties is forensic psychiatry and I wonder about the usefulness of hypnosis in helping witnesses remember accurately and in getting them and the accused to tell the truth.

Discussion by HELMUT RELINGER, Ph.D.

There are two important points you need to know about forensic hypnosis. First, while hypnosis does have the potential to improve the amount of accurate information a subject may recall, hypnosis is not a truth serum and does not guarantee that any additional memory will be accurate. Second, there are potential legal problems in using hypnosis in forensic situations which must be considered before hypnotizing a potential witness or victim of a crime.

A recent review of the scientific literature on hypnotic hypermnesia (Relinger, 1984a) revealed that hypnosis can enhance recall of meaningful material. This may be particularly true if the material was learned under stress, a point which has significant implication for forensic hypnosis, since much of the material to be recalled in forensic cases was learned in stressful situations. While research data are sparse because of the ethical restrictions on deliberately stressing research subjects, both case and clinical material suggests that hypnosis is most productive in situations where a) the subject was exposed to a trauma for which he is subsequently amnesic, or b) a subject was actively attempting to learn material in a highly stressful situation and was unable thereafter to recall that material. An example of the former is United States v. Awkard (1979), in which a prison inmate observed the knife murder of another inmate. Although initially amnesic for much of the ex-

40

perience, after hypnosis he was able to recall and identify all the inmates who participated in the murder (Kroger & Douce, 1979). Other cases in which subjects who were initially partially amnesic for the event were able to recall additional accurate information are available in both the scientific and legal literature (e.g., Schafer & Rubio, 1978). A case in which hypnosis allowed additional recall of material learned under stress is the Chowchilla kidnapping (People v. Woods et al., 1977), in which 26 school children and their bus driver were abducted at gunpoint. While the bus driver had attempted to memorize the license plate of the abductor's vehicle, he was unable to recall this information. Hypnosis allowed him to accurately recall two additional numbers, which then led to the arrest of the suspects. The suspected mechanism allowing such additional recall involves the notion that stress appears to affect retrieval more than encoding or registration, and hypnosis may counteract this stress-induced inhibition mechanism (Relinger, 1984a). Hypnosis has also been valuable as a memory aid in developing artists' sketches of suspected criminals. In State v. Stolp (1982), for example, the artist's rendering, done while the victim, in trance, described the assailant, was so accurate that the defendant was identified within three days by a man who had seen the sketch only once.

However, hypnosis is not a truth serum and does not guarantee that the additional information recalled will be accurate. Hypnotized subjects can voluntarily fabricate and lie while in hypnotic trance (Field & Dworkin, 1967). There is also scientific controversy as to whether hypnosis increases subjects' tendencies to involuntarily confabulate or produce inaccurate information (Diamond, 1980; Orne, 1979). Such confabulation seems to be more prominent in cases where age regression procedures, which are elaborate suggestions designed to convince subjects that they are actually re-experiencing the event, are used, rather than simple instructions to report everything that is accurately recalled. It has also been suggested that hypnosis unduly increases the subject's confidence in his or her memories (Dywan & Bowers, 1983), although these data are highly experimental in nature and not supported by more naturalistic studies (Relinger, 1984b). Further, Zelig and Beidleman (1981) suggested that hypnotized subjects are more responsive to verbal manipulations designed to implant memories that did not previously exist. However, more recent research has not supported this contention (Baker, Haynes, & Patrick, 1983). Yet, because hypnosis in no way assures that the recalled memories are true, anymore than memories reported in the waking state can be guaranteed to be true, the purpose of forensic hypnosis is generally to assist witnesses or victims of crimes in recalling additional information and/or clues that law enforcement agencies can then investigate, rather than validating the accuracy of reported memories.

One must also keep in mind that there are potential legal problems in using hypnosis in forensic situations. Because of the current scientific controversy around the question of whether or not hypnosis may increase a person's tendency to confabulate, numerous state courts have placed restrictions on the use of forensic hypnosis. Failure to be aware of these can have serious legal consequences and may render a witness or victim of a crime legally incompetent to testify in that case. Consultation with the attorney handling the case is absolutely essential before forensic hypnosis is undertaken.

A number of procedural guidelines for forensic hypnosis have been developed to attempt to minimize any potential contamination and potential consequent legal problems (e.g., Orne, 1979; Relinger & Stern, 1983). Following are some appropriate guidelines from Relinger and Stern (1983):

I. Credentials of the hypnotist
   A. Hypnosis should be conducted by a professional who is licensed to practice psychotherapy and hypnosis.
   B. The hypnotist should be viewed as an expert in clinical hypnosis and have at least three years' experience in this area. Experience in teaching hypnosis and affiliations with professional hypnosis societies are desirable.
II. Conduct of the hypnotist
   A. Prior to the hypnotic session.
      1. The hypnotist should have had no previous involvement in the case and should not have had previous contact with the subject.
      2. Fees for services should be set in advance.
      3. The hypnotist should not be verbally informed of the details of the case. Rather, he should request a typed statement outlining the event, place, and timeframe of the situation to be recalled while the subject is in trance.
      4. Upon initial contact by the referring party, the hypnotist should inform that party as to the undesirability of representing hypnosis in unrealistic terms to the subject. The referring party should be instructed to inform the subject that:
         a) Hypnosis may or may not be helpful in enhancing recall.
         b) Hypnosis will be conducted by a licensed health professional.
         c) The subject need not give consent until all questions about hypnosis have been answered by the hypnotist.
         d) Refusal to be hypnotized will not be regarded as uncooperative behavior.
   B. During the hypnosis session.
      1. Hypnosis should not be done immediately after the subject has been interrogated by police or other investigative personnel. The subject should be allowed a reasonable rest period (approximately 30 minutes) before the hypnosis session.
      2. All contact between the hypnotist and subject should be video-

taped, with both people fully visible at all times. Only the hypnotist and the subject should be in the room during the session. Investigative personnel may watch the session via a one-way mirror or television monitor.

a) An exception may be made when an artist's sketch is desired. The artist should be allowed to question the hypnotized subject under supervision of the hypnotist. This should occur in a separate session, with no other interrogation occurring. The session must be videotaped with all three people visible.

b) An exception may also be made if the subject is a child who refuses to be parted from the parent. A parent may be allowed to sit with the child after having received instructions in how not to influence the child's communications. All three people must be visible in the videotape.

3. The hypnotist should conduct a Mental Status Exam prior to the actual hypnosis to assure that the subject is competent and is not experiencing any psychological disturbance which would contraindicate use of hypnosis.

4. The hypnotist should provide a brief explanation of the hypnotic procedure to the subject, indicating that hypnosis often allows people to visualize and recall events more clearly than while they are in the waking state. All of the subject's questions should be answered and misconceptions clarified. The hypnotist then should request written consent to commence the hypnotic procedure.

5. All induction and deepening techniques available to the hypnotist may be used, except suggestions directly related to the recall process. That is, the subject should not be told that his or her memory is like a videotape, that he has perfect recall powers while under hypnosis, or anything else which could pressure the subject to report inaccurate information. Rather, the subject should be instructed to visualize and report everything he can accurately recall about the event and the situations leading up to it, with no detail too small to be unimportant. Leading questions, presuppositions, or any other verbal manipulations are not allowed while the subject is in trance. The hypnotist may encourage the subject to report anything and everything he can accurately recall.

6. Consequent to this free-recall phase, the hypnotist may ask open-ended questions about the events reported. Investigative personnel watching the session may submit a list of open-ended questions to the hypnotist, who will then read these questions to the subject. Since no verbal manipulations are allowed, it is the hypnotist's responsibility to screen and rephrase inappropriate questions.

7. At the end of the hypnosis session, the subject may be instructed

to recall everything that transpired under hypnosis unless this is therapeutically contraindicated. If so instructed, the subject should be told that he will be able to differentiate the information recalled under hypnosis from that remembered before hypnosis.

C. After the hypnosis session.

1. Since more than one session may be required to achieve a suitable trance, the hypnotist should not have contact with the subject between sessions, and all sessions should be videotaped.

2. The hypnotist should not accept the subject as a patient for psychotherapy until the case has closed. If therapy is indicated, the subject should be referred to another therapist.

III. Conduct of the referring party

A. Hypnosis for the purpose of enhanced recall should be done as early in the case as is possible.

B. At the time of the initial referral, the referring party should not reveal detailed information about the case to the hypnotist. Rather, information should be communicated prior to the hypnosis session, according to the guidelines delineated in section II.A.3.

C. The referring party should not misrepresent the powers of hypnosis to the potential subject. Descriptions should be confined to the information outlined in section II.A.4.

D. The referring party should have a written record of the potential subject's full recollection of the event prior to the hypnosis session.

References

Baker, R. A., Haynes, B., & Patrick, B. S. (1983). Hypnosis, memory, and incidental memory. *American Journal of Clinical Hypnosis, 25,* 253–262.

Diamond, B. L. (1980). Inherent problems in the use of pretrial hypnosis on a prospective witness. *California Law Review, 68,* 313–349.

Dywan, J., & Bowers, K. (1983). The use of hypnosis to enhance recall. *Science, 222,* 184–185.

Field, P. B., & Dworkin, S. F. (1967). Strategies of hypnotic interrogation. *Journal of Psychology, 67,* 47–58.

Kroger, W. S., & Douce, R. G. (1979). Hypnosis in criminal investigation. *International Journal of Clinical and Experimental Hypnosis, 27,* 358–374.

Orne, M. T. (1979). The use and misuse of hypnosis in court. *International Journal of Clinical and Experimental Hypnosis, 27,* 311–341.

People vs. Woods et al. No. 63187ABNC (Alameda Co., Cal., December 15, 1977).

Relinger, H. (1984a). Hypnotic hypermnesia: A critical review. *American Journal of Clinical Hypnosis, 26,* 212–225.

Relinger, H. (1984b). The critical issues in forensic hypnosis: Confidence and confabulation. Paper presented at the meetings of the American Society of Clinical Hypnosis, San Francisco.

Relinger, H., & Stern, T. K. (1983). Guidelines for forensic hypnosis. *Journal of Psychiatry and Law,* Spring, 69–74.

Schafer, D. W., & Rubio, R. (1978). Hypnosis to aid the recall of witnesses. *International Journal of Clinical and Experimental Hypnosis, 26,* 81–91.

State vs. Stolp, 33 Ariz. 213, 650 P.2d 1195 (1982).

United States vs. Awkard, 597 F.2d 667 (9th Cir. 1979).

Zelig, M., & Beidleman, W. B. (1981). The investigative use of hypnosis: A word of caution. *International Journal of Clinical and Experimental Hypnosis, 24,* 401–412.

$\underset{A}{\overset{Q}{\partial}}$ 8   The Validity of Memories Retrieved in Hypnosis

Question:

> How can I tell if memories retrieved in hypnosis, or any other hypnotic productions, are real or manufactured to please the hypnotherapist?

Discussion by MARTIN T. ORNE, M.D., Ph.D.

When an individual in hypnosis is encouraged to recall a past event which he does not recall completely in the waking state, he is likely to produce a considerably more vivid form of recall, and if the incident involved emotional trauma, he is likely to relive the event displaying intense affect. It is quite common for the individual in hypnosis to describe what is occurring with extensive details, many of which would be known only to an individual who was in fact there. In a therapeutic setting, and even in some other contexts, the individual may feel considerably relieved after the hypnotic session, and not uncommonly, psychopathological symptoms related to the matters recalled may be ameliorated or totally alleviated.

Because of the dramatic display of affect, the myriad of additional details brought forth, and the psychological improvement, there is a tendency for a therapist as well as lay observers to assume that these hypnotic memories are in fact historically accurate. This assumption is not justified. Typically, memories from different periods in the patient's life are combined; further, fantasies, beliefs, and fears may be mixed with actual recollections. While the "memories" represent a psychologically meaningful truth useful in treatment, they should not be confused with historically accurate fact. There is no way by which either the hypnotist or the subject can determine which aspects of these recollections are accurate and which aspects represent anachronistic memories dating from other times and fantasies which never oc-

45

curred at all. Neither the plausibility, nor the nature of the affect, nor the subjective conviction of the patient can be accepted as meaningful evidence for the historical accuracy of the recollection. Furthermore, a patient may show a dramatic improvement from working through pseudomemories which have no historical basis. It should be emphasized that reliving past events in hypnosis may seem so vivid and so convincing that not only lay individuals but also highly trained clinicians may be deceived.

Because of these difficulties, the American Medical Association has taken an official position on December 5, 1984, which states that hypnosis does not result in increased reliable recall, that under some circumstances additional details may be remembered, some of which may be accurate and others inaccurate, and that recognition memory is not aided. For these reasons, the AMA has indicated that previously hypnotized witnesses should not give testimony in court concerning the matters about which they have been hypnotized. If hypnosis is used at all, it should be strictly limited to the investigational use of the technique and a number of guidelines must be followed to minimize the likelihood of a miscarriage of justice.

Q&A 9   The Veracity of
Ideomotor Signals

Question:

I am intrigued by demonstrations I've seen of ideomotor signals and would like to use this method in my work, but how do you know if information derived from ideomotor signals is true?

Discussion by MICHAEL J. DIAMOND, Ph.D.

For the practitioner of clinical hypnosis, the issue of *veracity* is far less pertinent than that of *utility*. As with all clinically obtained data, the clinician is unlikely to know whether the patient's disclosures accurately reflect external or consensual reality. The clinician's task focuses primarily around the search for experiential or psychic reality; that is, obtaining narrative as opposed to historical truth (Spence, 1982). Whereas both experimentalists and forensic workers may direct their activities toward the investigative process per se, the clinician aims to discover the patient's *unique* experience (Erickson & Rossi, 1979). Thus, the therapist is concerned with recognizing the patient's internal world of *meaning*, be the referent psychological events, nonverbal or verbal behaviors, affects, cognitions, somatic processes, or symptoms.

Ideomotor signaling (Cheek & LeCron, 1968) is a particularly useful technique in that it enables a patient to respond in nonverbal as well as less voluntary ways to questions or suggestions typically presented by the hypnotist. These reactions may, however, be responses to internal questionings, associations, or experiences apart from any external stimulation. The procedure has additional value in providing trance-ratifying opportunities (Erickson & Rossi, 1979) resulting from the patient's experience of dissociation. The primary clinical advantage of this technique lies in its enabling a wider breadth and range of response, freeing the patient from the task of having

47

to translate internal experience into communicative forms more often associated with ordinary, waking-level ways of processing reality. Thus, preverbal, sensory, or preconscious experience need not be translated into imagistic, verbal, or more consciously active motility. The patient becomes "freer" to spontaneously represent internal experience and consequently to disclose it less encumbered by the secondary processes of logical thought, spatial representation, and the like. In turn, "deeper" (i.e., less preconscious or conscious) representations of experience can be more easily yielded.

Assessing the veridicality of these ideomotor representations is beyond the scope of the clinician's skills. Unconscious mental processing is highly complex and it would be a credulous oversimplification to treat less voluntary forms of communication as unequivocally representing psychic "truth." The unconscious is a repository of so much of the psyche — from the higher more creative faculties, to the ego's protective mechanisms, the censorship and ideals of the superego, as well as representations of more primitive instinctual impulses, archetypal residues, and less important mnemonic experiences, in addition to the primary process contradictions, distortions, and defensive as well as creative operations executed outside secondary or conscious-level processing (Freud, 1915).

Ideomotor signals needn't be taken at face value. It is, however, useful for the clinician to assess how actively the patient unconsciously or involuntarily participates, in contrast to the seemingly more conscious, voluntarily-produced finger movements. The clinician as observer might take into account the speed of the finger movements, the jerkiness versus the smoothness of the movements, the time taken to respond to questioning (i.e., Does the patient seem to be "thinking" about how to respond or, alternatively, "letting it happen?"), and/or the extent to which the finger response is congruent with other apparent trance-related physiological functions (e.g., slowed breathing, altered verbalization, modified muscular movement, and the like). Regardless of the results of this assessment, the ideomotor signal provides "grist for the hypnotherapist's mill"; for example, the apparently more voluntarily produced finger movements may indicate the extensiveness of the patient's resistances or defensiveness in a particular area, which may suggest further strategies for therapeutic intervention. Thus, whether the finger movement is an indication of a "deep" (i.e., substantially removed from conscious control) response or not, it continues to have value as an alternative means for the patient to communicate to the therapist and, ultimately, to one's own self. The search for psychic truth, in contrast to external or historic truth, is facilitated by the employment of this captivating hypnotherapeutic technique.

References

Cheek, D. B., & LeCron, L. M. (1968). *Clinical hypnotherapy.* New York: Grune & Stratton.

Erickson, M. H., & Rossi, E. L. (1979). *Hypnotherapy: An exploratory casebook.* New York: Irvington.
Freud, S. (1915). The unconscious. *Standard Edition, 14*: 159–215. New York: Norton.
Spence, D. (1982). *Narrative truth and historical truth: Meaning and interpretation in psychoanalysis.* New York: Norton.

$\underset{A}{\overset{Q}{\scriptstyle\mathcal{E}}}$ 10 Past Lives Regression

Question:

I've been both repulsed and intrigued by the little I've heard about past lives regression, an idea which must assume the reality of reincarnation. Is this just a lot of foolishness, or is there any validity to it?

Discussion by CAMPBELL PERRY, Ph.D.,
JEAN-ROCH LAURENCE, Ph.D.,
ROBERT NADON, M.A., &
LOUISE LABELLE, B.A.

Reincarnation is a belief held by many educated and intelligent people. As with the Christian belief in an afterlife, it is not amenable to verification by scientific standards. This does not mean that it is a mistaken belief — only that the proper tools are unavailable to settle the matter decisively, one way or the other. Believers may continue to believe whatever they wish, but as Burnham emphasized a century ago, there are severe difficulties in claiming scientific backing for this particular belief. In fact, much of the current debate about reincarnation is remarkably similar to that of over a century ago.

By the mid 19th century, the spread of the spiritualist movement, both in North America and Europe, led to a general interest in Oriental

The paper was prepared while the first author was supported by Natural Sciences and Engineering Research (NSERC) of Canada Grant No. A6361 ("Errors of Memory in Hypnosis"), and the second author was in receipt of an NSERC 5-year Post Doctoral Research Fellowship at Concordia University. The third author was supported by a Doctoral Fellowship awarded by Social Sciences and Humanities Research Council (SSHRC) of Canada. The continued assistance of NSERC and SSHRC is acknowledged gratefully.

philosophy and in metempsychosis (the belief in reincarnation). This enthusiasm for spiritualism paralleled a decline in interest in hypnosis, particularly in Europe, where reports of reincarnation became characteristic of mediums. By contrast, the scientists of the period sought to explain spiritualist phenomena in naturalistic terms.

Burnham (1889) stressed the role of paramnesias (i.e., pseudo-memories) in the creation of experiences of reincarnation; indeed, he stated that "pseudo-reminiscences give rise to the belief in metempsychosis" (p. 432). His review of the literature on memory led him to conclude that illusions of memory were an important aspect of normal cognitive functioning and were particularly present in individuals with vivid imagination (p. 445). He emphasized that reports of metempsychosis should be evaluated in the light of the individual's life-experiences, and should not be accepted automatically as matters of fact.

Burnham's reasoning was adopted by the Swiss psychiatrist Théodore Flournoy in his classic book *From India to the Planet Mars* (1900), where he related the case of Mrs. Smith, a medium who, in a hypnoid state, relived incidents in the prior incarnations of three different persona. Although space does not permit a review of this case, Flournoy's attitude parallels the main points of the present paper. He wrote:

> For me, these (Mrs. Smith's narratives of her Hindo life) are only memories of her present life, and I don't see anything supernatural in all this; although I have not succeeded yet in finding a key to this enigma, I know it exists, and I will point later to two or three clues that indicate that Mrs. Smith's Oriental knowledge may have a quite natural explanation. . . . For the spiritists, quite to the contrary, the memories awakened in somnambulism are nothing less than memories of Mrs. Smith's previous life and this titillating explanation . . . benefits from the fact that I am incapable of proving that it is not so. As one can see, there is a major misunderstanding on the question of methodology. (pp. 232–233, translated from the French edition, Flournoy, 1900)

This problem remains at the core of many current discussions of reincarnation, particularly when it is elicited by hypnosis, as is currently quite common.

The publication of Bernstein's (1956) *The Search for Bridey Murphy* began a vogue for books on reincarnation in which a hypnotic age regression technique is used to uncover an apparent previous life or lives. Thirty years later, this trend continues to flourish with an important additional emphasis. In recent decades, hypnosis has achieved considerable scientific status, and the dust jacket descriptors of such hypnosis-and-reincarnation books imply strongly that "science" (via the medium of hypnosis) has provided ironclad support for the hypothesis of reincarnation. This impression is reinforced by the fact that two recent books on this topic (Fiore, 1978; Wambach, 1979) have been authored by individuals possessing doctorates of psychology. Thus, the publisher's dust jacket description of *Encounters With the Past* (Moss with Keaton, 1981) includes the statement that it provides "astonishing accounts of hypnotic regression"; likewise, Wambach (1979) is "an astonishing investigation into cases of people taken back to previous existences" and Ramster (1980) involves "actual stories of Australian men and women who have revealed past lives under hypnosis." For Fiore (1978) it is stated that "reincarnation therapy . . . is helping people discover the roots of present day problems through hypnosis."

Inspection of these recent representative publications in this area reveals an underlying common assumption that material obtained in hypnotic age regression can be taken as literal truth. Unfortunately for proponents of this view, the scientific data indicate otherwise.

The Nature of Hypnosis

Although there is disagreement among the leading investigators of hypnosis as to its essential nature, there is also much consensus. Hypnosis is a situation in which a person sets aside critical judgment, without abandoning it completely, and engages in make-believe and fantasy (Gill & Brenman, 1959; Hilgard, 1977). The ability to do this is differentially distributed within the population, with approximately 10–15% of individuals being highly responsive to a hypnotic procedure (i.e., capable of suggested posthypnotic amnesia), a further 10–15% minimally responsive, and the remaining 70–80% moderately responsive to varying degrees (Hilgard, 1965). Further, this characteristic appears to be quite stable (Perry, 1977). Given these stable individual differences, the extent to which a person can experience what is suggested in the hypnotic situation may lead to major alterations, even distortions, of perception, mood and memory (Orne, 1980).

The nature of the make-believe and fantasy required for successful hypnotic performance has increasingly been emphasized in recent decades. It has been referred to variously as imaginative involvement (J. Hilgard, 1979), believed-in imaginings (Sarbin & Coe, 1972), and involvement in suggestion-related imaginings (Spanos & Barber, 1974). A similar notion is proposed by Sutcliffe (1961) where he characterizes the hypnotizable person as deluded in a descriptive, nonpejorative sense, and views the hypnotic situation as providing a context in which subjects who are skilled at make-believe and fantasy are given the opportunity both to do what they enjoy doing and what they are able to do especially well. Recently, Wilson and Barber (1983) provided data consistent with this accruing picture; they characterized the highly hypnotizable person as a "fantasy addict." They report of these individuals that "on fantasy they can do anything—experience a previous lifetime, experience their own birth, go off into the future, go off into space and so on" (p. 343). Further, their fantasies are described as having hallucinatory intensity, so that 85% of them reported that they often confuse memories of real events with memories of fantasies (in contrast to 24% of control subjects who furnished comparable reports).

Research data of the last two decades are quite consistent with this emerging viewpoint; briefly, they indicate that abilities such as imagery/imagination, absorption, dissociation, and selective attention underlie high hypnotic responsivity in yet undetermined combinations (see Perry & Laurence, 1983, for a summary of these data).

Given this conceptualization of hypnosis, it should be expected that any material provided in age regression (which is at the basis of reports of reincarnation) may be fact or fantasy, and is most likely to be an admixture of both. In particular, several problems have been identified in the clinical and experimental literatures of hypnosis which indicate that great care should be exercised in evaluating the verbal reports of hypnotically age regressed subjects. These are the issues of confabulation, memory creation, and inadvertent cueing; in addition, there is some evidence that reincarnation reports may serve the subject's current psychological needs.

Age Regression: Confabulation, Memory Creation,
Inadvertent Cueing and Psychological Needs

Although some authors (Reiser, 1980) consider confabulation to be a form of deliberate lying, it is in fact a tendency of the hypnotized person to confuse fact with fiction and to report fantasied events as actually having happened. It should be noted here that this tendency is not unique to hypnosis; it can and does occur in everyday experience. Much clinical and experimental evidence was collected in the last century demonstrating that the memory system is prone to confabulation and a variety of memory alterations (see Laurence et al., in press). An early experimental report was provided by Stalnacker and Riddle (1932) in which subjects were hypnotically age regressed and then asked to recite poems learned in childhood. When their hypnotic performance was compared with waking baseline performance, the subjects appeared to show a dramatic increase in recall of the poems. When examined carefully, it was found that there were increases in productivity which could be accounted for almost entirely in terms of confabulation. Subjects were found to have improvised appropriate phrases to "fill in the gaps" for what was imperfectly recalled. Nevertheless, the subjects reported that this confabulated recall was veridical.

In a classic study, Orne (1951) also found evidence of confabulation. He provided a number of instances; for example, one subject, asked during age regression who his first grade teacher was, replied "Miss Curtis." Posthypnotically, he identified her as his seventh or eighth grade teacher. Another subject, regressed to a situation in the past where he had taken the Rorschach Test, insisted that some cards that were, in reality, colored were achromatic, and vice versa. This subject had participated in a longitudinal study of the Rorschach in 1935, 1937, and 1942. In 1935, at age six, he had not given an M response to card 3, but he had given it in 1942 at age 13. In his regression to age six, he provided an M response. As Orne pointed out, this instance is typical of the confabulation process: "the response, which was remembered and was given, had been taken from the memories of a far later stage of development, namely, the age of 13, and was fitted into the suggested situation at the age of six" (p. 222).

There have also been both clinical and experimental demonstrations of the creation of a pseudo-memory, which subsequently comes to be believed as veridical. Clinical demonstrations of this were provided in the late 19th century by Janet who, on occasion, used deliberately created fantasied memories to successfully treat patients. His perhaps most famous case involved Marie (see Ellenberger, 1970, p. 364 for an account of this case in English). Marie suffered from, among other things, blindness in one eye, which she believed was congenital. Janet established somehow that the blindness had developed, along with an impetigo on one side of the face, at the age of six, as the result of her having to share a bed with another six-year-old girl who had an impetigo similar to the one Marie developed subsequently. Her impetigo was successfully treated by orthodox dermatological means, but the "blindness" persisted into young adulthood. Janet removed the blindness by regressing Marie to the night in question and suggesting that the other small girl did not have an impetigo; after two attempts, vision was restored and persisted posthypnotically. This report constitutes the first known attempt to implant a pseudo-memory, during age regression, in the successful treatment of a hysterical symptom. An additional example of memory creation was provided by Bernheim (1888/1973, pp. 164–165). Interestingly, the wheel was reinvented (as is common in the history of hypnosis) when Baker and Boaz (1983) reported the successful treatment of a dental phobia using similar techniques. In this case report, they suggested that a traumatic dental incident, which had actually occurred, was actually pleasant. The implantation of the pseudo-memory was sufficiently successful to permit major dental surgery some months later.

Other evidence that it is possible to deliberately create a pseudo-memory for a fantasied event was provided recently by Orne in a televised demonstration (Barnes, 1982). Here it was suggested to a female subject that she would regress to a night of the previous week for which she had no recall of having dreamed or of having been awakened. In hypnosis, Orne suggested that she was awakened by three loud noises. A week later, she maintained that she had been awakened by the noises and stood by her hypnotically elicited report even when presented with a tape recording of her prehypnosis recollections of having slept soundly on the night in question, without interruption. This observation has been tested experimentally by Laurence and Perry (1983), who found that such belief and confidence in the reality of a suggested pseudo-memory could be elicited in approximately 50% of highly hypnotizable individuals.

All of these data suggest that, if pseudo-memories can be elicited deliberately, they can, as equally, be elicited by inadvertent cueing. This has been shown in the legal, investigative utilization of hypnosis by police (see Laurence, Nadon, Nogrady, & Perry, in press), and it can be found also in the experimental literature of hypnosis. Orne (1982) recounts the interesting case of True's (1949) experimental study of hypnotic age regression, in which it was found that 92% of subjects regressed to the day of their tenth birthday could accurately recall the day of the week on which it fell. The same was found for 84% of subjects for their fourth birthday. This dramatic finding could not be replicated by a number of investigators. When Orne asked True how he had obtained his data, it transpired that *Science* magazine, in which the report had appeared, had altered his procedure section without his prior consent.

It became apparent that True had inadvertently cued his subjects, since he followed the quite unusual procedure of asking subjects: "Is it Monday? Is it Tuesday? Is it Wednesday?" etc., and he monitored responses by the use of a perpetual desk calendar that was in full view. Further evidence that True unintentionally cued his subjects is provided by the finding (O'Connell, Shor, & Orne, 1970) that in a group of actual four-year-old children, not one knew the day of the week.

A similar state of affairs can be found in the reincarnation literature. Wilson (1982) reported that hypnotically elicited reports of being reincarnated varied as a direct function of the hypnotist's beliefs about reincarnation. In comparing the reports of two British lay hypnotists, he noted that, for both, most of their clients remained British when a hypnotic age regression procedure was used to induce a prior life. Further, such hypnotically elicited reincarnations did not extend beyond the 16th century. The hypnotists differed though in one major respect — one of them elicited reincarnations nine months after the death of a previous persona; the clients of the other often took as many as 70 years before a new persona emerged.

There were further differences when these two British practitioners were compared with the reports of clients of three other hypnosis reincarnationists (one Welsh and two Americans). Their clients reported prior lives in Ancient Egypt and Tibet and there was "a distinct silence from less fashionable civilizations such as the Hittites, the Assyrians or the Scythians" (Wilson, 1982, p. 90). Clearly, demand characteristics (Orne, 1959) play a major role in fashioning the type of reincarnation report that a hypnotized subject provides. As will be seen, however, reports of reincarnation cannot be dismissed entirely in terms of the alternative hypothesis of demand characteristics.

A final problem in evaluating the reports of reincarnation by hypnotically age regressed subjects is provided by Kampman and Hirvenoja (1978). Two subjects were regressed to a previous life on two occasions separated by a seven-year interval. For the first subject, five different reincarnated personae were found on the first occasion and seven different ones on the second occasion seven years later. Not one of the seven personae found on the second occasion matched any of those found on the first. For the other subject, eight personae were produced on both occasions, and an additional four of them on the second one. The authors concluded that the current needs of the individual were reflected in the reincarnated personae that they reported, in terms of both realistic details reported and emotional experiences. Taken together, these observations suggest that reports of reincarnation should not be taken at face value; it is important to evaluate both the beliefs of the hypnotist *and* the needs and beliefs of the hypnotized subject who reports an experience of reincarnation during age regression.

Three Attempts to Document Cases of Reincarnation

Although most reports of reincarnation show no evidence of an attempt to verify hypnotically elicited verbal reports by independent means, a few do. The very first report (Bernstein, 1956) involved quite major attempts, by the media, to verify the hypnotically regressed reports of Ms. Virginia Tighe of Pueblo, Colorado. She reported that, in a previous existence, she was Bridey Murphy, who was born in Cork, Ireland in 1778, and died in 1864 by falling down stairs and breaking some bones in her hip. The year of her death coincided with the year that the Irish first began to take census records; thus investigators of her claim were obliged to search primarily through church records.

Despite extensive attempts, no evidence was ever found that Bridey Murphy, her father, Duncan Murphy (a Protestant Cork barrister), or her mother, Kathleen, existed at the time. There was no record found of her having married a Catholic, Sean Brian Joseph McCarthy in a Protestant ceremony when she was aged 20, and indeed, no evidence of his existence. She recounted that they moved to Belfast, where McCarthy attended law school and eventually taught law at Queen's University. Again, no evidence was found for these events. They were remarried in a Catholic ceremony during this period, at St. Theresa's Church by Father John Joseph Gorman. There is no record of the second marriage, and none of either the Church or the officiating priest. Ducasse (1970) points out that none of these points has ever been established, but argues that the evidence supports the reality of Ms. Tighe's hypnotically elicited recall. This conclusion was based, however, on a number of smaller details which were verified, though often circumstantially.

By contrast, it has been reported (Gardner, 1957) that a Chicago newspaper found a Mrs. Anthony Corkell, an Irish widow who had lived across the street from Ms. Tighe during the latter's childhood. Interestingly, Mrs. Corkell's maiden name was Bridie Murphy. Further, a high school teacher recalled that Ms. Tighe was highly active in the school drama society and was particularly impressive playing Irish roles. These, and other points raised by Gardner (1957) may suggest a number of alternative interpretations of this case. From a strictly scientific perspective, however, a failure to find evidence for an hypothesis, in this case one of reincarnation, does not mean that the hypothesis is false — simply that the primary evidence has not been found. This is especially so, given that the investigation was conducted by the news media, rather than by scientific investigators.

The same can be said of a Canadian case (Stearn, 1969) in which an Ontario high school girl, Joanne McIver, emerged as Susan Ganier in a hypnosis session conducted by her father. Her verbal report was that she was born in 1819, that her parents were Catherina and Mason Ganier, that she had a brother called Ruben, and that she lived at Massie, Ontario. She married a farmer, Thomas Marrow, who died in the late 1800s as a result of accidental stabbing by a pitchfork. She died, a childless widow, in 1903.

As with Bridey Murphy, some minor aspects of her recollections were verified independently. There was a village called Massie at the time which consisted of 200 residents and a horseshoe factory; it no longer appears on maps, though the name was still used by local residents at the time of Stearn's report. In addition, her father located an 80-year-old man who signed an affidavit that he had known a Susan Marrow. Further, in hypnosis, Susan mentioned that the local post mistress at a neighboring village of Anan was named Mrs. Speedie; her tombstone was located in the local graveyard.

As with Bridey Murphy, also, no evidence for the existence of Susan Ganier, Thomas Marrow, and her immediate family has ever been found; this is attributed to the fact that a fire at the Town Hall of nearby Owen Sound in the late 1880s destroyed most of the local records. Again, the lack of positive evidence for reincarnation renders this case neutral with respect to the reality of such phenomena.

A final case (Roby, 1975; Stevenson, 1976) involved Dolores Jay, wife of the Reverend Carol Jay, who, when hypnotized by him, became Gretchen Gottleib. She reported that she was the daughter of the Burgermeister of Ebeswalde, now in East Germany. Despite her father's social prominence, she did not attend school and could not read or write. She was murdered at age 16 by a group of soldiers during a period of religious conflict. In this case, records of both the Church and the village, dating from 1740, indicated that there never was a mayor of Eberswalde called Gottleib; in fact, no Gottleib family was ever listed in the Church records.

There is, however, one highly intriguing aspect to this final case. In response to her husband's questions in English, she replied in German, a language she denies ever having learned. Accounts of her linguistic fluency in German vary; Stevenson (1976), while noting errors in grammar, rated her German as "responsive"; that is, in his opinion she could give sensible answers to questions posed in German. By contrast, Roby (1975) a German-speaking U.P.I. journalist, characterized her German as at a Berlitz level. He noted, however, that she used words that were current in German a century ago which have since become archaic, as well as contemporary words that were not used a century ago. This puzzling issue of language acquisition leads to one final observation concerning hypnotically elicited reincarnation.

Source Amnesia and Reincarnation Reports

The phenomenon of source amnesia has been documented in some recent experimental reports (Evans, 1979; Evans & Thorn, 1966). It involves the tendency of some highly hypnotizable subjects to learn little known facts in hypnosis (such as the color of an amethyst when it is heated) and to be subsequently amnesic to the hypnotic context (or source) in which it was learned. Its occurrence is limited to highly hypnotizable subjects and its incidence has varied across studies, from 33% (Evans, 1979) to approximately 50% (Laurence et al., in press).

There are two reports in the reincarnation literature where a source amnesia hypothesis was investigated in an attempt to provide an alternative explanation of reincarnation reports. Hilgard (1977) describes a case of a college student who was hypnotized at a party and found himself in 19th century England, with a particularly detailed knowledge of the royal family. He became convinced that his experience was of genuine reincarnation. On careful interview that did not involve hypnosis, however, it transpired that, years earlier, he had studied the British royal family intensively, but had forgotten that he had done this. In the meantime, his interests had moved from literary to scientific pursuits.

Earlier, Lowes Dickinson (1911) reported to the British Society for Psychical Research the case of a woman who, when hypnotized by a physician, produced very detailed material suggesting that she had lived a prior life during the reign of King Richard II of England towards the end of the 14th century. She manifested detailed knowledge about members of the royal court and of the customs and costumes of that period. In the course of using a planchette (a type of ouija board) in Lowes Dickinson's presence to communicate with her previous persona, the source of this information was determined. The detailed knowledge of 14th century England had come from a book by Emily Holt entitled *The Countess Maude*, which she had read at the age of 12 years. This was confirmed in a subsequent hypnosis session. While these two reports are disappointing for proponents of reincarnation, they testify to the complexity of human cognitive processes. They indicate that quite complex material can become disassociated (Janet, 1889/ 1973) from the mainstream of consciousness, only to be retrieved and experienced as subjectively real when a procedure such as hypnosis is employed. Indeed, careful questioning of Mrs. Jay may have uncovered the source of her degree of fluency in German.

It is important that the main focus of this paper is understood. The authors are not in any way seeking to criticize the *belief* in reincarnation, which, as with a belief in an afterlife, is considered to be an acceptable belief. We criticize explicitly, however, the position that science has verified the truth of this belief. In order to verify the hypothesis of reincarnation, it would be necessary to demonstrate that hypnotically elicited verbal reports of reincarnation phenomena cannot be interpreted in terms of such alternative hypotheses as demand characteristics, implicit cueing, subjects' present-life beliefs/needs and source amnesia.

Most reports of these phenomena do not even attempt to examine their data in terms of these alternative hypotheses. On the few occasions when this has been done, such artifacts tend to have been found. The lesson from this may well be that it is important never to take verbal reports at face value, particularly when an age regression technique is employed. At the same time, there is evidence to suggest that reincarnation therapy may be helpful to some patients. In order to evaluate this final point, it is instructive to return to "animal magnetism," from which what we now call hypnosis developed. Franz Anton Mesmer believed that there was an invisible magnetic force or fluid in the atmosphere which he could harness and accumulate in his body and then transfer to the bodies of sick people. Although the existence of animal magnetism was never demonstrated, there is no question that Mesmer was able to obtain both cures and major alleviations of physical illnesses that had defied the attempts of the medical profession of this period. To argue as some do (Fiore, 1978) that therapeutic success with reincarnation therapy supports the hypothesis of reincarnation, is merely to return to Mesmer and to make a fatal link between effects and presumed causes.

References

Baker, S. R., & Boaz, D. (1983). The partial reformulation of a traumatic memory of a dental phobia during trance: A case study. *International Journal of Clinical and Experimental Hypnosis, 31,* 14–18.

Barnes, M. (Oct. 1982). *Hypnosis on trial*. London: British Broadcasting Corporation television program.

Bernheim, H. (1973). *Hypnosis and suggestion in psychotherapy*. New York: Aronson. (Originally published in 1888)

Bernstein, M. (1956). *The search for Bridey Murphy*. New York: Lancer.

Burnham, W. H. (1889). Memory, historically and experimentally considered. III. Paramnesia. *American Journal of Psychology, 2*, 431–464.

Ducasse, C. J. (1970). Bridey Murphy revisited. In M. Ebon (Ed.). *Reincarnation in the twentieth century* (pp. 84–112). New York: World Publishing.

Ellenberger, H. F. (1970). *The discovery of the unconscious: The history and evolution of dynamic psychiatry*. New York: Basic Books.

Evans, F. J. (1979). Contextual forgetting: Posthypnotic source amnesia. *Journal of Abnormal Psychology, 88*, 556–563.

Evans, F. J., & Thorn, W. A. F. (1966). Two types of post-hypnotic amnesia: Recall amnesia and source amnesia. *International Journal of Clinical and Experimental Hypnosis, 14*, 162–179.

Fiore, E. (1978). *You have been here before: A psychologist looks at past lives*. New York: Ballentine.

Flournoy, T. (1900). *Dés Indes à la planète Mars*. Paris: Editions du Seuil.

Gardner, M. (1957). *Fads and fallacies in the name of science*. New York: Dover.

Gill, M. M., & Brenman, M. (1959). *Hypnosis and related states*. New York: International Universities Press.

Hilgard, E. R. (1965). *Hypnotic susceptibility*. New York: Harcourt, Brace and World.

Hilgard, E. R. (1977). *Divided consciousness: Multiple controls in human thought and action*. New York: Wiley.

Hilgard, J. R. (1979). *Personality and hypnosis: A study of imaginative involvement* (2nd ed.). Chicago: University of Chicago Press. (First published in 1970)

Janet, P. (1973). *L'Automatisme psychologique*. Paris: Centre National de la Recherche Scientifique. (Originally published in 1889)

Kampman, R. & Hirvenoja, R. (1978). Dynamic relation of the secondary personality induced by hypnosis to the present personality. In F. H. Frankel & H. S. Zamansky (Eds.). *Hypnosis at its bicentennial: Selected papers* (pp. 183–188). New York: Plenum.

Laurence, J.-R., Nadon, R., Nogrady, H., & Perry, C. (in press). Duality, dissociation, and memory creation in highly hypnotizable subjects. *International Journal of Clinical and Experimental Hypnosis*.

Laurence, J.-R., & Perry, C. (1983). Hypnotically created memory among highly hypnotizable subjects. *Science, 222*, 523–524.

Lowes Dickinson, G. (1911). A case of emergence of a latent memory under hypnosis. *Proceedings of the Society for Psychical Research, 25*, 455–467.

Moss, P., with Keaton, J. (1981). *Encounters with the past: How man can experience and relive history*. Middlesex, England: Penguin.

O'Connell, D. N., Shor, R. E., & Orne, M. T. (1970). Hypnotic age regression: An empirical and methodological analysis. *Journal of Abnormal Psychology Monograph, 76* (3, Part 2), 1–32.

Orne, M. T. (1951). The mechanisms of hypnotic age regression: An empirical study. *Journal of Abnormal and Social Psychology, 46*, 213–225.

Orne, M. T. (1959). The nature of hypnosis: Artifact and essence. *Journal of Abnormal and Social Psychology, 58*, 277–299.

Orne, M. T. (1980). On the construct of hypnosis: How its definition affects research and its clinical application. In G. D. Burrows & L. Dennerstein (Eds.). *Handbook of hypnosis and psychosomatic medicine* (pp. 29–51). Amsterdam: Elsevier/North Holland.

Orne, M. T. (1982). Affidavit to the State Supreme Court of California on People v. Shirley (mimeo).

Perry, C. (1977). Is hypnotizability modifiable? *International Journal of Clinical and Experimental Hypnosis, 25*, 125–146.

Perry, C., & Laurence, J.-R. (1983). Hypnosis, surgery, and mind-body interaction: An historical evaluation. *Canadian Journal of Behavioral Science, 15*, 351–372.

Ramster, P. (1980). *The truth about reincarnation*. Adelaide, Australia: Rigby.

Reiser, M. (1980). *Handbook of investigative hypnosis*. Los Angeles: LEHI.

Roby, E. F. (Feb. 3, 1975). Another life emerges from "Gretchen's" mysterious past. *Montreal Gazette, Women's Entertainment, Classified*. p. 21.

Sarbin, T. R., & Coe, W. C. (1972). *Hypnosis: A social-psychological analysis of influence communication*. New York: Holt, Rinehart and Winston.

Spanos, N. P., & Barber, T. X. (1974). Toward a convergence in hypnosis research. *American Psychologist, 29*, 500–511.

Stalnaker, J. M., & Riddle, E. E. (1932). The effect of hypnosis on long-delayed memory. *Journal of General Psychology, 6*, 429–440.

Stearn, J. (1969). *The search for the girl with the blue eyes*. New York: Bantam.

Stevenson, I. (1976). A preliminary report of a new case of responsive xenoglassy: The case of Gretchen. *The Journal of the American Society for Psychical Research, 70*, 65–77.

Sutcliffe, J. P. (1961). "Credulous" and "skeptical" views of hypnotic phenomena: Experiments on esthesia, hallucination and delusion. *Journal of Abnormal and Social Psychology, 62*, 189–200.

True, R. M. (1949). Experimental control in hypnotic age regression states. *Science, 110*, 583–584.

Wambach, H. (1979). *Reliving past lives: The evidence under hypnosis*. New York: Bantam.

Wilson, I. (1982). *Reincarnation?* Suffolk, England: Penguin. (Originally published as *Mind out of Time?*, London: Gollancz, 1981)

Wilson, S. C., & Barber, T. X. (1983). The fantasy-prone personality: Implications for understanding imagery, hypnosis and parapsychological phenomena. In A. A. Sheikh (Ed.). *Imagery: Current theory, research, and application* (pp. 340–387). New York: Wiley.

Q&A 11 Permanence of Hypnotherapeutic Treatment

Question:

> I feel uncomfortable using hypnosis because symptoms seem to reappear with distressing frequency after they were presumably resolved. Is this generally the case?

Discussion by DAVID LIPSCHUTZ, Ph.D.

The question strikes me as akin to the old line, "When did you stop beating your wife?" Both are rhetorical. Although phrased as questions, implicit in each are a statement and a point of view. In the one it is that the one questioned is a wife-beater; in the other it is that hypnosis is transitory, superficial and ineffective. And, because both questions are really declarative, taken at face value they force a response that is either acquiescent or apologetic. Since neither is acceptable to me, I choose instead to take the two statement/questions head-on.

It has been my experience as a psychotherapist that when used appropriately (i.e., with the right patient and the right problem), hypnosis is at least as effective and as likely as any other psychotherapeutic technique to lead to a return of symptoms. This does not sound like much of a claim for hypnosis, but it is the best that can be made. Despite what the proponents of insight therapy, desensitization, counterconditioning, biofeedback or any of the dozens of other modalities proclaim, symptom recurrence is always a possibility. Likewise, there is no single, sure, foolproof royal road to recovery for all patients. And this, I believe, is the main point: Hypnosis cannot be singled out as somehow intrinsically faulty or deficient because patients sometimes suffer the return of symptoms or the treatment is sometimes ineffective. In the larger context, these are failings common in some degree to all psychotherapeutic techniques.

In regard to this whole question of symptom recurrence and the effectiveness of hypnotherapy, there is a phenomenon I have often observed that is worth mentioning. It concerns some so-called "failures."

In my work with college students who have test anxiety, there have been numerous instances where positive results have seemingly faded and the original condition (anxiety) has reasserted itself. Upon close study and over a prolonged period, I have found that this condition was itself transitory and that lasting benefits reappeared. Control of anxiety and its debilitating effects can apparently be gained through hypnosis, then lost, and then spontaneously return.

I have witnessed this same phenomenon with phobic cases. Common to all has been effective control or cure, followed by a reappearance of symptoms (e.g., obsessive thinking, anxiety, compulsive behavior), followed in turn by a disappearance of these symptoms.

I offer these experiences as partial refutation to the blanket charge against hypnosis that its effects are transitory and illusory. How often might we ourselves, as practitioners, underrate its effectiveness and write off as failures cures that may perhaps only become evident after the termination of treatment?

I can cite case after case of impressive results achieved by my patients through the use of hypnosis, but perhaps a closer clinical look at one case would be instructive of its effectiveness and permanence.

Florence, a 36-year-old mother of two, recently remarried after having been a widow for ten years, was referred to me by her physician. An agoraphobic in every sense of the term as described by Papalia and Olds (1985), she rarely left her home. On those few occasions when she did, to go shopping or to a restaurant or movie, she was invariably seized by overwhelming panic and anxiety, manifested by such symptoms as shortness of breath, hyperventilation, dizziness, profuse sweating, and rapid heartbeat. An overwhelming sense of impending death from heart failure would take hold of her and she would be gripped by panic. "The strain on my system is enormous," she said, "it feels like any moment I am going to collapse and die." She had, in fact, been taken by ambulance to hospitals at least four times after losing consciousness in public places. Other times she had gone to the emergency room because she believed she was dying.

The obsessive-compulsive aspect of Florence's disorder is best illustrated by her description of a typical evening at home. Because of her fear of being alone should she need help, she went to elaborate lengths to insure that someone was always with her. As her husband was a fireman, periodically working the night shift, this would involve feeding her 11- and 14-year-old sons as late as possible to delay their bedtime, pressing them to watch television late into the night, and, if they fell asleep, staying in continuous telephone contact with her mother.

The depth of Florence's dread and morbid apprehension can be gauged by her own words: "Even with the kids keeping me company, every time I hear a siren I look outside to see if the ambulance is going or coming. I keep worrying, will one be here if I need it? If I'm dying, will it get here on time?"

A troubled and anxious state, so characteristic of agoraphobia, had affected other aspects of Florence's life: She suffered insomnia; she found it difficult to relate even to her few close friends; her relationship with her husband was increasingly strained; and she hovered over her children, overprotecting them from imagined calamities.

Florence's treatment presented more than the usual problems. Just getting to my office was one of them. At first she came accompanied by her two sons and with a friend who drove her. The simple act of conversing privately with a stranger in unfamiliar surroundings put a great strain on her and she evidenced it in bodily signs with facial tics, continual movement and frequent sudden inhalations. In addition, all of the myths and bugaboos surrounding hypnosis hung in her preconscious. Most of the early sessions were devoted to lowering Florence's anxiety through explanation, answering questions and building a trusting relationship.

At home, Florence practiced Jacobson's (1938) relaxation techniques frequently and diligently, soon becoming very skilled. This led to a first attempt at induction, which served by its failure to teach me a valuable lesson. It was that I could not use many of the usual catch-words commonly used during induction (e.g., "drifting down," "deeper," "breathing getting slower"). All had highly charged emotional and morbid connotations for her. So, too, did the act of eye closure.

To meet the former problem, I learned to substitute "neutral" and less threatening words; to meet the latter, Florence simply kept her eyes open. Only afterwards, when she began feeling sufficiently secure to experiment did she close them, and then I instructed her to open them whenever she felt anxious and needed to reassure herself that she was in control.

By the third week I was able to induce a relatively deep trance. Using imagery that Florence found relaxing, I sought to build her feelings of mastery and control in anxiety-producing situations. A beach scene and floating on a low-flying cloud were her favorite scenes. Gradually, using Wolpe's (1961) principles of desensitization, I introduced image-specific situations arranged in a hierarchy. The reduction in anxiety that resulted carried over effectively to Florence's real-life situations and she was able to shop, go on bus and subways, and socialize. The more she did, the more confident and free of symptoms she became.

Once implanted, the effect of the imaginal desensitization procedure generalized into other of her problem areas. She began to sleep better, to tolerate being alone, to obsess less and less on morbid topics and, in her estimation, "to feel one hundred percent better mentally and physically." After eight weeks of therapy and for the first time in 12 years, Florence was almost entirely free of the agoraphobic syndrome. At this writing, 22 months after termination of therapy, she remains almost symptom-free. ("Every once in a while in a new situation," she reports, "I will feel anxiety building up, but I am able to control it now.")

I have gone into detail in the preceding case to emphasize the potency and effectiveness of hypnosis in treating pathological symptoms. There has been virtually no return of symptoms and, after almost two years, the likelihood of return is small.

To summarize, on the basis of this rather typical illustrative case and my clinical experience, hypnosis is not merely a palliative but often a cure, and symptoms treated by hypnosis do not necessarily return.

References

Jacobson, E. (1938). *Progressive relaxation*. Chicago: University of Chicago Press.

Papalia, E., & Olds, W. (1985). *Psychology*. New York: McGraw-Hill.

Wolpe, J. (1961). The systematic desensitization of neuroses. *Journal of Nervous and Mental Disease, 132*, 189–203.

SECTION III Preparing for Hypnosis

Almost every human endeavor is influenced, for better or for worse, by the manner in which the participants have been prepared for the event. Almost every thoughtful practitioner, no matter what his position in the healing arts, is aware of this. In matters as simple as prescribing a pill, patient compliance is enhanced if the patient is informed of the reasons for the pill being prescribed, the benefits expected, and if he is given reassurance about any possible side-effects. The prescriber's enthusiasm, or lack thereof, has such a powerful influence on the ultimate effectiveness of the prescription that all researchers have learned that *double* blind tests are required to yield any valid information about the worth of the pill compared to a placebo.

In matters as complicated as major surgery, the mental preparation of the patient has much to do with his/her anxiety prior to surgery and the rate of recovery following it. This same principle applies to all other procedures, including the use of hypnotherapy.

But where does preparation begin when we use hypnosis? It seems that some patients are adequately prepared at the time they make the first call for the first appointment. Perhaps prior experiences, readings, talks with friends who have been hypnotized, or fertile imagination have given them an accepting or even an enthusiastic attitude. What the patient hears over the phone when he or she calls for the appointment, the appearance of the office, the appearance and mannerisms of the therapist all contribute to the patient's attitude when hypnotherapy is suggested. Beyond this, the manner in which hypnotherapy is brought up has a powerful effect on the patient's acceptance.

In this section some of the more important aspects are discussed, ranging from general approaches useful for the average patient to specific approaches applicable to patients who present particular problems. Although our contributors offer specific words to be used for those particular problems, the careful reader will notice that the authors' respect for and consideration of the patients' concerns are as important, perhaps, as the words used.

$\underset{A}{\overset{Q}{\varepsilon}}$ 12 Presentation of
Doctor and Office to
Facilitate Hypnosis

Question:

I know that the way in which a doctor presents himself to patients is important in establishing hypnotic rapport. I imagine that the office setting, the attitude of the staff, and other factors are also important, but I've never heard them discussed. What can you tell me about this?

Discussion by JEFF STONE, D.M.D.

It is my opinion that hypnosis begins long before a doctor has contact with the patient. The events surrounding the person's calling for and scheduling an appointment, arriving at the office, viewing the reception room, and meeting the staff constitute the beginning steps of hypnosis. I also believe that the time between a person's calling for the appointment and finally meeting the doctor presents an opportunity to facilitate treatment and establish a satisfying and cooperative relationship with the patient. On the other hand, these preparatory events can be handled in such a way that the patient becomes difficult for both doctor and staff.

The doctor who is a family friend, spending hours counseling and treating the patient throughout his life, is rapidly disappearing. The health care fields and offices are not what they used to be. The reality is that few of us can answer our phones, supply our offices, and do all the required paperwork without trained assisting staff. Although they bring problems of their own, staff allow us to treat more patients by freeing us from the business tasks.

All of us at times are forced to use answering services or answering machines, but when a caller in distress reaches a trained staff person, a valuable opportunity exists. If the same person reaches an impersonal answering machine or an uninterested answering service, he or she may never call again. This patient needs a person on the line who can develop a positive, hypnotic context that will help reduce apprehension and set the stage for effective treatment.

When we make the decision to have assisting staff members, it is essential that we are aware that they are the main conduit between us and our patients. Furthermore, since they will usually be the first ones to communicate with our patients, assisting staff must be trained to speak in a positive hypnotic manner. If we neglect to do the training, it becomes a toss-up whether a positive, negative, or neutral relationship will result.

Let's consider what occurs when a person is making an appointment with the doctor. First, he is probably experiencing physical distress with an accompanying emotional component. People normally are reluctant to see a doctor unless they are in pain. If they do not have a doctor with whom they are familiar, it is more likely that the appointment will be postponed as long as possible. The longer the person delays seeking treatment, the greater the chances the symptoms will become acute. The more acute the symptoms, the higher the degree of stress. At some point the patient is forced to focus his attention on his problem. The level of stress that the patient has been experiencing is directly related to the depth of trance the patient has probably already entered. If he is not already in trance, his potential for easily entering one is strong.

Although there are many definitions of hypnotic trance, I consider it to be a receptive state on a continuum of consciousness. In fact, I generally categorize hypnosis into two basic forms. One form is the formal patient-doctor trance, where both patient and doctor are aware of its use. The second, informal type utilizes the patient's existing level of trance. During informal hypnosis, the patient is not consciously aware of its use.

When stress becomes a factor, the level of trance is likely to deepen. The patient in greatest need of an appointment is often under the most stress and is likely to be the most suggestible. His thinking processes tend to be literal, direct, and somewhat paranoid. He tends to move slowly and hold new body positions, even though they may be uncomfortable. His facial muscles are flattened out, his eyes are opened and it seems he does not focus on objects. Speech tends to be slow and without inflection. These are all signs of hypnotic trance.

It is interesting and sometimes important to note how far patients have traveled to reach your office. By this I am referring to how patients have decided to call *your* office as opposed to another doctor's office. If they are referred by a satisfied patient or a fellow doctor, the stress level tends to be lower and the trust level higher, since they have a recommendation and some second-hand knowledge of your staff, how your office functions, and most important, how you relate to your patients. Patients who come from phone book referrals and neighborhood walk-ins tend to be a little more difficult than the previous group, but they have had the opportunity to do some screening of you and your office. They have either gained information from your written office description or are already comfortable in the neighborhood in which you practice. This screening and information process is the first step in reducing stress and facilitating the development of a positive hypnotic context.

An entirely new and more difficult group of patients has developed in the last few years. They come to your office as a result of direct advertising and marketing. These patients are often the most skeptical, have usually waited the longest to call, have at best very little knowledge of your office, and thus have the highest stress. They arrive with a deep need to be cared for, and high levels of apprehension and discomfort. These patients are at a pivotal stage. Their first contact with your office is the most critical.

Your staff can develop either a positive or a negative hypnotic context. Assuming a negative hypnotic context is developed, let's look at what the results might be. Experience has taught me that a new patient, during the initial phone conversation, may choose not to make an appointment at all, or he may accept an appointment but not show up. Frequently, he may arrive late and/or display hostility towards both you and your staff. He may also find reasons, consciously and unconsciously, for not responding favorably to treatment. He may simply allow you to treat his emergency and never return. On the other hand, if a positive hypnotic context is developed, the patient's subconscious is working with you to facilitate the treatment and produce a more successful outcome.

In my general dental office, staff members have the first contact with new patients. In other offices this may vary, but something useful can apply. I train my staff to speak in positive hypnotic context. We find this increases patient cooperation and trust on both conscious and unconscious levels. It facilitates my treatment by reducing environmental stress, and most importantly, it starts building a relationship that works for the patient. I find that treatment is more successful, with fewer postoperative problems, when the patient feels comfortable on both a conscious and unconscious level, allowing him to truly accept my help.

Let me demonstrate how our office handles the first phone contact. When a new patient calls, he or she must be given at least five minutes of uninterrupted attention. In general, all phones are answered in the following way: "Good morning, Dr. Stone's office. This is Margie. How may I help you?"

These sentences contain: first, a positive greeting; second, an identification to let callers know they have reached the correct office; third, the first name of the person answering so that personal contact is established; and fourth, and most importantly, the question, "How may I help you?" The "how" implies that I am going to help, the "may I" implies that I am going to help you with your permission, and that all that is required is for you to tell me what you need. If a staff member does not have adequate time to spend with a new patient, she acknowledges this and asks permission to return the call within a specific period of time, not to exceed 15 minutes.

I feel that the patient has extended himself, often under stress, and deserves a response as soon as possible. To delay this response begins a negative hypnotic context, indicating that we are too busy to help him. If the patient cannot wait, our staff member delays her responsibilities in order to work immediately with him. During this five- to 10-minute conversation, besides obtaining name, address and phone number, Margie listens to the patient's needs and fears and jots them down for future reference.

If the patient is in physical discomfort, Margie evaluates the severity of the problem and attends to this first. Under all circumstances, a person's emergency need, whether real or imagined, must be a priority. Margie at this point will interject suggestions similar to the following: "Dr. Stone has helped many of our patients with similar problems." "Many patients are surprised how comfortable it is." "How did you find out about us? From your description, you've certainly contacted the right office." These sentences contain numerous positive suggestions, both direct and indirect. We assume the patient is in trance and speak to him as one would to a person who is highly suggestible.

If the patient is not in discomfort, it does not mean that he is not under stress and thus not in a suggestible state. Margie will still include positive suggestions, both direct and indirect, within the conversation.

When the patient arrives for the first appointment, Margie is sitting facing the reception room. To the staff as well as the patients, it is the "reception room" because its function is to receive, not to keep people waiting. I find this name change has engendered a corresponding attitude change. My staff and I become uncomfortable when patients are kept waiting more than 10 minutes.

Margie leaves her desk, establishes eye contact, and greets the patient by name as he enters the room: "Welcome, Mr. Jones. How well are you today?" This is not a casual greeting. The eye contact, the recognition of Margie's voice, and the use of his name begin transferring the telephone relationship into the office. Margie continues by asking, "How easy was it to find our office? Would you like coffee or tea?" Having previously referred to her notes from the phone conversation, Margie becomes more specific in her questions about how the patient is feeling. She also discusses the patient's fears, keeping the communication open while learning more specifics. Later, when the patient is moved by Anne to the operatory, this personal information is transmitted via Margie to Anne and me. This informs us what areas need specific attention for this patient.

During this introductory conversation, Margie automatically includes the name of Anne, our dental assistant. Where appropriate, she will repeat suggestions similar to the ones used in the initial phone conversation, interjecting my name and any staff person's name that the patient will meet during that appointment. She often uses photos from our bulletin board to introduce us and shares our recent newsletter to help acquaint the patient with our practice.

Using a personally written newsletter is new to our office, and I believe it will be valuable. We are using it to introduce our staff, communicate what new treatments are available, and give an overall impression of our commitment to patient care. It also allows us to communicate and answer many questions for all our patients simultaneously. The newsletter will be published on a quarterly basis.

Our reception room's bulletin board contains two important items. One section of the bulletin board contains the "Patient-of-the-Month," and the remainder has photos from our most recent Flying Doctors trip into Mexico. The "Patient-of-the-Month" section is comprised of before and after photographs of a dramatic cosmetic change in a patient's smile. These photos clearly show to patients what is possible and what we are capable of doing. The Flying Doctors section shows photos of our staff volunteering our professional care to the villagers of Sonora, Mexico. Our volunteer service in Mexico has a powerful impact on both staff and patients. It demonstrates to our patients, many of whom have origins south of the border, that we are committed to patient care regardless of financial rewards. It also opens up lines of communication. The excitement generated by the staff's participation in these trips has been infectious throughout our office. Many patients have offered unsolicited donations and assistance to this organization.

During this introductory period, patients are asked to fill out their medical history form. If questions arise, Margie will suggest, at some point, that Anne can respond to that question more effectively, and asks if the patient is willing to discuss it with her. Only rarely does she receive a negative response. If a negative response does occur, Margie continues to reinforce the transfer of trust from herself to Anne. For example, patients will ask, "Is the injection painful?" Although Margie can easily respond to this, she may choose this vehicle to transfer the patient to Anne. When it becomes appropriate, Anne enters the reception room. Margie will introduce her to the patient and Anne will establish physical contact by either a handshake or a guiding touch on the shoulder. This helps prepare the patient for physical contact encountered during treatment.

In our communication with our patients, wherever possible we refrain from direct commands. For example, we ask, "Would you please come this way?" or "Would you please fill out this form for the doctor?" Although there is an implied request, we always wait for patients' responses rather than assume they will say yes. This establishes on many levels that the patient is still in control. Except for a few carefully worded statements, each staff person can develop her own style of positive hypnotic communication. For example, Anne has a down-home style of expressing herself that makes everyone feel comfortable. As with formal hypnosis, natural abilities can enhance any methodology, so look to your staff's natural assets and strive to incorporate them.

Anne then brings the new patient into the operatory and seats him while continuing to discuss subjects other than dentistry. She will later log personal information onto our data sheets for future reference. At some point I unobtrusively join the conversation, making every effort to keep the patient at ease. I seat myself directly across from the patient at eye level, introduce myself making eye contact, and shake hands to reinforce the use of touch. At this point I begin reviewing the patient's history, preferably without interruptions. Realistically, interruptions do occur and I always request the patient's permission to leave the room. This respects his emotional rights, maintains a positive hypnotic context, and creates mutual respect.

An example of the effectiveness of developing a positive hypnotic context is demonstrated by one of my recent patients. He is a 31-year-old male presenting with a chief complaint of severe needle phobia and repeated fainting on injections. Margie, during her phone conversation with him, discussed this problem while interspersing positive hypnotic suggestions. She included, "You might be pleasantly surprised . . . ," "I used to have a problem with injections, but it no longer occurs with Dr. Stone," and "We have helped many people like yourself become comfortable."

Prior to his arrival, Margie had made Anne and me aware of the situation. Margie reinforced the positive hypnotic suggestions and carefully introduced the patient to our office prior to introducing Anne. Margie knew that under no circumstances, except an emergency, was I to be interrupted during this appointment. She adjusted the office schedule to allow an appropriate time.

Anne was prepared with a topical anesthetic and a 30 gauge needle. She knew that extra care was needed to keep the instrument setup and the syringe out of the patient's view. We were now fully prepared to treat this patient, knowing that this appointment would play a major role in his attitude toward his future appointments.

This patient was so well prepared by my staff that most of my hypnotic work was already done. I did a basic eye closure technique with suggestions that he would notice what was around him but that it didn't have to bother him at all. With each exhalation, he would allow as much tension to drift off as he would like. I explained to him that this experience was his own and that I was simply a guide; that there was nothing to bother him, nothing to disturb him, and nothing to do except to continue to become more comfortable. I spent approximately two minutes prior to giving him a mandibular block injection. The patient was so relaxed that I couldn't even detect contraction of any facial muscles during the injection. After the procedure, he was very surprised that he had overcome his phobia. All subsequent visits were handled easily. I believe this behavior can generalize to another dentist if he is treated carefully.

Subliminal hypnotic communication can be an extremely effective tool. This form of communication occurs whether we are aware of it or not, but once we develop awareness, we can use it for constructive ends. One example to consider is the effect your college degrees have if placed where patients can see them. These degrees provide both a very strong direct suggestion that you are an authority in your field and a more subliminal suggestion that you are a good practitioner. The majority of patients get a strong placebo effect from the proper placement of diplomas and awards.

Another interesting communication is the way doctors write prescriptions for analgesics. I was taught to write "prn pain." This suggests on many levels that pain is expected. In hypnosis we usually avoid use of the word "pain" and replace it with "comfort" or "comfortable." I now write "Take as needed for comfort" on my analgesic prescriptions.

Patients are often influenced by many things seemingly too obvious to even mention, such as the way the office looks, the way we dress, and so on. In our office, the manner in which we dress and even the magazines available in the reception room are carefully chosen to allow the patient the greatest degree of comfort. For example, we keep only recent issues of magazines, implying that our techniques and everything else about us are likely to be up to date.

Preoperative and postoperative instructions are another area of consideration. Standard procedure is to mention the possibility of numbness of lip or tongue, infection, bleeding, and swelling and pain following extractions. We are presently trying something different. We suggest that patients may be surprised how comfortable they are and they might notice one side more than the other. Although we write prescriptions "prn comfort," we suggest patients don't spend the money to fill the prescription because they probably won't need it. There is the important issue of informed consent, of course, but each of us must evaluate for ourselves the legal risks involved versus the effect of negative hypnotic suggestions to our patients.

Although most of us are not psychologists, we still can attend to our patients' basic needs. We can work to develop the most positive hypnotic relationship possible, so that patients can be treated in the most effective and comfortable ways. This is good for patients and good for us.

Q&A 13 Describing Hypnosis to Patients

Question:

> Although I've used hypnosis for many years, I'm never sure what to tell patients about it. I use all the words I've learned — relaxation, focused attention, unconscious mind, right hemisphere, etc. — but I'm embarrassed by them since I'm not sure I believe them myself. What is a good and accurate way of describing hypnosis to patients?

Discussion by HERBERT MANN, M.D.

Tremendous progress has been made in establishing hypnosis as an effective medical procedure for treating a vast array of emotional conflicts, psychogenic and psychosomatic disorders. However, despite intense interest in hypnosis as a therapeutic modality, outmoded ideas and misunderstandings persist. The striking character of the trance state, with its bewildering phenomena and aura of the unreal and supernatural, serves to foster its use by charlatans, stage hypnotists, and healing ministries. The attitude of the general public is markedly influenced by the exploitation of hypnosis as an entertainment medium and as a mystical pseudo-religious rite. Therefore, at times it is incumbent upon therapists to discuss the true nature of medical hypnosis, to dispel erroneous beliefs, and to offer a realistic program for the utilization of hypnosis in therapy.

Before deciding upon a good way to describe hypnosis to patients, perhaps one should consider why one wants to give them a description in the first place. There are those practitioners who never describe it, leading their patients into hypnotic trance without telling them that this is what is being done. At the other extreme there are those practitioners who give a full and complete description without being asked, thus expending considerable time, but perhaps accomplishing little more than the establishment of their own expertise on this subject. There is no body of evidence to indicate that one extreme is superior to the other.

Between the two extremes are those practitioners who ask the patient if there is anything he or she would like to know about hypnosis and then give an explanation in accord with the patient's request. If no questions are asked, this could be considered an indication that the patient is signifying his/her readiness to enter the trance state. Any unrequested explanations would merely serve to jeopardize that readiness. My own preference is to meet the needs of each patient, to answer any questions, and to emphasize the fact that hypnosis is not a stereotyped ritual that involves sleep, but rather a special kind of communication.

Among the more frequently asked questions are: What is it? How does it work? Will I do those outrageous stunts I've seen at stage shows? Are you sure I'll wake up again? Following are some of the ways I describe these and various other aspects of hypnosis.

For those who wish to know what hypnosis is, I describe it as a special state of awareness and heightened suggestibility. It is a form of communication that increases motivation and the ability to control psychophysiological responses and behavior. It is a pathway to the subconscious mind, the seat of emotions, feelings, sensations, and habit patterns.

To dispel any aura of the mystical, I explain that hypnosis is a natural phenomenon experienced in everyday life. For example, self-hypnosis may spontaneously develop while engrossed in a movie. Absorbed in a television program, a sports enthusiast may become oblivious to his wife's presence or her comments about a new dress or hairstyle. People in church, eyes focused on the cross, and lulled by organ music or the minister's voice, frequently experience daydreamy trances, drifting off into states of mental and physical relaxation.

Unfortunately, the general public's exposure to hypnosis is usually limited to its misuse by stage hypnotists and pseudo-religious faith healers. This leads to concerns about losing control and being under the influence of another. To allay such concerns I define hetero-hypnosis as a unique type of interaction between two people, a hypnotist (therapist) and a subject (patient). This relationship is entirely voluntary. There can be no hypnosis without the co-operation of the patient. Control of the trance state rests with the person being hypnotized. In hypnosis the patient may accept, reject, or modify suggestions. He may be immobile or move about, he may maintain a serious attitude or smile, giggle, or laugh; he may communicate verbally and/or nonverbally; and he may terminate the trance at any time if he so desires.

Performing under dramatic circumstances, stage hypnotists and religious healers attract naive, highly suggestible subjects who are prime candidates for somnambulistic behavior because of their distorted expectations and belief in the omnipotence of the hypnotist. Under those circumstances, these self-selected subjects do respond to suggestions as if they had no will of their own. In a professional environment, however, the therapist neither selects his patients nor surrounds himself with the drama of the stage or ministry. Consequently, somnambulism is relatively rare during early stages of treatment.

Patients who expect to behave like subjects on the stage are often disappointed and disillusioned when they do not achieve deep levels of trance and the expected loss of awareness of what is going on about them. They may even complain that they were not hypnotized because they were aware of their surroundings and heard everything said by the therapist. Blame may be directed toward the therapist for being incompetent or toward themselves for being unhypnotizable. I explain that if they could not hear the therapist they could not follow his suggestions, and if the subjects on the stage were not aware of their surroundings, they could not leap upon a table, stretch out between two chairs, or do whatever else was demanded of them.

When indicated, this easily leads into a discussion of other common misconceptions about hypnosis, the most common of which is that it is a sleep state, with no more awareness than that experienced in normal sleep. I point out that the hypnotized patient does not lose his ability to hear, but he does learn to become less and less involved with extraneous sounds and distractions and to focus more attention on suggestions of the therapist. Because of this, background noises gradually diminish and may even fade away. As the trance deepens there will be a tendency to accept ideas and experiences that will effect appropriate changes in responses and behavior. Far from being asleep, however, the patient will learn to communicate with the therapist verbally and nonverbally. In that way, the stage is set for the patient to talk about emotions and feelings at a subconscious level of awareness.

To further differentiate between hypnosis and sleep, I tell patients that eye closure is not an essential part of trance. With open eyes they can continue to develop deeper levels of trance and respond just as well as with eyes closed.

Another misconception that may cause some anxiety and resistance is a fear of remaining in trance in the event of the sudden illness or death of the hypnotist. Assurance can be given that the hypnotic relationship is a cooperative one. If anything occurs to disturb that relationship, within a few minutes the patient will come out of the trance. Along the same line, some patients worry about drifting out of range of the hypnotist's voice, especially if they are regressing to a period of their lives prior to the time that they first met the therapist. They can be reassured that the therapist's voice will go with them wherever they are, and, in any event, they are in control and may return to the present time and place whenever they wish.

If the patient wonders if he will remember the information he gave during the trance, I assure him that amnesia, the inability to remember what transpired, is actually quite uncommon. Most experimental evidence points to the fact that remembering or forgetting depends partly upon the expectations of the subject and largely on the need for retaining or discarding memories. Posthypnotic amnesia, when indicated in therapy, may be induced selectively by appropriate suggestions, but again, the suggestions will be followed only if the subject has no objections to them.

In laying a foundation for hypnotic techniques, I teach patients, in simple terms, how and why we behave as we do. We all function at two levels of awareness, the conscious and the subconscious. The conscious mind is the intellectual mind, the part of the mind that was used by the patient in deciding to make an appointment with the therapist. The subconscious mind came into play as the patient entered his automobile and, without conscious effort, performed all those intricate tasks of driving his automobile while thinking of the approaching appointment.

The subconscious mind automatically controls most of our activities, our emotions, feelings, sensations, and habits. Throughout our lives we are exposed to new learnings and experiences that become imprinted in the subconscious mind. For example, early in life, we learn at an intellectual, conscious level how to count, how to add, subtract, and multiply. Through repetition, the subconscious becomes imprinted with that information so that we find ourselves automatically proficient in dealing with those learnings. In the same way, the subconscious mind is responsible for the ease with which we automatically tie a shoe lace, button a shirt, nod our heads when thinking positively, frown when confused, or clinch our fists when angry.

Habits that we develop are, for the most part, extremely useful to us. In doing many things automatically, we save a great deal of time and energy. Occasionally, we find ourselves with a habit pattern that we would like to modify or eliminate. Hypnosis is a pathway to the subconscious and can be utilized to make appropriate changes in behavior. In a state of heightened suggestibility we focus attention on new ideas, new learnings, and new experiences that are imprinted in the subconscious and become automatic responses.

Before, or sometimes after, all the above explanations, some patients wonder about their ability to be hypnotized. I assure them that hypnosis is a learning process and that any intelligent person can cooperate in developing a trance state. Testing patients for hypnotizability is an academic exercise that is of little or no help in determining how a patient will respond within a therapeutic relationship. A patient who scores low on standardized, impersonal receptivity tests like eye fixation may respond very well to an informal, naturalistic, indirect induction technique. If a therapist assumes that a poor response to standardized induction procedures indicates the patient's inability to use hypnosis effectively, the patient may become the victim of a self-fulfilling prophecy. Hypnotizability is an ever changing phenomenon contingent upon intrapsychic and interpersonal relationships that vary with each hypnotic session.

In summary, hypnosis should be presented as an art of interpersonal relationship that arouses and activates introspection. It is a special state of awareness that increases the capacity to respond to ideas. It is a technique that offers the opportunity and freedom to accept help in changing behavior and certain physiological processes. It lends itself to the type of psychotherapy that involves guidance, reassurance, persuasion, and the rediscovery of forgotten aspects of one's personal history, all done in an atmosphere of genuine interest and enthusiasm.

Q&A 14 Patients Fearful of Hypnosis

Question:

Occasionally I see a patient who is afraid of hypnosis but for whom I think hypnosis would be beneficial. What is the best way of dealing with a patient like this?

Discussion by ALEXANDER A. LEVITAN, M.D., & RONNA JEVNE, Ph.D.

Patients vary in the degree and specific nature of their reluctance and fear. Most anxiety is grounded in one of several sources: misconceptions, unfamiliarity, negative expectancy or vested interest.

The most common *misconceptions* of patients prior to their experiencing hypnosis for the first time include:

a) The expectation that the patient will be asleep, and thus, unaware of the proceeding.
b) Something is "done to" the subject by the operator.
c) "Control" is surrendered to the operator.
d) Certain patients may be unable to come out of trance.
e) Hypnosis can cause the revelation of personal secrets against one's will.

The patient may feel totally *unfamiliar* with the experience of hypnosis and consequently be apprehensive. When the mystery is dispelled through discussion or association with familiar experiences, anxiety is reduced. For example, it is useful to point out to patients seeking hypnotherapy for the first time that they already know how to use self-hypnosis by virtue of the fact that their unconscious mind operates to block awareness of needless sensations, such as the shoes on their feet, the glasses on their head, or the watch on their wrist. Patients perceive that their skin has not ceased to feel these objects, but their unconscious mind has chosen not to bring these sensations to continuous conscious awareness. They can then be told that this is analogous to the use of hypnosis to turn off the sensation of pain or to reduce the need to smoke or to experience anxiety under certain circumstances.

An alternative experience association which has been well received by hypnotherapy patients is that of going to the movies. When seated in a theater surrounded by many other people, an individual can choose to focus his attention either on the other theater patrons or on the screen, shutting out awareness of the surroundings. The movie patron may find himself laughing or crying, oblivious to the reactions of his neighbors. The patient may be advised that this may occur in hypnosis as well. It may also be pointed out that the individual is usually fully awake during the viewing of the movie, just as he is in hypnosis. Despite careful attention to the movie, it is still possible for an individual to have extraneous thoughts occasionally entering his mind without necessarily detracting from the enjoyment of the movie. So, too, it is possible to have one's thoughts wander from the specific imagery employed in hypnotherapy without compromising the outcome.

Lack of familiarity with the therapist is also a source of anxiety. Within the patient's mind are such questions as: "How does this person see me?" "Can he or she be trusted?" As the patient feels more familiar and comfortable with the therapist, anxiety is reduced.

Negative expectancy can occur in several ways. It is important to recognize that the hypnotic induction begins when the possibility of hypnotherapy is raised in the mind of the patient. The success of hypnosis is reduced when it is suggested as a last resort, as in: "We've tried everything else. I doubt that it will work, but if you wish, I know someone who practices hypnosis." Under these circumstances a negative suggestion has already been implanted in the subconscious of the patient.

Alternatively, a referral originating with, "I'd like you to see Dr. X who has been very successful in using hypnosis to help patients with your problem," builds positive expectancy.

Prior negative experiences or associations also contribute to negative expectancies. For example, a 70-year-old woman with advanced cancer was reluctant to engage in hypnosis because of her earlier experience with polio. She stated that 25 years previously she had become very discouraged at her inability to will her legs to function once again. She expressed resentment towards health professionals who had encouraged her to hope for and work towards an unrealistic goal. She wished to avoid another failure. With therapy she learned to accept the premise that it was permissible for her to fail in this instance.

Patients familiar with someone who tried hypnosis unsuccessfully may also have a diminished expectation of success. It is helpful in these circumstances to point out that it's true that hypnotherapy does not work for everyone, but it does work for most people. The patient, the time, the place, the circumstances, and the hypnotherapist are all different, so there is an excellent chance that the outcome will also be different.

Many patients have a *vested interest* against success. This may take a series of forms.

Patients receiving considerable secondary gain from their symptoms may fear that hypnosis will strip them of these advantages. The classic case is that of the worker's compensation syndrome. If the patient's symptoms are relieved, financial and emotional benefits may be jeopardized.

In other instances the threat of the loss of support or respect of valued others may be substantial deterrent. This may take the form of disapproval by family, professional group, or even God. A family member who feels hypnosis is "silly," a colleague who feels it is "unprofessional," or a belief system that interprets portions of the Bible as a directive not to engage in hypnosis—all are powerful pressure against hypnosis.

Resolving Patients' Fears

The preinduction discussion is usually the most important aspect of resolving fears related to hypnosis. During the interview the therapist will do well to focus on three objectives: 1) creating a sense of safety; 2) building credibility; and 3) encouraging involvement.

The patient needs to feel, "I am valued here. This is a person I can trust. This person cares." Good communication cannot be overemphasized. Listening not only to what is said, but also to what is expressed through body language, contributes to the rapport that is the foundation of the therapeutic relationship. Clarifying concerns and issues in ways that affirm the value of the person's perceptions and experiences builds trust. The verbal and nonverbal language of helping and caring conveys, "You are valued. I can help. We can be partners." After greeting the patient with a solid handshake and making the patient comfortable, the therapist asks open-ended questions to help establish rapport. For example, sharing of concerns can be encouraged with such questions as: "How can I help you?" "What understanding do you have of hypnosis?" "What, if anything, makes your symptoms better or worse?" "What do you know about hypnosis?"

Paraphrasing and reflecting feelings assure the patient that he has been heard and understood. For example, "That must have been very difficult for you." "It must be frustrating for you to have suffered so long." "You seem encouraged by this recent step."

Affirming the patient's beliefs also builds rapport and provides an opportunity to normalize his or her experience. For example, "I'm pleased you bring some skepticism. That suggests you are open to new experiences." Or, "You've done well to come despite your reservations. Many of our patients begin with some questions."

Carl Rogers reminds us that the core of the helping relationship is unconditional positive regard, warmth and empathy. As the therapeutic relationship builds, the patient begins to feel, "It is okay to be myself here," or "This is a place where I can be me."

Credibility builds as the therapist demonstrates confidence without a need to control the patient. Paradoxically, the therapist's credibility and the patient's commitment may be increased by the suggestion that this may not be the preferred time for hypnotic treatment. The therapist may create opportunities to weave in stories of patients with similar symptoms who responded well to hypnotic treatment. If appropriate, the patient may be offered an opportunity to talk with other hypnosis patients. This can be arranged by having successful patients in the waiting room as new patients present themselves.

Regardless of the approach to creating positive expectancy, the therapist must avoid defending hypnosis or its outcomes. The patient needs to experience that not only is hypnosis under his control but also the decision to participate is freely his.

Involvement intensifies as the patient senses that this experience will lead to more control without loss of valued beliefs or relationships. Interest and willingness also increase as the patient experiences that this is truly a "joint" adventure and he is part of a "team." For the patient arriving with the misconception that hypnosis is an easy cure-all and something "you do to me," additional time must be taken to inform him of the cooperative aspects of hypnosis. Reassurance and information diminish the fear of failure. The anticipation of success heightens involvement.

The methods of creating a sense of safety, credibility and involvement are many and varied. However, most are some form of the following:

1) *Communication skills.* These skills (paraphrasing, open-ended questions, reflecting of feeling) cannot be overemphasized in the initial building of the therapeutic relationship.
2) *Information.* Educating the patient about hypnosis assists in correcting misconceptions and contributes to a positive expectancy.
3) *Reparenting.* Healthy parenting incorporates two basics — reassurance and permission. Because the therapist is an authority figure he or she is in a position to exert influences similar to an effective parent. Reassurance and permission are conveyed both verbally and nonverbally. Disclo-

sure during the preinduction discussion gives clues to the specific needs for reassurance and the permission needed to proceed with effective hypnotherapy. If a patient encounters difficulty relative to the time commitment necessary for self-hypnosis, granting permission to take time for oneself may be helpful. Paradoxically, reassurance that it is acceptable to hold on to symptoms and to return to therapy when they become unbearable may dispel fear and grant permission simultaneously. The latter is a combination of reassurance, permission, and a double bind.

4) *Double binds.* A double bind consists of offering an apparent choice between two alternatives, either of which will have a positive result. An example might be, "You may feel ready to begin hypnosis today or you may want to phone for your first appointment tomorrow." Another example could be, "I'm unsure if you want to give yourself total relief today or if you want to do that gradually." The patient is offered a choice but by implication the end result will be a health-promoting behavior.

5) *Reframing.* In reframing, a patient is given an alternative way of perceiving a situation or idea. The patient who feels responsible for everything and everyone can be taught to see how irresponsible it is to let his health be undermined. A very "macho" man can more easily accept taking time for practice when he perceives that it takes a great deal of strength to discipline oneself to practice daily. Pain can be perceived as a signal rather than a threat.

6) *Indirect hypnosis.* Indirect hypnosis is not a specific technique but a way of inducing an altered state and delivering suggestions in such a fashion that resistance is minimized. It is assumed that permissive or indirect suggestions, which do not appear to be direct commands, are less likely to arouse conscious attention, and thus resistance. The use of metaphor or storytelling is a common indirect approach to achieve change. Often the story can be so nondirective that the patient will spontaneously lapse into a trance and accept the embedded suggestions.

To demonstrate the aforementioned techniques, let us take one of the most commonly expressed fears and examine the various alternative approaches to its resolution. Patients frequently express the belief that hypnosis allows someone to "control your mind." Patients can be given the *information* that this belief often comes from performances by stage hypnotists. It can be pointed out that participants in stage hypnosis wish to perform and thus will behave as directed by the stage hypnotist whether they are truly in a hypnotic state or not. Further, the stage hypnotist carefully selects his subjects in order to choose the best performers.

In a clinical setting the relationship is entirely different and subjects are *reassured* that nothing will be done to embarrass them, particularly since there is no audience to observe them.

It is further pointed out that all hypnosis is really self-hypnosis. Should the therapist drop dead while teaching the patient self-hypnosis, the patient will not remain in trance indefinitely. Instead he or she will come out of trance and act appropriately.

It is also pointed out: that patients are always free to affirm their own control at any time (*creating safety*); that it is even fun to do so (*reframing*); that the therapist is interested in having the patient gain more control over his or her life (*reassurance*); and that hypnosis is a way of gaining more, not less, control over life (*information*).

Patients can also be told of other patients who had similar problems who used self-hypnosis to resolve their problems (*credibility*). Relating a story about someone daydreaming or watching TV while still being alert to important sounds such as the smoke detector or doorbell indicates that it is permissible to switch control to a more automatic part of our consciousness (*permission, use of metaphor*).

In sum, effectiveness in dealing with a patient who is afraid of hypnosis is related to: 1) understanding the nature and source of the fear; 2) establishing a sense of safety, credibility, and involvement which is the foundation of an effective therapeutic relationship needed for hypnotherapy; and 3) being familiar with and competent in using alternative induction techniques, especially indirect hypnosis.

Patients Skeptical
About Hypnosis

Question:

How can you persuade skeptical patients, of whom I see a large
number, that hypnosis would be beneficial for them?

Discussion by HAROLD P. GOLAN, D.M.D.

In considering skeptical patients, it is important to realize that the skepticism could be 1) a logical response to prior experiences, 2) a basic personality trait, or 3) a means of defending oneself against fears that may be either
conscious or unconscious. Each of these situations would be managed differently.

The therapist should remember that the patient has gone through several
thought processes before he ever arrived on the practitioner's doorstep. First,
the patient has realized that a problem or illness exists. Second, he must have
perceived that the problem or illness is his or her problem or illness. Third,
he knows that the problem or illness may be helped by professional treatment. Only then does the patient approach the doctor. No matter how skeptical the patient may be, he has come to the conclusion that some treatment
may help his situation. The practitioner must realize at this point that the
patient can be treated easily if the proper key is found to the skepticism.

At times, the skepticism can be viewed as very reasonable, in terms of
the patient's prior experiences. For instance, he may have had a frightening experience with hypnosis from watching a stage demonstration or seeing a nonprofessional use it as entertainment at a party. In those instances
it is probable that the subjects acted foolishly, as if they had lost control and
the hypnotist was totally in command. If this is the case, it should be explained that the person who has volunteered to go up on the stage wants
to be a part of the performance, and that in more usual circumstances no

one will do anything under hypnosis unless he or she wants to. Hypnosis can teach patients more control, rather than less, and they will not surrender any willpower to another. Their privacy will be respected, and they need not answer any questions unless they are willing to do so. They will not be unconscious; they will hear and understand everything, and can terminate any session at will. They should have no doubts about being unable to arouse or awaken. I like to give several examples of how they have already used hypnosis in their lives, such as complete relaxation as a baby and daydreaming.

Another reasonable source of skepticism is the well meaning but misinformed opinion of friends, family, or health professionals. Many physicians, especially psychiatrists, as well as many psychologists and nurses, have been taught by respected instructors that hypnosis is a foolish undertaking. They have been told that its benefits, if any, are transient, and that its dangers are significant. This may lead to a "poisoned referral," one in which the referring specialist has said, "I will send you for hypnosis, but I doubt that it will help."

In this instance, the patient must be reassured that hypnosis is a normal, natural, physiologic phenomenon. I have patients wiggle their toes in their shoes, and then ask if they feel their shoes. Next, I ask why they didn't feel their shoes a moment ago. They will answer that they weren't paying attention or thinking about their feet, and correctly so. I explain that the body has the ability to make itself anesthetic to their shoes, wristwatch, jewelry, or clothes all through the day, and it is this quality of their own body and mind control that I am going to teach them to use for their own treatment.

A character trait, such as defiance or suspicion of anyone in a position of authority, may be the source of the skepticism. It is important in such cases to make the patient realize that by resisting treatment and delaying cure, he may be aggravating his medical, dental, or psychological problem. He can be told that whatever the reasons for his skeptical thoughts, they are unimportant in comparison to his situation at the moment. His body is his most important possession; he needs his body to live, and he needs a healthy body to live happily. The therapist then emphasizes that self-preservation is the first rule of life; this usually removes that particular resistance.

It may happen that the patient resents some physical appearance or mannerisms of the therapist. The patient then uses skepticism to resist the hypnotic process. (Conversely, the therapist may dislike some characteristics of the patient.) This results in lack of rapport, which in turn causes the patient to throw doubt or suspicion on the hypnotic process.

Skepticism, as mentioned earlier, may also be used as a defense against certain fears; the fear of revealing too much, the fear of failure, and the fear of success are a few examples. The fear of revealing too much is not limited to concern that the therapist will learn forbidden secrets; it also includes the concern that the patient may learn too much about himself or that repressed feelings which are too traumatic may come to the surface.

An illustration of the fear of success might be those patients who claim that they wish to stop smoking, but inwardly they do not, and they will then use skepticism as a means of sabotaging the efforts of the therapist. Likewise, there are many other symptoms, which, though painful in themselves, do provide some payoff to the patients, so that, at least on an unconscious level, there is a reluctance to have them hypnotized away. The therapist will almost surely meet with failure unless these resistances are recognized and resolved.

The patient with low self-esteem will have perceived himself as having failed many times in the past and will not want to risk another failure. The fear that hypnosis won't work represents the possibility of failing again, so skepticism may help defend against that threat. Ego-strengthening is the solution here; the patient must be made aware of his potentialities.

The therapist must keep all of the above-mentioned reasons for skepticism in mind when a skeptical patient presents for therapy. Each doubt or question must be separately addressed and explained away before any therapy is started.

An example of a doubt impeding the progress of hypnosis may help explain how to review a situation in which a patient did not say anything until asked, but presented body language which expressed doubt and suspicion about the whole hypnotic process. This 22-year-old patient had had a surgical operation for correction of a prognothic mandible (jutting out of the lower jaw) which was cut, repositioned with bone grafts, and splinted in position for six weeks. After that she became refractory to all things dental. She became hysterical at the approach of a mouth mirror or a throat stick. Patients such as these need removable splints or permanent bridgework to hold the bite in its proper position. She could not bear to have anything intrude into her mouth.

I was called into consultation by the dental intern who was responsible for making the previously mentioned restorations. The patient agreed to treatment, whereupon we took the usual emotional history and explained hypnosis in a preconditioning talk. During the entire explanation she had her arms crossed tightly about her body, her forehead was wrinkled, and her whole general appearance was one of forbidding non-acceptance. I realized something was bothering her and asked if anything about the procedure was troubling to her. It is at junctures like this that the therapist must have the ability to recognize the patient's doubts, whether they are expressed verbally or nonverbally, as in this instance.

She asked if she would have to answer any questions. When I reassured her that her thoughts would be private and she could keep them that way, and that the whole process was very permissive, it was quite amazing to see her drop her arms into her lap and nod her permission. A successful hypnotic induction and treatment followed.

Most patients will have some doubts and questions. Certainly each skeptical patient will have doubts or questions. You, as a therapist, can refer back to one of the major causes mentioned, answer, explain, and even induce your patient so that he or she may enjoy the benefits which hypnosis can bring them. Be kind, gentle, and patient with skeptical patients, as they need more time to understand your explanations. Remember, they have already realized you can help them. All you have to do is find the key that unlocks their trust. Then therapy can proceed at the patient's own pace.

16 Patients Who Claim
They Are Not Hypnotizable

Question:

What can I say to a client who claims he is not hypnotizable and
that several people have tried unsuccessfully to hypnotize him?

Discussion by JOAN M. MURRAY-JOBSIS, Ph.D.

First of all I ask the client to tell me more about himself: to tell me what
his past experiences with hypnosis have been and to give me details about
the hypnotists with whom he has worked. What were the credentials of the
former hypnotists? Were they clinicians or entertainers or just friends? What
were the circumstances under which the earlier hypnosis experiences were
attempted? Why had people tried to hypnotize him? What kinds of techniques were used? Were they situations where the client was challenging
people to hypnotize him, or where they were challenging him? Was he in
a safe setting, or did he feel exposed and vulnerable? Had he in the past been
seeking hypnosis or did he find himself the unwilling participant in an hypnotic induction?

   In general, I try to find out as much as possible about the client's previous
experiences with hypnosis, why he had engaged in hypnosis, what kind of
inductions were attempted with him, and why he felt that they were unsuccessful. It is possible, of course, that the client never actually initiated
the hypnotic sessions in the past; if so, his lack of cooperation would not be
surprising. Secondly, the client may not have interpreted the hypnosis session correctly. It is possible that he was actually achieving hypnosis without
realizing it. In addition, there may have been other variables affecting the
past hypnotic experiences, such as whether or not the client was feeling uncomfortable in the earlier settings or whether he had personality differences

with the earlier hypnotists. In summary, I would try to find out all the details and circumstances surrounding the client's past "failures."

I then ask the client more about his perception of hypnosis and try to find out whether or not his understanding of hypnosis was realistic. Hypnosis isn't as dramatic as most people think; that is, it is not the way it is frequently presented on television. The person being hypnotized is not unconscious or unaware. Typically, the hypnotic subject is totally aware of what is going on around him and is also able to remember everything when he comes out of trance. Further, even though the person being hypnotized gives over temporary leadership to the operator/hypnotist, the hypnotic client is really in control. At the bottom line, the subject can always reclaim control and come back out of trance if he really wants to. I usually point out to patients the ultimate control they have by giving the following dramatic example: "If I were working with a client in hypnosis and were suddenly to have a stroke, the client would not remain floating off in trance. He would, of course, be able to come out of trance and take care of the situation."

Having obtained all possible information concerning the client's past difficulties with and perceptions of hypnosis, I then try to mitigate and reshape those perceptions. I help the client perceive hypnosis as a nonthreatening experience, emphasizing that he is in control and is able to maintain awareness both during and following hypnosis. This helps reduce any threat that the client might feel in relationship to hypnosis, and it also minimizes any false expectations of hypnosis being an enormously dramatic experience. Thus, if the actual hypnosis falls short of such dramatic expectations, the client is less likely to perceive himself as not hypnotized. In short, discussion includes an attempt to reduce the threat element of hypnosis and to reduce false expectations, so that the client can perceive himself as hypnotized when he is indeed hypnotized.

Next the client's motivation for coming to therapy and for requesting hypnosis is assessed. Is he really looking for successful hypnosis and for some relief from a symptom or problem? I point out to the client that everyone can be hypnotized, with the possible exception of persons who are so severely intellectually retarded that they are unable to concentrate for any length of time. Everyone has the potential capacity for hypnotizability — the only variable affecting success is motivation or willingness to be hypnotized. In pointing out that conflict or ambivalent feelings about hypnosis and fears or concerns over control struggles can interfere with success, I stress that being able to achieve hypnosis basically depends on a cooperative effort and that it takes the two of us working together to help the client achieve a trance. The client can be hypnotized only if he wants to be hypnotized, and I can help him learn to be hypnotized only if the two of us work together.

The client is then given some description of how I would work with him in hypnosis, basically describing an initial relaxation induction. I tell him that most people find such relaxation induction very comfortable and explain that there are very many ways of going into trance and that we will work with a series of induction messages until the client finds a comfortable way of simply drifting into trance. It is important to emphasize that there is no "one correct way" of entering into trance or experiencing trance.

The client's fears concerning hypnosis should be explored. Some clients fear loss of control. Others fear that hypnosis may allow some unacceptable part of themselves to emerge if they don't maintain their own conscious control and censor themselves. Occasionally clients fear the emergence of psychosis if they allow a lowering of their conscious controls. In response to these fears I discuss the fact that people do not easily become psychotic and that hypnosis doesn't produce accidental psychoses. This is a good time to remind the client that his feelings are acceptable, just as all feelings are acceptable. However, even in hypnosis the client possesses a degree of control, monitoring and self-censoring if he chooses to maintain it.

Some more severely disturbed clients may fear loss of control as a possible forerunner of loss of identity and of autonomy. In dealing with these fears of loss of autonomy, I stress again the fact that the client always retains control and the capacity for monitoring and keeping in contact with his own sense of autonomy. In addition, the client's sense of control and autonomy is reinforced by emphasizing that he is learning autohypnosis and that he is learning to enhance his own mastery and self-control. Clients who are worried about autonomy and control issues can open their eyes any time they want to and can even leave their eyes open if they really need to, maintaining an eyes-open trance. However, maintaining a trance with eyes open takes quite a bit of effort because an individual then has to work at blocking out extraneous visual stimulation even as he maintains the trance. Most clients, when they are permitted to open their eyes, discover that it is simply easier to have the eyes closed and to go on comfortably with an eyes-closed trance. However, the permission to open the eyes seems to allow clients a greater sense of control and a greater reassurance that they are not going to lose their sense of self and their autonomy. In addition, as I remind clients, when and if they open their eyes they can reassure themselves of the constancy and of the separateness of the two of us. There is no need to fear either abandonment or merger. We can keep our relationship and our individual autonomy constant and stable.

I let clients who are concerned about autonomy know that I will let them regulate the distance between us. Some clients seem to like the reassurance of knowing that I am sitting very close to them or even touching some part of their hand or arm. Other clients seem to want the reassurance of knowing that I am on the other side of the room in another chair and that I will keep my distance. The client's preferences about the closeness or distance should be respected.

Another major issue to be explored in dealing with clients who claim they are not hypnotizable is the possibility of a control struggle between client and therapist. Some clients may be acting out a struggle over control with the hypnotist that may come from previous control struggles with authority figures, usually beginning with parents. In such cases the client may not be concerned over autonomy issues or losing control, but instead may be concerned over who is going to be dominant or powerful in the hypnotic relationship. If the client seems to be engaged in a struggle for control, I try to emphasize again that hypnosis really is a cooperative effort, and that hypnosis is a tool, a technique that can benefit people. It is a skill that can be learned and that can provide a powerful technique for helping to alleviate symptoms and solve problems in life. Thus, I attempt to shift the client away from a control struggle and into a cooperative mindset, helping him to feel "we are a team" working together to help him learn how to accomplish hypnosis for his benefit. Although this cooperative alliance may be described very simply and concisely, I am careful to behave in such a way that the client perceives me as not trying to dominate him, compete with him or overpower him. This process of defusing a potential control struggle between client and therapist can be the most difficult element in creating a working alliance for hypnosis with a resistant client.

In summary, these are the steps in dealing with a client who claims he is not hypnotizable: obtain a thorough history of previous "failure," attempt to redefine hypnosis in a realistic and acceptable fashion, mitigate fear issues surrounding hypnosis, and then reduce control struggles and emphasize cooperative efforts.

Q&A 17 Clinical Usefulness of Hypnotizability Tests

Question:

Do hypnotizability tests have any use in clinical practice or is their value restricted to research settings?

Discussion by SHELDON COHEN, M.D.

The answer is a resounding, equivocal, "Yes, but." As part of our attempt to understand the universe in which we live, we continually attempt to classify and measure. As anyone who has worked in a laboratory can attest, even "objective" measurements can be highly variable, sometimes difficult to reproduce, and often subject to markedly differing interpretations. The problems are compounded exponentially when one moves into the measurement of emotional and behavioral reactions of human beings.

It is altogether understandable and natural to ask of any technique: "For whom is this method applicable?" "How do we determine what characteristics or attributes make it more or less likely that a given individual will respond positively?" It is out of these concerns that a succession of tests of hypnotizability (defined by Webster as "susceptibility to hypnosis") has been devised.

These tests are each comprised of a number of items indicating either a physical or psychological response to a suggestion. The physical responses include items such as the raising or lowering of an arm, immobilization of an arm, eye closure, swaying, etc. The psychological components may include amnesia, "hallucinations," responsiveness to posthypnotic suggestions, time distortions and age regression. Tests have been named after the institutions in which they were developed (Stanford [Weitzenhoffer & Hilgard, 1959] and Harvard [Shor & Orne, 1962]), the individual (Barber [Barber

95

& Wilson, 1978/79]), or by acronyms (HIP and ACE). All of these tests appear to have some shortcomings, requiring too much time, detracting from the clinical work at hand, or not seeming to fit the needs of a particular situation. Consequently, there are continual attempts to develop new tests and to move away from procedures which are not applicable in a clinician's office. When I was a journal editor, I could count on the postman to bring the "hypnotizability test of the month" from an author unhappy with the standard repertoire and convinced that he had found *the* answer to the clinician's dilemma.

There is a puzzling paradox. There is a very large corpus of literature about tests of hypnotizability, and many of the most original, productive researchers and clinicians have devoted significant portions of their professional careers to developing and refining tests of hypnotizability. They are quite convinced about the utility of the tests, differing only in *which* tests are useful.

Yet, one measure of the value of a procedure is its utilization by those acknowledged to be leaders in the field. Until his death in 1980, Milton H. Erickson stood out as the leading practitioner of hypnosis. He delivered innumerable lectures and participated in wide-ranging teaching conferences. In addition to being a very prolific writer, he was the founder of the *American Journal of Clinical Hypnosis*, which he edited for ten years. However, careful reading of the four volumes of his collected papers (Erickson, 1980) and Zeig's *A Teaching Seminar with Milton H. Erickson* (1980) fails to reveal any utilization by Erickson of standardized hypnotic testing. He undoubtedly was aware of the degree of responsivity whether it was arm levitation, posthypnotic suggestions, amnesia, or some other form of compliance, but he did not undertake to quantify such responses. Consequently, as one would expect, the large number of clinicians influenced by Erickson or those who espouse "Ericksonian techniques" have expressed little interest in formal testing.

How much do clinicians who report their cases in the literature utilize tests for hypnotizability? A survey was made of volume 24 of the *American Journal of Clinical Hypnosis* (July 1981–April 1982). The 13 articles devoted to clinical topics covered areas of grief, enuresis, amnesia, fugue states, learning problems, phobias, sexual dysfunctions, and dysphonia. They were straightforward, clear-cut presentations of common clinical problems with the authors emphasizing innovative, therapeutic approaches. One author utilized formal testing procedures. It is quite possible that the other 12 may have employed a test of hypnotizability but did not include it in their reports. However, the techniques reported seemed to indicate that most of the authors proceeded directly with an induction procedure without quantifying the depth of hypnosis, and then moved on rapidly with their therapeutic techniques.

A group of experienced clinicians were queried about their use of tests of hypnotizability (Cohen, 1982). Thirty-seven (82%) of 45 physicians, clinical psychologists, and dentists answered a survey given at a workshop in which they were teaching hypnosis to fellow professionals. Thirty percent reported current usage of tests of hypnotizability, 24% had abandoned them, and 46% had never used tests of hypnotizability. The only test used routinely was the HIP, employed by three (8%) of the clinicians. Another three (8%) used standard tests frequently (one each SHCS:Adult, HIP, BSS), with others reporting infrequent use of standardized tests, use of their own personal tests, or use of a single item from a standardized test. In the opinion of the majority of these clinicians, the tests were not generally indicated or helpful. Some believed they might even produce an antitherapeutic bias. The data lead to the conclusion that none of the tests of hypnotizability has yet proved its efficacy to even a significant minority of clinicians.

As noted earlier, the writings of Erickson and others indicate very little use of tests of hypnotizability by clinicians who publish their experiences. Likewise, a survey of some of the leading teachers of hypnotic techniques showed that most of them tended not to employ tests of hypnotizability, or at least not the full formal tests. To continue to determine the *actual* use of tests of hypnotizability by practitioners, whenever the question comes up in such a group, I ask about their use with their patients. To date, all groups have reported the same experiences as previously described.

Although there may be some positive correlation between hypnotizability and certain therapeutic gains, the reverse does not hold true. That is, there is no indication that low hypnotizability necessarily means that a given individual will not respond therapeutically. In my opinion, this is the major reason that most clinicians do not use the tests. Some clinicians have stated this as their reason, i.e., their feelings that they might have a negative bias toward instituting treatment with a patient who is not a good responder. I know of no clinician, including those who have developed or espoused tests, who would advocate withholding hypnosis from a patient simply because he or she scored low on a hypnotizability test.

A clinician who has become familiar with the major tests of hypnotizability and the very convincing arguments by their proponents may well feel that he is somehow or other remiss in not using such a test. Certainly at one time I began to wonder where I was deficient, since I did not routinely employ any of these wonderfully scientific measuring instruments. It slowly dawned on me that the proponents, by virtue of their major focus on testing, had a volume of experience that few, if any clinicians, could hope to match. It also became apparent that because of the tremendous amount of time invested in the testing, there was a concomitant emotional investment, so one could not expect the proponents to be "objective" about the applicability of their own tests. Though I have and continue to have tremendous respect and admiration for the developers and refiners of the tests, I heaved a sigh of relief when I realized my therapeutic capacities were no less because I did not find these tests relevant to my practice.

When all is said and done, the clinician ultimately asks himself the question, "How important are the tests of hypnotizability or the need to know about hypnotizability for my practice?" Mott (1979) notes that there are literature reports of a significant correlation between hypnotizability and pain reduction in the laboratory and that individuals who are more hypnotizable are more likely to gain relief from pain, migraine headaches, posttraumatic headaches, and asthma.

On the other hand, Barber (1977) reported that 99 out of 100 dental patients were able to use hypnosis as the sole anesthetic agent in undergoing dental operative procedures. In a follow-up article (Barber, 1980) he gives examples of patients who scored very poorly on standard scales of hypnotizability, yet responded quite well therapeutically with naturalistic, nonauthoritarian techniques. This would certainly seem to indicate that the most important consideration is the therapeutic alliance, with the technique of therapy being dependent on the therapist's making the necessary emotional contacts with the patient.

Since the formal tests are frequently used in research publications, some of a clinical nature, anyone using hypnosis should be familiar with the parameters of each test to be able to evaluate research reports intelligently. Certainly, all readers will want to try out the several clinical tests and decide for themselves what utility they have in their own practices. Beyond that, I suspect that each reader will have his or her own favorite method of induction and will use the patient's responsivity to the induction process as a rough measure of "hypnotizability."

I employ several different techniques, relying on a "feel" as to what seems right for the patient at a particular time. Most of the time, I use a simple handclasp as an initial induction-testing procedure. I have been using it for so long that I am not sure which of my teachers to credit as my model. It would not surprise me if some enterprising historian found that the technique had been used hundreds of years ago. I ask patients to clasp their outstretched hands tightly together, with palms pressing, and then to stare quite intently at one thumbnail of the outstretched hands. I tell the patient that the hands will be squeezing together tighter and tighter, as if they were in a vise; then, before they know it, the hands will feel as though they were stuck together and will not come apart even if they try to move them apart. At the appropriate time, I tell the patients that they might try to move them apart, and then I score, on the patient's chart, a rough approximation of the response from 0 (no response) to 4 + (hands clasped together so tightly the patient cannot move them at all). With a patient whose hands remain together, I give suggestions for lid heaviness and eye closure and move on with the induction process. I have found this to be simple and effective but certainly would not imply that it is necessarily any better than any other test with which the reader may be familiar. Basically, any of the items listed in the different tests may be used, but most people find that one of the tests involving motor functions will work satisfactorily, and as more experience is gained with that particular item, the clinician may fashion his own rough measure of "hypnotizability."

References

Barber, J. (1980). Hypnosis and the unhypnotizable. *American Journal of Clinical Hypnosis,* *23,* 4.

Barber, J. (1977). Rapid induction analgesia: A clinical report. *American Journal of Clinical Hypnosis, 19,* 138–147.

Barber, T. X., & Wilson, S. C. (1978/79). The Barber suggestibility scale and the creative imagination scale: Experimental and clinical applications. *American Journal of Clinical Hypnosis, 21,* 85.

Cohen, S. B. (1982). Clinical uses of measures of hypnotizability. Presented to the American Psychiatric Association, Toronto.

Erickson, M. H. (1980). *The collected papers of Milton H. Erickson* (E. Rossi, Ed.). New York: Irvington.

Mott, T. (1979). The clinical importance of hypnotizability. *American Journal of Clinical Hypnosis, 21,* 263.

Shor, R. E., & Orne, E. C. (1962). *The Harvard Group Scale of Hypnotic Susceptibility, Form A.* Palo Alto, CA: Consulting Psychologists Press.

Weitzenhoffer, A. M., & Hilgard, E. R. (1959). *Stanford Hypnotic Susceptibility Scales: Forms A and B.* Palo Alto, CA: Consulting Psychologists Press.

Zeig, J. K. (1980). *A teaching seminar with Milton H. Erickson, M.D.* New York: Brunner/Mazel.

SECTION IV *Inductions*

Some of the most commonly asked questions at hypnosis courses have to do with inductions and this topic is where a lot of anxiety about doing hypnosis is played out. Textbook authors are well aware of this and usually devote one or several long chapters to different induction methods and different ways of determining their success or failure.

Our contributors address most of the important questions about inductions: which ones to use, how long they should go on, how to know when and how deeply a patient is hypnotized, what to do about patients who don't get induced, how to use spontaneously occurring trances, and how to reintroduce hypnosis at another time.

A good example of the differences among practitioners that we mentioned in the introduction to the book can be seen in the first two discussions, where Zilbergeld and Golden have somewhat divergent positions on choosing inductions. An even more striking contrast is manifest in comparing these two responses with that expressed by Edelstien in his paper in the Methods section on selecting techniques. His view is both radical and simple: all inductions work about equally well for most people so it doesn't make any difference which you use. As we said earlier, those who expect unanimity here will be disappointed. But keep in mind that the three contributors have each used hypnosis for many years and each has been successful in helping many clients achieve the state we call hypnosis. Different viewpoints and practices are not necessarily a barrier to effective hypnotic treatment.

$\underset{A}{Q}_{\&}18$ Choosing Inductions

Question:

> I am confused about inductions. Does it make any difference which you use, whether you mix them (e.g., deep breathing plus going down stairs plus relaxing imagery), or what tone of voice you use?

Discussion by BERNIE ZILBERGELD, Ph.D.

I also used to be confused about inductions. My first exposure to hypnosis was with Milton Erickson and I assumed I would get similar results only by doing everything, including inductions, the way he did. But this was very difficult since he used many different inductions. How was I supposed to know which one to use? My insecurity wasn't helped by the fact that the hypnotherapist I went to for consultation on returning home from Erickson's had copied Erickson's confusion technique on two sheets of paper, which he read word for word to clients. That reinforced my idea that there was a right way to do inductions and a wrong way. So I also made a copy of the confusion technique and read it to the first client I saw afterwards. Unfortunately, being a blunt and straightforward person, I was very uncomfortable with all the confusion and became far more confused than the client, who ended up asking me if I was all right. I wasn't. I decided I had to think through this business about inductions.

The most important question is: What is the purpose of an induction? The answer I came up with is simple and has been of immense value. An induction is merely a transition between where the client is and the state of greater receptivity we want to get him into, the state called hypnosis. We hypnotherapists believe, with good reason, that it will be easier to obtain certain information and to increase the patient's receptivity to therapeutic

103

suggestions if we can move him into a less defensive, more open, stronger place, what we call trance or hypnosis. Induction is nothing more than what it takes to move him from A to B.

Once I accepted this idea, life became a lot easier. For one thing, I could see that sometimes no induction at all was necessary because the client had already moved into the state I wanted him in. For instance, one client started talking about an event many years ago, a birthday that was not celebrated, and as she did, it became clear from her posture, gestures, and affect that she was more there than here in the office with me. In other words, she had regressed to the time of the event she was describing. Prior to my new realization of the purpose of inductions, I probably would have done what I had seen several therapists do: after letting the client finish describing the event, inducing hypnosis and then trying to regress her to the event. This makes as much sense as the scene often repeated in hospitals, where patients are awakened to be given sleeping pills. But clearly such is not necessary. My client had inducted and regressed herself. All I had to do was encourage her to stay with it and then introduce some suggestions to help free her of this event which had ever since then contributed to her sense of not being a worthwhile human being.

It frequently happens in therapy, any kind of therapy, that the client, with no suggestion from the therapist, goes into a hypnotic state. It makes good sense to be aware of this when it happens and to exploit it for the client's benefit. Why not make use of what's already there? I believe this is the best kind of utilization therapy. But it can be used only by those who understand that inductions are not something that has to be done by the therapist or be under his control, who realize that induction is only a means to an end and not an end in itself.

How do you know when the client has entered hypnosis by himself? This is not an easy question to address because the answer depends on how you define hypnosis. For myself, I assume that absorption and involvement are signs of what I want. In the example given above of the woman describing her birthday experience, it was clear that she was wrapped up in the event as she was talking about it. Her eyes were glazed, she seemed to be paying no attention to me, and her posture suggested that she was actually experiencing the feelings surrounding the earlier event. Any time a client seems inner involved or preoccupied this is an indication that he is in hypnosis or on his way there. He should be encouraged to stay with the experience, the idea, the feeling, just as we encourage clients to go with or stay with relaxing imagery or so-called deepening procedures.

Another indication of spontaneous trance is when the client looks at me intensely, with great expectancy, a look commonly seen when people are engrossed in plays and movies and when teenagers view their idols. I used to feel very uncomfortable when clients looked at me this way and was tempted to yell at them, "Why are you looking at me that way? Do you think I can tell you how to solve your problem?" But I've learned to exploit the state they're in by saying something like, "Now I'm going to tell you something of great interest, something that will help you feel better about yourself," followed by whatever suggestions seem appropriate.

Of course, clients sometimes have interesting ideas about inductions and then it makes sense to utilize what we are given. I recall an older male patient who reported being hypnotized many years ago by a therapist who used a swinging pendulum. Since I didn't have a pendulum in the office, I suggested we try another method. No way, the patient asserted, the only way to be hypnotized was by watching a swinging pendulum. So I suggested he fantasize the pendulum or recall the time when it had been used. Again he refused. There had to be an actual swinging pendulum for him to watch. I finally realized that I needed to comply with his desires. So I rigged up a primitive pendulum, a large washer at the end of a piece of string, and had it ready for our next session. He was delighted and quickly went into trance.

Perhaps this example is the best way to set the stage for my next point, which is simply that since an induction is no more than the way from A to B, anything that will transport the client on that road — a car, a bus, a train, a boat, a plane, or anything else — is what is right. Swinging pendulums are fine for those who want them. Eye closure works well for most people, so they close their eyes on their own or I tell them to close them. But some clients are too frightened to close their eyes, so I tell them they *should* keep their eyes open. My clients usually sit on a reclining chair and before induction I suggest they might want to push back on the chair to recline further. This works well for many, but some prefer to sit upright so I tell them that is exactly what they should do. One man was so concerned about reclining that I went to another room and brought back a straight-backed kitchen chair to help him remain bolt upright. He was taken by my concern and induction was no problem. We used the kitchen chair for several sessions and one day he said he'd like to try the reclining chair; he liked it and never again used the straight chair.

In line with this emphasis on going along with the client's desires is the equally important point of not offending the client or making him feel worse. Chances are good, for instance, that a phrase commonly used in inductions, "and you're feeling heavier and heavier," is going to be anything but relaxing for a client concerned about weight. Common sense dictates finding another phrase. Similarly, a client with respiratory ailments such as asthma will probably not do well with inductions that require deep breathing. And the therapist will be well advised against suggesting to an agoraphobic that she is "floating in space" or to a claustrophobic that he is "ensconced in a cocoon of relaxation."

Some hypnotists have inductions they use most of the time because their experience is that these procedures work with most people. Some beginners are so nervous that they memorize one or two inductions and get upset if they forget their lines or can't use what they've memorized. Other people, like my consultant years ago, have copies of inductions on their desks from which they read to clients.

While I have a few pet inductions, I use them sparingly. What I do instead is ask patients how they relax themselves or if they have any fantasy or experience of a very peaceful event or scene. The information in their responses is what I use for induction. Often patients come up with scenes such as those in hypnosis textbooks: lying on the beach in Hawaii is a very common one with my patients, followed by being in a meadow, a grove of trees, or near a stream or lake. Sometimes the answers are different; one very busy and very wealthy client said the most relaxing experience he could imagine was being in a hotel room in New York City, knowing he had no work to do and wouldn't be bothered by phone calls, looking forward to a lazy breakfast and wandering about the town. I'd never heard this one before but used it nonetheless.

Aside from working for the patient, the induction must also be within the comfort level of the therapist; if it isn't, it won't work for the patient. As I indicated earlier, I am not skilled at or comfortable with confusion techniques and consequently they don't work for me. If the client relaxes with a scene that is not comfortable for the therapist to deal with, I think the therapist would be best advised to find out what other relaxing scenes or methods the client has.

As I work in the San Francisco Bay Area, a number of my clients have meditated or had relaxation training, autogenic training, or experience with biofeedback. Whenever this is the case and the experience was a positive one, I ask patients to do what it is they know how to do — meditate, relax themselves, and so forth — while I observe and make simple comments such as, "That's good, more and more relaxed," followed by therapeutic work when they're ready.

My comments about inductions may be more easily understood if I give my understanding of hypnosis. Much of the public and many hypnotists, even some who talk otherwise, believe hypnosis is something the therapist does to the client. The therapist inducts the client into hypnosis and then does something powerful and wonderful to make the client feel better, behave differently, and so on, and that's that. While I believe there are such cases and even have had some of my own, I doubt they are the rule. One-shot hypnotic cures are rare and many of them end in relapse. I consider hypnosis primarily as a coping skill, something the therapist can teach the client about but which the client will then have to use on his own, perhaps for the rest of his life.

Given this understanding, it makes sense to use what the client already knows and is comfortable with. If the client can get relaxed by visualizing a scene from his childhood, I would rather use my time to teach the client how to better use the scene than in an attempt to teach him some new scene or some other way of relaxing. After all, it's the client who's going to have to imagine the scene day after day, month after month. Why not go with something that's accessible, available, and comfortable? It's better and certainly more efficient to use in the office the kind of induction that the client will use on his own when doing self-hypnosis.

Because of the way I think about induction and hypnosis, the first two parts of the question — what induction to use and whether to mix inductions — become moot points. I choose inductions in accord with the notions already set forth. As long as they work, I know they're right. Mixing inductions is not an issue because I don't recognize standard inductions. A standard induction is only an induction that worked for someone who then wrote it up. My only interest is getting the client more receptive to suggestion, and whatever that takes is my standard induction for the day with that client.

Some readers may be aghast at my answer because they have been trained to do long inductions following a set routine. My own feeling is that inductions are basically a waste of time — what I want to do is get to the therapeutic questions or suggestions — so the less time spent on them, the more efficient the therapy. I am, after all, a therapist, not an inducer of trances. I have witnessed therapists do 20-minute, 30-minute, and even 60-minute inductions, but I can't understand the point of such extravaganzas even after long explanations by the therapists. The most common answer is that long inductions are required for really deep trances, and often an article of Erickson's is quoted where he talked about a very long induction, but my experience is that deep trances are unnecessary for the vast majority of the clients.

Since most therapists are paid by the hour, I think it irresponsible to use a 30-minute induction when the same results could have been accomplished in five minutes. I think some therapists use long inductions because it makes them look good and feel important. Why other therapists use them is beyond me. Erickson hypnotized me a number of times and although the content varied, the approach was always the same: long and boring. He would always reach for a picture or artifact on his desk and go on endlessly about it, boring me into trance. I have no understanding why he did this because I am a very good hypnotic subject and would have entered trance a lot quicker if he had just told me to do so, something he did with some clients and subjects.

A lot of the differences in feelings about trance can be accounted for by Daniel Araoz's distinction between the old hypnosis and the new hypnosis. In the old hypnosis, trance is considered a thing in itself and is surrounded by all manner of rituals and requirements. It is practiced by those who often use tests of susceptibility (to determine if the patient can indeed be inducted into hypnosis) and sometimes tests of depth as well. The hypnotist is given a large role in this scheme of things—he is the one who conducts the tests, determines susceptibility and depth, and gets the patient to go into trance—and comes out looking like a very busy and important fellow. In the new hypnosis, tests of any kind are rarely used. The assumption is that almost anyone can be hypnotized if the therapist will observe carefully and wisely use what patients present. The hypnotist's role is minimized, especially regarding induction. If the patient spontaneously enters trance, so much the better; the therapist can save his energy for the infinitely more important work of using hypnosis to best advantage.

Although there is probably some correlation between age of therapist and membership in the old hypnosis club, it would be a mistake to assume that every hypnotist over the age of 40 or 50 belongs to this outfit. Erickson is considered the founding father of the new hypnosis and practiced it at an advanced age. As usual, however, it is difficult to make sense of what Erickson did. Why did he use long inductions with me and with others seem to dispense with inductions altogether, simply saying, "Go into trance"? David Cheek is another old master who has in recent years apparently given up using inductions. In two recent demonstrations, involving a total of four subjects, Cheek simply gave the subjects a short talk about ideomotor signals and then asked questions to which the subjects replied with finger movements. There was no question that the subjects became hypnotized during the process and no question that the experience was emotional and helpful to at least two of them and also to several people in the audience. What all this suggests, I think, is that you don't have to be young to use the new hypnosis and, more important, that the importance of lengthy inductions or any inductions has been vastly overemphasized.

I consider it crucial, however, to get feedback from clients regarding the effectiveness of whatever inductions are done. There are several types of feedback. As I do an induction, I observe what is happening with the client, but unlike many of my colleagues I am often unsure how to interpret changes in breathing, in posture, and in demeanor. To make up for my ignorance, I feel free to ask. I may say something like, "Keeping your eyes closed and moving as little as possible, please tell me what's going on with you now." I must admit I am often surprised by the responses. Sometimes I am almost certain the client is experiencing difficulty or distress and his answer is, "This is wonderful. I've never felt this good." At other times, the response is not positive. The client is having difficulty listening to me, certain thoughts keep intruding, or he is wondering what is the point of the procedure. I take these answers seriously and deal with them immediately.

Another type of feedback comes after the hypnosis is ended. I always ask questions about how it felt to determine the degree of involvement in suggested images. Also, to ensure that clients feel free to complain about things they didn't like or weren't helpful, I always ask, "Was there anything disturbing, anything you'd like different?" The information obtained here is invaluable. Sometimes a client will say he had trouble with a particular word, phrase, or image I used — which I immediately make note of — or that the order of presentation should be changed or that while I was prattling on about a certain image (almost always one I got from the client), he was involved with a different one.

I usually make tapes of hypnotic work for clients to listen to at home and I always request feedback about them. Here again, the reactions are extremely useful and immediately incorporated into the next session's work.

My feeling about tone of voice is about the same as my feeling about inductions generally. Whatever works is fine. Obviously most people will not respond well to being yelled at, but other than saying to use common sense and be respectful of the patient, I don't think there are any rules to follow. Some therapists' voices change dramatically when they do inductions; they speak almost in a whisper and in a monotone. Many clients find this relaxing. On the other hand, I have seen good hypnotists induce trance very quickly without making such changes.

I am one of those therapists who has a special voice for hypnotic induction and work. I speak much more gently than usual and in a monotone. I don't do this deliberately, but it is what happens. This has had an important benefit for many of my clients. They develop a conditioned response to my change of voice. As soon as I start speaking in my "hypnotic voice," they start going into trance. Sometimes this has surprising results. Recently, without my knowledge, my voice changed in anticipation of doing hypnosis with a client I had seen several times before. I was going on about something or other without looking at the client while I fumbled with my tape recorder. When I turned to the client, ready to begin induction, she was already far gone.

There are clients, on the other hand, with whom I am careful *not* to let my voice change in my usual way. These are clients, men and women, who have expressed fear of intimacy — and it is clear that a gentle whisper can feel very intimate — and a few women who have expressed sexual feelings for me. With all these clients, I make an effort to keep my voice at a normal level and tone.

In conclusion, inductions are simply means rather than ends. Since it is the end of greater receptivity that we are or should be interested in, whatever method serves to get the client there in the most efficient way is what we should use. The point of therapy, including hypnotherapy, is to help people change and not, as some clinicians seem to think, to promote understanding or to demonstrate fancy and long-winded inductions.

$\underset{A}{Q}$&19 Another View of Choosing Inductions

Question:

> I am confused by all the induction methods I've read about. How does one know which will be more effective with a given patient?

Discussion by WILLIAM L. GOLDEN, Ph.D.

I will describe four approaches for choosing an induction most likely to elicit a favorable response: 1) trial and error; 2) capitalizing on the expectations, preferences and past experiences of the individual; 3) Ericksonian techniques; and 4) the hypnotic skills training approach.

Trial and Error

There are wide differences in how individuals respond to the various hypnotic induction procedures. For example some are extremely responsive to suggestions of lightness and hand levitation, while others show no response whatsoever. Nevertheless, the latter may be responsive to some other procedure, such as eye fixation. One method for selecting the most effective procedure is to experiment with several different inductions and thus discover which one results in the best patient response. One problem with trial and error is that negative expectations may develop if the hypnotist begins with the "wrong" method for that patient. Failure has the potential of decreasing the confidence of the patient in the hypnotist as well as in his or her own hypnotic ability. These failures can interfere with the patient's response to subsequent hypnotic procedures. Therefore, it would be preferable if the hypnotist could make the "right" choice immediately.

There are several ways in which the hypnotist can lessen the impact of a failure experience on the patient's receptivity to other hypnotic induction procedures. If the therapist is skilled and confident in employing a number of inductions, his credibility as an authority is increased. As such expertise is demonstrated, the patient will trust and believe in the hypnotist even if they together go into a few blind alleys.

However, patients could still doubt their own hypnotizability, and care should be taken to avoid such negative evaluations. One method for reducing this danger is to inform patients in advance that failure to respond to *some* procedures is to be expected, but others will meet with success, and so some trial and error is necessary in order to find the right one for them.

Capitalizing on Expectations and Preferences

The patient is an excellent source for information about what inductions are most likely to be effective. Hypnotic induction is easiest when the patient has had a positive hypnotic experience. If a patient was successful with a particular induction on another occasion, then the hypnotist would be wise to employ the same procedure. I typically ask for detailed accounts of what the patient experienced, what techniques were used, and how he or she reacted to them. Sometimes I modify the method of the previous hypnotist as a result of the patient's feedback. Keep in mind that although the basic induction of a previous hypnotist may have been effective, the patient may still have been dissatisfied with the previous treatment. Therefore, I ask what he or she liked and disliked about the previous method. For example, a number of patients who have sought hypnosis for weight control reported that, although they responded well to an eye fixation method of induction, they were annoyed when the previous hypnotist suggested, as part of the induction, that their bodies would feel heavy. Hence, my modification is to employ an eye fixation induction but without giving suggestions of heaviness. I suggest that only their eyes will feel heavy. (I would recommend not giving suggestions of heaviness to any patient with a weight problem. Hand levitation and suggestions of lightness or a relaxation method might be employed instead.)

I also think it is important to recognize the therapeutic relationship in hypnotherapy. I have often seen hypnotherapy trainees proceeding correctly as far as techniques are concerned but failing with patients because of interpersonal factors. They lack rapport and warmth or fail to instill trust and confidence in patients. Therefore, I also ask my patients what they liked and disliked about the style and approach of the previous hypnotist. Was the previous therapist too authoritarian, too passive, not directive enough, too distant, etc?

Other patients may have had hypnotic-like experiences, which provide the clinician with helpful clues in selecting an appropriate induction. Many patients have had positive experiences with meditation and with relaxation procedures, or have learned self-hypnosis from a book or from a record or tape recording. In addition, natural "autohypnotic" experiences can provide clues as to what induction might be effective. For example, one patient disclosed that when she was a child her bedroom window faced a clothesline and she listened to the sound of the sheets flapping in the wind to lull herself to sleep. The image of sheets flapping in the wind proved to be an excellent induction for her. Images for relaxation can be selected in a similar manner. I ask patients to recall when they felt very relaxed and to describe the situation in as much detail as possible. Later, I describe these scenes in vivid detail as part of an hypnotic induction.

Another way of deciding on the right induction is to inquire about expectations. What does the patient think will be effective? What method has the patient seen being used on someone else? What has the patient heard about hypnosis from friends? What does the patient expect hypnosis will be like? The rule of thumb is to match the method to the expectations of the patient. You can also evaluate the preferences and expectations of patients by describing several induction procedures, such as eye fixation, hand levitation, counting, and relaxation methods and then asking which one the patient prefers and thinks will be most effective.

Ericksonian Techniques

In Milton Erickson's approach to hypnosis (see Erickson & Rossi, 1979; Erickson, Rossi, & Rossi, 1976), hypnotic induction is accomplished through the utilization of the patient's own associations and response potentials. Erickson felt that standardized hypnotic inductions interfere with patients' responsiveness because they do not allow enough flexibility. He emphasized the importance of "joining" the patient and starting with and utilizing whatever the patient presents. The therapist "paces" i.e., gives suggestions that match the patient's behavior and experiences. When the therapist's suggestions match the patient's already occurring behavior and experience, the patient becomes more responsive to subsequent suggestions. Then the therapist can be more directive and take the lead. As Bandler and Grinder (1975) point out, there are two types of suggestions that involve pacing: 1) suggestions that describe the patient's ongoing observable behavior; and 2) suggestions that describe the patient's ongoing nonobservable experience.

The first type of pacing depends on the hypnotist's ability to be perceptive and notice small changes in the patient's ongoing behavior, such as the patient's breathing pattern, muscle tone, and posture. The suggestions are timed so that they are accurate descriptions of the patient's behavior, for example, suggesting that the patient "breathe in" as the patient actually inhales and suggesting that the patient "breathe out" as the patient exhales. Another example is to suggest to a patient who is in the process of shifting to a more comfortable position, "and as you sink more deeply in the chair. . . . " Leading occurs when the therapist adds "you can become more comfortable and start to relax all over."

The second type of pacing depends on the hypnotist's ability to give suggestions that will accurately describe the patient's private experience. This is possible through the use of indirect suggestions. There are several types of communication devices involving different forms of indirect suggestion that increase the likelihood that the hypnotist's suggestions will match the patient's private experience:

Open-ended suggestions. Erickson emphasized the importance of being permissive and allowing patients choices in their response to hypnotic suggestions. Open-ended suggestions, such as those involving generalizations, encourage individuals to project their own unique associations and meaning into them, thereby maximizing the likelihood that there will be some sort of response to the suggestions. Here are a few examples of open-ended suggestions that allow a great deal of freedom in how an individual will respond:

> You may be aware of a certain sensation. (Bandler & Grinder, 1975, p. 19)

> We all have potentials we are unaware of, and we usually don't know how they will be expressed.

> You may be aware of some changes during the week.

Suggestions involving several alternative ways of responding. One example of how Erickson increased the likelihood of response in an individual was to give suggestions that provided several alternative ways of responding. One of Erickson's inductions covering all of the possible ways of responding to a suggestion for hand levitation is the following:

> Shortly your right hand, or it may be your left hand will begin to lift up or it may press down, or it may not move at all, but we will wait to see just what happens. Maybe the thumb will be first, or you may feel something happening to your little finger, but the really important thing is not whether your hand lifts up or presses down or just remains still; rather it is your ability to sense fully whatever feeling may develop in your hand. (Erickson, Rossi, & Rossi, 1976, p. 78)

Suggestions such as this allow the individual freedom in how to respond.

When choice is given, there is less resistance. Also, under conditions where there are alternative ways of responding, the individual is more likely to relate to at least one of the choices.

Suggestions involving multiple tasks and alternative ways of responding. Erickson often made use of suggestions that involved multiple tasks. For example, he would assign absorbing tasks such as asking a patient to imagine listening to music while, at the same time, he would give other suggestions. According to Erickson, suggestions that involve multiple tasks reduce the likelihood of resistance, because the individual becomes more receptive to suggestions when confused or distracted by an absorbing task (Erickson & Rossi, 1979).

Some research from social psychology demonstrates the effectiveness of using distraction and multiple tasks in reducing resistance. Festinger and Maccoby (1964) found that simple distraction can overcome resistance: Two groups of college fraternity students were required to listen to a tape-recorded speech about the "evils" of college fraternities. During the presentation, one group of students was distracted while the other was not. The distraction was a highly entertaining silent film. Festinger and Maccoby predicted that the group that was engaged in the two tasks simultaneously would show more attitude change because their minds were too occupied for them to have an opportunity to build up resistance against the speech. Indeed, the group of students who were distracted underwent significantly more opinion change against fraternities than did the nondistracted group.

Applying Ericksonian principles, I have found that an eye fixation induction is more likely to be effective when it involves multiple tasks and allows patients alternative ways of responding. I have found eye closure occurs rapidly when I do not focus on eye closure but instead assign the patient the task of eye fixation while I suggest relaxation, changes in breathing, etc. The following induction illustrates these principles:

> "You can pick a spot, any spot will do, and keep on staring at it. If your eyes should wander just go back to the same spot. Just keep on staring at it until your eyes become tired of it. Then you can close your eyes and enter a peaceful relaxed state. While you stare at that spot you may notice some interesting phenomena. Some people experience a blurring of their vision, while for others the spot moves, pulsates, or disappears. The really important thing is for you to notice whatever it is that you experience and to enjoy it. . . . And while you continue to focus on that spot you can let yourself sink into the chair and begin to relax. . . . "

Truisms. Truisms are indirect suggestions (simple statements of fact) that cannot be denied. They do not direct the patient to do anything or have any particular type of experience. A truism only says that it is possible to have a particular type of experience:

People can usually relax more easily with their eyes closed.

When we are tired, our eyes begin to blink slowly and sometimes close without our quite realizing it. (Erickson & Rossi, 1979, p. 23)

Many people find it very relaxing to imagine being in a pleasant, peaceful place.

Indirect suggestions such as truisms may be effective because many patients become anxious or threatened whenever they perceive that they are expected to perform in a particular manner. Often they try too hard to respond to direct suggestions, which then makes them less responsive. Other patients seem to rebel whenever they feel that someone, including a therapist, is trying to control them. The advantage of the truism, as well as other indirect suggestions, is that it is difficult for patients to perceive that indirect suggestions are actually being directed towards them. Then, once these patients relax their guard and lower their defenses, they are more likely to respond.

Conversational postulates. Conversational postulates are indirect suggestions that state "You can" or ask "Can you?" experience a particular phenomena, feeling, or sensation. Conversational postulates are very permissive in their wording. Like other indirect suggestions, conversational postulates do not directly command the individual to do anything. They only suggest possibilities. Therefore, if the patient does not respond to these indirect suggestions, the failure to respond does not have an adverse effect on the credibility and influence of the hypnotist, nor does it result in self-blaming on the part of the patient, since no response was required.

Bandler and Grinder (1975) provide the following guidelines for constructing conversational postulates:

1) Identify a suggestion you want to give, e.g., eye fixation.
2) Form a command out of the suggestion, e.g., "Focus your eyes on that spot."
3) Rephrase the command into a possibility, e.g., "You can focus your eyes on that spot."
4) Or form a yes/no question out of the command, e.g., "Can you focus your eyes on that spot?"

Erickson has shown that it is possible to induce hypnosis by asking a series of questions. (See Erickson and Rossi, 1979, pp. 29–30, for Erickson's induction procedures for eye fixation and hand levitation where all of the suggestions are questions.)

Hypnotic Skills Training

Several hypnotherapists with a cognitive-behavioral orientation have developed programs for teaching individuals how to be more responsive to hypnotic suggestions (Diamond, 1974, 1977; Gargiulo, 1983; Golden, 1982; Golden & Friedberg, in press). These programs employ cognitive-behavioral principles and techniques such as modeling, imagery training, self-talk, reinforcement for incremental improvements in hypnotic responsiveness, and training in how to block out negative competing thoughts such as "This won't work" or "I'm not going to be able to respond." These methods have, in fact, been found to increase hypnotic responsiveness (Katz, 1979).

I typically teach hypnotic skills to most of my patients prior to having them experience an hypnotic induction. My reasons are twofold: 1) Hypnotic skills training can provide me with information about how a given patient responds to different types of suggestions, which will help me in deciding which induction procedure to use; and 2) hypnotic skills training will enhance the patient's responsiveness to hypnotic suggestion in general and will therefore increase the effectiveness of any hypnotic induction procedure.

Hypnotic skills training is conducted in the following manner: First a series of suggestions is selected. Any of the traditional hypnotic susceptibility tests can be employed. However, instead of using the tasks from hypnotic susceptibility scales as tests, they are modified into *practice exercises*. The patients are shown how to respond to them. For example, to produce hand levitation, patients are instructed to select appropriate strategies, such as imagining holding a helium balloon and employing self-suggestions of lightness. If the patient has difficulty, the therapist may serve as a model of demonstrating how to respond to suggestions for hand levitation through the use of appropriate strategies. The therapist might say something like,

> I'm able to produce hand levitation by imagining a giant helium balloon under the palm of my hand. I imagine its shape, its color, its texture, the feeling of buoyancy that it produces in my hand. This is the strategy that I use but you can use any image and suggestion that will work for you. Then I give myself suggestions that my hand is feeling light and buoyant, and that it feels like lifting. I suggest that it will start to lift, starting to lift, lifting, lifting. Notice that I repeat the suggestions many times, as often as needed in order to get a response. And if any

stray thoughts like "this won't work" enter my mind I just block them out or say 'Stop!' to them and refocus my balloon image and the suggestions of lightness.

The therapist can also help a patient having difficulty by asking, "What is going through your mind during the exercise?" This question helps identify distracting thoughts that interfere with hypnotic responsiveness. Once these competing thoughts are identified, the therapist teaches the patient how to block them by either refocusing on the appropriate image and suggestions and/or using thought stoppage, i.e., thinking, "Stop!"

Usually, I have my patients experiment and practice producing hand heaviness and lowering, hand levitation and hand lightness, and arm catalepsy. I may also employ other exercises such as Chevreul's pendulum. I attempt to order these exercises so that the easiest suggestions are experienced first. However, I have learned there is no universal order. For example, although hand heaviness is one of the easiest for many patients, some patients may find it is easier to respond to suggestions for hand levitation or arm catalepsy. Others find it easiest to produce a magnetic-like force between their hands that pulls the hands together or that forces them apart. These individual differences are exactly what I look for in determining what type of induction might be most appropriate for a given patient. So, if a patient responds well to suggestions of lightness, I employ hand levitation for inducing hypnosis. If, however, a patient responds better to suggestions for heaviness, I induce hypnosis via eye fixation and closure.

References

Bandler, R., & Grinder, J. (1975). *Patterns of the hypnotic techniques of Milton H. Erickson M.D.* Cupertino, CA: Meta Publications.

Diamond, M. J. (1974). Modification of hypnotizability: A review. *Psychological Bulletin, 81*, 180–198.

Diamond, M. J. (1977). Hypnotizability is modifiable: An alternative approach. *International Journal of Clinical and Experimental Hypnosis, 25*, 147–166.

Erickson, M. H., & Rossi, E. L. (1979). *Hypnotherapy: An exploratory casebook.* New York: Irvington.

Erickson, M. H., Rossi, E. L., & Rossi, S. L. (1976). *Hypnotic realities.* New York: Irvington.

Festinger, L., & Maccoby, N. (1964). On resistance to persuasive communications. *Journal of Abnormal and Social Psychology, 68*, 359–366.

Gargiulo, T. (1983). Influence of training in hypnotic responsivity on hypnotically suggested analgesia. Unpublished doctoral dissertation, California Coast University.

Golden, W. L. (1982). *Self-hypnosis: The rational-emotive approach.* (cassette recording). New York: Institute for Rational-Emotive Therapy.

Golden, W. L., & Friedberg, F. (in press). Cognitive-behavioral hypnotherapy. In W. Dryden & W. L. Golden (Eds.) *Cognitive-behavioral approaches to psychotherapy.* London: Harper & Row.

Katz, N. W. (1979). Comparative efficacy of behavioral training, training plus relaxation, and sleep/trance hypnotic induction in increasing hypnotic susceptibility. *Journal of Consulting and Clinical Psychology, 47*, 119–127.

Q&A 20 Duration of Inductions

Question:

In my introductory course on hypnosis I saw demonstrations of inductions that took 20–30 minutes, and others that took less than five minutes. In general, how long should an induction take?

Discussion by BILLIE S. LAZAR, Ph.D.

The hypnotic induction helps the patient make the transition from the waking state to hypnosis. With most patients, the induction takes no more than five minutes. However, the length of the induction may vary from several seconds to an entire session, depending on several factors. These include the responsivity of the patient, the particular techniques used, the patient's previous experience with and expectations about hypnosis, the demand characteristics of the situation, expectations of the therapist, and the meaning of hypnosis to the patient.

The clinician must keep in mind that the primary purpose of hypnotherapy is the treatment of the patient, rather than the production of the hypnotic state. When to stop the induction if the patient does not go into hypnosis is a matter of clinical judgment. Rather than prescribe "how long an induction should take," let us examine some of the factors that influence the length of the induction and consider the issue of when to stop if the induction is unlikely to be successful.

The particular technique used may influence the length of the hypnotic induction. On one hand, the induction may be well-defined and distinguishable from hypnosis and from the waking state (e.g., Gill & Brenman, 1959). On the other hand, the induction may be subtle and barely noticeable (e.g., Erickson, 1958, 1959).

When hypnotizability scales are used, the induction takes place within a prescribed time range, depending on the particular scale and the responsivity of the subject. For example, the Stanford Hypnotic Susceptibility Scale, Form A (Weitzenhoffer & Hilgard, 1959) allows 15 minutes for the eye closure induction. Some subjects may go into hypnosis within two minutes, while others may require the entire 15 minutes. (The subject is considered to have passed the item if the eyes close before a direct suggestion to do so is given.) On the other hand, the briefer Stanford Hypnotic Clinical Scale for Adults (Morgan & Hilgard, 1975) allows about five minutes for the induction, although this induction (suggestions of relaxation with eyes closed) does not assess when and whether the subject goes into hypnosis.

Beyond an initial assessment, I generally do not use the standardized hypnotizability scales, but, rather, techniques selected to fit the needs of the patient. In contrast to standardized scales, once the patient responds to the induction, the induction is ended and deepening or other techniques begun. Patients capable of ideomotor phenomena, intense and vivid imagery, and hypnotic analgesia usually need no more than two or three minutes for the induction. On the other hand, patients who cannot do any one of these phenomena may vary in the time needed for the induction. The induction typically takes less than one minute and at most five minutes. If the patient shows no sign of responding to the induction within about five minutes, I generally shift to another technique or discuss with the patient his or her reaction. If a partial response occurs, I continue as long as the patient's response progresses. The criterion for ending the induction, either because the patient goes into hypnosis or does not respond, is not time, but the response of the patient.

A rapid induction may work within minutes or seconds *if the patient responds*. For example, the postural sway technique may help a highly hypnotizable patient to go into a deep trance within two minutes. Similarly, the fractionation technique may take less than one minute. On the other hand, induction techniques such as eye fixation or arm levitation may be structured so that the subject does not go into hypnosis for five to 10 minutes or continued even after the subject goes into trance. An induction which suggests that a patient will be hypnotized after the therapist counts to 40 will take longer than one which suggests that hypnosis will result by the count of five.

With some patients, the therapist may choose to prolong the induction to ease the transition between the waking state and hypnosis. For example, a patient previously hospitalized with a diagnosis of borderline personality was referred for hypnotherapy because she feared and refused routine but necessary medical procedures. She felt that hypnosis was a magical tool and that fantasies and thoughts really happened. The initial induction, an eye fixation technique, took approximately five minutes, during which time the patient was told she could open her eyes at any time as well as talk and describe her thoughts and feelings.

The length of the hypnotic induction may depend on the patient's previous experience with and expectations about hypnosis. For example, if a patient has previously experienced long inductions, then he or she may need long inductions to go into hypnosis.

A patient with previous experience may be given a posthypnotic suggestion to go into hypnosis on cue, in which case the induction will take several seconds. Other patients with previous hypnotic experience may be hypnotized using a revivification technique, where the patient is told to recall a previous comfortable hypnotic experience. In good hypnotic subjects suggestions such as, "Recall the last time you were comfortably hypnotized and allow yourself to experience those comfortable feelings," may result in a trance state in less than a minute. Some subjects with previous experience go into hypnosis spontaneously. For example, in an introductory hypnosis course, an excellent subject (capable of positive and negative hallucinations) served as a practice subject for several students and was observed to go into a medium trance state upon sitting down in a chair in the room.

The demand characteristics of the situation and the expectations of the therapist may affect the length of time needed for the hypnotic induction. Research (e.g., Rosenthal, 1966) has shown that experimenter expectations influence a range of behaviors, from performance on tests to the turning of planaria. The therapist may suggest, either directly or indirectly, the length of the induction.

The meaning of hypnosis to the patient may influence the length of the induction. If the patient views hypnotherapy as potentially removing a symptom which he or she needs, then the patient may resist the hypnotic induction and take a longer time, if he or she goes into trance at all. A longer induction time may communicate the patient's wish to move slowly in treatment. For some patients, the induction may be experienced as similar to the symptom for which the patient seeks relief, and the patient may resist going into hypnosis. For example, a patient with a flying phobia sought hypnotherapy. After approximately three minutes of seemingly minimal response to an induction technique involving sensory imagery, the patient interrupted and noted that the induction felt as though he were flying. Subsequent techniques involving imagery of mastery rapidly resulted in a hypnotic state.

In general, hypnotic inductions take no more than a few minutes, although the time may be lengthened to accommodate certain patients or shortened for others. Although the patient's responsivity is a major factor in determining the length of the induction, other facets of the hypnotic context, including particular technique used, expectations about hypnosis, previous experience, and the meaning of the hypnotic situation to the patient also play a role in determining the length of the induction. When to end the induction if the patient does not respond involves clinical judgment. If the patient clearly does not respond after a few minutes, the therapist should switch to another technique or talk with the patient about what is going on.

References

Erickson, M. H. (1958). Naturalistic techniques of hypnosis. *American Journal of Clinical Hypnosis, 1*, 25–29.

Erickson, M. H. (1959). Further techniques of hypnosis — Utilization techniques. *American Journal of Clinical Hypnosis, 2*, 3–21.

Gill, M. M., & Brenman, M. (1959). *Hypnosis and related states.* New York: International Universities Press.

Morgan, A., & Hilgard, J. R. (1975). Stanford Hypnotic Clinical Scale for Adults. In E. R. Hilgard & J. R. Hilgard (Eds.). *Hypnosis in the relief of pain.* Los Altos, CA: William Kaufman.

Rosenthal, R. (1966). *Experimenter effects.* New York: Appleton-Century-Crofts.

Weitzenhoffer, A. M., & Hilgard E. R. (1959). *Stanford Hypnotic Susceptibility Scale: Forms A and B.* Palo Alto, CA: Consulting Psychologists Press.

$\underset{\underset{A}{\&}}{Q}$ 21 Using Spontaneous Trances

Question:

> In several discussions I've heard it said that formal inductions are not necessary, that one should simply utilize the spontaneous trances patients go into. How is this done?

Discussion by JOHN F. CHAVES, Ph.D.

Traditionally, it has been assumed that a hypnotic state is necessary in order to elicit responses to suggestions of the sort normally included as a part of a hypnotherapeutic intervention. However, for many years now, the literature in experimental hypnosis has clearly demonstrated that motivated subjects who have been suitably instructed can respond to suggestions to the same degree as subjects who have had a prior hypnotic induction procedure (Barber, Spanos, & Chaves, 1974). Moreover, the unhypnotized subjects' reports of their subjective involvement in the experience in responding to the suggestion parallels the involvement of the hypnotic subjects. Thus, the degree to which these subjects characterize their responses as involuntarily is comparable to hypnotic subjects.

The above findings have been obtained across a wide variety of subject populations involved with various kinds of suggestions. Even pain control by suggestion is as feasible without hypnosis as with hypnosis (Chaves & Barber, 1974, 1976). The pivotal issue is whether or not a suggestion has been administered (Evans & Paul, 1970). Thus, in achieving pain control direct suggestions for pain control are more important than suggestions that the subject is entering a hypnotic state. As Barber has noted, we have consistently erred by underestimating the base level of responsivity to suggestion in nonhypnotic subjects. Clinically, this observation has great import.

Among other things, it means that suggestions accompanied by appropriate cognitive strategies can be used under a wide variety of circumstances in which a formal hypnotic procedure may be inappropriate or unacceptable to the subject.

Next, let's turn to the question of enhancing the probability that subjects will respond to suggestions administered outside of the hypnotic context. Viewed from the standpoint of hypnotic state theory, one could attempt to identify signs of "spontaneous trances," presumably reflecting episodes of heightened responsivity to suggestion. Viewed in this way, the critical question becomes: How can you identify subjects who are experiencing spontaneous trance? Unfortunately, there is no ready answer to this question, in part because the denotation of critical terms such as "trance" is unclear. Typically, the occurrence of these spontaneous "trances" is inferred from the response of subjects to suggestions. This leads to an unsatisfactory tautology, however, since you only know that the subject has been in a spontaneous "trance" because he responded to the suggestion you've administered. Others have used the notion of "spontaneous trances" to explain why subjects respond to any suggestions that are administered outside of the hypnotic context. This interpretation has criticized elsewhere (Chaves, 1968). It is sufficient to note here that this notion of spontaneous "trance" is too broad to be of any real value.

Viewed from the cognitive/behavioral standpoint, the task is somewhat different. Rather than assuming that response to suggestions requires a "spontaneous trance," we instead focus on those factors, both intrinsic and extrinsic to the therapeutic intervention, that affect the probability of responding appropriately to suggestions (Chaves, 1985a, 1985b). This includes the patient's preconceptions regarding the nature of the therapeutic transaction, the phenomenological network in which the patient's problematic behaviors are embedded, as well as verbal and nonverbal interpersonal cues that can help set the stage for responding to the suggestion.

The patient's attitudes and expectations regarding the therapeutic intervention and the patient's perceived capacity to benefit thereby are often critical. Accordingly, an appropriate foundation can frequently be laid by conveying a strong positive attitude towards the patient's ability to respond to suggestions and a conviction that the patient will find it possible to respond appropriately. Dialogue with the patient to minimize competing negative thoughts or images can also be valuable in enhancing probability of response to suggestion (Brown & Chaves, 1980).

It may be instructive to consider how spontaneous hypnosis may be experienced from the viewpoint of a sophisticated participant. The following comments were obtained from a Ph.D. clinical psychologist who had been professionally trained in the use of clinical hypnosis and had been a patient of mine.

During an early hypnosis session, Dr. Chaves used a metaphor to the effect that the ideas he was introducing would soon begin to blend with my own thoughts, almost as if a new "fabric" of ideas were being woven together. This fabric would evolve into a new entity in which it would be hard to tell where certain of my thoughts ended and his began. Knowing that the alternatives being proposed were healthier than those I was accustomed to was a comforting thought.

I believe the metaphor of a "fabric" consisting of indistinguishable threads of consciousness — his and mine, substituting rational where there was once irrational — also serves nicely as a metaphor for what I later came to realize was a frequent quality of the therapy which could be called spontaneous hypnosis. There were definite moments in which trance vs. non-trance states were by and large indistinguishable. There were numerous moments when I felt myself paying so much attention, feeling so open and eager to listen, almost as though each exposure solidified concepts that had been introduced in or out of hypnosis. I knew precisely when this was happening and commented more than once about it. I finally got to the point that I no longer wondered, "Would we do hypnosis today?" because frequently what transpired, I felt, was hypnosis.

The type of cognitive restructuring therapy that was taking place, specifically within the context of hypnotherapy, as well as psychotherapy in general, has the potential to result in the patient's experiencing a level of consciousness that could be classified as hypnosis.

Some might call this indirect hypnosis, but I would not because I think it happens without even the intent of the therapist. Rather, it may primarily result from client variables operating within a trusting therapeutic relationship. I believe this happens in any psychotherapy when the client truly feels the support and effectiveness of therapy, and particularly when alternative ways of living seem not only possible but attainable. Although I do not believe psychotherapy is usually conceptualized as having such similarity to hypnosis, I believe there are many moments when an effective psychotherapy involves spontaneous hypnotic states.

As the above narrative makes clear, patients exposed to a hypnotic intervention that is presented within a cognitive/behavioral frame of reference describe experiences which resemble the reports of spontaneous hypnosis solicited from patients being treated with more traditional types of hypnotic intervention. The pivotal variable in spontaneous hypnosis is providing suggestions that are consistent with the patient's phenomenology within the context of a trusting therapeutic relationship.

References

Barber, T. X., Spanos, N. P., & Chaves, J. F. (1974). *Hypnotism, imagination, and human potentialities.* New York: Pergamon Press.

Brown, J., & Chaves, J. F. (1980). Hypnosis in the treatment of sexual dysfunction. *Journal of Sex and Marital Therapy, 6,* 63–74.

Chaves, J. F. (1968). Hypnosis reconceptualized: An overview of Barber's theoretical and empirical work. *Psychological Reports, 22,* 587–608.

Chaves, J. F., & Barber, T. X. (1974). Cognitive strategies, experimenter modeling and expectation in the attenuation of pain. *Journal of Abnormal Psychology, 83,* 356–363.

Chaves, J. F., & Barber, T. X. (1976). Hypnosis and surgery: A critical analysis without applications to acupuncture analgesia. *American Journal of Clinical Hypnosis, 18,* 217–236.

Chaves, J. F. (1985a). Hypnosis in the management of phantom limb pain. In T. Dowd & J. Healy (Eds.). *Case studies in hypnotherapy* (pp. 198–209). New York: Guilford.

Chaves, J. F. (1985b). Hypnosis in the management of behavioral components of Prader-Willi Syndrome. In T. Dowd & J. Healy (Eds.). *Case studies in hypnotherapy* (pp. 301–309). New York: Guilford.

Evans, M. B., & Paul, G. L. (1970). Effects of hypnotically suggested analgesia on physiological and subjective responses to cold stress. *Journal of Consulting and Clinical Psychology, 35,* 362–371.

$\underset{A}{\overset{Q}{\mathcal{E}}}22$ Depth of Trance and Susceptibility to Suggestion

Question:

How can I tell when someone is in a trance? How do I know when they are deep enough to be susceptible to my suggestions?

Discussion by SEYMOUR HOLZMAN, Ph.D.

First, it is useful to differentiate between a spontaneous trance and an induced trance. People spontaneously go in and out of trance states many times throughout their daily lives, without others' or their being aware of it. Recognizing the process in yourself makes it easier to recognize it in others. For example, while waiting for a train or bus, you may drift into an elaborate personal fantasy. Your eyes will be open as usual, but in your "mind's eye" you may be seeing all sorts of things that are not apparent to anyone else. It is only when the train or bus arrives that you resume seeing and attending to what is actually in front of you. This would be considered a spontaneous trance.

Another example is listening to someone's conversation, but suddenly not hearing it, perhaps for just a brief interval, while other thoughts, feelings, or images absorb your attention. Conversely, while you are talking to someone that person's eyes remain open, but you're aware that those eyes are focused on some far distant scene and the person's face has taken on a glazed look. In another moment or two, attention is focused on you again.

There are countless other everyday examples. However, it is not readily discernible when someone is in a spontaneous trance, except for his inattentive or somewhat unseeing look. Some therapists, when recognizing this in the office, will quietly tell the patient to close his/her eyes and then procede with whatever hypnotic work is indicated, thereby eliminating the need for a formal induction.

126

When working with a client specifically to induce a trance, the therapist most likely will find that the client has a favorable mental set, especially if the induction process has been explained beforehand. Although there are no absolute criteria to verify an induction, there are rather typical responses indicative of success: The eyes blink, close, reopen, and then close completely, followed in most instances by a rapid fluttering of the eyelids. Muscles go loose and limp and generally remain quite motionless. The shoulders sag, as the lower jaw does at times, and facial creases seem to smooth out. Breathing becomes easier and steadier. If the patient obtains a truly deep state, a circumoral pallor may be noted.

Following suggestions for awakening, the client may report distortions of time, sensory experiences, or bodily sensations. For example, "Gee, that session felt like it was only 10 minutes long." "It felt like I was so heavy (light, or floating)." "It felt so great I didn't want it to end." "I was surprised that I could ignore that fire engine going by." Reactions like these can serve as further evidence, presumptive, that a trance was achieved.

Some hypnotherapists, in order to convince the client, and perhaps themselves, that a trance has been established, may offer "challenges" to their clients. A "challenge" may consist of suggestions that the client's interlocked fingers are stuck so tightly together that they cannot be pulled apart, that eyelids are closed so tightly that they cannot be opened, or that the client's hand becomes so light that it floats up to the person's face. I do not get involved with challenges. Any attempt by the anxious hypnotherapist to verify that a trance has been induced is usually unnecessary and unproductive. Whether or not the client has entered a trance is not nearly as important as whether the client is prepared to make behavioral changes that are in his/her best interests.

In my therapy sessions for specific problems like excessive anxiety, overeating, or smoking, I am not as concerned about the depth of trance as I am that clients collaborate with me in formulating suggestions that they would want to hear in a hypnotic state and that are ego-syntonic for them. While the stage hypnotist may be preoccupied with depth of trance so that he may demonstrate the "irresistible" power of hypnotic suggestions, my task as a hypnotherapist is to develop trust, cooperation, and a therapeutic alliance in order to achieve mutually agreed upon goals. In order to promote this collaboration, I review with my clients a variety of pertinent suggestions that I have formulated in working with previous clients who had similar problems. This review of suggestions that I have used with others can sometimes stimulate the production of fresh suggestions, or modifications, which otherwise would not have occurred to either of us.

This entire process of joint collaboration to produce acceptable and ego-syntonic suggestions may serve to avoid resistance to the hypnotherapy. I am not imposing my suggestions on the client; rather, he or she has agreed to the suggestions that sound right and has chosen to hear these while in a relaxed, hypnotic state. I also recommend making an audiocasette for the client to take home to replay. The frequent relistening to this tape, after the hypnotherapy session is over, and the reinduction of a hypnotic state with each relistening, can promote imprinting of the agreed upon suggestions. A good example of this imprinting occurred with one client who was convinced that nothing much had happened in our session because she did not feel hypnotized. Nevertheless, she reported several weeks later that she found herself repeating, while driving her car, a slogan that we had agreed upon concerning her excessive anxiety: "I don't want it, I don't need it, and no more self-defeat."

My experience, therefore, has been that it is not so much the depth of trance that determines susceptibility to suggestions as the acceptability and ego-syntonicity of the suggestions. What also determines susceptibility to suggestions is the trust that has developed during this joint collaboration, which may encourage a readiness to take risks in trying out new behavior, rather than automatically continuing with previously unproductive and unsatisfying behavior.

It is frequently stated that those who seem to benefit most from hypnotherapy are capable of achieving either a light or medium trance. My own understanding of this paradoxical phenomenon is that those who can readily achieve a deep or somnambulistic state are so adept at repression and spontaneous amnesia that they automatically repress or develop amnesia for hypnotic suggestions. Those who are capable of a mild or moderate trance are not automatically repressing the suggestions and are therefore better able to integrate those suggestions that they consider useful, desirable, helpful, and appropriate.

Q&A 23 Importance of Depth of Trance

Question:

How can I tell how deeply hypnotized a client is and under what circumstances is depth of trance an important issue?

Discussion by JILL BOND CAIRE, Ph.D.

Depth is generally associated with the degree of disengagement from the external environment, narrowed focus of attention, and enhanced responsiveness to suggestion. Notions of depth have been determined by testing groups of individuals and grading the difficulty they exhibit in experiencing or producing certain phenomena. For example, eye closure is something most subjects are able to experience; thus it is graded as an "easy" or "light" trance phenomenon. Responses more difficult to produce and experienced by fewer subjects, such as amnesia and age regression, are rated as characteristics of "deep" trance.

There are many methods of ascertaining depth, depending on how accurately you wish to assess it. Clinicians most often test depth by giving subjects suggestions which are progressively more difficult to demonstrate, e.g., eye closure, postural sway, inability to unclasp hands or open eyes, and hallucinations. Formal scales, such as the Stanford Scales of Hypnotic Susceptibility, which were developed for experimental purposes, are also available; however, it is not at all clear what *therapeutic* purpose is served by the administration of such tests.

It is important to keep in mind that so-called depth of trance, often used synonymously with hypnotic suggestibility, is not static or linear in nature. Depth varies between individuals and also within an individual at different times. Most subjects experience fluctuations within a given session in degree

129

of engagement in internal processing and response to suggestion. Even well-trained hypnotic subjects experience these fluctuations. Individuals also vary in their capacity to experience certain kinds of phenomena. One person may be able to experience amnesia but not hallucinations, while for another person it may be just the opposite.

In clinical work, the primary reason for testing depth is to predict the client's potential response to suggestion. A second reason is to give the client a feeling of confidence in his or her capacity to respond to suggestions. For most clinical purposes a satisfactory level of depth or disengagement will be demonstrated by a slower, deeper pattern of breathing, passivity of facial muscles, and positive response to suggestions of eye closure.

It is a great mistake to assume that capacity for depth and the achievement of therapeutic goals are identical. Most beginning hypnotists are fascinated by the phenomena associated with deep trance and wish to observe them whenever possible. However, as clinical experience is gained, therapists discover that, while certain phenomena are frequently associated with depth — hallucinations, amnesia, loss of perceptual references, and certain kinds of automatic behaviors — the accomplishment of therapeutic goals does *not* depend on the capacity to produce these phenomena. In practice, one observes that very capable somnambulists may fail or have limited success in therapy and that some very "poor" subjects (those who do not attain great depth and even fail formal tests of hypnotic suggestibility) may achieve remarkable results. As Wilson and Barber (1983, p. 377) note, "Whether an individual is an excellent hypnotic subject in that he or she responds profoundly to *classical* hypnotic suggestions is not correlated with his or her responsiveness to *therapeutic* suggestions to lose weight, stop smoking, become relieved of back pain, and other ailments."

For clinicians it is much more useful to focus on therapeutic goals than on depth of hypnosis or the kinds of phenomena exhibited. Hypnosis in and of itself is not therapeutic; rather, it is a medium whereby therapeutic goals can be accomplished. While hypnosis is a state of mind in which individuals are generally more receptive and responsive to suggestion, the success of any suggestion depends on a correct understanding of the client and the utilization of his or her motivation and resources to accomplish a particular goal. A totally alien suggestion is not likely to be accepted by the client regardless of depth of trance.

The first steps toward designing successful suggestions include taking a thorough history of the problem, ascertaining the client's previous attempts at resolution, and assessing the client's coping skills, resources, and reasons for wanting to change. Next, the client's ideas about hypnosis need to be investigated so that misconceptions can be corrected. Most clients have had at least some exposure to hypnosis or quasi-hypnosis through the media. What they have seen or read is usually very dramatic, whereas response to hypnosis in clinical situations is usually much more subtle, especially when habits and attitudes are the focus of change. When clients express a wish for "proof" of hypnosis, it is always good to redirect their attention toward *observing the results* of the suggestions in the ensuing weeks. In this way the goals of the hypnotic interaction are the primary focus of both hypnotist and client, and such a situation is the most conducive for success.

Reference

Wilson, S. C., & Barber, T. X. (1983). The fantasy-prone personality: Implications for understanding imagery, hypnosis, and parapsychological phenomena. In A. A. Sheikh (Ed.). *Imagery* (pp. 340–387). New York: Wiley.

Q&A 24 Clients Who Can't Concentrate or Who Become More Anxious During Induction

Question:

> There are two types of patients who create special problems for me: those who seem unable to concentrate during the induction and don't go into trance, and those who get more anxious when I give suggestions for relaxation. How do you handle cases like these?

Discussion by WILLIAM FEZLER, Ph.D.

When somebody "can't" be hypnotized, I hypnotize them anyway. I explain to the patient that hypnosis, by definition, is a state of increased concentration. It is a state he or she learns to go into. Hypnosis, like concentration, is not an all or none state; it is a matter of degree. You are never so deep you can't go deeper. The most advanced master on the face of this earth has barely scratched the surface of the dimensions in awareness possible with hypnosis.

The important point is that anybody can be hypnotized. Patients, therefore, should not be concerned if they *feel* unable to concentrate in the beginning. That is why they are in my office. They are there to learn to concentrate, to go into a state of deep concentration, namely, hypnosis. Also most likely they are doing much better than they are giving themselves credit for doing. I always commend them on how well they did, saying they definitely were hypnotized. This in itself is a suggestion to enter hypnosis the next time it is attempted.

It can be seen from what I am saying that within the model I use for hypnosis, there is no such thing as a patient who can't concentrate during induction or is unable to go into trance. There are only patients who *believe* they are unable to do so. The job of the hypnotist is to change this belief.

132

That has been one of the primary uses of hypnosis from the beginning—to get patients to believe they can do something that they previously thought they couldn't. Belief is the father of the deed. When you believe you can do something, you can. As Henry Ford said, "Whether you believe you can or whether you believe you can't, you're right!" When you believe you are a non-smoker, non-drug abuser, non-drinker, you are. What you believe is what you become.

It is therefore imperative to never reinforce the patients' beliefs that they can't concentrate or can't go into trance. By making such statements as, "Everybody can be hypnotized," or "You definitely were hypnotized," or "You did much better than you realize," you reinforce patients' belief in their own hypnotizability, a belief that leads to deeper hypnosis each time it is done. Hypnotizability is like IQ. It is not absolute. It is a term that merely applies to patients' *present* level of development. Both IQ and hypnotizability can be increased with training.

When patients complain about how poor they believe their concentration to be or express their belief that they weren't hypnotized, I point to observable signs that they did indeed achieve a hypnotic state. It is good to routinely make positive comments concerning their rapid eye movements (lid flutters), masklike quality to their features, deep, regular breathing, and relaxed muscles. I tell them that all these physical manifestations are proof positive that they assuredly were hypnotized. Invariably, a patient will reply, "But I didn't 'feel' hypnotized. I then explain that initially a hypnotic state may be very difficult for a newcomer to discriminate—but it is very apparent to an observer. *I* could see that the hypnotic state was present. These validations, again, are *suggestions*, not statements of fact. You tell patients that they were hypnotized, not necessarily because they were, but because you want them to *be*. In time the suggestion will become reality. You say, "Your lids are getting very, very heavy," not because they *are* heavy, but because you want them to *become* heavy. You say, "You definitely were hypnotized," not necessarily because the patient was, but because you want him to *become* hypnotized.

If patients continue to protest that they don't feel anything, I reassure them with, "In time there will be no doubt in your mind that what you experience in a hypnotic state is different from what you feel at a nonhypnotic level. As you progress, your present hypnotic state will become your normal, everyday state and your then hypnotic state will be deeper than anything you have yet to experience." It is important that the patient determine the quality of the hypnotic state not by what he or she *expects*, but by how it is different from the normal, waking state. When asked to make this comparison, when asked simply to discriminate a *difference*, patients often realize that indeed they were hypnotized. They did enter into a plane of consciousness that was different from the state in which they first entered my office.

Another good technique to use on patients who claim they don't go into trance is to retell the classic story of Pavlov and his dog, relating it appropriately to *learning* hypnosis. The tale goes something like this: "I know you feel like nothing happened, but it did. You did very well today. What you accomplished was a hypnotic state, a state deep enough to eliminate the problems you came here to solve. Are you familiar with the story of Pavlov and the dog? (If the patient nods yes I still tell the story to refresh the memory.) Pavlov got a dog to salivate to the sound of a bell by pairing a bell with food 50 times. After the 50th pairing of food and bell, the dog salivated to the bell without the food present. What is remarkable is that on the 49th pairing, there was no more salivation to the bell than on the first. But on the 50th, presto! — the dog salivated. To an observer it looked like nothing was happening. But this wasn't true. Learning was taking place. Each time you practice hypnosis, it is a conditioning trial just like each time Pavlov paired food and bell. It may seem to you like nothing is going on, but this simply isn't so. You are learning to go into a hypnotic state. And after a certain number of practice sessions, you definitely will feel differently. There will be no doubt in your mind that you absolutely were hypnotized. Until that time it may *seem* as if nothing is happening. But it is. Each trial or session is necessary to click into that state. You just aren't aware until it happens. Many people want to skip the first 49 trials and only do the 50th, as they may want to play the Warsaw Concerto without first learning the scales, or master calculus but skip arithmetic. What you did today was great. It was a conditioning trial that ultimately will take you into an altered state of consciousness we call hypnosis, a state of increased concentration you will have no doubt that you are in."

In reference to the second part of this question, patients sometimes report feeling anxious when given suggestions for relaxation. Normally, I try to wait this period out. It is usually a nervous reaction like giggling at a funeral or laughing during a love scene. After a few sessions patients get used to the suggestions for relaxation and stop being inappropriate.

However, if the condition persists or is especially problematic, the practitioner can change the wording in the induction. Suggestions for "numbness," "limpness," "heaviness," "woodenness," can be substituted for "relaxation." I often use other positive sensations as substitutes, such as, "Feel a warm wave beginning in your toes, washing through your legs, arms, stomach, chest, neck, around your jaws, eyes, forehead, scalp." On occasion, the law of paradoxical intention is effective. In this paradigm, you suggest exactly the opposite sensation you wish to produce. For example, you might say, "Every breath you take, you become more and more tense, more and more anxious." This technique has reportedly been used successfully with resistant patients who do the opposite of what they are told. Personally I prefer to find positive sensory substitutes, such as warmth, euphoria, lightness, floating, to substitute for the word "relaxation."

Q & A 25 Using Cues to Reinstate Trance

Question:

Would you explain how a "cue" is used to reintroduce trance at the next visit?

Discussion by GEORGE GOLDBERG, D.D.S.

There are various approaches to the reintroduction of hypnosis. Briefly stated, the process is facilitated by using posthypnotic suggestions before ending the first trance. These suggestions may be designed to enhance a feeling of relaxation when the patient next returns for a visit, to strengthen the subject-therapist relationship, or to actually induce a trance when some specific cue is given.

Some therapists will use cues like, "When you return to this office and see me lay my pipe on the desk, your eyes will become heavy and you will reenter this state that you are now in." The cue may be, "When you are in this office and we intend to use hypnosis, I can merely put one hand on your shoulder and you will be able to go into a trance again." Any word, phrase, or action may be chosen by the doctor and incorporated into the posthypnotic suggestion.

Those methods, though effective, are not my style. In my dental practice my initial induction is so simple and efficient that I merely repeat it for reinductions, although I, too, use posthypnotic suggestions during the first induction to enhance the reinduction.

On the first visit I say, with great confidence and expectation, *"Close your eyes, relax, and go deeper."* No other embellishment is needed. To deepen the level of hypnosis I raise the patient's arm, assure myself that it remains elevated without my help (a cataleptic response), and then say, "As your arm goes down slowly to your lap, you will go deeper and deeper." This may be repeated two or three times for further deepening. It may also be varied slightly by first raising one arm, then the other, and then both.

I usually end the first induction with simple posthypnotic suggestions. I state, "The next time you come into my office and sit down in my chair, you will no longer have any reservations and will be more deeply relaxed." I compliment him on being such a fine, relaxed patient. (I believe this step enhances both the patient's self-esteem and the doctor-patient relationship.) I continue with, "You will gradually open your eyes and you will feel better than you felt all day. Now gradually open your eyes. How do you feel? Fine. Allow me to support your arm as you come out of the chair because you will feel a floating sensation when you make your first steps."

The patient looks and feels surprised when he makes his first step and he really does require support. The support given by the doctor, this simple physical contact, is very comforting to the patient. Because physical contact is often so reassuring, I frequently place my left hand on the right shoulder of the patient during the initial induction.

When the patient returns for the second visit, he will have been "conditioned" by the first visit. His reservations and resistances will have diminished, and his concentration, motivation, imagination, visualization, and expectations will have been enhanced. He is ready to dissociate to escape from both mental and physical pain, and is also willing to age regress, if necessary, to give up the repressed or painful memories stored in his subconscious.

On the second visit, then, to reinduce hypnosis, I merely say, "*Close your eyes, relax, and go deeper than you did before.*" I use reverse arm levitation to deepen the trance, as described for the first induction. I may also ask the patient to imagine a meter registering from 1 to 10, with 1 being very light relaxation and 10 being very deep. I ask, "Where would you consider yourself to be?" The answer is often lighter or deeper than I would have expected. If I wish to deepen relaxation, I repeat the arm levitation and the meter imagery.

Perhaps a few cases will help illustrate what I have been describing, and will also demonstrate variations that may be used with young children.

A four-year-old child, crying bitterly, was brought into my office by his mother. As soon as he sat in my chair, I spoke soothingly to him for a few moments, and then, with an authoritative voice, said, "*sleep.*" His mother and I were both surprised, but that's all it took for him to appear to be fast asleep. After all, that was the best way for the youngster to escape the ordeal he imagined lay in store for him. In a case like this, where the entire formal induction consists of one word, a "cue" is superfluous.

A second case is that of a six-year-old girl. On her first visit I asked, "What

TV program do you wish to watch?" She responded, "Mickey Mouse." I said, "Close your eyes and watch Mickey Mouse." I asked if the program was in color or black and white, and she told me it was in color. I said, "Now raise your left hand as long as you see Mickey Mouse. The clearer you see the picture the more you'll enjoy it." Her hand was raised, she smiled as if enjoying herself, and I proceeded to fill a cavity and follow that with a prophylaxis.

The induction on the second visit was essentially the same, and by the third visit, when I merely said, "Close your eyes and watch Mickey Mouse," she would raise her hand without being told to do so.

I believe this simple technique works so well in my practice because the patients have strong motivation; they do not want to suffer pain. I present no challenges to them and do not even use the word "hypnosis" to either the child or the mother, for I do not want that word to bring up questions or resistances. Instead, I use surprise. I ask the patient to concentrate on an imaginative picture, and the ensuing distraction and dissociation permit me to do my work with no discomfort to them.

One final case will illustrate how I might use a posthypnotic suggestion at the end of the first trance to facilitate entry into trance at the next session. More importantly, perhaps, it illustrates how a dentist can use hypnosis to help remove a long-standing fear of dental work.

A 46-year-old man contacted me on the phone, stating that he was referred by his dentist to discover why he had such difficulty in accepting a novocaine injection. He wanted his wife to come with him, not for support, but because she had a similar difficulty. When faced with the possibility of an injection, each would develop anxiety, a cold sweat, heart palpitations, and throbbing temples.

Both were highly motivated patients and had high expectations because their referring dentist had oriented them well. A good referral like this always enhances a positive doctor-patient relationship, which might even be called "waking hypnosis."

I took a detailed dental history from both patients, and then had him sit in my dental chair while she sat in another chair in the same room. I said, "Close your eyes and relax deeper." I paused a while, then asked, "How old are you?" He replied, "Four years old," showing spontaneous age regression. I asked his wife the same question, and she responded, "Five years old."

Further questioning revealed that both of their problems were similar. Neither had been well oriented by their parents or by their dentists to their first dental visits as small children, and each had reacted with alarm, shock, screaming, and fussing when given their first novocaine injections. By their second visits they were already conditioned to fear of the injections. Now, as adults, they required reconditioning under hypnosis.

I explained to them, as they remained in trance, that neither their parents nor their dentists had realized that they should have received a better orientation for accepting the injections. I said that now that they were older, they could better understand what had happened to two very young patients, and added, "When you both awaken, you will remember what happened in the past, and you will no longer fear your dental visits. All you will do is close your eyes, take a deep breath, and as you exhale, you will relax more deeply."

The inductions and reinductions I have described are rapid and easy. To the inexperienced hypnotherapist they may seem magical, but I assure you they are not. They are based upon an understanding of eleven important factors: motivation, expectation, conditioning, the doctor-patient relationship, ego-building, sensory cues (visual, auditory, and kinesthetic), role playing, imagination, concentration, dissociation, and distraction.

The patient enters the office with motivation, expectations, and frequently with conditioning. Any of these might be strong or weak, positive or negative. It is one of the doctor's tasks to be certain that each of them becomes strong and positive. The doctor-patient relationship is enhanced by soothing words and actions, as well as by the ego-building techniques employed. Imagination directed via appropriate sensory cues, concentration, and perhaps even role playing is utilized in producing the hypnotic state, and that in turn fosters the distraction and the dissociation that permit the hypnosis to achieve the results desired.

SECTION V Methods

Of hypnotic methods there is no end. To list and discuss them all would take a book at least the size of this one and there are a number of such books available. In a sense, this whole book is also about techniques. In almost all the sections, contributors discuss a variety of hypnotic methods they use to work with a variety of problems. We did not attempt to be comprehensive in this section. Instead, we used questions commonly asked about choosing techniques, self-hypnosis and tapes, effective hypnotic language, amnesia, age regression, post-hypnotic suggestion, ego state therapy, result imagery, ideomotor versus verbal responses, and so on.

This section includes two more examples of how differently experienced clinicians can view the same issue. On the question of what to do about a patient falling asleep during hypnosis we have one response from a psychoanalytic perspective (Smith) and another from an Ericksonian position (Greenleaf). These two discussions could not be more different, yet as far as we know each is effective for the therapist using it. On the question of whether to discuss hypnotic experiences with patients, Wineburg gives a definite yes. But as is accurately stated in the question he addresses, some therapists, especially those trying to induce amnesia, go out of their way *not* to discuss hypnotic experiences. Yet here again, therapists from both camps report effective work.

$Q_{&A}26$ Selecting Hypnotic Techniques

Question:

With so many hypnotic techniques available, it's easy to become overwhelmed with choices. How do you select which methods to use?

Discussion by M. GERALD EDELSTIEN, M.D.

The rich profusion of hypnotic techniques, coupled with the paucity of instruction on how to think systematically about using them, makes this a frequent and important question. Experienced therapists, primarily by dint of that experience, have evolved methods that work for them. This evolution is often long and cumbersome, but the process can be shortened significantly by logically organizing available techniques and desired goals.

First there are three times in which techniques are used: pre-induction, induction (including deepening and awakening), and post-induction. Perhaps it is semantically inaccurate to consider the pre-induction period for "hypnotic" techniques, but the establishment of rapport and the introduction to the concept of using hypnosis are so important that I feel they should be included. Instead of describing that phase here, I shall refer the reader to other papers in this book, specifically those written by Mann (Question 13) and Golan (Question 15).

Next, it is important to realize that, after the induction, there are only two things that *can* be done with hypnosis: the giving of suggestions, and the uncovering of repressed data. Basically, there are only two types of suggestions, direct and indirect, and although there are a multitude of uncovering techniques, a mere three will give the practitioner virtually all the flexibility he needs. With that brief outline in mind, let's proceed to see how techniques are selected.

140

The first goal, after taking an adequate history, establishing rapport, etc., is to induce a trance. Zilbergeld (Question 18) addresses this issue nicely, but I shall add a few brief comments. I believe the choice of techniques here should depend primarily on what feels most comfortable to the therapist, since most of the common techniques will work for most patients. There are a few patients, however, who do need something different, and here knowing a few other techniques can be useful. For example, the patient who is made more tense by suggestions for relaxation should be given a technique that does not involve relaxation, at least in the early phase; the patient who is frightened by eye closure should not be given suggestions for eye closure.

There is no evidence that any induction technique is superior to any other, unless one believes, as I do, that faster is better than slower. In this book are excellent examples of extremely rapid inductions, as described by Goldberg (Question 25) and Ewin (Question 52). Baumann (Question 71) describes a simple and effective induction with children, and Kohen (Question 70) describes an indirect technique with an acting-out teenager.

Likewise, there is no evidence that one deepening technique is superior to others, and almost all authors agree that "deepening" is a grossly overrated activity, since almost all therapeutic work can be done effectively with patients in a light to medium trance. All that needs to be said about "awakening" is that it should be slow enough that the patient is not unnecessarily startled, and rapid enough that no great expenditure of time is involved.

Assuming that suggestions are to be given after the induction, the first consideration is whether to use direct or indirect suggestions. Let's look at the direct ones first. Direct suggestions will usually work if: 1) the patient has the basic potential to fulfill the suggestion (for example, do not suggest, "When you awaken you will have a photographic memory and can leap over tall buildings"), and 2) there are neither conscious nor unconscious resistances to it. The probability of the suggestion's working is increased by: repetition, increased motivation, imagery involving one or more of the five senses, and the therapist's confidence in the technique.

It is generally easy to know if the patient has conscious resistances to the suggestion, but the unconscious ones, by their very nature, are unknown to the patient so he or she is unable to tell the therapist of them unless uncovering work has been done. One approach is to try direct suggestions, and if there are not adequate responses, assume that unconscious resistances exist. Working on that assumption, the therapist may then either try indirect suggestions or employ one of the "uncovering techniques" described below to analyze and deal with the resistance.

Direct suggestions may be given in a permissive style, "Perhaps you'll find that it's easier to . . . ," or in an authoritarian style, "Tomorrow at 2:00 you will do what I have told you." If the authoritarian style works, it certainly increases the prestige of the therapist and future suggestions are more likely to be successful. Conversely, if it doesn't work, prestige is lost, the patient's belief system is weakened, and therapy may become more difficult. This is only one of the reasons that today most therapists prefer the permissive style. The permissive style also generates less resentment and resistance from the patient and allows the patient to respond to the suggestions at his/her own pace.

Repetition of the suggestion is said to increase its effectiveness, but unless the therapist enjoys performing like a parrot, he need not repeat it more than once or twice, instructing the patient to continue repetitions at home, either by using self-hypnosis or by listening to a tape prepared by the therapist. There are some indications that the latter method is more effective.

Motivation to be rid of bad habits, neurotic problems, physical distress, etc., is usually high enough that specific efforts are not needed to increase that motivation. This is not universally true, however, particularly when the patient is strongly ambivalent about changing something that has been comfortable or even pleasurable to him/her for a long while. For example, a patient may wish to stop smoking, but has enjoyed the feel, taste, smell, and giving-the-hands-something-to-do aspects of smoking; understandably, the desire to stop will be countered in part by a wish to continue this satisfying but dangerous habit. Motivation, then, can be heightened by hypnotic suggestions that make the habit less desirable ("you will be more and more aware of all the disgusting and dangerous aspects of smoking," with elaboration of those aspects), or by suggestions that make stopping the habit more desirable ("you will have a feeling of pleasure and pride in making this intelligent decision, and you will find that you have more energy, more vitality, that your sex drive becomes stronger," etc.), or even better, by combining those two kinds of suggestions.

It is also said that combining imagery with a direct suggestion makes the suggestion more effective, and although I know of no studies that show that this is true, I suspect it is. A simplified example of this involves using hypnotic imagery to stop bleeding after a tooth extraction. Instead of merely telling the patient, "Make the bleeding stop," the dentist might say, "Every blood vessel in the human body is surrounded by a layer of muscles. They encircle those blood vessels like your fingers could encircle a garden hose. As they squeeze tighter and tighter, they close off the vessel so that no blood can flow through it. Imagine those muscles surrounding the blood vessels in your tooth socket and squeezing so tightly that all the bleeding stops."

The imagery, when used to control some physiological process, may involve seeing the organic structures change, as in the example above, seeing the desired result ("in your mind's eye you can see the skin on your hand becoming smooth and healthy again as that rash slowly fades away"), or a combination of seeing both the process of change and the end result. When I offer images of physiological structures undergoing change, I prefer to describe or even draw a picture of those structures before having the patient enter a trance.

When imagery is used to help change behavior, the subject may be asked to imagine him/herself performing in the way he/she wishes to perform ("You see yourself standing at the speaker's platform delivering your presentation with comfort and confidence and are pleased that all those important people are there to hear what you have to say"). The therapist may describe the behavior in detail, or the patient may be asked to simply imagine behaving in the desired way. In my own experience, the patient frequently has trouble imagining doing it well on his own until therapy has progressed beyond some initial stage.

Actually, it seems to me that when we use imagery to change behavior, what we are really doing most of the time is using it to change the feelings that led to that behavior, as in the example above. Here, it is true that a description of a better behavior was given, but an important part of the imagery involved *feelings* of calmness, confidence, and pleasure.

When images are used to augment suggestions to change feelings *per se*, a variety of techniques may be used. When working on feelings of fear, desensitizing images may be used. Having the patient imagine a gradual increase in exposure to the feared object or situation (progressive desensitization) is a very gentle, but very long and boring approach. Having the patient imagine being fully exposed to the dreaded stimulus (flooding or implosive desensitization) is traumatic to a mild degree and for a brief period of time, but is more quickly effective. With a fragile patient, it would be better to avoid too much therapeutic trauma, but the trauma may be mitigated by *distorting* the image. For example, the therapist can suggest that the patient is seeing the event through the wrong end of a telescope, on a very tiny TV screen, etc.

To alter feelings of anger or grief, the patient can be allowed to see him/herself expressing that anger or grief on a magic TV screen that no one else can see, and the direct suggestion can be added that each time this screen is watched, the old feelings will fade away more and more, making room for new and better feelings.

When the suggestion is for the desired change, and the imagery lets the patient imagine this occurring, I suspect that the specific suggestion or imagery is relatively unimportant, and the therapist's confidence in the technique assumes greater importance. My own experience may serve as an example.

Over the years I had learned a large number of techniques for dealing with pain. Some of these were simple direct suggestions: "As you become more deeply relaxed, the pain will fade away and disappear," or, "All the pain that was in your elbow will settle into your little finger, and since it's in that one small spot, it won't bother you nearly so much," or, "That pain will change into a funny little tingling sensation." All of those suggestions worked sometimes, and none of them worked all the time.

I had also learned a number of techniques that involved imagery of different sorts: "As you slip that magic stocking over your leg, it will cover all the pain," or, "As you see your brain exuding its own natural narcotics, the endorphins, . . . " Again, they all worked sometimes, but never always.

I was left feeling indecisive, not knowing how to choose one technique or another, nor which one to attempt with any given patient. Understandably, I never had a great deal of confidence in any of them. One day, however, it dawned on me that it really should make no difference which one I used, so I'd settle on just one, pretend that I was confident in it, and give it a sustained trial. (I also made tapes so my patients could have the suggestions repeated at home.) My results have been much better since that time, and I no longer need to pretend that I am confident.

In the final analysis, I believe that most of the time imagery is more important than the direct suggestion. The imagery should show the end result that is wanted, the process of change that produces that result, or a combination of the two. The direct suggestion need only say that this will occur. If this is true, then selecting a specific suggestion or a specific image is not a major problem. If the therapist already knows some that he or she has learned, they will probably work well. If the situation is one for which the therapist does not already know some suggestions and images, he can invent new ones, following the principles mentioned above.

Between direct and indirect suggestions there is an interesting hybrid, illustrated by a simple technique sometimes used for patients suffering from an acute burn. The therapist might say, "Close your eyes, relax, and go someplace where you were cool and comfortable." The suggestion itself is direct, the imagery is very loosely structured, but the main effect comes from the unspoken and very indirect suggestion, "If you're someplace where you're cool and comfortable, you can't be here, hot and hurting." This type of suggestion need not be limited to patients with acute burns, and the reader should let him/herself imagine other situations in which a similar sort of suggestion would be useful. I believe it is this ability to imagine how to use variations of old techniques in new situations that enables the therapist to become free of obsessively learning a thousand different techniques.

When it comes to indirect suggestions, I must plead incompetence. I've never been able to get them to work as well for me as other techniques do. I therefore refer the reader to that section of this book that deals with Ericksonian hypnosis. I will mention, however, a few thoughts and suspicions about this form of therapy.

Indirect suggestions have the very distinct advantage of generating little or no resistance; because the patient is not *told* to do something, he cannot refuse to do it. For reasons I don't understand, unless my suggestions are rather clear and direct, *my* patients don't follow them. I, therefore, prefer to use direct suggestions, and if the patient displays resistance, which is not too common an occurrence, we deal with that resistance, learning something valuable in the process.

If indirect suggestions are to be used, it is theoretically important for the therapist to have a clear understanding of the patient's problem, the underlying dynamics leading to that problem, the patient's past history, current life style, strengths and weaknesses. All of that information should somehow go into the formulation of the indirect suggestions. Theoretically, it is not sufficient to memorize one of Erickson's metaphors that was used for a specific problem and then repeat that metaphor with any patient who has a similar problem. In actual practice, it is probably true that if patients share the same problem, they may also share similar enough past experiences, etc., that the same metaphor may work for a certain percentage of them. That would be the lazy therapist's way out, however; more individualized metaphors would demand a great deal of time, thought, and caring on the part of the therapist.

I believe that the psychological or psychosomatic symptoms a patient displays are the result of: 1) a "bad habit" that once arose from some emotional need that is no longer present; 2) a still continuing effort to deal with subconscious conflicts; 3) a normal reaction to some very real and easily recognized trauma (like grief arising from the death of a loved one); or 4) the result of a physiological process—a noncontroversial example might be the anxiety and restlessness of someone who drinks 12–15 cups of coffee per day.

The bad habit and the normal reaction, if one chooses to treat a normal reaction, can be expected to respond to suggestions, direct or indirect, with no particular search for, or attention to, underlying, subconscious factors. If the symptoms are a continuing effort to deal with subconscious conflicts, however, it is my belief that either those conflicts must be brought to light (and here we would use the uncovering techniques) or the indirect suggestion must help the patient resolve that conflict. The patient, responding well to an indirect suggestion, might never be aware that a subconscious conflict was resolved, but the therapist, by careful planning or pure luck, must have given an indirect suggestion that addressed the conflict. Please note, I said the therapist "must have given . . . ," but I do not know that this is so; this is one of the speculations I have about what it takes to make an indirect suggestion effective in this type of case.

So now we come to uncovering techniques. I have a strong preference for these. They enable a patient, usually in only a few sessions, sometimes in only one, to discover the original source of his problem and to formulate, with or without my help, constructive solutions. Thus, the patient is fully aware of his/her own participation in the therapy and does not leave with the feeling that the therapist performed some sort of miracle while the patient rested comfortably in trance.

I use only three uncovering techniques; ideomotor responding, age regression, and ego state therapy. At times I use them in combination, at times I use special variations of them (for instance, I believe the affect bridge is a particularly valuable variation of age regression), and at times I suspect it doesn't make much difference which of these techniques is used, for it is possible that in many instances any of them would suffice. I have described these techniques in detail (Edelstien, 1981), have written about ways to facilitate age regression in Question 29, and know that a number of other articles in this book refer to those techniques, so rather than attempt to describe them here, I will tell how I make a preliminary decision as to which one to use.

Ideomotor signals, nonvoluntary movements of the fingers to signal yes or no in response the therapist's questions, are believed to represent nonverbal communications from the subconscious. Psychophysiological symptoms are believed to represent exactly the same thing (for example, bruxism might represent the message, "I've got to grit my teeth and bear it," or globus hystericus might represent, "I can't stand to swallow that crap you keep feeding me"). It seems logical, therefore, to use ideomotor signals when one is investigating the origin of this type of symptom.

When the patient has a strong feeling that causes problems, and the source of that feeling is not known, then the affect bridge is my favorite technique. For example, if a patient has a phobia toward dogs, the affect bridge can take him back to the *very first time* he ever had that feeling, and almost always it can then be seen how and why the feeling developed. Using this technique bypasses the need to use ideomotor signals to learn when and where the trouble originated, and then the need to use a more standard age regression, but therapy could be conducted very well in either manner.

For almost any other problem with an unknown origin, I prefer to use ego state therapy. Newey (Question 37) describes an interesting variation of ego state therapy in which he has the patient respond via ideomotor signals rather than verbally. I prefer verbal responses, not only because I feel I can obtain more information more quickly, but also because I prefer to give patients more opportunity to elaborate on their answers than they can do with only a yes or no response.

This, then, describes how I make my initial decision about which uncovering technique to use. If the one I chose initially does not seem to work out well, I merely state, without blaming the patient or myself, "This doesn't seem to be working now, so we'll try something else," and switch to one of the other techniques.

As I mentioned earlier, the techniques may often be interchangeable. If, for instance, a patient were complaining of severe headaches, the therapist could: 1) use ideomotor signals to learn the origin of this somatic symptom, 2) use the affect bridge to go back to the origin of that feeling (the headache) or to the origin of the feelings that caused the headache (probably repressed anger), or 3) use ego state therapy to talk with that part of the personality that causes the headaches.

In summary, once the therapist understands how to augment suggestions, how to create imagery, how to decide between direct and indirect suggestions, and when to use uncovering techniques, the choice of which technique to use is not very difficult. If the therapist does not already know a technique to use with a particular case, utilizing the principles mentioned above makes it much easier to invent one.

Reference

Edelstien, M. G. (1981). *Trauma, trance, and transformation*. New York: Brunner/Mazel.

Q&A 27 Hypnotic Communication: Is It Necessary to Accentuate the Positive?

Question:

> I've heard it said that it's bad to use negative words like "pain" and "tension" with hypnotized patients because such terms are likely to be taken as suggestions to bring about the negative state. It's best, I've heard, to use only positive terms such as "greater comfort" and "more peace and calm." Is there any validity to these ideas?

Discussion by JOSEPH BARBER, Ph.D.

This question suggests that there are abstract, simplistic rules that define effective hypnotic language. This is not so. What language is appropriate when using hypnosis depends on much broader clinical issues — in particular, issues of treatment goals and treatment strategy. In the example of grief, for instance: Is it best for the patient to deny the pain of loss or to come to terms with it? Does it best serve the patient's life to be unaware of the pain of grief temporarily, or will that temporary dissociation only prolong the grief process? Would the patient's needs be better served by offering support for going through the painful process? Might regression (hypnotic or otherwise) to past experiences of successful coping with loss be helpful? (Is hypnosis even necessary in the treatment of a particular problem?)

The key to determining the choice of treatment of any symptom (including treatment of physical pain or psychological pain) is in identifying the meaning and function of the symptom. If the pain is telling us something significant, then we ought not ignore it. Most often, physical pain signals biological threat to the organism. A patient requesting treatment of abdominal pain should be physically examined to determine the cause of the pain. Abdominal pain may signal the existence of a serious condition (e.g.,

148

appendicitis) that requires prompt and adequate curative treatment — not palliative treatment of the pain. Similarly, if the psychological pain signals something of a psychological nature that needs attending to, that pain ought not be ignored, either — an assessment of the causes of the distress and of possible curative treatment is in order. If it is determined that the patient needs to face the problem, there is no need to avoid language that accurately describes the problem (e.g., "loss," "pain," "grief," etc.).

If the clinician assesses the problem and determines that the patient needs to be relieved of pain (or anxiety, or sadness, or whatever is the distressing experience), *then* it may be technically useful to avoid language that calls up the to-be-avoided experience. Using physical pain as an example, it is often helpful, as the question suggests, to focus on the desired *comfort* rather than the existing but undesirable *pain*. While just hypnotically stating a word (e.g., "pain") does not magically or automatically evoke the experience of pain or even make it more difficult to manage, it may often be the case that "accentuating the positive" is a helpful strategy. There are exceptions to this principle, however. Some patients will be so aware of the *absence* of the words describing the pain that their response will be to hear them anyway, as if they had actually been stated. For such patients, obfuscation or circumlocution needs to be avoided in favor of a straightforward confrontation of the problem.

In summary, whether the clinician focuses on the problem or facilitates distraction or even dissociation is determined by an understanding of what the patient needs. This is obviously true of any clinical treatment — medical, dental, or psychological — and is not uniquely relevant to the use of hypnosis.

Q&A 28 Creative Self-Mothering

Question:

I've recently heard of a technique called "creative self-mothering." It sounds intriguing and I'd like to use it in my work. Can you tell me more about it?

Discussion by ELIZABETH McMAHON, Ph.D.

Creative self-mothering refers to a process in which the patient dissociates into a child-self and an adult-self and then relives part of childhood with the adult-self giving ideal parenting to the child-self. I first heard this therapeutic maneuver described by Joan Scagnelli (1982) in a seminar on psychotherapy with severely disturbed patients. She spoke of using this technique with borderline and schizophrenic patients and seemed to be using the process to help the patient construct a healthy ego.

This approach to renurturing has several advantages. It makes it clear that the patient has control over the experience. The patient's ability to make constructive change is emphasized. The patient's knowledge about his or her childhood and needs is utilized. Having the patient do the reparenting circumvents the problem of patients who cannot imagine their parents doing or saying what the patient wishes had been done or said. Finally, it seems easier for the patient to fantasize his/her own adult-self as present in the past than to imagine the presence of another person as Milton Erickson's (Erickson & Rossi, 1979) patient did in the "February Man" case.

The "February Man" case involved a pregnant woman who feared that unhappy childhood experiences might impair her ability to adequately mother her own child. Erickson spent hours obtaining the depth of trance he felt was necessary. He then had her regress several times to various ages, hallucinate the surroundings appropriate to that age, see him present in those

150

surroundings, and discuss with him what was happening at that time in her life. Amnesia was suggested and the discussions were accepted by her as real childhood experiences until the end of the therapy, when the amnesia was lifted. While Erickson's work is fascinating, given the constraints of my own practice and skill, I prefer an approach which doesn't involve hours of hypnotic training for the patient, elaborate constructed hallucinatory experiences, and extensive amnesia.

Since hearing about self-mothering, I have used it successfully with patients who are not borderline or psychotic but who do suffer from chronic lowered mood and low self-esteem. The patients with whom I use this technique tend to be harshly critical of themselves. They may give histories of overt, dramatic parental rejection or of chronic criticism by their parents, implying that the patient was never quite good enough. Very often, they were molested as children. Since we are discussing creative self-"mothering," I will speak of the patient as "she." To use this renurturing approach with men, I would change the terminology so that the male patient interacts with his child-self as an ideal father.

Self-mothering is introduced after the patient has identified things in her childhood which she wishes had been different. In introducing this technique, I stress that her parents did the very best they could based on their knowledge and abilities. The patient enters trance and is instructed to visualize herself as an infant. Then, while continuing to see her infant-self, she is told to go back to that time as she is now and mother that infant.

Having the patient visualize herself as an infant helps circumvent the internalized self-criticism and self-hatred and taps into the powerful biological urge to protect and care for babies. It is acceptable to feel loving and tender toward an infant. The patient may hate herself as an adult yet still feel that as an infant she is innocent and lovable.

I encourage the above feelings, using the wording I learned from Joan Scagnelli: "And of course that little child is lovable because ALL children are lovable and if the mother couldn't love that child, it was clearly a problem in the mother and not in the child." I continue talking with the patient until this general premise seems to be accepted. Then I give an open-ended suggestion that the patient redo whatever aspects of her childhood would be important for heightened self-esteem. For example, "And the adult (patient's name) as mother can do whatever is needed to make that little child (patient's name) feel loved and cherished. All the things that should have happened, can happen now."

In addition to the above suggestion, I usually talk while the patient is working in hypnosis, giving suggestions and emphasizing those aspects of childhood experience which the patient most needs to integrate or redo. For example, I emphasize how lovable the patient's infant-self is:

And as you see that tiny, innocent baby, you know how inherent-
ly lovable she really is. Feel her soft skin. Perhaps you can even
smell that beautiful, fresh baby scent that is so appealing. Maybe
she is looking at you with a loving, trusting look in her eyes. She
has a birthright to happiness. Hold her close to your body so that
she feels your protecting love and knows that she is safe. Cuddle
her and tell her in your own words everything that she needs to
hear. Perhaps you want to tell her how precious and wonderful
and beautiful she is. And as you marvel over how tiny and perfect
she is, you may notice her beautifully formed hands and fingers.
And maybe you want to let her know that she is unique. That
nobody else in the entire history of the world has ever had exactly those fingers and those fingerprints. And that, similarly, she
has her own unique potentials and abilities and thoughts and feelings which you are going to help her develop and enjoy.

As you can see in the above excerpt, I try to increase the patient's involvement in the experience by focusing on different sensory components of the
fantasy. I also suggest nurturing actions and ways to view the child-self. I
may encourage the patient to experience the situation first as the mother and
then again as the child: "And now as that young infant, feel your mother's
loving arms, warm and soft and comforting, holding you close to her body.
Feel her love surrounding you. Hear her tell you all the things that you need
to hear. Feel how much she loves you." I may suggest that the patient repeat
this experience until she feels completely satisfied both as mother and as
child. I frequently suggest that patients repeat this experience in self-hypnosis
at home so that they can continue the therapeutic work between sessions
and increase the effectiveness of our time together.

Obviously, the focus of the experience can be varied to meet the patient's
needs. With some patients, one may review all of childhood. With others,
one may focus just on childhood experiences regarding anger, sexuality,
autonomy, learning, or emotional intimacy. With a patient who views
herself as passive and helpless, I may review the process of realizing she has
control over her body and review how she learned to first sit up, and then
stand, and finally, triumphantly, to walk independently. I talk about how
the process was long and sometimes painful, but she kept trying even though
she fell time and again. I encourage her as parent to praise the perseverance
and strength and eventual success of the child and to give her child-self multiple messages that she (as parent) is confident that she (as child) can succeed.

The patient may have had a traumatic experience which is still affecting
her current life, such as a rape, a molestation, a physical assault, or even
just an embarrassing or shameful memory. She can reexperience the situation, intervening as the mother to help her victimized younger self integrate

the trauma in a less destructive way. She may even be able to fantasize an alternative memory and practice how she would feel and act if the trauma had not occurred. It can then be suggested that she no longer needs to let the past interfere with her future and that she has the ability now to act in the way that she has practiced in fantasy.

Some patients resist self-mothering because they feel it is a betrayal or criticism of their parents. Such patients may protest, "My parents did the best they could. They really loved me. I don't blame them." With these patients, it is especially important to emphasize that I accept that the parents did their best. And that since they did love the patient, wouldn't they want her to be truly happy and achieve all her God-given potential? I might see if the patient would agree that since she knows her parents loved her, doesn't she think that her parents would want to have given her everything she needed if they had only known, as she can know now, what she needed? I might suggest that the parents wanted their little girl to be happy and that by nurturing her little-girl-self, she is, in fact, carrying out her parents' fondest wishes and hopes.

Conversely, some patients are bitterly unhappy about their upbringing but are hopeless about the prospect of change: "What happened, happened. That's the way it is. I can't change what happened. So there's no use in going back over it." With these patients, I agree that we can't reach the physical young child and change what happened to her. However, I point out that we carry inside of us the young child that we were and that the emotional needs of that child are still alive inside today. In this sense, there is a very real child who is still pleading for love and mothering and it is this child within that they will mother.

For patients who can't imagine themselves as infants, I am indebted to Letitia Ward (1983) for sharing with me the following approach. The general topic is introduced by suggesting, "Let's talk about babies." In the ensuing discussion, the therapist begins to learn what the patient finds appealing in infants. The next step is to move to a more specific query: "Have you known a baby you really liked?" If the patient says she has, she is encouraged to share specific details about that child. If the patient says that she has not, she is asked to fantasize what someone whom she likes now was like as a baby, again emphasizing concrete details. The third step is to ask the patient if she has seen baby pictures of anyone in their family and to explore what was endearing about the pictures. And the final step is to ask the patient if she has seen baby pictures of herself.

The therapist can then discuss with the patient how lovable and endearing the patient was as a small child. The patient can be guided to feel toward herself the same tender feelings she had toward other babies by weaving into the description of her own infant-self some of the descriptive words or phrases she used earlier in describing those babies.

I have found that self-mothering provokes a powerful emotional response in patients. They frequently cry while imagining the suggested scenes. For many patients, it is a great relief to be permitted to feel tender and nurturing toward themselves. Patients report that they like and accept themselves more. Self-blame begins to be replaced with empathy for one's self. Ego-strengthening suggestions which might be disputed if given directly to the patient may be accepted as descriptive of "the child" being mothered (and, of course, in this way be integrated into the patient's self-image). The patient has control over the process and at the same time is open to positive suggestions from the therapist. In summary, I find self-mothering to be a benign, flexible, effective tool in psychotherapy and hope you will enjoy using it with your patients.

References

Erickson, M. H., & Rossi, E. L. (1979). Case 16, the February man. In *Hypnotherapy: An exploratory casebook* (pp. 461–476). New York: Irvington.

Scagnelli, J. (July, 1982). Seminar on psychotherapy with severely disturbed patients given during the American Society of Clinical Hypnosis' intermediate workshop, San Francisco.

Ward, L. Personal communication, December, 1982.

$\underset{A}{\overset{Q}{\cancel{\&}}}$ 29 Age Regression

Question:

I think age regression is a useful technique but have not been satisfied with the results I've gotten with it. Can you describe some good ways of facilitating age regression?

Discussion by M. GERALD EDELSTIEN, M.D.

Probably the most important factor in facilitating age regression, or any other hypnotic technique, is conducting the sessions so that the patient has a sense of trust in the therapist and relative comfort with the techniques that are to be used. Other authors in this book have discussed both of these issues, so I shall limit what I have to say on those topics.

With most of the techniques I use, I give an explanation of what I wish to do before asking the patient to participate in it. I rarely give specific reassurances unless the patient indicates, verbally or nonverbally, that there is some hesitation about what I have proposed. When that occurs, I merely ask what is troubling the patient. With age regression, the two most common concerns are reexperiencing some traumatic event or discovering some forgotten "sin."

If the patient expresses concern about feeling again the painful affect that was present the first time the sought-after event occurred, I readily admit that this not only could happen, but very likely will happen. I hasten to add, however, that I will be watching the patient closely, and if I see signs of any real distress, I can bring him/her back, easily and quickly, to the deep and pleasant relaxation that had been enjoyed in prior trance experiences. I also add, quite honestly, that in 30 years of experience I've never had a patient be significantly upset for more than a very short while, and even that has been infrequent.

155

If the major concern is discovering some forgotten sin, I admit that this is also a possibility, but extremely unlikely. It has been my experience that the patients who are concerned about having done something evil in the past are the ones who are least likely to have done so. The perpetrators of genuinely outrageous behavior usually have vacant lots where conscience should have grown, and are not likely to be concerned at all, especially if the statute of limitations has run out.

I modify that reassurance by stating that to the *child* who may have committed some misdeed, the wrongdoing very likely seemed to be a terrible event, but to the adult who will be looking at it now, it will be trivial. An example or two may be given, like that of a woman who saw me because of terribly low self-esteem. She went back to early childhood and reported stealing some article or other from a store. Ever since then she had felt like a cheat and a thief and had believed that no good person could ever love her. After this discovery, she mailed an anonymous money order to the store and felt good about herself for the first time in many years.

There is a real possibility that this reassuring explanation of mine could be a prehypnotic suggestion that "you won't learn anything bad about yourself"; thus, it might preclude the revelation of serious misconduct that did occur. Since the material that patients *do* reveal, however, turns out to be therapeutic, I don't spend a great deal of time worrying about that possibility.

To further facilitate age regression, some therapists offer theories about our minds storing every sight, sound, and experience that has ever occurred, and about hypnosis offering a method by which we can recall anything that ever happened to us. Frankly, I doubt that that is so, but I do have a begrudging admiration for those people who can boldly declare the truth of an unprovable hypothesis. At the very least, this display of confidence probably does aid the patient in giving responses that seem to be real. Whether or not they're historically accurate is another matter.

Once the patient is prepared to try age regression, the therapist must then decide upon a method to obtain it. There are many methods, of course, including indirect, Ericksonian techniques, although I have never found a need for anything so complicated.

Some therapists have patients "practice" age regression by first going back to some rather recent, pleasant experience, and on successive tries going back further and further, eventually to some distant and perhaps unpleasant experience. I have not found that to be necessary.

Some therapists set very specific times to which the patient is to return ("you will go back to your seventh birthday party," or, "you will go back to the very first time you experienced this fear"). Others will be less specific ("you will go backward through the years until you come to an event that was very important in creating this problem"). I use the former technique, and don't remember ever trying the latter, so I cannot offer a comparative opinion about them.

Some therapists use techniques involving imagery ("you will see yourself tearing pages off a calendar backwards, first today, then yesterday, and back and back until you are back to . . . , " or, "you will see yourself riding backward on a train; each telephone pole that you pass represents a year, and as you go further and further back into time . . . , " or, "you will see yourself on a magic carpet that carries you over space and backwards through time until . . . "). The techniques I use do not involve imagery, although I find imagery helpful with almost all the other hypnotic work I do.

My reasons for using age regression are twofold: one, to bring the patient back to an event he already remembers so he can master it in one way or another; the other, to uncover material that is not currently available to conscious memory. An example of the former would be something like this, "When I count backwards from three, you will be in your apartment again, on that night the intruder broke in and attacked you. You will not feel the physical pain, but you will live through the whole experience in just ten seconds of my time. Three, two, one, zero, back there again." (Something like this would be done as part of a desensitizing process to help the patient master the residual terror.)

When I'm dealing with a troublesome feeling of unknown origin, I use the technique known as the "affect bridge." This is a very simple technique, although it does not always work, as is true of all the other techniques. The patient is told, in trance, to let himself experience the feeling then and there, perhaps not in its full intensity, however. When the feeling is experienced, as confirmed by some signal from the patient, I say, "Hold onto that feeling. We will use it as a bridge to the past, and as I count backwards from ten you will travel backwards in time and space to the very first time you ever experienced that feeling. Ten, nine, eight, going back further and further, seven," etc.

This will usually get the patient back to a very specific time in his/her life. The specificity I request is "the very first time. . . . " Since I generally do not know the exact date, or may not even know the approximate age at which something traumatic happened to the patient, this method is very handy and circumvents the need of other exploration to learn *when* the event occurred prior to doing the age regression.

The other method I use is one that is taught by David Cheek. He has evolved a remarkably simple and effective technique for age regression, and it does not even require the formal induction of a trance, although the patient almost always goes into a trance during the process. My description of his technique is probably colored by my own style and experience, but I believe it comes pretty close to what he does.

After interviewing the patient, perhaps quite briefly, but long enough to sense that a good rapport has developed, I select a target symptom. The patient is given an explanation about ideomotor responses and is then asked, in a tone that clearly implies that the therapist fully expects the fingers to respond, "Now let's see which finger will move for 'yes'? Good, now let's see which finger will move for 'no'?"

Only a few questions are then used, perhaps along these lines: "Is this problem the result of something that is troublesome in your subconscious mind? Did it first get started a long time ago? Did the disturbing incident occur before the age of 12?" A few more questions are asked to learn the approximate age of the patient when the event happened; let's say it was when the patient was eight or nine years old.

The patient is then told, "Now, let your *subconscious* mind reorient itself to when you were eight or nine years old, very shortly before this incident occurred. When it has done that, let your "yes" finger give me a signal." Usually, there is a 10- to 30-second delay before the signal is given by the patient. The therapist continues, "Good, now let it go from the subconscious into the conscious mind, and when that has happened, let the finger signal me again." There may be another 30-second delay before getting the signal, but once the signal is given, the patient seems to be age regressed and responds accordingly. At no time is a formal induction used.

I wish to pause here to offer what I think is a very important warning. Age regression may take the patient back to a highly emotional time in his/her life, almost always one that was traumatic enough that repression occurred. If the therapist is not skilled in dealing with the emotions that might be released, age regression should not be done unless one simple precaution has been taken in advance. The patient can be asked, via ideomotor signals, "Would it be too disturbing to go back to the time this trouble first began?" If this answer is "yes," I advise not doing the regression at that time.

There is another warning I wish to offer: Do not take too literally the responses given by the regressed patient. I have found all such responses to be very helpful therapeutically, but I have not always believed their historical accuracy. The three papers by Diamond, Perry, and Relinger in Section II all speak to this issue. If age regression, or other hypnotic techniques, give us responses that are not historically accurate, this should not be considered a criticism specific to hypnosis. There is no other known method of inquiry, including psychoanalysis, in which one can be certain of the responses when an individual is asked to tell about events that happened many years ago.

Generally, we believe the responses obtained in any form of inquiry if: 1) the answer is consistent with other information we have; 2) it is consistent with our personal views of the universe (we would discount, "A little pink lady from Venus gave me the TV set I was accused of stealing," but some therapists, with a different view of the universe than my own, would accept explanations that came from a "prior life" to which the patient had "regressed"); and 3) if it is consistent with our therapeutic model. Some analysts, for example, may not believe that being bitten by a dog would be the source of a dog phobia; they would believe the fear of dogs represents a displacement of castration fears. I would not believe the dog phobia came from being killed by a pack of wild dogs during some previous life.

Although I would not believe the historical accuracy of this prior life experience, I know, from several cases I have treated, that revelation of such experiences is almost always therapeutic, and I do not know what that means. I suspect it means that the prior life experience symbolizes, in one way or another, important experiences that have occurred in this lifetime.

When age regression is attempted, the results might produce a full "revivification," in which the patient acts and talks like a child of whatever age would be appropriate to the regression, or there might be a lesser result like, "Now I remember what happened." The latter may be disappointing to the therapist who was expecting a full-blown regression, but the information obtained can be useful anyway. The result might also be, "Nothing's happening; I'm still here in your office." This, too, is disappointing, and not useful at all, unless it becomes a take-off point to explore the reasons for the resistance to the suggestion.

In summary, regression may be facilitated by making the patient comfortable with the therapist and the planned procedure, and by having the therapist become comfortable and familiar with one or a few of the techniques. The information obtained from the regression will almost always be helpful, but judgment should be exercised as to whether or not the information can be believed.

Q&A 30 What to Do When a Patient Falls Asleep in Hypnosis

Question:

What do I do when a patient falls alseep in hypnosis? Should I awaken him, continue giving suggestions in the hope they'll be heard even if he is sleeping, or what? And what does it mean that he falls asleep in the middle of hypnosis?

Discussion by ERIC GREENLEAF, Ph.D.

I'm going to begin my answer by drifting rapidly away from the question. . . . Let me tell you about a fellow who consulted me for hypnotherapy because he was unable to fall asleep: The man arrived at my office in a haggard condition caused by too many nights tossing and turning without any happy effect except the rustling sound made by his bedclothes as he moved about. I asked some questions about the problem he had — its duration, his fruitless attempts to solve it and so forth — but soon turned to the question of when he was most easily able to sleep. He told me somewhat sadly that when he was driven around in a moving car he soon dozed off and remained asleep until the car stopped moving.

To deal with his problem, I offered to tell him a story while he sat comfortably in his chair. He wouldn't have to do anything, just let me take him here and there as his mind moved through the images of the story. In the tale, I described a man enjoying being driven through the countryside in a car. Unhappily, the swiftly passing images of the countryside were soon replaced by dreamlike mental images, because the poor fellow had fallen asleep, not to awaken until the car stopped, and his friend said, "Well, here we are." I spun the tale, my client dozed off with a smile on his face, woke with my words, "Well, here we are," thanked me, and reported later that week that sleeping was no longer a problem.

160

Milton Erickson's hypnotherapeutic approaches employed "drifting rapidly away" for many different purposes. I used it here in order to give me some time to think about an answer and to allow my mind the play required to lure the fish to a strike. I drifted right to the story of the fellow who couldn't sleep. Well, by this time you might see that I am employing several typical methods developed by Erickson to induce in the listener (or reader) that state of "unconscious search" held by many to lead to satisfying resolutions of personal dilemmas. That is, I have moved the discussion away from problems and towards solutions. This is an invaluable aid in hypnotherapy, especially if we, like many "systemic" thinkers in the field of psychotherapy, hold that attempts at solution often perpetuate or constitute the problem!

While talking of a solution, I have given an example of a solution for the opposite problem from the one posed: "How to put 'em to sleep," replacing "How to wake 'em up." Again, a therapist following Erickson's approaches would seek to use what the client already knows in order to help him discover means to accomplish that which he thinks he does not know. *Utilization* is the term Erickson uses to describe this maneuver. In the example of the fellow who can't fall asleep, I was able to utilize his experiences of easily and helplessly falling asleep in cars to help him apply himself to the problem state occasioned by attempting without success to fall asleep in bed. Accomplishing this task in hypnotherapy was aided considerably by the patient's belief that car riding and sleeping were different acts, and by his surprise at finding that (aided by the device of a bedtime story) they could have similar outcomes. And again, as a therapist, I was listening for, or noting, those naturally occurring features of the patient's life which might best help him if applied to those unnatural states that he has brought to me for discussion and resolution.

Another thing which helps the therapist and his client in hypnotherapy is a practice often called "stacking up metaphors." Simply, there is a better chance for the fellow to sleep if the promise of hypnosis (a sort of sleep) is stacked up with an imagined experience of sleep (riding in the car) and with the situation in which he is being told a story (in order to be put to sleep). Helpless sleeplessness is then replaced by helpless sleepiness. What to call this sort of reversal of a symptom into a solution, I do not know. But I do hope something similar occurs in the reader who, asking to be told how to awaken a sleeping patient, is told first how to put a waking patient to sleep.

Think about this too: In the story about the fellow who couldn't sleep alone there is a format for suggesting that he wake. He was told that when his friend would say, "Well, here we are!" he would awaken. This suggestion tied together the friendship which allowed helpless sleep and the therapeutic hypnosis (a type of sleep) with a naturalistic reference to childhood situations in which travel ends with a declaration and proceeds through a set of questions: "Are we there yet?" The discomfort of the ride and the

anticipation of arriving at a happier place are echoed in the exchange between the patient and therapist.

Anyway, to be direct for a moment, it is always useful for a hypnotic
"operator" to "anchor" signals to behaviors which are to be expected from
the client. As Erickson was fond of remarking, "We all do this, so can you."
Typically, physical signals, such as arm levitation or arm lowering, are used
to deepen or lighten trance. Snapping fingers or making with a Bronx cheer
have been used to equal effect. Come to think of it, an ounce of prevention
is worth a pound of cure, so: if you, the therapist, are concerned about the
patient's falling asleep during hypnosis, you might avoid some troubles by
instructing the patient that hypnosis differs from sleep and that, should he
feel sleepy, he is to snap himself awake into a hypnotic trance. Those practitioners who liken hypnosis to sleep ought to provide their clients with
signals for awakening or with the interesting and well-documented information that even anesthetized patients have reported what they heard while
asleep when later hypnotized. An added instruction might be that if the person falls asleep he will awaken at, or within, a specified time period, say
"within five minutes," or "when you have finished a long dream," or whatever.

Still, mistakes can happen, can they not? And what if one forgets to provide signals, instruct the client, suggest times or events cued to waking? What
if he or she tries all this stuff and none of it seems to work, and the patient
falls asleep and bids fair to stay asleep through lunch?

If some such thing happens, please try to remember the sense of the words
of the great psychiatrist Harry Stack Sullivan. He claimed that the therapist
is "a serious student of practical aspects of human personality and living."
So, practically speaking, what can be done with a heavy sleeper? I would
suggest loud, abrupt speech or noises, gentle or ruder shaking of available
parts of the body such as hands or feet, bright lights, cold compresses or rapid
movement of furniture. A ringing telephone, when all else fails, has been
known to awaken heavy sleepers, as has the cry of the sleeper's infant child
(if the client has his infant child close by).

What I am attempting to say by all this is that it will help the therapist
to use his or her store of commonsense information as a useful guide to
psychotherapeutic situations. By this platitude I do not mean for the therapist to provide commonsense advice or explanations to patients (they have
already received this in plenty from their friends and families). No. I mean
rather the sort of common sense Erickson showed when he was presented
with a man who thought himself to be Jesus Christ. Erickson said that he
understood the man had experience as a carpenter, and, since the fellow
couldn't deny the point and maintain his identity, the carpenter allowed
himself to be engaged in various useful woodworking projects around the
hospital where he lived. The integration of isolated, symptomatic or helpless-

ly endured actions into the stream of one's life, with oneself and others, is a sometimes salutary outcome of the playful isolation, play-acting, operator-subject framework and of the idea of hypnosis itself.

What could this sort of statement mean, if anything? Well, for one thing, complex statements can be confusing. They cry out for clarification, and their employment in the induction of hypnosis is thought to be useful in focusing the client's attention on that inner search for clarification and coherence which he requires to resolve his difficulties in living. In another way of thinking about such things, complex sentence construction can be held to be a sort of projective test device upon which the reader can throw his or her mantle of meaningful conclusion. This is not, to be sure, the reason my sentences are at times obscure. No. I am only searching for a way in English to express something delightful, common and mysterious. That is, the observation that matching the form of the solution of a psychotherapeutic dilemma to that of the problem provides a powerful therapeutic effect. Erickson might, for example, employ an obsessive routine to hypnotize an obsessive man, or, in the example of Jesus Christ which I noted, use a man's play-acting of a character to enable him to play a useful part in the social world. The pretense of hypnotist-operator is a sort of shared delusion which both patient and therapist participate in, even though therapists often report the experience of trance while doing inductions, and, of course, patients often report the absence of trance in similar circumstances.

By using the words "pretense" and "shared delusion" I mean to apply some of the rude tugs or loud noises I spoke of earlier as commonsense aids to waking sleeping patients as a spur to drowsy readers. Zilbergeld, in Question 18, speaks of being hypnotized by boredom, and, later, by rote. Perhaps I can induce a trance HERE by hyperbole.

I'll put it this way: Hypnosis is a human state, all right. People claim to know if they are "in it" or not, even if they can't characterize it. But it is not a state like Nebraska is a state; nor is it a state like hypertension is a state. To be in hypnosis is more like being, say, in a state of confusion, or in love. And, if you please, the "methods of induction" of this state are more like following rules of social procedure than they are like following rules of chemical analysis. So that, to learn what to do in hypnotizing someone is like learning to play baseball or to chat at a cocktail party or to tell a joke. And to the extent that these learnings are shared by our patients, or that they can be instructed in them, we can mutually agree that hypnosis "has happened."

To return to the question one last time: If we ask "What if a patient falls asleep in hypnosis?" we assume that sleep and hypnosis are different and incompatible. If we assumed they were the same (as when hypnosis is thought of as a sort of sleep), we would continue giving suggestions to the patient. If we imagine they can coexist, we may comfortably speak of sleep with hypnosis or hypnotic sleep. Our and the patient's assumption of what hypnosis "is" will determine our actions and their reception by the other in the same way as our sense of what game we are playing will determine whether we stand still on hitting behind the batsman (as in baseball) or run if we do so (as in cricket). As a fortune cookie I was given many years ago suggested, "Guide yourself accordingly."

$\underset{A}{\overset{Q}{\&}}31$ Another View on Sleeping Patients

Question:

What do I do when a patient falls asleep in hypnosis? Should I awaken him, continue giving suggestions in the hope they'll be heard even if he is sleeping, or what? And what does it mean that he falls asleep in the middle of hypnosis?

Discussion by ALEXANDER H. SMITH, Ed.D.

I believe the question as it is asked carries with it a subtlety about what hypnosis is, how the therapist construes its activity, and in particular, how the therapist and patient affect one another.

The central question here of both practical and theoretical significance is *why* the patient has fallen asleep. I would like to consider this from the "outside in," dealing first with the realities of the patient's condition and then with more interpersonal and intrapsychic considerations.

Basically, if the patient has fallen asleep he or she must have been tired. How come? What is going on in the patient's life that would render him/her unable to engage in the give and take of the hypnotic process? Is he or she overworked, depressed? If so, from what circumstances? Sometimes spouses or parents and family have unwittingly contributed to the patient's distraction by starting an argument the night before the patient sees "that doctor" (Smith, 1981). The patient may be taking on extra work along with the work of hypnosis. If so, one should inquire as to these circumstances. What seems to be the context? Does the patient feel he or she can't receive without paying for it with more work? Or does the patient "arrange" later hours the night before the scheduled session? It is important not to jump the gun and assume that the "resistance" is in the service of some destructive or eroticized motive now defended against through sleep. While that configuration of needs and defenses may indeed be the case, it is better to assume a delayed, neutral, fact-finding attitude about the context of the sleep. Whatever the reasons given, I believe it is more helpful to accept those reasons as the best the patient can presently give, keep them in mind, and attempt to see where they fit into the larger picture. It is seldom helpful to confront the patient's motives about circumstances such as this where most of the motivation remains inaccessible.

Patients will vary in their preconscious perceptions about the role of sleep in hypnosis, despite previous orientations from the therapist. One patient may believe that sleep is the essence of hypnosis, and allows himself to drift off, almost as an achievement to be handed to the therapist. Another patient might view having fallen asleep as an enormous failure and may even feel hopeless about ever being helped. Since the unconscious perceptions about sleep vary, it is important to remain calmly, kindly alert to the conscious and preconscious constructions about sleep, the patient's feelings about it, and how it seems to be affecting the present course of treatment.

If the patient were a child, I would be more concerned about home circumstances and whether basic adequate nutrition and correct sleeping conditions prevail, or whether there is tension, chaos or other interfering conditions that do not allow the child the "average expectable environment" in which to grow up. Further, I would be more alert to the presence of problems at home or to actual anxiety, depression or other psychopathological conditions. Although my experience with children is limited, my sense is that they find hypnosis an enhancing and engaging process and that they rarely fall asleep.

The second part of the question — "Should I wake the patient up?" "How do I prevent it?" — not only states some concern about what to do, but also implies some anxiety on the part of the questioner. This brings into focus the hypnotic relationship.

The patient needs to be awakened when it is time to go. Before that, the therapist must consider whether it would be useful to allow the patient to snooze or to attempt to reengage him around what made him so "tired." Generally, I would elect to rouse the patient and to check out what is going on. Should I touch the patient while I do it? Why not? It is no different from waking up one's kid sister, a person on the bus, one's grandmother, etc. If the therapist feels some hesitation about rousing the patient, he should ask himself, "Whom do I imagine I am waking up?" Most likely the therapist has some countertransference anxiety that has been activated. The point here is that the expected conduct of the hypnosis is to proceed along the usual lines, i.e., if the patient is asleep, it is *not* hypnosis. What does it mean to the patient that the therapist awakened him? This must be considered too.

After rousing the patient, I would help him become reoriented and simply say, "You seemed to have fallen asleep . . . what was your experience before that?" The patient's response will enable the therapist to discern some of the unconscious meaning about the sleep. If the patient says, "Oh . . . yeah . . . I guess I did. Wasn't that the idea though?" then the therapist might begin to wonder about passive/aggressive distancing or even schizoid defenses, because the patient may have departed from a two-person system of relational work to a one-person system that excludes the therapist.

Not all such sleeping states in hypnosis represent paranoid anxieties on the part of the patient. Other patients may unconsciously equate sleep with a merger fantasy of the earliest kind in psychological development. Here the patient is not trying to get out of the clutches of a fantasied destructive therapist but instead is attempting to reunite with an omnipotent, idealized parental imago. In this instance the wish is not defended directly but is "acted out" with the therapist. The therapist must carefully sort out these issues because the anxiety and wishes can occur together in condensed form.

Higher level developmental issues also may be condensed with earlier ones or become the major organizing need at the moment. According to Fromm (1984), oedipal fantasies are part of the hypnotic relationship. The transference paradigms that develop around the hypnosis and the part the sleep response plays vary.

In summary, the sleep response must be understood in context. Does sleep represent a normal response to tiredness? Does it represent the patient's compliant response to the belief that hypnosis is sleep? Or is sleep a resistance to therapy or a transference reaction? These are questions I would attempt to answer from the verbalizations and style of delivery of the patient and from my own affective response to him.

After the patient has been awakened I would return to interviewing him around the conscious aims of treatment, reassuring him about having fallen asleep and about the future possibility of using hypnosis. I would work in an "upward" direction, saying, "You must have needed to fall asleep," or "Your unconscious found sleep to be the best choice at the time." To a more resistant patient I might say, "That seems like it was a rather creative thing to be able to do. What would you have hoped for?" If the patient were to give a distancing statement like, "just sleep," I would think about staying with that level of interaction, perhaps just paraphrasing or repeating the words exactly. This can assure the patient I am not going any faster or deeper than he desires. It also gives me a chance to think on my feet. So I might say, "Mmm, just sleep . . . " and wait. Usually the patient will elaborate because the energy required in self-defense has been freed up by the therapist's adopting a redundant, non-stimulating posture. If the patient were to say nothing else, I might speculate "upward" — "Well, at least you know how to take care of yourself in that department" or, "Do you need more sleep?" or something else that communicates conditions of safety and "holding" of the patient's transitional reality.

References

Fromm, E. (1984). Theory and practice of hypnoanalysis. In W. Wester & A. H. Smith (Eds.). *Clinical hypnosis: A multidisciplinary approach*. Philadelphia: Lippincott.
Smith, A. H. (1981). Object relations and family systems: Toward a reconceptualization of the hypnotic relationship. *Psychotherapy: Theory, Research and Practice, 18,* 54–67.

$\underset{A}{\overset{Q}{\mathcal{C}}}$ 32 The Longevity of Posthypnotic Suggestion

Question:

I've heard that posthypnotic suggestions can last for years, coming into play long after therapy and therapist are forgotten. Yet I've also heard that I'll be lucky if they last for 20 minutes after being given. What is the truth? How long do posthypnotic suggestions endure?

Discussion by GEORGE MATHESON, Ph.D., C.Psych.

The historic and anecdotal records of hypnosis abound with reports and tales of the effects of posthypnotic suggestion. Among the stories of the unusual or coercive nature of some of these suggestions are examples of their enduring nature. For example, an unverified and undoubtedly fictitious story involves the man (or woman?) trained through posthypnotic suggestion to go into a "deep trance" at the sound of a specific song. Supposedly, while he was driving the car one day the music began on the radio and a trance ensued, with a resulting serious car accident. Of a more reliable nature are the examples reported by Erickson and Erickson (1941) of posthypnotic performance after periods lasting in time from months to four and five years. They even comment about the use of a posthypnotically defined stimulus to induce hypnosis more than 20 years after its last occurrence.

The possibility that suggestions may have an enduring quality has led some therapists and texts on hypnosis to specify that suggestions given in hypnosis must be canceled or "removed" before ending the trance. However, this somewhat mechanical view of suggestion is generally questioned by most clinicians, who in practice experience many occasions when posthypnotic suggestions are ineffective or last only briefly. Perry (1977a, b; Duncan & Perry, 1977) has shown that only 2–3% of highly responsive subjects dem-

onstrate long-persisting suggestions. Thus, while some posthypnotic suggestions may last for many months or years, most have a much more limited
life span before they are assimilated, canceled by the subject, or simply forgotten.

The durability of posthypnotic suggestion depends on the nature of the
suggestion and the role and importance of the suggestion to the patient/sub-
ject. Regarding the latter aspect, it is well-known that the theatrical suggestions of the stage hypnotist, perhaps to tie one's shoe at the snap of the
hypnotist's fingers, has little lasting effect for most subjects. In contrast, the
posthypnotic training of a relaxation response is likely to be integrated by
the patient and maintained much longer.

Considering the nature of the posthypnotic suggestion, we find that durability is affected by the unconscious mechanisms of memory. Experience and
scientific examination of memory show that material is remembered better
and longer when it is relevant, presented in a meaningful manner, and presented repeatedly or for a long enough period to be perceived and encod-
ed. For example, a random series of numbers will be remembered better
and longer when there is a reason to retain the information, when a mechanism exists to give it meaning (i.e., a mnemonic system), and when it is
repeatedly offered. For instance, most people remember their own license
plate or phone number better than others that they only see briefly.

In a similar way, posthypnotic suggestions are more likely to endure if
they are offered in a context in which they have purpose or meaning, if they
are clear and succinct, and if they are offered several times to be embedded in memory. Compare the following:

> You can feel just as comfortable whenever you want, or feel like it.

with this:

> And in just the same way that you can enjoy your relaxed feel-
> ing right now, just like that feeling, and just as deeply as this re-
> laxing . . . is the way you can feel when you lie down on your
> bed tonight, . . . or the way you can feel when you sit down in
> your chair in your office . . . and the way you can feel when you
> sit down in this chair in this office next time. So that all you need
> to do is to lie down on your bed, or sit in your chair or just sit
> down again in this chair. That will be all you need to do to begin
> to go very deeply and very comfortably relaxed, just as you are
> right now.

The latter suggestions for relaxation are meaningful in that they are integrated into the ongoing experience, are specific to the nature of the response,
time and place, and are given repetitively in a pleasant conversational way.

The availability of the identified stimulus for the response and the provision of time limitations will also influence how long the suggestion remains effective. If the stimulus to trigger the posthypnotic response is of a recurring nature (e.g., "whenever you sit down in the dentist's chair and look up at that soft comfortable light"), then the suggestion is likely to have ongoing effect. If the stimulus is only available once, then the response will not be maintained and will fade.

Also, the actual posthypnotic suggestion may contain some definition of its time span. For instance, "while working on this paper, and only *this* paper, you will . . . " is limited to a short length of time, as is the clinical suggestion *"for as long as you are seeing me* in treatment and for only as long as you are seeing me, you will. . . . " In contrast, some suggestions are designed to be long-standing or to continue indefinitely. Depending on other factors, they may remain effective for a lifetime (e.g., "long after you have stopped seeing me you may continue to notice that whenever you . . . ").

Future orientation, as described by Erickson (1954), can also enhance the endurance of the posthypnotic suggestion. Basically this procedure involves the disorientation of the subject in time and then the systematic reorientation by projection into the future. As soon as the new orientation has been secured, "observations" (i.e., suggestions) can be made regarding the continuing experience or behavior of the subject in ways that are consistent with the previous posthypnotic suggestions. This method of a future-oriented hypnotic process is frequently employed in the treatment of habit disorders such as smoking, overeating and drinking, where the suggestion must endure for treatment to be successful.

Finally, amnesia must be considered. Amnesia plays a role not only in the strength of a posthypnotic suggestion, but also in the definition of its nature. Some writers define posthypnotic suggestion in such a way that amnesia is quintessential to the phenomenon. Erickson's definition (Erickson & Erickson, 1941), for instance, included "the absence of any demonstrable conscious awareness in the subject." However, others have minimized the importance of amnesia. Orne and his colleagues (Sheehan & Orne, 1968; Nace & Orne, 1970) have demonstrated the compulsive nature of posthypnotic behavior even when the subject is aware of the suggestion and of the expected behavior.

In summary, there is no "shelf life" to posthypnotic suggestions. Endurance depends on many factors, including meaningfulness, clarity, repetition, time definition and the benefit to the patient.

References

Duncan, B., & Perry, C. (1977). Uncancelled hypnotic suggestions: Initial studies. *American Journal of Clinical Hypnosis, 19*(3), 166–176.

Erickson, M. H., & Erickson, E. M. (1941). The nature and character of post-hypnotic behavior. *Journal of General Psychology, 24,* 95–133.

Erickson, M. H. (1954). Pseudo-orientation in time as a hypnotherapeutic procedure. *Journal of Clinical and Experimental Hypnosis, 2*, 261–283.

Nace, E. P., & Orne, M. T. (1970). Fate of an uncompleted post-hypnotic suggestion. *Journal of Abnormal Psychology, 75*(3), 278–285.

Perry, C. (1977a). Uncancelled hypnotic suggestions: The effects of hypnotic depth and hypnotic skill on their posthypnotic persistence. *Journal of Abnormal Psychology, 86*(5), 570–574.

Perry, C. (1977b). Variables influencing the posthypnotic persistence of an uncancelled hypnotic suggestion. *Annals of New York Academy of Sciences, 296*, 264–273.

Sheehan, P. W., & Orne, M. T. (1968). Some comments on the nature of post-hypnotic behaviour. *Journal of Nervous and Mental Disease, 146*(3), 209–220.

Q&A 33 The Importance and Role of Posthypnotic Amnesia

Question:

What is the role of amnesia in hypnosis? If it is necessary for effective hypnotic psychotherapy, what are good ways of obtaining it?

Discussion by FREDERICK J. EVANS, Ph.D.

Posthypnotic amnesia is dramatic because of the ease with which it can be induced in some deeply hypnotized subjects. The hypnotist suggests that, upon awakening from hypnosis, the subject will be unable to recall any of the hypnotic experiences, usually until an appropriate cue word is given. Although it probably does not occur spontaneously, the suggestion for amnesia may be implicit or it may occur because the patient expects to be amnestic for the hypnosis material. The subject with amnesia will typically report that the hypnosis experience was discontinuous with normal, waking life. Even when a subject recalls some of the experiences, he may have considerable difficulty, sometimes showing confusion about the sequence of events or about such details as whether a suggestion of arm rigidity involved the left or right arm.

It seems incongruous that some people could have so much difficulty describing what they had been doing during the preceding few minutes. Indeed, this incongruity has led some investigators, who reject verbal reports as unreliable, to mistakenly dismiss posthypnotic amnesia as simple compliance, role playing, or due to other strictly motivational influences. How-

This report was supported by the Carrier Foundation, Belle Mead, New Jersey, 08502. I wish to thank Kenneth Mathisen, Ph.D., for his helpful comments and Christine Makin for her technical help.

ever, recent research has shown that the amnesia cannot be breached in spite of strong pressure to do so.

It is obvious that posthypnotic amnesia is not merely some form of forgetting; nor does it involve a functional ablation of the hypnotic experiences (Cooper, 1972; Evans, 1980; Hilgard, 1965). At the appropriate word, most of the forgotten material can be recovered quite easily. The easy reversibility of amnesia (Nace, Orne, & Hammer, 1974) indicates that any forgetting is, at best, temporary. Indeed, the amnesia is usually partial rather than complete, particularly in the typical person with moderate hypnotic capacities. The existence of material recovered after the reversibility cue (rather than the amount recalled) might be the only indication that amnesia has occurred.

Posthypnotic amnesia appears to be similar to other functional amnesias observed in the clinic, the laboratory, and the psychopathology of everyday life. The experience is like forgetting where one has laid down the car keys, blocking an acquaintance's name at a cocktail party, the tip-of-the-tongue phenomenon, or the difficulty people have in remembering their nighttime dreams. Historically, posthypnotic amnesia has been viewed as similar to the memory disturbances observed in clinical cases of hysteria, fugue, dissociative states and multiple personality, and the islands of memory often observed in Korsakoff's syndrome. There is no recognizable disturbance of central nervous system functioning. Furthermore, the essential intactness of the critical memories during the amnesia period is evidenced by their eventual recovery, as well as by subtle hints of their presence and availability in other cognitive operations such as relearning or recognition.

Posthypnotic amnesia has been studied intensively using the sophisticated methodology of cognitive psychology, particularly focusing on amnesia as a retrieval deficit as the subject struggles to recall difficult-to-remember experiences. Much of the research on posthypnotic amnesia has been reviewed by Cooper (1972), Evans (1980), Hilgard (1968) and Kihlstrom and Evans (1979).

A somewhat different phenomenon from posthypnotic amnesia is *source amnesia*, in which subjects are able to recall information learned a few minutes before and during hypnosis, but are unable to recall *where* and *when* they learned that new knowledge. The content is recalled, but the context is forgotten, much in the way dissociated symptoms exert influence on waking mentation without conscious awareness (Evans, 1979).

Procedures for Facilitating Posthypnotic Amnesia

Posthypnotic amnesia is a difficult suggestion even with deeply hypnotizable patients. There is considerable emphasis on good memory in our culture, and patients may be concerned about cognitive deficits associated with their psychopathology. Even a temporary memory lapse may be anxiety-provoking to some people. The popular misconception that the hypnotized person will not remember what has occurred during hypnosis reinforces the automaton-like stereotype of what hypnosis might be like. Therefore, if post-hypnotic amnesia is deemed necessary, the patient must have a comfortable feeling about hypnosis and about his ability to voluntarily control cognitive processes in an area that may already be of some concern.

A typical amnesia suggestion, similar to those in the standard hypnosis susceptibility scales is:

> You will have difficulty in remembering all the things I have told you and all the things that you did or felt. In fact, you will find it to be so much of an effort to recall any of these things that you will have no wish to do so. It will be much easier simply to forget everything until I tell you that you can remember. You will remember nothing of what has happened until I say to you: "Now you can remember everything!" You will not remember *anything* until then. (Weitzenhoffer & Hilgard, 1962, pp. 23–24)

This kind of direct suggestion may be useful in early experiences with hypnosis, preferably involving measurement sessions divorced from clinical intervention, but clinical use may require additional reinforcement and practice. Standardized procedures provide clues as to how difficult it was for the patient to remember and how the amnesia was experienced. Comments such as "it was like trying to recall a dream" or "it was there, but vague" or "it was on the tip of my tongue" will give direction to later training on amnesia. Three procedures to help the patient experience amnesia will be described briefly; these involve focused attention on memory, guided imagery, and a specific amnesia.

Focused attention. The focused attention approach to inducing posthypnotic amnesia primarily involves forgetting by benign neglect. Typically, several suggestions will have been given during the hypnosis session, and one of these will be chosen as a very important experience. A suggested hypnotic dream is especially helpful because of the association between hypnosis and sleep and personal familiarity with dream recall difficulty. After the dream, or at the termination of the hypnosis suggestion, it is suggested that:

> It is particularly important that you remember to tell me that you had a dream. You might find this surprisingly difficult to do because sometimes the experiences of hypnosis later seem vague and fleeting. However, no matter *how* difficult it is for you to do so, it is *especially* important that you remember to tell me

about the dream. If you choose, you may prefer not to tell me what you were dreaming about; this is not important. What is important is that you try your hardest to remember that you had a dream and to tell me what the dream was like. Often, the experiences of deep hypnosis are difficult to remember subsequently, but it is especially important that you try as hard as you can to remember the dream. I don't care if you remember anything else as long as you remember about the dream.

This suggestion obviously involves a paradoxical intent because it gives the subtle message that it is all right to forget, but the focus is shifted to the difficulty of recalling even one specific item. Most patients, of course, are eager to tell the hypnotist about the dream. In the process of elaborating on the dream it is highly likely that the patient will ignore several other aspects of the hypnotic experience. By carefully leading the patient, indicating another suggestion (e.g., "by the way, you didn't tell me about your experience lying on the beach"), the therapist will confirm, through the patient's surprised reaction, that at least the beach had receded into the background and had been momentarily forgotten. Once the patient accepts that there were memory lapses it is relatively easy to explain that amnesia is another suggestion that hypnotized people can experience and that it is not a permanent memory loss.

Guided imagery. Guided imagery can be used to facilitate amnestic experience. For example, if it is suggested that the patient is enjoying himself relaxing in the sun, lying on the deck of a sailing boat, images in several modalities can reinforce the pleasurable feeling:

. . . as the boat glides through the water, you lie there, enjoying the warmth of the sun, listening to the sails flapping as the breeze stiffens. You may gradually become aware of a change in the weather. You feel the shadow of some clouds, and your body cools as the sun disappears. As you look towards the dock, you notice that it is beginning to get a little foggy or misty, and though you know it is still safe, you can experience the mist, and you begin to develop the sense that as the fog thickens, it begins to blanket the sails. Just as the fog blankets the boat and the tranquil landscape, so, too, a fog will begin to envelop and descend across your mind, so that gradually the fog will begin to blanket your mind, just as it blanketed out the sails and the boat. As this fog settles across your mind you will find that your mind will seem as if it is blanketed by a fog, a fog that you cannot easily penetrate until such time as I tell you "now the fog has lifted."

And, of course, while the fog has settled over your mind, you will not be able to remember anything at all that you have been experiencing during hypnosis. Of course, when I tell you "now the fog has lifted," everything will come back to you, and it will be as clear and as vivid as anything could be.

Specific amnesia. Sometimes specific amnesias can be very compelling to a patient and provide an experience that teaches flexible control over memory processes. For example, it is suggested that on a television screen the subject will see numbers from 1 to 10 randomly displayed.

As you begin to count the numbers aloud you will find that one of those numbers has been erased, and it is gone. It has disappeared from your counting system. You can't find the number "six" anymore, it is gone from your counting system, and in a little while, as you search for the numbers on the television screen and read them out to me, you will be able to find all the numbers . . . 1, 2, 3, 4, 5, 7, 8, 9, 10 . . . just like that.

Teaching a specific amnesia for specific neutral information may later provide the basis for teaching the patient to block out for therapeutic purposes specific real-life experiences that he may want to forget for a time period. It is especially useful as a method to teach the patient he has control over memory processes.

Clinical Applications of Posthypnotic Amnesia

It is relatively rare that posthypnotic amnesia is either necessary or even appropriate in clinical applications. Normally, work that has been done under hypnosis can be readily accepted by the patient, and unless the session is threatening psychodynamically, there is little reason why the patient should have amnesia for his/her hypnotic experiences. Occasionally, posthypnotic amnesia might be important to convince a patient that he or she has experienced deep hypnosis, even though it might not be necessary for specific therapeutic purposes (e.g., analgesia for surgery). There are at least three situations where it may be appropriate for the patient to be able to develop an amnesia: for ego-threatening material; for contractual alliances; and for effective use of posthypnotic suggestions.

Posthypnotic amnesia as a defense mechanism. Hypnotic procedures such as age regression, dream recall, and abreaction may be used to uncover specific material possibly relevant to the patient or the treatment plan. The sudden recollection of traumatic events may be psychodynamically threatening to the individual, and he may not be able to cope with the material in the normal waking state. For example, under hypnotic age regression a patient recalled, with appropriate affect, that she had been sexually abused by a grandfather during her early childhood. It was the therapist's judgment that she was psychologically not prepared to integrate this material into normal waking experience. Her ability to have posthypnotic amnesia for the revivified experience provided a defense mechanism allowing time for further psychotherapeutic effort before the implications of the memory had to be integrated into ongoing normal waking reality testing.

There is a critical balance that must be evaluated by the therapist because amnesia (even if developed for spontaneous defensive purposes) will dissipate over time. When amnesia is induced to help protect the individual's ego against threatening memories, some of the amnesia will dissipate over time. The threatening, anxiety-provoking material will gradually become available to the individual, either through sudden "insight" memories following the therapeutic session or in the guise of dreams and nightmares. The patient must be in a position to understand that this process may occur and to tolerate the material if in fact it becomes conscious. Certainly under these circumstances a patient must feel comfortable in contacting the therapist if the material begins to break through the amnestic defense and becomes threatening. The use of posthypnotic amnesia to provide an artificial method of defense against ego-threatening material requires clinical skill and judgment.

It should also be pointed out, of course, that there is no evidence that the revivified or abreactive material is based on real-life events that actually occurred unless subsequently confirmed by independent evidence. Hypnotically recovered "memories" are usually an inseparable mix of real-life happenings (source amnesia) and confabulated fantasy. The intensity of the abreaction or the vividness of the revivifications is irrelevant to their veridicality. However, for the sake of therapeutic endeavor, it may not really matter whether the patient has been sexually abused as a child; what is relevant is that, even if fantasy-based (in part), this is currently pertinent to the psychodynamics.

Posthypnotic amnesia as a contractual defense. A similar defensive use of posthypnotic amnesia may be involved when a patient learns mastery skills and self-control of symptoms or life experiences before he is ready to use these skills in normal daily functioning. For example, a patient with chronic pain who is involved in compensation or litigation procedures may initially be unaware of his own resources to control his pain and may further be unwilling to try to exert such control. Under hypnosis, he may be able to develop adequate control over pain, even though in the waking state it is obviously clear both to the patient and to everybody else that giving up the pain will jeopardize compensation and/or court claim. Perhaps the patient unconsciously knows that damages, etc., cannot be won in a pain-free condition. It may be necessary to establish a special contract with the patient that he has the resources to control the pain, but the choice about when he wants to do so is exclusively his. The choice as to when to have pain need not be a threatening experience to the patient. The ability to control pain may be established under hypnosis with an accompanying suggestion for amnesia that prevents the patient from being threatened about utilizing these pain reduction mastery skills in the normal waking state·until such time as he is ready to do so. Of course, when a contract exists between a therapist and a patient that one can remain amnestic for otherwise important mastery skills, it will become a critical therapeutic issue as to how and when a patient is able to use these mastery skills in a normal waking state. The patient may not be able to develop self-control and mastery until he knows the amnestic mechanism is available to him as needed.

Amnesia and posthypnotic suggestion. Many clinicians and most patients believe that amnesia is necessary for a posthypnotic suggestion to be carried out successfully. Posthypnotic suggestions can have a dissociative compulsivity independently of whether the person remembers them (Nace & Orne, 1970). If the patient can accept that the compulsive drive to carry out a posthypnotic suggestion does not need to be protected by an anmestic barrier, then posthypnotic behavior is no longer contingent on an equally difficult suggestion to forget the origins of the suggestion itself. Thus, for an effective posthypnotic suggestion to a smoking patient that the cigarette will be aversive and no longer pleasurable, it is not necessary that the patient have total amnesia for the fact that the suggestion has been given. Of course, a patient's expectation that amnesia is necessary for these suggestions to work may need to be honored by the therapist. It might be necessary for the patient to develop amnesia even if it is not necessary for the therapeutic process itself.

References

Cooper, L. M. (1972). Hypnotic amnesia. In E. Fromm & R. E. Shor (Eds.) *Hypnosis: Research developments and perspectives* (pp. 217–252). Chicago: Aldine-Atherton.

Evans, F. J. (1979). Contextual forgetting: Posthypnotic source amnesia. *Journal of Abnormal Psychology, 88,* 556–563.

Evans, F. J. (1980). Posthypnotic amnesia. In G. D. Burrows & L. Dennerstein (Eds.) *Handbook of hypnosis and psychosomatic medicine* (pp. 85–103). Amsterdam, The Netherlands: Elsevier.

Evans, F. J., & Kihlstrom, J. F. (1973). Posthypnotic amnesia as disrupted retrieval. *Journal of Abnormal Psychology, 82,* 317–323.

Hilgard, E. R. (1968). *The experience of hypnosis.* New York: Harcourt, Brace, Jovanovich.

Kihlstrom, J. F., & Evans, F. J. (1979). Memory retrieval processes in post-hypnotic amnesia. In J. F. Kihlstrom & F. J. Evans (Eds.) *Functional disorders of memory.* (pp. 179–215). Hillsdale, NJ.

Nace, E. P., & Orne, M. T. (1970). Fate of an uncompleted posthypnotic suggestion. *Journal of Abnormal Psychology, 75,* 278–285.

Nace, E. P., Orne, M. T., & Hammer, A. G. (1974). Posthypnotic amnesia as an active psychic process: The reversibility of amnesia. *Archives of General Psychiatry, 31,* 257–260.

Weitzenhoffer, A. M., & Hilgard, E. R. (1962). *Stanford Hypnotic Susceptibility Scale, Form C.* Palo Alto, CA: Consulting Psychologists Press.

Q & A 34 Self-hypnosis

Question:

How should I instruct clients to enter self-hypnosis and use it to achieve their goals?

Discussion by BRIAN M. ALMAN, Ph.D.

There are seven basic steps in helping patients use self-hypnosis. I shall list them and then show how I incorporate them in my work.

1) The patient must acquire a realistic understanding of what self-hypnosis is.
2) Therapeutic goals must be clearly defined.
3) A trance is induced.
4) A post-hypnotic suggestion is given and/or a tape is made to help the patient reenter the hypnotic state.
5) Appropriate suggestions are developed for use in making desired changes.
6) Posthypnotic cues are used to reinforce these suggestions.
7) Frequent practice is encouraged.

When clients request self-hypnosis or when the therapist thinks it would be an appropriate therapeutic technique, the first step is to place the method in proper perspective, eliminating misconceptions and ensuring that the clients see self-hypnosis as a learning experience and a naturalistic approach to change. I also ask for their ideas on self-hypnosis — what they have heard, read, and imagined — and I may suggest they read my book, *Self-Hypnosis: A Complete Manual for Health and Self-Change*.

As an aid in understanding hypnosis as a natural event, I encourage clients to recognize related experiences they bring into the office. Specifically, what experiences have they had that were absorbing, involving, relaxing, meditative or spiritual? With the information they provide regarding previous trance-like experiences, I ask them to close their eyes and recall those experiences, suggesting that they already know a great deal about self-hypnosis, or use their material to induce a comfortable hypnotic state or to deepen it if it is already present.

As an example, I once saw a client who reported that mountains have always been a source of revitalizing feelings and some reflection. Her favorite part is walking through the trails and looking for animals, which she often spots. Her presenting problem was low self-esteem and anxiety and depression. My words to her were as follows:

"Self-hypnosis is nothing more than allowing yourself to get as comfortable as you like, taking a few deep satisfying breaths and spending two or three minutes slowing yourself to a comfortable, relaxed pace . . . much the way clouds do around the mountains . . . just slowly drifting by . . . and of course, the mountains are a pleasing location in which to feel comfortable, at ease and even actively curious about what will happen, perhaps like right now you may be too. . . . When you go to the mountains, there is the question: will I find what I'm looking for? You are looking for many things . . . and staying open helps.

"Sometimes at home you may find stresses or worries and even feel weakened and all the time knowing a different trail may be much better or even realizing that a river near the mountains may feed the trees and all the different kinds of animals and trees need different foods . . . so all people too need different ideas, foods, approaches, and even strengths. The strengths have an inner voice that is always available to you with a deep refreshing breath . . . that guides you to stronger, healthier choices . . . and to know when it's time to look for more nourishment from the mountains, the environment, even a view to the outdoors and anytime this is strengthening in your self-hypnosis, at home or at work.

"Certainly your experience now is different from your past experiences and future ones, too, and knowing the past feelings of revitalization from the mountains and the choices of trails to follow . . . all offer you new ideas and new applications of self-discovery, self-confidence, and self-control . . . yours, designed by you and available when you want." This was followed by suggestions for returning to self-hypnosis when she wanted and for awakening.

This technique is what Milton Erickson called utilizing past successes. If clients have been effective in the past at reaching some quality state, they can use those successes to develop self-induced trance. I use whatever words clients use. Some regard the self-hypnotic state as a trance, some as a receptive state, and some use terms such as effective state or self-change state.

The words are not important. What is important is continued practice in entering, leaving, and reentering that state.

At this point, I might say to the client, "Now that you have some understanding of self-hypnosis, how do you feel it might assist you in dealing with your particular situation?" I gauge from their remarks whether they are being realistic or not. Since many clients believe that hypnosis is a magical, one-shot cure, I often find it useful to make this comment: "From our previous conversations I know that you are familiar with [something from their experience which requires a process of building skills and progressive development] and you know that when you first began to play tennis [or whatever they are familiar with] you needed to practice quite a bit in order to build your skills. In the same way, self-hypnosis must be practiced regularly in order for you to develop new skills. You may find you are able to learn in a very short period of time, or it may take as long as a week or two before you begin to notice some small change."

I would elaborate on this metaphor, drawing as much as I could from their own previous experiences with some skill that required practice and time before they noticed results. This sort of preparation helps clients develop positive but realistic expectations. Even though clients may not be in a trance during this dialogue, I am planting suggestions in an informal hypnotic setting.

As an example of this process, I once saw a client named Julie who weighed 275 pounds and had had many failures at dieting. She had tried all the pills and all the diets and had been to many physicians. She often lost some weight but quickly regained it. In response to earlier questions I learned that she had played cello in her high school orchestra and had been quite proud of that accomplishment. Though she no longer played cello, I used that experience to help her gain perspective on what we would be doing. My suggestion took this form:

"You probably remember when you first began to play the cello in grade school, you didn't even know how to hold the bow or where to place your fingers on the instrument. You may have even felt at that time that you could never learn to play as well as others you had seen playing cello. But you began by first learning about the instrument, how to hold it, how to tune it, where to place your fingers to play the basic notes, and you had to practice perhaps several hours a week, perhaps once or even twice a day.

"Gradually, you learned to play simple scales, perhaps a simple melody or two. You may recall that there were times when you felt frustrated and wanted to quit, but you were glad later, when you were playing on stage with the orchestra in high school, that you continued practicing even when you felt you were making no progress. Because during those times when you felt that practicing was not getting you anywhere, actually it was helping you in such a small way you weren't aware of it. And what a good feeling it was when you were able to play complete concert pieces and everyone applauded and you felt proud of your accomplishment.

"As we progress and practice with self-hypnosis to help you gain a similar feeling of pride of accomplishment, you will be practicing and working on small goals at first. Perhaps our first goal will be to eliminate only one unhealthy eating habit, perhaps learning one good eating habit. That may seem to you a very small step, much as learning how to tune the cello had seemed like only a small step toward learning to play. But we know that small steps build on one another and soon we can notice a change, perhaps a small change, perhaps a significant change."

I immediately build on these comments by talking about practice with self-hypnosis. I encourage clients to work 15 to 20 minutes once or twice a day, five or six days a week, for several weeks. Often I make tapes of their hypnosis experience in the office to help with their practice at home.

I also have clients write a description of their problems and current situation. This helps me learn about the problems, where they began, how they affect the clients' lives and other people's lives, and how they affect their perception of the world, themselves, and their abilities.

Once we have the necessary materials — an understanding of the current situation and a list of desired changes — we are in a position to create positive, ego-strengthening suggestions. I usually have clients develop the suggestions with my help. I convey the suggestions to them in the office after they've put themselves in a trance; at home they give the suggestions to themselves. They are given permission to open their eyes during trance and look at the list of positive suggestions they have written out beforehand.

Posthypnotic cues, a powerful extension of the trance state, are an important part of self-hypnosis. One of the most valuable uses of these cues is to reinstate the self-hypnotic trance. During an office session I may suggest, "Whenever you wish to return to this pleasant, relaxed state, all you need to do is take several deep, satisfying breaths and recall the cool tingling feeling you have right now in your fingers or perhaps in your entire hand. Yes, anytime you wish to regain this relaxed, comfortable feeling, just take several deep breaths and imagine how relaxed you can be."

Post-hypnotic cues for change can be associated with almost anything, e.g., a word, a feeling, or a behavior. When the client thinks of the word, has the feeling, or does the behavior, the suggestion goes into effect.

To return to my client Julie, I gave her post-hypnotic cues that she reinforced in her self-hypnosis to help her abstain from eating between meals during the day. My words were as follows:

"You may recall, Julie, that the refrigerator door has a handle on it. That handle can of course be an aid to opening the door. It can also be an aid in closing the door. But it can serve another purpose. That handle can be a reminder to you that *you* can have a handle on your appetite. There are times during the day when you know that opening the door of the refrigerator is appropriate, at your regular mealtimes. But during the rest of the day that door handle can represent to you an opportunity to get a better handle on yourself. You can take a look at the door handle, pause, take several deep breaths to relax and remind yourself that you do have a handle on your appetite. That's right, that handle can be a constant reminder of your own control, your own handle on your goals. By closing your eyes for just a moment, taking several deep breaths, you can imagine the door to your feelings of hunger closing."

It is important to have clients reinforce daily such posthypnotic suggestions until the cues are firmly implanted in their unconscious and have the desired results. Here again it may be necessary to explain that practice is needed before goals are achieved.

Self-hypnosis is a collaborative effort. As much as possible, I have clients work with me to develop the suggestions and cues that will be used. As time goes on and clients become more proficient at using hypnosis, they do more of the work of creating suggestions and cues.

Just about everything that can be done in heterohypnosis can also be done in self-hypnosis, so there are as many techniques as anyone might need. I often use rehearsal imagery, having clients imagine themselves acting and being as they would like to act and be, and imagining the successes they would like to have. In trance they can also recall their usual and self-defeating ways, from which we build bridges (with that word as the cue) to the new, positive behaviors they desire.

Since my experience is that the unconscious works best on its own, I encourage clients to let go of the trance work and move on to the next activity of the day without consciously reviewing what went on in trance. There is a need for regular practice with self-hypnosis but when the practice for the day is finished, clients should go on to other things.

One of the great benefits of self-hypnosis is shortening the duration of psychotherapy. I recall a 42-year-old client, depressed most of her life and greatly distraught about her marriage to an alcoholic manic-depressive who refused treatment of any kind. She was suffering tremendously. Most therapists would agree that years of therapy, perhaps combined with antidepressant medication, would be required to get her life in order. But I taught her self-hypnosis and we often used imagery based on her love of horses, with her imagining flying to health on winged horses. It was hard work and she usually spent two hours a day using self-hypnosis. But in five months she was much improved and her life was in much better shape. She probably saved herself four years of therapy.

The best therapy is often self-therapy, provided clients have the proper tools to work with. Self-hypnosis is one of the best of these tools and gives real meaning to the idea that those who want help need to look within themselves. Self-hypnosis can be practiced anywhere, any time for a few seconds, a few minutes, or longer without special props or equipment. Those who practice it are able to take the changes they create in trance and extend them, through posthypnotic cues, to the rest of their lives. Learning self-hypnosis is like learning to be one's own inner voice, one's own therapist.

$Q_{\&}^{A}35$ Making Hypnosis Tapes for Patients

Question:

Some therapists use hypnosis in the office but never make tapes for patients or instruct them in self-hypnosis. Other therapists almost always make tapes and ask clients to listen to them at home. What are the advantages and disadvantages of these two patterns?

Discussion by D. CORYDON HAMMOND, Ph.D.

There are several advantages of teaching patients self-hypnosis, with or without using tapes. First, it reduces dependency and promotes independence. Second, the patient may feel an increasing sense of self-mastery and esteem because of having skills for self-management. Third, patients can make more rapid progress through regularly doing something for themselves at home (such as self-hypnosis), rather than waiting for a once-a-week appointment.

However, we have limited information concerning the use of tapes for self-hypnosis versus self-hypnosis without tapes. Despite the widespread use of cassette tapes to assist patients in doing self-hypnosis, there have been no published reports comparing tape-assisted self-hypnosis with self-directed self-hypnosis. The published studies so far have only compared self-directed self-hypnosis with heterohypnosis (Johnson, 1979; Ruch, 1975; Shor & Easton, 1973) or extensively examined "self-initiated" self-hypnosis (Fromm et al., 1981), in which excellent subjects received minimal coaching on how to enter and use hypnosis.

However, I recently reported the results of a study comparing self-hypnosis with and without tapes (Hammond, 1984). The findings consistently favored the use of tapes. Tape-assisted self-hypnosis produced greater ability to concentrate, less distraction with extraneous thoughts, greater depth of trance, and more changes in body perception (e.g., distortion, loss of awareness, heaviness, floating). While not as pronounced, there were tendencies for subjects doing self-hypnosis with tapes, as compared with self-directed self-hypnosis, to rate their hypnotic experience as more enjoyable and to experience better auditory and kinesthetic imagery. When using tapes for self-hypnosis, subjects also more clearly felt that they were in an altered state of consciousness that they perceived as different from the waking state.

The results of this study and my clinical experience support the value of making individualized tapes for patients. However, this study used inexperienced subjects who were just beginning to use self-hypnosis. Repetitive use of a limited number of tapes may become boring, producing less concentration and satisfaction. In fact, in clinical practice some patients say that after numerous experiences with a self-hypnosis tape they have memorized the tape and feel bored. For this reason, I often prepare several tapes for a patient. Additionally, however, from the beginning of their practice, I strongly emphasize practicing self-hypnosis without a tape at least 50% of the time. I believe that patients should possess skills to flexibly and independently use self-hypnosis whenever they need it, not simply when a tape player and suitable tape are available.

Another factor that I have found important to take into account is the length of the tape. Some patients prefer 20-to-25-minute tapes, but experience has shown that many patients find this to be too long and that such lengthy tapes discourage them from doing self-hypnosis. I find that many patients prefer 5-to-15-minute tapes. Here, as with everything else in therapy, it is crucial to suit the treatment (or the tape) to the patient.

It also seems possible that tapes may be of more benefit to patients early in their self-hypnosis training and become less important with experience. I recently followed up a group of premenstrual syndrome patients who had attended eight hours of group training in self-hypnosis. At the conclusion of each of the four training sessions, members received a copy of a self-hypnosis tape made by me. The tapes averaged a little more than 20 minutes each. At the end of the training, patients rated the use of the self-hypnosis tapes as being much more beneficial than doing self-hypnosis without a tape. However, a six-to-eight-month follow-up revealed no relationship at all between earlier ratings of the usefulness of the tapes and the subsequent frequency of using the tapes in self-hypnosis. At follow-up, patients were using the tapes less than four times a month, but were doing self-hypnosis without tapes almost 14 times per month.

Thus, tapes for self-hypnosis may to some degree be rather like training wheels on a bicycle that can be phased out with experience and practice. Nonetheless, the little evidence we have so far suggests that tape-assisted self-hypnosis may be valuable at the beginning of hypnotherapy, just as training wheels are initially in learning to ride a bike.

References

Fromm, E., Brown, D., Hurt, S., Oberlander, J., Boxer, A., & Pfeifer, G. (1981). The phenomena and characteristics of self-hypnosis. *International Journal of Clinical & Experimental Hypnosis, 29,* 189–246.

Johnson, L. S. (1979). Self-hypnosis: Behavioral and phenomenological comparisons with heterohypnosis. *International Journal of Clinical & Experimental Hypnosis, 27,* 240–264.

Hammond, D. C. (Nov. 10, 1984). Self-hypnosis: A comparison of two methods. Talk at the 27th Annual Scientific Meeting, American Society of Clinical Hypnosis. San Francisco, California.

Ruch, J. C. (1975). Self-hypnosis: The result of heterohypnosis or vice versa. *International Journal of Clinical & Experimental Hypnosis, 23,* 282–304.

Shor, R. E., & Easton, R. D. (1973). A preliminary report on research comparing self- and hetero-hypnosis. *American Journal of Clinical Hypnosis, 16,* 37–44.

Question:

When using ideomotor signals my patients usually give valuable
information. But if I suggest, "Your unconscious will be able to
respond verbally instead of through your fingers," I don't get
valuable answers. Why is this?

Discussion by ERIKA WICK, Ph.D.

The question reports an intriguing phenomenon. The hypnotized subject
responds meaningfully when permitted to respond nonverbally, but does not
give valuable answers when expected to respond on a verbal level. How can
this be explained?

Before an explanation can be given, more questions have to be asked, to
put the occurrence into perspective. The key questions are:

1) Does this phenomenon *always* occur when a subject is asked to switch
   from an ideomotor response pattern to a verbal response pattern?
2) What are the related conditions: the therapist, the client, and issues in
   communications, such as the wording of a request or suggestion, specific
   therapeutic strategies, the material to be explored, or the subject's hypnotic state?

Before dealing with the mode-switch refusal we have to ask: Do all patients at all times stop giving useful answers when asked to switch from a
nonverbal to a verbal response pattern? The therapist who posed the question seems to find that patient productivity stops when the mode is switched.
Other therapists do not find that this effect can be generalized. They find
that many patients make the transition easily. Some subjects in fact are most

productive when they are first allowed to identify their therapeutic target for the session by means of ideomotor responses and then are given the opportunity to elaborate verbally on selected focal points: on elicited memories, fantasies, or other experiences.

However, with some patients it is necessary to discuss this type of therapeutic strategy before it is practiced so that they may understand the procedures and can agree to them. A client's agreement to a strategy puts him/her into the role of collaborator, cuts down on resistance, and ensures success or, in difficult cases, at least enhances its probability.

Most hypnotherapists encounter some forms of blocking or resistance in the course of their therapeutic work. Rarely, though, is a resistance phenomenon so consistent that it appears with every client and each time the specific strategy is used. In the case of the therapist who asked the question, it is suggested that he or she investigate the issue further to find out whether he or she provokes the productivity refusal. More generally, we should remind ourselves that the patient's refusal to cooperate productively is not always a negative move impeding the therapist's work. It can, instead, be an expression of the wisdom of resistance, which is a protective force that pushes the brakes when the therapist moves faster or into more dangerous territory than the client can handle at the given point in his/her development. Keeping the pressure-cooker effect of hypnosis in mind, it is important that the therapist be sensitive to the slow-down messages the patient is posting.

What are the reasons for and/or the conditions under which patient cooperation and productivity stops when a mode-switch is suggested? And what can be done to prevent it? Of the many possible contributing factors the following two are selected for discussion: 1) communications, and 2) the material to be explored.

In no therapeutic interaction do communications have to be worded as carefully as they do when a client is in a hypnotic state. The patient in the receptive state of hypnosis seems to be in need of communications that tune in to what he or she can and wants to be receptive to. The therapist needs to be aware of the subject's level of openness and vulnerability, which tends to reveal itself to the hypnotist from its flip-side, namely, as defensiveness. Communications that the patient rejects easily provoke various forms of resistance, including an aggressive/defensive snapping out of hypnosis.

With this in mind, let us first look at the communications as they were offered by the therapist who posed the question regarding the decreased patient productivity after a suggested response mode switch. The therapist said to the patient: "Your unconscious will be able to respond verbally instead of through your fingers." The patient thereafter was unable to give valuable information.

When speculating why this might have happened — assuming the outcome was communications related — a number of possibilities appear that should be brought into focus:

a) poorly understood terminology and/or concepts;
b) patient feeling bypassed;
c) patient resenting jargon;
d) asking for more than the switch request reveals.

a) Poorly understood concepts or terminology. Tom, the patient, has no clear understanding of what exactly the unconscious is and what is expected to happen when the unconscious responds. He is not familiar with the term and does not have a clear idea of what is expected when the unconscious starts verbalizing. He feels scared, uncomfortable, maybe inadequate, and prefers to be a nonresponder over responding in a way that would give away his ignorance about the concept of an unconscious or how it functions. If asked whether he knows what is meant by his unconscious, Tom is likely to answer affirmatively or say something like "sort of," rather than ask for clarification. He feels vulnerable and easily embarrassed, especially when he feels that his intelligence may be questioned. To this patient, responding simply in the words that come to his mind seems to have nothing to do with the unconscious that was invoked in the therapist's request. This patient does not know how the unconscious would be expected to respond.

Alternative: The therapist getting no positive response from his patient should reword his request, phrasing it so that the instructions give the patient a clear understanding of what the therapist expects him to do.

The following is a request option that indicates what is expected by the therapist, if the unconscious offers its responses verbally. It does not mention the word "unconscious," preventing any negative reactions to that word on the client's part. The therapist may say:

> Instead of having your fingers give me response signals, you will find it equally comfortable to let words respond. You will allow them to flow automatically any way they wish to appear. You will allow them to flow by themselves without getting involved in what they are saying.

b) Bypassing the patient. Bruce feels bypassed by his therapist's request that the unconscious do the answering rather than the patient himself. He may feel the therapist is in some mysterious way splitting the person up, dividing him against himself. Being unable to tolerate this feeling of being torn apart into a divided self, he stalls and offers resistance. It may feel to the patient as if the therapist were creating a new therapeutic alliance including the professional and the unconscious, at the exlusion of the client as a full person.

Alternative: The therapist discusses the planned strategy with the client before embarking upon this venture, and after having explained the reason for this approach obtains the client's agreement and cooperation.

c) Professional upmanship and jargoning. Liz sees her therapist as a professional who is attempting to enhance and polish his professional halo by using jargon, instead of plain English, especially if the therapist might have overused terms like "unconscious" and "ideomotor responses." This client has most likely been sensitized to the professional jargon syndrome by previous exposure to professionals where she contracted her "allergy" to technical in-group talk. She responds with resentment which gives rise to her resistance.

Alternative: The therapist meets the client on her level of communications and gains instant cooperation.

d) Asking for more than one switch. The therapist requests a switch from a hand-signal response mode to a verbal mode. Jim offers no resistance. However, when the questions arrive they require full-sentence and sometimes multi-sentence answers. Jim reacts to the incongruence between the therapist's explicit single-switch request and the fact that what he had agreed to suddenly turns out to involve two changes: namely the announced mode switch *plus* a switch from a yes/no response to a tell-me-a-tale response. The patient is willing to remain productive on the yes/no basis, but feels pushed unfairly to explore issues in greater depth without having been consulted about his readiness.

Alternative: The therapist getting no positive response from her client when asking for full-sentence answers may consider rephrasing her questions so that they may be answered with a simple one-syllable affirmation or negation, analogous to the questions she asked when eliciting ideomotor responses. Initiating verbalizations by imitating the yes/no ideomotor response pattern can be useful. Once the client has adjusted to this response mode other one-word answers can be requested, resulting in key-word responses. Key-word responses usually lead to a spontaneous and natural developmental progression. One-word mini-responses harmoniously grow into full-sentence answers and eventually multi-sentence in-depth report responses.

The therapist's other alternative is to be more explicit in his communications. If he specifies the full implications when requesting the switch from an ideomotor to a verbal response mode, he will prevent the development of the form of resistance that evolves when a client resents the unfairness experienced in an unannounced double switch. Being unable to counter what happened verbally without abandoning the hypnotic state, the patient feels forced to push the brakes.

Communications issues are by no means the only reason why a therapist may encounter resistance to switching from the ideomotor to the verbal response mode. One of the many other reasons is because a client is not yet ready to deal with the material to be explored. The fact that he or she gives valuable information when allowed to transmit the answers by means of an automatic noncognitive response mode, namely, by ideomotor action, but not when asked to respond verbally, gives the therapist an important message: The patient is willing to share uncomfortable information with the hypnotist as long as he himself does not have to take note of it.

Major underlying issues here are:

• *censoring*, which may pertain to an array of concerns, including morality, self-esteem, social respectability, avoidance of emotional pain,
• defensive patterns of *memory access manipulation*: storage, bypass and recall (forgetting, not remembering, bypassing, posthypnotic amnesia, storage deficit), and
• *automatic behavior*.

It is possible, for example, that Bert's resisting the therapist's request to switch from ideomotor to verbal responding makes sense. He does not want to know the information revealed by his ideomotor responses; he has even less desire to get involved in cognitively connecting to the issues at hand, delving into them and possibly finding out that he is not able to disconnect from them through posthypnotic amnesia, which works perfectly for him as long as he functions within an automatic response mode.

Bert is willing to let the therapist know where the crux of his problem is, but he is not yet able to face up to it himself. He entrusts the therapist with major pieces of information, believing that the trusted other will not feed it back to him or confront him with it until (and even then only to the degree that) he is ready for it.

As far as Bert's conscious recall is concerned, the gates of his memory have not allowed him any access to censored information, while at the same time they are permitting important messages to slip by the censoring gate for use by someone else. Hand movement signals bypass censoring and memory storage more easily than do verbal responses.

The explicit agreement Bert has with his therapist permits the patient to invoke the principle of posthypnotic amnesia and to be unable to recall what finger movements he made or whether there were any at all; if he does remember having made movements, they need not be recalled as connected to any of the questions asked by the therapist. In this way the patient gets his message across to someone else without himself getting involved on the cognitive level in any of the content issues.

The more the ideomotor responses are truly automatic, which by definition they should be, but in reality not always fully are, the more censoring is unnecessary. The censoring function helps the *conscious* ego to avoid hurt, conflict, guilt feelings, loss of self-esteem, embarrassment, etc., but appears unconcerned about how *unconscious* material measures up to an individual's value system and other standards applied by the person's conscience (understood here as a broad mechanism relating to various standard categories and not restricted to more issues), as long as it remains on the unconscious level.

Automatic behavior, though, is monitored in some way too. The monitor, the neutral function which is the precursor of the conscience, will shift our attention state and allow the censor to get into gear when necessary. The monitor provides us with a subliminal co-awareness, from which we can start getting involved, i.e., interfere in automatic developments, if it is warranted.

As an alternative the therapist can discuss the projected switch from ideomotor to verbal responses ahead of time. She announces that the last set of questions prior to making the switch to verbal responses will pertain to various topics covered with ideomotor responses and will explore which topics the patient is willing to deal with in depth on a verbal basis.

TABLE
Favored Functioning and Processing Modes

nonhypnotic state	hypnotic state
Dominant brain-hemisphere function, left-brain?	Nondominant brain-hemisphere function, right brain?
Rational response patterns	Emotional response patterns
Aristotelian logic	Psycho-logic
Higher cognitive functioning	Primary level processing
Linear thought organization; linear perception	Global thought organization; global (intuitive) perception
Verbalization (linear)	Nonverbal expression
Control over input and outflow	Automatic input and outflow
Volitional retrieval from memory	Involuntary recall (extreme: obsessive inflow)
Language coded retrieval	Experiential recall coding
Censor barrier at conscious-unconscious threshold	Relatively uncensored conscious-unconscious exchange flow
Active involvement	Receptive mode
Ideally non-regressed state	Regressed state
Reality boundaries	Omnipotence, fantasy
External world related	Inner world absorption (self, other, focal goal)

There are many possible valid answers to the question of why a subject in a hypnotic state may prefer to communicate nonverbally rather than verbally. A speculative but nevertheless empirically supported answer may be found in the functioning and processing modes that hypnotic and non-hypnotic states favor. When the two modes are juxtaposed a picture emerges that, on the hypnotic side, supports nonverbal communication (see Table).

When we look at some of the functioning and processing modes favored in hypnotic and nonhypnotic states, it becomes understandable that (and why) a subject in a deep trance may simply prefer not to communicate verbally. The client who has two goals, namely to reach a hypnotic state and to make therapeutic progress, may feel such comfort in achieving the first goal and enjoying the state of harmony that the second goal becomes more distant and loses its urgency. Not wanting to have the present equilibrium disturbed, the subject resists switching to functioning in a verbal mode. The verbal mode threatens to alienate the client from his trance state and to put him/her in touch with the reality issues that brought the individual into therapy in the first place. While the various reasons for resisting the switch to verbalization discussed previously are all significant in individual cases, there seems to be a shared experience among hypnotized subjects, having reached a given level of receptive absorption that translates into "Please, do not disturb me."

Q&A 37 Ego State Therapy With Depression

Question:

I've been fascinated by demonstrations of and what I've read about ego state therapy. I also have lots of patients who suffer from low self-esteem and serious depression. How can ego state therapy be effectively used with these problems?

Discussion by ANTHONY B. NEWEY, Ph.D.

The connection between negative self-image and depression is widely accepted. It makes sense that people who feel badly about themselves are less likely to lead satisfying lives and more likely to be depressed than those who feel good about themselves. Defective self-image is a primary factor in two major theories of depression, those of Jacobsen (1971) and Beck (1976). Beck's formulation has attracted widespread attention in recent years. Studies have shown his cognitive behavior therapy approach to be at least as effective as medication in the treatment of depression. Beck argues that measures to modify "cognitive distortions" in self-image are an essential part of treatment.

Hypnotic ego-strengthening techniques (Hartland, 1971; Stanton, 1977) have a similar purpose of creating more positive feelings about the self and life directly with hypnotic suggestion. I have not seen any actual data on the effectiveness of structured ego-strengthening methods. While they undoubtedly have some effect, I do not use them. My focus is on other issues which I believe are more fundamental in the treatment of depression and lead to more significant and enduring change.

Jacobsen and Beck define a causal role for self-esteem, with Beck focusing on self-feeling which is consciously perceived. But the relationship between depression and self-esteem cannot be just one way. Individuals who function effectively in the world also feel good about themselves *after* the fact, as a result of what they have experienced. Positive self-regard is not a fixed quantity but has to be reinforced over and over again through action. It is precisely this capacity to act which is blocked in the depressed person. We know that fear disturbs and inhibits behavior, as Sullivan (1953) in particular emphasized. I believe this is the central problem in the psychology of depressives. They carry unconscious fears which prevent them from responding authentically and thus cannot obtain for themselves an adequate sense of satisfaction from living.

Suppose that a young child in a high chair is trying to refuse some unwanted food and is yelled at and slapped for resisting. It may take only one such experience to leave that child badly frightened and permanently wary about asserting himself against parental wishes. The potential consequences for inhibiting behavior later on in life are apparent, but by then the reasons are likely to be buried deep in the psyche. Experience with a number of patients has convinced me that such hidden fears are crucial in depression. There may be any number of them which are partly or completely unavailable to awareness. It is these fears which need to be located and removed, a task for which hypnotic methods are exceptionally well suited.

The approach I use is derived from the ego state therapy model of H. H. and J. G. Watkins (1982), whose position draws upon Paul Federn's concept of the ego as differentiated into "states." The Watkins define an ego state as a "set of behaviors, perceptions, and experiences bound together by a common principle and separated by a boundary from other such states." Such dissociated segments of personality have an autonomous existence and can influence an individual's experience in varying ways, sudden mood shifts being a common example. An ego state appears to be similar to Jung's (1970) notion of the unconscious complex: an "agglomeration of associations" that, Jung said, forms a "little personality of itself." In Jung's words, "the complex upsets the breathing, it disturbs the heart . . . when you want to say or do something, unfortunately a complex interferes with this intention, then you do or say something different from what you intended."

An ego state is a kind of partial personality, and the individual functions as if he or she were a family of states. These normally unconscious states or parts can be brought to the surface in hypnosis and usually can describe their origins in the patient's history, their effects on conscious experience and behavior, and the nature of their interactions with other parts. Conflicts embodied within or arising between them are the genesis of neurotic symptoms. The Watkins' treatment method employs extensive direct interaction between therapist and particular parts while the patient is in trance, very much like the hypnotherapy of alternating multiple personality.

My own approach evolved from that of the Watkins but differs in some important particulars. First, my focus is on identifying and resolving fears. Second, I find communication with parts more efficiently handled with ideomotor signals than with two-way dialogue. Finally, while the Watkins have not proposed the existence of universal kinds of states, I have found it useful to think in terms of generic types.

While nothing should be assumed without confirmation in each situation, one can expect to encounter the following kinds of states or parts:

Child parts: These are dissociated parts of the person which have childhood origins. They are usually traceable to specific incidents that were in some way painful. Most were created before the age of five, and parts that existed at birth are sometimes encountered. The most important parts in this category have to do with fears of rejection or punishment. Others may be sad, angry, hurt and so on.

Parent parts: Usually there are two, a "mother part" and a "father part." Parent parts are typically judgmental and punishing, but they are usually distinct from each other and play separate roles in the patient's emotional life. They are the main source of conscious guilt and self-criticalness.

The "Strong Part": What I call the "Strong Part" is, I believe, an innate, universal dimension of self which has to do with the capacity for clarity and directness of response. While child and parent parts result from experience, the Strong Part always is present prior to birth. It grows as the person matures and is itself without fear. In the depressed person, the Strong Part will inevitably be found to be prevented from acting freely and openly.

Low self-esteem in depression has two components. On the one hand are negative self-judgments coming from parent parts and, on the other, unconscious fears which block the person (specifically, the Strong Part of the person) from acting in ways that yield positive self-feeling. Most frightened parts report themselves holding on to one or both parent parts, as if like real children they would rather have aversive contact than none at all. It is this pattern, in fact, which gives the parent parts the power they have. They use fear to inhibit behavior while simultaneously criticizing and punishing. I believe all neurotically depressed patients are caught in this bind.

It follows from this model of depression that the removal of fears should both free up behavior and reduce negative internal judgments so that positive self-feelings can develop in a natural way. My treatment approach follows a simple logic. It starts with assessment of reported or observed overt behavior, moves to hypnotherapeutic exploration and intervention at the unconscious level, and then returns to the conscious level to note results. This approach is used throughout therapy in an ongoing process of successively identifying and removing buried fears, one after the other. The same question is asked continuously: How is this person *not* behaving fully and naturally? What responses are missing or seem constricted? Whenever there is an indication that the patient's capacity to act is impaired, there is a possibility that one or more fears (frightened parts) are involved, irrespective of his or her reasoning about it.

As an example, I am seeing a chronically depressed but functioning single woman who recently returned from vacation feeling tense, fatigued, and dispirited rather than refreshed. She had gone with her older sister and her sister-in-law, both of whom had wanted to do a lot of sightseeing. The patient accompanied them though she had really wanted to spend her time on the beach. When asked why she hadn't done the latter, she said that her companions made her feel something was wrong with her for wanting to stay by herself and that "I'd rather go along than create problems." This was her style in her job as well, where she had always been very hardworking and uncomplaining regardless of the demands placed upon her. The question is obvious: Was there something below the surface that wouldn't let her say "no" forcefully?

A short series of ideomotor questions revealed that she was unconsciously quite angry about having felt denied and coerced. The anger was held in by a frightened part which was born when the patient was about two. One evening she had heard her parents arguing and had gone to see what was the matter. Her father, who had been drinking, told her to leave the room and blew up at her when she refused. What was worse, he stayed angry and did not kiss her goodnight as he normally would, so she had gone to bed unhappy and worried about her relationship with him. Her feelings about this incident did not go away. They made her afraid to say no to him and in her adult life continued at an unconscious level to keep her from asserting herself. This was particularly true in situations involving authority, which her sister had always represented to her.

I always use the Strong Part as a therapeutic agent acting, as it were, from within. Contact with this part is made early on. There are different ways to achieve this. One can ask for an ideomotor signal directly from the "part of the person which has no fears," or one can look for evidence that the patient sometimes acts in an uncharacteristically strong way, a sign that at those moments the part is appearing publicly. The key task is to confirm the Strong Part's presence and take whatever steps are needed to ensure that it is free to move about internally.

Problems in this step are not uncommon. Parent parts may attempt to interfere or it may be that the Strong Part doesn't know where it is or how to move. Guided imagery techniques are often helpful. A Strong Part reporting itself to be lying in the dark, for instance, can be asked to stand and turn slowly until it sees a line or point of light that would indicate the presence of a door. I have found that if I ask enough yes or no questions about the Strong Part's situation, I get enough information to devise a way to help it move about internally.

Frightened parts are approached in much the same way as actual children who need protection and comfort. When one enters the inner world in which parts exist and inquires about them, they almost always report themselves to be in the same circumstances which produced them in the first place. Thus, they may be in high chairs where they were punished for not eating or in cribs where they cried and no one came to pick them up. In most cases there is a feeling of being cut off from contact and all alone. The other typical finding is that frightened parts are holding on to at least one parent and are therefore subject to continual negative and threatening treatment.

After I learn something about each frightened part and where it is, I enlist the assistance of the Strong Part to find it, separate it from the parent part, and take it to a safe place where the parents are barred. This step is ordinarily straightforward and itself takes little time. To illustrate, the following is an excerpt from the session in which I took care of the fear about assertion in the depressed woman mentioned earlier. The patient is hypnotized and responding only with finger signals: Y = yes; N = no.

THERAPIST: Is the one with the fear in her room?   Y

Is she in the dark?   Y

Does the Strong Part (who is male) know about her?   Y

Does he have any feelings of anger toward her?   N

Would he go to her room and signal 'yes' when he's there?   Y

Would he open the door, go in, turn on the light, and then signal?   Y

Does he see her?   Y

Does she seem in any way afraid of him?   N

Would he then pick her up gently and hold her?   Y

Now I would like him to separate her completely from the father part and signal when he has done so.   Y

Finally, would he take her to a place where the father part cannot follow ever and see that from now on she is protected and cared for, that she is never yelled at, and that she never goes to bed feeling bad again?   Y

Is she feeling better already?   Y

Much better?   Y

I asked the Strong Part about anger because sometimes this part is angry at a frightened part for confining it and will make the fear worse if it approaches. This can produce conscious distress for the hypnotized patient as well. I have found that I can tell the Strong Part what happened initially to create the fear and point out that the patient as an infant or child couldn't have reacted any other way. With this understanding, the Strong Part is always willing to "not be angry anymore," and I can then safely proceed.

In the above example, the patient took one deep breath but otherwise had no particular conscious feeling, and after many such experiences I've concluded that there is no necessity for the fears to come into consciousness at all. Strong affect frequently does emerge in this kind of therapy, but fears for the most part are removed entirely at the unconscious level. Occasionally a parent part may obstruct or even reverse the process. When this happens one can be sure that some other fear is being manipulated and must be attended to first. Otherwise, with rare exceptions the same basic maneuver produces rapid, full and permanent resolution. With surprising frequency the effect on the patient's behavior is almost immediate, and, if I go back weeks or months later to check on its status, the fear is still gone.

A week after the quoted session the patient told me that she had been "losing her temper." At work she had refused a request that her staff do a project over a holiday, on the phone had "almost yelled" at someone who wanted special treatment on a report, and one day had felt so close to "exploding" that she had gone drinking after the office closed to calm herself down. She said she knew she was overreacting but was getting tired of people taking her willingness for granted and that she "couldn't control herself."

I don't cite these reactions as adaptive. The patient has much more to do before she will be on her feet psychologically. The point is that shortly after the hypnotic intervention there was demonstrable evidence of the beginning of a shift away from her traditional super-cooperative and self-defeating style. In hypnosis we found that the fear was now feeling "entirely secure" and the Strong Part of her had in fact been freer to express itself (along with other anger which had different sources). Patients hardly respond so visibly every time they leave my office, but in my practice as a whole I see this phenomenon all the time. Often without realizing it themselves, they report or show in the session this week behaviors and/or feelings which are unequivocally related to last week's therapeutic work. I have verified the connection between some overt change and the removal of a fear on numerous occasions.

Longer term, the results that patients achieve tend to be quite significant. Mood and energy levels increase; compulsive (e.g., overeating) and psychosomatic symptoms fade; emotions are experienced and expressed more clearly; natural capacities which may have been absent for years reappear, such as playfulness; and patients move simultaneously towards more self-direction and greater interpersonal involvement. With all of this comes marked reduction in guilt and self-derogation and increasingly positive feelings about self and life's possibilities.

Therapy for the patient can be quite intense. It is not well suited to highly resistant patients or those with poor ego strength or pronounced borderline characteristics. Excluding, in addition, those who are simply too depressed to enter into an active treatment relationship at all, so far as I can tell it is appropriate for anyone with a neurotic or psychosomatic diagnosis. Duration is not necessarily short-term. I have seen depressed patients for periods ranging from a few months to well over two years. The latter may seem extended by current standards, and perhaps it is. At the same time, the goal can entail a very broad change in a patient's capacity to function, and the status of treatment is, in effect, under continuous review. If progress is not being made, it is impossible not to know it. Both therapist and patient know pretty well that things are moving steadily forward, and there is never a feeling that one may be engaged in a therapy struggle that isn't in the end going to make much of a difference.

For the therapist, the work by its nature is energy consuming. Considerable activity is called for, there is a great deal of detail that has to be kept track of, and cathartic kinds of emotional experiences are frequent. Also, of course, one has to deal with resistance which can be stubborn and other sorts of complications and obstacles. Discussion of such issues is beyond the scope of this paper. Like all difficulties one faces in psychotherapy, a way has to be found around them. In my experience, with the ability to find out what is happening unconsciously at any point and to call upon the Strong Part as an inner ally, a way around always exists.

References

Beck, A. T. (1976). *Depression: Clinical, experimental, and theoretical aspects*. New York: Harper & Row.

Hartland, J. (1971). Further observations on the use of "ego strengthening" techniques. *American Journal of Clinical Hypnosis, 14*, 1–8.

Jacobsen, E. (1971). *Depression*. New York: International Universities Press.

Jung, C. G. (1970). *Analytical psychology: Its theory and practice*. New York: Random House.

Stanton, H. D. (1977). The utilization of suggestions derived from rational-emotive therapy. *International Journal of Clinical Hypnosis, XXV*, 18–26.

Sullivan, H. S. (1953). *The interpersonal theory of psychiatry*. New York: W. W. Norton.

Watkins, H. H., & Watkins, J. G. (1982). Ego-state therapy. In L. E. Abt & I. R. Stuart (Eds.). *The newer therapies: A source book* (pp. 137–155). New York: Van Nostrand Reinhold.

$\underset{A}{Q}$ 38 Using Result Imagery With Sex Problems

Question:

I see a fair number of sex problems but my success with them is not as good as I'd like and relapses are common. I've had courses and read the usual books, but the problem remains and I was wondering if hypnosis could help. I use hypnosis with other problems but so far not with cases of sexual dysfunction. The one specific I can offer is that several clients in the past year said, even while they were making some progress, "But I still feel impotent (or unsexual or frigid)."

Discussion by BERNIE ZILBERGELD, Ph.D.

There's no doubt in my mind that hypnosis can be a powerful supplement to the usual techniques of sex therapy. I think of hypnosis as a focused state of awareness, which is also the way I think of good sex. When one's attention is narrowed to erotic sensations in oneself and one's partner, one is fully present, really there, able to appreciate, enjoy, and go with the feelings. Under these conditions, rarely are there problems (unless, of course, there are physiological complications, an issue I don't deal with here). The body is free to do what it knows how to do — become aroused, respond to stimulation, become erect and engorged, and to have orgasm.

When, on the other hand, one's attention is not on what is happening, but is distracted by concerns, worries, and questions (what sex therapists call spectatoring), the trance isn't present and one often can't function or enjoy.

Good sex is simply an erotic trance. Although sex therapists don't know enough about hypnosis to use the term, they are basically trying to establish or reestablish trance, to free their patients of worries and other distractions so they can attend to what is going on in the moment. The fact that a focused state of awareness is essential to both hypnosis and sex is a good reason for using hypnosis to treat sex problems. What a client experiences in trance in the office or when practicing at home is what he needs to learn to experience during erotic activity.

To continue in this vein a moment longer, orgasm is probably the ultimate trance. For a few seconds, one's attention is forcibly riveted to a small portion of one's being. The sensations are so strong it is almost impossible to think of other things or to be distracted. I've heard people describe all sorts of things they were thinking about during sex, but I've yet to hear anyone say they were thinking about something else at the moment of orgasm.

There are many ways to integrate hypnosis and sex therapy, most of which are capably covered by Araoz (1982). For the rest of this paper, I will pick up on the client statement given by the questioner because I think sex therapists, and therapists working with a wide variety of other problems, often ignore the change in self-concept that has to accompany a change in behavior. The lack of attention to this issue often leads to failure and relapse. For convenience, I will use examples throughout of men with erection problems. Obviously, the same principles and methods apply to other complaints.

It is a truism that we construct views of ourselves that guide our behavior (and sometimes conflict with it as well). Men with sex problems, for instance, come to think of themselves as "not being a real man," "not having what it takes," "being a sexual failure," and as "being impotent." Over time these self-thoughts or concepts become deeply embedded and resistant to change, even in the face of real changes. I have had many clients who said "but I still feel impotent" even when they were not impotent in their last two, five, 10, or 20 encounters.

Sometimes all that is needed is more successes and time to allow behavior to influence the self-image. As the man continues to see that he's functional in sex, he in effect reconsiders the image of himself as impotent and starts seeing himself as sexy and potent. But such reconsideration and the construction of a new self-image can take many months unless the therapist does something to speed up the process. The client is very vulnerable during this time. Since his self-image has not caught up with the change in behavior, it's as if he says to himself: "How can I, a sexual failure and impotent man, have this erection and be enjoying sex?" This translates to a doubt about his abilities and he will be watchful of anything that confirms the old self-image. If he doesn't get an erection one time or notices that it's not as hard as he thinks it should be, the image will immediately reassert itself. "See, I'm still impotent and don't have what it takes. The erections I had in the last few weeks were only flukes."

On the other hand, a man with a realistic but positive sexual self-image has less trouble when he doesn't perform as he would like. Because he sees himself as manly, sexy, and potent, the lack of an erection one time can be easily dismissed. "Guess I'm too tired tonight or too concerned about work. We'll try again tomorrow." Whereas he can dismiss the lack of erection as a fluke, the man with the impotent self-image will dismiss the presence of erection as a fluke.

There are other cases where the successes seem to have almost no influence on the image of impotence. The self-image is so entrenched that changes in functioning seem unable to affect it. Men like this are likely candidates for relapse because sooner or later they will fail to function as well as they would like. This will be taken as evidence that they are really still the way they were (impotent), which in turn will reinforce that image and soon put an end to their functioning.

I hope I have said enough to make a case for the importance of dealing with self-images in therapy — and not only sex therapy. Most clients build an identity or image based on their problem: "I'm alcoholic," "I'm a fat person," "I'm incompetent," "I don't have what it takes (in this job, in bed, in relationships)." Therapists seem to know this in a vague way and some of their efforts go into trying to change the image. Therapist statements such as, "Maybe this accomplishment at work will help you see you're not as inadequate as you thought," and "I hope this successful experience will show you that you're more intelligent than you give yourself credit for" are commonly heard.

But there are more intensive and systematic ways of helping a client to alter his view of himself, and that is where hypnosis can be beneficial. I'm thinking specifically of what some have called result or goal imagery, where the client in a relaxed state imagines over and over again having accomplished his goals and what his life would be like given that accomplishment. Most of the emphasis in imagery work is on process, the ways the goal will be accomplished ("imagine yourself feeling very calm and comfortable, yet highly aroused as you get into bed and reach for her"). Process imagery is of course important, but result imagery is also important and often overlooked.

Goal imagery assumes that the desired results have already been achieved. You're not trying to get an erection or have good sex or be a good lover. All those things are taken for granted. You are a confident, skillful, fully functional lover, with lots of pleasure and lots of good experiences behind you. You fully anticipate a wonderful time whenever you think about having sex with your partner and whenever you make or respond to the first sexual move. (The last three sentences are often given verbatim to clients in trance.)

The client is then instructed to imagine how he would feel, be, and act in different situations given that he has achieved his goals. For example, "Imagine how you would feel when your partner makes a sexual invitation. Imagine the thoughts that would go through your head, the feelings you would have, and the sensations. Imagine how you respond." While this is perhaps the most relevant image, it's far from the only one that should be used. Depending on the case, other possibilities include how one would feel and what one would say and do when male friends in the locker room or at the water cooler talk or joke about sex, when one meets new women at the health club or at work, when a woman one knows (but not one's partner) acts flirtatiously at a party, and when one's partner starts a conversation about sex after they've finished love-making.

I usually start result imagery near the beginning of therapy, often before process imagery. This way, the goals are made concrete and help motivate the client through the inevitable rough spots in treatment. It also alerts me to problems because it frequently happens that there is difficulty with some of the result imagery. The client cannot imagine being functional in bed or cannot imagine feeling equal to the other guys when they talk about sex, and that helps me determine what needs work. It's also the case, at least in my experience, that changing self-image is a longer process than changing behavior, so I want to give it as much time as it needs.

A case example will illustrate how I use goal imagery. Greg is a business executive in his forties who had never felt comfortable in sex, had never experienced more than sporadic episodes of good sex, and had never had a romance that lasted more than a month or two. He frequently didn't have erections in sex and that, he thought, accounted for his anxiety about sex and relationships. I wasn't so sure about his explanation.

Because of several years experience with meditation, he was able to easily enter trance. In the second session, I asked him to imagine having achieved his goals of being fully functional sexually and being in a good relationship with an intelligent, attractive woman. He was unable to get even a glimpse of it. I then asked him to imagine having just had a satisfying sexual experience with a woman. Even though he had had a few such experiences, he couldn't remember or imagine them clearly. I then asked him to imagine how he would feel talking with other men, knowing he was a confident and competent lover. He shook his head and blurted out, "No way I can feel good in that situation. I'm just not good enough to compete with them."

We used an affect bridge to get to the source of these feelings. It turned out that he was a sickly child and could not compete with boys his age, who generally shunned him. Instead of helping him to develop his skills, his mother kept him away from other children and at the same time constantly criticized his frailties. He felt smothered by her, but the idea that he wasn't as good as other boys sunk in deeply. Although he did moderately well in school and in business, the feeling that he wasn't a real man — and therefore wasn't good enough for women — was unaffected. To be capable of good sex, to be able to satisfy a woman, would mean overthrowing his whole view of himself, which explained why he said he felt uncomfortable, "not myself," on the few occasions when he had good sex.

This case was long (seven months) and involved, and I will confine my remarks only to those aspects relevant to our discussion of goal imagery. We started by recalling past successes (e.g., winning a spelling bee in high school, being able to fend for himself after his mother died) and pleasurable experiences (e.g., spending an afternoon at the beach). In each case, he was asked to get into the feelings as deeply as possible and to imagine himself having the same feelings in the future (what he would be doing in the future to feel this way was at first left open). As he got more comfortable with this exercise, the suggestion was changed to "feeling this way with a woman sometime in the future." Sexual activity was not mentioned for many sessions because it was too threatening. But gradually he was able to imagine himself feeling good talking with a woman and doing things with her, and to accept that she also felt good about the experiences. We also did process imagery and work on assertiveness, social skills, and communication.

He improved enough in a few months to get closer to a woman at work whom he liked but wasn't physically attracted to. This suited our purposes admirably because he had never really talked seriously to a woman and been able to hear what she had to say. This woman friend, without her knowledge, became my assistant therapist. I helped prepare him with imagery to get desired information from her. For instance, he wanted to know what she found appealing in men and so he imagined different ways of asking her about this. He asked many times in many ways, and her answers were always the same: sensitivity, compassion, warmth, sense of humor, and so forth. While he didn't think he was a star in all these areas, at least he had some of the qualities and could work on the rest. It started to feel as if maybe, just maybe, he could compete with other men. Maybe running fast and fighting and throwing balls a long distance weren't that important after all.

As he started to feel more confident and comfortable, the images were changed. He was asked, for example, to imagine a small group of women talking about him, saying how sensitive and warm he was, how comfortable it was to talk to him, and what a good mate he would be for some lucky woman. Later on, his sexiness was also included in this imagery, with several of the women saying how much they admired his slim body (which he had previously thought of as a symbol of his frailty and a liability) and how they'd like to go to bed with him. These images were easier for him to handle than those dealing with other men, but gradually he was able to comfortably imagine a group of men discussing him in ways that made it clear they saw him as one of them and as having many good qualities.

The breakthrough came unexpectedly and by his own efforts. One day at home, while he was imagining other men talking about him in positive ways, the image changed to their discussing him sexually. He imagined the man he most admired telling the other men: "Greg must be quite a guy to be with Kim [a woman unknown to Greg but clearly a sexy and very appealing woman]. I'll bet he's something in the sack. He's got the air of a man who's had lots of experience and knows what he's about. And I'm sure women are attracted by his confidence and slim body." The other men nodded agreement and starting making jokes about his sexual prowess. Women readers may find the macho feeling a bit much, but it has to be remembered that Greg had never gone through a macho phase and perhaps he needed to, if only in his mind. He felt very good about the imagery and it gave him a bigger lift than imagining the women talking about him.

Now he was ready to imagine having achieved his goals. It wasn't always easy, but he was soon able to imagine himself being a good, functional lover; being wanted and accepted by women; and having a good relationship, which turned out to be a difficult one. Given his experience of being overprotected and constantly criticized by his mother, he was fearful of what might happen to him in a close relationship. One of the images that worked well was of a friend seeking his advice about the friend's complaining wife. (The hidden assumption in this exercise is that Greg is looked upon by other men as someone who would know how to deal with this kind of problem.) In the imagery, Greg tells the other man how to stand up to his wife, using examples from his own, very successful, relationship. Greg's closing lines to his friend in this fantasy show how far he had come: "Relationships require a lot of compromise, but you can't let your wife restrict you so much and always be on your case. You have to let her know you have rights and that you don't have to put up with abuse. Charlotte (Greg's wife in the fantasy) and I used to have some of the same problems. She wanted to protect me from taking risks in business and was always complaining about something or other. But I let her know that while I welcome her advice, I have to make my own decisions. I also don't like constant complaints. It's too draining. She's changed her ways and our marriage is a lot stronger."

Greg was successful in making most of the changes he desired although he wasn't married when I lost track of him two years ago when he moved to another state. He was much more confident around women, his sex problem had completely disappeared, and after dating for several months, he moved in with a woman he loved (and she moved with him to his new job on the east coast). He wasn't completely free of the old self-image, but when it asserted itself, it felt "alien even though familiar. It isn't me anymore." About a year after therapy ended and Greg was doing well in his life, I asked him what about the therapy stuck out as being most responsible for his success. He named several things we had done and then said: "Mainly the constant imagining myself being the way I wanted. It helped me try on a new self and get comfortable with it, and that in turn made me feel more comfortable as I saw my behavior changing. I had a place to put the new behaviors and a way of making them understandable and like a true part of me."

Of course not all clients with sex problems are as deeply troubled as Greg was and not all of them change as dramatically as he did. But I have found few cases where result imagery has not been of service. Sometimes the issues or goals seem small compared to Greg's. For example, for men who don't want to do oral sex on their partners.(but the partners very much want this), I often do process imagery (fantasizing doing oral sex) in conjunction with goal imagery ("Imagine you're a man who enjoys performing oral sex on your wife. She loves when you do it and expresses her appreciation in many ways. What do you imagine some of these ways are? Can you imagine what she tells women friends about your sex life? How would you feel differently around her, around other women, and with men as they talk about sex?")

These images can make a difference. I recall one man who liked his wife "going down on me" but wouldn't consider reciprocating because that would signify she was the boss and because "it doesn't smell good." After failing in an attempt at process imagery, I tried goal imagery. He was so taken with the reputation he would have among women (he knew his wife talked about sex to her women friends) that he went to work, with no help from me other than goal imagery, to develop his oral skills. He now considers himself to "have the best tongue in California" and his wife is pleased.

As Greg said, result imagery gives a client opportunities to experiment with new self-images. In imagining himself being certain ways, he starts changing the way he looks at himself, which in turn allows him to change his behavior and to integrate those changes in a consistent and meaningful pattern. For the therapist, result imagery is useful both diagnostically and therapeutically, making success more certain and relapse less likely. It's a very versatile and helpful technique, with the added benefit of being relatively easy to learn and use.

Reference

Araoz, D. L. (1982). *Hypnosis and sex therapy*. New York: Brunner/Mazel.

Q&A 39 Using Intimate Trance to Increase Sexual Satisfaction

Question:

Is there any way that hypnosis can be used to enhance lovemaking in couples who don't have dysfunctions but aren't getting as much satisfaction as they want from sex? I heard a talk in which "mutual trance" was briefly mentioned, but I don't know exactly what this means or how to help people achieve it.

Discussion by CAROL RINKLEIB ELLISON, Ph.D.

The body's ability to harmonize with another's body at levels deeper than thought is astounding. Leonard (1983) pointed out that an activity as simple as reading aloud together can bring breathing, heartbeat, and even brainwaives into synchrony; mutual *erotic arousal* can involve even deeper nonverbal connectedness.

As partners focus more and more on sensations, emotions, mental images and each other in sexual interaction, a state I call "intimate trance" can unfold. Their movements and arousal synchronize and a rhythmic, continuous feedback loop is established; awareness of separateness merges into a sense of "oneness" or unity. Some couples report feeling so attuned while in this synchronous state that their nervous systems seem to become one; each knows what the other is feeling because he or she feels it too.

Learning to develop and maintain an intimate trance is a particularly useful way for a couple to enhance feelings of intimacy, pleasure and sexual satisfaction. Intimate trance can be useful in both relationship therapy and sex therapy. Developing this altered state of consciousness may increase the sexual interest of an individual with low sexual desire and for some couples is a useful technique for neutralizing performance concerns.

I have adapted some of the techniques I use for inducing trance in my

211

therapy clients so that couples can use them to facilitate mutual trance in their intimate times together. Couples can be taught exercises and techniques to shift their interaction from an active, outward-oriented, linear mode toward a receptive, mutual, couple-focused one. My therapeutic stance is "How can I use what I know about hypnosis and sex therapy to assist this couple in developing scripts and rituals to facilitate a shared trance and sensual and sexual pleasure?"

Not all clients are appropriate subjects for the intimate trance. A basic difference in style between individuals is that metaphorically described as right-brain dominance versus left-brain dominance. The left hemisphere is primarily linear in its mode of operation, processes information sequentially, and primarily deals in rationality and logical thinking; the right hemisphere is more holistic, relational and simultaneous in its mode of operation, processing information more diffusely than the left hemisphere and integrating many inputs at once.

The two hemispheres of the brain offer two very different ways of experiencing pleasure. According to Savary and Ehlen-Miller (1979), the will-powered left hemisphere channels pleasure that is active, energetic, and makes the body feel full of life and vigor. Such pleasure occurs when the physical body is happily active: running a race, driving a car, dancing, efficiently typing a letter, and so on. This is the kind of pleasure sought by those who talk about "getting into shape" and enjoying feats of strength. To stimulate an energetic "high" chemically, a left-hemisphere-dominant person might take amphetamines. Individuals seeking pleasure in this style are more likely to relate to activities designed to make the body feel more alive and euphoric — sexual athleticism and techniques for multiple or more intense orgasms, for example — than to the intimate trance.

In contrast, Savary and Ehlen-Miller say, the right hemishpere coordinates pleasure that is quiet, receptive and makes the body feel contented and at peace. Such pleasure comes when the physical body is relaxed and at rest, dreaming, for example, or sitting in a bath, being with a close friend, feeling secure, loved and the like — activities that allow one to flow rather than concentrate. People aim for this kind of letting go when they use alcohol or marijuana or have massages.

My working hypothesis is that individuals we would describe as right-brain dominant — those who seem to be most intuitive and comfortable in "going with the flow" — and those who operate comfortably in both modes will benefit most from instruction in creating the intimate trance. Those who operate almost entirely in the verbal-rational mode will probably be unable to relate to the concept and benefit more from other emphases in sex therapy.

Carla and Andy were a couple who through sex therapy became able to utilize the intimate trance. "What can I do?" Carla asked during their first session. "Andy rubs too fast and it feels like he's not paying attention — like his hand is out there moving all by itself, not connected to his head. It's like he doesn't know he's touching *me* — how it's feeling to *me*. I don't think he even notices how it's feeling to him. I wish I could make him slow down and notice what he's doing."

My first step in teaching Carla and Andy about the intimate trance was drawing their attention to other experiences they had had of mutual trance. Most people, even those who have not yet experienced an intimate sexual trance, have had experiences in which they have "lost themselves" and felt a sense of oneness with others. These may have occurred while dancing, singing or playing an instrument in a musical group, playing on an athletic team, reading a story to a child, giving or receiving a massage, animatedly talking with friends, or stroking a pet, for example. Andy regularly played basketball with a group of friends; Carla had sung in her high school chorus. Through these experiences and others they had had, each could relate to the experience of shared trance.

Therapy with Carla and Andy entailed providing them with *intertwined* smaller experiences that were building blocks in the larger process of forming a pleasurable, intimate connection with each other. Some were done individually, some as a couple. The following were among the techniques and concepts I used with Carla and Andy:

1) *Centering*. Learning to be centered was especially important for Andy, and I assigned centering exercises to both Carla and Andy. Centering is finding an inner sense of calmness, certainty, and strength. "One way to center yourself," I told them, "is to take several slow deep breaths, letting them be as effortless as possible. Let your tensions drain away each time you exhale."

I suggested they begin to form a habit of centering any time they felt off balance or began a new activity and that they find centering cues in their environment — e.g., the phone ringing, coming to a red light or stop sign while driving, the beginning of a TV or radio commercial — that reminded them to breathe slowly, evenly and effortlessly, and to purposefully let go of tensions.

2) *Forming intent*. Forming intent is like a mini-meditation in which you ask yourself, all in the flash of an instant: "Why am I (are we) here? What do I want to happen? What emotional state or quality of connecting would I like to create?" Forming intent need take only a moment and once learned can become a seemingly spontaneous habit.

"Forming intent is the most important step of all," I told Carla and Andy, "because it makes you aware of where you are, what you are doing, and why. Forming intent allows you to choose and direct the kind of sensual experience you want. On one occasion you might be making up after an intense argument in a mood of passionate reconciliation. At another time you might be focused on being nurturing and loving.

"Sometimes you will get sidetracked from the kind of experience you want to be having. If you do, you can always recenter yourself, recall the quality of experience you want, and make adjustments to get the situation back to how you want it to be. If you find yourselves getting stuck, we can talk about those times in our sessions together. Sometimes you will modify your intent as you go along; that's okay, too."

3) *Taking time for a couple transition from separateness to togetherness before sensual or sexual interaction.* One activity that was particularly effective for Carla and Andy in drawing attention from their daily tasks and the external environment to each other was taking their dog for an evening walk. Sitting down to talk, sharing wine, dancing, and building a fire and making popcorn were other activities they mentioned when I asked them what activities might work for them.

4) *Making a personal transition into the experience.* I encouraged Carla and Andy to do what each could to facilitate his or her own openness, arousal, focus, and potential to enjoy an experience. Personal preparation might include such relaxing activities as a shower or bath, stretching and a few deep breaths to facilitate both relaxation and sexual arousal, or moving to music. When energy was low, a snack or something to drink before sex could facilitate sexual pleasure. Personal transition may sometimes be done alone or sometime with one's partner; it might be done before, as a part of, or after activities of couple transition. A shower might, for example, follow a walk but precede sitting by a fire making popcorn.

5) *Sexual choreography.* An important therapist role is that of sexual choreographer, monitoring and modifying the timing and details in the scripting of the couple's sensual and sexual interaction. When Carla and Andy began therapy, Andy was typically undoing the trance-building of their couple time by shifting into personal preparation without maintaining contact with Carla. "It's so hard to get him to settle in and just stay there turning on with me," she said. "We have a glass of wine with dinner, then start getting close on the couch, and decide to head for the bedroom. The next thing I know, he's gone! He's locking the door, checking on the dog, brushing his teeth, rummaging in the dresser drawer for a condom.

"Why did he have to brush his teeth? We were already kissing. If he's worried about bad breath, it's already too late. By the time he comes back, I've lost all my turn-on and I don't feel connected anymore — or like having sex."

During one therapy session we discussed the mundane details that needed to be regularly taken care of at sexual times — locking the door, turning on their answering machine, making the fire or lighting the candles they sometimes used, making sure the dog was taken care of, preparing a beverage, putting a tape in the tape recorder — and the personal details — brushing teeth, showering, shaving, going to the bathroom, contracepting.

We discussed who took care of these details and when, the way taking care of these was in any way disruptive to the smoothness of their sexual process and their intimate trance-building, and solutions to the problems we discovered. Our intent was to create sexual experiences that would flow freely and without distraction. Some solutions were as simple as moving the condoms to a nightstand drawer next to the bed, and some much more complex because they involved power issues of who was responsible for what.

6) *Breathing exercises*. I prescribed a variety of breathing exercises for Carla and Andy. For example, I recommended that on some of the nights when they weren't engaging in sex they lie one behind the other for 10 minutes in a "spoon position," slowing, deepening and synchronizing their breathing. There are many resources both therapists and clients can use for additional exercises of this type; for example, Speads (1978), Jencks (1977), Rush (1973), and my own *The Intimate Way: Sexual Choreography* (in progress).

7) *Exercises for focusing attention*. "It's like his hand is out there moving all by itself, not connected to his head. I wish he would notice what's he's doing," Carla had said of Andy.

I frequently prescribe *massage* as an activity in which couples can experiment with focusing attention on touch and sensation and practice developing the intimate trance. Downing's classic, *The Massage Book* (1972), is a good resource for those who want to learn more about this important topic.

I sometimes direct couples in touching each other during a therapy session. During one session I had Andy lie face down on the massage table and instructed Carla in oiling his back. (I later had them reverse roles.) I gave Andy some suggestions for slowing and deepening his breathing and experiencing the table's support; then I turned my attention to Carla:

"Lay your hands quietly on Andy's back, centering yourself, slowing your breathing. Begin to synchronize your breathing with his. Now focus your attention in your hands. Deepen your awareness of Andy. How relaxed is he? How centered does he seem? Move your hands, slightly, in a gentle rocking motion. Experience Andy through your hands and take a few minutes to facilitate deeper relaxation for him.

"Now begin to slowly oil his back, applying the oil first to your hands and then from your hands to his skin; begin the first oiling stroke as he is exhaling. Keep your attention in your hands. Feel the differences in tension in his muscles, the variations in temperature, mold your hands to fit the contours over which they pass. Take your time.

"When you feel finished, stand quietly with your hands in place for a moment. Then slowly, gently, lightly cap his head, barely touching his hair. Very slowly return your hands to your side and stand quietly for a moment paying attention to what you are feeling. Andy, lie there for a few more minutes focusing on energy movement in your body and anything else you are experiencing."

When they were finished, we talked about what had gone on. I monitored the touching when it was occurring and made such comments to Carla as: "Close your eyes for a few minutes and see what that is like," or "Slow down a little and notice what you're feeling in your own body. Now recenter yourself and just stand again with your hands resting quietly on Andy's back for a little while, not moving them until you feel absolutely calm and ready. There's no hurry; the calmer you feel, the more Andy will sense your quietness and be pleasured by it."

Through this kind of work during therapy sessions I am often present and acting as a coach when clients first begin to consciously create mutual trances. I have found that supervising clients when they are actually touching each other is many times more effective than merely instructing them in how to touch each other at home, and often provides me with much useful information about behaviors that may have been blocking development of the trance state in their couple system.

8) *Touching to music.* A favorite tape played regularly during massage or sex can become a strong cue to enter the intimate trance and surrender to feelings of pleasure. Among compositions and artists I recommend are Paul A. Sutin's "Serenity," Ron Dexter's "Golden Voyage," and many of the compositions played by Paul Horn, George Winston, and Steve Halpern.

9) *Developing personal cues and rituals.* Couples can benefit from developing personal rituals that are preludes to sexual interaction — for example, putting on their favorite music — and personal cues that are invitations to sex and the intimate trance — for example, a special wink, phrase or touch. I weave suggestions into the therapy describing desirable responses these cues will elicit when the partners use them later in their sensual activities.

10) *Maintaining the trance state.* The hypnosis literature acknowledges that the trance state is a process that involves both coming up and going deeper, in and out of deeper and lighter states. Sexual responses also vary with stimulation and involvement. Men's erections and women's vaginal tumescence do not remain constant during sex, but, for most people, wax

and wane. Couples may need to be helped to recognize what is occurring when the trance lightens or sexual arousal becomes momentarily less intense so that they do not overreact to these changes and lighten the trance or diminish arousal even more. I advised Carla and Andy to take time to re-synchronize and reclaim the state:

"If the spell lightens or seems broken, recall that this lightening is often a natural occurrence and that you are there for mutual enjoyment and inti-mate feelings. Mention your feeling of separateness if you wish. Perhaps ask what is going on with your partner. If there is something you need to at-tend to, do so.

"Then caringly draw your attention once again to your pleasurable sensa-tions and continue. Improvise and reclaim your experience. Take a deep breath and lie quietly together a moment. Begin again to stroke each other. Caress. Pleasure. Enjoy.

"If thoughts or doubts intrude, let them pass by. They really don't matter. Don't stop to focus on them. You may not be able to stop them, but you don't have to focus your attention on them. You can talk about them later if you want to. Focus on your sensations. There is no need to plan what is going to happen next.

"Remain flexible. If a technique doesn't work, use another one. Just keep making shifts toward increasing your mutual pleasure and stay in tune with your partner."

11) *Imagery for mutuality and merging.* The following is an example of the kind of imagery I use with couples like Carla and Andy:

"Perceive your body as a continuous flowing river of warm energy. Sense it flowing between you. Slow down. As you lie there together, let your thoughts stop and intuitions, images, and impressions emerge. Experience the harmony between you as the sensations flow through and around your body. Let your movements be subtle and soft. Feel your aliveness. Work together in unison, united. Relax; surrender.

"Laugh joyously inside; delight in what you are experiencing. Extend your mind beyond the boundaries of your body to include your partner. Be calm, receptive, trusting. Pace and lead your partner's responses while at the same time being paced and led by them. Become for that moment no longer sep-arate. Experience through your body what your partner is experiencing and doing. Feel what you feel. Soar together to the height of aliveness."

Carla and Andy were basically a harmonious couple who liked each other and enjoyed doing many things together. Although Andy seemed very in-sensitive when therapy began, he took readily to the exercises and learned quickly to pay attention when he was touching Carla. After a few months of sex therapy, the intimate trance was a regular part of their sexual rep-ertoire.

I have trained several dozen couples to use intimate trances; the almost invariable result is increased sexual satisfaction. In a number of cases, an added benefit was that long-standing sexual dysfunctions were overcome.

References

Downing, G. (1972). *The massage book*. New York: Random House, The Bookworks.
Ellison, C. (in progress). *The intimate way: Sexual choreography*.
Jencks, B. (1977). *Your body: Biofeedback at its best*. Chicago: Nelson Hall.
Leonard, G. (1983). *The end of sex*. Los Angeles: JP Tarcher, Inc.
Rush, A. K. (1973). *Getting clear: Bodywork for women*. New York: Random House, The Bookworks.
Savary, L. M., & Ehlen-Miller, M. (1979). *Mindways: A guide for exploring your mind*. San Francisco: Harper & Row.
Speads, C. H. (1978). *Breathing: The ABC's*. New York: Harper & Row.

Q&A 40 Asking Patients About Their Trance Experiences

Question:

Since I'm curious what my patients experience in trance, I usually ask them about it as soon as it's over. But I notice that some authorities, notably Erickson and his followers, will do anything not to discuss the experience. They distract the patient by discussing other things or by abruptly ending the session. Is there anything wrong with what I do? Also, how can you know what the patient is doing in trance if you never discuss the experience with him?

Discussion by ELLIOT N. WINEBURG, M.D.

Following treatment by hypnosis, should the therapist discuss the session with the client? Referring to the ancient medical dictum, "Do not harm the patient," the answer is absolutely clear, based on my clinical experience. The practitioner's concern is to apply the safest form of treatment available and assure the health and functioning of the patient.

Problems following a session of hypnosis are rare. A problem that has been reported is a continuation of the trance state mediated by the patient himself long after the official termination of the hypnotic session. This can lead to hysterical-type symptoms such as paralysis or even depersonalization (Wineburg & Straker, 1973).

On the basis of our own experience at Mt. Sinai Medical Center in New York, we have initiated a careful discussion of the hypnotic experience prior to the actual session. Patients' preconceived notions of what can happen during hypnosis and afterward are explored, and any misconceptions are immediately negated. The patient is told that the procedure is safe, that the

219

session will terminate when the doctor says so, and that only therapeutic posthypnotic suggestions will follow.

The same clinical approach is observed after the session. The patient must be given a short time to raise any questions. The position of each hypnotic subject as an observer of his actual session is important in this consideration. Patients can have fears about what has gone on and these must be quickly allayed. Hypnosis long preceded psychotherapy as a form of treatment. Psychotherapy itself has always insisted on an open, two-way communication, and this certainly should occur after the hypnotic sessions is finished.

A great deal about the patient's prognosis is also learned from the frank discussion after the session. The patient may state that certain suggestions are idiosyncratic in this case. For instance, one patient found the command that the eyes remain closed to be very distressful; in fact, it was responsible for a modest amount of anxiety during the actual trance state in spite of a general suggestion for overall relaxation. A future hypnotic session with that individual would not include this very common form of induction.

At one time we videotaped a hypnotic session of a patient and then two weeks later made a second videotape of the patient watching her own session as she engaged in a frank discussion of each individual reaction that had occurred (Wineburg, 1974). A wide range of information resulted from this one patient's introspective analysis of the session. Material thus became available that in no way could be predicted from merely objectively observing the patient during that initial hypnosis.

The questioner states that Erickson does not discuss experience of the trance. In the carefully documented book *Hypnotic Realities*, Rossi and Rossi (1976) record an actual hypnotic session conducted by Erickson. At one point the subject "spontaneously opens her eyes and reorients to her body" and the implication is clear that the trance is over. At that point Erickson asks a number of questions concerning the patient's subjective experiences during the trance, e.g., "Now, what's happened to you? . . . Does it feel a half-hour has passed?" . . . "Do you know what you just said?" It would appear that Erickson did not refrain from discussing the trance state wth his patients.

The trained therapist who discusses each hypnotic session with the patient is in a far better position to offer an efficient and safe form of treatment. The questioner is absolutely right in making this posthypnotic discussion a part of each treatment session.

References

Erickson, M. H., Rossi, E. L., & Rossi, S. I. (1976). *Hypnotic realities*. New York: Irvington.
Wineburg, E. N., & Straker, N. (1973). An episode of acute, self-limiting depersonalization following a first-session of hypnosis. *American Journal of Psychiatry, 130*(1), 98–100.
Wineburg, E. N. (1974). Ann views her own session. Videotape on file at Mount Sinai School of Medicine, New York.

SECTION VI *Ericksonian Hypnotherapy*

Perhaps no figure since Franz Mesmer has put his stamp on hypnosis the way that Milton Erickson has. At the very least, it is clear that the current rennaisance of therapeutic hypnosis owes a great deal to Erickson's name and fame. For many people, what Erickson did constitutes hypnosis, or at least good hypnosis. Erickson's followers are many and they exert considerable influence in the field of therapeutic hypnosis. It is almost impossible to attend a hypnosis conference or read a hypnosis book or journal without coming across his name and accomplishments. And it has gone further than this, with a cult-like following having developed among some of his followers.

But not everyone is enamored of Erickson. There seem to be as many detractors as followers, though the former are not as vocal as the latter. Some doubt that Erickson really was as good as others think, an easy position to maintain since there are no independent assessments of the successes he wrote about. Some, as already noted, have tried Erickson's techniques on their own patients and experienced failure rather than success and concluded that Erickson was either a magician or a charlatan. Some others, having read about Erickson's work, have decided that whether or not it was effective, it is too time-consuming and too convoluted to be useful in their practices. Newcomers to hypnosis often take this point of view. The more they read of Erickson, the more confused they get. They either give up hypnosis altogether or use methods they can more easily grasp.

Still another group of clinicians, a fairly large one consisting of some opposed to Erickson and many not opposed, are concerned about the cult that has grown up around his name. They fear that the hero worship they see will negatively affect the whole field, leading to dogmatism, conformity, and a lack of progress.

Even among Erickson's followers, a kind of reassessment seems to be in the works. All the discussions in this section are written by people who identify themselves as Ericksonians, though some more strongly than others. Yet what comes through in many of the papers are caveats about mindless adulation and emulation. We find this anti-hero worship theme refreshing and certainly give it our blessing. Here is one place where the three of us agree: that whatever else he was, Erickson was the master pragmatist, always looking for a specific solution to a specific problem, ever wary of all-purpose solutions and panaceas. There was much good in his work, but it has to be remembered that what was effective for him may not be effective in other hands and with other patients and problems.

It also has to be remembered, and several of our contributors make the point, that Erickson's work is now shrouded in mythology. It is not true, for instance, that Erickson was always or mainly permissive. He could be a very authoritarian therapist. It is also not true that he spoke mainly in metaphors. He could and did say very directly, "Go into a trance" or "Do such and such," to certain patients.

In order that we not lose what is valuable in Erickson's approach, it is important that we not lose the man to the myths or judge hypnotists by how closely they follow Erickson. It is doubtful that he would have wanted to leave such a legacy.

Q & A 41 What Is Ericksonian Hypnosis?

Question:

I keep running across Erickson's name and techniques in books and workshops, but I'm not sure I know what his approach was. What exactly is Ericksonian hypnosis and how does it differ from other hypnotherapeutic approaches?

Discussion by MICHAEL D. YAPKO, Ph.D.

In recent years, the name Milton H. Erickson, M.D., has come to be associated with an approach to clinical practice that is unique and, in some ways, revolutionary. His methods of hypnosis and psychotherapy were so original and nontraditional that his work has become a focal point of health care professionals everywhere, as is evidenced by the huge attendance at international and national conventions honoring Erickson's work and by the many recent publications describing various elements of his approaches.

A keen observer of people, Erickson deviated from the traditional theory and practice of psychotherapy, believing that change did not necessarily require intensive analysis over a long period of time. Furthermore, he did not believe "insight" (knowing "why" a behavior or feeling exists) was necessary in order for change to occur. The result of his views was his brief strategic therapy which made extensive use of clinical hypnosis. This discussion involves a description of the principles and patterns evident in Erickson's use of hypnosis. It is by no means a conclusive analysis, but an orientation to the nature of Erickson's hypnotic work.

Principles of Ericksonian Hypnosis (The Utilization Approach)

Ericksonian hypnosis as a distinctive method is based on a number of principles implicit in the formula guiding Ericksonian interventions: "Accept and utilize." This is the essence of Ericksonian approaches, collectively known as the "utilization approach" (Erickson & Rossi, 1979). The formula and its associated principles are described in the remainder of this section. A succinct contrast between Erickson's approaches and those of traditional and standardized hypnosis is to be found in Table 1.

1) *Each person is unique.* While all acknowledge this in principle, the scripting of hypnotic approaches (i.e., the use of the same approach with different clients) precludes this recognition at the level of practice. Ericksonian approaches demand spontaneity and utilization of the client's unique resources, personal history, and specific responses to the clinician. Thus, prepared scripts that are "Ericksonian" are impossible to create.

2) *The client's experience is valid for him.* Through the acceptance of the client's experience as a valid product of personal choices, both conscious and unconscious, "resistance" can be utilized in the process. What is traditionally termed "resistance" is accepted as useful information describing the limits of client experience, rather than confronted or interpreted as undesirable.

3) *Each person relates to ongoing experience from his own frame of reference.* All people project meaning onto current experiences based on their own range of knowledge and past experience. Thus, idiosyncratic responses to hypnosis and psychotherapy are not only allowed, but expected and considered integral to the treatment process. The client's unique associations are the focal point of treatment; disrupting undesirable associations and building new, positive associations is the goal of the clinician.

4) *Join the client at the client's frame of reference.* One way the "accept and utilize" formula is manifested is in the clinician's accepting the client's views and experiences and utilizing them in the therapy. Using the language of the client is another such manifestation.

5) *The unconscious mind is rich in resources, positive in nature, and patterned from experience.* Unlike traditional views that characterize the unconscious as negative, random, and in need of healing, Erickson characterized the unconscious as a storehouse of valuable life-learnings that could be beneficial to a person when properly accessed (Zeig, 1980b). Thus, he assumed that each person already had the necessary resources for meaningful change. Erickson placed great faith in the unconscious to meaningfully guide one's life path, regulate the flow of information according to what one could effectively handle, and otherwise manage one's life. Erickson was confident that useful information made available to the unconscious hypnotically would be integrated in problem-solving ways, particularly when the information stimulated the right associations, i.e., the most meaningful thoughts and feelings, including memories, values, and so forth.

6) *Trance is naturalistic.* Unlike the traditional views of hypnosis as a special state that only some people are capable of experiencing meaningfully, Ericksonian approaches presuppose that all people experience trance spontaneously and routinely in the course of living, what Erickson called "the everyday trance." Ericksonian trance inductions and trance utilizations involve attention-absorbing yet gentle and natural conversational methods that stimulate the client's associational processes.

TABLE
General Principles Contrasting the Views of the
Major Models of Hypnosis

Variable	Traditional	Standardized	Ericksonian (Utilization)
Individualized approach?	No	No	Yes
Naturalistic concept of trance?	No	No	Yes
Naturalistic techniques?	No	No	Yes
Hypnotist's demeanor?	Authoritarian	Authoritarian or permissive	Authoritarian or permissive
Suggestion style used?	Direct	Direct	Direct or indirect
Degree of compliance demanded?	High	High	Low
How is power in the relation distributed?	Unequally in favor of the hypnotist	Unequally in favor of the client	Equally
Content or process oriented?	Content	Content	Either or both
Who can experience trance meaningfully?	Some	Some	All
Source of resistance?	Intrapersonal	Intrapersonal	Intra- or interpersonal
Reaction to resistance?	Confrontation or interpretation	Confrontation or interpretation	Utilization
Emphasizes trance depth?	Yes	Yes	No
Makes use of formal suggestibility tests?	Yes	Yes	No
Structure of process?	Linear	Linear	Mosaic
Relative value of insights?	Low	Low	Low
View of the symptoms' intentions?	Negative	Negative	Positive
Etiology of symptoms?	Intrapersonal	Intrapersonal	Inter- or intrapersonal
Symptomatic vs. dynamic approach?	Either or both	Symptomatic	Either or both
Recognition of secondary gains?	No	No	Yes
Characterization of the unconscious?	Negative	Negative	Positive
Role of the unconscious?	Reactive	Reactive	Active

Patterns of Ericksonian Hypnosis

It is difficult to understand Ericksonian hypnosis without considering the patterns of Ericksonian psychotherapy. This discussion, however, will focus only on Erickson's use of hypnosis.

Erickson's hypnotic methods have been described as indirect. In fact, many of Erickson's methods *were* indirect, but not exclusively so. Erickson could be, and often was, very direct and authoritarian in his manner, particularly when his patients were open and responsive with him (Yapko, 1983, 1984a). In general, however, Erickson's methods were indirect in that his goal was simply to *allow for the possibility of a response* rather than directly demanding one (Zeig, 1980a). Therefore, they suggest ways the client *might* meaningfully respond, and then accept and utilize the offered responses (Erickson & Rossi, 1979, 1981).

Ericksonian approaches to hypnosis have been characterized as "naturalistic," i.e., conversational. The ability to initiate a trance induction while engaging in natural discussion is a practical possibility directly arising from the recognition of trance states (i.e., states of concentrated attention) occurring routinely (Haley, 1973). In this approach, there is no need for overtly identifying the onset of hypnotic procedure; rather, the clinician simply involves the client in an interaction that is absorbing, building an internal focus on his potentials as well as subjective associations. This is the phase of trance induction, with underlying goals of facilitating less reliance on conscious processes (altering one's usual frame of reference) and building trance responsiveness. On the other hand, guiding the client's experience in therapeutic ways through the introduction of new information, new viewpoints, and other pattern-interrupting methods becomes the therapy phase, or trance utilization phase (Erickson & Rossi, 1979, 1981). In practice, the phases of hypnotic interaction are much less clearly defined than in more traditional, structured approaches (Haley, 1973).

One structure evident in most of Erickson's hypnotic patterns is the facilitation of both the trance state and the various trance phenomena through his naturalistic method. This involves describing interesting yet routine contexts in which trance responses may typically arise. It might simply describe a situation in which one spontaneously enters trance, while nonverbally emphasizing certain ideas ("marking" or embedding suggestions). For example, the entrancing qualities of watching a fire are described in the following induction process:

> This past winter was such a cold one and I often found myself so grateful for the simple pleasure of having a fireplace . . . fireplaces are so soothing in the wintertime . . . you may know that from your own experience . . . for *you can feel so warm and so*

comfortable . . . when you *take time to just sit quietly* and know
that *you can relax deeply* . . . and *be so comfortable* . . . and
you know how to *feel good* . . . and a fire can be so beautiful
to watch . . . and watching for *hours can seem like minutes* . . .
because the colors are *so absorbing* . . . and the patterns of the
wood burning at different rates in different spots is *so soothing*
to watch . . .

Building an internal focus and responsiveness to the clinician's guidance
is the goal of the trance inductions, and this may be accomplished through
a variety of methods, such as: 1) the revivification of previous informal
trance experiences as in the above example; 2) the revivification of previous
formal trance experiences ("You can recall in vivid detail what your most
satisfying experience with hypnosis was like . . . how you were sitting,
which relaxing images you saw," etc.); and 3) the use of negative suggestions
when wanting to utilize the resistance of a client responding in a contrary
manner ("You don't have to sit comfortably . . . and you don't even need
to think about allowing yourself the soothing experience of closing your eyes
and letting your mind drift," etc.) (Yapko, 1984a).

To facilitate a particular trance phenomenon, one might simply describe
a natural context in which the desired type of response occurs, creating the
possibility of that response in the client as he is encouraged to experientially
relate to the description (Zeig, 1980b, 1982). To facilitate age regression,
for example, one might offer the client the following:

Recently, I had the experience of visiting the town I grew up
in . . . and it was so very interesting to *go back in time and reexperience important memories from childhood* . . . *memories*
that had been long forgotten *drifted into awareness* . . . and it
was such a good feeling to *remember happy experiences* . . . an
early birthday party . . . a friend in school . . . an important
event that had a big impact on the kind of person I am today
. . . and *you can experience what that must be like* . . .

In this example, suggesting the possibility of an age regression, the client
is gently oriented to past experience in a way that is not personally threatening, thus reducing or eliminating the need for defensive reactions. The
possibility is created that the client may think of early childhood memories.
Which memory then becomes a specific focal point for interaction is a product of personal choice that is derived from a combination of personal, interpersonal, and situational factors (Yapko, 1984a). The client's choice is
accepted, and the information is utilized in whatever ways the clinician sees
fit.

As a general strategy for acquiring skills in Ericksonian hypnosis, recognizing trance phenomena as they arise in the course of daily living will provide numerous possibilities for naturalistically facilitating such trance phenomena with clients. Absorbing descriptions of the sensory details of the context in which the trance response is evident stimulates the unconscious associations in the client, allowing him or her to relate to the experience in a personal and idiosyncratic way (Zeig, 1980b; Watzlawick, 1978).

The primary vehicle for Erickson's indirect methods is the *anecdote*, commonly addressed in the literature on Erickson as the "therapeutic metaphor." Evident in the previous sample induction and utilization, the anecdotal method involves the telling of a story that will contain meaningful messages on multiple levels of awareness. Erickson observed that when clients present their problems to clinicians, they inevitably communicate on multiple levels; there is the surface meaning of their chosen words, but there is also an underlying reality concerning what the client "really" means or what the symptom "really" symbolizes (Zeig, 1980b).

Erickson believed that instead of attempting to promote conscious awareness for the deeper level meanings of client communications, thereby restricting oneself to only one level (and in his view, the most limited level) of the individual, the clinician can also communicate on multiple levels, some outside of conscious awareness. This is the basis for Erickson's anecdotal methods. Furthermore, the use of anecdotes to make a point allows the client to absorb the point experientially, in an interesting and usually realistic context of human experience. This makes the point far more real and emotionally significant for the client. Emotionally significant learnings afford one a greater opportunity for integration of information than do insignificant ones.

Anecdotes 1) encourage the client to actively identify with the story since it is introduced in a way that suggests it is relevant to the client's needs, 2) encourage the client to actively learn from others' experiences, 3) diminish or eliminate resistance because the client is encouraged to respond to the anecdote in whatever way is desired without the demand for a specific response, and 4) provide a memorable and meaningful way to integrate new learnings (Zeig, 1980b).

Anecdotes are used to induce trance, facilitate specific trance phenomena, suggest resolutions to problems, address a problem's unconscious underlying dynamics without encouraging or promoting insight, and for other such meaningful applications. While the indirect anecdotal method is certainly one of Erickson's key contributions to hypnotic procedure, there are other uniquely Ericksonian hypnotic patterns that are also worthy of brief consideration. These include the interspersal approaches and confusion methods.

The *interspersal approach* involves the use of specific words or phrases in the larger context of a routine conversation or therapeutic metaphor that are designed to facilitate the building of new associations within the client

(Erickson & Rossi, 1979; Erickson, 1966). Such words or phrases may be used singly or repetitiously to stimulate the new associations. If, for example, a clinician would want to facilitate the expectation of positive changes ("building expectancy"), the clinician can intersperse suggestions leading the client in that direction as in the following:

> You came here hoping that I might say or do something that would . . . *allow yourself to feel better* . . . and you didn't know just what I would say . . . or what I would do . . . and you forgot that you have already gone through *so many positive changes you're capable of* remembering . . . and *change is inevitable* . . . and you can't stop progress . . . you know you have changed . . . and *you can expect more changes* . . . without even working at it . . . you have a *change* of mind . . . a *change* of heart . . . a *change* of luck . . . and changes on even deeper levels . . .

Interspersed in this example are multiple references to the possibility and probability of change, in effect building a therapeutic momentum based on positive expectations. Evident in this example are other verbal strategies, such as presupposition, dissociation, indirect post-hypnotic suggestions, truisms, open-ended suggestions, and others (Erickson & Rossi, 1979). Such strategies are typical of the Ericksonian approach which emphasizes creative use of verbal as well as nonverbal patterns. Nonverbal patterns include the *"marking"* of suggestions, *modeling* (the clinician behaving in the manner desired of the trance subject, e.g., unmoving, fixed attention, the deliberate matching or mismatching of client nonverbals, etc.), and the use of varied *voice dynamics* to facilitate the integration of verbal messages (Yapko, 1984a).

The *confusion methods* are designed to disrupt the client's usual patterns for processing experience (Erickson & Rossi, 1979). It is well-known that when one is certain about something, it is very difficult to induce a change of attitude. Confusion methods are designed to create a state of uncertainty in the client as a means for introducing the possibility of change (Erickson, 1964). Confusion methods may involve the use of sensory overload (i.e., the use of multiple, complex ideas or sources of input that overwhelm the client's ability to consciously sort through it all), or pattern interruption (introducing a new behavior or idea that disrupts the client's usual sequence of responding, making it difficult or impossible for the person to attain his usual, dysfunctional outcome). Confusion methods disorient the person, facilitating an inward search (thus their utility in trance induction or trance utilization) to make meaning out of a seemingly absurd event. As the person becomes focused on making meaning of confusing ideas or demands, the deeper meanings of embedded suggestions can take effect. The clinician can intersperse meaningful suggestions throughout the confusing ramblings, giving those suggestions greater clarity and significance by the contrast with their confusing background. In the following example, a confusion method is employed for the purpose of facilitating hypnotic amnesia:

> . . . and after learning what you've learned about yourself today . . . you have an opportunity to decide at a deeper level . . . how much you'd like to remember . . . and your conscious mind can know at one level . . . and your unconscious can know at a deeper level . . . and you can remember what you'd like to remember . . . and remember to forget what you'd like to . . . and when you remember to forget what you'd like to forget to remember . . . you can remember to forget what you've forgotten to forget when you realize deeply that remembering to remember to forget that *no one has to remember to learn* what they came here to learn by forgetting to remember the memory of insignificant and *forgotten learnings that can mean a lot* . . .

As the client attempts to sort through the confusing suggestions surrounding remembering and forgetting, those very processes are accessed. The client can be trusted to choose what degree of remembering and forgetting will be the most beneficial for him.

Erickson did not promote a specific and detailed theoretical model of personality or clinical intervention. His view was an atheoretical one emphasizing the need to respond to the uniqueness of each individual. Thus, "Ericksonian hypnosis" as a method may be more easily characterized by the flexibility of the general "accept and utilize" formula than any specific hypnotic or psychotherapeutic approach. In my description of Erickson's work, emphasis has been placed on the clinician's assuming a flexible yet active role in guiding the course of treatment even when indirect methods are used. The many Ericksonian patterns involve a sophisticated use of linguistic and cognitive structures which requires an open-minded and careful analysis for the serious practitioner of clinical hypnosis. The broad range of verbal and nonverbal strategies evident in Erickson's work is lasting evidence of his many contributions to psychotherapy.

References

Erickson, M. (1964). The confusion technique in hypnosis. *American Journal of Clinical Hypnosis, 6*, 183–207.
Erickson, M. (1966). The interspersal hypnotic technique for symptom correction and pain control. *American Journal of Clinical Hypnosis, 8*, 198–209.

Erickson, M., & Rossi, E. (1979). *Hypnotherapy: An exploratory casebook.* New York: Irvington.

Erickson, M., & Rossi, E. (1981). *Experiencing hypnosis: Therapeutic approaches to altered states.* New York: Irvington.

Haley, J. (1973). *Uncommon therapy.* New York: Norton.

Watzlawick, P. (1978). *The language of change.* New York: Basic Books.

Yapko, M. (1983). A comparative analysis of direct and indirect hypnotic communication styles. *American Journal of Clinical Hypnosis, 25,* 270–276.

Yapko, M. (1984a). *Trancework: An introduction to clinical hypnosis.* New York: Irvington.

Yapko, M. (1984b). Implications of the Ericksonian and Neurolinguistic Programming approaches for responsibility of therapeutic outcomes. *American Journal of Clinical Hypnosis, 27,* 137–143.

Zeig, J. (1980a). Symptom prescription and Ericksonian principles of hypnosis and psychotherapy. *American Journal of Clinical Hypnosis, 23,* 16–22.

Zeig, J. (ed.). (1980b). *A teaching seminar with Milton H. Erickson.* New York: Brunner/Mazel.

Zeig, J. (ed.). (1982). *Ericksonian approaches to hypnosis and psychotherapy.* New York: Brunner/Mazel.

$\underset{A}{\overset{Q}{}}$&$42$ Evidence of
Erickson's Effectiveness

Question:

> I was a patient and student of Milton Erickson's, and my own experience and observations make me skeptical about whether he really got the results he and others say he did. His treatment of me was at best only partly successful and I sat in on several of his cases that seemed to me to be very qualified successes or outright failures, although Erickson never admitted this. Is there any evidence that he was as good a therapist (as opposed to a great hypnotist) as everyone seems to believe?

Discussion by D. CORYDON HAMMOND, Ph.D.

Erickson, like most clinical practitioners, primarily talked about his successful cases rather than his failures. Also, like most other clinicians, Erickson did not systematically follow up all of his patients to determine the long-term results of therapy. Thus, with Erickson and most other therapists, judgments about their effectiveness are based only on the potentially inaccurate perceptions of people who knew them. In a strictly scientific sense, we will never know the effectiveness rate of Milton Erickson. Nonetheless, there are some things worth saying.

The American Association for Marriage and Family Therapy (AAMFT) asks an interesting question of colleagues and supervisors who write letters of recommendation for membership applicants: "Would you refer a member of your own family to this person for therapy? In discussing this question with colleagues, most of them indicate that few of their peers merit such confidence. However, this was the kind of confidence that Milton Erickson inspired in many who knew him. Some of this confidence may be attributable to his charisma in public demonstrations and the fact that some of his techniques seemed so subtle and mystifying. But perhaps some of the confidence in Erickson may have been due to the fact that he actually was an unusually talented therapist.

Let us consider some of the characteristics of good therapy, one of which is that the treatment is individualized to the specific needs and requirements of the patient. There is some evidence (e.g., Holroyd, 1980; Nuland & Field, 1970) that the individualization of hypnosis encourages more successful outcomes. Alman (1983) found that some individuals respond better to an indirect, permissive approach, while others are more responsive to direct suggestion. Alman indicated that the number of subjects who were responsive to each approach appeared to be equally distributed. Not only may there be better outcomes when treatment is individualized, but other research (Lieberman, Yalom, & Miles, 1973) suggests that failure to individualize therapy may encourage psychological casualties and negative results. This seems relevant because Erickson strongly emphasized tailoring the therapy to the unique personality and needs of the patient. This is certainly not proof that *he* was a good therapist, but it appears to be an important characteristic of good therapists in general.

For decades there has been widespread agreement among therapists (e.g., Fiedler, 1950, 1951; Munroe, 1955; Rogers, 1957; Shoben, 1953) and a certain amount of research support (Truax & Mitchell, 1971) for the belief that qualities of respect, acceptance, caring, genuineness, warmth and empathy are related to positive outcomes. Erickson certainly seemed capable of manifesting many of these human qualities with his patients.

In my own struggle to separate the man from the myths about him, I interviewed many long-term associates of Erickson. A few of the comments by these individuals seem relevant to the question at hand.

Dr. Herbert Mann met Erickson in 1950, became a colleague and friend, and one of the 13 founding members (with Erickson) of the American Society of Clinical Hypnosis. Mann (Note 1) talked about some of Erickson's human qualities: "I think Erickson was an extremely compassionate man who wanted very, very much to help people. Erickson said that he didn't need a soft reclining armchair [for patients to sit in], that any chair was fine. What was important was the relationship that was established with the patient."

Unfortunately, much of what is being emphasized about Erickson are his techniques, rather than his emphasis on gaining rapport with patients (Hammond, 1984). But his human qualities were probably at least as important as his techniques in accounting for his therapeutic success. Erickson was willing to go well beyond the "call of duty" in helping his patients. His case studies are filled with examples of making home visits to patients, taking them out into the community (e.g., to a restaurant) on homework assignments, utilizing community resources for them, having them do yardwork for him, and even boarding a pet dog at his home. Because he was both caring and flexible, he was not restricted by artificial rules regarding his interactions with patients.

In his case reports, there are also frequent illustrations of the ways in which he would accept patient symptomatology and respond empathically, establishing rapport and "pacing" the patient. Dr. Bertha Rodger, a former ASCH President who knew Erickson for many years, said (Note 2): "Erickson felt that hypnosis was an interpersonal relationship, not just a ritual or a formula." It is also important to remember that he saw his techniques — often admired for their subtlety and power — as means toward situation-specific goals, and not as ends in themselves or as universally applicable. This is a point not always understood by those who advertise themselves as disciples and Erickson experts.

Erickson saw several patients briefly whom he then referred to Mann. "These patients would tell me that in their first visit with Erickson he would spend three to four hours with them. They didn't expect that. They thought that he was going to be like any other psychiatrist who keeps his eye on the clock and when the 50 minutes are up, that would be it. But time didn't really seem [to matter] much to him and he became so enthralled, so interested in their problems, that he just went on until he felt that he could interrupt the therapy [session] and make another appointment" (Note 1).

Despite the emphasis on understanding the patient and being respectful and empathic, it would be wrong to conclude that all Erickson did was "relate" to his patients. The establishment of rapport and understanding was only the beginning of his work. I believe that another reason for his success was that Erickson was a thoughtful clinician, willing to spend long periods of time thinking about and planning treatment. His therapy has been called both directive and strategic, and with good reason. Erickson saw it as his job, after collecting information from the patient, to decide how treatment was to be conducted, in terms of both general strategy and the smallest tactical details. This kind of work demands careful planning.

My interviews with long-term associates and a few former patients revealed a consistency of response. Everyone agreed that he was very dedicated, willing to invest enormous amounts of time with his patients (such as three- or four-hour initial sessions) and in thoughtfully planning their treatment. His widow once commented to me that, "There was no limit to the amount of time he would spend," and she mentioned the "endless hours" he would invest in preparing for a session. Erickson himself once indicated that he carefully prepared a 40- or 50-page script for eliciting different trance phenomena, that was later reduced to 20 pages, and then 10 pages, and then just two pages. Such compulsive preparation helped create a master clinician with maximum flexibility.

Regarding Erickson's great persistence, and referring specifically to a resistant female patient that Erickson treated, Mann (Note 1) told me: "Perhaps it was his personality that he did not want to fail; perhaps it was his drive to find out why he could not succeed; perhaps it was just the compassion of the man. He wanted to . . . help her. So he would spend all sorts of time. I have a feeling that after that first day [following an initial three-hour interview] when she left his office, I don't think he went to sleep that night until he spent a great deal of time analyzing what went on during those three hours. Most therapists would have thrown up their hands, and if they had made another appointment, they would not have given the case another thought until the patient came in the next day. But not Erickson! I have a feeling that he spent a long time rethinking every moment of that three-hour session. This, I think, is the reason for Erickson's success and great rapport. He did not give up! He was extremely analytical in trying to understand why he failed and why his patients failed . . . and then devising new directions and treatment strategies." How many of us are willing to dedicate so much time to our patients? How many of us spend even a few minutes before a session thinking about what we are going to do? Although we have no proof, it seems to make sense that a therapist who carefully plans treatment is likely to get better results than one who doesn't.

I believe that many myths are being perpetuated about Erickson (Hammond, 1984). When someone is overinterpreted and deified, it naturally makes people skeptical about his actual accomplishments. I have the highest respect for Erickson, but this does not restrain me from seeing him as human. He made therapeutic errors and he certainly failed with some patients. There were also shortcomings and limitations in his writings and research (Hilgard, 1984). But accepting his humanness does not stop me from acknowledging his exceptionally creative contributions and positive attributes.

Although we will never know exactly how successful Erickson was as a therapist, just as we don't know how successful any other therapists are, I think the weight of the evidence is that Erickson was one of the best. He had qualities that any good therapist would do well to emulate! He worked to convey understanding, was respectful and willing to accept patients where they were. He was not a "hypnotist" who believed in hypnosis or any other method as a panacea. Hypnosis was just one part of his work. He was an exceptional model of electicism, willing to use almost anything that might be helpful. He always attempted to individualize treatment to suit the patient's needs rather than attempting to fit the patient into the mold of the therapist's theory or favorite method. He was concerned with what worked and not with what fit or didn't fit this or that model of therapy. He was also uniquely dedicated to the patients he worked with and cared enough to devote enormous amounts of time to thoughtful treatment planning and introspective analysis of his own behavior. He was persistent, and resistance was not perceived as a problem of the patient, but as a challenge to his creativity and flexibility. I consider these to be qualities of excellence.

Reference Notes

1. Mann, H. Personal communication. November 18, 1983.
2. Rodger, B. Personal communication. September 1, 1984.

References

Alman, B. (Nov. 17, 1983). Bypassing hypnotic susceptibility scales. Paper presented at the 26th Annual Scientific Meeting, American Society of Clinical Hypnosis, Dallas, Texas.

Fiedler, F. E. (1950). The concept of an ideal therapeutic relationship. *Journal of Consulting Psychology, 14,* 339–345.

Fiedler, F. E. (1951). Comparison of therapeutic relationships in psychoanalytic, non-directive and Adlerian therapy. *Journal of Consulting Psychology, 14,* 436–445.

Hammond, D. C. (1984). Myths about Erickson and Ericksonian hypnosis. *American Journal of Clinical Hypnosis, 26,* 236–245.

Hilgard, E. (1984). Book review of the Collected Papers of Milton H. Erickson on Hypnosis. *International Journal of Clinical & Experimental Hypnosis, 32,* 257–265.

Holroyd, J. (1980). Hypnosis treatment for smoking: An evaluative review. *International Journal of Clinical & Experimental Hypnosis, 28,* 341–357.

Lieberman, M. A., Yalom, I. D., & Miles, M. B. (1973). *Encounter groups: First facts.* New York: Basic Books.

Munroe, R. L. (1955). *Schools of psychoanalytic thought.* New York: Dryden Press.

Nuland, W., & Field, P. B. (1970). Smoking and hypnosis: A systematic clinical approach. *International Journal of Clinical and Experimental Hypnosis, 18,* 290–306.

Rogers, C. R. (1957). The necessary and sufficient conditions for therapeutic personality change. *Journal of Consulting Psychology, 21,* 95–103.

Shoben, E. J. (1953). Some observations on psychotherapy and the learning process. In O. H. Mowrer (Ed.). *Psychotherapy: Theory and research.* New York: Ronald Press.

Truax, C. B., & Mitchell, K. M. (1971). Research on certain therapist interpersonal skills in relation to process and outcome. In A. E. Bergin & S. L. Garfield (Eds.). *Handbook of psychotherapy and behavior change* (pp. 299–344). New York: Wiley.

Q&A 43 Naturalistic Methods of Hypnosis

Question:

What exactly are naturalistic methods of hypnosis, what is their connection to Milton Erickson, how are they used, and what is their value?

Discussion by JILL BOND CAIRE, Ph.D.

Milton Erickson always liked to emphasize that hypnosis is the communication of ideas and he took an interest in discovering how many ways ideas could be communicated to and accepted by people. He was the first to describe naturalistic hypnosis as "the acceptance of the situation encountered and utilization of it, without endeavoring to restructure it psychologically" (Haley, 1967). Naturalistic techniques are most often used in situations where the formal use of trance may be inappropriate or unacceptable to the patient who, at the same time, is highly motivated to change.

It is important to remember that it is only in our western culture that hypnosis is associated with a quiet, relaxed demeanor occurring after soothing, repetitive stimulation. Other cultures may use very different methods of hypnotic induction, which might include vigorous movements to induce certain types of trance experience. Thus, to create or utilize a naturally occurring trance, it is not always necessary that the person appear to be "hypnotized." There are many entrances to altered states and more than one process in which ideas may be accepted into the mind. What we mean by hypnosis is an attempt to create a psychological condition whereby certain ideas may become more acceptable.

Too often when people hear the word "hypnosis" they think about controlling or being controlled, which is a total misperception and a discounting of the hypnotized individual's capacity to respond in unique and particular ways to suggestions. In my experience it is not necessary to induce a formal trance in order to use suggestion, but if the suggestions are going to be effective, they must be associated with the predominant patterns of functioning of the patient. Suggestions must be formulated in a manner that takes into consideration the unique personality and capacity of the individual, using words, tone, pacing and styles that are meaningful to the person. This does not entail simple mimicking of the person but a recognition of the person's individuality and real needs at the time.

There are also certain situations which enhance or create a receptivity that may not generally be present. For example, the conditions of hospitalization and nature of the reactions to serious illness generally serve to fixate a patient's attention and create a desire to find a satisfactory way of managing the threats associated with serious illness.

In summary, in order to use naturalistic techniques, one must have a willingness to accept the natural situation and natural abilities of the individual while inducing a shift in the perception of the individual. These ideas are difficult to articulate, but I hope the following examples will serve to clarify what I mean. The examples are drawn from my work as a counseling psychologist on a cardiac rehabilitation team. The main purpose of cardiac rehabilitation is to help patients recover to their maximum capacity in a manner that reinforces their self-esteem and reliance on their own resources for coping, an attitude which is necessary for optimal recovery. Naturalistic techniques allow the therapist to help patients to cope in a way that emphasizes the strengths and coping skills of the individual.

Three examples will be given illustrating the utilization of three different modes of presentation. The first exhibits the utilization of a patient's cognitive style, the second shows how an altered state of consciousness can be modified, and the third exhibits the use of a traditional hypnotic technique presented in a naturalistic manner.

The first case, although more dramatic than most, is an example of a fairly common reaction post cardiac surgery and also demonstrates the time constraints generally associated with in-hospital treatment. This patient was seen five days post aorto-coronary bypass surgery. He was a 63-year-old Caucasian male, a very successful businessman who had been married to the same woman for 40 years. Although all post-operative cardiac patients are seen routinely, I was alerted to this patient because of his demands that his caregivers tell him precisely when and to what degree his normal functioning would return.

When questioned about his reactions to surgery and his illness, the patient explained that work was the most rewarding part of his life and that he took great pride in the quality of his performance. He had, accordingly, given himself four months to regain his previous level of ability. He was frustrated by what he saw as incompetence or evasiveness of the medical team in not verifying his ideas about how he should recover. Although no direct threat of suicide was made, he expressed the belief that there was no use living if he could not function at his previous level. He described himself as a fascist politically, remarking that he was intolerant of others' disabilities, "people who are a drain on society should not be allowed to live," and, as this had been his philosophy in health, he would not change it now.

The patient had achieved a high level of success as the broker of a large real estate firm. He loved to travel and mentioned that he only appreciated the finest in food, wines and classical music.

Although the patient readily admitted to anxiety and distress, he thought that people who needed any kind of psychological help were weak. He clearly had no cognitive defenses to deal with disability of any nature. What he needed was an alternative perception of disability and a feeling of curiosity about what he might be able to enjoy despite limitations.

The first question to ask is, "What does this particular individual need to understand or learn in order to cope satisfactorily with the tasks associated with his stage of development?" In this case, the patient's coping skills had gained him considerable recognition and success in his professional endeavors but in no way prepared him for dealing with the increased losses and dependency of later years.

The decision about which types of suggestions to use to stimulate the patient's own patterns of psychological functioning is based on carefully observing the patient to determine what is meaningful to him. In the case of a resistant patient, the time taken for a thorough evaluation and history is of great importance. The patient's comments about his love of classical music and his highly refined taste in traveling became crucial in selecting appropriate suggestions and designing appropriate interventions. The patient might have been closed to psychological intervention, but he was open to listening to stories about people who were meaningful to him. The examples chosen were Beethoven's biography and a television special about Margaret Mead's travels. Beethoven's life story is one of remarkable adjustment to a profound disability. He went deaf at what might have been considered the prime of his life and entered a period of depression and loss of creativity until he was able to adjust to his limitation. His adjustment, of course, was as extraordinary as his talent. He developed the ability to listen and create the music in his own mind and went on to create what are now considered his greatest works. This story and the example of Margaret Mead gave me the opportunity to make many suggestions about how individuals could cope successfully with aging and disability. For example, I could quite naturally make the comment that, while I had always appreciated Margaret Mead's work, I was especially interested in her more mature insights as she returned to the places she had studied earlier. And it could be casually mentioned that of course she used a cane now and needed help out of the native boats, but that she nevertheless always showed a strong vitality.

No attempt was made to alter the personality, but suggestions were designed to integrate alternative ideas within the predominant personality structure. The patient's personality was such that he would spontaneously identify himself with these particular types of individuals, unconsciously and consciously. Through this identification he could enter a type of trance and receive all the benefits of the suggestions. He was left with the final suggestion that many people use their time in the hospital to think about the things that are really meaningful to them and that he too should have a great deal to contemplate. The following day the patient indicated that he had made a marked adjustment in his demands, saying that if he could only travel, he would be satisfied. During the course of his conversation, he also mentioned Beethoven's Ninth Symphony.

The second example concerns an unmarried man in his mid-thirties who had a mitral valve replaced. He had experienced considerable anxiety and ambivalence prior to surgery, but ultimately was prevailed upon by his brother to have the operation. He had an obsessional coping style and made an initial good adjustment to the surgery by attempting to be a cooperative, "model" patient. He developed obsessional ideation following an incident involving a bowel impaction approximately six days post surgery.

The trauma involved the patient's fastidiousness and his reluctance to be assisted by female nurses with his bowel functioning. While the patient was in the bathroom attempting to solve the problem for himself, his monitor began to indicate cardiac distress and the female intern insisted that he come out of the bathroom. When the patient refused, she threatened calling Security to force open the door if he did not come out voluntarily. He was humiliated, but came out and allowed the nurse to clear the impaction. The following morning he was having intrusive images regarding the incident and obsessively repeating what had happened to anyone who would listen. He was overwhelmed by feelings of shame and humiliation and was unsuccessfully attempting to deal with these feelings by affirming that he had tried to be a good patient, that he had always had regular bowel movements, and that all the nurses had said he was a good patient. These defenses were inadequate to resolve the threat to his self-esteem.

The patient was seen the morning after the incident. Initial attempts to calm him were unsuccessful. He was then given repetitive casual suggestions about the relief of getting things off one's chest. He was also offered the suggestion that each time he told the story he could become less and less anxious until finally the incident wouldn't bother him at all.

After some 20 repetitions he became calm enough for further interventions. These consisted primarily of reassurance that negative reactions were normal for people in his predicament and wondering about, and reinforcement of, positive coping skills. His primary defense was intellectualization, and questioning elicited that the patient was quite proud of his ability to deal with people. He was the head of a firm which dealt with the public and he supervised about 15 employees. Thus, speculations were made about the many kinds of difficult people and situations the patient had already handled, to which he could agree. These speculations were very simple questions about the patient's experiences heading an office. It was only necessary to redirect his attention to the management skills he used on a daily basis. These suggestions were interspersed between recitations of the traumatic incident. After some ten more repetitions, the patient reasoned that if he could now discuss the situation with the intern, he could understand that she had had her own reasons for her reactions. The patient speculated as to what these might have been. His self-esteem was restored and he was happy to notice that there were some visitors waiting to see him. The following day the patient reported that the incident no longer bothered him and that he had even been able to joke about it to the nurse.

Because of the patient's emotional distress, there was no opportunity to obtain a history or conduct a mental status exam before the intervention. The patient was tall and well-groomed but in an obvious state of panic. It was precisely because of this panic state that it was not necessary to induce a formal trance. The patient's state of mind served to make him more responsive to simple suggestions. The repetitive and simple suggestions were sufficient to direct his attention to his own resources that could be useful to him in resolving his trauma. It should also be noted that the therapist did not rush the patient, allowing him to fully utilize the suggestion that he could repeat the story until all of his anxiety was dissipated.

The third case involves a 65-year-old man who also needed a mitral valve replacement. Following his surgery he developed intrusive thoughts about having had his heart handled, "picked up and opened." These thoughts caused him great distress and agitation. He was also distressed by the knowledge that his previous condition could recur.

The patient was a tall, grizzled-looking man who had lived and worked all his life in the Midwest. He, his wife, and children had always dreamed of moving to California until gradually the whole family began to make the move. His two sons married and settled in California, and recently the patient and his wife also moved across the country in preparation for retirement. Shortly after he moved to California, he developed a heart infection which forced him to retire early with resulting financial loss. Further, he was unable to enjoy his plans for travel and recreation, as his heart condition prevented his going much above sea level.

Most patients cope with the tremendous medical advances by denying or filtering out much of the information given. This patient presented his situation as having been interrupted and overwhelmed by what had occurred just as he was overwhelmed by the medical information.

A very simple, unobtrusive induction of trance was accomplished by asking the patient to describe his life prior to his cardiac infection. People often enter a type of trance when recalling past events and this process was enhanced by repeating phrases of his recall of pleasurable experiences. When the patient was in a satisfactory state of reverie (as noted by his fixed posture and gaze), his experience was represented to him as being similar to one of the storms he had experienced in childhood. They seemed devastating at the time, but the crops were resown and soon the memory of that storm seemed so long ago, and the storm even became a topic of cheerful conversation once it was safely past. As these suggestions were given the patient was nodding his head in agreement. He was then projected into the future of new pleasurable experiences which he had so long looked forward to: his retirement, watching his grandchildren grow, fishing, and enjoying the beauty of the mountains. Many suggestions were interwoven with these phrases, such as how his memories of his illness and surgery seemed so distant and blurry and how thankful he felt for each day of pleasure. In this way the patient could encapsulate his experience of the surgery and place it in his memories, the way that other unfortunate unexpected phenomena had been placed during his childhood growing up on a farm.

In the above cases it can be observed how hospitalization and the nature of the individual reactions to illness and surgery can create an enhanced responsivity to suggestion. This situation provides an opportunity for the therapist to help the patient organize his experiences in a therapeutic manner. There is no "technique" that will work for all patients. Each patient is unique.

In the first case what was utilized was the patient's sense of uniqueness and his identification with extraordinary individuals. Without this, hearing stories of Beethovan or Margaret Mead would have been irrelevant to his experience. In the second case, what was crucial was finding an area in which the patient felt competent and in control. If the questions about management had not elicited this, it would have been necessary to continue probing. In the third case, because of the patient's presentation, it was possible to link the idea of the surgery with past experiences which, although they had been frightening, had been survived.

It is the therapist's responsibility to respect and utilize the patient's method of presentation in order to stimulate the patient's own patterns of psychological functioning. In this way problems can be met with already acquired learnings or ones that will be accumulated in the future. The Ericksonian principle of making small modifications which allow patients to discover and learn that they have the resources to deal with their problems is compatible with the goals of cardiac rehabilitation. The seemingly minimal role of the therapist helps patients to reestablish their self-esteem and reliance on their own resources for coping, an attitude which is necessary for optimal recovery.

Reference

Haley, J. (1967). *Advanced techniques of hypnosis and therapy: Selected papers of Milton H. Erickson, M.D.* New York: Grune & Stratton.

44 How Much Complexity and Indirection Are Necessary?

Question:

Is it necessary to go through all the effort and indirection Erickson went through to get decent results? I've been impressed by the writings about him, but the actual inductions and suggestions seem incredibly convoluted and time-consuming. Do I need to follow them to do effective therapy?

Discussion by MARC LEHRER, Ph.D.

I do not believe that you have to do work with hypnosis in a complex way in order to get good results. Your question about the necessity of using complex hypnosis inductions is frequently asked by participants in Ericksonian hypnosis training groups and by those who have been reading books about Milton Erickson's cases. I had the opportunity to attend many of Erickson's training seminars and to meet with him individually. In my opinion much that has been written about Erickson and (unfortunately) by him has tended to emphasize complex inductions while neglecting the practical and psychocultural reasons why such inductions were used or Erickson's use of less complex methods.

Erickson used simple inductions and direct suggestion and advice with patients in many situations. However, examples of his methods often are presented as being complex in his writings for several reasons in addition to the actual case work.

First, in his earlier articles and presentations he wanted to place his work on a different and more professional level from stage hypnotists and therapists who were known to use direct methods of hypnosis in an attempt to control individuals. During the time when he was developing his hypnotic techniques, the vast majority of persons with whom he worked either knew nothing about hypnosis or greatly feared its effects. This was due to the fact that a major source of information about hypnosis in the late 1920s and 1930s (and to this day) was carnival shows, stage hypnosis at state fairs, movies such as *Svengali*, and so on. Many people feared being controlled or made to do something stupid by a hypnotist, or opposed hypnosis because of religious beliefs. Physicians of the times held very prominent positions in the community and felt threatened by the challenge to their absolute medical authority by Erickson's claims for hypnosis. Considering the context, it is no wonder that Erickson used complex and indirect ways to distract, surprise, convince, and motivate patients to use hypnosis.

Then, too, Erickson was repeatedly challenged by physicians at medical meetings when he presented his work. During these "training under fire" circumstances, he became a master at hypnotic induction and influence. Later in his life, when he lost more and more power of his voice from illness and aging, he developed more refined metaphorical and indirect methods, which in addition distracted patients from his obvious infirmities.

Second, Erickson emphasized cases of unusual hypnotic responsivity to help convince disbelievers of the nature of hypnotic processes and of the power of the unconscious. Many of the "double bind" inductions, complex use of arm cataplexies, age regressions, hallucinations, time distortion, and amnesias were used for these purposes. I think it is unfortunate that the best video available of Erickson's work, *The Artistry of Milton Erickson, M.D.* (Monde Tape) (Lustig, 1975) emphasizes work with hypnosis and trance states in the most complex of ways to convince people of the power of hypnosis. Too often the result of this tape is to leave the viewer convinced that he or she could never use hypnosis in the way it has been demonstrated.

Third, many of the case examples Erickson referred to during the last years of his life were used as part of a process of teaching with metaphor. Thus, the majority of persons who were instructed by Erickson in the last years of his life were not only hearing about a case but were also being indirectly influenced by the complex metaphorical style in which he presented the case. This did not mean that Erickson did not use less complex methods when working with patients. Simple case stories with predictable outcomes just do not hold the attention of a group the way more unusual and complicated cases do.

I believe that we who are working with the patients of today need both a working knowledge of simple and direct hypnosis as well as complex techniques. Our situation is often quite different from what Erickson encountered in his work with patients. For example, many persons come to see me because of my identification with Erickson and my teaching of his methods. Frequently they have read something about him or about his methods of work with individuals and may be familiar with his case stories. These patients expect me to be indirect, metaphorical, and to give confusing or paradoxical assignments in connection with the "deep" hypnosis they feel is necessary to solve their problems.

Using what I consider to be good Ericksonian technique, I have found that some of my most effective work with such individuals has occurred when I have used simple and straightforward inductions coupled with direct suggestion and undisguised case examples of success. A number of my patients and trainees, however, tell me that when doing this I have been wonderfully "indirect." Is this an example of the patient using an "Ericksonian" technique on the therapist? I think it is more likely that our patients are becoming more sophisticated and knowledgeable about hypnosis and are also still dealing with some of the same old issues involving loss of control and developing a relationship with a therapist.

I would therefore advise you first to become experienced with the fundamentals of hypnosis. Basic inductions, learning to observe your patient in hypnosis, developing confidence in talking with patients in hypnosis, asking questions and using the ideas and associations that occur to you are all important. Spend time practicing age regression, reframing, dissociation, and ego-strengthening techniques. Develop your own source of trustable knowledge about how patients respond in hypnosis with you. It is at this point in your development as a hypnotist that you would begin to benefit most from some of the more complex examples of Erickson's work.

I would also recommend that you disregard the emphasis in many writings about Erickson which imply that using complexity or indirection is the only way to get past the "resistance" of the patient. It is not only Erickson's technique which accounts for his success with a patient. He also developed guidelines from experience of when to use a simpler approach and when a more complex set of hypnosis methods were required. I feel a more fundamental message from Erickson's constant exploration for new ways of using hypnosis is to be flexible, rather than complex, in your approach.

I also perceive a world coming where many persons have read books about Erickson and Neurolinguistic Programming and other such methods. These patients will soon tire of the all too frequent rehashing of patient examples that are used in many books and may in fact be more knowledgeable about the latest version of what Erickson was "really doing" than you are. Therefore, concentrate upon what you do well with hypnosis and use Erickson's examples to stimulate new ideas for yourself.

In sum, there clearly will always be a right time and place for the use of simple as well as complex methods in hypnosis. However, there is no law that says that "indirect" or complex metaphorical methods are better or more effective than "direct" methods. Erickson learned to work with direct methods and refined his techniques based upon his excellent observational skills, an inquisitive mind, the necessity of working with persons who feared being controlled, and many other psychological and psychocultural factors that influenced both him and his patients. We can most benefit from Erickson's clinical and teaching examples by using an approach that fits the needs of our patients.

Ultimately you must select the methods and styles of using hypnosis with your patients. If Erickson's pioneering work in both complex inductions and metaphorical techniques leads you to more sophisticated and effective methods of work with hypnosis, so much the better. If he just isn't your cup of tea, then dine elsewhere. There really are many other approaches to choose from.

Reference

Lustig, H. S. (1975). *The artistry of Milton H. Erickson, M.D.* Haverford, PA: Herbert S. Lustig, M.D., Ltd.

$\underset{A}{\overset{Q}{\&}}45$ Learning Erickson's Methods

Question:

When I try to emulate Erickson's methods, I usually get terribly confused and anxious. As a result, the therapy goes downhill. How can I learn what is valuable in his approach and still stay calm and do good therapy?

Discussion by BRIAN GRODNER, Ph.D.

This is a question (and a concern) that often arises when therapists are learning to use Ericksonian methods. These methods are not easily understood just from reading. They are different enough from many other therapeutic orientations to require some shifts in thinking, attitude and practice.

Too often Ericksonian methods are considered in a vacuum. They are perceived as "tricky" techniques worshipped for their power rather than merely means and possibilities. All of the techniques Erickson used were tools to implement therapeutic goals, not ends in themselves. If you keep in mind Erickson's philosophy, operating principles and assumptions, the methods he used will feel more natural and understandable and less arbitrary, disconnected and confusing. Let's look at some of these assumptions and operating principles.

Erickson's view of therapy is well illustrated by the story of his successfully returning a lost horse whose owner and home were unknown. Erickson walked the horse to the road, mounted him and started riding. Whenever the horse started to graze, Erickson would bring him back to the road. Finally the horse went down a drive and to the barn of a farm. The farmer came out and said, "Thank you. How did you know where my horse belonged?" Erickson replied, "I didn't know, the horse knew; my job was to keep him on the road."

Erickson believed that everyone has the resources needed to do what he or she wants — or at least the experience from which these resources can be built. Unfortunately, these resources are often blocked, hidden, or otherwise out of reach because of inhibitions, fears, expectations and incorrect assumptions about one's abilities.

It is our psychological or internal reality that most strongly influences our behavior and feelings and the use of our resources and limitations. Clients come to us with varying degrees of ambivalence, cooperation, defenses, intellectualization and so-called "resistance." The main questions often facing Erickson, and other therapists as well, are: How is this internal reality influenced? How can these resources be tapped and employed in constructive ways? Certainly a "you can do it," supportive attitude is not enough.

Erickson believed that an altered state of consciousness could be helpful, a state where limitations could be bypassed, new understandings and new perspectives developed, new solutions created, new behaviors implemented. This state where the rich repository of life experiences and unconscious wisdom may be tapped is often called trance. Erickson realized that you don't need a swinging watch or closed eyes to help clients enter hypnosis and use it successfully. After all, many clients come to therapy already using hypnosis, albeit negative self-hypnosis that promotes and reinforces their limitations and fears.

But a rote, structured use of hypnosis is not enough, because people are different in many ways. Although all therapists give lip service to this cliché, Erickson took it to heart. He believed that it was crucial to get a careful and thorough understanding of his patient. His assessment process, though not used to make traditional psychiatric diagnoses, was detailed and practical. He wanted answers to such questions as: What is this person's frame of reference and attitudes (about himself, about his problem, about therapy, about me)? What resources does he have that I can use to help him get where he wants to go? Will he respond to direct or indirect suggestions? Erickson, at times, used an indirect approach to bypass rigid limitations and evoke within people their own meaningful associations. He used syntax which had meanings on many different levels for the many different aspects of people's personalities.

Contrary to what many people now believe, Erickson could be authoritarian and direct, and he was with clients for whom he thought that approach fit.

Erickson tried to "get in synch" with patients, to accept and utilize their behavior, history and frames of reference. But to accept and use these things, you first have to discover what they are. Erickson was a master of sensory awareness, attuned to the verbal and nonverbal behavior of his clients. Unfortunately, Ericksonian strategies of assessment and information-gathering have been neglected in most of the literature and workshops on his work.

It follows from Erickson's attempt to accept each client on his or her own ground that treatment was always individualized. His flexibility allowed him the freedom to be creative.

Erickson was the ultimate pragmatist and the only thing that really mattered to him was how he could help this particular patient improve in a particular way. He could never be pigeonholed nor his techniques universalized, although many therapists are now busy trying to do just that. Erickson was always developing new methods because new clients presented different situations that required different responses. He didn't have a technique which he tried to force or fit. Erickson understood his client and used a technique which fit both his client's "personality" and the desired outcome.

You can think about some of these operating principles of Ericksonian therapy and hypnosis and utilize your knowledge of your client. Then you can try Ericksonian methods in a more systematic, logical, natural manner without the confusion that focusing on the technique itself usually causes.

A few simple examples may be helpful. Metaphors are not necessarily complicated stories told for the sake of confusion. At times, a client has assumptions and limitations about change in a certain area in his or her life. Let's say direct suggestions and increased understanding do not seem to work. You, as a therapist, want to help the client entertain different possibilities for change and bypass the content area where he is stuck with conditioned negative responses. A metaphor or story which is similar in nature to the client's situation but with a different content is a logical idea and may be successful. For instance, if a client is trying to do something and yet sabotaging what he is trying to do, sometimes just pointing out the dynamics will help, but not often. Describing in detail driving a car with one foot on the gas and one foot on the brake at the same time may help him to consciously and unconsciously understand both the pattern and possible ways around it.

The first step, then, is to begin with operating principles and goals and careful assessment. The second step is to go slowly and systematically with different techniques. The metaphor of driving the car can be elaborated upon, more specifically geared to the client, more or less indirect, and geared to unconscious understanding.

In hypnosis, you wish to imply and guide a client into a deeper trance through gentle implication rather than direct suggestions which he or she seems to resist. So you could say, "You might want to go into a deeper trance now or wait until you begin to be aware of a change in your breathing." A next step may be an emphasis in voice tone of the embedded statement, "go into a deeper trance now." The examples just given for implication of deep trance are relatively easy language to learn. Practice on the level of sophistication you're comfortable with in each area before going on. A more sophisticated version of this example might be: "You may be aware of the subtle changes in your breathing. I wonder whether or not you're aware of beginning to get ready to go into the deeper trance you find yourself comfortably entering into. Now . . . " Too often therapists jump too soon into greater sophistication than can be easily integrated.

At the beginning, arbitrary separation of different techniques is helpful. Choose one client with whom to practice a particular method. Prewrite an induction or metaphor (as Erickson did for many years). Then you can begin to integrate different methods and techniques. And, of course, there is no substitute for practice, both supervised and on your own, to increase comfort and competence.

Remember in therapy it is important to increase choice rather than take anything away. Give yourself the same break. You already have, I'm sure, knowledge and competence which don't have to be thrown away.

We know clients don't generally do well with negative motivation and self-deprecating and judgmental behavior. Neither do we!

You might tell a story to yourself about a coach on a softball team talking to a player about to bat in the bottom of the ninth inning and saying, "You're our last chance for the winning run. But you've struck out three times today, you're in a slump, there's a hitch in your swing, and the fans are booing you. Now go out and hit a home run for our team."

That story may make it easier to look at what you may be doing and how self-defeating most negative motivation is — how it gets in the way of providing the emotional foundation of confidence, encouragement and positive belief which supports change and growth in therapy and life in general. Can you get what you need from the metaphor and then rewrite it to more specifically fit your interests and what you are doing? What would be a vague yet positive ending for you?

Integrate Ericksonian methods into your own personal style and professional practice to find what's valuable for you about Ericksonian methods without losing what's valuable about you. What personal resources do you need to be more comfortable in using these methods? What do you need in order to implement those resources? Under what circumstances is it possible?

Learn to use hypnosis as a "hypnotic life style" and a tool for yourself. Use self-hypnosis and the support of others to help yourself access, mobilize, and use assets of confidence, calmness and fluidity while practicing Ericksonian methods. A personal hypnotic life style and creative flexibility in therapy are reciprocally encouraging.

And lastly, confusion might mean that you're learning something new, something that can't be neatly explained by what you've learned or experienced in the past.

Let me close with three questions: Can you be clear about your confusion, knowing how exciting it is to be experiencing something interesting and new? Can you be confused and relaxed at the same time? Have you read the Emperor's New Clothes lately?

$\underset{A}{Q_{\&}} 46$ Motivating Patients
to Follow Prescriptions

Question:

> How did Erickson get patients to follow his prescriptions? I tried
> a number of them with poor results. With a case of insomnia,
> I followed one of his published examples, telling my patient to
> work on a project he disliked when he couldn't sleep (Erickson
> had his patient wax floors, a task he hated). Unlike Erickson's
> patient, mine neither slept nor did what I told him. How could
> I have motivated him better?

Discussion by JEFFREY K. ZEIG, Ph.D.

When teaching psychotherapy, Milton Erickson rarely mentioned the idea
of technique. Only two major techniques were discussed in detail, the confusion technique (Erickson, 1964) and the interspersal technique (Erickson,
1966). Rather, he promoted the idea of "utilization."

Techniques are best derived from the patient, not the therapist. Whatever
technique the patient uses to be an ineffective patient can also be used by
the therapist to promote effective living. For example, if the patient speaks
schizophrenic "word salad" to distance himself, the therapist can use the
same method to promote an empathic relationship.

One of the main principles of Ericksonian psychotherapy is that patients
have within them the resources necessary for change. They do not need to
be taught anything new; rather, potentials that lie dormant need to be accessed and developed. Thinking in terms of technique is limiting. It is best
not to bend the patient to fit a preselected technique; rather, one should
tailor psychotherapy for each patient (Zeig, 1980).

The insomnia case is an example of ordeal therapy (Haley, 1984). Waxing
the floor was only part of an integrated treatment program. The process of

252

psychotherapy is most important. Interventions are most successful when there is proper "set up" and "follow through." Aspects of the patient's personality are used to seed interventions in small steps. Main interventions are not merely presented; rather, they are broken down into a number of small steps and the patient is asked to respond to each step. By the time the therapist and patient reach the main intervention, it is just another step in a chain of steps to which the patient has already agreed.

It is antithetical to the Ericksonian approach to provide a model of treatment. However, I can identify important treatment issues in the utilization approach:

1) Identify the resources (unaccessed strengths) in the patient.
2) Diagnose the patient's values, i.e., what the patient likes and dislikes (which are also resources).
3) Develop the resources by utilizing the patient's values.
4) Connect the developed resources to the problem, either directly or indirectly.
5) Step four is best conducted by moving in small steps, accessing trust and motivation throughout the process.
6) Drama can be used to enhance responsiveness to directives.
7) Seeding ideas prior to presenting them primes responsive behavior.
8) Timing is crucial. The process of therapy involves pacing, disruption and patterning. Resistance often results from inadequate attention to these processes.
9) The therapist must have an expectant attitude. Here are two examples:
    a) There is a story that may be apocryphal about an experimenter who asked a graduate student to conduct some research. The graduate student was to go into a room in which he would find two undergraduates and give one of them a dime and the other a dollar. No information was provided about which student was to receive the dime and which student was to receive the dollar.

       Unbeknownst to the graduate student, the experimenter met with each of the undergraduate students prior to the experiment: One was told that the graduate student would give him a dime; the other was told that the graduate student would give him a dollar. Of course, the student who expected the dollar got the dollar; the student who expected the dime got the dime (Zeig, 1982, p. 262). Even in these times of inflation, it is important to have one dollar expectations for one's patients.
    b) Schoen (1983) reported a case of a patient who had previous therapy but was unable to overcome a habit problem. After one year of visits to Erickson, the patient succeeded. When asked how he got over the problem, he indicated, "Erickson *believed* that I could conquer it."

10) Follow through. There are numerous techniques for following through. One technique is to practice the new behavior in the room with the therapist. Another is to have follow-up contact with the patient. A third is to have the patient practice the new behavior in fantasy.

Milton Erickson's therapy was a commonsense approach. He believed that patients learn best when they do things (Zeig, 1980). Therapeutic actions must be relevant to the patient and the patient's values.

References

Erickson, M. H. (1964). The confusion technique in hypnosis. *American Journal of Clinical Hypnosis, 6,* 183–207.

Erickson, M. H. (1966). The interspersal hypnotic technique for symptom correction and pain control. *American Journal of Clinical Hypnosis, 3,* 198–209.

Haley, J. (1984). *Ordeal therapy: Unusual ways to change behavior.* San Francisco: Jossey-Bass.

Schoen, S. (1983). NLP: An overview, with commentaries. *The Psychotherapy Newsletter, 1,* 16–26.

Zeig, J. K. (1980). *A teaching seminar with Milton H. Erickson, M.D.* New York: Brunner/Mazel.

Zeig, J. K. (1982). Ericksonian approaches to promote abstinence from cigarette smoking. In J. K. Zeig (Ed.), *Ericksonian Approaches to Hypnosis and Psychotherapy* (pp. 255–269). New York: Brunner/Mazel.

Q&A 47 Effective Use of Erickson's Interspersal Technique

Question:

I have unsuccessfully attempted on many occasions to use Erickson's interspersal technique. I tell shaggy dog stories modeled on his, weaving in therapeutic suggestions, but as far as I can tell, my clients don't get them consciously or unconsciously. What's the trick?

Discussion by PETER TILTON, M.D.

The first rule in applying this (interspersal) or any other Ericksonian technique is simply: *Do not try to be Erickson!* With that in mind, the most important step is proper and thorough understanding of the patient's problem by obtaining a good history.

Too often the inexperienced therapist, as well as the experienced therapist who is now attempting to become an "Ericksonian hypnotherapist," will indiscriminantly apply his techniques verbatim, thinking that the brilliance of his words will do the trick. This is done without careful consideration of the client's needs and attitudes.

In order to be successful it is important to understand the nature of a client's problem and its symbolic meaning. The presenting symptom must be analyzed as to whether it is a primary or secondary symptom. A primary symptom, one which can be considered an intrapsychic phenomenon (and which may require more long-term character reconstructive therapy) is more difficult to change than a secondary symptom, one which can be considered as secondary gain involving conflict with changes in the environment (interpersonal). These secondary symptoms will be more amenable to change by this technique or other brief therapy models.

From the history, the therapist should obtain useful knowledge about the client's way of thinking — his likes, dislikes, hobbies, habits, modes of expression (visual, kinesthetic, auditory), pleasures, and leisure activities. An understanding of the client's fantasy life, dreams and daydreams is equally important in planning strategy. It is helpful to understand the client's use of language (his choice of words, manner of speaking, etc.) and nonverbal communications, which can then be utilized in the formulation of therapeutic suggestions.

My second rule is: *Do what is simplest first!* Thus, one must consider all the possible alternatives for accomplishing therapeutic change. The therapist must ask: Why use this technique? Would another technique work better or more easily? Is the interspersal technique used out of laziness — is it easier to tell a nice story with interspersed suggestions and hope for change rather than do something that requires more effort? I would like to stress that the successful use of this technique requires work. Knowing the client's problem, his view of the world, his goals and how to meet them, and then formulating a story with the use of the interspersal suggestions take considerable time and effort, especially while one is gaining familiarity with the use of this technique.

Another helpful rule is: *The more resistant the client, the more need for indirection!* In his article on the interspersal hypnotic technique, Erickson (1966) states that he used this technique "to secure, to fixate and to hold a difficult patient's attention and to distract him from creating difficulties that would impede therapy." Thus, he interspersed the therapeutic suggestions among trance induction and trance maintenance suggestions to prevent unwarranted resistance by disguising the therapeutic suggestions, thus allowing the patient to move toward the desired goal in accordance with his need and behavioral potentials. This technique can also be successful in less obviously resistant clients, who can enter and remain in trance without the use of the interspersal technique for induction or maintenance, but still seem to have difficulty in achieving their stated goals and may be exhibiting more subtle forms of resistance.

Another important point to consider is that the client does not *need* to consciously understand the story or interspersed suggestions. Again, Erickson (1966) induced suggestions for amnesia so that the client would consciously remember the suggestions *not* at the termination of trance (so that the conscious belief systems would not interfere with the autonomous response to the hypnotic suggestions), but only *later*, after a successful change had taken place. I usually give open-ended suggestions to the effect that the client can remember what is necessary but it may be easier to forget and leave ideas of importance to the unconscious where it will continue effecting the change that the client desires. Then, whatever the client does consciously remember is in accordance with his needs. However, the only way to know if the client "got it" *unconsciously* is by assessing behavior change or symptom reduction after the hypnotic session.

Finally, Erickson (1966) stressed the importance of continued repetitions "until the therapist feels confident that the patient has absorbed the therapeutic suggestions adequately." I would add that repetition does not mean only two or three times, but perhaps 10 or 20 times in slightly different forms.

With these rules in mind, it is necessary to pick a topic and way of speaking that will be of interest to the client (hopefully based on ideas derived from the client's initial history). I usually use a metaphoric story that in itself has a message to the patient's unconscious (and conscious as well) that the desired change can be accomplished. In using a story with the interspersal technique it is important that the suggestions be ego-syntonic — that is, that they fit in with the client's image of himself and his world. In this way the therapist, by utilizing and stressing his client's strength in an indirect manner, creates a therapeutic milieu for change to occur (i.e., behavioral change or symptom reduction).

In the beginning it might be helpful for the therapist to write out the entire story, including the interspersed suggestions, with as many repetitions as deemed necessary. This will help the therapist to become familiar with this method. The therapist should then practice telling the story because this can be crucial to the success of the technique.

The interspersed suggestions should be given after a pause, with a shift in tone or emphasis, so that they are highlighted in the client's mind. However, the change (slower and more emphatic) must be subtle, so as not to distract the client from the main story; he should not linger on the interspersed suggestion but receive it unconsciously as a separate entity within a greater context.

A favorite story that I have developed is derived from a combination of ideas from Erickson's (1966) tomato plant and Pelletier's (1979) ego-strengthening tree. It provides a great deal of flexibility in allowing the therapist to be as *creatively responsible* as possible, utilizing any part or the entire life cycle of a tree to correspond to any aspect of the client's life cycle.

The following case presentation illustrates the use of the interspersal technique using my favorite story.

The client was an attractive 40-year-old female, a radiologist known slightly to me ten years earlier during my internship. She was referred by a nurse who knew of my work in hypnosis, ostensibly because of concerns about a possible nausea and vomiting post-anesthetic response to her upcoming hysterectomy (necessary due to enlarged fibroid uterus — a benign tumorous condition). She had had major surgery once before and experienced unpleasant nausea and vomiting post-surgically. Previously, in medical school, she had been hypnotized as a learning experience and found it to be a positive and pleasant experience. It was her hope that hypnotic suggestion could help her to have less nausea and vomiting and to be more alert and awake following surgery.

Hypnosis was induced by hand levitation with an explanation of the unconscious control of the hands and, thus, other physiological functions as well. The remainder of the hypnotic session was a rehearsal image of the surgical procedure from start to finish with typical suggestions for bleeding control, reduction of edema, waking from surgery alert with a good appetite and healthy rapid return of bowel and bladder function and optimum wound healing — in short, a successful experience. She also experienced glove anesthesia, which was to be used for pain control, and taught autohypnosis, which she successfully performed in my presence.

At the second and final session one week later and two weeks before the scheduled surgery, the client (successful with self-hypnosis) stated that her main concern now was her ability to return to normal sexual function. She felt that she was "closing a chapter in her life" (she had no children and now would no longer be able to bear any) and was concerned that the man with whom she was living, younger than she, would leave her if he wanted children. It seemed to me that she was having some doubts about her self-worth and ability to continue functioning as a woman brought about by this unexpected mid-life crisis. She was, however, a successful woman with a good sense of herself and her abilities; she now needed to get in touch with her inner strengths to help her overcome this life change.

It was felt that, because of her knowledge of medicine, human behavior and sexual function, simple reassurance, direct suggestion or imagery in hypnosis would not suffice. I believed that she could utilize her existing ego strength and unconscious potentials in an indirect manner to resolve this conflict. Based on the fact that there had been successful hypnosis at the previous session and a good relationship resulting in her revealing her deeper concerns without directly asking for psychotherapy, I decided that a metaphoric story with interspersed suggestions would be the best way to proceed.

The following is a short excerpt from this second session with the capitalized words being the interspersed suggestions spoken after a slight pause, more slowly and more emphatically.

The patient was hypnotized and asked to see herself kayaking (her favorite sport) down a river. She was asked to see "that magical tree over there on the river bank. . . . Go over to it and sit under it and notice that it has one fruit which . . . GIVES OFF MANY SEEDS WITH THE POTENTIAL FOR NEW LIFE, but in time that tree does, Nancy, . . . GO THROUGH CHANGES IN ITS LIFE, and as it . . . GROWS OLDER, the fruit also . . . GROWS OLDER AND CHANGES AND AS HAPPENS with all fruit . . . IT CAN SPOIL AND FALL from the tree and that tree can . . . FEEL THE LOSS AND ACCEPT THIS LOSS AND LET IT FALL because that tree . . . DOES KNOW THAT IT WILL CONTINUE GROWING AND CHANGING HAPPILY IN A NEW WAY and that tree . . . CAN BE PROUD OF ITS OTHER PRODUCTIVITY, PAYING MORE ATTENTION TO ITS OTHER ASPECTS, its leaves, its flowers and that tree . . . CAN REALLY ENJOY THE CHANGES IN ITS LIFE AND CONTINUE BEING PRODUCTIVE IN NEW WAYS."

These suggestions were repeated many times in similar fashion along with other interspersed ego-strengthening suggestions. Following this, the patient, when she felt ready, imagined herself back in the river and kayaking, "seeing herself in a new way." This was followed by a repeat hypnotic rehearsal of the surgical procedure (both to address the client's original problem and to distract her from the story and its meaning).

At the termination of the trance a general discussion of her use of self-hypnosis to control pain, nausea and vomiting was held. The patient casually mentioned that she liked the story but did not elaborate, nor did I.

Two weeks later, the day before surgery, I received two bottles of wine with the following note:

> I wanted to thank you for the instruction and suggesting an image that has been quite helpful in helping me deal with the psychological aspects; now I have only the mechanical aspects left.

In this case no psychotherapy was requested, although a problem was presented in such a way that the patient was asking for help in resolving her self-doubts and needed some reassurance that her life would continue to be fulfilling following the surgery and resulting life change. This technique stressed the client's healthy adaptive ego functions and helped her meet her own needs without the use of psychotherapy through the use of interspersing therapeutic suggestion with a metaphoric story in an ego-strengthening and ego-syntonic manner.

In summary, to be successful with this technique, the therapist should be able to 1) properly assess the client's problem, 2) understand the client's mode of thinking and use of language and image of himself and his world, and 3) use ego-syntonic suggestions interspersed repeatedly in a story that itself can have important meaning to the client. Practice by formulating and writing out the dialogue and the use of voice shifts are essential in delineating the suggestions to the patient's unconscious. But besides knowing *how*, it is equally important to know *why* and *when* to use the interspersal technique.

References

Erickson, M. H. (1966). The interspersal hypnotic technique for symptom correction and pain control. *American Journal of Clinical Hypnosis, 8,* 198–209.

Pelletier, A. M. (1979). Three uses of guided imagery in hypnosis, *American Journal of Clinical Hypnosis, 22,* 32–36.

Q&A 48 Choosing the Right Metaphors for Particular Clients

Question:

> The idea of indirection and talking to clients in terms of metaphors is very appealing to me and I've had some success working this way, but also a number of failures. How do you decide which metaphors are appropriate for a particular client?

Discussion by STEPHEN R. LANKTON, M.S.W.

Generally speaking, any therapy that uses metaphor as an intervention works strategically from available resources and builds needed resources with the client. This two-part procedure of determining available resources and estimating needed resources involves several factors, including: the *treatment contract* and *goals* derived from the *diagnostic assessment*, the client's *developmental age* and *developmental issues*, and the *client's life experiences* including the *client's own metaphors*.

The use of metaphor in hypnotherapy presupposes that the therapist operates from a strategic approach. The first consideration, therefore, is *always* the unique family and individuals, the treatment contract, and the therapeutic goal(s). Once goals have been tentatively established, the selection of interventions (particularly metaphors) is guided by all of the above considerations. The client's contract and the therapist's assessment are continually refined during therapy.

Several factors are involved in assessment, which can only be mentioned here: the structure of the family or social system, the stage of development of the client and client system, the psychological age of all individuals concerned, the available and needed resources, the pattern or function of the presenting symptomatic behavior, and the treatment contract.

A metaphor provides a context to convey a therapeutic learning. Therefore, the strategic therapist must be guided by the goals that have been set to fulfill the treatment contract. The process of changing concepts and imagery within the metaphor should be built around the expectation that the client will learn something that will challenge a held attitude, evoke an emotion, highlight a behavior, encourage a new self-image, etc. Since the actual change process is initiated within the listener from experience evoked by each particular metaphor, the metaphor should be carefully structured to increase the likelihood of accomplishing the specific outcome (attitude restructuring, emotion, behavior, self-image enhancement, etc.).

Such metaphors result from careful observation and feedback. Strategic therapists plan the process of imagery and concept change within each metaphor to conform to the treatment plan; they do not merely "free associate" ideas that may come to mind in the session (Erickson, 1980, p. 336).

The structures that we use to facilitate various therapeutic goals have been elaborated elsewhere (Lankton & Lankton, 1983; Lankton, 1985). Here I will summarize the major requirements for three of these protocols: attitude restructuring, affect flexibility, and behavior change. Again, in choosing metaphors, the concerns and goals of the particular client(s) must be stated first by the strategic therapist. The *content* of the metaphor can be selected to aid the identification and understanding of the client and subsequently be arranged to follow a *process* of change as outlined below. The following protocols simulate the manner of idea formation occurring in the "real world" and, as such, can be expected to help promote and create attitude, emotional, and behavioral learnings in therapy.

Attitude Restructuring

1) Create a story that examines the behavior or attitude in question from the protagonist's perspective.
2) Alternate within the story to examine the opposite behavior or attitude from the perspective of at least one other protagonist.
3) Conclude the story by relating the consequence(s) of each protagonist's behavior(s) and/or beliefs to the perceptions each held.

A metaphor of this type was used to challenge the attitude expressed by an unmarried male client. Part of his difficulty was that he was firm in his belief that a person from a broken home could not have a happy marriage. An attitude metaphor told to him concerned two high school girls that I had known. One was killed by her husband, who also took his own life, one week prior to our high school reunion.

The story explained that "Georgia" came from a happy home and viewed her future optimistically. Following this character development, the life of the second protagonist, "Sally," was elaborated. Sally was from an abusive family and her parents eventually divorced. This portion of the metaphor took several minutes and followed steps one and two above. The client could be expected to project his attitude in an attempt to predict the outcome that Sally was killed. Finally, however, the story ends with the revelation that Georgia, not Sally, was the victim.

In this example the client's attitude was evoked and then, presumably, confused or bewildered by the actual ending of the story. Having projected the incorrect answer to the dramatic end of the story, a client must certainly question where his thinking went wrong. Thus, he temporarily suspends his strongly held belief. Hence, he will be more receptive to new learnings in the therapeutic session.

Affect and Emotional Flexibility

1) Create a story that establishes a relationship between the protagonist and a person, place or thing that involves emotion or affect (e.g., tenderness, anxiety, mastery, confusion, love, longing).
2) Change the story so that it provides detail about the *movement* in the relationship (e.g., moving with, moving toward, moving away, orbiting, chasing).
3) End the story with a focus on details of observable behaviors and internal physiological changes of the main protagonist (and coincidentally of the listener) that result from the building emotion.

An affect metaphor that helps a client increase or build a sense of sadness might be told to a client who has not grieved a loss. Although several story *contents* would be possible, the following *process* of imagery change (in any story with which the listener is likely to identify) will increase the likelihood of a therapeutic success.

The character development initially paints the protagonist as positive and sketches a positive relationship (warm, friendly, loving, caring, understanding, etc.) between the protagonist and another person, place or thing. The second step in the process of the story must introduce movement, in this case, movement away from or separating the two. As this separation occurs, a listener will make sense of the changing imagery by experiencing a meaningful personal reaction.

The third step suggests that the story culminate with a focus on the bodily reaction of the protagonist and especially those changes that will be exhibited by the listener. Thus, the listener finds himself or herself experiencing aspects of the complex constellation of sadness built unconsciously and beyond the level of conscious resistance. The conscious awareness and identification with the drama of the story line will serve only to capture attention. The unconscious response is created by the movement of imagery in the story according to the protocol and the subsequent experience it evokes in the listener.

Behavior Change

1) Create a story that emphasizes the protagonist's goals rather than his/her motives, while detailing the protagonist's observable behavior related to the client's desired behavioral role.
2) Include within the story the details of the protagonist's internal attention and non-observable behavior used to support the actions he or she exhibits.
3) Before ending, extend the context of the story so that it is possible to repeat explanations of the desired behavior.

The metaphors that develop a sensitivity to some behaviors, for instance, the behaviors involved in asking for help, entail sharing a story that does little more than make a few specific behaviors explicit. The story might involve a man asking for help in a service station and again in a hardware store. The protagonist's motives would not be mentioned. His behaviors, however, would be explained in detail. These might include: standing with his palms upward, shifting his weight from one foot to the other, using a softened voice tone, dropping his gaze, using the words, "I need your help with this . . . , " etc. The man's internal experience at the time would also be explored. The story would either describe the same man in other situations or observe others asking for help with similar behaviors. Hence, the listener thinks of performing the behaviors but the metaphoric framework removes him one step from possible threat and reduces defensive resistance that may occur.

In summarizing these three basic metaphor process protocols, let me compare them to common experiences. The attitude metaphor follows the format of many of Aesop's fables, like "the boy who cried wolf" and many New Testament stories like the prodigal son or the story of the twelve talents. The affect format, found in innumerable stories from cinema, could be illustrated with the simple and well-known tale *Love Story*. In *Love Story* the relationship of the starring couple is first shown to be intensely close and loving; then, unexpectedly, the woman contracts cancer and dies. The viewers are left observing the grieved reaction of the other main character. The behavior protocol follows the format of the common television cooking and home improvement shows. Here there is no motive (such as to impress the folks or outdo the neighbors). Rather, the behaviors needed are displayed methodically and repeatedly.

Content for the Metaphor

The selection of metaphoric content is determined, in part, by the client's life experiences. The therapist would not be inclined to speak about ballet dancing to the physicist who has never danced. Neither would the therapist be likely to use a metaphor about nuclear physics with the high-school-educated dishwasher. One guideline for selecting content is the client's developmental age, as shown by vocabulary, values, gestures, manipulations for infantile gratification, and unresolved psychodynamic issues. The metaphorical content may involve vocabulary and issues that are relevant to the client's developmental successes.

If a client's developmental age is determined to be four to six years, the stories told might be about learning that is understandable to a six-year-old child. Nevertheless, this can be done so that clients are not offended. One method of safeguarding the client is to adjust the overall frame or introduction of the story to the needs of the client's conscious mind.

The conscious impact of a story can change radically when the introduction is varied. For instance, a story about a six-year-old child used to teach trust with a client with latency issues might be introduced in many different ways. One might begin, "You, of course, don't need to be reminded . . . , " and continue in that spirit with a resistant client. For the client requiring a challenge, the introduction and overall frame might be "I'm not sure you understand the learning conveyed in the story of. . . . " With a compliant client the therapist again must modify the introduction, saying, perhaps, "I wonder if you can fully appreciate how . . . , " and continuing in this provocative spirit throughout the session. Introducing the same story in different ways, then, will extend the usefulness of the particular metaphor to a wider range of clients.

Metaphors are open suggestions rather than closed or restrictive suggestions. They orient the listener toward an area of potential change and resources but they do not channel and specify a particular limited response. We must, then, consider how indirect suggestions (such as those represented in the delivery of a metaphor) are heard by a client. This can be noticed both in the lingering and thought-provoking aspect of the metaphor and in the client's here-and-now response to what is occurring in therapy. Using a trial-and-error approach, the strategic therapist attempts to make the material presented in the session as meaningful as possible. It ought to go without saying that the therapist does not know how the client will respond nor what meaning the client will derive from the metaphor until after the fact.

When presented with indirect communication, the listener responds to what is relevant and ignores that which is not. An excellent personal example comes from my last visit with Erickson before Christmas 1979. My wife and I casually mentioned that we did not see a Christmas tree (and implied that one should be present). During the course of the day that followed Erickson told many case stories, some of which I had heard before. Interestingly, when I left the office, I found that both Carol and I had developed a general amnesia for most of the stories. That evening we drove to a shopping center. It occurred to us that we might be able to get a tree and all the trimmings and take it to Erickson's office. We did so and he seemed pleased . . . and we were proud to have done it. Several weeks later we received the audiotapes of these final days and discovered, while listening, that he had told a long story about buying (among other things) a "tree and all the trimmings." He even detailed the particulars of the trimmings. They were the ones we purchased! The real learning is, however, that *we* were the only ones who bought the tree. Twelve others who had also been present did not buy trees. The suggestions were taken by those for whom they were relevant. If not relevant, suggestions are ignored. The client's experience determines what is heard and what response is given.

The thought-stimulating aspect of metaphor yields immediate or short-term responses, as well as lingering or long-term responses to meaningful stories. The immediate responses are noticeable as ideomotor changes in the client. These provide a bit of a barometer during the session against which the therapist can measure the connections being made by the client. Long-term meaning, however, is harder to measure. One personal incident concerns my return to Erickson's office after completing an assignment that involved seeking out and finding a boojum tree growing north of Squaw Peak. I was to find the tree and also "the creeping devils" (a horizontally growing web of cactus) that would be nearby. When I returned to his office the following day I was asked if I had, indeed, found the boojum. I answered yes. Then he asked, "And did you see the creeping devils?" I again answered affirmatively but with some reservation. I was not sure if the cactus I found was what he had meant by the term "creeping devils." "Remember that . . . , " he said expectantly, "There'll always be creeping devils nearby." He abruptly changed the topic . . . but the meaning lingers today, years later. The lingering meaning is, however, like a kaleidoscope. Each year the ambiguity seems to take new shape and deliver more meaning and learning than it did the year before. This type of growing or teleological unfolding is an important component of metaphor and indirect communication. It is the aspect that is most elusive and perhaps has the greatest impact. The most common reward of such communication may be the increased respect with which the client regards the therapy. It is difficult for clients not to notice how indirect techniques leave them free to appreciate the answers they formulate for themselves from within.

The therapist's experience also influences the choice of stories. I tend to discredit the notion that the therapist proceeds upon intuitive leads. Therapy employing metaphor is not a matter of "saying the first thing that comes into your head." Occasionally, one will hear that therapy proceeds throughout by telling a story that is only a result of the therapist's intuitive conception of what would be "good" for the client to hear. I hope it is obvious from this short essay that treatment planning plays the largest role in metaphor selection and design.

There is, however, a role for the therapist's intuition when formulating metaphor. Once the goal has been determined and the metaphor structured, intuition plays a role in the selection of appropriate content. The therapist must find a story that fits the strategic goals and also rests firmly within the therapist's skill and experience. It is a mistake to attempt to talk of auto racing, dog breeding, flower arrangement, etc., if the therapist knows nothing of these subjects. Intellectual knowledge is of very little use; knowledge rooted in sensory observation invariably proves to be the most useful kind for therapeutic metaphors. The most simple observation of nature, human or otherwise, often provides the foundation for a teaching story. In order to tell such a story, however, the therapist must have used his or her skills of observation. It is such a simple but important point: If you don't notice anything you don't have anything to say about it.

References

Erickson, M. H. (1980). The method employed to formulate a complex story for the induction of an experimental neurosis in a hypnotic subject. In E. Rossi (Ed.). *The collected papers of Milton H. Erickson, M.D., Vol. 3* (pp. 336–355). New York: Irvington.

Lankton, S. (1985). Multiple embedded metaphor. In J. Zeig (Ed.). *Ericksonian psychotherapy, Vol. 1: Structures.* New York: Brunner/Mazel.

Lankton, S., & Lankton, C. (1983). *The answer within: A clinical framework of Ericksonian hypnotherapy.* New York: Brunner/Mazel.

SECTION VII *Applications*

Applications of hypnotherapeutic techniques, in general, seem to be limited only by the limits of therapists' imaginations. Specifically, however, there are more stringent boundaries within which we must work. For any therapist, one of the most important boundaries is the extent of his knowledge about the condition with which he is working. For any given patient there will be a host of limitations, ranging from the practical considerations of time and money available to less well defined factors like an innate capacity to respond to a given suggestion.

The first question in this section, discussed by Mutter, demonstrates the exceptionally broad range of applications that are now possible. It is easy to imagine that there are still other applications that were left unmentioned, and still more that will be discovered in the future.

This section makes no attempt to discuss each and every situation in which hypnosis might be applied, but it is hoped that the range of applications discussed is broad enough that the principles involved can be generalized to meet the needs of other patients. This is an extremely important concept, for no therapist will reach his potential if he rigorously sticks to techniques already learned. To be truly successful, he *must* develop the ability to understand the basic principles and, utilizing those, improvise to meet the unique demands that patients frequently present.

$\underset{A}{\overset{Q}{\scriptstyle{\&}}}49$ The Many Applications of Hypnosis

Question:

I've occasionally used hypnosis to calm seriously anxious patients, but I've never relied on it for anything else because I'm not sure it works well enough to be worth the time and effort. Does it?

Discussion by CHARLES B. MUTTER, M.D.

Absolutely. Beside alleviating anxiety, hypnosis is used in many areas of medical, dental and psychological practice.

In dentistry, hypnosis has been found to be quite effective in the control of pain and healing. Quite often the dentist can use rapid induction techniques that will quickly relax the patient to the point that the pain threshold is increased up to 40%. In many patients, total pain control can be effected without the use of anesthetics. Posthypnotic suggestions are given to increase healing, reduce swelling, and prolong comfort without compromising blood supply. Other dental conditions such as gagging, bruxism, and temporomandibular joint pain have been effectively treated with hypnosis.

Hypnosis is often used with surgery and emergency medicine. As in dentistry, pain control, healing, resistance to infection, reduction of blood loss and swelling are affected by hypnosis. One excellent example is the use of hypnosis in patients with burns. Suggestions can be given to reduce fluid and electrolyte loss. If a burn is treated with hypnosis within 17 hours, excessive scar formation and resultant physical deformity can be greatly reduced. In severe burns, dressings must be changed daily. Hypnotic suggestions for pain control and time distortion can be given to increase comfort, save time and enhance healing potential. Similar suggestions can be given to patients undergoing surgery to reduce swelling and blood loss, increase healing and resistance to infection, and speed postoperative recovery. Quite often, patients can be discharged earlier and return to normal functioning more quickly.

Hypnotic applications to psychiatry and psychology have been used throughout the history of medicine. Besides treating anxiety effectively, hypnosis can be applied to all phases of psychotherapy for a wide range of disorders, including depression, psychoneuroses, psychosis in remission, personality and character disorders and sexual disorders. Hypnosis is currently considered the treatment of choice with patients suffering from post-traumatic stress disorders because of the rapidity of response and diminished duration of treatment. Generally, this condition requires two to three years of treatment using usual psychotherapeutic techniques, whereas hypnotic intervention, when effective, can accomplish this task in half the time. Hypnoanalysis is especially effective with many psychiatric disorders because it is a direct route to the unconscious mind and can often uncover repressed traumatic material within a very short period of time, in contrast with other forms of psychotherapy, which could take months or years of intensive treatment before meaningful material is uncovered.

Hypnosis has been used in the treatment of habit disorders such as smoking, obesity, bulimia, nail biting, thumbsucking, drug and alcohol abuse. Usually, substance abuse is a very difficult problem to treat. Quite often hypnosis can be used in conjunction with other forms of treatment to effect major breakthroughs and shorten the course of treatment.

The world medical literature is full of case histories where hypnosis has been used as a treatment modality. Much has been published on the use of hypnosis with pain, postoperative healing and reduction of postoperative complications. Hypnosis has been used with greater frequency in pain clinics with people having chronic debilitating painful disease. Such patients often suffer from anxiety and depression because they feel their body is out of control. Hypnosis is especially useful because it can break the pain/depression cycle and relieve both symptoms simultaneously. In addition, it often obviates the need for patients to take narcotics and reduces the possibility of drug dependence or addiction. Of great recent interest is the use of hypnosis in the treatment of cancer, not only as a means to alleviate pain, but as a direct intervention to combat this disorder in conjunction with other conventional forms of cancer treatment.

Hypnosis has a direct connection with the autonomic nervous system. Therefore, almost all psychosomatic or psychophysiological disorders such as asthma, migraine headaches, ulcers, colitis, hypertension, certain skin disorders, and many other conditions respond in some degree to hypnotherapeutic intervention. Many behavior modification techniques used with hypnosis are highly effective in symptom control.

The question of time and effort is important in the practice of the healing profession. Unlike other therapeutic strategies, hypnosis, when effective, is rapid, dramatic, shortens the course of treatment, and thus, is highly time- and cost-efficient. Not only is it effective in alleviating symptoms, but it also serves as an ego-strengthening device that gives the patient a greater feeling of mastery over his body. The beneficial results are often lifelong in duration. This tool is well worth the time and effort for there are almost no contraindications or adverse side effects when used by a skilled clinician.

Q&A 50 Contraindications to Using Hypnosis

Question:

> When talking to hypnotherapists, I get the impression that hypnosis can be used with any patient with any problem. But surely there must be some patients and some problems for which hypnosis is not well-suited. What can you tell me about contraindications to using hypnotherapy?

Discussion by PETER A. CARICH, Ph.D.

Briefly stated, there are only two contraindications to the use of hypnosis: its employment by an inadequately trained operator, and its use for inappropriate purposes.

Hypnosis is a phenomenon that can be induced easily by anyone who has some basic knowledge of trance induction. This knowledge may be obtained through formal instruction, but it can be acquired merely by reading a single book or by watching someone else inducing a trance. It's unfortunate that trance induction is so easily learned, for those who play around with it without a professional background in a particular discipline like medicine, dentistry, or behavioral science can cause problems to the one being hypnotized and possible harm to themselves. Hypnosis should be considered to be an adjunctive tool used by professionals trained in one of the above disciplines, and knowledge of induction techniques does not give a person expertise in the use of hypnosis as a therapeutic intervention.

According to Spiegel and Spiegel (1978), there is no evidence that the phenomenon of hypnosis itself is dangerous: "In our experience of using hypnosis with thousands of patients, we have had no case of a patient who became psychotic as a result of hypnosis" (p. 19). Conn (1972) states that there are no specific dangers unique to hypnosis, but dangers do lie in the areas of transference and countertransference. (Since those dangers exist in every form of therapy, physical or psychological, I will not elaborate on them here.)

Rosen and Bartemeier (1961) report that a few cases of dangerous effects followed hypnotherapy, mainly because poorly advised therapists or other unqualified people used hypnosis. There appears to be a consensus among many writers that the danger is not within hypnosis itself but in how it is used. Kroger (1977) states:

> The lack of documentation, personal bias, operator attitude, and hearsay evidence, together with the necessary warnings against the unwarranted current use of hypnosis . . . all contribute to exaggerated claims that hypnosis is dangerous. It is safe to say that hypnosis is the safest of all psychotherapies. (p. 386)

Kleinhauz and Beran (1981) believe there are two areas of risk involved with the use of hypnosis: 1) when a researcher uses hypnosis to accomplish experimental goals instead of therapeutic goals; and 2) when a practitioner does not recognize the potential danger involved with some particular treatment. Most practitioners have set goals that are within their range of competency, thereby eliminating this potential risk. The hypnotist who lacks professional training, however, may not be able to recognize or correctly interpret meaningful communications transmitted by the patient either verbally or nonverbally. Thus, the untrained person will not be able to react in a proper way to the patient's distress signals.

A case presented by Kleinhauz and Beran demonstrates the dangerous use of hypnosis by a person without knowledge in psychodynamics. During a hypnotic entertainment program, a girl in her mid-teens naively participated. After the program she remained drowsy. She had feelings of anger at the hypnotist which she had not expressed. Her condition became worse and gradually she went into a stupor. Her tongue collapsed into her throat, she began to gag, and was admitted to a hospital. The original hypnotist was called to see her, but despite his efforts, her condition worsened. She was in atasia abasia, and her eyeballs were rolled up into their sockets. She could neither speak nor identify people well known to her. She was retaining urine and had to be catheterized. Her blood pressure, pulse, and temperature were all normal.

Various medications were tried, but did not help. After a few days she still was not responding and had to be maintained on intravenous fluids. A series of tests were given to rule out organic brain disease: full neurological examination, EEG, EKG, spinal fluid test, cranial X-rays, and eye examination. According to her family, there were no previous signs of physical or emotional disorder.

After six more days dehypnosis was begun. Kleinhauz approached her and, with a restful and soothing voice, said, "I am a doctor, and a very good hypnotist, too. I know that you were hypnotized before. I am a much better hypnotist than the man who hypnotized you. If you are willing to let me help you, I will do so. If you want to do so, you can hear me. I will help you. Stay now in this restful condition."

At that point she responded to his voice, but to no other stimuli. Her first response was fluttering of the eyelids, and then, by opening and closing her lids, she was able to give yes and no answers to his questions. When her eyes were open, they were still rolled up into the sockets, and she failed to respond to any visual stimuli. Step by step, always allowing the patient to control the pace and to indicate a willingness to proceed, she was brought to see Kleinhauz's face, and then to perceive other visual stimuli.

In the same gradual manner, each of the other senses was brought back into function, and then she was able to start speaking again. Hunger and thirst were restored, and she began eating and drinking once more. She had total amnesia for the original hypnotic episode, but her memory was restored in a similar step by step fashion. The entire session lasted for four uninterrupted hours. It was felt that the essential part of the dehypnotic treatment was reestablishing her sense of self-control that had been so badly damaged in the prior hypnotic experience.

Kleinhauz and Beran state:

> . . . hypnopsychotherapy is a most positive expression of an appropriate hypnotic relationship, since the patient's welfare is the primary goal and the hypnotic state is a tool by which the patient expects to be helped. The focus is on the interactional process, and thus the tool becomes part of the therapy. (1981, p. 149)

Understandably, they believe that there is a greater chance of misuse of hypnosis when the goal benefits the operator rather than the subject.

Stage hypnotists frequently cause complications through their misuse of hypnosis. Many stage hypnotists perform the stunt in which suggestions of body rigidity are given under hypnosis; the stiffened subject is then placed between two chairs with his head on one and his feet on the other. The hypnotist then sits on the person's stomach or has a member of the audience stand upon it. Back injuries or aggravated hernias have resulted from this (Cheek & LeCron, 1968).

For 40 years Kroger has been a proponent of banning the use of hypnosis by stage persons. Many writers agree that such usage not only presents dangers to the subjects, but also creates a negative attitude toward hypnosis in general, causing many professionals and potential patients to view it with distrust and skepticism.

Another area of potential danger is the use of age regression by an unskilled person. This technique can open the proverbial can of worms; as a result, the subject may experience severe trauma if the operator is unable to help the subject adapt to the emotional impact of a past event that was suppressed but never reconciled.

I witnessed a very experienced and skilled therapist demonstrate the use of ideomotor responses and age regression during a training seminar for nurses. His subject, one of the students, became terribly upset when she age regressed to a traumatic period of her life. The demonstration had to be aborted so the student could be given individualized help with the released emotions. Fortunately, the operator had the necessary skill to deal with the situation himself, but I had to wonder about the wisdom of teaching these techniques to nurses who did not have a sound background in psychological matters. Incidentally, another student who was only watching the demonstration had such a severe response to what was going on upon the speaker's platform that she, too, required individualized help.

West and Deckert (1965) state that hypnosis in practice poses certain dangers:

1) *The danger of causing a recrudescence of symptoms in a patient whose illness is in remission or improving.* One example given was a schizophrenic patient who might be employing neurotic defenses to keep the psychotic symptoms at bay. Hypnosis could intensify hysterical, phobic or compulsive symptomatology.

2) *The danger of prolonging an illness or masking an illness while offering superficial relief.* Examples would be a patient who had severe pain from an infection, hypnosis being used to relieve the pain while the infection became worse, or a high school boy being hypnotized for relief of severe headaches (with some success) while an unsuspected brain tumor continued to grow.

3) *Creating excessive dependency.* Although dependency can occur in all psychotherapy, there is a possibility that it can occur much more rapidly with the use of hypnosis. There is also the possibility that because treatment with hypnosis is frequently more rapid than treatment without it, there may be less opportunity for the dependency to develop.

4) *Using hypnosis for sexual seduction.* William Bryant used to teach that he was certain that many young men had used hypnosis for this purpose, but that he was equally certain that they had wasted considerable time by resorting to hypnosis. This glib commentary may or may not be accurate, but it does not take into account an important issue: Although it is unlikely anyone could be *forced* into sexual activity through the use of hypnosis, the "victim" might engage in activity that would be refused, except for the convenience of having an excuse, "I would never have done that if I hadn't been hypnotized."

5) *Using hypnosis to enroll the patient in criminal activity*. Experts are split in their opinions about this possibility, but probably what is true for the preceding danger is also true here.

Do the "dangers" of self-hypnosis constitute a contradindication to hypnosis? We must realize that a person may enter an autohypnotic state by watching television, daydreaming, praying, meditating, etc. Cheek and LeCron (1968) state that a few psychiatrists believe that a patient might form fantasies with the use of self-hypnosis and experience difficulties because of their denial of reality. Of course, patients form fantasies with self-hypnosis; we teach them to do so, although we are apt to label them "images" rather than "fantasies."

Cheek and LeCron state that they knew of no one who has ever had a bad result or found any danger in self-hypnosis. Edelstien (1981) reports that one of his patients became so enthralled with the fantasies which she created when in self-hypnosis that she spent excessive time enjoying them. This interfered with her performance on the job and took precedence over her usual social activities. After a few months she became tired of doing that and started writing a novel based upon the fantasies she had created. There were no long-term difficulties.

Kroger (1977) suggests the following safeguards in teaching autohypnosis: Give accurate and precise instructions about how and when to practice; offer definite suggestions for termination; and know how to select patients for autohypnosis. Using those safeguards, Kroger states that he has used various methods of teaching self-hypnosis to hundreds of selected patients and as yet fails to see any dangers.

In summary, then, it seems that if the operator is skilled in his particular specialty, uses hypnosis only within the area of his expertise, and only for purposes that are genuinely in the best interests of the patient, there are no specific contraindications to hypnosis.

References

Cheek, D. B., & LeCron, L. M. (1968). *Clinical hypnotherapy*. New York: Grune & Stratton, p. 68.
Conn, J. H. (1972). Is hypnosis really dangerous? *International Journal of Clinical and Experimental Hypnosis, 20*, 61.
Edelstien, M. G. (1981). *Trauma, trance and transformation*. New York: Brunner/Mazel.
Kleinhauz, M., & Beran, B. (1981). Misuses of hypnosis: A medical emergency and its treatment. *International Journal of Clinical and Experimental Hypnosis, 29*, 148–161.
Kroger, W. S. (1977). *Clinical and experimental hypnosis*. Philadelphia: Lippincott, pp. 90, 103.
Rosen, H., & Bartemeier, L. (1961). Hypnosis in medical practice. *Journal of the American Medical Association, 75*, 128.
Spiegel, H., & Spiegel, D. (1978). *Trance and treatment: Clinical uses of hypnosis*. New York: Basic Books.
West, L. J., & Deckert, G. (1965). Dangers of hypnosis. *Journal of the American Medical Association, 192*, 9.

Q&A 51 Using Hypnosis With Patients With Seizures

Question:

> Is hypnosis contraindicated in a patient with seizures? If not, are there any special precautions that should be taken?

Discussion by DONALD W. SCHAFER, M.D.

Hypnosis is not contraindicated in a patient with seizures, nor do I know of any special precautions that need be taken with such patients, assuming there is a valid indication for hypnotherapy in the first place.

Conversely, there may be specific indications for hypnosis and self-hypnosis in at least some of these patients, since many of them can be helped to control or eliminate the episodes. I have a few prerequisites before attempting this kind of work:

1) The patient must have had a good neurological examination to rule out the possibility of tumor, vascular disorders, drug withdrawal, or other physical conditions that might require specific medical or surgical management.
2) The patient must have auras, those feelings or experiences that precede the actual seizures. Some patients describe their auras as flashes of light; others, as giddy feelings; still others have different descriptions, but in each case it is important that the patient have some way of knowing that a seizure is imminent.
3) The patient must have had the experience of aborting at least one seizure. It does not seem to matter if the attacks are of the petit mal or the grand mal variety, as long as there is a history of having had an aura and preventing the full-blown seizure from occurring.

If these criteria are met, treatment might be very simple. What I do is

279

learn how the patient aborted the one seizure, then teach him/her self-hypnosis and offer instructions so that the patient can use self-hypnosis to recreate the situation in which the attack was aborted. A brief case example illustrates this technique.

A 29-year-old unmarried man had a history of mixed seizures. Most were of the petit mal variety, but he had grand mal ones as well. His periods of unconsciousness from one type of attack or the other were frequent enough and long enough that he had developed a schizoid life style. He was unable to work, lived with his married sister, and had become very reclusive. He was on antiseizure medication, but he continued to have frequent episodes despite that. He was also in psychotherapy, and it was his therapist who referred him to me.

On careful inquiry I learned that sometimes he could abort his seizures by turning on loud music. He was an excellent hypnotic subject who could "experience" hearing loud music when this was suggested to him. I taught him self-hypnosis and instructed him that at the first sign of his aura he was to put himself into a trance and hallucinate the music. For all intents and purposes his seizures ceased. Follow-up more than a year later indicated that these good results were being maintained.

Patients with multiple personality disorder often have been misdiagnosed as having petit mal, temporal lobe seizures, fugue states, hysteria, etc. There are still many practitioners who do not recognize this disorder, and even deny its existence, so when they are presented with a patient with recurring episodes of amnesia they are inclined to misdiagnose and place the patient on antiseizure medication.

Antiseizure medicine is useless, of course, for the treatment of multiple personality disorder, but I did see one patient who had multiple personality and a seizure disorder as well. She had a nicely defined aura that enabled her to recognize the presence of an impending attack. She, like all multiple personality patients, was an excellent hypnotic subject. She was taught how to do self-hypnosis and how to call upon one of her other personalities to emerge at the first sign of an aura. Although I cannot explain it on any physiological basis that I know, this simple maneuver enabled her to remain seizure free.

This technique is not the only one that can be used with seizure patients. We know that when a patient is under stress, the chances of a seizure are increased. Any relaxation method that the patient can learn will help diminish his level of stress and thus improve his condition. Hypnosis and self-hypnosis are ideally suited for this and can benefit many patients.

"Analytic" techniques may also be employed. Since Charcot proposed the concept of hystero-epilepsy in the middle of the last century, we have known that many patients have a high psychogenic overlay to their epilepsies. Using hypnosis for dream work is one way to better understand the psychological problems that aggravate the illness, but my preference is the affect bridge (Schafer, 1981), which allows exploration of the origin of the seizures.

I recently heard of one lady with a seizure disorder, but without EEG changes, for whom this affect bridge worked very well. While in a hypnotic state she was asked to focus on the feelings that she had prior to a seizure. She was then asked to regress to the time that she first had those feelings. She went back to a period just prior to a surgical procedure she had had, and recalled a statement that she had misinterpreted as a prediction that she was going to die.

Perhaps there is still another way in which hypnosis might be used to help these patients, although I consider it highly speculative at this point. I cannot remember the source of my information, but I've heard that with hypnotic training a person can be taught to alter his/her brain wave patterns at the time of an impending seizure. This requires the use of a brain wave monitor, and might best be accomplished in a biofeedback setting.

I think it important to note that the patients in whom we are most interested are those whose seizures are not well regulated despite careful adjustments of anticonvulsant medication. The well regulated patients are unlikely to seek our help anyway, but if one should, I believe it would be unwise to offer hypnotherapy in place of a medication that is working well.

Finally, although I imagine that a seizure could be set off in hypnosis, I do not see that as a specific contraindication. I would advise against suggesting that the hypnotized patient have a seizure, not only because of the difficulties it would cause him, if the suggestion worked, but also because of the difficulties the therapist would face in dealing with it. At first glance it might seem as though this caution is absurdly obvious, but some therapists, when teaching pain control, have the patient increase his own pain and then diminish it; some, when teaching control of asthma, have the patient precipitate an attack and then relieve it. I would not use that technique with these patients. I myself have advocated "As-If-ECT" (Schafer, 1960) for patients who had previously had a good result from ECT and then experienced another breakdown similar to the one for which the shock therapy had been given. In doing so, however, I used hypnotic imagery to guide the patient through another series of shock treatments, step by step, *except* for the actual application of the electrical charge that caused the convulsions. Had I included that step I do not know if the patient would have convulsed or not, but it seemed senseless to take that chance.

References

Schafer, D. W. (1960). As-if electroshock therapy. *American Journal of Clinical Hypnosis, 2*, 4.

Schafer, D. W. (1981). The recognition and hypnotherapy of patients with unrecognized altered states. *American Journal of Clinical Hypnosis, 23*, 3.

Q & A 52 Hypnosis and Pain Management

Question:

> What are some of the techniques for using hypnosis to control pain and how effective are they? How does one select a specific technique for a specific patient?

Discussion by DABNEY M. EWIN, M.D.

There are many techniques for pain control with which a hypnotherapist should be familiar. As with analgesic medicines, a particular patient may respond to one and not another. Each therapist should become skilled and comfortable with at least two of these and know where to find information on the others when necessary. To answer these questions, I will give a short comment on several (with references to sources for more complete elaboration). Then I will go into some detail about those with which I've had most success.

Mesmeric passes by hypnotechnicians were all that Esdaile (1850) needed to get sufficient anaesthesia for 3000 surgical procedures. This takes one-half to four hours and is rarely used today, though some renewed interest is occurring (Pulos, 1980).

Direct suggestion in hypnosis consists of inducing a trance and giving the suggestion deemed most appropriate by the hypnotist. It is effective during the trance, but *chronic* pain usually recurs on arousal, making it only a little more effective than placebo. It is most useful with highly hypnotizable subjects and in *acute* painful situations. Because of its simplicity it may be used almost as a test of hypnotizability. As with placebo, it is not reliable for long-term relief of chronic pain.

The *interspersal* technique is a means of giving indirect suggestions interspersed in an irrelevant discussion. It is best exemplified by Erickson's (1966) rhapsody about a tomato plant while treating a cancer patient. Because the tomato plant is irrelevant to the patient's pain problem, he is not alert to mobilizing his resistance to change and his subconscious is given free rein with healing thoughts. This is quite effective in skilled hands.

Glove anesthesia can be produced by suggestion and then transferred to the involved area. This is relatively easy for short-term analgesia and may be a convincing demonstration of trance capacity for a skeptical patient (Crasilneck & Hall, 1975, p. 59). It is a form of direct suggestion.

Guided imagery with suggestions to resume the trance state when needed produced adequate analgesia in 99 of 100 consecutive dental patients in Barber's (1977) series.

Hypnoanalysis is my favorite approach for chronic pain, and it is not difficult. The techniques described by Cheek and LeCron (1968) and Barnett (1981) work well, even though Barnett says little about pain in his book.

Chronic Pain

Hypnosis is only part of the chronic pain clinic approach which includes physical therapy, nerve blocks, group psychotherapy, TENS (transcutaneous electric nerve stimulation), relaxation, movement and occupational therapy, medicines, etc., as well as surgery if indicated. With all this about one-third get well, one-third improve, and one-third are unimproved. A change in attitude engendered by hypnosis enables the patient to cope much better.

Constant pain is a special complaint that is heard often in pain clinics and may not be amenable to any treatment other than hypnoanalysis. Webster defines "constant" as "something that does not vary or change in an essential relationship," and this distinguishes it from other words that define severity or unresponsiveness to treatment, such as "intractable," "incapacitating," "chronic," "unrelenting," "unbearable," "excruciating," etc. When the patient says the pain is constant, never goes away, is continuous, always there, and "I live with it," the subconscious corollary is, "If I didn't have it, I'd be dead." This idea equates pain with life itself; therefore, the pain cannot be relinquished *completely* even for five minutes. The patient may admit to some variation of intensity, but will maintain vehemently that the pain (like life) is present all the time, even when asleep.

Physical pain is rarely, if ever, constant. Cancer pain can be completely relieved for several hours by medication. Arthritis has remissions or is relieved by heat, rest, and medicine. A patient with a ruptured disc will report that rest in a certain position gives relief. The therapist should ask the patient in the waking state, "Since this started, has there ever been *any* time when you were completely free of pain?" and "What about when you were asleep?" If the patient answers "no" to these questions, then the pain is more likely psychological than physical, and the patient may have a *constant pain syndrome* (Ewin, 1980).

Because self-preservation is the first law of nature, survival is more important than pain (i.e., being alive and in pain is better than being dead without it). When at an emotional level pain is equated with life, then as long as the pain is present death cannot have occurred, and the pain gives subconscious reassurance of this. Paradoxically, the therapist who proposes to end pain (life) is a threat to the patient, and the intuitive therapist will sense the limited trust extended and know that a direct attack on the pain with hypnotic suggestions will be rejected even in deep trance. The "grand indifference" of conversion hysteria is different from the defensiveness these patients show. They seem to know there is a cure and seek it hopefully, but faced with conventional treatment they heroically resist giving up control of the pain (life).

The *constant pain syndrome* is characterized by the simultaneous occurrence of three things (Ewin's triad): 1) *mental disorientation* in which the patient may have had a concussion, a drug overdose, a stroke, an anesthetic, or even a vivid dream causing him to be unable to respond or react in a normal way; 2) *fear of death* in which the experience is perceived as life-threatening; and 3) *pain*. Being mentally unable to deal with the perceived threat of death, the presence of pain is reassurance to the subconscious that he can't have died yet. When normal mentation returns, the subconscious clings tenaciously to the deeply imprinted idea that pain equals life, and changing this idea is the goal of therapy.

Discussion of these dynamics in the waking state will be rejected summarily and will mobilize the patient's defenses to maintain his pain (life). Treatment involves establishing rapport, regressing to the incident, expressing empathy and understanding of the value of the pain at the time, and making the point that "even though it seemed so bad then, we *know* now that you didn't die, don't we?" and insisting on a response to that question. Then, after asking the patient to use ideomotor signals to respond, the therapist asks, "Does the deepest part of your inner mind really know that you survived and are fully alive?" After getting a "yes" signal to that, the therapist says, "Since the pain was the only way you knew you were alive when it happened, it must have been very reassuring then, but now that you have recovered all the usual ways of knowing you're alive, do you still need the *pain* to prove you're alive?" The "no" signal to this leads to the clincher: "Since you don't need the pain any longer, and you came here to get rid of it, would it be all right to just let it go?" "Yes" to this is good news and bad news.

The patient has just agreed to abandon a life support system he has relied on for months or years. In my experience he invariably has second thoughts and paradoxically *increases* the pain on the evening of the day he agreed to relinquish it! He should be seen the next morning to vent his anger about "What the hell did you do to me?" which I counter with, "So you were able to make it worse. That's wonderful! It means you've taken control of your pain. If you can make it worse, you can make it better whenever you choose. Would you like to cut it in half right now?" He's in a bind because he just complained about the pain, so I put him right into trance and tell him to give a "yes" signal when it is half as intense as it was on coming to my office. Next I ask, "Would it be all right to have one minute of being completely free of pain, realizing it is better to be alive *without* pain than to be alive *with* pain?" Assent to this calls for an ideomotor signal when he is completely free of pain, and I time one minute for him. This leads to the suggestion that if he can do it for one minute, then whenever he's ready he can do it for two, four, eight, ad infinitum.

Some patients have so much secondary gain involved from pensions, social security, worker's compensation, liability litigation, or family manipulation that a sudden, miraculous cure would be embarrassing or self-defeating. Do not overtreat to satisfy your own ego. These patients need a suggestion that, "Knowing now that you can control your pain, whenever you are ready, you will be able to diminish your pain to a minimal and tolerable level, or turn it off completely at will." One of my patients, who for four and a half years was confined to his chair and bed (Ewin, 1980, Case 2), was on pension and social security at age 54. Follow-up three years after treatment revealed that he was comfortable at leisure, could play with his grandchildren, hunt and fish, but exertion such as attempting to mow the lawn caused pain and he had not returned to work. His solution was much better than total incapacitation!

Pain is a feeling (an emotion?), and pure pain without emotional overlay or conditioning is experimentally quite tolerable (Melzac, 1973, p. 27). Other feelings that increase suffering need to be explored (Ewin, 1978), since they provide overlay that can be moderated.

Nonacceptance is a problem because the pain is imposed against the patient's will. "Why me?" stands as a barrier to treatment, for the patient refuses to move on until that question is answered. There is no satisfactory answer, and I bypass it in trance by first interspersing into my induction "*pure* pain doesn't really hurt that much" and later asking for an ideomotor answer to "Would it be all right for you to experience a small amount of pure pain as long as it is at a tolerable level?" The patient who gives this permission feels he has regained some control and will extend that control to keeping the pain pure and at a tolerable level.

Fear of being the victim of some unusual or undiagnosable disorder mounts as weeks and months of inconclusive tests and differing medical opinions go on. In trance a positive ideomotor answer to "Is it all right to bring to consciousness any fears that you have?" will uncover these fears and allow the therapist to dispel them with the facts. The patient should be taught self-hypnotic methods of rejecting negative ideas in the future.

Negative interpretation of the meaning of the pain adds to suffering. The therapist should ask the patient to signal his answer to "Is there any possible good that can come out of this?" and if so bring it up to consciousness. Beecher's (1959, p. 165) battlefield studies in Korea showed that the severely injured soldier would often refuse analgesics, responding to his "painful" wound with " . . . relief, thankfulness at his escape alive from the battlefield, even euphoria," interpreting it as a "good" wound. Another question is, "What do you know about this condition?" which may get an answer like "I know that once a person hurts his back he never gets well." Such an idea must be removed.

Endless suffering is a threat that hangs over the chronic pain patient, and he may wonder if he can stand it indefinitely or if he will ever get relief. I intersperse "no pain lasts forever" in my induction at each visit, and after several visits it tends to be accepted.

Guilt and anger add greatly to suffering and should be brought out whenever pain results from an accident. If the patient was negligent, he feels stupid and guilty and the pain serves as subconscious punishment. If someone else is at fault, he blames that person and nurtures his anger in proportion to his suffering. Forgiveness of self treats guilt; forgiveness of another cures anger. If litigation is in progress, I point out that forgiving the *person* who injured him does not vitiate his legal right to recovery. Nonetheless, his anger is magnifying his own suffering and misery, while the object of his anger is unhurt. I assume the role of spokesman for my patient's adversary, apologize for the physical injury and hurt feelings, and beg forgiveness. He is not always ready to forgive right away, but when he does his suffering is greatly relieved and his ego boosted. He somehow feels a better person than before.

Negative suggestions must be removed. Quite often these patients will volunteer in waking history that the doctor said, "You have to learn to live with it." Taken literally (as the subconscious does), this means you must die to get rid of it, an idea that obstructs treatment. In trance this should be removed and replaced with, "You will find you can cope with it."

Identification with another person who had a similar pain needs investigation. Pain that started with the terminal illness of a loved one and mimics that person's pain is treated by bringing to consciousness the fact that the pain won't bring the departed back and that it would be better to keep the happy memories and lay aside the miserable ones. Having pain is an inappropriate way to mourn.

Surgery that unexpectedly failed to relieve pain should be reviewed in trance. Patients hear under anesthesia (and with concussions), and pessimistic comments by the surgeon are embedded like posthypnotic suggestions.

Details of the technique to uncover this have been described elsewhere (Ewin, 1984, p. 214).

Self-hypnosis is a useful adjunct to treatment and reinforces whatever progress has been made. Because everyone normally passes through a trance-equivalent state in going from the waking to sleep states, I have my patients give themselves suggestions or, better yet, use a tape at night just as they are falling asleep. Proponents of self-hypnosis as a discrete therapy (Alman, 1983) anecdotally report good results, which I assume are comparable to direct suggestions in hypnosis.

Acute Pain

In any acutely painful situation such as dislocated shoulder, fracture, burn, etc., the patient's fear focuses his attention into a trance-equivalent state and all that is needed for induction is to say, "I'm the doctor. I can help you. Will you do what I say?" When he agrees to do what I say without testing it, he has made a commitment as good as agreeing to carry out a posthypnotic suggestion. Then I say, "Just lie down here, close your eyes, take a deep breath, and as you let it out let all the tension go out of every nerve and fiber in your body." From there I go to some sort of imagery that the patient associates with laughter and dissociate the extremity if it is a fracture or dislocation. If the patient is burned, *early* hypnosis (first two hours) with the anti-inflammatory suggestion "cool and comfortable" will markedly attenuate burn depth (Ewin, 1978), and in burns over less than 20% of body surface a single trance will often eliminate pain until healed. In larger burns, repeated hypnosis will reduce requested narcotics by 50% (Wakeman & Kaplan, 1978). A detailed verbalization of emergency burn care has been published and should be reviewed by those treating burn patients (Ewin, 1984, pp. 221–225).

References

Alman, B. M. (1983). *Self-hypnosis*. San Diego: International Health Publications.
Barber, J. (1977). Rapid induction analgesia. *American Journal of Clinical Hypnosis, 19*, 138.
Barnett, E. A. (1981). *Analytical hypnotherapy: Principles and practice*. Kingston, Ontario: Junica.
Beecher, H. K. (1959). *Measurement of subjective responses*. Oxford: Oxford University Press.
Cheek, D. B. & LeCron, L. M. (1968). Pain: Its meaning and treatment. In *Clinical Hypnotherapy* (pp. 142–152). New York: Grune & Stratton.
Crasilneck, H. B. & Hall, J. A. (1975). *Clinical hypnosis: Principles and applications*. New York: Grune & Stratton.
Erickson, M. H. (1966). The interspersal hypnotic technique for symptom correction and pain control. *American Journal of Clinical Hypnosis, 3*, 198–209.
Esdaile, J. (1957). *Hypnosis in medicine and surgery*. New York: Julian Press. (Reprinted from the original *Mesmerism in India*, 1850)
Ewin, D. M. (1978). Relieving suffering and pain with hypnosis. *Geriatrics, 33*:87–89.

Ewin, D. M. (1980). Constant pain syndrome: Its psychological meaning and cure using hypno-analysis. In H. J. Wain (Ed.). *Clinical Hypnosis in Medicine*. Chicago: Year Book Medical Publishers.

Ewin, D. M. (1984). Hypnosis in surgery and anesthesia. In W. C. Wester, II, & A. H. Smith, Jr. (Eds.). *Clinical hypnosis: A multidisciplinary approach*. (pp. 210–235). Philadelphia: Lippincott.

Hilgard, E. R. & Hilgard, J. R. (1975). *Hypnosis in the relief of pain*. Los Altos, CA: William Kaufmann.

Melzac, R. (1973). *The puzzle of pain*. New York: Basic Books.

Pulos, L. (1980). Mesmerism revisited: The effectiveness of Esdaile's techniques in the production of deep hypnosis and total body hypnoanesthesia. *American Journal of Clinical Hypnosis, 22*, 206–211.

Wakeman, R. J. & Kaplan, J. Z. (1978). An experimental study of hypnosis in painful burns. *American Journal of Clinical Hypnosis, 21*, 3.

$\underset{\mathit{A}}{\overset{Q}{\mathit{\&}}}53$ Hypnosis With Psychotic and Borderline Patients

Question:

Is hypnosis appropriate for patients diagnosed as borderline or psychotic? If so, what type of inductions and suggestions work best and what kinds of safeguards need to be employed?

Discussion by ELGAN L. BAKER, Ph.D.

As clinical hypnosis has developed over the past two decades, alterations in technique have resulted in the application of hypnotherapy with a broadening range of patient populations and presenting problems. In many ways, this trend has paralleled developments within the general psychotherapy literature. In particular, considerable attention has been focused on the psychotherapy of primitive and severely disturbed individuals, including borderline and psychotic patients. Hypnosis has also been increasingly utilized in the therapeutic management of these patients. Appropriate utilization of hypnosis with severely disturbed patients requires careful consideration of issues related to susceptibility, trance induction, indications and trance utilization.

Susceptibility

More than 40 empirical studies have appeared in the literature since 1950 investigating the question of hypnotic susceptibility with borderline and psychotic patients. Most of these have compared the hypnotizability of schizophrenics to normals or other diagnostic groups on standardized hypnotic susceptibility scales. This research has consistently demonstrated that psychotics and borderlines are generally comparable to normal subjects and to neurotic patients in their susceptibility to hypnosis (Abrams, 1964; Baker,

1983; Greene, 1976; Vingoe & Kramer, 1966). Acute psychotics appear to be slightly more susceptible than chronics, schizophrenic and affective psychotic patients evidence comparable degrees of hypnotizability, and there is no evidence that pharmacotherapy significantly affects susceptibility scores (Baker, 1984). Most researchers have concluded that severely disturbed patients can achieve trance states with relatively brief standard inductions, although more clinical success is achieved with cooperative, motivated, and nonparanoid patients. Further, both literature review and clinical experience indicate that the judicious utilization of hypnotherapy does not precipitate unmodulated regression or dissociative experiences with these patients, nor does it interfere with reconstitutive processes. Rather, it can support ego functions and facilitate recovery and broad therapeutic gains (Baker, 1981, 1983; Fromm, 1984; Scagnelli, 1975, 1976).

Induction

Most induction strategies commonly used in clinical work may be effectively employed with borderline and psychotic patients (Kramer & Brennan, 1964). In general, permissive but structured inductions appear to work best. With severely disturbed patients, a variety of dynamic concerns need to be kept in mind during the induction process (Baker, 1983; Scagnelli, 1976). These include:

- *fear of loss of control*, which can be managed by permissiveness, reassurance, the use of non-authoritarian and open-ended suggestions and instruction in autohypnosis as soon as possible;
- *fear of closeness, boundary intrusion and merger*, which can be managed by providing clear and consistent structure, allowing the patient maximum freedom in determining trance depth, and supporting observing ego (self-observation and self-monitoring) functions;
- *fear of loss of the therapist* through abandonment or destruction, which can be managed by allowing patients to open their eyes at will during trance to confirm the therapist's presence and by providing clear limits and direct answers regarding the therapist's powers and abilities to care for the patient and to contain the intensity of affect and impulse; and
- *fear of loss of identity*, which can be managed by reassurance, suggestion, interpretation and directed imagery focusing on the guided process of growing, becoming and doing better rather than on totally positive observations or totally unacceptable messages.

Induction strategies which involve a combination of relaxation, guided imagery, and fantasy have been most efficacious, especially when feelings of comfort, security, continued body integrity and self-control are emphasized.

Indications

Hypnosis should not be attempted with borderline and psychotic patients until a therapeutic alliance has been established. Until this point, hypnosis may result in untoward regressions and abreactions which may precipitate negative transference and resistance sufficient to interrupt the therapeutic process. However, selected hypnotic techniques may be utilized with these patients early in treatment to manage the frequently intense, labile and negative transferences and to support the evolution of the working alliance (Baker, 1981; Fromm, 1984; Scagnelli, 1974, 1975, 1976). These techniques utilize circumscribed trance experiences and directed imagery to establish a positive internal representation of the therapist and to evoke and support the affective availability necessary for the development of rapport in psychotherapy.

Hypnosis can be helpful with these patients in: provision of ego support and mastery; management of disturbances in boundary integrity and identity; modulation and abreaction of disruptive affect; support of the therapeutic alliance; management of resistance; symptom amelioration; and support and stimulation of interpretive, working-through and integrative processes in the ongoing treatment.

Utilization

With borderline and psychotic patients hypnosis is most appropriately used as part of a more general intensive treatment regimen. It is most constructively introduced within the context of long-term, insight-oriented psychotherapy and may be utilized concurrently with antipsychotic medication. Therapists should realize that the introduction of hypnosis into the psychotherapy situation typically intensifies the transference in a rapid and dramatic fashion. Therefore, a viable working alliance and an essentially positive transference constitute the best environment for utilizing hypnotic strategies with these patients.

A wide variety of utilization techniques may be employed, including abreactive, supportive, suggestive, mastery-oriented and integrative approaches. Such strategies are typically incorporated into an integrated program which focuses on such goals as the support and restoration of the patient's capacity for object-relatedness; the stabilization of the therapeutic relationship and treatment process; the structuralization and support of a variety of ego functions, including reality-testing and impulse control; the modulation of specific symptoms such as hallucinations and delusions; and the facilitation of working-through in psychotherapy. A case example will illustrate some of these issues.

Eugene was a 19-year-old white male who became progressively withdrawn and dysfunctional during the first semester of his freshman year at
college. While at home for Christmas vacation, he became increasingly ob-
sessed with the cleanliness of his home and phobic of germs and contamination. He spent most of his time alone in his room, inspecting his clothing,
bedding and furniture for lice, maggots or other vermin. Shortly after returning to school, the patient became acutely psychotic and reported voices
accusing him of having various venereal diseases. The patient was seen shortly after his admission to the adult inpatient unit of a teaching hospital. He
was minimally verbal, uncooperative and fearful of physical contact with
other patients or staff. Eugene was reluctant to engage in psychotherapy.
During our third session hypnosis was introduced to support the security of
his boundaries, to enhance his sense of comfort with interpersonal involvement, to begin to contain the regressive pull of his impulses, and to reinforce the development of a positive therapeutic alliance. This was considered
to be an appropriate and necessary intervention to diffuse negative transference intrusions and to provide for a secure and gratifying experience of
involvement with the therapist. Hypnosis was introduced as an opportunity
to enhance self-control and feelings of safety.

The patient proved to be a good subject, and trance was induced utilizing a structured, yet permissive, relaxation induction. Following deepening with images which emphasized comfort and security, the patient was
encouraged to open his eyes to check to see that he and the therapist were
still there and that the treatment room remained the same as before he
entered trance. Eugene was visibly relaxed by this reassurance, which was
elaborated with observations regarding the consistency, reliability and
security of the environment and the emerging therapeutic relationship. At
this point, an arm catalepsy was suggested. The following vignette is taken
from this portion of the hypnotherapeutic work.

THERAPIST: Just feel how strong your arm is there. Each muscle connected
          to the other from your fingertips to your shoulder. Strong and solid
          and powerful. Focus on that feeling of strength, Gene. It's your arm
          and your body and your strength. Can you feel it?
EUGENE: (Nods head yes) It's there.
THERAPIST: That's right . . . the strength is there . . . and you're here. Here
          with me in my office. It's good to know that you can feel strong and
          safe here when we're together. You can feel a sense of power sufficient
          to help you feel secure for a while. It's *your* strength which you can
          use whenever you need to, whenever you want to so that we can come
          together and work together and help your sense of power and security
          to grow.
EUGENE: I'm afraid of germs and worms and other terms . . . that . . .

uh . . . scare and tear and bare . . . uh . . . me, see. (Laughs and shakes head)

THERAPIST: I understand. So let's just use your strength to weave a special cloth, a blanket . . . a suit of armor to protect you from intrusion or contamination. Just feel that strength expand to every part of you from the top of your head to the tips of your toes. As it does, imagine that you can see a beautiful, strong suit of armor in your mind's eye. Every part of you can be covered. Clean and safe.

EUGENE: Yes, I feel it . . . I do.

THERAPIST: Good. That sense of strength can be with you when we're together, and it can help you to feel safe when we're apart. It can help you know that each part of you is connected, just as it should be and nothing . . . *nothing* can get inside or come outside unless you choose for it to happen.

Following this work on boundary reinforcement, hypnotic imagery was utilized to support the patient's sense of security in alligning himself with the therapist. Such techniques proved useful in facilitating a sufficiently positive and strong working alliance to allow for continuing psychotherapy to evolve.

The use of hypnosis with borderline and psychotic patients appears to be generally safe, has varied clinical indications, and has been demonstrated to be useful as part of an ongoing program of intensive treatment. The clinical and empirical literature in this area continues to grow. Despite reports of clinical success, the contributions of hypnosis to the treatment of these patients has not been fully substantiated through careful and controlled research. Such research is now appropriate, necessary and imminent. In the meantime, the clinical use of hypnosis with these patients is best recommended to colleagues experienced both in hypnotherapy and in intensive psychotherapy with borderlines and psychotics.

References

Abrams, S. (1964). The use of hypnotic techniques with psychotics. *American Journal of Psychiatry, 18,* 79–94.

Baker, E. L. (1981). An hypnotherapeutic approach to enhance object relatedness in psychotic patients. *International Journal of Clinical and Experimental Hypnosis, 29*(2), 136–147.

Baker, E. L. (April 1983). The use of hypnotic techniques with psychotics. *American Journal of Clinical Hypnosis, 25,* 4.

Baker, E. L. (1984). Hypnotherapy with severely disturbed patients. In G. Pratt, D. Wood, & B. Alman (Eds.). *A clinical hypnosis primer.* La Jolla: Psychology and Consulting Associates Press.

Fromm, E. (1984). Hypnoanalysis with special reference to the borderline patient. *Psychoanalytic Psychology, 1,* 67–78.

Greene, J. T. (1976). Hypnotizability of hospitalized psychotics. *International Journal of Clinical and Experimental Hypnosis, 27*, 103–108.

Kramer, E., & Brennan, E. P. (1964). Hypnotic susceptibility of schizophrenic patients. *Journal of Abnormal and Social Psychology, 64*, 657–659.

Scagnelli, J. (July 1974). A case of hypnotherapy with an acute schizophrenic. *American Journal of Clinical Hypnosis, 17*, 1.

Scagnelli, J. (July 1975). Therapy with eight schizophrenic and borderline patients: Summary of a therapy approach that employs a semi-symbiotic bond between patient and therapist. *Journal of Clinical Psychology, 31*(3), 519–525.

Scagnelli, J. (1976). Hypnotherapy with schizophrenic and borderline patients: Summary of therapy with 8 patients. *American Journal of Clinical Hypnosis, 19*, 33–38.

Vingoe, F. J., & Kramer, E. F. (1966). Hypnotic susceptibility of hospitalized patients: A pilot study. *International Journal of Clinical and Experimental Hypnosis, 14*, 47–54.

Hypnosis in the Treatment
of Genital Herpes

Question:

A client told me she uses imagery to head off or mitigate herpes flare-ups. Is there evidence that hypnosis is a generally effective treatment for genital herpes? What hypnotic methods have been the most helpful?

Discussion by SOL S. GOULD, Ph.D.

Historically, herpes simplex has been treated in a variety of generally unsuccessful ways. A person with the disease often feels helpless and resigned to recurrences over which he or she feels no control (Himell, 1981). Hope has been given, however, that the factors that lead to recurrence can be identified and controlled, since, as Glogau (1980) and others note, herpes flare-ups seem to be related to stress.

The fact that hypnosis has been used to *produce* herpes simplex gives hope that it can also be used to help get rid of it or at least reduce its severity. Helig and Hoff produced herpes simplex in proved herpes virus carriers by hypnotically suggesting unpleasant emotionally stimulating situations (Scott, 1960). Herpes has also been produced by hypnotic suggestion in a 27-year-old soldier. Twenty-four hours later, an occurrence of one large blister and satellite smaller blisters about his lower lip was diagnosed by a skin consultant as herpes simplex (Ullman, 1947).

On the other side, there have been a number of reports of reducing the number and duration of herpes flare-ups by use of hypnosis. Scott provides a number of such examples and writes that emotional tension may precipitate flare-ups of the disease, which is of definite organic etiology. "In some way emotional reactions activate the virus that may be residing dormant in the host, or activates the cutaneous response to its presence" (Scott, 1960, p. 119).

One case in point is a 32-year-old single woman with a master's degree in education who contracted genital herpes approximately three years prior to her initial consultation with the author. She had lived with the condition flaring up once a month and lasting several days; however, at the time of consultation the condition had grown to a "full-blown attack," causing considerably more difficulty. The original condition was described as tiny blisters only two or three millimeters in size intermittently covering an area of one centimeter, while the full-blown attack was described as severe blisters completely covering an area over two centimeters wide. The blisters erupted and created an itching and burning sensation which also seemed connected, in her case, to a rash on her perineum and anus. This attack lasted two weeks and recurred only a few days after the previous episode. She had exhausted all available medical approaches and had referred herself for hypnotherapy as a last resort. She realized that stress was one of the trigger components of her attacks. During the evaluation session, she mentioned that she felt anger toward her previous boyfriend for giving her the infection. Her attacks were exacerbated by the fact that she had a new boyfriend and was afraid to tell him. She seemed overcome by fear and guilt and was buying time in their relationship so that she could tell her new boyfriend about the disease once she felt more confident.

Spiegel's Hypnosis Induction Profile (1974) was administered. The subject was judged to be a four, the highest possible score. The plan for hypnosis started with ego-strengthening suggestions (Hartland, 1971). A quiet period of two minutes then allowed the integration of these suggestions. Following the strategy of visualization used in cancer therapy (Simonton, Matthews-Simonton, & Creighton, 1978), suggestions were made of a strong cell structure, perfect skin, hormonal balance, cleanliness, and a cooling refreshed feeling in the area of the vagina and perineum. Imagery of internally controlled friendly white sharks was used to "devour" the virus. Since the patient also enjoyed water- and snow-skiing, imagery of cool breezes, white refreshing snow, and clean fresh water was incorporated into these images. She visualized herself forgiving and releasing her previous boyfriend of guilt, thereby allowing her anger to abate. Before the termination of the sessions, a posthypnotic suggestion of a "cool, quiet, pleasant, normal, healthy feeling" was imparted to the client. Each time she was hypnotized, she would be surprised at her delightful feelings of health. This session was reinforced by a third session within two days.

The therapy plan was to use a nondirective approach plus visualization. The client was taught to use self-hypnosis utilizing a breathing technique and hand levitation. A tape was made using general ego-strengthening suggestions, and another tape was made utilizing the patient's fantasy of water- and snow-skiing. She used the two tapes every night and enjoyed practicing the visualizations. The patient felt that hypnosis helped her acquire a more positive attitude toward herself and relief of guilt and blame, as well as an improved ability to cope with the unpleasant sensations. Following her ability to relax and lower her anxiety level, she was able to go for three months without a recurrence.

The second case is a 26-year-old married woman who contracted genital herpes approximately four years prior to the initial consultation. The initial lesion was one inch across and one-half inch wide, appearing on the buttocks. Before the patient referred herself to us, three occurrences were noted of the same size in a four month period. She came to the clinic to learn to lessen her anxiety, believing nothing could be done about the lesions themselves. The peculiar position of the lesion corresponded to an area of the thigh which comes in contact with toilet seats: she had never heard of contracting herpes in this manner. Since she had had no extramarital contact, she suspected that her husband was having outside contact; however, he remained asymptomatic. She was perplexed and distressed.

This subject was also judged to be a four on Spiegel's Hypnosis Induction Profile. Ego-strengthening suggestions were again used, after which a quiet period of two minutes was allowed to pass to integrate these suggestions. Visualizations of white healing lights were used during the first and second sessions. Suggestions of a strong cell structure, perfect skin, cleanliness, and tranquility in the area of the infection were used. She visualized herself bathed in white lights and traveling through concentric circles radiating peace and protection. She visualized herself being purified as she traveled through the circles until she emerged as flawless as a diamond, reflecting only clarity and light. Before the termination of the second session, a post-hypnotic suggestion of cleanliness and perfection was imparted to the client.

The second session was scheduled for reinforcement within a few days. The client cancelled her appointment for the third session, saying that the tape we had made for her was sufficient. She reported that she practiced the imagery techniques faithfully each night and that she experienced a feeling of "renewal" throughout her body. She did not experience a lesion for the next three years, and she had indeed forgotten about the herpes. After the three-year respite, however, she was involved in a serious auto accident, which resulted in major abrasions, contusions, and severe physiological problems. She was traumatized by the nearly fatal incident. Three days after the accident, the lesions appeared in the form of tiny blisters (1–2 millimeters) on the labia majora, covering approximately 2 centimeters. She had apparently inadvertently infected herself in this location. Only a physician's diagnosis could convince her that this also was genital herpes, since the size and severity were greatly diminished compared to the original episode. This was followed by two more exacerbations lasting four to five days with a one-day break in between. She had a great deal of anxiety caused by many other physical problems due to the accident. At this time imagery of internally controlled white sharks was added to the previous method used with this patient. Seven months passed since her last exacerbation, and she reported a greater feeling of control and generalized feeling of well-being and no return of herpes symptoms.

An example of the suggestions used would be:

> So very deep . . . from this point on all that you will ever have to do, to go into this very deep hypnotic state, is to take your signal breath, a very deep diaphragmatic breath and allow yourself to go very deep, very deep indeed . . . just give up to gravity. The long, slow, deep breath is your signal as you mentally think the word, calm . . . as you exhale, down . . . deeper . . . down, you can think and feel the word, calm . . . and as you exhale, exhale with the word c . . . a . . . l . . . m . . . c . . . a . . . l . . . m, allow it to become almost like a mantra and your body will automatically respond. As you breathe deep . . . go deeper and deeper and deeper . . . deeper . . . and now move the shaft of light from the sun. Let that shaft of light enter at your right hip and you can manipulate it, move it, gliding it, massaging your bones and everything between the outer skin and the inner bone is being healed, rejuvenated, and revitalized. You move that shaft of light all the way down to your toes, from the hip to the toes, to the hip bone.
> Feel that shaft of light moving it up and back in your left leg . . . it enters at the hip, going down . . . heavy, warm, relaxed . . . working down to your toes, a lightness or perhaps not even feeling anything at all, but a warm shaft of light that you can use in your imagination . . . you can move it up and back, moving it up and back . . . moving it up and back . . . and now, perhaps, you can feel that feeling of total calmness in infinite space . . . perhaps a floating or a soaring whatever feeling you have is OK. Whatever your thoughts, whatever your reaction, it is OK for you. Take the light of the sun and now bring it into your stomach area . . . move it around, feel the warmth . . . bring it into your pelvic area and feel it . . . feel every organ in your body and your pelvic area and every cell in the lower part of your body around your pelvic area . . . feel it deep . . . move that shaft of light, the white light which is warm and healing, warm and healing . . . feel it, every single cell, every area, totally, completely . . . healed . . . that shaft of light move it deep within the vaginal area . . . let it flood the area. It sanitizes, it cures

. . . every cell . . . between the vagina and the anus . . . get that shaft of light to massage the total area, cleansing, healing every single cell, rejuvenating, and destroying all viruses . . . destroying all viruses . . . destroying all the feelings as you represent them as the worms beneath the skin, do it until they are all dead, being destroyed by the beam of light which sanitizes, which cures, which heals and rejuvenates. Feel and imagine the light . . . take that light from the sun, move it around, move it around your thighs and both sides . . . feel that healthy, smooth, vibrant feeling, think and feel, think beautiful, warm vaginal tissue, massage it with the beam of light . . . healthy, vibrant, so very natural, so very perfect in every way. . . .

In both cases there was a significant reduction in general stress, a decrease in the subjective level of pain, and a clearing of skin lesions. These results are no flukes. I have follow-up data of at least 18 months for 24 patients treated with hypnosis for genital herpes. Seventy-four percent can be considered greatly improved. Forty-four percent experienced a 65% reduction in number of flare-ups and a 50% reduction in duration of flareups. Thirty percent had no lesions at all during the follow-up period, though at times a number of them did feel some itching in the genitals. There was a very high correlation between extent of improvement and amount of time using hypnotic techniques. Patients who improved the most (had no recurrence of lesions) did self-hypnosis at least five times a week, while patients who demonstrated considerable improvement but still had some flare-ups used hypnosis only during periods of great stress. Those patients who stopped using hypnosis altogether showed the least change.

On the basis of these results, my conclusion is that regular practice of self-hypnosis, using tapes of the patient's own healing imagery, is a highly effective method of treating genital herpes.

References

Glogau, R. G. (1980). How I treat herpes simplex. *Medical Times, 108*, 66–68.

Hartland, J. (1971). *Medical and dental hypnosis and its clinical applications.* Baltimore: Williams & Wilkins.

Himell, K. (1981). Genital herpes, the need for counseling. *Journal of Obstetric, Gynecologic and Neo-Natal Nursing, 10*(6), 446–449.

Scott, M. J. (1960). *Hypnosis in skin and allergic diseases.* Springfield, IL: Charles C. Thomas.

Simonton, O. C., Matthews-Simonton, S., & Creighton, J. L. (1978). *Getting well again.* New York: Bantam Books.

Spiegel, H. (1974). *Manual for hypnotic induction profile: Eye roll levitation method.* New York: Soni Medica.

Ullman, M. (1947). Herpes simplex and second degree burn induced under hypnosis. *American Journal of Psychiatry, 103*, 828–830.

$\underset{A}{Q_{\&}}$ 55 Hypnosis With Social Phobias and Stage Fright

Question:

A large number of patients I see suffer from some kind of phobic response, especially social phobias (fear of speaking to strangers, fear of asking for dates) and stage fright (fear of giving oral presentations in classes, meetings, or work groups). How can hypnosis be used to treat such patients?

Discussion by ARNOLD A. LAZARUS, Ph.D.

A variety of circumstances can induce phobic responses. In some instances, they are a product of ongoing conflicts and/or past traumatic events. In other cases, they are predominantly a function of social skill deficits. Consider a sensitive individual who was ridiculed by the teacher or group leader while giving a talk to a seminar or study group. Thereafter, he or she might be expected to avoid similar situations where such humiliation could ensue. A small number of social phobics report a specific trigger incident. For instance, a young man at a party felt nauseous and vomited before reaching the bathroom, making an embarrassing mess. Consequently, he became afraid of going to parties and tended to avoid public gatherings. On the other hand, a somewhat reticent 20-year-old man, whose social learning history revealed a paucity of adequate male roles, reported no untoward experiences, but anticipated that his fumbling, inept interpersonal style would most likely result in rejection were he to hazard the chance of asking someone out on a date. His was a pure anticipatory anxiety reaction; he had never placed himself in the position of risking actual rejection. In most social phobias, the major emphasis is on "What will other people think of me?" Hypnosis alone is unlikely to benefit those individuals whose fears are mainly due to gaps or lacunae in their social repertoires. These people tend to need

300

specific coaching, training, rehearsal, shaping, and modeling before confronting their feared situations. Nevertheless, hypnosis can play an important adjunctive role and might often be a major ingredient in a broad-based treatment package.

Phobic reactions are characterized by *negative anticipations* (the phobic sufferer invariably reports mental images of personal failure, if not catastrophic gloom and doom, when picturing himself venturing into the fear-laden area), and *persistent avoidance* (phobic reactions tend to endure because the patient does not consistently expose herself to the feared situations, and thus extinction cannot supervene). Effective treatment aims to replace negative anticipations with positive images (hypnotic procedures can prove especially useful in this connection), and to supersede the usual "cop-outs" and general patterns of avoidance. Most often, clients need to be encouraged to "take emotional risks" and to expose themselves, in a systematic and progressive manner, to their feared situations. As I shall underscore, hypnosis can play a crucial role in achieving each of these goals.

Kelly (1955) emphasized that *"a person's processes are psychologically channelized by the ways in which he anticipates events"* (p. 46). Clearly, if someone anticipates personal rejection or public humiliation, he or she will be inclined to avoid being placed in such invidious positions. Thus, one young man stated: "Whenever I imagine myself asking an attractive woman out on a date, I picture the Woody Allen line in which she looks me over and says 'Get lost, creep!'" With that negative anticipation, small wonder that he experienced a "fear of asking for dates"! This leads directly into one of the major treatment objectives: replace negative/failure imagery with positive/success imagery. In this regard, hypnosis can play a most useful role.

I have contended, for some time, that *before most people can achieve something in reality, they first have to be able to picture it in imagery.* The corollary is that if someone cannot picture himself or herself performing a specific act, it is probable that he or she will be unable to accomplish it in reality. Thus, an individual with a public-speaking phobia, when asked: "Can you imagine yourself standing in front of a group and remaining calm while giving a talk?" is unlikely to answer affirmatively. Virtually every event or experience is transposed into images and thoughts. Our beliefs and perceptions govern our affective responses. It is hypothesized that rapid/automatic thoughts or images occur between every activating event and the subsequent emotional response. Thus, to overcome irrational fears, the phobic individual's cognitions and images have to be accessed and modified. Many years ago, I used to employ standard systematic desensitization techniques. Patients in a deeply relaxed or hypnotic state would be asked to picture a hierarchy of events pertaining to their phobic situations. Step by step, in piecemeal fashion, each item would be counterposed by relaxation, again and again, until even the most frightening item failed to evoke anxiety. Like most therapists, I found this method exceedingly tedious and time-consuming. Consequently, instead of using formal desensitization, I began to employ a *negative effects* technique because of its rapidity and superior effectiveness. Here is a case in point:

Al, a 22-year-old college senior, was terrified of asking women out on a date. He was strongly attracted to Sue, a 20-year-old sophomore, and on one occasion, Al asked her out and they spent a pleasant evening together. Despite this successful and positively reinforcing event, Al had avoided asking her out again, although he claimed to be "in love" with her. He said: "You have no idea what it took for me to ask her out that one time. I psyched myself up for three weeks, and when I finally got round to asking her, I thought I was going to die. My heart was pounding so hard I was sure something would snap. . . . I felt lightheaded, I was sweating and shaking, and I must have looked like a nut case. I was amazed that she agreed to go out with me." I inquired whether Al had continued feeling anxious throughout the entire evening. He had not. "No," he explained, "for me the scary part is *asking* for a date. . . . Once that hurdle is passed, I'm just fine."

The initial therapeutic tactic was that of rational disputation or cognitive relabeling. I stressed that rejection *per se* was not necessarily a sign that he was unattractive, unappealing, unworthy, or defective, that people's tastes vary, and what some consider good-looking and worthwhile, others may find distinctly unpleasant. Thereafter, the *negative effects* technique was employed. Hypnotic instructions involving eye closure and deep muscle relaxation induced a sufficiently altered state of consciousness so that Al could picture various images clearly, vividly, and realistically.

THERAPIST: Now just settle back and continue relaxing like that. (10-second pause) Very good. Now I am going to ask you to picture a scene. Try to do so as vividly and as realistically as possible. (3-second pause) You notice that Sue is in the library reading a book. Can you get a clear image of her?

AL: (After about 10 seconds) Yes.

THERAPIST: Good. Now look at her, try to see what she is wearing, study her closely. (10-second pause) Can you tell me what you see?

AL: (Keeping his eyes closed) I see her sitting at a table in the Periodicals Room. There is nobody else in the room. (Pause) She is wearing a blue dress with a pink scarf. She looks very pretty.

THERAPIST: Excellent. Now here's what I want you to picture. You tell her how much you enjoyed your last date and you ask her if she would like to go out with you again. Can you picture that?

AL: (Squirming) Yes.

THERAPIST: Very well. Now picture Sue turning you down. She says, "Sorry, but I'm too busy studying for an exam." Can you imagine that clearly?

AL: Loud and clear!

THERAPIST: Now see yourself asking her if she would like to go out with you after the exam.

AL: Okay.

THERAPIST: She says, "I'll be too exhausted to go out." Can you picture that?

AL: It feels as if I'm getting the brush-off.

THERAPIST: Exactly! She's too polite to come right out and say: "Get lost, creep!" But you are getting the message. Sue would rather not go out with you. Now stay with that, and tell me what you have to do in order to emerge with your self-respect intact. Can you picture yourself saying or doing something that enables you to feel, let's say, rather disappointed, but hardly devastated?

AL: (After 15–20 seconds) I don't know. There were two thoughts. I could tell myself the things we have discussed, that this does not make me into a worm, that I just happen not to be her type. (Pause) The other idea was for me to come right out and ask her to level with me, to tell me to my face that she'd rather not spend time in my company. (He opens his eyes.)

THERAPIST: That's great! Let's take the rational thoughts first. Rejection often says more about the other person that it says about you. Sue's ideal man might just happen to be short, stockily built, brown-eyed, and have a heavy black beard. [Al is tall, slim, blue-eyed, and clean-shaven.] So if any woman turns you down, can you very seriously entertain the idea that this is probably simply because you are not her type, that it is no aspersion on your manhood or on your attractiveness and basic worth?

AL: I guess I can only really know after I've tried and been turned down.

THERAPIST: True. So when are you going to put it to the test? I'm eager to know the answer.

AL: You sound as if you'll be disappointed if I ask Sue out and she accepts the invitation.

THERAPIST: Well, that won't give us a chance to test out your ability to take rejection on the chin and to keep smiling. [I am being only slightly facetious.] It would be good for you to develop a mind-set that made you look forward to experiencing a whole string of rejections in order to toughen yourself up.

AL: Well, even if Sue says "yes," I'm sure there will be other opportunities. . . .

THERAPIST: I'm delighted to hear it. [Indeed, this implies that he fully intends to take the prescribed risks.] Why don't we turn to your second tactic now. Run that by me again.

AL: Oh, um, what I was thinking is that I could simply say something like,

"Look, do me a favor. If you'd rather not go out with me, just say so. This would save me a lot of time and energy, and it would stop me from pestering you."
THERAPIST: I like that. I can't wait for you to be rejected so that you can put it to the test.

The *negative effects* procedure zooms right into the pivotal fear and extinguishes the pain associated with it. There is no need for tedious hierarchies, or for the presentation of scene after scene. The use of hypnosis can augment the authenticity of this simple method, so that the client experiences the full impact of his or her feared consequence, but pictures an outcome in which the affective responses are no longer troublesome. The same effect, of course, can be obtained without hypnosis, simply by using muscle relaxation and imagery. In my experience, however, most clients fare better when they are told about "altered states of consciousness" and are given hypnotic suggestions as a prelude to the implementation of the technique.

When dealing with public speaking anxieties, the desensitization procedure, with or without hypnosis, can be very elaborate. Typically, one has the client imagining him/herself giving a presentation to one other person (such as a good friend) and then to two people (one good friend and perhaps one acquaintance). Thereafter, more and more people are added — colleagues, associates, and complete strangers — and step-by-step the client is enjoined to stay calm and relaxed as the group grows in size. Here again, I prefer to use the negative effects technique. A specific incident strongly suggested that the desensitization method left clients somewhat vulnerable.

A female executive whose job required her to make verbal presentations to several work groups had been treated, quite successfully, with systematic desensitization. Prior to this treatment, her level of anxiety, even at the thought of giving a verbal report to as few as three colleagues, was extremely high. Post-desensitization, she was able to perform her work requirement with minimal discomfort. She remained anxiety-free for several months until, during one of her reports, two of her superiors had asked pointed questions. My client felt that she was viewed as incompetent by the group, and suffered a total relapse. The desensitization had programmed in *success images* (she approached the situation with positive images in mind) but had not dealt with her basic dysfunctional belief — that it was a dire necessity for her to appear totally competent in front of a group.

Unlike implosion and flooding, the negative effects technique does not take the situation to an absurd position — one does *not* have the client imagining a scene in which an entire audience ends up jeering, or walking out, or hurling rotten tomatoes. Instead, the aim is simply to enable the client to feel that a less than sterling performance is perfectly acceptable. Here is an example:

Lisa worked for a large company, and it was her responsibility to deliver a verbal report each month to the governing board. She was in charge of symposia, and the board members required not only an update of the number of meetings each month, how many presenters and participants were drawn from inside and outside the company, the specific topics that had been covered, and various other basic statistics and facts, but also an appraisal of the educational impact of the symposia. While this chore seldom called for more than 5–10 minutes of Lisa's time each month, her degree of anticipatory anxiety was extreme. She always took at least 10 mg Valium 30–60 minutes before each such presentation to take "some of the edge off of my anxiety."

Lisa was most responsive to abdominal breathing to the slow rhythmic click of a metronome and appeared to enter a "hypnotic trance." She was then asked to picture herself presenting her monthly report to the board and not being able to answer some of their questions.

THERAPIST: Can you tell me what is happening?

LISA: Mr. Riley is asking me what we served for lunch and what the caterers had charged per head.

THERAPIST: All right. Now you don't have those figures. What happens from there?

LISA: I don't know. That's never happened.

THERAPIST: That's the point. I want you to imagine that you are in the meeting, and for some reason or other, you can't give Mr. Riley the data he is asking for. Can you see it?

LISA: (Pause) I can see it, and I feel like a complete fool.

THERAPIST: Now somebody else is asking you for some information, and you don't have that either. Think what that could be.

LISA: Mr. Thomas wants to know how much we collected from the sponsors.

THERAPIST: And you don't have those figures either.

LISA: Oh dear! (Remains silent, eyes closed)

THERAPIST: (After about 45 seconds) Can you tell me what is going on?

LISA: I had a lot of thoughts. First, I saw them asking for my resignation then and there, but I decided that this wouldn't be the way they would handle it. Then I thought about the things they'd say about me after I left the meeting and went back to my office. (Pause) I decided that the most likely thing was that they'd tell my boss how poorly prepared I was.

THERAPIST: Fine. Then what happens?

LISA: My boss asks me what went wrong.

THERAPIST: What do you tell him?

LISA: (Pause) I guess I could lie and say that I had a bad headache and was not feeling well.

THERAPIST: The good old illness cop-out. Would that work for you?

LISA: (Opens her eyes) I have to have some valid reason.

THERAPIST: Why? What's wrong with adopting the position that as a fallible, not totally perfect human being, you can screw up from time to time? Let's try something out. Please close your eyes again, take in a few deep breaths. (Hypnotic instructions follow for about two to three minutes) Now repeat this to yourself: "I give myself permission to be fallible." Keep saying that to yourself. (One minute pause) Okay, open your eyes. What happened?

LISA: It's a completely different way of seeing the world, of approaching things. Instead of feeling that I must excel, it speaks to the fact that if I give a poor presentation, I can apologize and try harder next time.

THERAPIST: Are you merely paying lip service to those ideas or can you really buy into them?

LISA: I think I can get there.

THERAPIST: As a homework exercise, will you do the self-hypnosis I showed you last time? When you feel relaxed and calm, picture yourself screwing up at work; see yourself not able to answer certain questions from the board, and instead of becoming upset, try to see what you have to do to remain calm.

It took several weeks before Lisa was able to persuade herself that it would indeed not be a complete indictment of her worth as an employee if she presented a far less than perfect account to the board. Her anticipatory anxiety diminished and she acquired a more adaptive — carefree — attitude in general. In each of the foregoing instances, hypnosis played a central role by fostering veridical imagery which, in turn, augmented the necessary cognitive shifts.

Reference

Kelly, G. A. (1955). *The psychology of personal constructs*. New York: Norton.

Q & A 56 Hypnosis With Agoraphobia

Question:

What hypnotic techniques can be used with agoraphobia and how effective are they? The underlying question is whether hypnosis is worth using with this debilitating condition.

Discussion by GERALD D. WINTER, Ed.D.

Agoraphobia is the most common and most disabling of all the phobias. It afflicts mainly women, usually in late adolescence or early adulthood. The main symptom is phobic anxiety or panic attacks, often evoked when away from home or another safe place, in crowds, or in a confined space. Because overarousal of the autonomic nervous system may be part of the clinical picture, relaxation or hypnosis often gives the patient a measure of psychophysiological control. However, it is important to note that the etiology of agoraphobia is not well understood and that agoraphobia itself is not a homogeneous condition. Each case has to be understood and treated on its own merits.

I will review four cases where hypnosis was the main element in treatment.

The first patient was a white, foreign-born woman in her late twenties. She reported that she had always been anxious and never felt comfortable in any situation with other people or in strange places. She was married at an early age to her childhood sweetheart. This stormy marriage ended in divorce when her husband was sentenced to prison for armed robbery. She then married his father, her father-in-law, and bore him a child. This man was an alcoholic who treated her well when sober but was jealous and violent when drunk.

She started having panic attacks and was unable to leave the house. Her family physician prescribed mild tranquilizers (Diazepam) and referred her to me when this medication didn't help. I had to make a house call because she was unable to go beyond her front door. Since she was very apprehensive about meeting me, I did not use hypnosis during the first session but instead tried to be supportive and gave her some breathing exercises to do.

At the second meeting, the next day, I induced hypnosis with a slow ten-count induction and she responded very well. I use this type of induction (counting from one to ten with suggestions of progressive muscle relaxation after each number) because it gives me an opportunity to see the progress of relaxation or lack of it. In this way, I can alter the count and suggestions to fit the needs of the patient. I gave suggestions that she would pleasantly anticipate going out into her yard, progressing further each time. I also suggested that she would take the energy involved in having her symptoms and redirect that energy to some positive and appropriate physical or mental activity. Some paradoxical suggestions were added to the effect that she would look forward to her panic so that she could learn to enjoy it.

I saw her three times a week for three weeks. Although she never looked forward to the panic attacks, she made steady improvement, going further and further out of the house each day. In the fourth session, she reported a setback, being unable to leave the house that day. I told her that success does not necessarily proceed in a straight line. Instead, after taking two steps forward, a step backward may have to be taken in order to reestablish homeostasis. She accepted this explanation and continued her progress the next day. By the ninth session, after having been weaned from her medication, she was able to go shopping and be with friends.

Her husband called the night after the ninth session to say I had done too good a job. His wife had not only left the house but run away to live in another city with one of his friends. She told him that now she could leave him and be with the man she loved.

There is an interesting postscript to this case. The woman recently called — nine years after I had seen her — to complain about a different problem. She is now unable to stay at home alone and always has to be out. This problem appeared four years ago and has been getting progressively worse. In the beginning she thought she could handle it on her own but now feels she can't. At first I thought that this was a different problem but after seeing her I discovered that it was an extension of the same problem. She has to be out only if she can be with safe people but staying at home is still her haven. A short period of treatment brought an alleviation of the severe symptoms, and we will be working, again, on a complete remission.

The second case involved a 30-year-old white woman who described herself as very nervous. Shopping had always been difficult but lately she had been unable to go even when accompanied by a friend or relative. She was referred by her physician after a course of tranquilizers and antidepressants had failed to effect a change.

Her husband, whom she feared, was against the use of hypnosis but her physician prevailed upon her to give it a try. She felt she had little to lose and defied her husband. He resented this, but let her go ahead because he was sure that she would fail.

She was a very willing subject who immediately went into a deep state of hypnosis. I felt that she was so uncomfortable with her anxiety that a rapid change was inevitable. This proved to be true. I suggested that she would look forward to her anxiety so she could learn to enjoy it. She felt this was foolish but agreed to go along. Before the next session, she went to the supermarket but couldn't get herself to go in. I asked if she could go in if she knew that my assistant and I would be there. She said yes. Hypnosis was induced and she was encouraged to attempt another shopping trip. Again, she was told that if by chance she panicked, she could learn to enjoy it. She was also reminded that my assistant and I would be in the store.

Her trip to the supermarket the next day was uneventful; there was no panic and no anxiety. After going to the store with her two more times, I suggested that she could now do this on her own, without my being in the store, and that she was beginning to enjoy the expectation of panic that did not occur. She was instructed, the first time out, to go to the market and then to come directly to my office. She followed my directions and reported an absence of panic or anxiety. Her sessions were then extended to once every two weeks with instructions to go shopping as often as needed. She knew that if she experienced any anxiety she could call and be seen. Eventually, her visits were extended to once per month. Soon after, treatment was ended by mutual agreement.

That was 13 years ago. I called her just prior to writing this paper to see how she was doing. She said that her symptoms were still in remission. She admitted to some brief bouts of anxiety but she is able to handle these herself. She remembers that if she does begin to panic, she will enjoy it, but for some reason the panic doesn't appear. She feels that this is a helpful tool for avoiding panic. Her attitude is positive and her expectancy of panic appears to have entirely disappeared.

The third patient, a woman in her late twenties, was experiencing a variety of psychophysiologic, psychological, and cardiovascular symptoms. After going from physician to physician she was finally diagnosed as having a heart problem (mitral valve prolapse syndrome) and was placed on Inderal. This helped alleviate some of her symptoms but not her extreme anxiety and panic. At the time of referral, her symptoms were becoming more severe and her chest pains were returning despite the medication.

The patient had always felt anxious and rejected. She married when young in an attempt to leave her unloving parents. Her anxiety did not abate, but she was able to work during the first years of marriage. The marriage was rocky and her parents continued to be rejecting. From her point of view, she had nothing going for her. When her anxiety became extreme or when she had an argument with her husband, she would run home to mother for a few days to try to get nurturing that she desired. This didn't help because her mother was incapable of filling her needs. Nothing worked for her, she felt more and more helpless, and the agoraphobia became full-blown after she became pregnant. Though she could leave the house with someone whom she considered safe, she usually panicked, became nauseous, and had severe chest pains, shortness of breath, and severe trembling.

She received medication for her heart problem, marital therapy from a family therapist, and hypnotherapy from me. I initially saw her three times per week. All the sessions included positive statements about the imminent alleviation of symptoms. She was told that her mind and body had brought on the symptoms and that they would know how to remove them. I suggested that hypnosis would facilitate recovery by reminding the mind and body that they could reverse themselves. I also asked her to repeat this statement 20 times before retiring at night and upon waking in the morning: "Positive feelings give me the advantages that I desire." Self-hypnosis was very difficult for her to do, so I made a hypnotic tape for her to listen to twice a day.

There was an immediate reduction in symptoms for a short period of time, probably due to the attention she was getting. When some of the symptoms returned, I gave my standard two steps forward and one step backward explanation, and in a short time she again improved. But then we reached a plateau. The trembling and shortness of breath eased considerably and, while the chest pains were there, they were less severe and of shorter duration. I tried different techniques, including paradoxical suggestions used earlier, but she remained where she was, improved but not cured.

As a last resort, I gave the suggestion that the body and mind must have misunderstood the directions they had been given and that a new method of implanting suggestions would be tried. She was told she would not consciously notice the difference but that this new method would certainly make her feel better. I used the same induction as before but made it slower and with more suggestions for relaxation, followed by a heavy dose of ego-strengthening suggestions. This seemed to break the impasse and her symptoms subsided further.

At the end of five months I spaced her visits to once a month with instructions that she could call and come in if she had problems. I received two calls over the next months that did not require her coming to the office. Slowly but surely her symptoms disappeared. Therapy was terminated at the end of 12 months.

At this writing, three years after the end of therapy, she is able to be alone without anxiety or apprehension. The chest pains that she experienced have now diminished to the point that she only takes medication about once a week instead of on a regular basis. There are still marital problems but these have improved and the marriage has a better chance of success than was previously expected. At this point, she has not been able to conceive without spontaneously aborting.

The final patient, a very attractive 18-year-old woman, was referred by the psychotherapist she had worked with for over a year. Her symptoms included difficulty in swallowing and breathing, dizziness, and panic. Her panic attacks had no definite pattern and appeared "out of the blue." A large number of therapists, from behaviorists to psychoanalysts, had been consulted over the years, but to no avail. The plan was for her to stay with the referring therapist and see me as an adjunct to her treatment.

I told her I had seen many cases like hers and that I had every reason to believe that her treatment would be successful. As a first approach, I gently placed my hand on her throat and told her that in a few moments, my hand would feel warm. When this happened, she was told that the warmth would penetrate and release the spasms that were causing her difficulty in swallowing and breathing. She had an immediate positive response and hypnosis was induced. I then told her that her own mind and body, which had brought on the symptoms, would know how to dissipate them. She underwent a dramatic change for the better. After three sessions her symptoms went into complete remission. But such "honeymoon" effects usually are not lasting, and sure enough, within a week her symptoms began to reappear. I gave her my two steps forward, one step backward routine, which helped considerably.

Her symptoms continued to abate until she began working at a new job. After two hours of work all of her original symptoms reappeared. Since the mere mention of paradoxical suggestions had negative effects, I continued using the "laying on of hands" plus direct suggestions for alleviation of symptoms. These methods were successful for a time but her symptoms always reappeared after a few months and we were back to square one with her treatment. Finally, after two years of therapy, there was marked improvement in the frequency, duration, and severity of her symptoms but she was still not asymptomatic. I suggested antidepressant medication, but she refused. She also refused the suggestion that she attend the Panic Clinic at Columbia Presbyterian Hospital as an adjunct to treatment.

My staff and I felt we had taken her as far as we could and that a referral was in order. We thought that she was manipulating her environment to avoid the responsibilities of growing up. Her symptoms allowed her to remain a child who would be taken care of. Though her father allowed her to work, he was just as happy to have her home to help with the cooking and cleaning. Her remaining a child meant that she could be free from any responsibility and not have to establish a male-female relationship.

I recently contacted the patient to see how she was doing. She said that she had done well with her new therapist for a while, but then slipped back to where she was when we concluded therapy.

Although the last case represents only minimal improvement, my staff and I have seen a large number of agoraphobic patients over the last 20 years who have been helped considerably with hypnotherapy. That is saying quite a bit, given the difficulty most therapists have in treating this complex and incompletely understood ailment. It is my personal belief, however, that we often need to be especially resourceful, as well as open to the inclusion of antidepressant medication, in the treatment of this malady.

Q&A 57 Hypnosis With Surgery

Question:

Although I've never used it this way, I've heard that hypnosis can be used pre- and postoperatively to reduce discomfort and aid in recovery. Is this true, and if so, how exactly is it done?

Discussion by ANDREW E. ST. AMAND, M.D.

The psychological impact of hospitalization with impending surgery varies with each patient, depending on experiential background and personality, the gravity (real or perceived) of the proposed surgical procedure, and the ambiance of the hospital. In essence, the hospital represents to the patient not only the "solution" to his physical illness ("all will be taken care of"), but also a new experience in which he is likely to feel anxiety over the "loss of control." Indeed, the most important psychological attitude characterizing the hospitalized peri-operative patient is this bipolar state of mind, dependence versus independence. The surgical procedure, by its very nature, adds an additional psychological charge. The patient's anxiety is often manifested as a need for reassurance from the anesthesiologist or anesthetist, the surgeon, the nursing staff and the hospital personnel involved in his or her care. Any method that can overcome conscious and unconscious fears, anxieties and apprehension, as well as provide the strongest possible reassurance regarding the outcome of the operation and the postoperative period, is of incalculable value to the patient anticipating surgery. Just sitting and listening to what the patient has to say, and then responding with reassuring words and satisfactory explanations of the anesthesia techniques proposed will alleviate or reduce anxiety without formal trance induction.

One of the greatest sources of anxiety in the preoperative patient is the anesthesia experience itself. Some patients look upon general anesthesia as a menacing or threatening experience, for it raises the possibility of not recovering or "waking up" or even death. Most anesthesiologists and anesthetists are aware of the fact that these anxious, frightened patients require larger than usual dosages of preoperative medication, or, more correctly, are resistant to the usual dosages. These patients also require more anesthetic agents during surgery. Excessive fright often produces grave results, and, in many instances, sudden death. Dr. John Finney used to say that if a patient felt sure he was going to die during an operation, he would not operate on him (Kulvin, 1966). I myself have witnessed this phenomenon, which I call the "Voodoo Phenomenon," on at least six occasions. Dying of fright is a real possibility.

Many anesthesiologists, upon encountering a patient with this attitude, refuse to administer a general anesthesia for an elective procedure. I recall the case of a 17-year-old girl in previous good health with unexplained lower abdominal pain. During the preoperative anesthesia visit, the patient's mother expressed an inordinate amount of interest and asked many questions regarding the cardiac monitoring that is maintained during anesthesia. In the patient's presence, the mother said that the patient's friend had died of cardiac arrest during anesthesia. The patient herself did not *seem* anxious. The following day a cystoscopic examination of the bladder was performed. During the ten minutes of anesthesia the patient had an alarming cardiac arrythmia, which reverted to normal sinus rhythm immediately after termination of anesthesia. Undoubtedly the mother's anxiety was communicated to the patient, resulting in an elevation of endogenous catecholamines, epinephrine and norepinephrine. This elevation was responsible for the arrythmias *after* the induction of anesthesia.

The anesthesiologist's or anesthetist's attitude, expression and manner can have a remarkable effect on the patient. Suggestions and explanations must be adjusted to the patient's capacity to understand. In establishing rapport with the patient, the anesthesiologist or anesthetist may knowingly or accidentally be employing the principles of hypnosis. The preoperative patient is usually quite anxious and tense and is in a state of *selective attention* during the interview. This selective attention or *focused consciousness* on the words, actions and suggestions of the anesthesiologist can be considered a form of waking hypnosis. Calm reassurance, adequate explanations and a confident manner contribute enormously to allaying the patient's fears. The hospitalization and the doctor-patient rapport achieved by the caring, unrushed, conscientious anesthesiologist establish a structured setting that results in the patient's being most amenable to suggestions. it is not uncommon for me to spend 30 minutes or much longer with a patient during the preoperative anesthetic visit to reduce the anxiety level of the patient. Suggestions such as, "You have an excellent surgeon and I'll be monitoring your body functions closely throughout the anesthesia, and you will be quite surprised how well you feel *when I visit you after surgery*," can have a calming effect on the patient. The suggestion, "when I visit you after surgery," implies, of course, recovery from the surgery and anesthesia.

Many preoperative patients are preoccupied with the post-surgical pain they expect to experience. Rudyard Kipling said, "Words are the most powerful drug used by mankind." I try as much as possible to avoid the use of the word *pain* and substitute "discomfort" or "hurt" or a "peculiar different sensation" instead. The suggestion is made that no matter what preconceived notions patients may have from hearing about the experiences of friends or relatives, they are going to be pleasantly surprised by how little discomfort they will have postoperatively. I explain that pain is a feeling and response, and therefore a subjective or *personal experience*. No two individuals respond the same way. "If you can't think positively, or believe or accept what I'm saying, why don't you think *neutrally*? You may be *pleasantly* surprised." Emphasis is placed on the italicized words. I point out, in a humorous manner when the occasion dictates, "Here you are thinking about and, to a certain degree, feeling pain and we haven't even operated on you yet. If you expect a great deal of pain following surgery your wish may be granted. If, on the other hand, you accept what I'm telling you and take a curious attitude and wait and see, you probably will be pleasantly surprised at *how little discomfort* you have." In other words, I spend time with the patient in this state of selective attention to promote a positive attitude, because a positive attitude can marshall inner forces that calm the patient preoperatively and lead to a smoother operative and postoperative course.

The comparatively brief preoperative anesthesiologist-patient encounter for emergency procedures can be facilitated by the calm, confident manner and voice of the anesthesiologist, which will reduce the patient's anxiety. I recall a late night emergency operation on a young woman severely ill with toxic ulcerative colitis, septicemia, high fever and bowel obstruction. The patient was *terrified* of the operation and felt impending doom. My unhurried, deliberately casual preparation and "small talk," conducted as though this was a simple appendectomy, apparently had a profound effect on her. Before being discharged from the hospital the patient confided in me that she was very frightened the night of the surgery, but because I had acted as though it were a routine, simple operation she "relaxed" (her word). I neglected to tell her that because of the gravity of her condition and the anesthesia risk it imposed, I was as concerned about the surgery as she was.

In many emergency situations the patient is already in a dissociated, hypnotic-like state. The anesthesiologist or surgeon can use this state of confusion and dissociation to suture lacerations, set fractures, or reduce dislocations with little or no anesthesia.

Thus far I have focused on the importance of suggestions during the preoperative interview. Anxiety specifically over the surgical procedure and the outcome, fear of the anesthesia itself, and fear of death can also be dealt with preoperatively using more formal trance induction. Occasionally, I am asked to see a patient with a pathological fear of anesthesia or of needles prior to scheduling the patient for elective or necessary surgery. Two or three office visits within a week or two are usually sufficient. Trance is induced and constructive suggestions given. The sessions are tape recorded and the patient is instructed to listen to the tape several times a day. Some of the suggestions I use are: "Today we employ the most modern and sophisticated surgical techniques with careful monitoring of your body functions during anesthesia." "Everyone in the operating room is working together as a well-trained team to see you *safely* through the operation." "Since your operation is necessary, isn't it nice to know and be assured that you will be attended to by a well-trained team of doctors and nurses." "As you learn these techniques of relaxation you are learning how to exert self-control over your body and make it well again." Emphasis is placed on open-ended suggestions. "*Soon*, you will be able to do the things that are within your ability." "You will be surprised how well everything goes and how well you feel" or "how little discomfort there is" or "notice that peculiar, different, yet not unpleasant sensation."

One patient with "fear of needles" whom I treated with hypnosis would actually collapse in shock at the sight of a needle. His blood pressure dropped abruptly and a diagnosis of "vago-vagal response" was made. The patient needed a lumbar laminectomy for a herniated disc. I saw the young man on two occasions within ten days. Trance was induced and general suggestions for relaxation, self-control, and ego-strengthening were used. The sessions were taped and the patient encouraged to practice self-relaxation with the tape several times a day. I administered the anesthesia and the surgical procedure was uneventful. The patient no longer had the pathological fear of injections. It is of interest to note that the patient's wife needed surgery six months later and had a similar, unreasonable fear of needles, though not as extreme as her husband's. At her request, I saw her once in the office and, through the use of hypnosis, was able to remove her anxiety.

A teenage diabetic was dependent on his parents to administer his daily insulin injections. He was able to draw the proper dose of insulin into the syringe, but he was unable to puncture his own skin. Following consultation and three hypnotherapy sessions the problem was resolved.

Hardly a year goes by that there isn't an urgent request for consultation and hypnotherapy for a patient requiring radiation therapy for a malignancy. These patients usually express fear of "being alone" in the treatment room and of being immobilized in a certain position for a short period of time. They deny claustrophobia. The last patient I saw had a huge, fungating, malignant tumor of the hypopharynx. The patient was treated using

hypnosis on two consecutive days and was able to start high voltage radiation therapy on the third day. Though the patient still had some anxiety,
he was able to complete the full course of radiation treatments.

The fretfully anxious preoperative patient can be calmed with any simple
relaxation technique. Using the trance state, the patient can be imprinted
with the suggestion that she/he will also be able to experience this degree
of relaxation postoperatively and minimize or even control discomfort. I try
to teach short, very simple self-relaxation techniques. The verbalization of
the technique I use most often is as follows:

> To learn a simple relaxation method, *prepare* yourself by con-
> centrating on two things *right now*. One, concentrate on the posi-
> tion your body is in, noticing the weight of your body in the
> chair, the back rest, the seat of the chair, the arm rests . . .
> noticing the position of your arms . . . your legs . . . the weight
> of your clothing . . . the texture and warmth of your clothing.
> . . . Be as comfortable as your conscious mind can permit you
> to be and, *second*, concentrate on your *normal* breathing pattern,
> not rapid breaths, not deep breaths, but your *normal* breathing
> pattern, paying special attention to the air as it leaves your lungs.
> So pay attention to the position of your body being as comfort-
> able as your conscious mind can permit you to be, and notice
> the air as it leaves your lungs. You will notice that by the third
> . . . or fourth . . . breath you exhale . . . that your shoulders
> and neck muscles will relax and that by the, oh, perhaps the sixth
> or seventh breath you exhale, the muscles in your face and fore-
> head will relax, and by the time you reach the tenth or perhaps
> the eleventh breath you'll notice that the eyelid muscles will relax
> and close, if they haven't done so already, and you'll experience
> a pleasant, harmless, floating sensation and then I'll begin.

I repeat myself starting at the sixth or seventh breath . . . etc. Rest assured that four out of five patients will have eyelid catalepsy and you can
proceed to deepen the trance and give constructive suggestions regarding
surgery, anesthesia and the postoperative course. The above induction technique is carried out *without looking* at the patient and in a very casual manner, usually while I am jotting notes in the patient's chart. This procedure
is simple and very effective. Try it on yourself now. The trance is terminated
and I then ask the patient to repeat the procedure in my presence without
a word from me. It is amazing how many patients will go into a trance spontaneously. The patient is then told that he or she will be able to carry out
this simple "mental gymnastic" following surgery and be *more comfortable*
and heal more quickly. Postoperatively, the same technique is used and the

patient is reminded that as the muscles relax there will be less tension on the incision and *much less discomfort.*

A difficult campaign involves the instruction of the recovery room nurses to avoid using negative or leading suggestions to the patients emerging from anesthesia. Suggestions such as, "It's all over now, Mr. Smith; you're in the Recovery Room," or "Are you having a lot of pain, Mr. Smith?" can be supplanted by "Everything went very well, Mr. Smith; you're in the Recovery Room," and "Are you *fairly comfortable,* Mr. Smith?" The practice of automatically placing an emesis basin next to the patient's head suggests that the patient will be sick to his stomach. If the anesthesiologist or anesthetist takes the time preoperatively to calm and reassure the patient, the incidence of postoperative nausea and vomiting will be greatly reduced.

Another postoperative use of hypnosis is the management of hiccups. Though not always successful, it is worth a trial of hypnotherapy. There is nothing to lose and much to gain.

Persistent vomiting following oral feeding for which no organic cause can be found may respond to hypnotherapy. After exploratory surgery a 42-year-old woman was found to have inoperable carcinoma of the pancreas. The patient was discharged on the tenth postoperative day. She developed persistent vomiting of solid food but not liquids. She was readmitted to the hospital and after appropriate studies no organic basis for her symptoms could be found. On consultation, I used the simple induction, described above, on the first visit. I then focused her attention on *how well* she was going to do, *day by day,* in conquering her inability to eat solid food and *even conquering* her illness. The attention was on getting well again using taped relaxation techniques many times a day and also determining in her mind to "fight" her illness. Not only was the patient able to swallow food and be discharged from the hospital a few days later, but she was also able to achieve a state of equanimity until the day she died at home three months later. The family was most appreciative of the use of hypnotherapy.

Anxiety and fear that a specific problem will occur postoperatively can result in reality. A teenager who had undergone a second stage operation on her spine for idiopathic scoliosis was apprehensive about the urinary catheter being removed. After the first operation, recatheterization was necessary for a short period of time following removal of the catheter. Her fears were realized when the catheter was removed after the second operation. She complained that she was unable to void. I was asked to see her as soon as possible to see if hypnosis would help resolve her problem and avoid recatheterization. With the mother's permission and presence, the youngster readily went into trance and was given the following suggestions: "It would be interesting to see how soon you empty your bladder after I leave. I wonder if it will be five minutes or 30 minutes. I'll be interested in your exact report." When I called 40 minutes later I found that the patient had voided 15 minutes after I left.

I have had numerous occasions to use hypnosis with terminally ill postoperative patients. Hypnosis and relaxation techniques were used to instill hope and a positive attitude, as well as to control unpleasant symptoms. Though certainly not always successful, those instances where hypnotherapy did help proved most rewarding. The cancer-riddled wife of a physician treated through hypnosis to control her discomfort was prompted to remark, "I still have some pain, but this I can live with." The patient and her husband were grateful for some degree of relief obtained through hypnotherapy.

Occasionally, I am asked to help a postoperative orthopedic patient undergoing physical therapy. Because of discomfort or fear of discomfort, the patient will "split" or restrict the range of motion of an extremity. The patient is first reassured that the wound is healed and then taught self-hypnosis. Suggestions used are: "Visualize your muscles relaxing and moving more freely . . . the strength in your muscles is increasing each time you exercise . . . the circulation is also improving and you feel more and more comfortable with time." Occasionally I use time distortion here; "each second represents a minute, each minute an hour," etc.

I have described some of the applications of hypnosis in the preoperative and postoperative periods that have been useful in my experience. Undoubtedly there are many more peri-operative situations where hypnosis may be of use. The preoperative anesthetic visit is unquestionably the most important occasion to use relaxation techniques. This may range from formal trance induction to simple, calm, reassuring words in a confident, positive manner.

Reference

Kulvin, M. M. (1966). Scared to death (letter). *Journal of the American Medical Association, 198*(1), 90.

$\underset{A}{\overset{Q}{\raisebox{-0.5ex}{$\mathcal{C}$}}}$ 58 Hypnosis and Stress Management

Question:

I run several programs to reduce and manage stress and have only recently realized that hypnosis might be a useful part of such programs. What hypnotic techniques would be of value?

Discussion by GEORGE J. PRATT, Ph.D.

In developing a stress management program using hypnosis you should first analyze the situation to determine the source of excessive stress. Since some stress is necessary for all of us to function, proper stress control does not mean the elimination of all stress. It is the excessive stress that we are concerned about.

People experience prolonged excessive stress as a result of many different sources: work, unemployment, changing sex roles, inner-city congestion, an unhappy marriage, and financial problems, to name a few. They also confront more catastrophic and sudden stress when, for example, a loved one becomes seriously ill or dies or a natural catastrophe such as a flood or fire leaves them homeless. People have many ways for coping with the excessive stresses in their lives. Alcohol and drugs are two of the more prevalent and more unhealthy ways of managing stress. Unfortunately, these methods can produce more health problems than they alleviate.

A much better, more lasting method of stress control is hypnosis and self-hypnosis. In a typical stress management program hypnosis is one modality, used along with proper nutrition, exercise, assertiveness training, a balance between work, love and play, and other cognitive strategies.

First let's explore the way excessive stress affects the body to better understand how hypnotic techniques can be used to defuse the negative effects of stress. Chronic stress—stress that occurs over a prolonged period and above the level of ordinary stress we all are accustomed to — is the most damaging.

Hans Selye, the renowned stress researcher, described the effects of chronic stress in what he called the "general adaptation syndrome" or G.A.S. (1956). This reaction to chronic stress has three stages — the alarm reaction, resistance, and exhaustion. During the last two stages, resistance and exhaustion, the body's immune defenses are progressively worn down and used up. Once the exhaustion stage is reached, the body is susceptible to disease that normally would not affect it.

The beginning symptoms of this damaging stage of stress exhaustion might be headaches, upset stomach, high blood pressure, skin eruptions, or tense sore muscles. If these early warning signs are not recognized and the underlying stress controlled, serious illness may soon develop.

Some people have a problem identifying where the "real" excessive stress is in their lives. Hypnosis can be very useful for those people in uncovering the stressing area. For example, a patient we'll call Bill came to therapy on recommendation from his physician, who had been treating Bill for gastritis. Bill's stomach inflammation was aggravated by his drinking. The physician recognized that until the emotional stress that was causing Bill to aggravate the condition was found and treated, the gastritis would persist in spite of the bland diet and medication.

Bill's history showed no particularly outstanding stressing agent and he was unable to see any special circumstances that would be producing excessive stress. Bill was open to using hypnosis to see if we could uncover any hidden stressing factors. After developing hypnotic induction and helping Bill relax within trance, we began exploring his present life. He was quite able to talk while in trance, but when he was asked about his family members his voice caught and his speech pattern became very deliberate and controlled. When asked specifically about his father, Bill thought for some moments before speaking.

It took several sessions before the entire story unfolded. Bill's father had beaten and abused him when he was a young boy. It was disguised as "discipline" for minor infractions at the time. However, as Bill became an adult his unconscious mind recognized the childhood beatings for what they were. Bill had repressed a tremendous amount of anger, which was constantly irritated by his present close proximity to his father.

With his trance awareness taken into his conscious awareness, Bill was able to deal directly with his stressful emotions and his father. His "nerves" calmed considerably and, after a confrontation with his father about the childhood events, Bill reported a much more relaxed feeling overall in his life.

This is an example of how hypnosis can be used to uncover the true causes of stress if they are unknown. Often age regression and uncovering techniques, such as ideomotor finger responses, are useful in determining the source of stress. Unconscious stress is insidious and if it remains hidden only the symptoms will be treated — never the cause.

In most cases, however, the cause of excessive stress is known. Pressure in the workplace, financial concerns and domestic discord are typical stressors mentioned by people seeking help.

Self-hypnosis can be taught to clients during heterohypnosis sessions and allows clients to carry the benefits of hypnotic modalities anywhere and to use the techniques whenever necessary.

Individuals can use self-hypnosis to develop more relaxation and relieve tension on their own. Whether one chooses to call it relaxation therapy, autogenic training, meditation or progressive relaxation is immaterial — the techniques are hypnotic.

First clients are asked to write a brief suggestion that incorporates positive images of a successful response to a stressful situation, for example, feeling relaxed and calm when a traffic jam makes them late for an appointment, or taking several deep breaths to unwind stress from a yelling boss or children fighting at the dinner table.

Next, clients develop a hypnotic trance by focusing their eyes on a spot on the wall or some other visual focal point just above their horizontal line of sight (this causes eye fatigue and enhances the development of trance). As they take slow, deep breaths and concentrate all their attention on the focal spot, they can imagine all their tension and tightness escaping with each outgoing breath. They might want to count backward from any number to one, with each slow count breathing deeply and imagining themselves become more relaxed. If their eyes have not closed by the time they've counted down to one, they may go ahead and close their eyes anyway. They can imagine themselves in their favorite place of relaxation or vacation. From this point — a light or medium hypnotic trance is most likely to have developed — they may give themselves the positive suggestions written earlier.

Perhaps the most powerful aspect of hypnosis for stress management is the use of posthypnotic suggestions and cues for dealing with stress outside of the hypnotic trance. These cues can be any action or image that can be associated with relaxation at or near the time of a stressful occurrence.

For instance, suppose a client, Harriet, becomes stressed from an annoying co-worker. She must work with that person, so little can be done to alter the situation, short of quitting. Find an action or symbol Harriet can mentally imagine that represents unwinding of that tension and stress — perhaps clenching a fist tightly as if gathering all the tension in the fist. Then, as she takes a deep breath and slowly exhales, she can release the clenched fingers and imagine the stress being released at the same time.

By practicing this technique while in trance and associating the release of the clenched fist with the release of tension, she is developing a post-hypnotic cue so that whenever she clenches her fist and gathers the tension there, she can release the tension and stress by relaxing her fist. Thus, after the suggestion and action are repeated a number of times while in trance, the same effects will occur later, outside of trance, while working with that annoying co-worker or involved in other stressful activities.

Often stress is associated with some sort of performance task. When that task is job-related the stress can become chronic, in a cycle of performance anxiety — stress — deteriorating performance — increased stress. Self-hypnosis can be very effective in breaking that stress cycle.

One client, a professional baseball pitcher, had endured a poor season. His pitching was off and even at spring training he was developing a great deal of performance-related stress. After teaching him self-hypnosis techniques, we developed a series of posthypnotic cues to allow him to relax while on the mound. As he took a deep breath and gently pulled on his hat brim, he imagined how he was exhaling the stress and at the same time "pulling" the stress out of his head and body through his hat brim. We added some cues for more focus on the ball and on his task of throwing it over the plate. He suggested to himself that as he threw the ball he was throwing it down a long pipe that inevitably led over home plate. While on the mound, he merely imagined a long pipe, a cue for him to throw the ball down the pipe to the plate. After six weeks of self-hypnosis practice daily with these relaxation and task specific cues, his pitching improved so much that instead of being returned to the minor leagues — as was his fear — he became a starting pitcher and had a relatively successful season.

After clients gain awareness of the stressors in their lives, they can develop suggestions and posthypnotic cues for dealing with both specific situations and unforeseen stressors. The clenched fist technique mentioned earlier is a very effective, general method for stress control that can be used in a variety of situations. However, if stress is caused by a particular situation that must be dealt with on an ongoing basis, more specific cues can be developed. For example, if clients are in a job that requires dealing with difficult customers, they might suggest to themselves that whenever they feel their tension level rising while on the phone, they will take a deep breath and snap a toothpick in half. The breaking of the toothpick can signal the breaking of the stress and the deep breath is a signal for renewal of their positive mood and understanding nature.

Suggestions such as these must be given over a number of trance sessions in order to firmly establish the posthypnotic cues. Self-hypnosis should be practiced at least 15 or 20 minutes a day five or six times a week.

Clients will probably notice a lessening of overall stress and tension very quickly, but it may be some time before the posthypnotic cues become effective. The longer the stress reaction has been taking place, the longer it will take to undo that reaction.

The effects of excessive stress are lessened by changing the client's perception and reaction to the stressing agent. Hypnosis can be effective in raising awareness of stressors and in altering one's reaction. If research continues to find more and more evidence that physiological illnesses are linked to excessive stress, hypnotic relaxation may prove to be one of the most valuable therapeutic tools available.

Reference

Selye, H. (1956). *The stress of life*. New York: McGraw-Hill.

Q&A 59 Hypnosis With Smoking and Overeating

Question:

I am thoroughly confused by what I've read about the benefits of hypnosis for smoking and overeating. I've read both that hypnosis is wonderfully effective and that it's not much good at all. Can you clarify this issue? If there are therapists getting good results with these problems, what are they doing?

Discussion by BRIAN GRODNER, Ph.D.

Hypnosis can be very effective in treating smoking, overeating, and other habit problems. There are therapists getting very good results in this area, although the many studies published and reviews of these studies (e.g., Johns, 1984; Katz, 1980; Mott & Roberts, 1979; Wadden & Anderton, 1982) have not reached definitive conclusions.

There are a number of problems with the research on hypnosis and habit control. For instance, rarely do the authors specify what was done under the name of hypnosis, so we really don't know what the treatment involved. As Katz (1980) states, "to report that a client was treated with hypnosis is like reporting that one used psychotherapy or medicine to effect a cure." Little is said about the subjective experiences of the subjects or even if they were in fact hypnotized.

Another problem with the research is that in the vast majority of studies hypnotic techniques were direct and standardized; the same direct techniques were used on all subjects. Barber's (1977) study on the use of indirect hypnotic strategies for pain control challenged many traditionally held beliefs about the effectiveness of hypnosis. He found that the overwhelming majority of subjects (however poorly they responded to susceptibility scales or direct approaches) were able to use indirect methods for successful pain

325

relief. This matches the belief of many clinicians that hypnotic susceptibility scales merely measure response to a particular set of stimuli and are not related to success in hypnosis or therapy. This idea has been supported by the research of Barber (1980), Alman and Carney (1980), and that of others. Of course, the individualization of clinical treatment should also increase the success of therapy.

Because of these and other problems with the research on the effectiveness of hypnotherapy with habit control, for now I have to accept my own clinical evidence and that of other therapists who are successfully treating smoking and overeating. I hope that in time the research problems will be cleared up and that controlled research will substantiate our claims and tell us exactly how effective we are and what areas need more work.

How does hypnosis help in habit control? Many clients believe that hypnosis works because of some inherent qualities in the hypnotic process. That is why clients come in and want the "one session zap" to lose weight or stop smoking. But the successful long-lasting zap is atypical. It is usually the result of someone already having made a decision, for example, to stop smoking. The client, however, because of his or her beliefs about how changes occur, may need some special process like hypnosis to legitimize or ratify the change.

Studies have shown that clients do better when they believe that hypnosis will *help* them change rather than do it automatically for them (e.g., Perry, Gelfand, & Marcovitch, 1979). To understand how hypnosis helps we must focus on how therapy works, what helps people change, how clients become motivated and able to make new decisions. How are patients persuaded to follow a medical regimen or believe they will get better? Hypnosis works by augmenting, strengthening, extending, or speeding up these processes.

A successful habit control program must be comprehensive. The nature of the habits must be understood within the context of the client's personality and life. Rarely have I encountered clients for whom a desired habit change did not relate to a desired change in life style or self-image. Therefore, issues of personality, life style, and personal motivation must be addressed.

Treatment should have a positive, not deprivation, orientation. Changes should be permanent, not temporary or short-term, and the quality of the client's commitment to change is important.

Therapy should be individualized and, in order to accomplish this, one must learn about the client. Information must be gathered about reasons for losing weight or stopping smoking, as well as reasons for not giving up cigarettes or overeating, history of habits, other attempts to stop, involvement of others, medical and health information, and so on. You must also gather specific behavioral information on eating or smoking, such as how much, when, where, and what, and the emotional and logistical context of the behavior. Is the habit a reaction or attempted solution to feelings of anxiety, depression, or boredom? Is the habit a means to psychological ends, e.g., obesity as a barrier to feared intimacy and sexuality or smoking as a barrier to loneliness or a way of feeling grownup?

Attention should be paid to client's traditions and beliefs, such as having to clean one's plate. The therapist should be prepared to share "tricks" and helpful hints while encouraging new habits. The therapist needs knowledge of such issues as nutrition, food substitution, calorie burnoff, metabolism and set point theory, and nicotine addiction. Goals need to be established and behavioral reinforcement needs to be used.

Perhaps most important for success are developing new attitudes and a new self-image as a non-smoker or slim person.

Hypnosis can be used effectively in losing weight and stopping smoking in many different ways. Here are some of them:

1) *Changing feelings and attitudes.* Hypnotic suggestions can be more comprehensive than just direct reminders to eat less or not smoke. What are some of the client's feelings and attitudes which are associated with, or relevant to, being slimmer or a nonsmoker? Examples are suggestions for cleanliness, being in fashion, and being proud of your body.

2) *Tapping into the client's unconscious and personal history for more complete information (perhaps by use of age regression) to more fully understand current drives and behavior.* Why the client has the habit, what benefits accrue from it, what early decisions prompted it, and what internal obstacles there are to change are some of the questions which may be answered.

3) *Accessing and mobilizing resources such as confidence and optimism.* One way is to recreate past experiences in which the client was confident. Extract the attitudes, behaviors, and feelings which were most significant at those times and help the client use them for his or her current habit control program.

4) *Changing physiological responses such as hunger pangs and withdrawal symptoms.* Hunger pangs can be relabeled as interesting stomach contractions rather than a signal to eat. To calm some of the symptoms of nicotine withdrawal the patient can hypnotically spray the skin (internally and externally) with a soothing emolient or relaxing agent. Many of the hypnotic techniques for pain control can be successfully adapted for this area as well.

5) *Reframing of current habit behaviors as positive attempts to meet needs and then developing alternative responses to meet these needs without the negative byproducts of the current habit.* The therapist needs to understand that clients are doing the best they can with the choices they believe are available to them. Accepting the intention or reason behind the behavior helps clients let go of particular (and problematic) solutions.

6) *Mentally rehearsing and planning successful responses to difficult situations,* e.g., a smoke-filled gathering, a party buffet.

7) *Direct and indirect suggestions for new behaviors and habits,* e.g., chewing more slowly.

8) *Using full sensory imagery of reaching goals with a sense of victory and*

pride. Hypnosis can pair the visual imagery of a goal being reached with the building up of good feelings, pride, and a sense of victory. This will increase motivation and help clients believe that the goal is attainable and worthwhile.

9) *Vivifying, strengthening and accessing of aversive strategies such as rapid smoking.* Hypnosis can be used to develop and recreate the aversive feeling in so strong a manner that it will be stronger than the positive feelings usually derived from the habit.

10) *Enhancement of other therapeutic strategies such as metaphors, dreamwork, and reinforcement.* Telling a metaphor or having a client be reinforced while in a trance can allow greater receptivity to your therapeutic message.

11) *Using symbolic images such as Pac Man eating up excess fat.*

12) *Posthypnotic suggestion.* Since the client has trouble controlling habits outside of your office, posthypnotic suggestions help generalize the suggestions to the client's everyday environment when he or she is not with you, e.g., "You may be surprised and delighted to find yourself savoring a cold fresh salad whenever you eat in a restaurant."

13) *Using self-hypnosis so clients can increase their sense of control and integrate their new behaviors and attitudes into the fabric of their everyday lives.* Self-hypnosis should be taught to clients as soon as heterohypnosis has been started. Clients should learn to deal with distractions because distractions have the same relationship to successful self-hypnosis as obstacles and stumbling blocks have to meeting one's goals. Clients should be taught to increase the speed and ease with which self-hypnosis can be used. This not only increases the practical effectiveness of hypnosis in the client's real world but allows more time during sessions for utilization (as opposed to induction) of trance states.

14) *Strengthening the new self-image and attitudes, which are the most important part of eating or smoking control.* We in effect ask clients to behave like nonsmokers or slim people when they are still predominantly smokers and overeaters.

Here is an *abbreviated* set of instructions for one way I use hypnosis to help people change their self-image: "Make a clear image of what you would look like if you were slim, wearing what you'd be wearing and doing what you'd be doing. Step into the picture seeing through your eyes, hearing through your ears and feeling in your body your slimness. You are *now* a slim person and as a slim person you think like a slim person, choose foods like a slim person, exercise like a slim person, etc. You are *now* and will always be a slim person. [Here I usually give signals to trigger and access this experience.] You might notice a layer of fat remaining on the outside of the slim you. This is just a time lag and the fat is not really a part of you anymore. It's like an antler ready to come off, but still connected, like fur ready to molt but still temporarily on the body. I don't know the way you will most easily see, hear, and feel the fat leaving. Maybe it will melt off or peel off or evaporate off or fall off or leave by a way specially meaningful to you as a slim person."

I use hypnosis and other Ericksonian approaches without a formal trance to accept and utilize clients' behavior while creating and vivifying special images to help them change. An example is the client seeking to lose weight who has a "need" to eat everything on his or her plate and frequently to finish what is left on the plates of others. A screening for such hard-core clients is to ask if it would be acceptable if someone else ate the food. If their response is positive, it is clear that habit or belief rather than hunger is the main influence.

Rather than preach to them (they already know they should stop and already give themselves a hard time), I might say, "I really admire your interest in ecology. I think it's great of you to sacrifice your health and looks, to use yourself as a garbage can rather than throw food out in the garbage and contribute to our solid waste removal problem. But how about doing it more completely and congruently? The next time and every time you're about to eat food just because it's there, would you take out a big plastic garbage bag and put it on. Wear it and then you can finish everything on the plate." This strong imagery is much more powerful than the effects of discussion. Clients invariably laugh and report later that this image came to them instantly whenever they were about to eat food they really didn't want.

Hypnosis can help create the internal and external reality in which a client is motivated and able to lose weight and stop smoking. In summary, the research may say "maybe," but creative clinicians who integrate hypnosis with a sound therapeutic approach tailored to the individual client are saying "yes." When properly used, hypnosis can be very effective in helping clients modify destructive habits.

References

Alman, B., & Carney, R. (1980). Consequences of direct and indirect suggestions on success of post-hypnotic behavior. *American Journal of Clinical Hypnosis, 23*(2), 112–118.

Barber, J. (1980). Hypnosis and the unhypnotizable. *American Journal of Clinical Hypnosis, 23*(1), 409.

Barber, J. (1977). Rapid induction analgesia: A clinical report. *American Journal of Clinical Hypnosis, 19*(3), 138–147.

Johns, M. (1984). Unpublished manuscript.

Katz, N. (1980). Hypnosis and the addictions: A critical review. *Addictive Behaviors, 5*(1), 41–47.

Mott, T., & Roberts, J. (1979). Obesity and hypnosis: A review of the literature. *American Journal of Clinical Hypnosis, 22*, 3–7.

Perry, C., Gelfand, R., & Marcovitch, R. (1979). The relevance of hypnotic susceptibility in the clinical context. *Journal of Abnormal Psychology, 88*, 592–603.

Wadden, T. A., & Anderton, C. H. (1982). The clinical use of hypnosis. *Psych. Bulletin, 91*(2), 215–243.

$\underset{A}{\overset{Q}{\underset{\&}{}}}60$ Using Hypnosis
With Habitual Aborters

Question:

> Women who have suffered more than four spontaneous abortions
> without delivering an infant are categorized as habitual aborters.
> Can hypnosis be used to help such women carry a pregnancy to
> term?

Discussion by DAVID B. CHEEK, M.D.

We have known for many years that emotional factors play a major part
in the physiological sequences terminating in a spontaneous abortion. Stallworthy, in England (1959), wrote a classic paper on the fact that almost
any form of treatment for repeated abortions will be successful if the physician is enthusiastic about a certain treatment regimen and conveys confidence that this will work.

Hypnosis combined with use of unconscious skeletal muscle responses
(ideomotor signals) gives access to unconscious factors causing some abortions, particularly those occurring repeatedly. Recognition of the origins permits the pregnant woman to become her own psychotherapist in preventing
the loss of a desired pregnancy.

There are definite organic factors that can cause abortions, and most
prominent among those would be: congenital anomalies of the uterus, lethal
genes in the embryo, viral infections causing severe defects in the conceptus,
nutritional deficiencies, and chemical toxins affecting the embryo during
the first eight weeks of gestation. If obvious organic factors have been ruled
out, then careful attention must be given to the remaining psychological
factors.

A woman who has had even one spontaneous or induced abortion will
approach the next pregnancy with some trepidation. It is hard for her to

plan for the birth of a healthy child. She may feel that she is not worthy of having a healthy normal child or that she lacks some quality of motherhood. She does not shop for baby clothes or a bassinet for she is afraid of "counting her chickens before they hatch."

Emotional Factors in Abortion

A thorough emotional history should be obtained in these patients. There are a number of factors that can have a crucial bearing on the success of a pregnancy; those that I have found to be particularly significant are:

1) A history of the patient's mother having had a serious illness or major emotional problem during or immediately after her pregnancy with the patient. There is a tendency for the daughter of such a pregnancy to assume guilt for her mother's difficulties.
2) Starting life feeling unwanted as an infant, or later, feeling unwanted as a girl. I believe that the understandings of babies at birth are imprinted and remain fixed, and that delivery room conversations, often misinterpreted, can form the bases of powerful, negative impressions.
3) A history of a serious illness during childhood, leaving the patient feeling inadequate because she was out of school or could not play like other children.
4) The death of a parent or parental divorce before the patient was 10 years old. This may cause the patient to feel responsible for what happened.
5) Parental concern if the beginning of menstruation is delayed past the age of 15 can make the child feel she is not normal and therefore cannot be sure she will have a normal child at term.
6) A history of abdominal surgery through a transverse or midline incision can make women overly concerned with their female organs.
7) Being sexually molested as a child can cause a woman to reject her femininity and feel hostility toward all males. Both forces mitigate against childbearing.
8) There may be unconscious guilt arising from an induced or spontaneous abortion, stillbirth, or delivery of an abnormal infant in the previous pregnancy.
9) Unconscious hostility toward the husband or any member of his family during the present pregnancy may cause the woman to subconsciously identify her baby with his family and may cause her to abort "his baby."
10) A history of severe menstrual cramps leading to the remark by parents or friends, "If you think that this is bad, just wait until you have a baby.

Intervention

In a retrograde study of abortion sequences some years ago, I found that more than half of the women started their bleeding and expulsive contractions during the night, usually between one and four in the morning. The majority of those who started during the day revealed, during age regression, their belief that the process really originated with troubled dreams repeated for several nights prior to the abortion.

Fortunately, thought sequences capable of causing abortion very rarely do so the first time around. They occur on repeated cycles of sleep and on successive nights of sleep. This gives the patient an opportunity to recognize that her sleep has been disturbed and to report this change in behavior to her doctor or midwife. Early intervention can prevent loss of a normal conceptus. The physician should know how to act at once during the first telephone call of alarm. It is far better in the case of a woman with a history of habitual abortion to check out the emotional background *before* the patient begins the pregnancy.

Even if the process of bleeding and consciously perceived uterine contractions has already begun, there is usually time to expose the emotional cause and help the patient stop the progress toward abortion or delivery of a dangerously premature infant. But intervention must begin at once and should not be delayed by admission of the patient to a hospital. It can be handled over the telephone, any time, at home or even long distance when the patient is on a vacation trip.

All pregnant women, regardless of previous history, should know how to recognize that their sleep has been troubled and be shown how to check their own subconscious reactions to threatening dreams and deep sleep ideation. Their first line of correction is to ask for an ideomotor response to the question, "Is there an emotional cause for this?" If the answer is a "yes" with a finger signal or movement of a Chevreul pendulum, they can ask, "Now that I know this, can I stop my bleeding (or cramps) and go on with this pregnancy?"

If the answer suggests an organic beginning or inability to stop the process, there is still time to make a telephone call to the doctor or midwife who is capable of inducing hypnosis over the telephone, searching for the causal experience, and permitting the patient to make her corrections for the sake of her baby.

Consider this example: A woman who has not been to your office but has been referred to you for obstetrical care calls at 3 p.m. on Sunday to say that she has an appointment next week but started to bleed slightly this morning and is now having cramps. She would have called earlier but she did not want to bother you. She reports that her last period started 10 weeks ago, that this is a planned pregnancy but she has had five previous miscarriages of planned pregnancies and she hopes that she might be able to carry this one. She is 30 years old and has been happily married for six years.

This is an emergency and you must act quickly if you are to be of help to her. You need not be concerned about her past history. She is frightened and is therefore already in a hypnoidal state. This enables her to respond strongly to positive, hopeful suggestions given honestly and authoritatively. We should use hypnosis permissively under peaceful circumstances but authoritative commands are necessary during an emergency.

Explain that you will show her how to stop this process but you need to know what has started this trouble. Say to her, "Let the subconscious part of your mind go back to the moment you are starting the bleeding. When you are there you will feel a twitching sensation in your right index finger. Don't try to recall what is going on. Just say 'now' when you feel that finger lifting up from where it is resting."

There is a double reason for this approach. Your words tell the patient that something can be done right now to prevent what has happened regularly before. The request for an unconscious gesture when reaching the moment that bleeding started centers her attention on what her finger might do and diminishes her acute attention to the contractions of her uterus and the fact that she is bleeding.

It probably will take less than 30 seconds before she says, "Now." You will probably notice that her voice is subdued, indicating that she has slipped into a deeper trance state. Say to her, "Let a thought come to you about what your subconscious knows has started your bleeding. When you know it your 'yes' finger will lift again and when it does please tell me what comes to your mind."

There may be another 30-second pause before she responds. Be quiet until she reports something like, "I'm asleep after lunch. I'm dreaming that the doctor is saying he doesn't think I will be able to carry my baby because of all the other ones I have lost. He says we can try some hormones to see if that will help."

You answer, "That index finger can represent a 'yes' answer to a question. Your middle finger on the same hand can represent a 'no' answer. This is like your nodding your head unconsciously when you agree with someone or shaking your head if you disagree. I want to know is this dream occurring *after* you have started bleeding?"

She answers, "My 'no' finger is lifting."

"All right. This is a dream and your subconscious knows the dream is the cause of your bleeding. Sadness and fear can make a uterus bleed even when a woman is not pregnant. Is your inner mind willing now to stop the bleeding and let your baby go on developing normally?"

The patient will usually find her 'yes' finger lifting for this question, but if she gets a 'no' or some other finger that might mean she does not want to answer, you must ask her 'yes' finger to lift when she knows why she feels this way. It is usually some feeling of guilt or defeatist belief system at work. Simple recognition permits her to remove that factor.

You conclude the telephone call with a deepening series of suggestions and directions to relax her abdomen, stop the irritability of her uterus and fall asleep for about 10 minutes after hanging up. You ask her to call you back in one hour with a report. Do not say any more about bleeding. Just ask her to call you in one hour. The statement often used by doctors is, "Give me a call if your bleeding continues or gets worse." Such a statement is interpreted as meaning the doctor expects her to bleed and she will do it. She has shown five previous times how well she can bleed and abort.

You explain that this does not mean she has to miscarry again. Bleeding occurs in 30% of pregnant women at some time during their pregnancy and has nothing to do with prognosis unless they become frightened.

This presentation is easily understood by a frightened patient. The statement of a way for communicating unconscious information is also telling the patient tacitly that discovery of the cause will permit correction of the problem. This diverts her total attention from the bleeding and uterine cramps to the more constructive area of what she can do to stop the trouble and get on with the pregnancy.

The questions and the subconscious review of significant events have led the patient further away from the thought that she might lose this pregnancy.

A marvelous protective action takes place by virtue simply of entering a hypnotic state at a time of crisis. Coagulation mechanisms return to a normal balance and all vegetative behavior is improved. There is no need to command bleeding to stop or the uterus to remain quiet but it helps the patient to make better use of these protective functions when you show respect for this phenomenon by saying, "Now this is something you dreamed. Would you agree that this dream does not need to threaten the life of your baby, that you have a right to stop your bleeding and get on with your pregnancy?"

Let us turn now to the special situation of habitually aborting women. Women who have had six or more successive abortions without birth of a living child at term generally consider themselves hopeless cases. Their chances of having a full-term child are thought to be less than 10%. By the time there have been six miscarriages a woman may have become so discouraged that she submits to a hysterectomy, which is often preceded by severe pelvic complaints.

I have had the privilege of working with five such women, one of whom was pregnant with her tenth trial. She was aborting when I first saw her. She had been molested by her grandfather when she was four years old, had wished she could be a boy, had become fat and developed excess body hair. She had married a man she knew to be homosexual. After the seventh abortion she divorced her husband and shortly thereafter married a delightfully masculine and thoughtful man. The early life imprinting, however, was not corrected. She moved away from San Francisco, lost the next four pregnancies, and finally had a hysterectomy and removal of an enlarged ovary. Thereafter she adopted a child, returned to her normal weight, and lost the excess hair on her body.

The remaining five all had living, normal infants at term, although they all had frightening experiences with bleeding one or more times during the first successful pregnancy. Each was taught how to obtain ideomotor responses to questions. They called at the first sign of bleeding or cramping. They were able to discover the source of their trouble and were able to stop their bleeding within minutes of our telephone questioning. All were eventually able to hallucinate delivery of their infant as they reached their sixth month of pregnancy. This is a very good prognostic sign. Three of the four who were able to have a living child were unable to hallucinate a successful ending at the time of their first pregnancy under my care. (See Table.)

TABLE

Case	Age	Abortions before therapy	Abortions after therapy	Living babies
W.C.	26	7	4	0
S.W.	32	8	1	3
V.F.	37	5	1	1
G.F.	28	6	0	2
G.S.	37	8	1	1

When caring for women who have had multiple abortions, the physician must be prepared for emergency calls at any time. It is important that such women know they can call on their doctor or midwife at any time. The knowledge that they are expected to telephone if they are frightened is often enough for them to solve their own problem without calling. But it is also of utmost importance to recognize that delay in offering help may result in enough damage to the circulation to the fetus to cause abortion in spite of therapy, as happened in three of these cases.

When a distressed, frightened patient calls, your first question should be, "Now let me see. What finger lifts for a 'yes' answer?" This takes the patient's attention briefly away from concentration on the bleeding or cramping. It also shifts her time perception to the last time you were using hypnosis and ideomotor questioning in the safety of your office. The next question should be, "Does your inner mind know that your baby is OK?" If the answer is "yes," the bleeding and cramps may stop without any further intervention. If it is a "no," you must ask your patient to go back to whatever gave her that silly idea that the baby is not OK and to bring the thought up to where she can tell you about it. The cause is usually constructed out of dream material or residual pessimism about the pregnancy being too good to be true.

Patients seem to know what they are able to do in a constructive way when they are pregnant. It is up to us who care for them to listen to remarks volunteered by our patients and to know how to search for troubled dreams and sources of pessimism. The results are rewarding when we are able to project our faith in our patients' being able to find solutions to their challenges.

Reference

Stallworthy, J. (1959). Habitual abortion. *International Journal of Fertility, 4,* 237–241.

$\underset{A}{Q}_{\&}61$ Using Hypnosis to Enhance Athletic Performance

Question:

I understand that many world-class athletes use visualization or hypnosis in their training. How is hypnosis used to enhance athletic performance?

**Discussion by GEORGE J. PRATT, Ph.D., &
ERROL R. KORN, M.D.**

The scientific rationale for the use of mental processes in physical performance dates back to Jacobson's studies (1932) of electrophysiology, demonstrating that when one imagines a physical activity, the muscles involved are stimulated. More recent research (Ahsen, 1976) indicates that actual neural growth occurs as a result of mental imagery. As for the enhancement of athletic performance, a number of studies give unqualified support for the facilitating effects of mental training.

Studies have demonstrated the effectiveness of mental processes in basketball free throw shooting (Hall & Erffmeyer, 1983), karate performance (Weinberg, Seabourne, & Jackson, 1982), and darts (Vandell, Davis, & Clugston, 1943). Charles Garfield, in an unpublished lecture, cited a 1980 study of world-class Soviet athletes who were divided into four groups based on the amount of physical training and mental training received. The group that received the most mental training demonstrated the greatest improvement and the group showing the least improvement was the one that received only physical training.

It must be realized, however, that hypnosis cannot turn everyone into a superstar. No amount of hypnosis will allow a weekend athlete to win against a seasoned champion. When boxer Ken Norton used self-hypnosis to prepare for the bout in which he beat Mohammed Ali, he was not sud-

denly transformed into a winner. He was already very good and the hypnosis simply helped him perform at his best. And that is what athletes need
to understand about hypnosis; at its best it can help them make the most
of themselves and perform at or near their peak.

Our work to enhance athletic performance can be broken down into four
categories: goal-setting, relaxation, concentration, and rehearsal.

Goal-setting

Specific and realistic goals must be set by athletes and coach or therapist.
Athletes should be encouraged to write down in what areas and to what
degree they wish to improve and over what length of time. As they write
down their goals, clients have the opportunity to reflect on them, which
helps develop realistic and incremental objectives; however, the therapist
must stand ready to help ensure that the goals are attainable.

A golfer, for instance, can be encouraged to choose as his or her first goal
something like improving by an average of three strokes in six weeks. On
the other hand, he or she should be discouraged from setting a goal of
winning a big tournament coming up in six weeks, since failure to win could
be ego-damaging and negate the progress up to that point. Even placing
third might be perceived as failure. Yet, if every six weeks of practice yielded
three more strokes off the average score, in several months the client's performance might be improved enough to win a major tournament.

A competitive swimmer's realistic goals might be developing a smoother
stroke first, then increasing speed by one-half of a second every two weeks.
Imagery of a smooth, gliding stroke pulling him or her forward could be
the first step. Gradually that stroke could become more and more rapid until
imagery of a paddle-wheel could be visualized speeding through the water.

Just as athletes do not expect a few days of physical training to yield
dramatic results, so they should not expect a few hours or days of hypnosis
to make them into world champions, unless they are virtually at that level
already, as was the case with Ken Norton.

Relaxation

Since physical tension is counterproductive to optimal athletic performance, relaxation is an important goal. Not only is relaxation preferable to
anxiety, but it is also the basis upon which greater concentration and rehearsal are built. (Before going further, a caveat is in order. Although the
importance of relaxation can hardly be exaggerated, it is theoretically possible for an athlete to become too relaxed, to the point where he or she is com-
placent and loses competitive striving. We have never encountered such a
situation but it is possible and the therapist or coach should be alert to it.)

Progressive relaxation and calming imagery are two very effective ways to release tension and anxiety, and both can be part of or lead to hypnotic inductions. Many of our clients tell us that tapes of the relaxation and induction experiences we create in the office are useful when they use self-hypnosis at home. We provide several posthypnotic cues in the office to facilitate self-hypnosis later — for example, suggesting that, whenever they wish to reenter this same level of relaxation and focus, they can count backward from 30 to 1 and imagine each number as a step closer to this same deep, comfortable level of relaxation.

Mental relaxation actually leads to greater mental alertness. This alertness is a positive feature and produces better physical and mental reactions and better physical coordination.

Concentration

Concentration on a physical activity can be enhanced with hypnosis, which is itself a process of focused attention. We have clients develop posthypnotic cues that lead to greater concentration. This work can take two directions. The first is to eliminate distractions. In nearly every sport the multitude of sounds, sights, and physical distractions surrounding the event can impede one's focus and performance. By preventing themselves from being distracted, athletes will naturally perform nearer their optimal level.

Posthypnotic cues can be developed for any sport. In golf, for example, this kind of suggestion might be used: "Before the game begins, the act of selecting which golf balls you will play with is much like selecting which sights and sounds you will play with. Only those elements necessary to playing the game well will be focused on." In baseball, suggestions can be given along these lines: "You know that you put on special shoes to play the game. These shoes are specially designed for a specific purpose. In the same way the shoes are focused to a purpose, you may know that as you put on those shoes you can begin to become more focused and concentrate specifically upon your activity and tasks within the game. Any time during the game you desire to have more concentration, merely thinking about your shoes and how they are focused to a purpose can allow you to become more focused in your performance."

By linking the desired result (elimination of distraction) to a part of the athlete's preparation, the therapist creates a posthypnotic cue for the desired response. Asking the client to relate the step-by-step process he or she goes through before competition will help in finding and developing such cues for a sport or activity with which the therapist is unfamiliar.

The second part of concentration is focus on the specific task which is the crux of optimal performance; for instance, kicking the ball accurately in soccer. Suggestions for concentration in a soccer player might include: "You know that the playing field is composed of lines and angles. You also know that the ball travels in a direction that is determined by the precise angle at which it is struck. You may find that you know, even without thinking about it, the precise angle at which the ball must be struck in order to travel to the desired place on the field. By taking a deep breath a few moments before you kick the ball, you can develop a deep concentration within you. That concentration can allow your foot to meet the ball at the exact angle you already know will cause the ball to go where you wish it to."

Such suggestions tie together images that are already familiar to the athlete with images of future actions that are related. Such cues are more easily accepted and more likely to develop the desired responses. For each task within a sport, the therapist should try to create and develop the desired responses. For each task within a sport, the therapist should try to create and develop several posthypnotic cues. In conversations with the client, information will be elicited that will enable the therapist to develop such related images. If, for example, the soccer player also enjoyed playing billiards, you might relate the angle of his kick to the carom of the billiard balls.

Taking material from the client's repertoire of experiences to create suggestions will make the suggestions more powerful and more successful. This takes time, but the investment of that time will yield better results than formula suggestions.

Rehearsal

Mentally rehearsing one's performance, as mentioned earlier, can be more productive than actual physical practice. Naturally, combining mental and physical practice can produce more complete and fully integrated behavior during play. Jack Nicklaus has related that he never hits a golf ball without first visualizing it landing exactly where he wishes. He often imagines a groove going from the ball to the hole and the ball following in that groove. Or he mentally sees the ball flying through the air and landing nicely near the pin.

There are two basic types of rehearsal imagery — process and result. Process imagery is imagining the various steps that must be undertaken to accomplish a given task. For example, a tennis player would imagine a proper swing of the racket and angle of approach on the ball — that is the *process* of making a successful serve. The player might then imagine the ball landing in just the precise spot on the court that would be most advantageous and then even imagine the *feeling* of elation that would accompany the game-winning point. That is *result* imagery.

Both process and result imagery are important. Further, clients should be reminded that imagery is not only visual. They should be encouraged to involve as many of their senses in the imagery as possible, including their emotional responses to successful processes and results.

Teaching clients to do self-hypnosis is perhaps the best way to have them perform mental rehearsals of their activity. We encourage our clients to imagine, while in self-hypnosis, each facet of their game. They can begin with the earliest preparations for play. While imagining lacing up shoes or donning clothing or equipment, they can also reinforce the posthypnotic cues associated with such preliminary actions.

One of our clients, a semi-pro baseball player, had a difficult time with performance anxiety. He was just fine in games where there were no particularly important spectators; however, if family or professional scouting agents were in attendance he would play terribly. We developed a set of posthypnotic cues that began in the locker room. In fact, the locker itself was a cue for him to pack away his tension and anxiety along with his street clothes.

He was reminded that the visor of his baseball hat was designed to shield his eyes from the sun and we used it as a cue to shield himself from the tension of spectators, whoever they might be. Tugging on his hat brim while at his second base position was a cue to shield himself from anxiety. Additionally, we developed cues that gripping the bat was giving him a better grip on his concentration. He was also encouraged to imagine himself catching ground balls and, when at bat, seeing the ball he hit travel long and straight. He was helped to imagine the wonderful feeling of a double, triple, or even a home run. By combining these process and result images, this player stopped making the mistakes his anxiety had produced and his continued mental imagery helped him improve his batting average. He is now playing for an American League team. We occasionally conduct telephone sessions to modify and reinforce his continuing self-hypnosis practice.

Another aspect of rehearsal involves recalling athletes' performance *after* a game. This after-the-fact rehearsal serves to analyze and improve their actual performance. While in a hypnotic trance they can recall details of specific actions. Their correct, successful actions can be examined and reinforced. Incorrect, unsuccessful actions can be replaced in the imagery with successful ones. This type of rehearsal should be done well after the game is over. Clients should be instructed not to try to analyze their performance during the activity. Paralysis through analysis can occur if they attempt to examine their actions during the activity. Analysis of their performance is best done at an unconscious level, later, while in trance.

The program of goal-setting, relaxation, concentration, and rehearsal coupled with posthypnotic cues can lead to greatly improved performance. Clients, however, should understand that results should not be expected in days, though that could happen. It must be emphasized that a program of regular trance work should accompany their regular physical workouts and practice.

References

Ahsen, A. (1976). Neural experimental growth potentials for the treatment of accidental traumas, debilitating stress conditions and chronic emotional blocking. *Journal of Mental Imagery, 2,* 1–22.

Hall, E. G., & Erffmeyer, E. S. (1983). The effect of visuo-motor behavior rehearsal with videotape modeling on free throw accuracy of intercollegiate female basketball players. *Journal of Sports Psychology, 5,* 343–346.

Jacobson, E. (1932). Electrophysiology of mental activities. *American Journal of Psychology, 44,* 677–694.

Vandell, R. A., Davis, R. A., & Clugston, H. A. (1943). The function of mental practice in the acquisition of motor skills. *Journal of General Psychology, 29,* 243–250.

Weinberg, R. S., Seabourne, T. G., & Jackson, A. (1982). Effects of visuo-motor behavioral rehearsal on state-trait anxiety and performance: Is practice important? *Journal of Sport Behavior, 5,* 209–219.

SECTION VIII *Hypnosis and Other Modalities*

Hypnosis is rarely used in its pure form. Other modalities are almost always connected to it, at least if one can agree that the "bedside manner" is the oldest, and certainly one of the most important modalities ever discovered. Those who have utilized hypnosis are well aware that their other areas of expertise are a critical factor in their successes with hypnotherapy, but non-users may not have this same awareness.

A few years ago an important psychiatric organization sent out a questionnaire asking, among other things, "What type(s) of therapy do you do?" Listed among the choices were psychoanalytic, insight-oriented, behavioral, hypnosis, etc. This demonstrated a clear lack of understanding about hypnosis, for it made it sound as though hypnosis were a treatment in and of itself, rather than a modality that can be used in psychoanalytic, insight-oriented, behavioral, and other therapies.

The above has been stated lest the reader be misled by the title of this section. But there were important questions about *how* hypnosis might be combined with, or incorporated into, other treatment modalities like chemotherapy, group therapy, family therapy, insight-oriented therapy, and biofeedback, and those questions seemed to deserve a section of their own.

This section deals specifically with those questions. Any therapist who prescribes psychoactive medications or treats patients for whom such medications have been prescribed should find the discussion of the effects of medication on hypnotizability and hypnotic responsiveness a valuable con-

343

tribution. Those who are doing group or family therapy may be stimulated to incorporate hypnosis into their current practices when they read the relevant papers, and even those who are not using group therapy may start considering it when they realize that what is described as a group technique for stress reduction could be modified to treat groups of people who want to lose weight, stop smoking, or deal with some other common problem. And, finally, since hypnosis and biofeedback have certain aspects in common, therapeutic goals being not the least of these, we have included a paper discussing those aspects.

$\underset{A}{\overset{Q}{\cancel{\&}}}$ 62 Effects of Psychoactive Medication on Hypnosis

Question:

> Do medications (antidepressant, antipsychotic, pain killers, etc.) affect how one should use hypnosis and what results can be expected?

Discussion by DAVID SPIEGEL, M.D.

The effects of psychoactive medications on the use of hypnosis can be examined from the perspective of both their target effects in reducing the symptoms of psychiatric illness and their side effects, such as sedation. The organizing conceptual framework that helps to make these issues coherent is a concentration model of hypnosis, understanding it as a form of aroused attentive focal concentration with a relative suspension of peripheral awareness. This focused ribbon of concentration is a matrix within which the other hypnotic phenomena such as perceptual alteration, involuntariness of motor control, temporal reorientation and compulsive compliance may occur. From this point of view the hypnotic experience is a high-level, complex cognitive process which requires intact concentration. Thus, in theory, any psychoactive medication which through its treatment effect removes impediments to concentration, such as hallucinations or severe anxiety, could potentially remove an interference with hypnotic experience. By the same token, any medication which hampers concentration by causing sedation or confusion would be likely to diminish hypnotic responsiveness.

There is little evidence that any psychoactive medication substantially enhances hypnotic responsiveness *per se*. Consistent with the concentration model of hypnosis, 10 mg of dextroamphetamine has been found to improve hypnotic performance, especially among low hypnotizables (Ulett et al., 1972). There are some studies which indicate an increase in hypnotizability with LSD (Sjoberg & Hollister, 1965) and cannabis (Beahrs et al., 1974). However, the actual increases in scores were extremely small and, clearly, any use of drugs with such profound cognitive and perceptual effects would not be indicated to enhance hypnotizability, especially since any increase in performance is likely to occur at the expense of a person's overall ability to control responsiveness.

While there is comparatively little systematic research on this issue, the few studies that have been done provide support for the distinction between target and side effects. For example, Gibson et al. (1977) demonstrated that diazepam, a classical antianxiety agent, given to low hypnotizable subjects, tended to enhance their hypnotizability scores, presumably by reducing anxious preoccupation. The same drug given to high hypnotizable subjects tended to diminish their hypnotic performance, presumably by sedating them and thereby hampering concentration. This tradeoff between target and side effects is a standard problem when using psychoactive, pain and other forms of medication, but clinical practice as well as systematic research indicates that when patients are sedated, for example, from the use of comparatively long-acting sedative hypnotics, their general impairment in concentration will be reflected in poor hypnotic performance.

The interaction between hypnotizability and psychopathology is a complex issue. Most studies report generally lower hypnotizability and the absence of very high hypnotizability among patients with psychotic disorders. Of eleven empirical studies conducted utilizing the Stanford type scales (Weitzenhoffer & Hilgard, 1959; Shor & Orne, 1962) between 1936 and 1978, six (Bartlett, 1936; Gill & Brenman, 1959; Barber et al., 1964; Webb & Nesmith, 1964; Lavoie et al., 1973; Lavoie et al., 1978) conclude that psychotic patients are less hypnotizable than normal comparison samples. One study (Kramer, 1966) concludes that psychotics are equally hypnotizable to normal comparison samples, and four conclude that psychotics are equally or more hypnotizable than normals (Kramer & Brennan, 1964; Vingoe & Kramer, 1966; Greene, 1969; Gordon, 1973). In only one of these studies (Gordon, 1973) was age controlled for, and since hypnotic responsivity and age are strongly correlated (Morgan & Hilgard, 1973), this is a critical control variable.

Studies of this issue with the Hypnotic Induction Profile (HIP) (Spiegel & Spiegel, 1978) are less ambiguous: All published studies show markedly lower hypnotic responsivity on the HIP among psychotic patients (Spiegel et al., 1975; Spiegel et al., 1982). Age was controlled for in the latter study. The mean HIP induction score (range = 0–10) of patients with schizophrenia, at 3.99, was little more than half the mean score of the normal volunteers at 7.23. These observations are consistent with Shakow's (1971) segmental set theory of schizophrenia. He views the fundamental deficit in schizophrenia as an inability to maintain a major set in the face of distracting minor sets. In this case, the major set would be the hypnotic induction, and the patient's failure to respond represents this incapacity to attend to the major premise. While it would therefore make sense that the use of antipsychotic medications might enhance the hypnotizability of these psychotic patients, the one study on the issue to date (Spiegel, 1980) shows only a nonsignificant trend in that direction (p < .3). These drugs have been reported to result in a nonsignificant lowering of hypnotizability scores in normal subjects (Beahrs et al., 1974).

Studies of the hypnotizability of patients with psychiatric disturbances other than schizophrenia and psychotic illnesses are extremely rare. One study (Spiegel et al., 1982) demonstrated that patients with generalized anxiety disorder, that is, severe anxiety lasting at least one month and requiring intensive treatment, was associated with extremely low hypnotizability scores on the HIP, comparable to those of schizophrenics in that study. Half of those anxious patients were on benzodiazepines, and their hypnotizability scores were higher than those of the patients not so treated (p < .07). Thus, in this case, pharmacologic treatment with benzodiazepines appeared to improve hypnotizability (which was still low even in the treated group). Such differences did not occur in the patients with unipolar and bipolar depressive disorders, whose hypnotizability scores were higher than those of the schizophrenics but still lower than those of the normal controls. One reason for this is that some but not all antidepressants are quite sedating and those patients given sedating antidepressants may have traded whatever impairment in concentration was related to their depressive preoccupations for sedation due to medication side effects.

The clinical guidelines which emerge from these data are that sound clinical assessment and judgment are the best guide to the combination of psychoactive medication and hypnosis. Patients who meet clinical criteria for anxiety in particular, and theoretically other psychiatric disturbances, may find that pharmacologic or other psychotherapeutic treatment of their condition will result in an enhanced capacity to respond to hypnosis. From a theoretical point of view, treatment would reduce interference with their ability to experience their basic hypnotic capacity. From a practical point of view, if a patient scores poorly on a hypnotizability scale or fails to respond to a clinical induction but shows evidence of marked anxiety, depression or thought disorder, retesting after appropriate treatment may yield different results. At the same time, a poor performance in an otherwise psychologically healthy individual may be explained by sedation due to medication.

This may actually be more of a problem with patients on pain medications, which are commonly sedating. Since hypnotic techniques are extremely useful in the treatment of pain (Hilgard & Hilgard, 1975; Spiegel & Bloom, 1983) and since the half-life of most potent analgesics is rather short, it may be important to instruct pain patients to time their use of self-hypnosis for pain control to occur before or after the peak sedative effect of an analgesic drug. One strategy that works well is to suggest to patients learning to use self-hypnosis that they attempt the self-hypnotic analgesia just prior to taking another dose of pain medication in an attempt to prolong the intervals between doses. In this way the use of self-hypnosis can be gradually increased at a time when the patient is least sedated, while the use of analgesic medication can be reduced.

The general place of psychotropic medication in relation to hypnosis is analogous to the place of hypnosis in the broader context of psychotherapeutic treatment: Both can facilitate a primary treatment goal. Psychoactive medication is appropriate insofar as it treats a primary psychiatric symptom. Hypnosis is appropriate insofar as it facilitates a sound treatment strategy.

References

Barber, T. X., Karacan, I., & Calverley, D. S. (1964). "Hypnotizability" and suggestibility in chronic schizophrenics. *Archives of General Psychiatry, 11*, 439–451.

Bartlett, M. R. (1936). Suggestibility in psychopathic individuals: A study with psychoneurotic and dementia praecox subjects. *Journal of General Psychology, 12*, 241–247.

Beahrs, J. E., Carlin, A. S., & Shehorn, J. (1974). Impact of psychoactive drugs on hypnotizability. *American Journal of Clinical Hypnosis, 16*, 267–269.

Gibson, H. B., Corcoran, M. E., & Curran, J. D. (1977). Hypnotic susceptibility and personality: The consequences of diazepam and the sex of the subjects. *British Journal of Psychology, 68*, 51–59.

Gill, M. M., & Brenman, M. (1959). *Hypnosis and related states: Psychoanalytic studies in regression.* New York: International Universities Press.

Gordon, M. C. (1973). Suggestibility of chronic schizophrenic and normal males matched for age. *International Journal of Clinical and Experimental Hypnosis, 21*, 284–288.

Greene, J. T. (1969). Hypnotizability of hospitalized psychotics. *International Journal of Clinical and Experimental Hypnosis, 17*, 103–108.

Hilgard, E. R., & Hilgard, J. R. (1975). *Hypnosis in the relief of pain*, Los Altos, CA: William Kaufmann.

Kramer, E. (1966). Group induction of hypnosis with institutionalized patients. *International Journal of Clinical and Experimental Hypnosis, 14*, 243–246.

Kramer, E., & Brennan, E. P. (1964). Hypnotic susceptibility of schizophrenic patients. *Journal of Abnormal Social Psychology, 69*, 657–659.

Lavoie, G., Lieberman, J., Sabourin, M., et al. (1978). Individual and group assessment of hypnotic responsivity in coerced volunteer chronic schizophrenics. In F. F. Frankel & H. S. Zamansky (Eds.). *Hypnosis at its bicentennial: Selected papers.* New York: Plenum.

Lavoie, G., Sabourin, M., & Langlois, J. (1973). Hypnotic susceptibility, amnesia, and IQ in chronic schizophrenia. *International Journal of Clinical and Experimental Hypnosis, 21*, 157–168.

Morgan, A. H., & Hilgard, E. R. (1973). Age differences in susceptibility to hypnosis. *International Journal of Clinical and Experimental Hypnosis, 21*, 78–85.

Shakow, D. (1971). Some observations on the psychology (and some fewer on the biology) of schizophrenia. *Nervous Mental Disorders, 153*, 300–316.

Shor, R. E., & Orne, E. C. (1963). Norms on the Harvard Group Scale of Hypnotic Susceptibility, Form A. *International Journal of Clinical and Experimental Hypnosis, 11*, 39–47.

Sjoberg, B. M., & Hollister, L. E. (1965). The effects of psychotomimetic drugs on primary suggestibility. *Psychopharmacologia, 8*, 251–262.

Spiegel, D. (1980). Hypnotizability and psychoactive medication. *American Journal of Clinical Hypnosis, 22,* 217–222.

Spiegel, D., & Bloom, J. R. (1983). Group therapy and hypnosis reduce metastatic breast carcinoma pain. *Psychosomatic Medicine, 45,* 333–339.

Spiegel, D., Detrick, D., & Frischholz, E. (1982). Hypnotizability and psychopathology. *American Journal of Psychiatry, 139,* 431–437.

Spiegel, H., Fleiss, J. L., & Bridger, A. A. et al. (1975). Hypnotizability and mental health. In S. Arieti (Ed.). *New dimensions in psychiatry: A world view.* New York: Wiley.

Spiegel, H., & Spiegel, D. (1978). *Trance and treatment: Clinical uses of hypnosis.* New York: Basic Books.

Ulett, G. A., Akpinar, S., & Itil, T. M. (1972). Hypnosis: Pharmacological reality. *American Journal of Psychiatry, 128,* 799–805.

Vingoe, F. J., & Kramer, E. F. (1966). Hypnotic susceptibility of hospitalized psychotic patients: A pilot study. *International Journal of Clinical and Experimental Hypnosis, 14,* 47–54.

Webb, R. A., & Nesmith, C. C. (1964). A normative study of suggestibility in a mental patient population. *International Journal of Clinical and Experimental Hypnosis, 12,* 181–183.

Weitzenhoffer, A. M., & Hilgard, E. R. (1959). *Stanford Hypnotic Susceptibility Scale: Forms A and B.* Palo Alto, CA: Consulting Psychologists Press.

$\underset{A}{Q}\!\!\!\underset{A}{}63$ Using Hypnosis in Groups

Question:

> I've used hypnosis with individuals, but don't quite understand how it can be used with groups of individuals. Can you enlighten me?

Discussion by JUDITH JANARO FABIAN, Ph.D., &
GERALD I. MANUS, Ph.D.

Perhaps one of the most exciting aspects of hypnosis is its enhanced capability in groups. Numerous factors which facilitate the process operate in such a situation. Although group pressures may be subtle, they are very powerful. A positive social milieu, a shared goal, motivation for participation, and confidence in the leader are all adjuncts for success. These aspects, implicit in the situation and in the empathic environment, need not be explicitly stated. Seeing others responding to suggestions reinforces changes within the individual, as the perception of others in a similar situation tends to validate the process, the contextual format, and the goal. Concurrently, there is a reduction of the anxiety that arises whenever new learning is required.

Kroger (1977) speaks of several other factors that account for the success of mass hypnosis. These include a feeling of "emotional contagion," identification, the mobilization of an inherent competitiveness, and a desire to please the leader. These aspects give the therapist a clear advantage in the process.

The size of the group is a significant factor only when it changes the attitude of the participants. For example, if individuals feel an indifference to their unique needs, or that communication with the therapist is inadequate, then the outcome may be affected adversely.

Most individuals want to be perceived as good, responsive participants, and have a strong desire to succeed. For them, compliance and susceptibility are increased. However, groups tend to have one or two dissident individuals among their participants who attain status by identifying themselves as non-responders. These individuals seem to acquire a certain amount of ego gratification in being "resistant," although they are putatively cooperative. Another small number of individuals are so anxious that they cannot focus as needed to enter a trance. They are afraid to deal with their own internal states of anxiety. They feel out of control and are convinced that focusing on their intrapsychic status will exacerbate the high level of arousal and confusion with which they live. These are the individuals who live in a constant state of painful discomfort and sleep only when exhausted, as they have no middle state of comfort. Sometimes these individuals cannot be treated in a group framework because they need to be desensitized to the experience in a slow, systematic, methodical fashion.

Hypnosis can be used in a group setting in a variety of ways. In a traditional format, patients may be hypnotized individually to deal with their individual problems while the other members observe and later discuss the experience. All members of the group may be hypnotized simultaneously and told to imagine what it feels like to experience what one particular patient is experiencing, thus greatly enhancing empathy. The whole group may be hypnotized and the session conducted in the usual manner, but with greater relaxation, and thus less defensiveness from the participants.

If the group shares a truly common goal, like stopping smoking, reducing stress, etc., the process may be somewhat different. We will offer a description of the latter.

We have been running stress reduction groups at Kaiser Permanente Medical Group in Fremont, CA, for the past three and one-half years. These groups are based primarily on relaxation and hypnotic techniques combined with cognitive restructuring. The course meets on a weekly basis, over a five-week period. The group size ranges from 15–30 patients who complete the program. Currently well over two hundred people have done so.

An important consideration is that this is a diverse group of patients who come to the department of psychiatry via different routes — all seeking mitigation of stress-induced symptoms. Most are referred by physicians or other health providers. Some are self-referred, having identified significant problems in coping with life situations. A large number are referred by former members. Participants in the stress reduction group include those who are interested in pain control, reduction of somatic symptoms and/or immobilizing effects of anxiety, concerns about habit or behavioral problems, help with phobic and panic symptoms, or a multitude of other problems.

Each series starts with a lecture on the physiological and psychological components associated with stress. Attention is paid to causes and effects of stress, the connection between stress and general life patterns, and methods of increasing health-maintaining behaviors. The didactic approach serves multiple functions: giving an overview and direction to the series, building up an expectation of success and diminishing the anxiety of the participants. At this stage the participants maintain a passive role.

In the next session we focus on relaxation training, which we view both as preparatory and as a part of the training in the hypnotic process (Edmonston, 1981). It is here that we require more active participation under directive guidance. We then extend and intensify the hypnotic experience initiated previously. We use muscle relaxation, autogenic training and visual and kinesthetic imagery. Suggestions are given for positive and enduring responses: "Open your eyes and remain alert and awake, while you continue to feel relaxed; this good feeling of calm and well-being will remain with you for a long time after." Participants are then taught a variety of ways to induce self-hypnosis. They are encouraged to practice any of the techniques most comfortable in meeting their unique needs. They are instructed to practice on a daily basis in order to reinforce the process and, more specifically, to begin to feel more self-sufficient.

We include a session on cognitive restructuring to help patients cope with their responses to environmental demands as well as their internal experiences. This session provides suggestions on interpreting experiences in an ego-syntonic way. A repertoire of cognitive responses is suggested. These suggestions are designed to enhance the ability to maintain control and to avoid inundation by anxiety. They give participants specific advice on ways to respond to life stressors, in order to help make changes in modes of coping.

Some examples of our suggested ways to cope and improve resistance to stress are:

1) Learn not to take everything personally — many things are not your fault or are not your responsibility.
2) Wait before you act on a situation — particularly if you are anxious. Be sure to give yourself time to calm down so that you can act effectively and appropriately.
3) Develop a buffer zone, i.e., a space of time or activity, between one stressful demand and another stressful demand, e.g., between work and home pressures.
4) Learn to accept what you cannot change, including organizations and other people.
5) Do not let your happiness depend on someone else's happiness or behavior.
6) Develop many alternatives for fulfillment in life, i.e., don't put all your eggs in one basket.
7) Surround yourself with as many social supports as possible, i.e., family, relatives, friends, etc., provided they are a positive influence.

8) Develop a list of effective things to do when you find yourself under stress. Tailor this to your individual needs; carry it with you.
9) If you are trying to communicate, don't put the other person on the defensive or else you will not be heard.
10) When criticizing someone, help them to retain their dignity.

The final session reviews and reinforces various levels of the hypnotic process. At this point, participants feel validated because they have identified parallel experiences with other members, as well as similar goals. In addition, during the course of the sessions, they have noted improvements in their own anxiety level and ways of functioning. They have heard other members report similar progress. This feedback process begins right after the relaxation training. It serves as a reinforcement.

The group initially appears quite diverse because each person views his or her problems as idiosyncratic and marked by unique symptoms. Yet, regardless of the source of the stressor, whether it be physical, work-related, or intrapsychic, the common response is anxiety, as well as similar dynamic patterns: feelings of impotence, isolation, and, above all, lack of control. The techniques we utilize, i.e., relaxation and self-hypnosis, help the individuals to experience a sense of power, control and effectiveness which is within their capacity. The cognitive component provides an opportunity to identify, discuss, and share awareness of common obstacles. Participants begin to notice that, although the stressors are different, the responses are similar. More important, the techniques seem to be effective despite different styles, personalities, or problems.

In order to solidify each of the experiences, we distribute printed material to aid training in the relaxation process and to provide suggestions for a cognitive repertoire of responses. We have also developed audiotapes offering the range of hypnotic cues for training and reinforcement purposes. These are distributed to participants who complete the five-session series. These tapes provide a source of continued support for those who may not have made the transition to internal cues.

We have collected data on cognitive and somatic symptom changes between the first and fifth sessions of our series using a 14-item cognitive-somatic scale developed by Schwartz, Davidson, and Goleman (1978). The cognitive subscales rate items such as concentration difficulties, thought intrusion, worry, imagination of negative events, and indecisiveness. The somatic subscales rate items such as heart palpitations, stomach tension, perspiration, immobilization and diarrhea. The data indicate statistically significant differences between pre and post testing. Individual items and total scores for the cognitive and somatic subscales exceed the probability level of .01, with most of the individual items exceeding the probability levels of .001. These results have been very supportive of our program.

Patients have reported very salient changes in their lifestyles and experiences. They have told us of decreases in alcohol consumption and smoking without specific directives addressed to these issues. They have noted positive changes in pain thresholds, such that arthritic pain and back pain have diminished, and, in some cases, disappeared, at least during the course of our sessions. Migraine headaches have decreased in frequency and intensity, and sleep difficulties seem to be ameliorated. People report fairly significant changes in interpersonal relations on the job and in their family life. Several individuals have been asked as to whether they were on some new magical potion that changed their personalities. We did have one "negative" report. One of our female participants claimed her sex life had faded away. It turned out that her husband felt uncomfortable awakening her after watching her make a hand gesture that put her into a deep sleep. The latter was rectified when she decided to talk with him about his intentions for the evening before making her self-hypnotic gesture.

In general, patient reports have been supplemented by physician feedback, reports of family members, and diminished use of psychotherapy. We recognize that most of the information we have deals with short-term change. We have not yet had the opportunity to investigate long-term outcome.

One of the most significant advantages of a group program of this nature, particularly in a health maintenance organization, is its cost-effectiveness. Individual treatment for the same objective would not only take vast amounts of time, but would also be less effective. Validation from those sharing discomfort tends to be much more believable and cogent.

Our findings strongly suggest the value of group experience in facilitating the hypnotic process and its therapeutic gains. We believe that the critical factors are a high level of motivation produced by internal or external stressors, a shared goal, a positive social milieu, confidence in the leaders and a supportive, healing environment. We find that even putatively dissident, resistant participants are often helped by the group process.

References

Edmonston, W. (1981). *Hypnosis and relaxation: Modern verification of an old equation*. New York: Wiley.

Kroger, W. S. (1977). *Clinical and experimental hypnosis* (2nd ed.). Philadelphia: Lippincott.

Schwartz, G. E., Davidson, R. J., & Goleman, D. J. (1978). Patterning of cognitive and somatic processes in the self-regulation of anxiety: Effects of meditation versus exercise. *Psychosomatic Medicine. 40*(4), 321–328.

$\begin{matrix} Q \\ \& \, 64 \\ A \end{matrix}$ The Use of Hypnosis in Couple and Family Therapy

Question:

I do a fair amount of hypnosis with my individual clients, but as my work has come to deal more with couples and families, I'm unsure of how to go about it. If I want to do hypnosis with one member of a couple or family, is it best to see him or her alone? Or should I just hypnotize the one with the others watching?

Discussion by BENNETT G. BRAUN, M.D.

In approaching the use of hypnosis in family or couple therapy, the two options that you have suggested are equally good depending upon the circumstances. However, it is important to note that the question should not be reduced to an "either/or" answer. You have many more options, each with different purposes and results. You can hypnotize an individual alone or with the mate watching. You also can hypnotize both members of a couple at the same time, and they can interact with each other and/or with you. The same options apply in family therapy. An individual can by hypnotized alone or with the family watching. The whole family can by hypnotized, and different members can participate or not depending on the issue at hand.

The purpose of family therapy with or without hypnosis is to work with the family system by working with each individual member's effect on that system. If you hypnotize one family member alone or in front of the other members, you are removing that member from the system by giving him or her special treatment. You risk making him or her the indicated patient and implying that he or she is the "sick" one in the family. Similarly, you may imply that he or she is the only one well enough to undergo hypnosis. You may be saying in effect, "Let's all meet Joe or Sally," rather than, "Let's treat all family members together and thereby work with the family system."

Isolating an individual from the system may interfere further with healthy family dynamics. When the whole family is hypnotized, some members may interact and some may not do so until a later time, just as in a therapy session without hypnosis. Hence, the hypnotic experience can fit into the continuity of ongoing therapy. If all are hypnotized together, no one is more special than anyone else, and the roles of secrecy and triangling are minimized.

On the other hand, some individual and couple issues are best worked with in a setting apart from the family therapy session. For example, if an individual wants to stop smoking, you may not want to use valuable family time for his or her treatment. Some family therapy issues are specific to the parents in the family, and these are best treated in a couple setting. For example, it may be inappropriate for a couple to work with the issue of infidelity when children of certain ages are present. Here you risk breaking the parent-child boundaries that family therapy helps to establish.

With issues that do not break family boundaries, I prefer to hypnotize all members of the family therapy session. I may use hypnosis to work on one family member's issue while helping the other family members identify with that member's problem. For example, a phobic may be inhibiting family functioning and consequently receiving direct and indirect anger from the others. I use hypnosis to help eliminate the phobia with desensitization techniques and to help the other family members empathize with the feelings of the phobic. By hypnotically recalling and building upon fearful experiences they have had, the others can be helped to understand the sensation of paralyzing fear. As a result, they become more supportive and active as participants in the therapy. They may even suggest ways of treating the phobia by drawing upon their knowledge of family relationships. So, hypnosis can be used to work with individual problems within the family setting when everyone participates by being hypnotized.

You prefaced your question by mentioning that you feel unsure of "how to go about" using hypnosis in the family and couple settings. Let me respond by reviewing the general advantages and problems involved in using hypnosis in these settings. Then I shall describe the guidelines and techniques that I tend to use in practice.

Unlike members of a general psychotherapy group, the members of a family or couple live in close contact with one another. Hypnosis, a dissociative state, encourages each member to perceive the therapy session as a time to disengage from daily conflicts. The relaxation that accompanies hypnosis introduces calmness into an escalating family system. Families which have sought therapy often have few recent shared pleasurable experiences, and hypnosis gives the family the opportunity to experience this under your guidance. Family and couple members relearn that good feelings can be experienced together. This in turn helps to build a mood of trust and cooperation, to increase rapport and mutual sensitivity, and to decrease defenses. In addition, hypnosis with projective techniques can be used to identify issues that are otherwise difficult for family members to bring up. When there is a lull in the therapy, hypnosis also can be used to keep it moving (Braun, 1984b).

There are problems and contraindications to using hypnosis as an adjunctive tool in family and couple therapy. However, the problems are relative to the skill of the therapist and to his or her knowledge of both hypnosis and family therapy. The therapist must be prepared to deal with abreactions and spontaneous age regressions. An abreaction in one member can be complicated by the presence of the other family members. Spontaneous age regressions, especially in teenagers, are common in family therapy because the presence of parents seems to stimulate regression.

The use of hypnosis is often inadvisable when a family member with a borderline or hysteric personality disorder is present. As repressed material emerges and defenses break down, it is thought that there is a risk of precipitating a psychotic breakdown in the borderline patient. The presence of the family combined with the sense of closeness from the shared hypnotic experience accentuates regression, intensifies transference, and may perpetuate a personal crisis for the hysteric patient. In general, crises of any kind that are not handled constructively by the therapist and family together may destroy the patients' newly gained sense of mastery and cohesion. This loss can be magnified when the crises are mishandled under hypnosis.

There are many hypnotic induction techniques that are well suited to family therapy. I try to choose induction techniques that keep the family together in timing and goals. For example, progressive relaxation techniques are good because all family members can work with their feet, legs, etc., at the same time. Color imagery and guided fantasy techniques direct family and couple members to concentrate on the same thing at the same time. The reverse blink technique works well as an induction method, but it does not require everyone to progress at the same rate. Family members begin with their eyes closed. Each time the therapist counts a number, they open and shut their eyelids (the reverse of a blink). Suggestions are made between counts to encourage deeper relaxation, to indicate that the person will relax more deeply with each count, and eventually to allow the eyes to remain closed. Different people will stop opening their eyes at different times, but all will end up relaxed with their eyes closed.

Once hypnosis has been induced, a variety of techniques can be used. I often continue with projective techniques. I might ask the family to imagine that they are watching their favorite television program, a technique that is especially engaging when children are present. A guided fantasy technique that I often use involves a PT boat. Each family member imagines he or she is a crew member on a PT boat with an important mission. The PT boat has to carry an urgent message to an aircraft carrier which has lost its communication system. The PT boat must warn the carrier that it is entering enemy territory and should change its course. Each person in the therapy session should have mental images of every crew member, from captain to sailor, performing his or her last-minute checks of the PT boat before it embarks on its mission. The PT boat moves away from shore and at first everything is going smoothly. Suddenly, one of the crew notices that the radar system is not functioning, a problem that should have been corrected on shore. Because it is too dangerous to continue without radar, the PT boat must abandon its mission. The crew members then are called before the commanding officer to explain what went wrong and whose fault it was. During the debriefing, they examine how they felt during the trip. A fantasy such as this one reveals information about family dynamics. All kinds of fantasies can be created and directed by the therapist depending upon the kind of information he or she would like to elicit.

Age regression can be used to explore past events. Remembering and examining past events can help bring them into a new and more constructive perspective. If a past event was not experienced by all members of the family, having someone relive it while the others attempt to experience it under hypnosis helps to create a shared event.

Identifying the interaction style of a family or couple helps to direct my choice of induction and projective techniques. Kramer (1968) defines four marriage sytles which can be generalized to describe family styles in ways that I find useful (Braun, 1984a).

The *united front* marriage or family is overtly harmonious and seeks treatment because one member, usually a child, is symptomatic. The family believes that the "problem child" needs therapy, and they do not seem to understand that this treatment must include the family as a whole unit. I tend to use relaxation techniques to build rapport and increase trust with this family style. I then use guided fantasy methods to get the family to reveal how members cooperate, handle stress and hostility, and cover things up.

The *overadequate/underadequate* marriage or family includes at least one member who is seen as capable, competent, and symptom-free and at least one member who is not fully able to care for himself or herself. When the "sick" partner in a couple begins to "get well," the other partner often develops symptoms as a result of this new stress. I may use the ideal self-image technique with these couples and families. One member creates two images of himself or herself, one as he or she perceives himself/herself today and one as he or she would like to be ideally. Obtaining feedback from other members is therapeutic because they usually see their family member as falling between the two extreme images. I also use direct and indirect suggestions to strengthen underadequate members and to support vulnerability in overadequate members. Hypnotic role reversal can be used so that the over-adequate members come to understand the sense of helplessness and frustration with which underadequate members live, and so that underadequate members come to realize that overadequate members feel isolated and lonely. Hypnotic role reversal provides another technique for encouraging mutual empathy.

The *conflictual* marriage or family is identified by open conflict such as fighting. It is important to break the cycle of fighting, create ways of making peace, offer opportunities for shared positive experiences, and facilitate empathy among family members. Hypnosis can be used as a tool for each of these goals. After using progressive relaxation techniques for hypnotic induction, I often proceed with two fantasy techniques. Fantasy can be used to help the family imagine what life would be like without any conflict at all, or it can be used to help the family imagine the conflicts escalating to gigantic proportions. When family members are asked to do the first exercise, that is, to minimize and eliminate conflict, they get in touch with how it feels to exist without fighting. When they create a fantasy of maximized conflict, they often become frightened and paradoxically act to reduce the conflict.

The fourth type of marriage or family style is called *mixed*. It represents a combination of two or more of the above types, and I combine the goals and techniques accordingly. As you can tell already, there are many ways to use hypnosis in couple and family therapy. Only your imagination limits its applications.

Now, let me say a few words about how to structure couple and family hypnotherapy. As with any therapy, you want to begin by establishing rapport and by gaining an understanding of the interpersonal dynamics among family members and between each member and yourself, the therapist. It is then important to conduct a formal prehypnotic interview. Here you give the family some concept of how hypnosis works in general and how you plan to approach this family unit's problem with it. It is also important to allay fears and clarify misconceptions about hypnosis at this point.

When you begin hypnotic work, you can divide it into five phases. In the *induction phase*, you help focus the patients' attention and concentration with specific induction techniques such as the reverse blink technique. In the *deepening phase*, you employ techniques to deepen the sense of being in trance and prepare the patients for the work phase. For deepening I might use a muscle relaxation technique, color imagery, or both. In the *work phase*, I tend to use projective and age regression techniques to allow specific information about family relationships to surface and to achieve some of the specific goals that I have already described for certain family styles. The *termination phase* ends the hypnotic experience and may include the use of posthypnotic suggestions. And finally, a *processing and debriefing phase* is an essential follow-up. Having time out of hypnosis to process the material helps the family members integrate their experience into the here and now. It is important in this phase to help the patients avoid the mistake of attributing the power of change to either the hypnotic technique or to the hypnotherapist. The power of change belongs to each patient, and hypnosis is best viewed as a helpful tool for or the context in which change takes place (Braun, 1980).

Let me conclude by commenting on a few practical considerations. When using hypnosis, take small obtainable steps. Avoid the urge to push ahead too quickly. Be aware that one family member may absorb the hypnotic suggestions you have directed to another when everyone is hypnotized. Similarly, if you are hypnotizing one individual with the others watching, one of the observers may go into trance too. So, always sit where you can visually scan every family member. Be aware that deeply relaxed or hypnotized patients are regressed and may be more concrete in their thinking. This regression may be an advantage in that it lowers critical thinking, defensiveness, and the repression barrier. However, if the hypnotherapist moves too quickly, he or she can create confusion, lose rapport, and jeopardize progress.

So, we have reviewed the general concepts of hypnosis and family or couple therapy. Keep these concepts in mind and then work as you would at any other time. You may be in trance or out during the sessions. Go ahead and good luck!

The author wishes to acknowledge Laurie S. Lipman for her assistance in the preparation of this paper.

References

Braun, B. G. (1980). Hypnosis in groups and group hynotherapy. In G. Burrows & L. Dennerstein (Eds.). *Handbook of hypnosis and psychosomatic medicine.* Amsterdam: Elsevier & North Holland Biomedical Press.

Braun, B. G. (1984a). Hypnosis and family therapy. *American Journal of Clinical Hypnosis,* 26, 182–186.

Braun, B. G. (1984b). Hypnosis in family therapy. In W. C. Webster, II, & A. H. Smith, Jr. (Eds.), *Clinical hypnosis: A multidisciplinary approach.* Philadelphia: Lippincott.

Kramer, C. (1968). *Beginning phase of family treatment.* Chicago: Kramer Foundation.

Q&A 65 Integrating Hypnosis With Insight-oriented Psychotherapy

Question:

My training was in insight-oriented therapy and I'm uncertain how to integrate my new training in hypnosis with my primary style of therapy. How can hypnosis be used to make insight psychotherapy more effective or efficient?

Discussion by JEROME M. SCHNECK, M.D.

In my experience, insight-oriented therapy is made more effective and efficient by using hypnosis with some patients. The availability of a variety of hypnotic techniques adds dimensions to therapy that can be potentially advantageous.

Diagnosis is not the central issue in determining whether or not hypnosis is employed. It can be used with a wide variety of patients. Basically, the incorporation of hypnotherapy into treatment rests with the clinical judgment and experience of the therapist. If a patient seeks insight-oriented therapy immediately, that can be started soon after an assessment, at times rapid, is made of the apparent personality of the patient. By mutual agreement, hypnosis may be delayed until such assessment is made during the first few nonhypnotic sessions. Assuming that hypnotherapy is then decided upon by the patient and therapist, it can be initiated at any point during the course of their contact. Hypnosis may consume various periods of time within each session. It may be used during a few or many sessions, or interspersed with nonhypnotic interviews. This permits evaluation of desirability and effectiveness of hypnosis versus nonhypnotic therapy for this particular individual. If hypnosis is not especially helpful when compared with nonhypnotic therapy, it can be discontinued temporarily or permanently according to the judgment of the therapist and with the patient's agreement.

Hypnotherapy may be employed in keeping with the theoretical orientation of the therapist. Hypnoanalysis, for example, would involve the fusion of a psychoanalytic orientation with hypnotic techniques introduced for additional potential advantage. A special advantage for some patients in using hypnosis is their ability to see familiar events and problems in perspectives broader and more enlightening than had heretofore been possible. Thus, additional insights are achieved. This, in my experience, is more important for most hypnotherapy patients than the traditional use of hypnosis to enhance recall of past events. The latter is often helpful, but also frequently unduly stressed.

Some hypnotic techniques employed involve the use of direct suggestions to enhance insights (although insights are often achieved spontaneously by many patients when simply evaluating their thoughts and emotions during periods of silent hypnotic relaxation), conversational exchange of patient and therapist during hypnosis leading to insights that are not attained in similar conversations without use of hypnosis, and hypnotic relaxation without comment, permitting at times a greater approach by the patient to self-understanding than can be achieved without hypnosis. Needless to say, the nature of the transference plays some role, lesser or greater, in promoting insight and change in patients, whether or not such transference is analyzed during or outside of trance. The analysis of the transference may occur spontaneously by the patient as insights develop or it may be promoted by comments offered by the therapist.

Free association may be used in hypnotherapy as in nonhypnotic treatment. Often insights come about spontaneously and more frequently during free association by patients in hypnosis. Long buried memories tend to come to the fore. They are more likely to be significant when they appear spontaneously, although direct suggestions for recall may also be helpful. The importance of such recalled experiences vary with patients, depending on the nature of their problems and the relation of the latter to the buried memories.

Most patients can become aware of spontaneous sensory and motor phenomena during hypnosis. These may be analyzed or bypassed, depending on the judgment of the therapist. Not infrequently, patients offer their own analysis. There may occur, for example, sensations of lightness or heaviness of the body or body parts, sensations of warmth or cold, tingling feelings, floating sensations, anesthesia of body parts, a sense of absence of body parts or of the entire body, and other experiences. There may be movements of head, arms or legs that have significance in relation to concurrent thought processes and which, when analyzed, contribute to additional insights.

Visual imagery may be spontaneous or induced (patient's eyes closed) with suggestions that the patient clarify problems and assist movement toward solutions of such problems or conflicts. Hypnotic dreams may be spontaneous or induced and they can have the quality in form and meaning of the patient's nocturnal dreams. They may be analyzed as nocturnal dreams are. I have also encountered hypnotic nightmares that appear spontaneously or on suggestion for clarification of important issues. Hypnotic suggestions may also be given for the greater recollection of nocturnal dreams.

Automatic writing and drawing may be induced (with the patient's eyes open or closed as circumstances require), and recollection of buried memories achieved in this way, or problems solved with greater ease than might happen otherwise. Regression and revivification may occur in hypnosis, spontaneously or on suggestion, and these may prove to be helpful. Some patients may be capable of experiencing visual hallucinations (eyes open) and auditory hallucinations for problem clarification.

Time distortion is another technique. It can be suggested or may appear spontaneously, a short time period such as minutes covering hours or days of actual experience. Prehypnotic suggestion (the opposite of the traditional posthypnotic suggestion) can be used with some patients. For example, a patient may be told prior to hypnotic induction that after entering hypnosis he will relive and gain insight into a particular experience. Hypnosis is induced but no verbalizations by the therapist need then ensue. When effective, insights are attained and helpful gains fostered.

I prefer to employ the simplest techniques, such as conversational exchange, free association, scene visualizations (patient's eyes closed), and hypnotic dreams, because they are more easily achieved by patients, require the least amount of time, and are often effective. Automatic writing or drawing and hallucinatory experiences are more difficult. There is no correlation between the difficulty of the technique and the therapeutic results. Some patients capable of achieving hypnotic hallucinations may make little progress in therapy. Others, by simply conversing in the hypnotic setting, may achieve great progress. Let us consider a few case excerpts.

A woman in hypnoanalysis for relief of recurrent anxiety episodes had her first induced hypnotic dream during the sixth session. The content was not specified by the therapist. She found herself in a subway train and felt that people around her regarded her with hostility. A man approached her. She ran through several cars of the train but finally the man cornered her menacingly and the dream ended. She then referred to the dream as a nightmare. She had attempted to wake up from it during hypnosis but had been unable to do so. She verbalized associations to the dream in hypnosis and concluded that the events reflected her feelings of inferiority, fear of people, and inclination to associate with persons she regarded as inferior to herself in order to master her anxieties and to "feel above them." She concluded that she projected her resentment of people on to those in her hypnotic nightmare and that they in turn viewed her with animosity. She said she realized that her fear of attack was related to her attempt to control men through her own sexual behavior.

During his hypnoanalysis and after a period of silence in hypnosis, a man reported a spontaneous dream. He had never known hypnotic dreams could occur nor had he heard of them. He was in an enclosure, like a deep well. It was dark but sunlight was seen through the opening at the top. He, the person in the dream, was "a little man" who started to climb the wall of the enclosure in order to get out into whatever the sunlight signified for him. His efforts were repetitive, as he got halfway to the top, returned to the bottom of his own accord, moved to another area, climbed again, descended again and continued the maneuver on and on. He associated, in hypnosis, to this dream by revealing that he was the man whose activity symbolized his pattern in life. He managed to reach certain heights, but instead of just slipping down he would actually discontinue efforts, retreat, and start again with repetitive compulsive actions, only to his detriment. He actually kept himself from reaching the top because of the masochistic components in his personality.

A woman sought hypnotherapy to lose weight, realizing that, while she would become more attractive to men if she were thinner, their attentions might disturb her. She achieved her major goal of weight loss, but while accomplishing this she revivified, when asked to have an experience that would further clarify her problem, an attempted rape 10 years before, when she subtly enticed a man who then almost beat her to death when she resisted. The fear and anxiety during the hypnotic revivification contrasted with a previously bland recollection. There was a hostile reaction, after the event, to her mother. This was not overtly related to the untold assault and was quite inappropriate at the time. She was astonished in hypnosis when she recalled meeting friends after the assault, making no reference to it, and behaving as though nothing had happened. The hypnotic setting exposed the isolation and displacement (reaction to her mother) of affect, her rebelliousness and her occasional self-injurious behavior. Especially in hypnosis there is often revealed not only repression, but the specific components of isolation and displacement and, in a variety of patients, mechanisms of condensation, symbolization, substitution, denial, reaction formation, projection, identification, introjection, and externalization.

A young woman entered hypnoanalysis because of feelings of anxiety and discomfort in some social relationships. As a child she had experienced sex play with a brother several years older. As an adolescent she developed a germ phobia focusing on doorknobs and water faucets as possible and specific sources of infection. She realized her fears were irrational. In a subsequent hypnosis session she spontaneously combined some memories. She recalled that her brother had told her, when she asked about the nature of the semen she saw when he ejaculated, that "it was what made girls pregnant." She then recognized in hypnosis that she had previously unconsciously identified sperm with germs, and that her fear of the latter was an unconscious extension of her fear of impregnation by sperm (semen). Her sexual anxiety and guilt were allayed.

An army veteran developed severe claustrophobia in a variety of settings, including subway stations and trains, making it necessary for him to leave stations on several occasions during long trips. During hypnotherapy he revivified an episode of being trapped in a trench when an army tank stopped above him, resulting in the walls of the trench collapsing. He had to be dug out, cried, and was in a panic. His contact with the therapist during revivification was so tenuous that he misidentified the therapist as an officer on the tank scene. In subway stations he had illusions of the wheels of oncoming trains looking like tank treads. In hypnoanalysis his closed-in feeling was linked to other traumatic physical entrapments, as well as feelings of being trapped in personal relationships prior to army service and in subsequent family settings.

Motor and sensory phenomena, often experienced spontaneously in hypnoanalysis, are often basic expressions of personality operations and understood as symbolic expressions of certain feelings and attitudes that may have been previously disguised. They may not be mentioned at certain times (but alluded to later) in an effort to suppress or repress associated ideation and affect. They may be influenced by specific transference components. A middle-aged man in hypnoanalysis said he could appreciate acquaintances briefly but soon became bored, aloof, and avoided close ties. When telling about a doctor he had seen, he felt as if he had turned his head in a direction away from me. He had not. He analyzed this as a belief that it reflected his rejection of me in order to avoid a close feeling in the therapeutic contact. Another patient had felt as if his head had turned in a completely opposite direction from one actually facing me. He analyzed this as a denial of homosexual transference feelings. For other patients it is a reflection of ambivalence toward treatment and a desire to run away. The first patient mentioned above said in hypnosis, "I feel very rigid and stiff." He analyzed this as a reflection of the way he felt in everyday life. A female patient once described the same sensations and identified them as a reflection of her latent homosexuality.

A young man was referred for treatment by a dean at his college following various thefts which the patient first admitted and later denied. He would be permitted to return to school only after successful treatment. In hypnoanalysis the patient recognized, when analyzing the events, that he had assumed blame for the theft in his masochistic attempt to hurt his authoritarian father and in an effort to increase his personal sense of worth by doing good, even though the nature and purpose of his actions remained known only to himself. In this case hypnotic procedures were technically simple, yet effective, showing that involved or complex measures are often not necessary. In hypnosis he experienced periods of silence followed by the revealing of events, thoughts and interpretations unknown to him otherwise. Toward the conclusion of treatment, after he had gained a good understanding of himself, hypnosis was discontinued and several nonhypnotic sessions followed. Eventually, on return to school, he did very well academically and in his personal relationships. He stopped getting into various difficulties to hurt his father, realizing he would be unable to change his father's personality. Their relationship then, in fact, improved. He realized his troublesome behavior had been disturbing his mother. The transference relationship was beneficial in that it involved a dual quality, the therapist seen as an authoritative figure identified with his father and as a helpful supporting individual whom he identified with his mother. This dual hypnotic transference feature has been encountered often with other patients as well. The transference in treatment is often intensified with the introduction of hypnosis, and the hypnosis itself is often identified with power, control, and authoritarian significance.

It is not possible within the confines of this brief account to describe the richness and variety of patients, treatment settings, and hypnotic measures available and alluded to above only succinctly. The cases presented reflect at least some of the possibilities for using hypnosis in insight-oriented therapy.

$\underset{A}{\overset{Q}{\&}}66$ Incorporating Hypnosis Into Long-term Psychotherapy

Question:

> My preferred style of psychotherapy is long-term and psychodynamically oriented. How can hypnosis be incorporated into it?

Discussion by ERIKA WICK, Ph.D.

There are a number of reasons why therapists may wish to introduce hypnosis into their strategies. Hypnotic techniques offer more than just shortcuts on a long journey. Hypnosis can shift a cumbersome, slow-moving therapy into a faster gear and get a therapeutic venture that got stuck back on track and rolling again. Also, clients who have grown tired of their no-end-in-sight therapy may find their interest rekindled when hypnosis brings new impetus to their long-term therapy.

In order to ensure success with hypnosis, the client has to be ready for its use, the therapist's personal and technical readiness has to be established, and a realistic therapeutic territory has to be selected.

Clients have to be ready for hypnosis and they also have to be prepared for its implementation. Caution is indicated when a patient's lack of therapeutic success coincides with the lack of desire to make progress, because the patient enjoys long-term therapy as a device for attention-getting and narcissistic self-mirroring, or because the client is determined to prove that despite his/her willingness to seek help, the presenting problem is insurmountable. In these cases, as well as where the use of hypnosis might trigger a major defense breakdown, the use of hypnosis should be evaluated carefully. Also, the use of the word hypnosis should be used with discretion. Some patients respond better to treatment if technique descriptions are used rather than the ill-defined term "hypnosis" (Levitt, Edmonston, & Wick, 1983).

The patient who is ready for hypnosis needs to be prepared for its implementation. This includes reaching an agreement on what is to take place in terms of therapist activities, such as the use of specific induction techniques, deepening techniques, or autohypnosis. Informing the client as to what he or she might expect to experience is a powerful way of enhancing the effectiveness of the hypnotic approach. Strong expectation suggestions minimize the chance for failure.

Of the many conditions which call for the use of hypnosis in long-term therapy, two shall be mentioned specifically. One arises when traumatic core issues have been identified and interpreted by the analyst. The dynamics are understood, the insights gained, but change does not follow: The cathartic effect is missing because client and psychoanalyst got stuck in the realm of reason. When this therapeutic constellation appears, employing hypnosis (or an emotional-experiential technique equivalent) is more than indicated; it is a must. The other therapeutic issue is the one Freud (1930) struggled with when he considered giving up hypnosis. His concern centered on recalling events neither patient nor therapist have any conscious knowledge of. Despite his mixed feelings about hypnosis, even to Freud attempting to achieve such a task *without* hypnosis "at first seemed to be a senseless and hopeless undertaking." Nevertheless, Freud decided in favor of using free association. His optimism proved justified only in some cases. For most cases, hypnosis remains the modality of choice, as the example to be cited will illustrate.

The following case demonstrates how the use of hypnosis changed the course of a long-term therapeutic venture. Major insight into the case could be gained only through information which on a conscious level was equally unknown to patient and therapist. Hypnosis permitted access to the missing information link.

Dan sought help for what he himself had diagnosed as a "normal" midlife crisis. The basic life tasks seemed to have been accomplished: Dan had achieved success in business as well as in his private life. All of his children were college educated, happily married adults, who had good relationships with their parents. His relationship with his spouse was comfortable although not particularly exciting. Life had peaked and held no further promise.

On the emotional side, Dan was prone to bouts of severe depression and at times to severe anxiety attacks. He remained overwhelmed with guilt feelings and generally struggled with inferiority feelings despite his good looks and his social and business success. He also suffered from psychosomatic syndromes, which could be incapacitating at times of special stress, as well as during his well documented, annual mid-winter depression, which peaked around Christmas and lasted into the third week in January. It was especially at this time of the year that he entertained thoughts of suicide, welcoming death and spending time composing tombstone inscriptions for himself.

His perspective of life was reduced to facing a slow decline and ultimately death. Merely to sit in God's waiting room had little appeal for Dan. At this time, the world still perceived him on the plateau of success and nobody would suspect him of having committed suicide if he died a reasonably staged "accidental death."

While Dan professed strong suicidal intentions and had the details of their implementation all worked out, he found himself a therapist instead of going ahead with his plans. It seemed as if he were seeking a witness to his pain and a parental figure who would approve of his plan and allow him to share the guilt over his suicidal intention. He firmly denied the existence of any latent hope that the premature end of his life could be avoided and that he might have other options.

Because Dan did not believe in hypnotic "hocus-pocus," initially no attempt was made to convert him to working with hypnotic techniques. When it became clear that the self-diagnosed mid-life crisis constituted a mere peak in his ongoing history of negative emotional experiences, psychodynamically oriented therapy was initiated. Dan was seen twice a week for several months.

According to the client's account, his childhood had been perfectly normal and uneventful, with the exception that his father died when he was three years old. The absence of his father had been compensated for, as the extended family provided several substitute fathers for him to whom he could relate positively. In fact, observing some of his childhood friends' situations, he did not feel deprived. Instead he felt blessed at times that he did not have to put up with someone like their fathers. In short, Dan could not find any connection between his current negative emotional experiences and the loss of his father. Despite the client's initial denials, his mid-winter slump eventually began to emerge as an anniversary reaction (Dlin, 1985), commemorating the depression he had experienced as a three-year-old after the death of his father, who had died at that time of the year. He may also have been conditioned over the years by his widowed mother to recapture the sadness and grieve the loss around the anniversary of the fatal event. Despite serious attempts to reach the world of the three-year-old and the aid of supportive photographs and "homework" talks with mother and siblings, Dan was unable to get involved in any significant experiences when he attempted to recapture the time when his father had died.

When the issue of his mother's reaction to her husband's death and its effect on Danny came up, the response was even more defensive. Dan could not come up with any negative memories regarding his mother. On the contrary, he had placed his mother onto such a pedestal of perfection that she appeared almost void of human qualities. She was described as the absolutely greatest woman who ever walked on this earth and as the woman whom Dan loves most in his life. In actuality, the patient sees "the woman he loves most in his life" about twice a year and calls her, if she is lucky, about once a month. Any negative feelings towards his mother were vehemently denied by the client.

A few additional avenues were explored without success. The client remained unable to connect his syndrome to any life events by memory or by reason. When, despite the patient's efforts to cooperate with his therapy, the core of Dan's problem remained elusive, it became necessary to consider therapeutic alternatives. Dan immediately rejected all behavioral routines.

At this point the client was persuaded to consider the use of noncognitive modalities. He was told that some relaxing, experiential techniques would allow him to move into the realm of hypnotic experiences, but that it would be left up to his control how far he wished to let himself go. Dan agreed to relaxation exercises in view of his psychosomatic complaints and was also willing to search for memories or any relevant emotional-experiential messages he might be able to obtain by way of imagery and age-regression. The physical relaxation exercises met with good results. Dan became much more relaxed and at that point felt encouraged to embark with positive anticipation upon his journey into the world of imagery.

The breakthrough came when the client was asked, while in a medium-depth hypnotic state, to *switch into the role of his mother* and identify with her. Dan's slight resistance to the role switch was overcome easily when the purpose was stated, namely, that it would allow him to observe little Danny. The role-switch was an immediate success: Mother's grief, despair and depression fit like a glove. Dan replayed what he had observed as a child: mother used her energy to hold back her feelings and to appear strong in the face of extreme adversity. She was unable to reach out to the children, for fear she might show her feelings. She played the role of a well defended inaccessible fortress.

The next step involved *switching back into being the little boy vis-à-vis the great mother*. Within no time the world of the three-year-old was reconstructed. Little Danny found himself in a world which was void of expression. He was being ignored by his grief-stricken mother, left to his own helplessness, confusion, anxiety and depression. There was no one to comfort him, hold him, share feelings with, explain, help him understand Daddy's death and whatever else was going on, such as why his mother would not talk to him. Mother was somewhat like a remote, invulnerable goddess, beautiful and strong. She "never broke down and cried." Pride, strength and "business as usual" were the family policy. Danny's mother was determined to make sure that the father's death would not interfere with her children's "happy childhood." But Danny, the sensitive little boy, and his siblings soaked up mother's real feelings by way of emotional osmosis. Depression, grief, despair and anxiety were both overwhelming and confusing, because they totally contradicted the officially proclaimed happiness policy.

There was more confusion. Danny looked towards his mother for closeness and reassurance, but all he got was "strength," silence and mother's self-absorption. There was no one to allow him to cry, to be warm and feeling. Danny felt so isolated, so rejected, so terribly punished. Yet, he did not know what he was being punished for. He suffered the rejections of the worst culprit without ever having been accused of anything. Somehow he surmised that, based on the extent of the punishment, his guilt had to be enormous. From the timing of the punishment he could gather that his guilt had some connection with his father's death. Soon things fell into place. The next time he and his siblings upset the mother she said: "If you are not good, you'll drive *me* into the grave, too." Now Danny knew that Daddy had died because he had not always been good and that mother punished him because Dad's death was his fault. Although he did not know what he had done wrong, he carried this horrendous guilt, that was commensurate with his experience of rejection and punishment.

Many times Danny tried to reach his silent, distant mother, pleading with her: "I am good, Mommy, I'll be good." When she laid down for a nap and closed her eyes, he was especially scared, since she looked so much like Daddy when he was ill and after he had died. He would silently sit on the bed clingingly hold on to her leg and occasionally repeat: "But I'll be good, Mom, I'll be good."

Based on the information retrieved in the hypnotic state, the key issues in Dan's problem complex could rapidly be identified and dealt with therapeutically. At the core of the client's problems was not the death of his father, but one of its major consequences. Although Daddy's leaving and incomprehensibly not returning left Danny undeniably with a loss, it was mother's way of coping with the fatal event that devastated him. The proud denial of painful emotions in favor of a "happy childhood policy" was a tough experience for the sensitive young boy who felt overwhelmed by the depression, guilt, hurt, helplessness and existential anxiety that permeated the house.

The following is a selection of a few focal points that emerged as targets for therapeutic intervention:

Relationships. Danny suffered from low self-esteem ("rejected" by mother and father). He developed a confused head-heart twisting style of relating to himself and others (do not acknowledge felt emotions; let your brain decide what you are supposed to feel) and a defensive, nonmutual way of interpersonal relating marked by clinging and dependency needs.

Guilt-assumption syndrome and depression. Mother's self-absorption/depression was experienced as punitive rejection. The (mother-)"assigned guilt" in the death of the father resulted in a severe "guilt-assumption syndrome" (Wick, Sigman, & Kline, 1971), commensurate with the severity of the punishment, which as a "guilt equivalent" (tit for tat), carried a message about the "crime." The burden of this never alleviated guilt overshadowed Dan's whole life, tuning it on the melancholic side (Zisook, Shuchter, & Schuckit, 1985).

Anniversary syndrome. The tortures of the anniversary reaction (Dlin, 1985) "hurt so good," since they were properly allocated, direct expressions of genuine feelings of grief over the loss of the father and over the "psychological loss" of the grieving mother. They represented non-twisted emotions (expressions of the heart) the head had never known about.

Raynaud's disease. On the psychosomatic side the denial of pain, psychological numbing and anesthesia by "freezing" or hibernating all express themselves well in Dan's development of Raynaud's disease. When Dan is stressed, anxious or upset, he chokes his blood vessels, his face freezes, his hands and feet turn bluish pale and ice-cold. Is he merely repressing painful emotions or is he also playing dead, identifying with his dead father, the man who took Mom, the warm and alive woman, with him into the grave and left the children with the distant, desparing, grieving widow?

Midlife crisis. The issue of the self-diagnosed midlife crisis was taken seriously. It was considered independently but also within the perspectives offered by the problems acquired in the first part of life.

Hypnosis offers many advantages that can be helpful within the framework of long-term therapy. The case selected demonstrates merely one of them, illustrating how hypnosis can facilitate access to nonverbally coded memories. In Dan's case the therapeutic modality switch made it possible to gain access to the core of the client's problem, which on the cognitive level was not readily available to memory recall, since it essentially had the quality of a non-event. In contrast to well-delineated traumatic events (e.g., burning fingers on a stove) or any definable happening, the negative counterpart, a nonhappening, such as the experience of mother's inaccessibility and self-absorption, is difficult to recall, especially if it occurred at a time when a child is too young to identify and adequately label what is going on. The way the child sorts out and understands what takes place is the same way the memory assimilates and codes the event for recall.

Considering the level of the young child's conceptualization capacity and his total inability to deal with abstracts, combined with his egocentric world perception, Danny's assimilation of the events was appropriate, although not correct in terms of what actually took place. The experience of maternal deprivation in full view of mother's physical presence was extremely confusing and from his egocentric perspective could only be understood as punishment. Bowing to the maternal wisdom and justice, Danny carried the "assigned guilt." From a cognitive coding viewpoint, the traumatic, confusing experience centered around a core of "nothing happened," which in its vagueness is hard to code for recall. Yet, this poorly storage-coded, vague "nothing," mother's remoteness, was retrievable via hypnosis.

The therapist had been ready to use hypnosis all along. The client became convinced that the long-term approach was not going to yield the hoped-for results. The therapeutic territory was right: psychoanalytic exploration techniques had turned infertile. Switching to nonrational, experiential techniques was indicated. The patient accepted the use of hypnosis at least in hopes of making changes on the psychosomatic level, expecting that relaxation techniques could help his physical condition. When he, however, found out that hypnosis enabled him to switch to a nonrational mode of thinking which permitted access to experiences he had been unable to retrieve along the usual memory tracks, he became intrigued with the use of the hypnotic modality and requested that hypnosis be made part of his therapeutic routine.

Fertile territory for excellent results with hypnosis exists in any therapeutic situation, including long-term therapy, that either demands a bypassing of the rational-logical thinking mode or at least allows goal achievement to be expedited by doing so. In fact, hypnosis is a natural enhancement of any type of psychoanalytic therapy.

It has been said that the psychoanalytic approach has a hypnotic quality inasmuch as patients' recall of memories is supposed to be exempt from rational scrutiny. Introducing hypnosis, from this perspective, does not constitute a qualitative therapeutic shift, merely a quantitative one. In hypnosis the receptive mode is retained, yet the receptivity towards and the absorption in incoming material such as memories, feelings, etc., are intensified. It makes sense (and it also "makes cents" in our cost-conscious, health-insured society) to expedite the patient's slow therapeutic efforts through a more efficient approach to recalling past life events, as well as allowing patients engaged in any type of long-term therapy to focus with hypnotic concentration on their here-and-now experiencing and working-through.

Turning back to the original question, "How can hypnosis be incorporated into long-term therapy?" let me counter it with another question: "How can long-term therapy be done *without* the benefit of hypnosis?"

References

Dlin, B. (1985). Presidential Address: Psychobiology and the treatment of anniversary reactions. *Psychosomatics, 26*(6), 505–520.

Freud, S. (1930). *Ueber Psychoanalyse.* Fuenf Vorlesungen gehalten zur 20jaehrigen Gruendungsfeier der Clark University in Worcester Mass. September 1909 (8th ed.). Leipzig: Franz Deutike.

Levitt, E., Edmonston, W. E., Jr., & Wick, E. (1983). Project enlightenment (defining hypnosis). *APA Division 30 Psychological Hypnosis Newsletter.*

Wick, E., Sigman, R., & Kline, M. (1971). Hypnotherapy and therapeutic education in the treatment of obesity: Differential treatment factors. *Psychiatric Quarterly, 45*(2), 234–254.

Zisook, S., Shuchter, S., & Schuckit, M. (1985). Unresolved grief among psychiatric patients. *Psychosomatics, 26*(6), 497–503.

$\underset{A}{\overset{Q}{\mathcal{C}}}$ 67 Biofeedback and Hypnosis

Question:

Is there any benefit from combining hypnosis with biofeedback and can biofeedback be used to determine hypnotizability or depth of trance?

Discussion by IAN WICKRAM, Ph.D.

Combining biofeedback with hypnosis appears to have clinical value in at least two areas: increasing response to hypnosis and generating powerful but temporary placebo effects to alter presenting symptoms. The value of using biofeedback to assess hypnotizability and depth of trance is not as clear.

First, it is convenient to distinguish between the trait and attitudinal-motivational components of hypnotic behavior. It appears that the trait or ability component is relatively stable and resistant to modification, while the attitudinal-motivational aspect is fairly resonsive to alteration (Diamond, 1977). Elsewhere (Wickramasekera, 1977) I have presented data demonstrating that hypnotic behavior can be at least temporarily increased by individualized training procedures using EMG and theta feedback training.

Biofeedback instruments are useful for people who are skeptical or analytical about hypnosis, on the one hand, or excessively fearful, on the other. EMG biofeedback provides a highly credible and quantitative entry into hypnosis for the skeptic and a convenient and self-controlled method of learning to "let go" for the fearful. For the fearful it helps develop tolerance of the unusual subjective perceptions and sensations (lightness, floating, spinning, tingling, numbness, body expanding and contracting, etc.) that are typically associated with the moderate to deep hypnotic experience. The fearful client discovers that he can exit the unusual subjective experience whenever he chooses and return to it when he chooses, gradually getting

374

used to the unusual sensation of "letting go" that frightens many people away from hypnosis.

For skeptics the objective and quantitative changes that occur on a strip chart recorder or digital integrator (which quantifies the EMG signal for preselected time periods) encourages the belief that something important, verifiable, and "real" is going on during EMG training, even if they do not at first notice changes in their personal subjective experience such as numbness and tingling. In other words, biofeedback keeps the skeptic comfortable, task-involved and goal-oriented.

For people with superior hypnotic ability and those who have experienced hypnosis as a comfortable and credible state, *immediate* EMG feedback may be intrusive and disrupt their ability to relax (Qualls & Sheehan, 1981). However, *delayed* objective feedback of physiological change (looking at a strip chart recording after hypnosis) can powerfully increase their sense of self-efficacy and keep them task-oriented.

Biofeedback may be most useful for subjects with low or moderate hypnotic abilities. The biofeedback instruments can be used to train or shape a pre-sleep state (low physiological arousal) that will be rather reliably associated with profound subjective changes that will convince skeptical and unmotivated patients that something important is going on.

In training patients to use EMG feedback, it is crucial to maintain their sense of involvement and excitement with the use of immediate or delayed feedback devices such as strip chart recordings; otherwise the experience can be deadly dull and simply an exercise in boredom. Much biofeedback practiced in university laboratories loses its appeal for patient and therapist because the incentive properties of reinforcing events are ignored (Honig, 1966). Mechanistic repetitions of behavioral procedures and technical operations (presence or absence of feedback *per se*) will not guarantee an increase of hypnotic ability. The clinician should place the procedures in a larger context of meaning that can sustain ego involvement and motivation to produce an alert low arousal state and a feeling of self-efficacy.

In the area of assessing hypnotic ability, the use of biofeedback devices is promising but unproven. I have made several clinical observations that relate to this. Many people with high hypnotic ability are able to make large temporary changes in several of their physiological functions with minimal or no training. This is particularly true if they are low on neuroticism (Eysenck, 1960). These people can drop their baseline frontal EMG level by 5 to 15 microvolts.

A subset of people who are high both on hypnotizability and neuroticism are unable to alter their physiological function without extensive training. I have found that people of high hypnotizability who are prone to catastrophize (Ellis, 1962) during transient stress have *higher* EMG baselines than people of moderate or low hypnotic ability, and are less able, during a stressful episode, to drop their frontal EMG with brief relaxation instructions.

People of low hypnotic ability can seldom demonstrate large changes without some prior relaxation, biofeedback or meditation training. The sum of these observations suggests that those persons who have had no prior training, but who are able to reduce a frontal baseline EMG of 15 to 20 microvolts to 5 to 8 microvolts by simply closing their eyes and relaxing, are probably above average to superior in their hypnotic abilities.

Engstrom's data (1976) suggest that people who have a high density of alpha waves in their eyes-closed EEG baseline condition are probably good hypnotic subjects. However, there are generally more problems with artifacts in measuring EEG with moderately priced biofeedback devices, so EEG monitoring is not recommended for routine clinical purposes.

The use of biofeedback to measure depth of trance is problematic unless one defines depth in terms of changes in biological functions, e.g., EMG, vasodilation, density of theta or alpha in the EEG, etc. These changes may all be produced in superior hypnotic subjects given specific suggestions for changes in these specific functions. But these changes do not guarantee that subjective alterations (e.g., spinning, floating, euphoria) indicating greater depth will occur. In the superior hypnotic subject it may be possible to get a profound subjective sense of depth while biological measures indicate high arousal or tension. If the depth of trance is defined primarily in terms of subjective changes, no reliable physiological correlate has been reported.

A second clinical use of EMG and heart rate biofeedback instruments is to determine if your patient is relaxing in an objective physiological sense. It is possible to have a patient report profound subjective relaxation in the absence of any changes in EMG or heart rate measures. If you think that the variables that control the patient's symptom (e.g., headache pain) are in fact physiological (e.g., sustained muscle spasm in head, neck or upper back), then using hypnosis to simply alter the patient's subjective perception of sensory stimuli may produce a temporary reduction of pain based on the placebo effect but no sustained reduction of the headache. If the placebo effect of pain reduction is, as I think, a conditioned response (Wickramasekera, 1980) and is not supported by reduction in the underlying muscle spasm, the symptomatic remission is likely to be only temporary and followed by "placebo sag" or extinction. The headache pain will return in a few days or weeks. Therefore, the benefits of combining biofeedback with hypnosis are that it enables you to "cash in" on two powerful placebos: 1) the mystique of hypnosis, and 2) the high credibility of biomedical electronic instrumentation. More important, it enables you to direct your interventions at the presumed underlying mechanism of headache pain, the muscle spasm.

References

Diamond, M. J. (1977). Issues and methods for modifying responsibility to hypnosis. *Annals of the New York Academy of Sciences, 296,* 119–128.

Ellis, A. *Reason and emotion in psychotherapy.* New York, Lyle Stuart, 1962.

Engstrom, D. (1976). Hypnotic susceptibility, EEG-alpha and self regulation. In G. E. Schwartz & D. Shapiro (Eds.). *Consciousness and self regulation: Advances in research.* New York: Plenum.

Eysenck, H. J. (1960). *The structure of human personality* (3rd ed). London: Methuan.

Harsher-Towe, D. (1983). Control of EMG activity in subjects demonstrating high and low levels of hypnotizability. Unpublished doctoral dissertation, Virginia Consortium of Professional Psychology.

Honig, W. K. (1966). *Operant behavior: Areas of research and application.* New York: Appleton-Century-Crofts.

Qualls, P. J., & Sheehan, P. W. (1981). EMG biofeedback as a relaxation technique: A critical appraisal and reassessment. *Psychological Bulletin, 901,* 21–42.

Wickramasekera, I. (1977). On attempts to modify hypnotic susceptibility: Some psychophysiological procedures and promising directions. *Annals of the New York Academy of Sciences, 296,* 143–153.

Wickramasekera, I. (1980). A conditioned response model of the placebo effect: Predictions from the model. *Biofeedback and Self-Regulation, 5*(1), 5–18.

Wickramasekera, I. (Aug. 1983). A model of people at high risk. Paper presented at the International Stress and Tension Control Society, Brighton, England.

SECTION IX *Hypnosis With Children and Adolescents*

Although hypnosis has been used with children and adolescents for over 200 years, the topic is still largely neglected. The available literature is sparse and the number of clinicians using hypnosis with children few. Many health professionals, including a number of hypnotherapists, seem to think that hypnosis is not appropriate for youngsters and that children are not hypnotizable.

Yet the facts belie these beliefs. Given their closeness to internal imagery and their readiness to pretend or make-believe, children as a group are more responsive than adults to hypnosis. A child who has imaginary playmates or pets, who acts as if someone no longer there really is there, who sees him or herself living in a different place, or who gets deeply involved in what he or she will be as an adult — such a child is clearly manifesting a number of characteristics of what we call hypnosis. The ease with which children are receptive to hypnosis can be easily gauged by simply asking them to watch a favorite television program in their heads or to imagine being on another planet doing whatever is done there. Most children and most adolescents love to fantasize and to pretend, to imagine that things are other than what they seem, and that is a great deal of what hypnosis is.

The three papers in this section contain a number of fascinating case studies of the use of hypnosis with young people. We hope they will encourage others to consider using hypnosis with their young clients and patients, for it is a shame that such a natural technique (for children) and such an effective one is so little used.

379

Question:

> I've used hypnosis extensively with adults and now sometimes get requests to use it with children, which I have no experience doing. I guess I'm so adult-oriented that I can't even conceive of what a case of hypnotherapy with a child would look like. Can you give some examples, particularly of the techniques that are effective with children?

Discussion by DANIEL LUTZKER, Ph.D.

It is commonly accepted that children tend to be very good hypnotic subjects. Reasons put forth to explain this include the child's capacity for flights of fancy, a relative absence of inhibition, a greater capacity for eidetic imagery and a reduced capacity for critical judgment. Whatever the reasons, hypnotic work with children can be very beneficial to the patient.

As with any other age group, trust and rapport are critical to the establishment of a therapeutic relationship. In addition, when working with children one must be cognizant not only of the usual variables but also the level of the child's development — his vocabulary, his ability to understand the need for the procedure, and his experiential world. Some case illustrations may help to clarify this:

Case 1. Nocturnal Enuresis

Alan was eight years old when his mother brought him to see me. He had been enuretic for the past four years. Attempts to find a medical cause had proved futile and psychotherapy had led to no change. Obvious stress factors were the birth of a younger sister about a year before the onset of the

381

symptom and a chronically upset household. The parents bickered constantly, as did the siblings. To make matters worse, the family was economically
marginal, in part because the father tended to be neglectful of his business.

The initial hypnotherapeutic approach was to attempt symptom removal
by way of guided imagery. Alan was asked first if he would like to stop
wetting his bed. He answered "yes." (It is surprising how many children are
unconcerned about their enuresis.) I told him that there was a way to do
this — a way that involved using his imagination. Would he like to try this?

"What do I have to do?"

"All you have to do is to picture in your mind things I am going to describe
to you. What you think has an effect on what happens inside your body.
What happens when you think about something good to eat? Close your eyes
and picture yourself eating something really good. (Alan closed his eyes and
soon licked his lips.) What is happening inside your mouth?"

"It's getting all watery."

"Right! When you think about eating something good, your body gets
ready to do that. Your body acts as if you really were eating. What we are
going to do now is to try to get your body to stop wetting your bed while
you're asleep. Are you ready to begin?" (Alan nodded and hypnosis was
induced using visual imagery.)

"It feels so good to be so relaxed and at ease that you may wish to sink
down into a deeper and deeper kind of relaxation, letting yourself drift off
into a very dreamy condition, similar to going to sleep. When you're in this
nice dreamy condition, picture yourself standing outside of your own body,
looking down at yourself relaxing in your very special place. You can feel
very pleased to see how cozy and comfortable you look. As you stand there,
I'd like you to imagine the part of you that's outside of your body beginning to grow smaller, getting smaller and smaller and smaller, shrinking
down to a very, very tiny size . . . getting so tiny that in a little while you'll
be small enough to enter your own body. When you're small enough to enter
your own body, picture yourself doing that. You can enter at whatever point
you wish, by whatever way you like. Once inside the body you can enjoy
a very pleasant and a very interesting trip traveling through the body to the
part of the body that controls peeing. As you might know, pee travels
through the body and is stored in a special place called the 'bladder' until
you are ready to get rid of it. When you want to pee you open a valve on
the bladder — like turning on the water in the sink — and let the pee out. Then
you shut the valve again. Most people do this only in the daytime but
some people have trouble keeping the valve shut at night. To help you keep
the valve shut at night I'd like you to attach it to a timer. First, I'd like you
to find the valve that controls peeing. When you find that valve, I'd like
you to imagine yourself attaching a timer to the valve. Set the timer so that
when you go to sleep it will shut the valve tightly to keep any pee from

coming out. Set it so that it keeps the valve tightly shut until a few minutes after you wake up in the morning. In this way you can keep from wetting your bed because every night the timer will automatically shut the valve when you go to sleep and will keep it shut until after you wake up in the morning."

This procedure worked very well for the first week. In the middle of the second week Alan began to wet his bed again. After some reflection I concluded that I had not taken sufficient account of the child's world. Instead I had taken adult concepts and experience and imposed them on the patient. Valves, timers and bladder are not the stuff of childhood. I could do better.

An interview with the mother led to the discovery that Alan was a "nut on Star Wars." He loved anything that had to do with it, knew the names of all the characters and had numerous toys derived from this series of motion pictures. A new strategy was devised.

In the next session Alan was asked to picture himself in a spacecraft, getting ready to blast off to a "Star Wars planet." We held a countdown from 10 to zero. Alan raised his arms up and began to steer his spaceship, heading for another planet in a far off galaxy.

"Picture yourself now approaching the planet . . . slowing down your engines . . . getting ready to land. See yourself setting your spaceship down gently on the planet . . . a soft bump — perfect landing! Picture yourself now taking off your seatbelt, opening the door and climbing out. A short distance away there's a big building with a sign on it that says 'Hall of Science.' A man is standing on the steps — a famous scientist — and he is waving to you. Picture yourself walking over to the Hall of Science and shaking hands with the man. He says, 'Alan, I'm so glad you could come. Let me show you my laboratory!' Picture yourself going into the Hall of Science with the man and walking down the hall with him, going to his laboratory. When you go into the laboratory you can see many interesting things going on. The scientist says, 'Alan, I have just invented a device that cures bed wetting. I want you to be the first one to use it!' Picture yourself getting seated comfortably in a chair while the scientist attaches wires to you with a special paste. He says, 'When I throw this switch a pleasant current will run through your body and in a few seconds you will be totally cured of your bed wetting.' Picture the scientist throwing the switch. A nice pleasant feeling comes over you and in a few seconds you are cured! When you are cured, picture yourself helping the scientist to remove the wires. Picture yourself thanking him for helping you. Then you shake hands and leave the laboratory, returning to your spaceship."

Alan thoroughly enjoyed this fantasy trip. His ability to be truly involved in it was evident from his smiling, his "steering" of the space craft, and his removal of the wires. He stopped wetting his bed and was still dry five years later.

This case illustrates a partial success which was turned into a total success by improvement of the mental imagery and a change in strategy. The imagery used at first did not capture the child's imagination as effectively as the "Star Wars" imagery. His enthusiastic involvement in the latter scene was very evident. Secondly, there was a deliberate attempt to make the experience ego-enhancing by placing the patient in control of a spacecraft, by having him warmly received by a famous scientist and by giving him the distinction of being the first person to undergo a revolutionary new form of therapy.

Another difference in the two approaches is that in the first case a method of control was employed which involved machinery. The machinery had to be functioning daily and had the potential to break down. The second approach involved a permanent cure in which nothing could go wrong. In fact, the patient was placed in a position which virtually demanded a permanent cure. Note the instruction, "When you are cured, picture yourself helping the scientist to remove the wires." Thus Alan could not proceed with the fantasy until the cure was effected.

Alternative explanations can, of course, be offered. The practice effect of a second session and Alan's familiarity with me may have also played a role.

Case 2. Brittle Diabetes

Brittle diabetes refers to a diabetic condition which is not controllable through drugs and diet. Sugar levels in such patients fluctuate wildly and unpredictably, often leading to medical emergencies.

Betty was a 13-year-old brittle diabetic referred by the head of the department of pediatrics in a large hospital. He had read an article I had published on the use of hypnosis in various medical conditions (stroke, cancer, Freidrich's ataxis, multiple sclerosis, burns, etc.). He asked whether hypnosis could aid in the control of diabetes. I replied that I really did not know but I would be willing to try.

The patient resented being sent to "a shrink" because "I'm not crazy." She was violently opposed to hypnosis and admitted to being frightened by the whole idea. This she did by a nod of the head in answer to a question. In fact, Betty said almost nothing but spent the entire first session crying softly.

I replied that I really was not the least bit interested in whether she was crazy; I was interested only in her diabetes. As her tears continued to fall, I explained that I had been doing some very exciting things with people who had a wide variety of physical ills and that most of them had shown improvement. Her doctor thought that perhaps I could help her too.

She said nothing but appeared to be listening so I went on. I told her about the 60-year-old man who was confined to a wheelchair, his entire left side paralyzed by a stroke. After eight weeks of hypnotherapy and medical treatment he was able to walk unassisted. She still said nothing so I explained my "theory" about how this works.

"If you think at all, your vocal cords vibrate; they get ready to speak. If you think about doing something — say picking up this pen — the muscles needed to do this tense a little. Your body responds to your thoughts. This is done unconsciously. That is, you don't have to think about it, you just do it. You don't have to think about which muscles to move in order to walk. You just walk.

Now consider this. If you cut your finger your body repairs the damage. You produce new blood cells, new skin tissue, new muscle cells — whatever is necessary. How much of each does the body produce? Exactly the amount required — no more, no less. You never wind up, for example, with extra skin hanging down from where the cut had been. How do you manage to do this? I don't know. But somewhere in the body is the knowledge required — a knowledge that we are not generally aware we have.

Now let's put these two facts together. The body knows how to repair itself and the body responds to thoughts. If we become ill and we think about getting better, this may increase the likelihood that we *will* get better. Doctors have known this for a long time. They talk about patients having the will to live — or giving up the will to live. In recent years there have been some very interesting studies published which suggest that cancer can be combatted in this way. My own work with a whole bunch of different diseases suggests the same thing. Whether it works with diabetes I don't know — but I want to find out. Are you willing to work with me?"

Betty made no reply.

"You've got nothing to lose. The worst thing that can happen is that it won't work, in which case you'll be no worse off than before." I waited. Betty's lips moved. Very softly she said, "I'm scared."

"I can see you are very tense," I said. "Let me show you how to relax." I did an arm drop induction and was pleased to see that there was much less resistance than I had anticipated. Then I had Betty visualize a pleasant, very special place of her own choosing in which to relax. After a few moments of relaxation I had her return to the present place (my office). I asked how she felt and she replied, "Better." I told her that relaxation is the first step in hypnosis and that the hypnotic experience is a very pleasant, relaxing one. However, since she was afraid of hypnosis, we would only do relaxation.

Betty's mother was interviewed. She told me that the diabetes had severely hampered her daughter's functioning. She was unable to attend school and had to be tutored at home. She was unable to go anywhere alone. She had no friends. Every year there was at least one hospitalization. It soon became apparent that there was a degree of symbiosis here. Betty was tied to her mother. Her mother was tied to her too. She spent very little time away from Betty and when she did she worried until she got home.

The next session was cancelled because of a hospitalization. In the following session I talked with Betty about her lifestyle — about how her diabetes hampered her, about what her future might be. We also practiced another "relaxation exercise," but avoided "hypnosis." Betty told me that her sugar levels were always measured at either zero or + 4 (the highest rating) and never in between. I asked whether it wouldn't be possible to narrow that range. She asked, "How could I do that?" I replied, "By using the power of your mind to influence your body." Without using "hypnosis," I induced a relaxed state in Betty. Using the same guided imagery employed in the case of Alan, I had her go into her body and enter the "control room" of the brain. There she located the controls that regulated sugar levels and adjusted them so as to fluctuate within a narrower range. After accomplishing that, she returned to her "special place," grew back to full size and integrated herself with her body again.

At the next session Betty excitedly reported that for the first time in her life she had measured her sugar level at + 2! Encouraged by this success we had another "relaxation session," repeating what had been done the previous week. This time we taped the session so that she could reinforce the suggestions daily. There were three more sessions which were devoted partly to practice and partly to more traditional psychotherapy. Betty's sugar levels fluctuated between 0 and + 2 with several readings of + 1 occurring during this three-week period.

Therapy was interrupted early in June by summer vacation. The family would be away at their summer home until Labor Day. The mother promised to call me in September. However, she failed to do so. I made a follow-up call in late October. The mother said, "You wouldn't believe it's the same kid. Not only is her diabetes under control, but she's going to public school, she's joined a girls' organization and she's playing soccer!"

The case was closed and the mother promised to call me if there were any problems. I never heard from her again.

This case illustrates one of the ways to overcome resistance as well as a means of introducing a theory about the ability of the mind to influence "involuntary" body processes. I have had two other cases of brittle diabetes, one of which was treated successfully. The other was not. In addition, there have been many other cases with various somatic problems. The next two cases are good examples.

Case 3. Aplastic Anemia

Aplastic anemia is a condition in which the body ceases to produce blood cells. When the existing supply of blood is exhausted the patient dies. Medical intervention is successful in about half of the cases. The causes of this condition are obscure. The treatment involves close monitoring of the patient, blood transfusions and chemotherapy.

The patient, Steve, is the 15-year-old adopted son of my oldest friend. His father was familiar with my work because we had had many discussions about it. I had also hypnotized both his mother and his cousin in the past. Thus, Steve was comfortable both with the hypnotist and with the concept of using hypnosis to combat disease. He was eager to try this route to recovery.

Steve's doctor was not familiar with hypnosis but she supported the notion wholeheartedly on the grounds that it couldn't hurt and it might help.

Steve is an extremely intelligent and inquisitive youngster. He learned all he could about his illness and instructed me in regard to what had to be done. On some occasions we needed to work on producing one kind of blood cells. On other occasions we worked on a different kind. Sometimes he had fevers and we worked on bringing his body temperature down. Sometimes he was nauseous and we worked on that.

The method was to induce a hypnotic state through visualization. He would picture himself lying on a beach on Grand Cayman Island, his favorite vacation spot. Then we would proceed with deep relaxation and guided imagery to get him into the "control room" of the brain. He would then make the adjustments necessary to produce the desired result. I made him a variety of tapes to use for his various symptoms. Soon he began to disregard the tapes, employing instead his own original thoughts. He was the most inventive and self-motivated subject I had ever had.

Although there were many ups and downs, moments of despair and periods of exhaustion for all of us, Steve had a full recovery. He is back home, attending school and engaging in his usual activities although he is still being treated on an outpatient basis.

The case of Steve was included for three reasons. First, to indicate that hypnosis can be used to treat numerous conditions and symptoms. Secondly, I wanted to make the point that the hypnotist is only an adjunct to the therapy. Once he had grasped the basic idea, Steve was able to treat himself. Finally, it was because of Steve that I met Dougie and I especially wanted to tell you about Dougie.

Case 4. Leukemia

Dougie is a cute four-year-old who was sharing Steve's hospital room. He has been hospitalized several times because of leukemia.

Dougie was a very frightened child. He insisted on having one of his parents with him at all times. He showed great anxiety whenever anyone approached him. His parents complained that he never slept.

One night I had gone to work with Steve. I drew the curtain separating the two boys and proceeded to do an induction. When I finished my work with Steve, Dougie's father emerged from behind the curtain. "I want you to see something," he said. He pulled the curtain back. There lay Dougie, fast asleep with his TV set on.

His father explained. "He was watching TV and doing a puzzle when he heard you talking to Steve. He began to listen in and pretty soon he was asleep. If you can, would you make a tape for Dougie? He's going to be discharged soon and I'd like to have a tape I could use at home. He never sleeps like this!"

I hesitated. From what I had read and heard, children under the age of seven tended to be poor subjects. On the other hand, here was indisputable proof that this is not always the case. "Let me think how I might approach this," I said. "Tell me a little about Dougie. What is he interested in?"

"He loves the super heroes, especially He-Man," he said.

"That gives me an idea," I said. "Let me work on it and I'll see you tomorrow."

The next day I gave it some thought. Dougie didn't really know me, although he had seen me several times. Would he be frightened if I approached him? He's only four years old. How long is his attention span? How much can he comprehend? After some thought I decided to make a tape for Dougie without going through the process of meeting, establishing rapport and inducing a hypnotic state. Instead, I created a personalized story which went like this:

"Hi Dougie! My name is Dan and I'm here to tell you a very special bedtime story. What makes it a *special* story is that it's all about *you*. So what I'd like you to do is to close your eyes and imagine yourself walking down a path that goes through the woods. But this is no ordinary woods. This woods is made up of special trees that grow candies and toys. There's a lollipop tree, a gumdrop tree, a teddy bear tree — all kinds of trees with all kinds of toys and good things to eat. As you walk through the woods you can eat anything you wish. You can take any toys you want. Also, there are many animals in the woods, all of them friendly, and you can stop and pet them if you wish. After a while you might get a little tired from walking, so picture yourself settling down for a nice rest beneath a gumdrop tree — or whatever tree you like. Just as you settle down for a rest you see some people coming. Why, it's He-Man and Superman and some of your other favorite super heroes! They come up to you and talk to you. They ask you to tell them about yourself. So you tell them how sometimes you get sick and sometimes you have pain and sometimes you can't sleep. He-Man says, 'We can help you! You just go to sleep and we will sprinkle a magic dust on ourselves to make us very tiny. When we're very tiny we'll go into your body and beat up all those bad germs that make you sick. Then we'll throw those germs completely out of your body.'

"And so you let yourself get very, very sleepy and have a nice nap. While you're asleep you can picture He-Man and your other super hero friends sprinkling themselves with the magic powder and growing smaller and smaller. When they're very tiny picture them going into your body and finding the bad germs. You can enjoy watching them beat up the bad germs. Picture them throwing all the bad germs out of your body. When they are finished getting rid of the bad germs, He-Man says, 'Now you can go to sleep, Dougie, and have a real good rest. When you wake up in the morning you can feel stronger and healthier. Good-night, Dougie!'"

I gave the tape to Dougie's father. The next day he told me, "Dougie loved it! He got real interested in the story and went right off to sleep."

Dougie was discharged the next day. Two weeks later I made a follow-up phone call. Dougie had been asking for the tape every night and always slept through the night after hearing it.

This case is a departure from formal hypnosis. Because of the patient's extreme youth I felt it would be better to induce a hypnotic state in a manner more natural and familiar to him. A four-year-old knows what a bedtime story is. He knows that following a bedtime story one goes to sleep.

Young children are also very narcissistic. To capture his interest I told him "a very special bedtime story," a story that is "a *special* story" because it's all about *you*." What could be more interesting?

Then I introduced elements that would appeal to young children — candy, toys, friendly animals, and finally, super heroes. Could a child want much more?

The super heroes, as we all know, exist to help us in our struggles against evil, embodied in "the bad germs that make you sick." The super heroes can do for Dougie what he cannot do for himself. They can vanquish the bad germs. With allies like these, need the child worry?

Unfortunately, I lost track of this case. Dougie's family lives in another state and I have had no other contact with them. I don't know how he is going so far as leukemia is concerned. All I know is that at last report he was sleeping well.

Case 5. Hysterical Paralysis

Ira was referred by his pediatrician. He had been "driving his parents crazy and driving me crazy too," the doctor said. He presented first with one illness, then another. Now he had a total paralysis of both legs. "Medically, there's absolutely nothing wrong with him. You're my last hope."

The patient was 10 years old at that time. He lived with his mother and stepfather. He had almost no contact with his father and regarded the stepfather as his real father. The mother felt that perhaps his symptoms were related to his father's lack of interest in him. She had contacted the father, who made a perfunctory telephone call to Ira but showed no real concern.

At the first appointment I saw only the parents, obtaining the usual history and discussing the possibility of utilizing hypnotherapy. When I saw Ira sitting in my waiting room at the next session I asked him to come into my office. "I can't," he said with a smile, "I can't walk." His parents began to get up to carry him into the office. I signaled them not to, "If you can't walk," I said, "you'll have to find some other way to come into my office."

Ira looked confused. He looked first at one parent, then at the other but he got no response. "Perhaps you could roll into the office," I suggested. Ira liked this idea. He slid onto the floor and rolled into my office. Then he pulled himself up into a chair. We discussed his paralysis and he showed the classic "belle indifference" of the hysteric. I considered different strategies and decided on one that I felt would lead to the least resistance. Instead of explaining that physical symptoms could have psychological origins, I chose to treat his paralysis as an organic illness. I told him that his doctor had referred him to me because of the very interesting work I had been doing in treating physical ills with hypnosis. I explained my theory about the brain's ability to direct the body to take just the right steps to effect a cure. I cited examples from some of my cases. Ira was very interested. He agreed to try it. From there we proceeded into hypnosis via visualization of a special place and then used the out-of-body technique to get Ira into the control room of his brain. There he made the adjustments necessary to instruct the body to repair the damage in his legs. I had him imagine the legs getting stronger and stronger. At the end of the session I told Ira he could leave.

"But I can't walk," he protested.

"Your legs are stronger now," I said. "Why don't you try? I think you can do it!"

Very dramatically Ira pulled himself up to his feet. "I'll fall," he said.

"So you'll pick yourself up," I countered.

Ira proceeded to walk, very slowly and deliberately, placing his hands on the wall for support. I encouraged him by saying, "Good! I knew you could do it!" He proceeded to the waiting room door. When I opened it his parents looked at him in amazement. He staggered into the waiting room and collapsed in his mother's arms.

As they prepared to leave Ira raised his arms sideways so that he could use a parent on each side for support. I told him, "No, I want you to walk to the elevator. Now that your legs are getting better you need to exercise them."

Prior to the next session I gave some thought to ways of improving upon what had already been accomplished. I devised a new strategy.

At the next session I was advised that Ira had been walking with great difficulty and was still weak. He tired easily. I assured him and his parents that he would soon be walking perfectly.

This time I took Ira on a different kind of mental trip. I had him visualize a 50-story building. Then I asked him to picture himself standing by the elevator with me, on the 50th floor. When the elevator opened we stepped inside and rode down to the first floor. I counted the floors as we descended and as we descended Ira went into a deep state of relaxation. When we reached the first floor Ira was in his "deepest possible state of relaxation." When the doors opened we walked down the hall to a laboratory, where Ira was going to receive a new treatment which would cure his condition.

"Picture yourself getting seated comfortably in a chair. Next to the chair is a machine which was designed specifically to cure the kind of condition you have. There are wires attached to the machine. Picture yourself attaching the wires from the machine to each of the joints in your legs. Attach one wire to each ankle, one to each knee and one to each hip. When all the wires are attached, I'd like you to signal me by raising one finger (pause). Good! Now I'd like you to notice the switch on the machine. When you turn the switch on, a gentle electrical current will pass through your legs. The nerves in your body, as you might know, run on electricity. What this machine does is to increase the electricity in the nerves, just like you would recharge a battery. When your nerves are recharged, you will be able to walk normally again. When you are ready you may turn the switch on."

Ira made a motion with one finger. I continued, "Feel a pleasant current traveling through your legs, restoring strength to the nerves and the muscles. You can continue to enjoy this feeling for as long as it takes and when your legs are fully cured you can turn the machine off."

I waited. In a short while Ira extended one finger and made a downward motion with it. "Are you cured now?" I asked. He nodded. "Wonderful! Now you can disconnect the wires."

At the end of the session Ira got up and strode out into the waiting room. His parents rejoiced.

"Now I want you to be sure and do some walking every day to keep those legs strong and next week I'll race you down the hall to the candy machine. The loser has to buy candy for the winner!"

Ira won.

This is not the end of the story, however.

Ira's mother was eager to learn *why* he had developed his paralysis. Ira too thought that was a good idea. In the next session we sought an answer.

Ira was hypnotized and was told, " . . . it feels so good to be so relaxed and so at ease that you may wish to continue to relax deeper and deeper, letting yourself drift off into a very deep sleep. As you drift off into sleep you can have a dream — a dream that will give us some clues about why you were unable to walk. Later on, after you have had your dream, you can return to a fully alert state and remember the dream in great detail. I'm going to be quiet now so that you can enjoy your sleep and dream as long as you wish."

In a few minutes Ira reported the following dream:

"I was in a boxing ring and I was beating up a lady. Everybody was cheering. I really beat her up. After the fight I went outside and there was a big crowd and everyone was asking me questions. (What kind of questions?) Like, 'How did you do it?' and somebody held up a newspaper with a headline that said, 'Ira wins $50,000 in big fight!' (What happened next?) That's it. I was a big hero and that was the end of the dream."

I asked Ira if he could get any meaning out of the dream. He couldn't, so I became more specific.

"Can you describe the lady you were fighting with?"

"Yeah. She was short, not exactly fat but not thin. She had dark hair."

"Did she resemble anyone you know?"

Ira grinned. "My mother," he said. We went on to discuss Ira's relationship with his mother. He resented her nagging, her overprotectiveness, her irritability. He also resented having to share her with his stepfather, although he was genuinely fond of the man. "Sometimes, I wish it was only me and her again," he said.

We moved from here into conventional psychotherapy and parent counseling. Because I have an ongoing relationship with Ira's doctor, I can report with certainty that there have been no hysterical symptoms in the past four years. There have, of course, been ups and downs in the relationships within the family.

Ira's case involves several different kinds of psychotherapy. In addition to hypnotherapy there was behavior modification, parent counseling and insight-oriented psychotherapy.

When I first encountered Ira he told me he couldn't walk. His parents were ready to carry him into my office. The first thing I did was to counsel the parents not to do this, not to reinforce Ira's paralysis through secondary gain.

My next step was to present Ira with a problem and throw the responsibility for his problem onto Ira. He had to get himself into my office somehow. Since he did not have a solution, I offered a suggestion. He could roll into the office. Thus, he got into the office unassisted. Also, he had taken my first suggestion.

Next I decided to treat Ira as though he had an organc condition. This had the advantage of minimizing resistance since I was not attacking his illness as being "merely psychological." I provided him with a rationale to explain how he could get better. We went through the process in fantasy. Then I gave him the suggestion that he had already profited from the first session ("Your legs are stronger now").

At the end of the formal first session Ira was given verbal reinforcement ("Good! I knew you could do it") when he produced the desired response.

I again counseled the parents not to help him. ("No, I want you to walk to the elevator. Now that your legs are getting better you need to exercise them").

In the second session there was a shift in strategy. Since I understood that Ira was oppositional and manipulative, I felt it was important for him to be in control of his treatment, as he had been in the first session. However, I wanted a permanent cure. The solution was to create a bind — a situation in which he had no choice but to cure himself (" . . . when your legs are fully cured you can turn the machine off"). I was prepared to stay as long as necessary. Ira could not end his session without being cured.

Positive reinforcement was given verbally for accomplishing this. Then, with a view toward preventing possible regression, I offered an additional reward (" . . . next week I'll race you down the hall to the candy machine. The loser has to buy candy for the winner!"). I offered a competition with a prize which Ira would win only if his legs were functioning well.

Finally, after the symptom was abandoned, we achieved insight. This was done by a) inducing a dream which was predetermined to be related to the symptom, b) creating perfect recall, and c) then analyzing the dream. In one session we discovered that behind Ira's symptom lay dissatisfaction with the relationship with his mother, not with his father. Knowing this we were able to go to work on the problem.

Q&69 Hypnosis With Very Young Children

Question:

> I work with a lot of children ages three to six and want to know if hypnosis can be used effectively with them. Children of this age don't have the cognitive skills necessary for some kinds of inductions.

Discussion by GARY R. ELKINS, Ph.D., &
BRYAN D. CARTER, Ph.D.

It is possible for children in the three-to-six-year age range to profit from the use of hypnotically-based interventions. However, the extremely short attention span of children in this age range is a contraindication for the more formalized and directive induction techniques. Our experience has been that adult-oriented inductions such as progressive relaxation or traditional deepening suggestions are unlikely to be productive with young children. Indeed, such techniques may generate anxiety in the preschool child. Successful induction methods must be in keeping with the child's developmental level and cognitive capacity.

Developmentally, a preschool child has an extremely rich fantasy life in which primary process thinking plays an active role. Preschool children may readily slip between the worlds of fantasy and reality, often intermingling material from both domains. This primary position of fantasy in the life of the preschooler should be explored and utilized in the therapist's attempt to produce a hypnotic state with the child. Needless to say, the rapport between the therapist and the child is a crucial element in developing a therapeutic relationship on which hypnotherapeutic interventions can be based. A review of hypnotic suggestibility in children by Chapman, Elkins, and Carter (1982) demonstrated the high correlation between the child's ability to relate to adults in a comfortable manner and his/her receptiveness to hypnotic suggestion.

Pre-induction talk should be focused on building rapport and gathering information about the child's likes, dislikes, imagery abilities, and social environment. The therapist should spend preliminary sessions working with the child in a somewhat traditional play therapy modality. This enhances the child's trust in the therapist and allows the therapist to become aware of the child's interests and use of imagination in fantasy play. During this stage, the parent may be involved to increase the transference and to provide information about the child. The parent may also reinforce the therapist's suggestions and confidence in the process. All of this is directed toward setting the stage for hypnotherapeutic interventions and interchange.

The therapist may describe the process of hypnosis to the child or a more informal induction may be used. In many respects, however, hypnosis in the preschool child is actually an extension of the degree of rapport between the therapist and child. Since play is one of the primary modalities and concerns, it is the perfect vehicle for implementing therapeutic suggestions. The practitioner may engage the child through storytelling, use videotapes or books, or speak to the child through a stuffed animal or doll. Two case examples are presented which illustrate the integration of hypnosis in management and therapy of preschoolers' medical and psychological problems.

The patient (J.L.) was a four-year-old girl who had been admitted to the pediatric unit of a medical center due to the acute onset of severe pain in her right hip. Examination and tests revealed that she had a septic infection in the hip joint which required emergency surgery in order to drain the abscess. Needless to say, the acuteness of this situation did not allow for good emotional preparation for hospitalization and surgery. Following the surgery, the patient was put in a single room where she had to be placed in traction while the incision and hip joint healed. After two days, she became extremely socially withdrawn and resistant with hospital staff. Her only response to nursing personnel was "no" to virtually everything. She frequently refused food, refused to make eye contact with staff and attendants, and rapidly regressed in her behavior. She refused to use a bed pan, but when it was removed would immediately wet or soil the bed. When the consultant was called in to deal with this crisis, the patient was lying in her room and two nurses were attempting to change her I.V. The patient was actively fighting them as they searched for another position on the vein in which to insert the needle for the new I.V. She was obviously an extremely frightened and traumatized little girl.

The nurses left the room and the therapist spent some time trying to talk directly to the patient. She actively resisted this, looking away and refusing to say anything but "no." The therapist then picked up a stuffed animal at the end of her bed and began to talk to it about the little girl. Gradually, material was brought up with the stuffed toy about how scary and frightening it must be to be in the hospital and to have painful things done to you while your mommy and daddy are away. The stuffed animal talked back to the therapist about these feelings and how angry he was that his parents were not there with him. After a short while, the patient rolled around in her bed and looked at the therapist and the stuffed toy while they were having this conversation. It was obvious from her body tone and facial expression that her fearfulness and anxiety had decreased significantly. Shortly after that she began to spontaneously speak, verbalizing, through the stuffed toy, her own responses to the therapist's questions and conversation.

Gradually, the therapist worked in material pertaining to how the stuffed animal could relax when he had his I.V. changed and how, if he relaxed and thought about something pleasant, something warm and comfortable, the I.V. being put in probably would feel no more painful than a little bee sting. After this was discussed for a while, the therapist and the stuffed toy began to joke with the patient about the color of her hair and other things in the room, amusing her with a number of absurdities. The patient brightened and giggled in response to this part of the interaction. Shortly thereafter, the nurses reentered the room and the patient was able to instruct the nurses in how to put the I.V. into the stuffed toy's arm. After that she readily cooperated with the changing of her own I.V. with minimal demonstration of discomfort or anxiety.

In working with this young patient, at no time was a formal induction utilized, but instead the patient was able to focus on talking through the stuffed animal as a way of developing coping responses to her frightening situation. At all times during this interaction, the therapist actively joined with the patient in her dialogue, helping her develop coping responses and positive visual images about her experience. The change was quite dramatic, and from the time of the initial consultation, the patient became extremely cooperative with a number of noxious procedures during the course of her hospitalization. She became quite verbally outgoing and friendly with the nursing staff, who developed a strong attachment to her during her hospitalization.

M.L. was a five-year-old girl with several intense fears and phobias. Over a three-month period, she had become increasingly fearful at night. When the lights were turned out, she perceived the objects in her room as taking on ominous forms which frightened her. She would run out of the bedroom telling her parents that the picture of the clown on the wall looked mean and evil and that the toys on the shelves looked scary.

The parents tried removing objects from the room; then, however, the patient was afraid of the dark and shadows in the room. The parents tried to calm her without success and the patient requested that they stay awake in her room until she was asleep. While it was apparent that the patient was receiving considerable secondary gain in the form of attention, it was also obvious that her fear was very genuine and at times she was terrified.

Prior to the beginning of hypnotherapy, the parents were asked to put a rheostat on the light switch in her bedroom so that the patient could control the brightness or dimness of the lighting. Marks were made on the dimmer switch and the goal of moving the dimmer switch down one notch in brightness each night was set. This gave the patient some control over the darkness of the room. The patient was seen for individual therapy. M.L. was playing with a doll and the therapist began to tell the patient a story about the doll that involved "going for a walk at night in the forest." As the story progressed, M.L.'s gaze became fixed, her motor activity and respiratory rate decreased, and she became more relaxed. It was suggested that the doll was able to "feel happy" by noticing how nice and quiet the darkness was. In the story there was a "strong, brave tree" that responded to the doll with supportive and encouraging statements. The therapist suggested that she could be as brave as the tree and the session was completed.

During the next several weeks, the patient was seen weekly and the induction and similar suggestions were repeated. The parents observed that the patient readily played with her own dolls at home, sitting in the same relaxed posture on the floor and repeating the therapeutic suggestion utilized in the session. The parents praised M.L. for her progress and provided her with special treats as she improved. During the third week, her fearfulness of the dark and of the objects in the room rapidly subsided to the point where she had the lighting rheostat set on the lowest setting and she was able to sleep alone without difficulty.

These cases demonstrate the responsiveness of preschool children to hypnotherapy. A hypnotic state was achieved by each child within the context of play and storytelling directed toward task mastery. The major emphasis was on the development of a warm and trusting relationship that formed the basis for suggestions and producing an altered state of consciousness. The absorption that young children show in their play is a ready testimony to their hypnotizability. However, hypnosis with young children does differ considerably from that of adolescents and adults.

It should be noted that no attempt was made to suggest to the children that they close their eyes. While eye closure may be important in adult hypnosis, it may cause discomfort or resistance in the preschooler. Children of this age often prefer to keep their eyes open and perhaps to attend to some object. Further, young children are likely to move about during the induction or become involved in play or other activities. It is the challenge to the therapist to creatively involve the child without rigidly adhering to expectations of hypnotic behavior on the child's part.

In utilizing hypnotic techniques with young children, the developmental level of the child must also be considered. Certainly, the period from three to six years is a time of rapid cognitive, social, and physical change for the child and children can vary considerably in this regard. Review of the child's developmental history and skills can be helpful in planning the therapeutic process. The child hypnotherapist experiences greater success by adapting an approach to the child which is integrated with the child's play and fantasy.

References

Chapman, R. A., Elkins, G. R., & Carter, B. D. (1982). Childhood hypnotic susceptability: A review. *Journal of the American Society for Psychosomatic Dentistry and Medicine, 29,* 54–63.

$\underset{A}{Q_{\&}}70$ Hypnosis With Acting-out Adolescents

Question:

I work a lot with acting-out adolescents and wonder if and how hypnosis can be used with them.

Discussion by DANIEL P. KOHEN, M.D.

Hypnotherapy has been used effectively with a variety of behavioral problems in adolescents, including delinquency (Ambrose & Newbold, 1958; Baumann, 1970; Kaffman, 1968; Mellor, 1960) and hyperactivity (Braud, 1978; Omizo, 1980). In a study comparing the effectiveness of biofeedback and progressive relaxation on hyperactivity (Braud, 1978), adolescents treated with biofeedback *and* relaxation showed the greatest improvement, with decreases in irritability, explosiveness, impulsivity, and aggression, and an increase in frustration tolerance.

Although clinicians often turn to hypnotherapy only as a last resort in the management of behavior problems in adolescents, reports on its usefulness tend to be positive *if the patient personally experiences distress* and thus *is motivated to change,* and if the parents/family are able and willing to cooperate in the treatment. If the problem has evolved into character pathology — manifested, for example, by ego syntonicity and little associated anxiety — treatment by any method is difficult if not impossible (Gardner & Olness, 1981; Mellor, 1960). Baumann (1970) notes specifically that teenage drug abusers were more likely to succeed with the aid of hypnosis when there was a perceived and expressed need to change due to a belief in the potential for harm.

Rapport Development and Information-gathering

It is crucial that a positive and trusting relationship be established between therapist and patient. The therapist must focus on sensitively getting to know the teenager and understanding his perceptions of his problem before considering intervention techniques, hypnotic or otherwise. The therapist must be careful to create a relationship in which he is viewed as an ally, friend, and coach, rather than as yet another of the variety of adults against whom the adolescent may be rebelling or resisting. Since many adolescents have already been to a number of therapists and programs before encountering the hypnotherapeutically-oriented clinician, the process of rapport development may require several hours.

When to introduce hypnosis depends upon the therapist's understanding of the patient and on whether the therapist wants to use hypnosis as an aid in history-taking. Mellor (1960) has emphasized the value of ideomotor signals in data-gathering as well as in treatment. Ideomotor signals may help the patient circumvent emotional blocks to the expression of important ideas and feelings.

In delineating the adolescent's acting-out behavior, it is mandatory that both therapist and patient understand precisely what is happening that is "not working," what the patient believes about the causes of his problems, and what beliefs and expectations he has about change. Honest responses to such inquiries may come during a first conversation or not until later, when rapport has been sufficiently developed.

The most important thing the therapist needs to understand is to what extent the patient is motivated to change. Understanding this will also help build a positive approach and prevent the disappointment of early "failure." Success must often be measured in small increments which are defined, visible, and palpable, and upon which the teenager may build in order to keep growing.

The therapist should also know that teenagers with behavior problems are struggling in their quest for autonomy, their development of mastery, and their development of self. Many have experienced repeated failures in getting their needs met and many feel that they have experienced nothing they can consider a success, either in school, at home, in a job, or with friends. The therapist must understand and greet the teenager "where he is," being careful to assess not only cognitive development, but also social, emotional, and psychosexual development, in order to best create an effective relationship.

Induction Techniques

In determining the most appropriate induction technique, it is necessary to know the patient's developmental level. The immature adolescent may easily benefit from techniques normally used for younger children (Gardner & Olness, 1981). With other adolescents, any of the variety of adult inductions should be considered.

Since many teenagers are skeptical of hypnosis, awareness of external validation of change is very helpful. The visual observation of arm levitation and reverse levitation, for instance, is at once exciting, powerful, and reaffirming while experiencing a first trance. Pointing out simple bodily changes is also beneficial and can be used to build the trance (e.g., "you probably already noticed how slowly you are breathing now and that's a good sign that you're teaching yourself this new idea really well . . . and you may have noticed your eyelids fluttering . . . and how still you've let your muscles become *just from focusing your mind this way*"). Similarly, the use of biofeedback devices demonstrating self-regulation of physiologic processes is effective in validating to the patient that verifiable changes are occurring and that he is in control of them. This also helps build the patient's confidence.

Favorite place imagery in association with progressive relaxation is very effective for many adolescents. In the course of even a first interview, the therapist can easily identify with the teenager what he or she enjoys, what is fun, what he might do when there are no obligations, as well as the details of these experiences. By carefully selecting the language in this conversation, the therapist may also begin to set the mood and create an expectancy that control is possible, specifically through the cultivation of imagined experiences. Thus, I often ask directly, "What do you do for fun?" or "What do you do to feel good *when you need to*?" Emphasis is placed on "when you need to" in order to begin to create the expectation that they already know how to create comfort for themselves when they need to, but may have never given (full) conscious attention to it until *now*.

This helps to demystify hypnosis and to give control to the patient. The therapist is flattering the patient by indirectly acknowledging that he believes the patient already *does something* positive, and then implying that the awareness of this may be used to effect control in other areas. I may then ask, "What makes you decide to do something to relax or calm yourself *on purpose*?" The implication is that they *do* have that control and that it may be cultivated. The next step may be to link their usage of these techniques to the circumstances or behaviors which are undesirable. Thus, the one who feels controlled, put down, or angry when disciplined may "get control" or feel "comfort" or "relief" by going to her bedroom, putting on headphones, or staring out the window. This spontaneous, self-decided and described relaxation treatment may then be built upon as the favorite place imagery in a hypnotherapeutic plan.

Similarly, one may ask, "How long does it take for you to feel good?" or "to stop feeling lousy?" or "to begin to mellow out?" Such inquiry not only provides information, but also directly implies that this "calming" or "mellowness" *does happen* because they *make* it happen, even without planning

or thinking about it. This also affords the therapist the opportunity to compliment the patient and in the process reinforce the development of a positive
relationship.

Using Hypnosis in Medical Examinations

I frequently do physical examinations for teenagers temporarily residing
in a halfway house. These adolescents, some of whom are runaways, have
a number of problems, including drug abuse, prostitution, school failure,
physical or sexual abuse, and conflicts with parents. Most of them are anxious because of the uncertainty of their immediate as well as perhaps long-
range futures, and because of the coerciveness of "having to come for a physical."

A self-report personal/health history is completed prior to a nursing intake interview, following which the teen is seen by the physician. While the
overall goal is to identify any immediate physical needs, sufficient time is
allotted for more relaxed conversation, and for identification of long-term
concerns raised by the patient, nurse or physician. Asked about health concerns, the teenagers often indicate that they have difficulty dealing with
stress or name a variety of somatic concerns, including recurrent headaches,
abdominal and/or chest pain, nervousness, or difficulty getting to sleep. The
intake form also specifically identifies favorite activities, and asks that teens
identify ways that they already have of handling stress.

Often I find it helpful to continue conversation about favorite activities
and self-control and comfort while easing from the history into the physical
examination. "Why don't we continue talking while we get going with the
checkup, so we can save time?" Then, as the patient sits on the examination table, I may ask directly something on the order of "Did you ever notice"
or "I'm *sure* you have noticed before" (a compliment) "that there is a natural
tendency for the shoulders to go down . . . as you . . . breathe . . . out"
and I ask the patient to "just pay attention to that and notice that with your
slow breathing while I listen to your lungs." I may ask as I auscultate the
posterior lung fields, "Isn't that interesting how those muscles do that *because* you want them to?" and I may add to the relaxation during expiration
via a small amount of pressure from my hand on the tops of the shoulders,
timed to my verbalizations as well as to the patient's exhalation. Then, as
I continue to listen, I build on this naturalistic induction by saying, "What's
really interesting is that you can *build* on this *yourself*, you can kind of let
that natural kind of relaxing grow or spread . . . each . . . time . . . that
. . . you . . . breathe . . . out . . . slower . . . and . . . slower . . . and
. . . easier." Pacing these to the patient's breathing . . . "and you don't even
have to try, *you can* just *let it happen* and enjoy it *because of how easily
you give yourself comfort this way when you really need and want it. And
I will just continue checking various parts of the physical examination, add-

ing "and you don't even have to pay attention as I finish the checkup, I'll let you know if I need your help with anything special . . . in fact, you may want to imagine, if you haven't started to already, that you are somewhere else." And here I would add mention of one or two of the favorite activities of the patient learned about in the pre-trance/pre-exam conversation.

At this point it is often simple to offer nonthreatening and potentially powerful suggestions that the patient may easily use: "Perhaps you are already daydreaming that you are _____ or doing something else that you like doing (the choices offered here are particularly important for the teenager seeking and needing a sense of control) . . . and while you do it you know that it can be just like when you daydream for yourself . . . only it's good to learn *now* that *you can create it this way* . . . and when you need it you can build it like you're *doing* . . . *BECAUSE* (patients, especially teens, need a *reason* to be willing to accept/carry out the hypnotic suggestion) you're the boss of your body . . . by using your mind this way you can make changes occur JUST THE WAY YOU'RE MAKING YOURSELF RELAX THIS WAY WITHOUT EVEN TRYING (validating the belief) . . . by letting your mind relax (repeating what the patient is doing and reinforcing the ability to be able to do again) in some easy nice way by thinking something you really enjoy doing . . . and it's so easy . . . (pause) . . . and it gets even easier each time that you practice (posthypnotic suggestion for value of subsequent practice, introduction of concept of practice to pique the patient's interest and attention) . . . *BECAUSE* EVERYONE KNOWS (therefore of course *he* must know) that every time you practice something it gets easier and better . . . and that's how you got to be so good at (whatever you know they said they do well) . . . and so it sure is nice to know that this *simple way* of giving yourself relaxed feelings all the way down to your . . . by the way, how far down is it now? . . . that's good . . . and it can be even faster and better each time that you do it. . . . So, even if you don't exactly need it, it *might* be fun and valuable and a good gift to give yourself two or three or four times each day for a few minutes BECAUSE each time that you do it for five or 10 minutes it feels so good, . . . so relaxed . . . so controlled. After you do it for a while (incentive) you *may* (choice) even discover that if you want to work on something special you can use it for even more than relaxing . . . like I knew a guy once who wanted to get better at playing basketball, so every time he would practice his relaxing *this* way he would use some of the time to see himself in his mind just shooting free throws over and over again, and he would see exactly how he stood and looked and held his arms and hands . . . and he told me that he got to be a better free throw shooter that way . . . in his mind he would see each one go in and then he'd check out how he'd done it . . . *because he decided to use his mind to help his body*". And I might tell several simple quick vignettes of others who used similar techniques this way.

If the patient comes out of trance during the series of suggestions, I continue the same kind of explanations in somewhat less hypnotic language. As I conclude the physical, I casually ask patients to tell me what that was like, what they thought of it, what they liked and didn't like, and *when* (continuing my expectancy) they thought they would practice the same kind of thing for themselves. Patients often describe the sensations as similar to others they have experienced, as when they have meditated or been "high" or when they have done warmup exercises for a school team, or in dance or acting classes. This familiarity allows for the enhancement of both trust and self-control and permits the next step as well, i.e., the suggestion that they incorporate this first in a routine of some kind, and then toward control of some aspect of the problem in question.

I often portray this to the patient as a matter-of-fact suggestion at the end of the hypnotic experience, and repeat it in the immediate post-trance period as a reinforcing, so-called "waking suggestion." I might note, for example, "I'm not sure exactly how you want to apply this to solve *some* of what is going on in your life these days, but I would be happy to help you to use it to solve some problems however you want to do that. I don't know if you simply want to use it to not feel so angry for so long, or if you want to use it to understand your feelings a little better, or if you want to use it to just get that nice high feeling without having to pay for or get the side effects of the chemicals, or what. . . . I can't decide those . . . and I can't solve the problems, but I can be a good coach with you and am willing to do it . . . so why don't you think about it and let me know when you're ready . . . and exactly what it is you want to accomplish . . . and we can then discuss it some more. . . . "

The approach described allows for the concept of self-control and seeds the belief that it can occur. I ask patients to practice self-hypnosis a couple of times a day in order to "get used to how good you can help yourself feel" and to begin to notice the range of different kinds of good feelings you can create . . . ," while at the same time instructing them to "not expect it to be the same and terrific each time. "Sometimes your practice will be better than others . . . " I ask them to decide between now and a vague "next visit" whether they will use the same or different images, and invite them to keep a record of experiences as they practice, noticing differences in feelings as well as in physical responses. Implicit in all of these suggestions, of course, is that they are in charge and that I have certain expectations and believe they can progress.

Building on what feels good seems to be a key to helping the patient to create further successes. Rather than accepting "failure" with this approach, the therapist should work to identify that aspect of the patient's experience/practice that was good, positive, valuable. Even if the patient begins a follow-up session with "I tried it and it didn't work . . . I couldn't do it . . . ," the fact that he has come back and is willing to discuss it indicates that motivation remains. The therapist should review the details of their efforts to find ways to focus and reinforce positive responses. Patients may want to utilize an imaginary scale, e.g., 0–10, to measure or rate their particular problem/concern, be it wheezing, unhappiness, pain, anger, sadness, fear. By using these analogies, e.g., to a 12-inch ruler, the patient may begin to develop a willingness to view the problem in relative, and therefore *changeable*, terms, rather than in absolute, all or none, terms.

Case Discussion

D. was a 17-year-old male who was admitted to the adolescent psychiatry unit for diagnosis and treatment following continuing difficulties at home with "acting-out," characterized by poor grades in school, some fighting, truancy, and general difficulty in getting along with others. His parents had run out of ideas and he had been admitted initially with a consideration of possible psychiatric disorder. Initial evaluation indicated no real difficulty with reality orientation, but a low sense of self-esteem that was apparently inappropriately compensated by peculiar acting-out and ineffective attention-seeking behaviors. A sometimes explosive affect was noted. An official diagnosis of "character disorder" was made. A program of milieu therapy on the inpatient adolescent unit was begun with emphasis on 1) adherence to rules of the unit with a strict hierarchical system of rewards/punishments for appropriate/inappropriate behaviors; 2) personal involvement in individualized treatment plans and goals; 3) group therapy; and 4) individual psychotherapy.

A week into D.'s treatment program I was contacted to see if hypnosis would be of value as an adjunct in the management of his enuresis. He had been wetting the bed "ever since I can remember," had had a variety of medical interventions "tried" with little or no success, and at age 16 had recently had urological investigation about which he remained quite angry. He recalled with anger the discomfort and violation he felt at cystoscopy and at being given a command "like an animal" to "VOID!" This had not, in his perception, altered the enuresis in any way. He remained on three medications, (Tofranil, Cystospaz, and Valium) for the enuresis, and in spite of this and keeping a calendar, he continued to have accidents. He said he "can't stand the regimentation of being reminded or having to take the medicines and I have accidents when I'm on it anyway, especially when I'm under stress like if I'm worried or have a test . . . wow!" and then added some self-deprecating phrases. Examination for organic causes for the enuresis revealed no abnormalities.

I arranged for the physician who had admitted him to introduce me to D., and I was presented as someone who knew a lot about enuresis and teenagers and might be able to show him some things to help himself be dry. He acknowledged both embarrassment and lack of knowledge, as well as a desire to be dry, and we arranged to meet the following day. In getting to know each other in the first hour we discussed the details of his enuresis as noted above, the variety of interventions that had not worked, his shame, anger, and disdain, as well as his sense of helplessness about this problem.

During our initial conversation about genitourinary anatomy and basic physiology of urination D. was intrigued and accepting of the notion of utilizing his brain or "inner mind" to do something about this problem. He was told, for example, that the brain is always awake, constantly sending signals to the right places at the right times, even when his body is asleep. Evidence for this was intriguing to him in terms of heart beating, breathing, turning over, kicking off sheets when warm, all of which are directed to occur by the "master computer" of the brain. Indirect, "waking suggestions" were given, repeating that "it's good to know and realize that the *brain is the boss of the body*, sends messages to every cell, is of course in control of everything" so "it's just a matter of training the brain to get the signals going back and forth the right way." His predictable response of interest was to inquire how that could be accomplished, and we spoke of relaxation and imagination as ways to unlock the brain and allow it accessibility to reprogramming and making changes occur, through practice. He was eager to move ahead.

I learned of his recent interest in the Bible (New Testament) and spiritual matters and he learned accordingly of my experience in spirituality (Old Testament) and my beliefs in the similarities of spirituality to the relaxation/imagery experience. This also piqued his interest. He described favorite activities as including reading books, lying outside, and going on hikes, and was interested to hear my description of hypnosis as an alternative form of awareness that we are spontaneously in and out of all day. Utilizing the imagery he had given me, and prior to beginning the trance, I told him that hypnosis and self-hypnosis are like when we focus our concentration and feel good in doing so and shut out outside stimuli, "like the high, good feeling we may get when we pray, you know?" He agreed.

"Well, self-hypnotizing can be just that way, and then the only different thing about it is that when you get to feeling that way, you can use that feeling when your mind is *comfortable* and *safe* and *controlled* and *open* to *train yourself* (enhancing his control) and teach yourself to do certain things that you may want to do differently or better . . . like having dry beds, or like having a better golf game, or doing more concentration on a test, like that. . . . " As he was told this, D. developed a spontaneous light trance with eye fixation, focused attention, and slowed breathing. I invited him to begin (from the already light trance) by closing his eyes, having reassured him that I would sit where I was and he would be where he was, and I would talk to him.

Induction was continued and deepening accomplished with focus on breathing in and out and specifically with inviting him to breathe in comfort and breathe out tension. Because of his basic concerns about self-control, his low self-esteem, and his general skepticism of adults, I interspersed suggestions throughout for personal control and responsibility, ego-strengthening, and positive self-esteem. Deepening continued with imagery of being outside, asking him to be aware of sounds, weather, and people with him, to feel the softness of grass, and the warmth of the sun, to see the sky, etc. Progressive relaxation was then added, noting "many people find that their self-hypnosis feels even better as they allow muscles to relax progressively. Some begin at their feet, and relax upwards; some begin at their scalp and go down. . . . I don't care which you decide to use for your comfort . . . you can let me know many things while we do this, because you're the *boss of your body*. Some people like to talk, others to nod, or others like to raise a finger as a signal." He raised a finger and head and neck flopped forward, relaxing. "Remind yourself that in hypnosis everything that occurs is, of course, a help to you, that this is up to you with me as a coach . . . and as the relaxing spreads down your body you may even be learning and moving along faster than what I'm saying or slower or at the same speed. I don't know when the relaxation will move all the way, or whether it will go down the right side or the left side of your body first . . .but I do know that as this occurs you can be *proud* (ego-strengthening) of how fast you're learning to help yourself . . . and you can wonder how exactly you might apply this interesting and comfortable feeling to solving that problem you used to have even more . . . "

He was asked specifically to signal with his finger when he was relaxed throughout his body, and then again when he thought his mind was ready to give messages internally to his bladder. He paused for 15–20 seconds and then raised a finger. He was told first in the second person and then in the first person: "When you get ready for sleep, and when you practice this self-hypnosis before bed, tell yourself that before you go to sleep you will walk to the bathroom, send the message from the brain to the bladder to relax the bladder so all the urine can go out in the toilet where it belongs, then let the bladder close, and walk back to your bed. As you get into your nice, warm, dry bed, remind yourself to have a wonderful night's sleep and especially to have a good and pleasant dream; and remind your wide awake brain that during the night, if your bladder should fill up with urine, the bladder will send the message to the brain that the bladder is full, and the brain then has two choices. It can decide to wake you up so you can walk to the toilet, urinate in the toilet, return to your dry bed and sleep the rest of the night in a dry bed, OR the brain can decide to send a message back to the bladder to stay full, closed through the night, awaken in the morning in a nice comfortable dry bed, and *then* walk to the bathroom, urinate in the toilet and feel proud." He was then told the same series of suggestions as a reminder in the first person, "So, say it to yourself this way, 'when *I* go to bed . . . ,' etc." and then asked to take a moment to do it for himself in private silence. Following this he was told that he should remind himself how good he feels when he wakes up proud and happy in a dry bed in the morning, and then to finish the self-hypnosis exercise by a message to himself to have a nice dream.

The trance suggestions were completed with double bind suggestions about how I didn't know how *fast* he'd be dry, that it could be a few days or as long as two or three weeks, but that the more he practiced the better he'd get.

Following the first trance experience he described paresthesias of his feet and numbness of the hand, and said he was "interested" and happy but "too relaxed." I complimented him on his trust and excellence. By mutual agreement, he began to practice self-hypnosis three times a day and succeeded in accomplishing dry beds very quickly. To our surprise the psychiatrist discontinued his medications the first day.

On follow-up three weeks later D. had no problem with accidents. He had been dry except for one or two occasions in the past three weeks, and was pleased and content. He was quite anxious, however, about a growing discomfort in an ingrown toenail on his left great toe. Associated infection had developed and the pediatrician recommended that this be treated by surgical removal of the ingrown nail. This suggestion kindled a panic in D., who in response began to demand angrily that this procedure be done under general anesthetic, shouting how he hated (and feared) needles, needed to be asleep, etc. In discussing this he told me of his great fear of needles and, in a typically histrionic, dramatic manner, how he would refuse and fight the procedure. When the suggestion was made that he might be surprised to know that he could use his self-hypnosis for control of this discomfort, his anxiety turned to curiosity and interested calm.

He went into hypnosis spontaneously and was taught a simple pain control technique, by reliving the after-injection experience of dental anesthesia, gradually dripping and oozing that hypnoanesthetic from his jaw into one hand or the other, feeling it become numb, and then "testing it by pinching it as hard as you like because you want to notice how much you can change the usual feelings." He was also then instructed to practice transferring this first to one foot and then to the other one where the *easy* surgery would be. Finally, multiple suggestions were given that, "I don't know when it is time to do this whether you make the toe numb or the whole foot . . . whether you will want to watch your success or not watch, and whether you will want to just leave your foot there in hypnosis or whether you'll stay there in hypnosis and watch or not watch . . . whichever you do you can be proud and enjoy how surprised the other people will be who probably don't believe you can do this . . . "

After two of these 30-minute preparatory hypnotic sessions for control of anxiety and pain, D. underwent surgical removal of the ingrown toenail with the aid of local anesthesia and hypnoanalgesia/hypnoanesthesia. During practice sessions he was taught, as noted, the transfer of recalled dental anesthesia to his toe. Multiple ego-strengthening suggestions were given during both practice and the procedure itself. These were given to reinforce his ability and self-confidence and to accomplish the specific desired goal of toenail removal without severe pain or loss of control, *and* to build general self-esteem. These included: "It's nice to know that you have the ability to not let the discomfort bother you. . . . You can use your memory and self-hypnosis so well that that toe can feel numb and anesthetized, what a good feeling you give yourself . . . imagine how proud you will be. . . . I don't know whether you're more proud of this or of the dry beds. . . . It's good to discover the ability *within you* that you have . . . to use this to solve problems, and give yourself comfort and control when you need it . . . it's good to be the boss of your body . . . and to know that you can use this special talent and ability in other ways that you may need in the future."

In D.'s circumstances hypnosis had specific application and value in the amelioration of a daily habit problem which had undoubtedly been a source of sadness, helplessness, and low self-esteem both in childhood and throughout adolescence. In solving the problem *he proved to himself that he could master aspects of his personal behavior*, something that neither he nor most of the adults in his life had previously believed possible. His demeanor and approachability improved on the inpatient unit and his response to individual and group psychotherapy was quite positive. He made plans for returning to school and getting a job. The ability to have his toenail removed surgically without general anesthesia or panic seemed to be of similar direct and symbolic value to D. His affect became manifest now as pride and bravado as he described his success and freedom from pain to his peers on the adolescent unit. After a total of six weeks in the inpatient unit, he was discharged and returned home. He adjusted well to work and completed high school.

References

Ambrose, G., & Newbold, G. (1958). *A Handbook of Medical Hypnosis*. Baltimore: Williams and Wilkins. pp. 147–197.

Baumann, F. (1970). Hypnosis and the adolescent drug abuser. *American Journal of Clinical Hypnosis*, *13*(1), 17–21.

Braud, L. W. (1978). The effects of frontal EMG biofeedback and progressive relaxation upon hyperactivity and its behavioral concomitants. *Biofeedback and Self-Regulation*, *3*(1), 69–80.

Gardner, G. G., & Olness, K. N. (1981). *Hypnosis and hypnotherapy with children*. New York: Grune & Stratton.

Kaffman, M. (1968). Hypnosis as an adjunct to psychotherapy in child psychiatry. *Archives of General Psychiatry, 18*, 725–738.

Mellor, N. H. (1960). Hypnosis in juvenile delinquency. *G.P., 22*, 83–87.

Omizo, M. M. (1980). The effects of biofeedback induced relaxation training in hyperactive adolescent boys. *Journal of Psychology, 105*, 131–138.

X *Therapists' Qualms
and Special Problems*

It is apparent to any interested observer that far more practitioners have taken courses in hypnosis than are now using it. This attrition rate, of unknown magnitude, is most likely due to the various qualms that practitioners have in regard to the uses of hypnosis.

The qualms may be internally or externally generated, and may be of conscious origin or hidden in the unconscious, extractable only by penetrating self-contemplation or by more formal therapy. Whatever the origin, and wherever the qualms might dwell, it is a tragic waste of a learned technique to use it sparingly or not at all because of those qualms.

In this section the various authors have made important contributions to assist the therapist in dealing with some of those elements that might interfere with a more frequent and more enjoyable use of hypnotic techniques. The issues discussed range broadly from fears of failure to fears of success, from concerns about sexual arousal in the therapist to concerns about sexual arousal in the patient, from fears of nonresponsiveness to fears of excessive responsiveness. Ethical issues are discussed, as are specific problems that have occurred or are intimidating simply because they might occur.

Perhaps it's wise for therapists to refrain from embarking on therapeutic ventures if they are unfamiliar with the disease processes requiring therapy, but if they are qualified to treat the illness without hypnosis, almost certainly they could treat it safely with hypnosis, and often more effectively. Doing anything effectively depends largely on having a certain base of

411

knowledge, practice, and confidence in one's abilities. Here, though, it is easy to run into a serious dilemma; much of our knowledge comes from experience and practice. The conscientious therapist may find it uncomfortable to "practice" without a sense of confidence in what he or she is doing. Confidence is achieved primarily by prior success, and prior success is often the result of knowledge and practice. This vicious cycle can be broken only by a certain degree of courage, and it is hoped that among the papers in this section there will be some that enable the reader to acquire the courage needed to expand his/her area of expertise in the use of hypnotherapy.

Q&A 71 Is It Necessary to Tell Patients You Are Using "Hypnosis"?

Question:

Many therapists and dentists do hypnosis without telling the patient that's what they're doing. Is this ethical? I thought patients have the right to know what methods are being used, but then I hear that hypnosis is more effective if it's snuck in without announcement. I'd like to hear how the courts, the APA's, insurance companies, and some hypnosis experts feel about this.

Discussion by FRANZ BAUMANN, M.D.

First, let me say that I'm a medical practitioner, not an attorney, and I would not venture to offer any legal opinion about how the courts would feel about anything. Neither have I read any serious discussions about the ethics of using hypnotic techniques without first telling the patient. What I have to say, then, is based upon my being a pediatrician who has used hypnosis for over 25 years. What I will discuss has worked well for me, and from what I gather my colleagues have had similar experiences.

I believe it is entirely ethical to use hypnotic approaches without first telling the patient. Milton Erickson, one of the most respected of all hypnotherapists, has been described as inducing hypnotic states in a number of patients without their knowing what he was doing. As a matter of fact, at times they did not even know that therapy was being started. Never have I heard any expert express criticism of this activity.

It is important to realize that I do not "do hypnosis." I _use_ hypnosis, when appropriate, as one of the tools of my trade. At times I use hypnotic techniques, such as direct or indirect suggestion, or relaxation exercises, without a formal induction of trance. Since there is no clear scientific definition of hypnosis, I—or anyone else—would be hard pressed to say if this is hypnosis or not. The surgeon must tell the patient that he intends to remove an appendix or some other part of the anatomy, but he need not specify that he intends to use hemostats, Allis clamps, or other specific tools of his trade. The psychotherapist need not inform the patient that he intends to use interpretations, clarifications, or behavior modification techniques. I feel that the same is true regarding hypnosis.

However, there is a difference of opinion as to whether or not the patient should be told. Some experts always tell the patient, partly because in their opinion it is the more ethical thing to do, and partly because they contend that if we ever expect the general public to accept hypnosis with greater ease, we should speak of it easily ourselves, rather then using euphemisms like "relaxation." Other experts do use the euphemisms, contending that this reduces apprehension and resistance, and therefore the patient has more ready access to the benefits of the trance state.

For myself, if the patient has been referred to me specifically for hypnosis, there is no issue. We discuss hypnosis and any apprehensions the patient may have about it. I attempt to dispel any misconceptions; in particular I make it clear that I cannot make the subjects do anything they are unwilling to do, but I might be able to help them do and enjoy those things that they wish to do. I point out that all people have been in a state of hypnosis spontaneously without being aware of it; daydreaming, meditation, yoga, and many other activities resemble it in many ways. I specify that patients come to me to gain control, not to give it up to another person. I inform them that I am teaching them a new skill, one that they must practice at home.

If an adolescent has not been referred specifically for hypnosis, I might say, "I'd like to teach you a new way to just let go and concentrate, a way that you can learn and enjoy." Learning is the business of children, and they accept that concept. I feel that I am not so much hypnotizing them as inviting them to learn a new skill. If asked, "Is this hypnosis?" I answer, "Yes, really, and doesn't it feel good?" I believe that this strengthens the patient-physician relationship.

In regard to the courts, and again, reminding you that I am not a legal expert, it is conceivable, but unlikely, that difficulties might arise. If, for instance, the patient belonged to a religion that forbade hypnosis, and hypnosis was used without informing that patient, and he later discovered it, there would be the possibility of trouble. If the patient had been told, "I'll teach you a new way to relax," perhaps the argument would turn on whether the patient had become relaxed or had entered hypnosis, and I do not know how the courts would decide that.

There is also the possibility that a disturbed patient could claim that he was hypnotized without his consent, and that he continues to feel that he is under the influence of the hypnotherapist. I believe most experts would agree that the hypnosis was not the source of his feelings of being influenced, but the ways of God and the courts are mysterious to behold.

There is another caution that should be included here. If the patient has been the witness to a crime, and the case is still pending, it would be inadvisable to use hypnosis, as hypnosis or as "relaxation," for anything in any way connected to the crime. For instance, do not desensitize the patient to the trauma incurred by witnessing the event, for in some jurisdictions this would then disqualify him as a reliable witness.

In regard to the insurance companies: Most of them do not recognize hypnosis as a paid benefit at this time, although hypnoanesthesia is usually covered. I believe the physician should bill for his services as "extended office visit." The psychiatrist and psychologist should bill for "psychotherapy," and the dentist should bill for whatever procedure he might have done. I do believe the word "hypnosis" should appear on the statement, even if no specific charge is listed for it, in order to make it better known to patients and insurance companies. When I am questioned about why I work with hypnosis, I usually answer that it shortens treatment and reduces costs.

One final word — there are, I believe, good reasons for using hypnosis without first telling the patient about it, but getting more effective results is not one of those reasons. Those who use "guided visual imagery" therapeutically report that their results are the same whether or not a trance was formally induced; I know of no studies that show that when hypnosis is "snuck in" that it is more effective; in my own practice, it seems that the results are just as good either way.

Q&A 72 Patients Experiencing Negative Affect in Hypnosis

Question:

> Sometimes a patient in trance appears to experience a great deal of negative affect: muscles tense, breathing is labored, face is contorted, and there may be moans or cries. Should I bring her out of it, encourage her to experience her feelings, ask what is going on, or what?

Discussion by MARC LEHRER, Ph.D.

Here are the guidelines that I use for dealing with situations where the patient may have strong emotional reactions while in hypnosis:

1) Remain in emotional contact with your patient. Be non-evaluative. Do not initially withdraw in an attempt to analyze the situation.
2) Start to form an impression of what is occurring. Ask questions, make guesses. Clarify the situation as well as you can while giving the patient the possibility of staying with the emotional situation.
3) Be reassuring and make positive reframing statements. Your patient needs to know that you are confident that the situation can be dealt with.
4) Make clinical interventions and be prepared to modify your responses depending upon the patient's reactions. Use reframing and ego-strengthening. You are reinforcing the idea that your patient is a capable human being. On a secondary level you are indirectly suggesting that your patient can deal with any future emotional states while working with you.

I'll clarify each of these areas with comments and follow with some clinical examples.

Guidelines

Remaining in contact with your patient. The best way to do this is to monitor both large, obvious reactions and small, less often noticed reactions (sometimes called minimal changes) that the patient is making while in hypnosis. If you do this, you are less likely to be surprised by a patient's sudden emotional reaction. You often can see signs of stress before they reach the patient's awareness or before they turn into moans or tears. If you talk with your patient about what you see, you are remaining in contact and your patient will learn to trust your observations. I tell my patients I will support them in what they need to do. They get the message that it is all right to continue.

Start to form an impression of what is occurring. Ask questions and notice how your patient responds. Are there only more tears or movements, head nods or shakes to signify yes or no, responses with words, other facial or body cues, meaningful affect? As I get more information, I want to discover if the patient is experiencing a memory or a disturbing visual image or thought or just an overwhelming feeling. I ask, "What's happening now?" (asking for immediate experience), rather than, "Tell me what's happening," (asking for a more complete description involving past actions and meanings that may remove the patient from the experience). The patient who has spontaneously age regressed ("big man . . . scared") or who can only report a feeling ("blackness . . . horrible blackness") can talk more easily about the immediate experience than about everything that has occurred.

When training therapists to use hypnosis I find that this step is often most difficult for those who feel that they have to completely understand a situation to make a response to a patient. If the patient is unable to speak it is often helpful to tell the patient to breathe. I might say, "That's right, just keep on breathing . . . (look for compliance), that's better, now breathe some of it out . . . , that's good, what's happening now?" Sometimes I may continue in this way for several minutes, sometimes for longer (several hours in one of my cases), until the patient can relate what is occurring. The goal of the therapist is to maintain rapport with the patient while obtaining information.

I should also mention that sometimes while the therapist continues to maintain rapport (using the above examples of breathing, for instance), the patient may be proceeding to work out the difficulty at another level. Under these circumstances the patient primarily needs a psychologically safe environment and a lack of interference from the therapist. For this reason, I am not concerned if I don't get a verbal response as long as the nonverbal signs seem to show a lessening of affect and expressions of relief or satisfaction.

I believe that the hypnotherapist needs to trust in positive signs that indicate the patient's unconscious processes are at work.

Reassure the patient. By this time you have established contact with your patient. The patient is listening to you while continuing to react (often called a mixed state of hypnotic attention). You have provided some relief and/or contact for the patient and are psychologically perceived in the role of a supportive, helpful person. In this heightened moment of contact what you do or say is likely to function as a posthypnotic suggestion. If I have little or no information about the problem the patient is experiencing, I say, "I'm here and I'll help you work this out." If I think the patient has made some progress or a new realization, I say, "It's about time you started to work that out." If the patient is indicating little or no progress, then I say, "Starting (or dealing with) the process of change is often the hardest part. Let's think together about what needs to be done next." (Joining with the patient and adding some positive expectation). Notice that each of the above reassuring statements joins with the patient, adds some positive expectation, and functions as a positive posthypnotic suggestion and positive reframing of what has been accomplished.

Make clinical interventions. Age regression, positive reframing, and hypnotic suggestion are probably the most important interventions for the beginning hypnotherapist to master. The patient who appears distressed may be spontaneously regressed to a previous traumatic incident or upset by a sudden new awareness of a disturbing situation. An example of a powerful age regression intervention with reframing that can be useful in these circumstances is the following: Use the partial contact you have with the patient to suggest that the patient go back and observe the traumatic event from the perspective of the more knowledgeable (and therefore somewhat wiser) present-day self. This creates a partial dissociation and will help reduce some of the affect. Once there, direct the present-day self to suggest something helpful to the age regressed self. I have had hypnotized patients suddenly recall forgotten traumatic incidents of 50 and 60 years earlier. I have then directed them to have conversations with themselves, with long-dead parents, and with relatives and schoolmates whom they have not seen for many years. This type of age regression intervention is based upon diffusing the disturbing affect using dissociation, followed by reframing to prevent old patterns from re-emerging. I also use variations on affect bridging if the patient is unaware of any content associated with the traumatic feeling states.

There are also times when it seems that the patient is truly stuck in the painful experience. I recommend that the therapist first attempt to get the patient's permission before forceful alerting procedures are attempted. For example, "Bill, you have been struggling for a while now and it looks to me that you are getting really tired. I think it would be best if I helped you come out of hypnosis for now so you can get a chance to build up your energy. Is this all right with you? . . . Just nod your head up and down if it is. Yes, good, well in a few moments I'm going to speak a little louder, and then with your permission touch and hold your arm. That will be a signal to you to prepare to come out of hypnosis by beginning to open your eyes. Then the relief will come. Ready . . . all right . . . , etc."

Contraindications and Pitfalls

1) If the patient does not have good reality-testing or is unable or unwilling to maintain concentration or contact with the therapist, it is unwise to allow affect to build to explosive proportions. In these instances highly structured suggestions and reorientating the patient to the outside world is advisable. This may be done by forcing the patient to recall a detail in your office, your name, his or her name, or other reality-based details. Avoid touch in these situations until ambiguity is lessened and rapport is reestablished. For example, a suicidal patient who was in hypnosis for ego-strengthening suddenly reported weakness in his knees and moaned about his helpless situation. I used authoritarian suggestions directing him to "breathe down through your knees and through the floor!" Soon I had taken his arm and held him up while we walked around my office as I repeated, "Notice the strength returning." After about 10 minutes he began to feel better. Beginning hypnotherapists are often apprehensive about situations where the patient must be forcefully alerted. In contrast, I have found that patients who are alerted in this manner make good recoveries.

2) Be careful of establishing a relationship of manipulation, dependency or control over a needy or impressionable patient. It is all too easy to do this when the patient is alerting from hypnosis after working through a traumatic recall or incident. I am careful to congratulate my patient on what a fine job he or she has done and deemphasize my role.

3) The time factor needs to be considered. Other patients may be waiting while you are dealing with your patient's distress. Under most circumstances it is all right to tell your patient that you will return in a few moments, need to make a brief call, tell other patients of the delay, etc. Give your patient a message of confidence in being able to handle the difficulty of the situation (if you believe this to be true). Another strategy that I have found to be helpful when time is a factor is to suggest that the patient finish only a part of the problem now. Further hypnotic suggestions for continuing to work on the problem in bland and disguised dreams can also be given. I ask such patients to call me on a regular basis before our next appointment to tell me how well they are doing (an indirect suggestion for doing well).

Case Examples

The patient was a woman with a fear of taking airplane flights. I was using GSR biofeedback to monitor her fear responses. She had fast and strong emotional reactions (from the GSR monitoring and observed changes in breathing, skin color and muscle movement around the eyes.) While using hypnosis for diagnostic exploration about her condition, I asked her to explore the reasons she had moved to San Francisco. There was a fast rise on the GSR, followed by small twitches around the eyes and breathing changes (*remain in contact with your patient*). From these signs I guessed that she would soon begin to cry (*form an impression*). I quickly made the suggestion that she honor the feelings from her eyes (*be reassuring*). She then began to cry. My intervention resulted in her considering a message from the tears rather than feeling that they were still one more failure before her impending air journey. She then reported while in a mixed hypnotic and tearful state that she realized that she felt rootless living in San Francisco. I was then able to give her the suggestion to consider looking for her roots while observing the countryside below (*make clinical interventions*). She sent me a postcard following the flight she took the next day, reporting that the journey was without fear and that she had the curious sensation of feeling her feet "planted firmly on the floor" of the airplane.

A 62-year-old woman called for an appointment because she felt a great sigh every time she tried to relax and could not continue. Initial interviews showed her to be intelligent and without any signs of serious mental disturbance. She did, however, greatly fear these sighs. As she was going into trance I watched for the occurrence of the sigh. I saw breathing changes starting. I then forcefully said, "Now thank that sigh!" (*reframing*) She had a great sigh and then continued with her eyes closed. I asked her what was happening now. She said, "I'm five years old. My mother is in the fields and working hard. My father is sick. I try to help my mother by making lunch with the wood stove but get soot all over the kitchen. My mother comes in and sees the mess. She thinks that I have been playing and slaps me really hard on the face." She suddenly opened her eyes and said, "And you know, I've never forgiven her for that!" We later continued in hypnosis with age regression and reframing. She was then able to relax at home and learned to use the smaller sigh that occurred as a hypnotic deepener.

$\underset{A}{\overset{Q}{\underset{\sim}{}}}73$ Patients Who Are Intellectual and Analytical Even in Trance

Question:

What can I do with clients who are almost totally "left brain" in orientation? Even in what appears to be the hypnotic state their productions are intellectual and analytical, not much different from when they *aren't* in trance. The intuitive, unconscious side of them just does not emerge. I wonder if they even have such a side.

Discussion by JEAN HOLROYD, Ph.D.

In working with clients I consider several factors: the client's responsivity to hypnotic tasks, the problem(s) we are addressing with hypnosis, and my own countertransference. While this question is phrased in terms of individual differences in hypnotic response, adequate resolution requires consideration of aspects beyond mere clinical interaction. Let me take them in reverse order of the way I listed them.

When a patient is slow to respond to hypnosis I am inclined to feel something between inadequacy or anxiety and urgency, particularly if treatment is being sought for a very serious condition. Aside from the fact that I share most people's desire for success, I am aware that "low hypnotizables" elicit less involvement from hypnotists, even in standardized testing situations. Hence I am concerned that I remedy my own attitude lest I participate in self-fulfilling prophecy. Over time I have learned that the best way for me to handle my own performance anxiety is to do self-hypnosis, giving myself direct suggestions that I'll be comfortable working with this person, creative in my approach, etc. Occasionally I begin the work in a light trance (in contrast with hypnosis situations involving highly responsive subjects, where I may readily slip into trance while working with a patient).

The next thing to consider is whether hypnosis is actually necessary for the problem we are addressing. Perhaps we can finesse the situation by using behavioral treatment or biofeedback. Perhaps only a very light trance is necessary. Here I usually resort to an economic model: What type of therapy can produce the best results with the least investment of time and money? Many problems for which hypnosis is sought are readily treated with other, allied treatment approaches, and most patients accept a recommendation to adopt the method most likely to succeed. I would say that the problem becomes more critical when hypnosis seems to be the treatment of choice because some of its characteristics potentiate treatment, notably the characteristics of dissociation and heightened suggestibility.

Pain and some psychosomatic disorders are types of problems for which hypnosis is particularly useful. A patient seeking hypnosis for a severe pain problem, for whom other approaches have not worked, should be helped to develop the maximum hypnotic response of which he or she is capable. If the problem is severe enough and other methods won't do, then both patient and therapist must be willing to invest time and effort in developing the best response possible. Note that we are no longer talking about whether the patient is intellectual, analytical, left-brained, or in any way observably different from what s/he is in the waking state. We are talking about assisting him/her to develop the maximum responsivity to tasks involving dissociation and suggestion.

In terms of improving the patient's response to hypnosis I follow several broad guidelines:

1) Start where the patient is — Milton Erickson's utilization principle. There have been repeated demonstrations that people may need to work with someone who is very sensitive to their individual and complex needs before they "get the hang of" hypnosis.
2) Use language and an *attitude* that are as permissive as possible. It is more than a matter of phrasing or sentence construction. It is a matter of making as many options for dissociative experience available as possible.
3) Educate patients extensively and intensively about their hypnotic experience, with verbal instruction, practice experiences, modeling responses, etc.
4) Involve patients as active directors of their own experiences. This may entail having them describe their imagery while I join in to add little details they might want to include (as opposed to the guided imagery type of induction many of us undertake) or having them practice self-hypnosis mini-exercises as suggested by the works of Morris (1974) or Ruch (1975).
5) Mutual hypnosis, or having them hypnotize me, sometimes helps them set aside their analytical approach.
6) Working with them when they are "in extremis" because of pain or severe-

ly disabling illness sometimes creates a motivational shift — a kind of "any port in a storm" response that facilitates a satisfying dissociative experience for them.

7) Use of easy psychomotor automatisms (eye closure, a combined arm drop and arm levitation procedure) helps provide confidence that they can experience trance phenomena.

8) Ask them in a permissive way simply to set aside that critical, evaluative part of themselves for a bit while they go through the experience.

I realize that in answering the question I slipped sideways into answering a related question, "What do you do if someone has difficulty going into hypnosis?" In returning to the original question, and taking all of the foregoing into consideration, I would say that I would not be much concerned if patients' productions were "intellectual and analytical, not much different from when they aren't in a trance." If they *themselves* expressed the wish to experience more of their intuition and unconscious processes, I would help them to identify those parts of their experience that are most "unconscious" or intuitive, and then give them additional experience in that area in order to build confidence and help them feel more secure. Someone who has labeled himself or herself as "too intellectual" may be delightfully surprised to realize that arm levitation is completely non-intellectual and that the preconscious mind-body connections can be explored and developed to give him or her a better appreciation of "unconscious" processes. Another person who can experience olfactory sensations/memories in imagination might be gratified to learn that the "smells" can carry him back in time, like an affect bridge, to important experiences or events he had forgotten. Only after the client feels successful, having identified some areas of his/her own experience that are intuitive and "unconscious," would I introduce tasks that might otherwise be challenging and reinforce a negative self-concept.

The techniques for increasing capacity for nonconscious involvement are myriad in hypnosis: hypnotic dreaming, affect bridge, guided or nonguided imagery tasks, automatic writing, psychomotor signaling, nonverbal interaction with the hypnotist, etc. After helping the client to set aside the self-definition of being too "left-brained," I would begin exploring some of these standard techniques, going at a pace that would permit a successful experience rather than providing a challenge that the client couldn't meet. For example, if the client were able to experience any kind of imagery at all, I would have him undertake many self-directed (in my presence) imagery involvement activities of a very simple nature (e.g., describing to me what his or her bed felt like, what he himself looks like in the mirror) before moving to sequential imagery, as in guided imagination. Then, if he could imagine walking down a path, or entering a meadow, I would have him gradually add his own details. When he himself is providing most of the description, he can be led to appreciate that the details came from some part of the back of his mind. From that, the client can be introduced to more imaginative guided affective imagery, and then on to hypnotic dreaming. The main principle I follow derives from operant learning theory, which stresses learning without failure and "shaping" responses that are not initially part of an organism's repertoire.

Finally, the hypnosis part of my psychotherapy may be central or peripheral. Because this is a book on hypnosis I have answered the question in terms of how hypnosis might be useful. However, in practice I might elect to approach the problem with some other kind of psychotherapy, rather than hypnosis, if the problems and the client's characterological development indicate that another type of therapy is needed.

References

Morris, F. (1974). *Self-hypnosis in two days*. Berkeley, CA: Intergalactic Publishing.
Ruch, J. C. (1975). Self-hypnosis: The result of heterohypnosis or vice versa? *International Journal of Clinical and Experimental Hypnosis, 23*, 282–304.

Question:

> An occasional patient goes into hypnosis and then will not re-
> spond to questions or suggestions. What does this mean? What
> can be done to prevent it? And how is the situation best managed
> when it does occur?

Discussion by ROBERT SIGMAN, Ed.D.

I take the position that a patient is treated not *with* hypnosis but *in*
hypnosis — that this clinical specialty is not itself a treatment but rather a
conduit for delivering some more organized system of therapy: behavior
modification, psychoanalysis, transactional analysis, gestalt therapy, what
have you. Given this view, it is apparent that nonresponse to therapist intervention, however occasional, represents some degree of breakdown in the
overall therapeutic rapport. To a behavior modifier, nonresponse might suggest some snag in the reinforcement contingencies; to a researcher, the possibility of a confounding intervening variable; to a psychoanalyst, resistance.
Whatever the underlying theoretical orientation, such interruption is best
viewed not as a random occurrence but as a signal that perhaps crucial
psychological data are leaking out of the dyadic pipeline.

Hypnotically, this situation arises almost always because of *excessive*
deepening, where emphasis on technique overshadows the purpose of treatment. In short, the patient who, without hypnosis, would be saying "I don't
know" or "I can't remember" can withdraw, with therapist assistance, into
a hypnotic cocoon where the regression is in the service of not the ego but
of intensified repression.

Often this resistance is to long-standing emotional issues. Sometimes it
is to transferential arrangements within the therapeutic relationship itself.

For example, if being hypnotized is experienced as being under the control of an all-powerful figure, then it is reasonable to expect fearful, covertly angry reactions; additionally, the very passive or masochistic may experience the perceived omnipotence as being sexually gratifying. Such patient distortion occasionally manifests itself in the style of withdrawal to which we are addressing ourselves.

By way of case illustration: Dr. A., a highly experienced eclectic therapist had recently undertaken a specialty in clinical hypnosis and was being supervised in the management of Mrs. B., a well-educated, mildly depressed 35-year-old woman whose presenting problem was chronic moderate obesity. Rather than building a hypnotic relationship, he was using hypnosis in a decidedly instrumental fashion, i.e., a formal arm levitation induction at the beginning of each session with as much deepening as possible. He took the fact that Mrs. B. was capable of classical trance alterations as an indicator of success and was waiting for the pounds to roll off under the diet/exercise regimen he was "recommending."

At a particular session, after she had lost 11 of the 25 excess pounds, he suggested that she imagine herself "at the desired weight, looking and feeling as attractive as she wished." For the first time, there was no feedback. Despite the nonresponse, he ended the hour with a posthypnotic reinforcement of the suggested image.

In supervision Dr. A. was directed to bypass the induction and simply to inquire about the prior meeting. Mrs. B. reported that his suggestion had been blocked by a spontaneously occurring image of a very vivid glacier, along with a salty taste in her mouth that persisted throughout the intervening week; further, she had become fearful lest the "program" not work due to her failure to comply.

Astute clinician that he was, Dr. A. began exploring both the transference and the sequels to his suggestion. While he used no formal induction and no deepening beyond the enhancement of her own visual imagery, there began to emerge a history of very early sexual abuse (including fellatio) by her tyrannical father. In the ensuing year of treatment, Mrs. B. more than lost the 25 pounds and changed her whole style of food intake to a much more wholesome pattern. In addition, there were significant gains in the quality of her life both maritally and professionally. As illustrated, a nonresponse, properly managed, can be woven into the fabric of therapy; overall, however, they are best avoided.

The following are two conceptual guidelines that will discourage the nonresponse dilemma. 1) Remember that there is no significant correlation between hypnotic depth and clinical productivity. Experienced hypnotherapists report that some of their most effective work is done in relatively light states, where there is less likelihood of the hypnotic process obscuring the dynamic material. 2) Always know the metaphorical meaning the patient attaches to being in a trance state. For some it is to be free and safe; for others it is to be overpowered. Actually, there are myriad meanings, each of which the therapist must know.

Given all of the above, should there, nevertheless, arise the impasse on which this question focuses, there are two steps to be taken: 1) Bear in mind that anything that can be induced hypnotically can be removed hypnotically. Simply direct your patient to let his or her attention return to the room feeling very fully aware. 2) Make dynamic use of the event in subsequent sessions. It contains within it rich and potentially curative information.

Q&A 75 Discomfort With Hypnotic Failures

Question:

> Although I realize I have failures with other approaches, I feel more uncomfortable and embarrassed when my hypnotic techniques don't work. What suggestions do you have for explaining failure with hypnosis that would alleviate my discomfort and that of that patient?

Discussion by CLORINDA G. MARGOLIS, Ph.D.

A simple *explanation* to the patient would be: "It seems that something is interfering with our ability to get this to work at this time." That explanation would then be followed by an exploration of what the interfering factor might be.

A more complete answer to the question, however, depends on how one understands the nature of hypnosis and its uses. The question is, in fact, loaded. In a way, it's based on the antiquated notion of the hypnotist as a strong authority figure, almost invariably male, who, by virtue of his will or by the mere magic of the trance, simply hypnotizes the problem away. Such a view prevails among the relatively uninformed public. Unfortunately, it also persists among clinicians, particularly among those who are just learning hypnotic techniques and are unfamiliar with the complex features of hypnotic practice.

Most therapists who use hypnotic techniques already have sufficient skills to maximize the likelihood of success, almost independently of their particular theories of hypnosis or its therapeutic uses. Very often, however, both hypnotist and patient anticipate immediate favorable results and are disappointed when this instantaneous gratification is not achieved. But this arises from a mechanistic view of the therapeutic situation and doesn't take into account the complexities of the patient's inner dynamics or his/her relationship with the therapist.

If the induction fails, the patient may even be secretly pleased, if he or she believes that only weak-minded people can be hypnotized. If therapeutic suggestions fail, this could be a happy but secret confirmation that one's problem is insoluble. Such "failures" may embarrass the therapist who does not appreciate the concept of resistance or know how to deal with it.

But such embarrassment is unnecessary and unhelpful. I see no reason why hypnotherapists should set themselves up for this kind of failure or discomfort. Unsatisfactory results may be minimized by prior preparations, which are always possible except in real emergency situations. These preparations would include: getting to know the patient well, understanding the problem in depth, knowing the strengths and deficiencies of the patient, offering explanations of the hypnotic process, and perhaps even negotiating a therapeutic contract.

Even with these preparations, hypnotherapy, like all other forms of therapy, may still fail, and the assessments of those failures are always relevant. Failures may occur in facilitating a hypnotic state in a patient, in achieving positive responses to hypnotic suggestions, or by eliciting unexpected and unwanted behavior during and following the hypnotic session.

Understandably, the first two sorts of failure may cause embarrassment and even defensiveness in the therapist, as well as disappointment and even indignation in the patient. But these negative feelings really point to a more profound and perhaps unrecognized emotional interaction between two people engaged in an obviously intimate relationship.

The third sort of "failure" has more to do with the complexity of the hypnotic and therapeutic relationship itself. For example, a patient may, on occasion, actually experience an increase in pain after leaving the office, where hypnotic suggestions were given for pain reduction. One therapist, seeing this as a failure, may decide not to use hypnosis again, thus scaring himself and the patient away from further attempts. Another therapist could reframe the experience, stating, "I'm sorry that you suffered, but now at least we know that hypnotic intervention can influence the intensity of your pain. If it can increase the intensity, it can also decrease it, so now we'll have you practice doing both." A third, more analytically inclined, would proceed to explore the meaning of the pain and/or the removal of it. Experienced hypnotherapists can tolerate paradoxical responses and continue to explore hypnotic interventions.

Once we appreciate that hypnosis is not simply a technique or set of techniques for removing symptoms from a patient, the authority picture begins to dissolve and we can construe it as a form of therapy that requires a sustained, sometimes profound, form of cooperation. Its success depends in some way on the complexity of human personality, on multiple levels of consciousness and experience, and on the therapist's ability to help the patient access parts of him/herself. Our awareness of ourselves and our internal and external environments are constantly changing, subject to sudden shifts of attention, thought, stimuli, feeling, and activity.

In helping patients move into hypnotic trance, the therapist helps them enter altered states in which, directed and encouraged to attend to particular stimuli and to ignore others, they may reinterpret their own experience and thereby reduce or eliminate particular difficulties. We may, for example, help a patient change his/her mood from discouragement to hope, in order to facilitate changes in thought processes. Or we may give suggestions to help a patient increase his/her energy level or distract attention from pain. But in general we are providing patients with the opportunity as well as pertinent exercises for mastering new ways of coping with their own problems.

So seen, hypnosis provides a therapeutic instrument that depends entirely on a working relationship between therapist and patient. Even the process of discovering the most effective hypnotic suggestions for a specific patient's presenting problem presupposes a distinctly cooperative venture. Dealing with other problems that may emerge during the course of therapy requires precisely the same sort of cooperation.

Imagine, for example, using imagery with a patient who presents with chronic pain. During hypnotherapy it is found that the pain masks a depression due to an experience of impotency. Here, the pain is misleading, and as trust develops the impotency problem is raised. If this is handled appropriately, depression disappears and pain itself is managed more comfortably. Certainly, as the therapeutic picture changes, as hypnotic goals are adjusted to changing information, the notion of simple success or failure linked with the authority model becomes irrelevant. Nevertheless, there remains the question of how to assess ambiguous results of treatment for problems that the patient may not acknowledge. Two brief cases may clarify the issue.

A very attractive 40-year-old woman came to me for hypnosis because she could not find some jewels that she had taken from her safe deposit box. She had had them reset, had worn them, and because of her fear of burglary, had hidden them in several different places in her house. She also mentioned that she was in the throes of a divorce and was drinking more than usual.

She recalled that after driving home from a party four months earlier, she had fixed herself a drink, had taken off her jewelry, and had wandered around the apartment wondering where she should hide them this time. The next time she wanted to wear them, three months later, she could not find the jewels and methodically took apart her four-room apartment. She repeated the process several times before requesting hypnosis.

I hypnotized her on two different occasions. Following the first session, she remembered more about the evening in question, how upset she had been following the party, some details about her clothing, and even an impression of having put the jewels in a jewelry pouch. Other details surfaced, which she discussed with some affect, but she did not remember where she had put the jewels.

In the second session she reported having had no success in finding the jewels, despite a strong, but obviously false, sense of their being in the glove compartment of her car. Under hypnosis we explored this feeling, but nothing emerged that seemed relevant to the missing jewels. I suggested in various ways that she should let her unconscious mind help her find them. When she left, she called her insurance agent and set up an appointment for a few days later. When he arrived at her apartment he suggested they look one more time. She took him directly to her bedroom closet, pulled out her shoeboxes, remarking that she had looked through these many times already. As she looked in the first box, she put her hand in the toe of one shoe and pulled out the pouch of jewels. They were both surprised and delighted. The next day she called to tell me the news and thanked me for trying to help her. She did not appear to credit our hypnotic sessions with any part of the favorable outcome.

The second case was a 26-year-old engineer who had been burned over 47% of his body in a gasoline fire, and was being treated in a burn unit where I served as consultant. During debridement procedures, in which the dressings were changed and dead tissue cut away, the patient did not cry out or make any sounds, although the staff believed him to be suffering enormously. They asked me to see him because they were persuaded that his stoic behavior might be countertherapeutic.

When I talked with him, he readily admitted that debridement was very painful, and indicated that he was willing to learn hypnotic techniques or any other techniques that might help him. I taught him hypnosis over two sessions. I gave him the suggestion that when he received his medication prior to debridement procedures, he would put himself into a hypnotic trance and travel to other places where time would pass quickly because he was enjoying himself. He developed satisfactory imagery for himself and reported liking the experience.

During our third session he said he did not want to be hypnotized again because he wanted to handle the pain by himself. He explained that he was a mountain climber and a skier and might be expected to have to deal with pain again from time to time. He didn't want to be dependent on anyone but himself for pain management. Almost as an afterthought, he said he had found a way to handle the pain by himself. He told me that when he received his medication in preparation for debridement procedures, he imagined he was taking a trip somewhere, where he could enjoy himself and make the time go by very quickly. By concentrating in this way, he felt he could now handle the pain entirely by himself. It was perfectly clear that he was completely amnestic about the work we had done together; nevertheless, it was important that he continue to feel independent. I was enthusiastic about his achievement and entirely supportive of his efforts to master the situation. I did not see him again.

These two cases demonstrate some of the difficulties inherent in identifying success or failure using hypnosis. Both cases were handled in such a way that hypnotic success was never on the line. Rather, emphasis was placed on a positive therapeutic outcome. Hypnotizability was not formally assessed in either case, but there was strong evidence that the burn patient had been hypnotized, was able to use self-hypnosis for pain control, and had become amnesic with respect to my hypnotic suggestions. In the first case, the patient had reported feeling relaxed, as well as surprised at being able to recover further information about her experience, but she questioned whether she had actually been hypnotized.

In neither case was the issue of hypnotizability important to the hypnotherapeutic process itself. Hypnotic suggestions were offered without regard to the nature or depth of the patients' trances. Their responses to suggestions helped them mobilize their own resources and solve their own problems. Both were successful, but neither would have credited hypnosis, although I believe that hypnosis played an essential role in each instance. If one had not found her jewels or the other controlled his pain, the results would have been disappointing in part, but not embarrassing, for the very nature of the cooperative effort could still be a valuable, even therapeutic encounter.

In short, viewing hypnosis as a holistic approach to human problems, not as a set of techniques applied in routine fashion to isolated problems, encourages a collaborative effort between therapist and patient that has its own distinctive therapeutic features. The following suggestions may help reduce the likelihood of overstressing the success-failure issue during hypnosis:

1) Instruct patients about the nature of hypnosis.
2) Know each patient well.
3) Teach hypnosis in a permissive way before giving hypnotic suggestions relating to the presenting problem.
4) Match suggestions to the needs and resources of the patient.
5) Be prepared to change the direction of hypnotic suggestion if the patient resists or if needs change.

Patients Who Become
Sexually Aroused in Hypnosis

Question:

I'm afraid of using hypnosis for sexual problems because in one
case where I did the woman patient became very aroused and
felt very vulnerable. I, as a man, felt very uncomfortable with
this experience. Are there ways around this?

Discussion by DANIEL L. ARAOZ, Ed.D.

The possibility of sexual arousal when we "think" of sexual matters is always
there, in and out of hypnosis. By sexual arousal I mean the noticeable physiological changes, sensed especially in the genital areas. Concretely, the man
senses, at least, the beginning of penile erection; the woman senses, at least,
the beginning of vaginal lubrication and/or clitoral awareness. In sex hypnotherapy, among other things, we try to foster positive hypnotic (i.e., mental) experience, such as rehearsing more enjoyable sexual activity or reliving past sexual encounters of a positive nature.

   In one of my books (Araoz & Bleck, 1982), many scenarios are listed for
the purpose of arousing interest, fun and playfulness in sex, so that sexual
activity at home can improve. However, some authors, such as Macvough
(1979), intend to produce sexual arousal in the therapy session. Since I consider healthy human sexual activity in our culture generally to be a private
and intimate experience, I am very much against the intentional eliciting
of sexual arousal during the therapy session. The treatment session should
teach the individual client techniques to be used privately, not provide a
setting for sexual activity. If the couple is seen together, which is preferred
for sexual problems when people are in a relationship, sexual arousal in the
session should never be the goal. In general, then, we must be clear that any

sexually arousing mental activity during the therapy session must be directed to its practice at home.

When dealing with a client of either sex, young or old, the therapist must be prepared for the possibility of sexual arousal. It is our professional responsibility, in accordance with every ethics code in existence, to direct the client's imagery to a real or possible sexual partner, never to the therapist. The issue of sexual activity between client and therapist has been discussed *ad nauseam*, and there is no way to justify it. It is always a transgression simply because, by definition, client and therapist do not deal in terms of equality. One requests the other's assistance because of a perceived inability to deal alone and effectively with a problem. The expert is not "a date" and should never allow himself to be placed in that position. The moment he becomes a date, he loses his role as expert and, consequently, stops assisting the person. In so doing, he is breaking the initial, implicit contract of the client-therapist relationship.

If the client does not have a sexual partner and cannot think of someone in that role, a hypnotic approach may not be appropriate. The sexual problem presented for treatment will have to be redefined, probably as one of self-esteem, inadequate emotional development or something else. In other words, the presented sexual problem is, in this case, a manifestation of a more fundamental psychological dysfunction, which requires other than sex therapy. To proceed with the latter could easily trigger images and feelings with the therapist as their object. Incidentally, because of this, sex surrogates should be used with great prudence and only after careful evaluation of the patient to be sure that the problem is not more a psychological than a sexual one.

Let us turn now to some practical ways of handling sexual arousal during hypnotic treatment of sexual dysfunction. First, techniques for couples in therapy will be presented; later, instances of sexual arousal or its possibility with individual patients will be discussed and the interventions to be used will be explained. In both cases, the general technique integrating sexual feelings experienced during the therapy session and the whole process of change is what I have called a somatic bridge (Araoz, 1984).

At those times when couples have felt sexually aroused by a hypnotic technique used in therapy, I have suggested to them that I can leave the office for a few minutes to give them a chance to be alone. This offer has made most couples decide that they want to continue with the therapy session without that interruption. In a few cases they have welcomed my giving them a few moments of privacy, but in over 25 years no couple has wanted to have sexual intercourse in my office. The moments spent alone seem to give them an opportunity to plan a more enjoyable sexual encounter in the immediate future.

Another way of handling the sexual arousal of a couple during the session is to interject suggestions to the effect that this current arousal is merely a sample of the new level of arousal they can enjoy, and to encourage them to feel the same urge and desire when the circumstances are right for good sex. The following is a verbatim transcript from a recorded session with a couple in which the husband "had lost all sexual desire."

During the second session he became very sexually conscious of his wife. The therapist said:

> Increase your relaxation even more. To be sexually aroused you must be relaxed and think of the next time you two will be alone, able to enjoy sex. Do you focus on that? . . . Your present desire grows even stronger. You're alone. The circumstances are right and you will have one of the best sexual encounters in your life. Get into it. Because you're now turned on to each other, you will be able to be more turned on when the circumstances are right. Look forward to it. Enjoy the prospect of it. You'll be so turned on, so relaxed with each other, so playful. You'll love making love. . . .

A third technique to be used when a couple becomes sexually interested in each other during hypnotherapy is to interrupt the sexual imagery and suggest that it can continue later when they are alone. The difference between this and the previous approach is that here you actually stop the sexual imagery, whereas in the preceding technique you continue it, but in reference to their future sexual activity.

If one of the spouses finds himself/herself turned on sexually, not to the other, but to someone else, two possibilities present themselves; both are to be handled delicately and expertly. First is that the imagined partner represents qualities desired in the spouse. If both partners recognize this, with the therapist's help, this spontaneous intrusion becomes therapeutically useful. However, if the imagined partner cannot be seen in this way, there is a strong probability that the sexual problem is really an indication of a relational deficiency, requiring couple therapy, rather than sex therapy, with or without hypnosis.

When a person is not involved in an ongoing sexual relationship, there still might be sexual problems. The gamut ranges from premature ejaculation due to excessive arousal to lack of arousal in superficial sexual encounters, with many other difficulties found between these extremes.

Such a person being treated hypnotically might become sexually aroused. Should this occur, it is necessary to offer reassurance that this is a natural reaction and to give hypnotic suggestions to thank the inner mind for this signal of health and normalcy.

Another technique, especially with people complaining of infrequent sexual arousal, is to retrace the development of this problem in the therapy session, "as if we were going over a play in slow motion during a sports program on TV." In this way, the client has an opportunity to become aware of possible dynamics at work in the sexual arousal pattern. It is often helpful to use a modification of the Watkins' ego state therapy (Araoz, 1985; Watkins & Watkins, 1979). The client may then discover that there is a "part" of him sabotaging his conscious desire to improve his sexual functioning.

If the client's sexual feelings during the therapy session involve the therapist in any way, the former may become very frightened. (I assume the therapist is experienced enough to handle this situation.) It is important in this case to focus on the sexual drive, rather than on its target. This was the case with an elderly (70-year-old) male patient whose problem was lack of sexual interest, but who experienced sexual feelings towards his therapist, a highly trained, middle-aged woman. The following excerpt is taken verbatim from that session.

> Welcome your sensations and feelings. They are part of you. They are finally coming back. Your body is reminding you of that side of you which was hidden for quite a while since you became a widower. Focus on your sexual feelings now and be happy they are still there. They are good. Now check how it feels to think about enjoying sex with Nancy (a lady friend who was interested in him). Not yet? OK, put your feelings back inside you now. But you know they are in you. One of these days you'll surprise Nancy with your desire to be sexual with her, as she wants . . .

As can be noticed, the therapist was fully accepting of the client's sexual sensations and feelings. She gently changed the object of those feelings, introducing Nancy, his lady friend. Towards the end of the session the client was able to visualize himself with Nancy.

However, when the individual client who has no sexual partner is sexually aroused by the presence of the therapist, whatever hypnotic procedure was being used should be interrupted. Instead, the client should be encouraged to think of someone he could consider as a sexual partner. When the client chooses someone, the therapist proceeds hypnotically, introducing that person in the imagery.

It may happen that the client does not come up with any possible sexual partner. In that case the client is encouraged to think of someone he considers a "sex symbol" and to focus his hypnotic imagery on that person (Araoz, 1982). After this, he may be able to imagine someone with whom he could possibly have sex, and then one proceeds to the previous situation.

A Clinical Vignette

The couple were two professional people previously married to different partners, with grown children living on their own. They had attended a couples' intensive weekend with Dr. Richard Stuart a few months previously, which had solidified their relationship. They were committed to one another and planned to get married. Their problem was that he was now "more loving than sexual" to her, as he put it. She assured him that this did not bother her, and that the current pattern of having sex "only" several times a week was fine with her. He claimed that he was afraid "due to his age" (he was 55) that the diminution of his sexual desire was "the beginning of trouble."

I will describe only one pertinent aspect of the case, which has to do with his sexual arousal during the session. During one of their early therapy visits, I was guiding them in erotic imagery when he became very upset. When asked what it was, he hesitated and, after several tentative statements, requested that she leave him alone with me for a while.

While she was in the waiting room, he told me with great feelings of guilt and nervousness that in the midst of the erotic imagery the picture that kept coming to him was that of his fiancée's older daughter (24 years old at the time), and that he felt very aroused by it, although he had never thought of her sexually before. He accepted my reassurances, but felt very upset at the sharp sexual images involving the young woman and the strong sexual arousal, including an erection, he had experienced in the session. He judged that telling his fiancée the truth could trigger long-term problems, and that not telling her could damage the relationship.

I suggested that he plan to tell her, but not immediately, and that he try the erotic imagery a few more times before telling her. Since I usually see partners both together and individually in the very first session, subsequent sessions are not anticipated as always being conjoint, and thus the fiancée did not feel surprised at my request to wait outside while he and I spent some moments together. We practiced the erotic imagery once more together that very same day and the image of his fiancée came to him without any difficulty.

Depending on our theoretical points of departure, we might speculate differently as to the meaning of this occurrence, but it would be difficult to make any scientifically sound statement about it. The explanation the client found satisfactory and with which his fiancée agreed when he told her three sessions later was this: He became sexually aroused and recognized that he was not too old, as he feared. "I could even make it with that girl," in his words. On the other hand, because he felt uncomfortable with his sexual feelings in my office, his inner mind changed the object of the arousal to one that would upset him and thus force him to interrupt the experience, as, indeed, happened.

This vignette illustrates, first, the delicate issue of sexual arousal in therapy and the different nuances it can take. Second, it points to the most important aspect of my whole response to the question posed: Don't panic! No matter how the client may experience sexual feelings or who the object of those feelings might be, the therapist can remain in control and truly help the client if he knows that the sexual arousal is just one aspect of what is going on in the client's subconscious mind. The therapist who does not allow the sexual arousal to distract him from the ultimate goal of helping the patient, according to the way the problem was defined and the therapeutic goal was set, will consider it another step in the sex hypnotherapy process. The content (sexual arousal) is never as important as the process or context (personal change towards self-fulfillment).

References

Araoz, D. L. (1982). *Hypnosis and sex therapy*. New York: Brunner/Mazel.

Araoz, D. L., & Bleck, R. T. (1982). *Hypnosex*. New York: Arbor Press.

Araoz, D. L. (1984). *Self transformation through the new hypnosis*. (Cassette series and manuals). New York: BMA Cassettes, Guilford Press.

Araoz, D. L. (1985). *The new hypnosis*. New York: Brunner/Mazel.

Macvough, G. S. (1979). *Frigidity: What you should know about its cure with hypnosis*. Elmsford, NY: Pergamon.

Watkins, J., & Watkins, H. (1979). The theory and practice of ego-state therapy. In H. Grayson (Ed.). *Short-term approaches to psychotherapy*. New York: Human Sciences Press.

Question:

> As a woman therapist, I'm nervous about using hypnosis with
> male patients. It seems too intimate (they're reclining as if in
> sleep, I'm sitting close, talking in a whisper, and they "wake up"
> in my presence), almost as if I'm a lover. How can I feel better
> about this?

Discussion by SHIRLEY SANDERS, Ph.D.

This question is an important one, for it represents one of the many problems that make beginning hypnotherapists feel uncomfortable with their
newly learned techniques. It is certainly not unique to the female therapist,
for many males feel the same discomfort in treating women patients, and
either sex may experience the problem when dealing with homosexual patients.

In order to feel better about this, the therapist should understand some
of the historical antecedents for this concern, have a clear understanding
of the role of the therapist, know where some of the currently held myths
and misconceptions had their origins, and be aware of the generalized effects of gender on hypnotic susceptibility.

The role of the hypnotherapist is a very complicated one, regardless of
sex of the therapist. As in any psychotherapy relationship, the hypnotherapist
has an ethical responsibility to help the patient meet certain goals. Specifically, the therapist has the goal of helping the patient to help himself, without
exploitation or abuse. Culturally, it is important to point out that in the
history of hypnosis, there were concerns about the possibility of seduction
under hypnosis, as reported in the first report of the French commission of
enquiry. This commission concluded that such practices may have an in-

jurious reaction upon reality (Bailly, 1888). The therapist was an active male viewed as possessing power, and the patient was viewed as a passive female who was the recipient of the power of the therapist. According to then-held beliefs, "Women are always magnetized by men. . . . This physician is a man, it does not deprive us of our sex. . . . The danger is reciprocal. The magnetic treatment must be dangerous to morality, while proposing to cure disease which requires prolonged treatment, pleasing and precious emotions are excited" (p. 4).

Mesmer used hypnosis around 1780 and was presumed to have magnetic powers. According to his theory of animal magnetism, illness was caused by a misdistribution of animal spirits in the body and it was the task of the therapist to redistribute these animal spirits to heal the patient. In France at that time, society was very protective of women and viewed the passive receptiveness of the female patient to be a form of sexual abuse imposed by the hypnotherapist. Even 100 years later, hypnosis is described as having a substantial impact on the female. For example, Charcot (1886) described a woman who talked of nothing but her hypnotist until she ran away from home to live with him.

Other claims were made by women who had something to gain from the allegation that they had been seduced while under hypnosis. For example, one young woman accused her lover, who was in deep trouble with the law, of hypnotizing her and then suggesting that she lure the bailiff into her apartment, that her submitting to the bailiff would free him of his difficulties (Perry, 1979). It would appear that this woman wanted to blame her indiscretion on hypnosis.

Freud (1924) pointed out that unconscious wishes and fantasies were operative in determining behavior (although out of awareness), when conflicts between the unconscious wishes and conscious morality were strong. While Freud himself believed that hypnosis distorted the transference and abandoned its use, at the present time hypnosis is viewed differently.

Indeed, in the '60s and '70s much attention was directed to the question of whether hypnosis is a cause or external force. According to Conn (1972), hypnosis cannot be considered "a cause" or an external force. Rather, he describes it as "an adaptation, a folie à deux, an alibi, a neurotic compromise, a ritualized regressive masochistic maneuver to obtain gratification of unacceptable wishes and to avoid superego condemnation" (p. 1). The "danger" in the use of hypnosis is the same danger that accompanies every psychotherapeutic relationship. In such a relationship, the motives, goals and wishes of both the therapist and the patient are important. During hypnosis the subject experiences a temporary displacement of feelings, the transference, onto the hypnotherapist. This displacement contains central personality and emotional attitudes originally formed early in life, regarding early bonding experience. The importance of transference and the relationship between doctor and patient appears to be significant in the hypnotherapy situation. At the same time, countertransference, i.e., the therapist's reactions to the patient, which are grounded in the therapist's past experiences, is just as important. While we will look more carefully at the concepts of transference and countertransference in the hypnotic relationship, first let us turn to therapeutic goals.

Hypnosis, being an interaction between two people, must be viewed in the context in which it is used. In clinical application, the context is one of healing, not abuse or exploitation of the patient. The therapist has the goal of helping the patient to help himself. Indeed, the responsibility of the therapist is an ethical one, the guiding ethic being that the goal of all therapy is self-knowledge leading to change. In line with this, letting the patient be in charge of his own conduct is ethical and important. The healer's role is not a sexual one, but, rather, a nurturing one. That is to say, the hypnotherapist is supportive, providing a catalytic role in the patient's self-understanding and self-growth. The tone of voice may be soft and soothing, *which is quite distinct from sexual seduction*. The pace of speech may be slow and rolling, again more a lullaby than an invitation to sexual activity. Even touch can be used in a healing, soothing, nonsexual way.

However, the goal of hypnotherapy is not merely to nurture the patient or simply to remove symptoms. The important point is that the patient be given a clear, unambiguous message that the relationship is one based on helping the patient to help himself, not to be confused in any way with sexual intent. The interaction of transference and countertransference is particularly important in maintaining clear communication.

All therapy, including hypnotherapy, requires rapport. According to Ellenberger (1970), the nature of rapport stems from the anticipation of love. Indeed, the nature of transference-love is self-evident, since treatment evokes this feeling and the therapist's job is to help the patient free his capacity to love. Fromm (1968) points out that the hypnotic context fosters infantile dependency transference, with the therapist cast into the role of the omnipotent parent. It may also stimulate an oedipal transference with fantasies of seduction or competition.

Some patients may harbor unconscious wishes to seduce or be seduced by the therapist. In this case, the patient may attempt to project his own sexual meanings and wishes onto the hypnotherapist. It is important that the hypnotherapist be aware of such patient projection.

Then we may encounter the neurotic, masochistic woman seeking therapy for the need to be overpowered. In these situations, the patient projects her own sexual wishes onto the therapist, whose task is to clarify the interaction, interpret the patient's projection of sexual meanings and wishes, and refocus on the tasks of therapy: helping the patient to help herself.

Gill and Brenman (1959), Fromm (1968), Wolberg (1967), and others discuss the importance of countertransference, i.e., the motives and unconscious reactions of the therapist. As a woman therapist who utilizes hypnosis with male patients, it is important to follow the rules of effective, competent psychotherapy. In this light, the therapist must realize that the patient's behavior may take on a frankly sexual form, even professed love. The patient may wish to exert power over the therapist. In male-female relationships, sexuality frequently is used by certain male patients as a way of diminishing the female. Overt declarations of love by the patient may actually be a test for the therapist. The patient may want the therapist to provide necessary limits and boundaries, or the patient's resistance to treatment may provocatively intensify the perceived love towards the therapist and exaggerate his wish for sexual dominance.

Freud's rule of therapist abstention is important. It is not permissible to gratify the patient's wish. The patient's desire and longing are allowed verbal expression in fantasy in order to explore and clarify the emotion and increase motivation for the therapeutic work. If the patient's advances were returned, it would be a defeat for the treatment in that the patient's only success would be expressing in action what should be remembered and discussed. Instead of love, the patient seeks substitute gratification. Gratification based on transitory acting-out is an illusion, an illusion that cannot be satisfied. Thus, the therapist must recognize the illusory love, but not indulge it.

As a way of staying on task, the therapist must keep in mind four perspectives: the therapist's own unconscious wishes, the patient's unconscious wishes, society's mores, and the therapeutic task. In doing so, we help the patient decide, choose, commit and bear the burden of human freedom.

Female therapists use hypnosis less often than male therapists. Women psychotherapists comprise almost one-third of all psychotherapists, yet they comprise only 18% of the membership of the American Society of Clinical Hypnosis (Sanders, 1985). One hypothesis is that even today hypnosis is viewed among female therapists as mainly a masculine-dominated, authoritarian and controlling approach to patients and that women therapists fear such authoritarian control. A second hypothesis is that women are less likely to seek out hypnosis training because there are relatively fewer opportunities to gain knowledge of more permissive techniques. This, however, is changing.

Traditional therapists and traditional hypnotherapists replicate the dominant, more powerful, more knowledgeable, healthier male therapist stereotype and the less powerful, helpless, dependent, needy female client expectation. This stereotype is partly related to socialization practices. Men are socialized to experiment with power, aggression and assertion. They may have unrealistic expectations about hypnosis. They may believe that to be hypnotized is to be an empty robot who does everything one is asked or to be rebellious and sarcastic as a way of holding on to personal identity. They may confuse dependency with intimacy and intimacy with sexuality. Surely there are more ways of being intimate than through sexuality. For example, the therapy hour is intimate in that painful feelings are expressed and shared with the therapist.

A more egalitarian perspective holds that the power inherent in the role of the therapist not be abused and that the therapist not behave in an arbitrarily or unnecessarily authoritarian manner. Rather, the power of the client is emphasized. The egalitarian therapist recognizes the contradiction of sharing ideas and feelings with the client and decreasing power differences, while still maintaining the genuine authority and objectivity required by the role of therapist.

Finally, it is important to look at the studies on hypnotic susceptibility and sex of the therapist. In such studies, the sex of the therapist has not been a significant factor in determining the response of the subject to hypnosis (Weitzenhoffer & Weitzenhoffer, 1957). Relationship factors are more important. In studying hypnotic susceptibility, Coe (1976) found that the sex of therapist did not affect the hypnotic responsiveness of subjects or distort their responses. Hedberg (1974) also found that sex of the hypnotist was not important, while Levitt and Baker (1983) confirmed the importance of the relationship. Along these lines, Nash (1984) found that, within the relationship, perceived power of the hypnotist was an important factor. Diamond (1984) points out that hypnotherapy skills are a function of the hypnotist's ability to create a facilitating holding environment for the patient's internal experience. Thus, relationship and skill are the essentials in carrying out hypnotherapy.

References

Bailly, J. S. (1888). *A secret report on mesmerism or animal magnetism.* New York: D. Appleton and Co. Quoted in R. E. Shor & M. T. Orne, *The nature of hypnosis: Selected readings.* New York: Holt, Rinehart and Winston, 1965.

Charcot, J. M. (1886). *Oeuvres complètes* (9 Vols.). Paris: Aux Beureaux du Progrès Médical.

Coe, W. C. (1976). Effects of hypnotist susceptibility. *International Journal of Clinical and Experimental Hypnosis, 24,* 281.

Conn, J. H. (1972). Is hypnosis really dangerous? *International Journal of Clinical and Experimental Hypnosis, 20,* 61.

Diamond, M. J. (1984). It takes two to tango. Some thoughts on the neglected importance of the hypnotist in an interactive hypnotherapeutic relationship. *American Journal of Clinical Hypnosis, 27,* 3.

Ellenberger, H. F. (1970). *The discovery of the unconscious.* New York: Basic Books.

Freud, S. A short account of psychoanalysis (1924). *Standard Edition,* vol. 19. New York: Norton.

Fromm, E. (1968). Transference and counter-transference in hypnoanalysis. *International Journal of Clinical and Experimental Hypnosis, 16,* 77.

Gill, M. M., & Brenman, M. (1959). *Hypnosis and related states*. New York: International
  Universities Press.
Hedberg, A. G. (1974). The effect of certain examiner and subject characteristics on respon-
  siveness to suggestion. *International Journal of Clinical and Experimental Hypnosis, 22*, 354.
Levitt, E. E., & Baker, E. L. (1983). The hypnotic relationship: Another look at coercion,
  compliance and resistance. A brief communication. *International Journal of Clinical and
  Experimental Hypnosis, 31*, 125.
Nash, M. R. (Oct. 1984). Measuring the transferential aspects of the hypnotic relationship.
  Paper presented at the Annual Meeting of the Society for Clinical and Experimental Hyp-
  nosis, San Antonio, Texas.
Perry, C. (1979). Hypnotic coercion and compliance to it: A review of evidence presented in
  a legal case. *International Journal of Clinical and Experimental Hypnosis, 27*, 187–218.
Sanders, S. (1985). Membership in ASCH. Unpublished survery.
Weitzenhoffer, A., & Weitzenhoffer, G. B. (1957). Sex, transference and susceptibility to hyp-
  nosis. *American Journal of Clinical Hypnosis, 1*, 15.
Wolberg, L. R. (1967). *Hypnosis in psychoanalysis and psychotherapy*, New York: Macmillan.

Q&A 78 Handling a Patient Who Doesn't Come Out of Trance

Question:

I had an alarming situation several years ago and haven't used hypnosis since. A patient went into a very deep trance and though I assumed he was out of it and okay when he left the office, his wife called the next day to say he was acting bizarrely. He was "spaced out," unable to concentrate, and seemed oblivious to his surroundings. She was afraid to let him go to work. I made a house call and he seemed to be still in deep trance. I got him to come out of it with some effort, but my confidence was badly shaken. What did I do wrong? Is there a way of preventing such incidents?

Discussion by HELEN H. WATKINS, Ph.D.

The therapist in this case seemed to assume that because of the severity of the patient's reaction the therapist "did something wrong." It is to be regretted that this experience caused the therapist to lose confidence in the clinical use of hypnosis and cease using it. Such a happening is uncommon but not unheard of among seasoned hypnotherapists. It seems logical to me that such a reaction is much more likely to happen with a short-term client who has come to therapy for a narrowly defined hypnotic purpose, such as to stop smoking. In such a case the therapist is likely to concentrate on the client's smoking history rather than other psychological facets of his/her personality. However, I myself have never had such an experience with a client seeking to stop smoking.

There is insufficient information to determine whether the therapist did anything "wrong." Prevention may lie in obtaining a more detailed history of any previous hypnotic or dissociative experiences, or in more carefully

445

controlling the induction procedure. Checking with the client on each step of the induction may have elucidated the desire to escape into a deep trance.

The first reaction for any practitioner confronted with such circumstances is not to panic, but immediately to contact the patient and continue therapeutic work, first by removing the hypnotic state with calm and firm dehypnotizing suggestions which are continued until it is clear that the patient has returned to a full state of alertness. Then one should inquire about the patient's feelings and experiences. Questioning may reveal some particular reason why the patient "chose" to dissociate at that time, perhaps a fear of what might be revealed under hypnosis, anxiety at loss of control, a threat from sexual impulses, etc. J. G. Watkins (1954, 1963) has discussed a number of these "transference" reactions.

It is also possible that the patient is so highly hypnotizable that dissociation is a natural occurrence. In that case hypnotic inductions are not indicated, but teaching the patient not to enter the dissociated state would be indicated. I recall one patient who was constantly entering the trance state at inopportune moments. With the cooperation of one ego state, we worked out a plan wherein he could remain alert by tightening his fist. To contact this ego state (and others), all he had to do was close his eyes for a few moments and that part of him was available to speak to me.

Since there is a possibility that the patient may be a borderline psychotic or given to frequent dissociating, psychological testing (Rorschach, MMPI, TAT, etc.) might be indicated to determine whether his personality is in the normal-neurotic range or in danger of a more drastic disintegration. If the latter is the case, then hypnosis should probably not be used in the therapy. (It should be noted that even these cases have been successfully treated hypnotherapeutically, but should be undertaken only by very experienced therapists.)

Sometimes the patient has found the hypnotic experience so pleasant that he does not wish to come out of it. The therapist, in this case, merely needs to let the patient know that his needs are recognized but that this is not an appropriate response, and that the therapist and patient will explore this matter together at the next session. Again, it is important that the therapist not panic but reassure the patient that he does not consider the behavior weird.

Assuming that one is not dealing with a truly borderline individual, then an entirely different approach becomes possible and from a more optimistic perspective. That is to regard the experience as a promising one that opens up new channels for treatment. Quite possibly the therapist has touched upon an underlying dissociated state during the hypnotic experience. Such a dissociated state had some purpose, some need, some relevance to the therapy. It may be an actual entity with its own feelings, thoughts, needs and purposes, thus, an "ego state." In that case it can be interviewed under hypnosis to understand its function within the economy of the total personality. These techniques are described in my and my husband's writings as "ego-state therapy" (see Watkins & Watkins, 1979, 1981, 1982). If it is a true ego state, then its reluctance to disappear gives evidence of its need to be contacted and to express itself to the therapist. Hypnosis is therefore strongly indicated as a therapeutic technique to allow this part of the personality to emerge.

Under such circumstances the dissociation manifested by the patient can be converted into a therapeutic asset, and a whole new approach to treatment becomes possible. Instead of viewing the incident as a catastrophic and alarming occurrence, the therapist can see it as an opportunity to deal with the patient's personality conflicts more significantly.

References

Watkins, J. G. (1954). Trance and transference. *Journal of Clinical and Experimental Hypnosis, 2,* 284–290.

Watkins, J. G. (1963). Psychodynamics of hypnotic induction and termination. In J. M. Schneck (Ed.). *Hypnosis in modern medicine* (pp. 363–389). Springfield, IL: Charles C Thomas.

Watkins, J. G., & Watkins, H. H. (1979). The theory and practice of ego-state therapy. In H. Grayson (Ed.). *Short-term approaches to psychotherapy* (pp. 176–220). New York: National Institute for the Psychotherapies and Human Sciences Press.

Watkins, J. G., & Watkins, H. H. (1981). Ego-state therapy. In R. J. Corsini (Ed.). *Handbook of innovative psychotherapies* (pp. 252–270). New York: Wiley.

Watkins, J. G., & Watkins, H. H. (1982). Ego-state therapy. In L. E. Abt & I. R. Stuarts (Eds.). *The newer therapies: A handbook* (pp. 137–155). New York: Van Nostrand Reinhold.

Q&A 79 Terrifying Imagery in Hypnosis

Question:

> Each time I try to use imagery with one of my patients, she immediately has terrifying images in whatever sensory modality I'm using. How can I manage this?

Discussion by RICHARD HOREVITZ, Ph.D.

The spontaneous development of frightening imagery in hypnosis is not altogether rare. It can develop for a number of reasons. Clinical management depends on an accurate assessment of its origin.

In order to discuss management, I will outline four different sorts of problems that can lead to the development of frightening imagery. With each I'll propose a simple conceptual understanding and the corresponding management strategy. Probably none of these problems actually occurs in isolation. In practice a combination of strategies is frequently called for.

1) Relaxation problems. Although rarely studied in detail, over the years numerous investigators have reported that relaxation *per se* can be a source of extreme distress in a small number of patients (e.g., Norris & Fahrion, 1984).

In these cases we presume that reduction in the level of chronic and constant muscular and autonomic hyperarousal itself leads to the problem. Presumably signals of decreased arousal and dramatic drops in tension levels produce novel neural messages that the brain can neither interpret nor integrate without dramatic conscious representation.

Conceptually this is parallel to sensory deprivation experience. When the central nervous system is deprived of its normal load of sensory and motor stimulation, experimental subjects first lapse into trance-like states and then gradually develop multimodal hallucinations (Herron, 1957). With extremely tense individuals, relaxation functions as sensory deprivation from interoceptive, nociceptive, and proprioceptive sensors, as well as reducing visual and auditory stimulation. The reduced signal flux is fancifully elaborated by the brain in an effort to piece together what is happening.

The management strategy is rather simple. As Braun (1980a) suggests, slow stepwise procedures with small incremental goals allow for a gradual reduction in tension levels without the problems of dramatic dropoffs. When these problems occur in my work, I typically substitute methods high in perceived control and low in focus of mental activity for direct hypnotic procedures. Jacobson's (1938) progressive muscle relaxation, its abbreviated versions (Bernstein & Given, 1984), autogenic relaxation (Norris & Fahrion, 1984), and EMG biofeedback can all be used to accomplish this goal.

2) Dissociation problems. Hypnosis involves more than a relaxation component; it involves dissociation of the normal hierarchical organization of control functions. Excellent hypnotic subjects can readily develop an altered state of consciousness which includes the ability to alter the perceptual, cognitive and affective dimensions of experience.

Excellent hypnotic subjects show exceptional talent for becoming imaginatively involved with suggestion. Thus, their personal experience is quite often influenced by their hypnotic talents. Barber refers to the most adept hypnotic individuals as fantasy-prone personalities (Wilson & Barber, 1983). In their study of these individuals, Wilson and Barber found them to be absorbed in private imaginative events much of the time, reporting frequent "paranormal" experiences and long histories of profoundly realistic fantasy life.

These people have exceptional life histories and, as Josephine Hilgard (1979) has shown, an unusual incidence of severe punishment or abuse in childhood. Recently, Lynn and his colleagues found this to be true among 50% of a large sample of highly hypnotizable college students (Nash, Lynn, & Givens, 1984).

Often, when introduced to formal hypnosis, these highly exceptional talents can develop profound trance depth characterized by dissociation, archaic involvement, heightened transference, diminished generalized reality orientation and cognitive distortions. This can become extremely frightening because fantasy material, somatic or sensory hallucinations, or dissociated imagery can be experienced as very real. Excellent subjects tend to become deeply absorbed in the compellingly real quality of their experience, including literal acceptance of hypnotic suggestions (Bowers, 1978; Sheehan, 1979). Many unintended situational, interpersonal, and subjective elements can become woven into the imaginative fabric.

When exposed to conventional hypnotic inductions these subjects can occasionally develop frightening imagery because they experience too little control of the situation, too little control over the direction of events, too little control over the depth and richness of experience, and too little connection with the therapist.

The appropriate management strategy then consists of giving more: more control, more communication, more feedback, more input. Enhanced communication is the most successful strategy in my experience. With very gifted subjects I greatly increase the amount of shared planning, goal definition, strategy identification, imagery preferences, identification of potential problems, identification of subtle clues and meanings prior to the use of trance. I discuss with them therapeutic tactics and especially modes of communication to be employed during the trance experience.

During trance work, I review what we have discussed prior to induction. With the most gifted subjects I encourage the use of both ideomotor signaling, especially for emergencies, and direct verbal communication during trance. Eventually these elaborate precautions are no longer necessary with most patients.

Occasionally a very gifted subject is also very fragmented internally. When this is the case I teach simple stepwise procedures, such as autogenic relaxation exercises, before any trance work at all. With patients who have had a history of abuse, I emphasize self-hypnosis, allowing them a great deal of freedom to fluctuate in and out of trance as they need.

3) Relationship problems. There are three general sorts of problems that I see under this heading: problems in the personal relationship with the therapist aggravated by the hypnotic experience; problems in relationship and intimacy heightened by the hypnotic relationship; fears of abandonment activated by the hypnotic experience. All of these can lead to the development of terrifying imagery. I will discuss them separately.

a) The struggle for control: The manner in which hypnosis is used in contemporary psychotherapy represents an alteration in the therapeutic relationship. Often the therapist is directive and even manipulative. It is easy to overlook the interpersonal implications of these changes. If you have established a pattern of asking your patients how they feel or think and then utilize hypnosis in a way that tells them what they are experiencing, you have dramatically altered the balance of power and very subtly altered interpersonal boundaries. Since "archaic involvement" is a characteristic of the hypnotic relationship, this change and the accompanying negative affect are rarely mentioned by the patient (Shevrin, 1979).

Confusion at boundaries and struggles for power can be manifested in terrifying experiences for patients. Since these terrors begin with the hypnotic relationship, management begins here. Fostering self-control of mental, physical and physiological processes, as well as involvement in the interpersonal issues, can alleviate the confusion, which is itself a valid therapeutic aim (Budzinski & Stoyva, 1984).

b) Core interpersonal problems: The terrifying imagery experienced by your patient may represent pervasive core conflicts surrounding relationships, trust and intimacy. Patients who are functioning at very primitive levels ("borderline," severely narcissistically disturbed, histrionic, and passive/aggressive patients) can develop problems in hypnosis of this sort. Expertise in working with these patients is the first consideration. Hypnosis can be effectively used, as Elgan Baker has shown (1982, 1983).

Similar problems of negative imagery can also develop in the treatment of patients who have been severely traumatized sexually, physically or emotionally. Not uncommon with multiple personalities (Braun, 1980b; Horevitz, 1983; Kluft, 1982), problems with hypnosis also have been reported in working with rape victims, holocaust survivors, witnesses to mass trauma, etc. The fearful imagery has to do with the relationship threat of hypnosis, not with the content of the memory. Whatever the source of the need for protection against intrusion, great care is needed before proceeding with hypnosis. Feelings of boundary protection, internal cohesion, and self-mastery can be developed in ways discussed earlier.

c) Object loss problems: While some people experience the heightened sense of empathy associated with the hypnotic relationship as intrusive and threatening, others are much more focused on the hypnotic experience itself. For some of these people, the requirement to become absorbed in their own inner experience is itself frightening because it means the loss of feelings of connection to the therapist and the "real world." This sense of isolation yields frightening fantasies of loss, death, separation, mutilation, dramatic conflagration, or experiences of dizzying vertigo. Even when these patients are encouraged to communicate in hypnosis, they can experience the loss of "parts" through hypnotic self-absorption.

The commonsense advice, if you are dealing with problems like this, is not to use hypnosis in the first place (i.e., avoid the problem). Or, if you already have, quit before you get into more trouble. But that leaves unanswered what to do if you are in the middle of trouble. I see it as a twofold task. First, help the patient maintain contact with you and his/her own body. Second, assume that everything the patient says is literally true, as in a game, and find some creative way to work it through. This is something like what Jung (1929) meant by active imagination. It requires active intervention on the therapist's part to help the patient get off the mountain top on which he is stranded, or to find the lost body parts, etc. In this way it is like playing a fantasy game with a child who intuitively knows the rules of his own game, cannot tell them to you but can tell you whether or when your suggestions will work.

4) Unconscious content problems. It is possible that significant therapeutic issues are represented symbolically in your patient's imagery itself. The imagery can relate to dynamic, historical or transferential issues. Hypnosis is typically understood by patients as a force able to unlock the unconscious mind, or a mental truth serum. The threat of breaking amnestic processes can produce horrifying imagery directly or indirectly expressing the material involved.

Management depends on identifying probable sources of the problem through careful interviewing outside of hypnosis. If there is some material that is protected in this way, hypnosis can be introduced first for relaxation or as a continuation of other relaxation techniques. Then ego enhancement techniques can be used along with ideal-self techniques to build the inner resources to deal with the material itself.

References

Baker, E. L. (1982). The management of transference phenomena in the treatment of primitive states. *Psychotherapy: Theory, Research, Practice, 19,* 194–198.

Baker, E. L. (1983). Resistance in hypnotherapy of primitive states. *International Journal of Clinical and Experimental Hypnosis, 31,* 82–89.

Bernstein, D. A., & Given, B. A. (1984). Progressive relaxation: Abbreviated methods. In R. L. Woolfolk & P. M. Lehrer (Eds.). *Principles and practice of stress management* (pp. 43–69). New York: Guilford.

Bowers, P. G. (1978). Hypnotizability, creativity and the role of effortless experiencing. *International Journal of Clinical and Experimental Hypnosis, 26,* 184–202.

Braun, B. G. (1980a). A cause of biofeedback failure. *American Journal of Biofeedback, 3*(2), 179–180.

Braun, B. G. (1980b). Hypnosis for multiple personality. In Wain H. (Ed.). *Clinical Hypnosis and Medicine.* Chicago: Year Book Medical Publishers.

Budzinski, T. L., & Stoyva, J. M. (1984). Biofeedback methods in the treatment of anxiety and stress. In R. L. Woolfolk & P. M. Lehrer (Eds.). *Principles and practice of stress management.* New York: Guilford.

Herron, W. (1957). The pathology of boredom. *Scientific American.* (Reprinted in S. Coopersmith (Ed.). *Frontiers of psychological research.* San Francisco: Freeman, 1966.

Hilgard, J. R. (1979). *Personality and hypnosis: A study of imaginative involvement* (rev. ed.). Chicago: University of Chicago Press.

Horevitz, R. P. (1983). Hypnosis for multiple personality disorder: A framework for beginning. *American Journal of Clinical Hypnosis, 26,* 138–145.

Jacobson, E. (1938). *Progressive relaxation* (2nd ed.). Chicago: University of Chicago Press.

Jung, C. G. (1929). *Contributions to analytic psychology.* New York: Harcourt, Brace.

Kluft, R. P. (1982). Varieties of hypnotic interventions in the treatment of multiple personalities. *American Journal of Clinical Hypnosis, 24,* 230–240.

Nash, M. R., Lynn, S. J., & Givens, D. L. (1984). Adult hypnotic susceptibility, childhood punishment and child abuse. *International Journal of Clinical and Experimental Hypnosis, 32,* 6–11.

Norris, P. A., & Fahrion, S. L. (1984). Autogenic biofeedback in psychophysiological therapy and stress management. In R. L. Woolfolk & P. M. Lehrer (Eds.). *Principles and practice of stress management* (pp. 220–254). New York: Guilford.

Sheehan, P. W. (1979). Hypnosis and the process of imagination. In E. Fromm & R. L. Shor (Eds.). *Hypnosis: Developments in research and new perspectives*. New York: Aldine.

Shevrin, H. (1979). The wish to cooperate and the temptation to submit: The hypnotized subject's dilemma. In E. Fromm & R. L. Shor (Eds.). *Hypnosis: Developments in research and new perspectives*. New York: Aldine.

Wilson, S. C., & Barber, T. X. (1983). The fantasy-prone personality: Implications for understanding imagery, hypnosis and parapsychological phenomena. In A. A. Sheikh (Ed.). *Imagery: Current theory, research and applications*. New York: Wiley.

80 Danger That
Hypnosis Will Cause Harm

Question:

I'm concerned that patients could become psychotic as a result of hypnosis, or that they could become worse because of the recovery of painful memories with which they are not prepared to cope. Are there such dangers, and if so, how can I guard against them?

Discussion by JOHN W. HEDENBERG, Ph.D.

In all of my experience with hypnosis, I have never seen an instance of any patient (mine or a colleague's) becoming psychotic as a result of hypnosis. There are, of course, many warnings, often with rather dire overtones, about this in the hypnotic literature. I have no doubt that it is possible for an unfeeling and hostile hypnotist to trigger great discomfort (even acute anxiety, rage, or fear) in a subject or patient, if that hypnotist tries to *force* that person to behave or communicate in a way discordant with the person's personality structure and interests. However, a hypnotist of that kind is, by definition, *not* doing hypno*therapy*. He or she is, rather, attempting what has become known as "brainwashing," an exceedingly hostile endeavor which has no place whatsoever in any of the healing arts or professions.

Unfortunately, in the earlier days of hypnotic treatment, when it was considered that the doctor was the authoritarian and infallible expert, whose judgments and orders any well-behaved patient was supposed to accept meekly and unquestioningly, too many patients *were* stressed in that way. Under such well-intentioned mistreatment, some of them did, indeed, flee into psychotic behavior. That behavior was then interpreted as an effect of hypnosis *per se*, rather than as the effect of insensitive mishandling on the part of the doctor. It was also (rather unimaginatively) seen as a totally bad thing, to be avoided at all costs, without recognition that it was a very effective way for any hard-pressed patient to bring the hypnotic "treatment" to an instant halt. There have been very few more effective ways, throughout recent medical history, to give genuine pause to a doctor than by becoming psychotic!

Fortunately, I believe, such outcomes are totally unnecessary. Over the years, I have learned a great respect for the ability of any and all persons to protect themselves, consciously and/or unconsciously, against experiencing *anything* in hypnosis that they cannot handle safely. No patient I have ever seen has been unable either to ignore an inadvertently overdirective or frightening suggestion or to let me know in some other direct or indirect way that he/she refuses to go along with it. When one finds, in a particular case, that a patient either is simply not responding in the suggested way or is becoming uneasy, that patient is communicating that one had better back off. At such times it pays to take as much time as necessary to gently explore the basis of that failure to accept the suggestion — always with full respect for the patient's need to protect and defend.

All patients should be granted the right to set their own speed of progression in their therapy. It is wasteful of time and effort for both patient and therapist to attempt to do too much too quickly. With constant respectful watchfulness for where and in what ways one might be treading too heavily, there is no need ever to come close to tripping off any psychotic behavior — even when working with quite unstable patients whose outward everyday behavior and thought are permeated with self-defeating patterns. Such patients have a great deal of change to accomplish before they can live more satisfying lives. They know, at some deep level, that they cannot do all that changing too fast; they will therefore defend themselves against being too rushed by the hypnotherapist, using any conscious or unconscious means at hand. If we hypnotherapists respect that ability fully, and do not trample it, we will be operating as first-rate therapists should.

Being a person whose much-preferred style of interpersonal interaction is friendly and permissive, I have never tried to test the limits of that innate protective strength in hypnotic subjects or patients. However, I suspect that those limits (if indeed there *are* any) lie far beyond my ability or willingness to "push" or "crowd" a subject or patient. Indeed, I am convinced that in almost all life situations the therapeutic effectiveness of hypnotic interventions increases as *less* directive authoritativeness is used.

The only exceptions are "life-or-death" emergency situations in which time is of the essence. An example might be an automobile accident resulting in serious injuries to people, at which a hypnotically skilled person might arrive. In such a situation kind but very *firm* suggestion by that person would be essential for maximum probability of rapidly stopping bleeding, preventing full-blown shock, and in general saving lives. It is generally a waste of time (and harmful to good rapport with a patient) for a therapist engaged in *non-emergency* psychotherapy to try to use hypnosis as a "brute force" tool to bring about some change in a patient that he/she believes the patient "should" have.

A somewhat related issue is that of using hypnosis with a patient who is *already* psychotic. The principle was stated above that psychotherapeutic suggestion with *any* patient should always be permissively respectful of the patient's view of his/her world in any case. It can be added that hypnotic work with already psychotic patients should be very carefully arranged to avoid overstressing the special weaknesses of such patient, who in general cannot handle issues of intimacy and close interpersonal relationship. Provided such care has been wisely used, psychotic patients can be worked with effectively using hypnosis.

81 Dealing With Overly Compliant Patients

Question:

> What should I do about patients who seem determined to please me, even in trance? I've had several who produce textbook responses in age regression, affect bridge, and ego state therapy, yet no real change takes place. I don't think they are deliberately faking and I do believe they experience trance, but something is wrong.

Discussion by JOHN W. HEDENBERG, Ph.D.

It is a fact that a good many patients (though by no means all) will at times behave as though they had a need to compliantly please the hypnotherapist with whom they are in hypnotic rapport. They generally do this without awareness of doing so, by unconsciously generating a response that there is reason to believe the therapist will accept with approval (whether verbalized or not). When this is taking place, in response to some suggestion or request by the therapist, the resulting production is apt to be far more contaminated than the therapist might prefer with content that is not necessarily relevant to the patient's own genuine and legitimate psychological needs. While such responses are not useless to the therapist in his/her task of seeking to aid the patient, it is wise to exert reasonable effort to minimize that kind of difficulty.

    Patients, like all people, are enormously complex — far more so than can be described fully in any finite number of words. Those who are (sometimes) compliant in the way mentioned may have a variety of out-of-awareness reasons for it. One may be that of avoiding or postponing feared change by seeming outwardly to cooperate beautifully in the work, while inwardly preventing the desired result. Such a tactic is always good for at least *some* delay, since it cannot be detected at once. Whenever nonproductive compliance is encountered, it behooves the hypnotherapist (as with other more obvious defenses against too rapid work) to back off and try to find out what might be blocking readiness for change.

In general, however, it is usually the case that whatever the reason for the compliant but unproductive behavior, it cannot be dealt with by conscious reasoning with the patient. He or she sincerely does not understand it, and does not know what to do to transcend it. Nor does the therapist have a complete understanding of all the possible factors involved. In such situations, the difficulty is best avoided or minimized by presenting verbal and/or nonverbal suggestions in ways that baffle or confuse the patient's conscious thinking long enough to allow time for unconsciously generated responses to occur. This is much easier to say than to do, of course, if the therapist tries to do it in a consciously reasoned way (a task somewhat akin to lifting one's self off the floor by the bootstraps!).

Experience has made it quite clear to me and to some colleagues that much better results are obtained in such instances by making no attempt to generate ambiguous suggestions through rational thought. Instead, it has been much more profitable to allow a moderately deep trance state to develop in me, while I am intently focused on the patient and his/her presenting appearance and behavior. Within a short time, I find myself actively talking (or nonverbally behaving) in some fashion that focuses the patient's attention on a search for relevant meaning for him/herself in what I am doing and/or saying. While his/her conscious thought is attempting to "reason" it out, there is time for the unconscious thinking to arrive at conclusions and decisions and to implement them in some effective way. Under these circumstances, the responses are usually much richer and more productive than those following any consciously generated suggestions of mine.

Let me illustrate briefly. When I work in this mode with a patient I might find myself doing or saying a wide range of things. I might find myself telling a story or anecdote about some friend or family member. I might find myself gazing, with interested expectancy obvious to the patient, at his hand, or at my own (after which one or the other or both is apt to levitate). I might find my hand very gently touching his/hers in a way that somehow brings about a gush of tears and the releasing outpouring of a long-forgotten painful or humiliating incident. I might find myself rambling on about something that both of us are puzzled about, but which in some remarkable way elicits some constructive alteration in the course of events at the moment. There seem to be innumerable ways that my unconscious (whatever that is!) can find to resolve difficulties that baffle my conscious self.

It should be unequivocally stated here, however, that in using this just-described method the therapist must be able to feel confident in trusting his own unconscious to provide wisely what is required. Without that confidence, it is much safer for the therapist (and hence for the patient) if the therapist sticks to doing whatever can be done using ordinary conscious, rational thought in generating suggestions. That trusting-in-self confidence is gradually acquired through much experience by the therapist in learning, through his *own* hypnotic life experiences, that it is justified. Beginning practitioners of hypnotherapy are well advised to refrain from attempting such things with patients until they have developed their own self-trust sufficiently. With patience and steady continuing exploration of self-hypnotic capacities, that will come to pass.

Until that more advanced capability is attained, there is no need to be particularly concerned when certain patients seem to be too compliant for the therapist's comfort. Therapy can still be conducted, even if only by the time-honored heuristic rule applicable in *every* field of endeavor, "When what you're doing isn't working, back off and carefully try something else."

$\underset{A}{\overset{Q}{\&}}$82 Hypnotic Communication: How Literal Is the Unconscious?

Question:

> I've heard that the unconscious takes things very literally and that makes me uncomfortable using hypnosis for anything more than light relaxation work. How do other hypnotherapists get around this problem?

Discussion by STEVEN J. LYNN, Ph.D., &
DAVID C. FRAUMAN, Ph.D.

This comment reflects a number of important concerns that clinicians have about using hypnosis in their clinical practice. Given the almost mystical powers that are ascribed to hypnosis, it is not surprising that some clinicians view hypnosis as the "royal road to the unconscious" and think of the hypnotized client as a passive automaton who responds to suggestions in a purely literal manner. Relatedly, some clinicians believe that hypnosis alters thought processes to preclude rational, reality-bound thinking and fear that hypnosis can unleash primitive, affectively charged experiences that defy regulation and control by the hypnotist. It is not surprising that clinicians who hold such beliefs might be reluctant to integrate hypnotic procedures into their clinical practice.

Before we address the concerns implied by the above, let us consider why suggestions proffered in the context of hypnosis can produce profound alterations in subjective experience. Hypnotic suggestions often orient the client to relax physically and mentally, to focus attention directly on the hypnotist's communications and away from the environment and current concerns, and to engage in fantasy and give free rein to the imagination in accord with suggested experiences such as age regression and diminished pain sensitivity. The hypnotist's soothing and relaxed tone of voice and altered speech patterns tend to reinforce more explicit suggestions and help to define the experience of hypnosis as one that is very different from waking reality.

Hypnotic suggestions often invite the client to adopt an alternative frame of reference. For example, the hypnotist might suggest that the client think, feel, or act "as if" he or she were a child or to act "as if" the hypnotist were making contact with a hidden part of the self or the "unconscious." As Barber (1985) has noted, when the procedures are defined as hypnosis or self-hypnosis, the therapist can relate to the client in a more relaxed, personal, meaningful, uninhibited, and imaginative way than is generally possible in a typical two-way conversation. Suggestions for increased fluidity of associations, for the utilization of creativity and problem-solving abilities, and for the experience of comfort, security, and decreased inhibition can facilitate the client's adopting various alternative roles, examining problems, feelings, and maladaptive thoughts from new perspectives and using imagery and cognitive rehearsal to consolidate new learnings.

Unless competing or disruptive thoughts and feelings inhibit absorption in suggestion-related imaginings, clients may experience compelling alterations in subjective experience. However, hypnotic subjects do not typically respond to suggestions in a purely literal manner, lose contact with "reality," or become passive automatons. For example, we have never encountered an adequately "rested" client who literally fell asleep immediately following a suggestion to do so. Clients are aware that falling asleep would preclude their responding to subsequent suggestions and therefore violate one of the central demands of the hypnotic situation — to be a responsive subject. Likewise, age regressed clients who have compelling affective experiences associated with childhood do not necessarily abandon their adult reality orientation or cognitive capacities and relinquish their ability to process information as an "adult." Further, during hypnosis, clients do not lose contact with external reality. Responsive subjects are vitally attuned to the hypnotist and his or her communications. They manifest the ability to respond to suggestions that are both subtle and complex.

Hypnotized clients' cognitive processes appear to be active and goal-directed rather than passive and literal. Responsive hypnotic subjects' creative imaginings clearly demonstrate their active attempts to fulfill the requirements of hypnotic suggestions. Sheehan and McConkey (1982) have demonstrated that hypnotized subjects exhibit distinct cognitive styles in their responses to suggestions. While some highly responsive subjects attempt to think and imagine along with the hypnotist's suggestions in a literal manner, other equally responsive subjects' imaginings are more idiosyncratic and independent of the hypnotist's suggestions even though they remain consistent with the goals of the suggestion.

We have observed that clients' needs, goals, and defenses often transform the meaning of therapeutic suggestions. Clients' responses to suggestions reflect their interpretation of suggestions, their tendency to elaborate upon suggested ideas and experiences with personally meaningful images, fantasies, and associations, and their reluctance to respond to suggestions that are ego-dystonic. Recognition of the role of resistance in hypnotherapy and of the diversity of clients' interpretations of and responses to suggestions has contributed to the tendency to use non-authoritarian, permissive suggestions to minimize resistance and promote a spectrum of potentially therapeutic responses. Because clients tend to relate to hypnotic suggestions in a personal rather than a literal fashion, it is important to individually tailor suggestions to the client's unique situation and personality dynamics.

One reason for some clinicians' belief that the hypnotist can communicate directly with the unconscious is the use of ideomotor finger signaling to communicate with the hypnotist (Cheek & LeCron, 1968). The therapist might suggest something like the following: "I will now speak to your unconscious. Your unconscious can signal me by lifting the index finger of your right hand to indicate 'yes.' When this happens, your finger will rise by itself." Clients are often convinced that their motor responses are involuntary. The client's responses may supplement or even contradict when the client reports on a "conscious" level. However, for the reasons elaborated below we would argue that it would be a mistake to conclude that such reports and behavior actually reflect unconscious responses or the ability of hypnosis to bypass conscious processes and communicate directly with the unconscious.

First, research in our laboratory (Lynn, Nash, Rhue, Frauman, & Stanley, 1983; Lynn, Nash, Rhue, Frauman, & Sweeney, 1984) and related research conducted by Spanos and his colleagues (e.g., Spanos & Gorassini, 1984; Spanos, Weekes, & de Groh, 1984) indicate that although hypnotized subjects often experience their suggestion-related responses as involuntary, such experiences are influenced by a number of factors. For example, passively worded suggestions such as, "Your finger will rise by itself," foster the illusion that the finger is responding automatically. Furthermore, subjects' preconceptions about hypnosis, their conception of the hypnotist as a powerful figure, and their suggestion-related fantasies and imagery all contribute to the experience of their own responses to hypnosis as involuntary "happenings" that occur without their conscious control.

Second, as Hilgard (1985) has pointed out, reports given in response to suggestions for "unconscious" finger signaling that contradict "conscious" reports may reflect ambivalence rather than a direct accessing of unconscious material. For example, ambivalence may be expressed by the client's answering "yes" to the question, "Do you hate your mother?" despite denial of such intense feelings while the person is "awake." Indeed, given the cultural stereotype of the hypnotic subject as passive and the hypnotist and hypnotic procedures as "powerful" and capable of evoking unconscious or repressed material, it is not surprising that some clients might experience a diminution of responsibility for thoughts, feelings, and actions and reveal information they ordinarily would not. A number of our clients, who requested hypnosis to uncover the details of their childhood histories of parental abuse, expressed related concerns. That is, careful exploration of their motivation revealed that they were in fact in touch with their past but were ashamed to share the details of their history without the support of hypnosis. A parallel to this situation can be found in some clients' tendency to communicate certain feelings to their therapist through their reports of dreams. Because such clients view their dream as the author of the script, and because their dreaming "unconscious" experienced the rage directed toward a parent, for example, they experience a diminished sense of responsibility for their feelings and feel freer to communicate them to their therapist.

Third, as we mentioned earlier, susceptible clients are adept at fantasizing and imagining and can readily adopt the metaphor of their personality or consciousness being composed of distinct parts (e.g., conscious vs. unconscious) when the hypnotist directs them to conceptualize themselves in this manner. Indeed, one of the hallmarks of the good hypnotic subject is cognitive flexibility and the ability to assume multiple perspectives and adopt multiple roles with attendant subjective experiences when requested to do so. The therapist's request to speak to the "unconscious" conveys the expectation that it is possible to contact hidden or unintegrated aspects of the personality and have a dialogue with them. Thus, when hypnotized clients respond to this request, they are responding to a suggestion and striving to fulfill their expectations about what is required by the hypnotist's communications. Thus, responding in the context of the metaphor that it is the unconscious relating to the hypnotist can be viewed as consistent with responding to other hypnotic suggestions rather than as indicative of a literal ability to circumvent conscious processes.

The suggestion to speak to the unconscious can, however, have therapeutic value. It places demands upon the client to explore hidden motivations and ambivalent feelings and to generate alternative conceptualizations of the personality and behavior. However, it is important to keep in mind that the gamut of defenses, displacements, condensations, and symbolizations are often evident in hypnotized clients' verbalizations and responses to suggestions, just as they are in non-hypnotized subjects' "memories, dreams, and reflections." In neither instance are unconscious dynamics simply "revealed" to the therapist; rather, they must be inferred by their diverse symbolic expressions.

The clinician is probably ill served by rigidly dichotomizing conscious and unconscious mental processes. While clients differ in their ability to articulate different levels of awareness (Wachtel, 1985), it is often impossible to distinguish conscious from truly unconscious manifestations. Hence, what is conscious and what is unconscious may actually be a pseudo-issue. A more central issue is whether "new information," including verbalizations and manifestations of cognitive and affective processes, contributes to an understanding of the psychological and behavioral dynamics crucial to problem or symptom resolution. This parallels the observation that clients' "insights" can be useful to the extent that they facilitate therapeutic objectives, independent of their ultimate "truth value" or their source in conscious or unconscious mental functioning.

We have attempted to argue that the unconscious does not "take things very literally" and that hypnosis per se does not provide the therapist with an unclouded window to the client's unconscious or "brings up unconscious mental functioning." While hypnosis can stimulate primary process thinking and promote a concentration of the client's awareness on imagery and fantasy, this rarely occurs apart from expectancies that arise out of the hypnotic context and the hypnotist's implicit and explicit suggestions. However, an issue that is of crucial importance to the hypnotherapist is the regulation of the sometimes profound affect and intense subjective experience that can be associated with hypnotic procedures.

We shall present a case study of an anorectic woman (treated by S.J.L.) that will illustrate some of the ways in which hypnosuggestions can be used to augment the therapist's control over ideational and affective processes. We selected this case because it underscores the importance of anticipating the emergence of affective material and incorporating suggestions to enhance the client's sense of comfort, security, and mastery. It is particularly germane to our discussion in that suggestions were employed that invited the client to interact with different "parts" of herself.

Mrs. B. is a 24-year-old married mother of a four-year-old boy. She presented with the cardinal symptoms of anorexia nervosa and a history of two hospitalizations following periods of food restriction. At the start of therapy, Mrs. B, 5'5" tall, weighed 88 pounds. After six months of twice weekly, insight-oriented psychotherapy and close monitoring by her physician, she was able to stabilize her weight for a two-week period at 120 lbs. However, Mrs. B still occasionally abused laxatives and continued to experience depression, anxiety, food preoccupations, and diminished self-esteem. In addition, she continued to manifest a tenuous sense of self, pronounced dependency needs, perfectionism and fears of abandonment and rejection. Her tendency to use splitting defenses (e.g., rigid propensity to dichotomize experience into mutually exclusive categories of good versus bad, right versus wrong, and should versus should not) also created difficulties for her. These personality trends and defensive operations reflected the dynamics central to anorexia nervosa and the organization of her character at the borderline level of development.

Hypnosis was incorporated into the overall treatment because it was felt that hypnosuggestions could help her to relax, imagine, and maintain control of her thoughts and impulses. Further, Mrs. B. had positive associations with hypnosis. Indeed, earlier in treatment she had approached the therapist about using hypnosis to help her to achieve greater control over eating. She was assured that the procedures would be carried out in a stepwise fashion and at a pace that she would be able to control. She was also informed that she would not receive suggestions until she indicated a readiness to respond. The suggestions were presented to her in terms of self-hypnosis; the therapist's main function was described as that of guiding and facilitating relaxation and the creative use of imagination. Before the first suggestion to simply relax and feel happy and content was presented, it was stressed that Mrs. B. could resist any suggestions, if she so desired, and that she could open her eyes and comment on the proceedings at any time if she felt it would promote the process of therapy.

The therapist began with "easy" suggestions and only moved to more demanding suggestions when it was felt Mrs. B. would be responsive and after she indicated her willingness to attempt to imagine or respond to the suggestion. The first session was devoted to encouraging feelings of physical and mental well-being while self-hypnotized. In addition, suggestions were delivered along the lines of encouraging her to permit herself to "feel more and more a sense of control, security, a letting go as you begin to experience a sense of the possibility of relaxing while letting yourself begin to enjoy a sense of feeling of being in charge of your life, as you go deeper and deeper, if you would like to, when you would like to, in your self-hypnosis." Similar suggestions were also delivered at the start of subsequent sessions.

Mrs. B.'s feelings of "very deep relaxation" were physically "anchored" by helping her to associate these feelings of equanimity and control with the unobtrusive gesture of touching together the thumb and index finger of her right hand. She was informed that, with practice she could use this anchor to relax and attain calmness and a heightened sense of control both in and outside of her therapy sessions.

In the next session, Mrs. B. experienced no difficulty having a fantasy accompanied by feelings of relaxation and well-being and selecting a favorite place associated with feelings of happiness and relaxation. Following these two suggestions, she was able to describe a pleasant beach scene with which she was familiar, and she was encouraged to practice returning to the beach scene at home when she wanted to feel relaxed and comfortable. This scene was also "anchored" and added to the imaginal and physical associations linked with the gesture she learned the previous session.

During the third session, feelings of self-deprecation were elicited in response to the suggestion to "have a fantasy about yourself, and describe the feelings that you experience." Mrs. B. visualized herself as "fat and ugly," as she imagined herself consuming only a few bites of cereal. She was asked to shift her attention from this discomfiting image to the peaceful beach scene, and to let herself use her abilities to "move with her imagination" to comfort herself and demonstrate that she did, indeed, have control over her thoughts and, hence, her feelings. With some prompting, Mrs. B. was able to do this and to anchor these feelings, along with a sense of mastery for breaking a long-standing chain of thoughts and feelings and replacing painful, anxiety-laden thoughts with more adaptive imagery and thoughts.

During the next session, Mrs. B. was asked to fantasize about a specific problem or conflict area. She fantasized that she was more assertive in stating her needs and in asking for help from her husband. This proved to be difficult but not extremely anxiety-provoking. When the suggestion was made for her to visualize herself asking for help from her husband, Mrs. B. reported being "scared and embarrassed." After reaffirming Mrs. B.'s desire to master the situation, the therapist suggested that, if she wished, he could be there in the fantasy, standing beside her. When Mrs. B. was encouraged to fantasize about the scene again, and after she changed the therapist's position in the fantasy from holding her hand, to standing beside her, to standing behind her, Mrs. B. reported that she felt the safest with the therapist standing beside her but invisible to her husband, "like a guardian angel." The session ended with practice returning to the beach scene, with suggestions for self-confidence, self-control, and positive coping in everyday life. The therapist-related imagery was invoked at later points in the therapy when the therapist vacationed, in order to help Mrs. B. better tolerate separation and counter feelings of abandonment.

During the next session, Mrs. B. was asked to visualize the various ways in which her life would be improved when her difficulties were resolved. In her fantasy of the future, Mrs. B. envisioned herself as a slim, accomplished, assertive and respected physician. She imagined she could make decisions without feeling compelled to consult others, and she felt a sense of pride in being able to "take charge" around the home. This suggestion was repeated as a short motivation-building exercise at the end of the subsequent hypnosis sessions. It is important to note that prior to this session, Mrs. B. had been reluctant to entertain a "career" as anything other than that of a housewife, although she felt extremely frustrated devoting her "total energy" to this pursuit.

During the next session, two approaches were taken to facilitate Mrs. B.'s examination of her assertion deficits from multiple perspectives. While fantasizing about an instance of nonassertive behavior, Mrs. B. was asked to verbalize her associations to the words "weakness," "strength," "good," "bad," "wrong," "right," and to the first names of her husband and her son, who were part of the scenario she envisioned. The second approach required Mrs. B. to verbalize possible solutions to her assertion difficulties. While engaged in fantasizing, Mrs. B. was asked to verbalize her associations to "holding it in" and "letting it out." At this point in treatment, Mrs. B. was able to disclose a sharply demarcated split in her experience of herself and her presentation to others. It became clear that she could act in a more assertive manner when she enacted her "masculine self," a self that she described as strong, sleek, never hungry, never approval-seeking; she stated, "He doesn't need anybody, he doesn't need anything, he never cries, he helps me be strong, he doesn't need food, friends, love, *anything*." In contrast, she found it almost impossible to be assertive when she was her "feminine self," a self that she described as weak, fat, a pig, needy, and dependent; she stated, "She needs everybody and everybody's approval." This revelation was accompanied by considerable apprehension that the therapist would reject her because "I'm so crazy." After being reassured by a discussion of the need to better understand and explore the issues raised by the emergence of this important new material, Mrs. B. relaxed noticeably and was able to achieve a comfortable level of relaxation following suggestions to practice the anchoring excercise, return to the beach scene, and fantasize about her life in the future.

During the next session, Mrs. B. was encouraged to enact, in fantasy, an interaction between her two "selves." She was asked to verbalize the dialogue as the two selves confronted each other and to empathize, as a third party, with each self in turn. Considerable affect accompanied this fantasy, and the therapist responded with suggestions for calmness and equanimity. Twelve sessions were needed to more fully explore her intense ambivalence about each of her "selves" and the childhood origins of her ambivalence. These sessions proved to be a pivotal point in the therapy.

Age regression suggestions were used to elicit a great deal of clinically significant material. Mrs. B. was informed that her ability to have a meaningful age regression experience depended upon her willingness to fantasize, imagine, and reexperience the events and affective states of childhood. She was further informed that she would never fully sever her link with the present and that she could simply open her eyes and immediately "return" to the present or she could gradually reorient herself to the present at any time she chose. Mrs. B. also was told that she would retain her "adult" ability to initiate commentary on her experiences and communicate with the therapist without its interfering with her experience of age regression and that she would be able to converse with the therapist when he tapped her left shoulder. Nonverbal cues (a tap on the right shoulder) were also established to facilitate rapid reorientation to the present.

Before each experience of age regression, the therapist asked Mrs. B.'s permission about whether she would be comfortable proceeding. To ease her anticipatory anxiety, she was also asked whether she would like to imagine the therapist's presence in the scene envisioned. Prior to Mrs. B.'s describing scenes of being abused as a child, it was suggested that she watch the scenes on a television in her imagination and that she control her affective response with the use of imaginary dials that regulated her emotional distance from and degree of identification with the "main character" (herself). Anchoring techniques to facilitate calmness and equanimity, well-practiced in earlier hypnotic sessions, were also incorporated into her experiences of age regression. On a number of occasions when it was desirable to dilute the affective charge of the recalled events prior to terminating hypnosis, suggestions were given for Mrs. B. to let her emotional associations and memories of the incidents gradually fade from her consciousness like a dream, "until the dream is no longer a part of your awareness."

These techniques appeared to facilitate Mrs. B.'s ability to discuss her abuse as a child at the hands of her stepfather, her early vows to be "tough and never cry or show pain," her anger toward her passive mother, her jealousy of her male siblings whom her stepfather accorded privileges because they were male, her fears of being overwhelmed by anger and her feelings of powerlessness in the presence of her stepfather, and her feelings that she was never "good enough" to be openly loved by either parent.

During the last two sessions in this series, Mrs. B. was first encouraged to enact in vivo a confrontation between her two "selves" and then to role play an assertive situation with her husband, with the therapist enacting her husband's part. She was able to engage in the first role play and to better understand how her two "selves" corresponded to representations of her parents (stepfather = male, mother = female) and reflected, in part, her ambivalence about identifying with either parent. In the second role play, it became quite clear how her fantasies of annihilating others with her anger and of being annihilated by her husband's uncontrollable fury related to her conflict about assertion.

In the course of her three-year treatment, this material was worked through and Mrs. B. achieved a largely successful resolution of her ambivalence, significant improvement in her level of self-acceptance and interpersonal satisfaction, and completed two years of undergraduate course work in premedical studies. When she terminated therapy, she still expressed some concern about her weight and ruminated about food during times of stress; however, she had achieved a stable weight for the past year.

It is important to note that at no point in Mrs. B.'s treatment were her "two selves" conceptualized as separate entities residing within her. While the therapist used hypnotic techniques that on occasion required that Mrs. B. act "as if" her personality were divided into warring factions, he was careful not to reify the client's terminology and self-conceptualization as a split human being. This is not to say that the client's conflict and ambivalence were minimized or ignored. Quite the contrary, helping Mrs. B. develop a coherent sense of self unencumbered by debilitating conflict and ambivalence was a primary objective of therapy. In closing, hypnotic procedures can be productively used to maximize treatment gains by ameliorating anxiety that is associated with negotiating the rough terrain of self-exploration and the demanding process of psychotherapy.

References

Barber, T. X. (1985). Hypnosuggestive procedures as catalysts for psychotherapies. In S. J. Lynn & J. P. Garske (Eds.). *Contemporary psychotherapies: Models and methods.* Columbus, OH: Merrill Press.

Cheek, D. B., & LeCron, L. (1968). *Clinical hypnotherapy.* New York: Grune & Stratton.

Hilgard, E. R. (1985). Conscious and unconscious processes in hypnosis. In D. Waxman, P. C. Misra, M. Gibson, & M. A. Baske (Eds.). *Modern trends in hypnosis.* New York: Plenum.

Lynn, S. J., Nash, M. R., Rhue, J., Frauman, D., & Stanley, S. (1983). Hypnosis and the experience of nonvolition. *International Journal of Clinical and Experimental Hypnosis, 31,* 293–308.

Lynn, S. J., Nash, M. R., Rhue, J., Frauman, D., & Sweeney, C. (1984). Nonvolition, expectancies, and hypnotic rapport. *Journal of Abnormal Psychology, 93,* 295–303.

Lynn, S. J., Snodgrass, M., Hardaway, R., & Lenz, J. (1984). Hypnotic susceptibility: Predictions and evaluations of performance and experience. Paper presented at the Meeting of the American Psychological Association.

Sheehan, P. W., & McConkey, K. (1982). *Hypnosis and experience.* Hillsdale, NJ: Erlbaum.

Spanos, N., & Gorassini, D. (1984). The structure of hypnotic test suggestions and attributions of responding involuntarily. *Journal of Personality and Social Psychology, 46,* 688–696.

Spanos, N., Weekes, J., & de Groh, M. (1984). The "involuntary" countering of suggested requests: A test of the ideomotor hypothesis of hypnotic responsiveness. *British Journal of Experimental and Clinical Hypnosis, 1,* 3–11.

Wachtel, P. (1985). Foreward. In K. Bowers & D. Meichenbaum (Eds.). *The unconscious reconsidered.* New York: Wiley.

Q&*A* 83 Can Hypnotized Patients Be Persuaded to Do Almost Anything?

Question:

I'm nervous about using a method that I've heard can be used to get patients to do almost anything. What is the evidence that a person will do things under hypnosis that he or she wouldn't do otherwise?

Discussion by WILLIAM L. GOLDEN, Ph.D.

Many leading authorities (e.g., Erickson, 1939; Le Cron, 1964) have maintained that hypnosis cannot be used to make people act against their moral principles. In contrast, other experts (e.g., Estabrooks, 1943; Weitzenhoffer, 1953) have claimed that hypnosis can be used under certain conditions to get people to do things that they would not ordinarily do. Estabrooks (1943), for example, reported the case of an amateur hypnotist named Nielson who employed hypnosis to induce a subject to commit a murder. Marcuse (1959) reported a similar case. Yet hypnotherapists routinely tell their clients that they cannot be made to do things under hypnosis that is against their will. How legitimate is this claim?

Several attempts have been made to investigate whether hypnosis can or cannot be used for antisocial purposes. Watkins (1947) used hypnosis to induce a soldier to assault an officer and in another experiment demonstrated that an army intelligence agent would divulge secret information under hypnosis. Schneck (1947) reports the case of a soldier who went AWOL in response to hypnotic suggestion. Wells (1941) found that subjects could be induced to steal small sums of money from their friends. He also reported being able to induce amnesia in these subjects.

Rowland (1939) compared hypnotized and nonhypnotized subjects in order to test whether hypnosis was capable of inducing subjects to engage in behavior that could be dangerous to self and others. The subjects were ordered under hypnosis to touch a rattlesnake, which they were told was a piece of rubber. The safety of the subjects was protected by means of a special invisible glass shield which prevented them from actually touching the snake. Three out of four subjects complied with this suggestion. In another experiment, two subjects were instructed under hypnosis to throw sulphuric acid at the experimenter, whose safety was protected by invisible glass. Both subjects complied with the instruction. As a basis of comparison, an informal control group of 42 nonhypnotized individuals were asked to pick up the snake. Rowland reported that 41 out of the 42 subjects would not even come close to the snake's cage.

In a replication of Rowland's experiment, Young (1952) instructed subjects to pick up a poisonous snake and throw nitric acid at an experimental assistant. Young found that seven out of eight subjects complied with the instructions in the hypnotized state, but refused when they were instructed in a nonhypnotized state.

Not all of the researchers got their subjects to engage in dangerous and antisocial behavior. Estabrooks (1943) failed to replicate Rowland's (1939) findings. Nevertheless, Estabrooks did succeed in getting subjects to forge checks while under hypnosis. He explained the discrepancy as resulting from his having expectations different from Rowland's. Whereas Rowland expected his subjects to engage in dangerous behavior in response to hypnotic suggestion, Estabrooks did not. According to Estabrooks, the expectations of the hypnotist are conveyed to the subject, so that, if the researcher expects subjects to resist hypnotic suggestions to engage in dangerous and/or antisocial behavior, they will resist. These biases and expectations of the experimenter are inadvertently conveyed to the subject in very subtle ways, such as a tone of voice. Estabrooks offered the same explanation to account for Erickson's (1939) report that he was unable to induce hypnotic subjects to perform unacceptable and harmful acts such as receiving or giving an electric shock, lying, playing pranks on others, and undressing for a complete physical examination, even though the subjects did many of these things in the normal nonhypnotic state. All of the subjects had hypnotic experiences with Erickson prior to their participation in his informal experiments, thereby giving them ample opportunity to learn of his own beliefs about hypnosis as well as his expectations about how they would respond.

On the basis of his review of the research on hypnosis and antisocial behavior Estabrooks concluded that hypnosis could be used for criminal purposes. Weitzenhoffer (1953), on the other hand, has said that hypnosis alone is incapable of inducing subjects to commit antisocial acts. After carefully reviewing the studies, Weitzenhoffer observed that most of the investigators who were successful in getting subjects to engage in antisocial acts first produced perceptual alterations on the subjects, thereby disguising the true nature of the requested behavior. For example, Wells (1941) succeeded in getting subjects to steal money from friends by telling them under hypnosis that it was their own money. Rowland (1939) and Young (1952) convinced subjects to reach for the snake after giving them the suggestion that it was a piece of rubber. Weitzenhoffer concluded that the perceptual alterations prevented the subjects in these studies from perceiving that their actions were dangerous or antisocial. If Weitzenhoffer is correct, then, although it may not be possible to induce individuals to hurt themselves or commit crimes through direct suggestions, it may still be possible to get compliance by preventing the subjects from being aware that they are doing something dangerous or illegal. For example, a subject may resist a direct hypnotic command to jump off the roof of a building, but jump in response to a hallucination created through hypnotic suggestion that he or she is diving into a pool of water.

A complete empirical test of this hypothesis in a naturalistic setting is, of course, impossible. If the researchers obtained positive results they would be guilty of criminal acts and the reward for their positive findings would be a prison sentence. Furthermore, as Orne and Evans (1965) pointed out, when positive results have been obtained under protected laboratory conditions, the results may have had nothing to do with the ability of hypnosis to produce antisocial behavior; rather, they may be due to demand characteristics of the situation. They proposed that there are demand characteristics operating in experiments investigating the possible antisocial use of hypnosis. Subjects have certain expectations about psychologists and experimental investigations that are created by the setting itself, i.e., demand characteristics of the situation. Subjects naturally expect that the investigators are reputable and will not have them do anything that is really illegal, immoral, or dangerous to themselves or others. Therefore, they feel safe in complying with any task suggested by the experimenter. Even the naturalistic experiments, such as Watkins' (1947) demonstration that hypnosis could be used to get an intelligence agent to reveal secret information or to get a soldier to attack an officer could be explained by demand characteristics, i.e., the soldiers could have perceived that they were expected to engage in the suggested behavior, that protective measures would be taken, and that there would be no punishment for responding to the hypnotic suggestions.

Orne and Evans (1965) conducted an experiment in which they examined whether nonhypnotized subjects would respond to instructions to engage in dangerous and antisocial behavior at the same frequency as hypnotized subjects when the demand characteristics were the same for both groups. They were critical of the controls used in Rowland's and Young's experiments, pointing out that Rowland did not exert the same pressure on the informal control group as he did on the hypnotized group of subjects. Likewise, Young did not exert the same amount of pressure on the subjects in the nonhypnotic condition as in the hypnotic condition. Therefore, in the Orne and Evans study equal pressure to comply was exerted on the hypnotized subjects, nonhypnotized subjects and simulators. Orne and Evans found that the hypnotized subjects did respond to the instructions to touch a rattlesnake (five out of six) and throw acid at an assistant of the experimenter (five out of six). However, they also found that approximately the same number of subjects in the nonhypnotized group responded to the instructions of the experimenter to reach for the snake (three of six) and throw acid at the assistant (five of six).

Levitt et al. (1975) obtained similar results. They found that equal numbers of hypnotized and control subjects (simulators) responded to instructions to engage in objectionable acts such as cutting up an American flag and mutilating a bible. However, they also elicited a greater degree of noncompliance (26%) from both the hypnotized and the control group subjects than earlier studies. Levitt et al. postulated that the greater resistance was due to the nature of the objectionable tasks that they employed in their study. They pointed out that, since the subjects really destroyed the bible, there was no way that they could think they were being tricked or protected by the experimenter.

Orne and Evans (1965) concluded that the operation of demand characteristics in psychological experiments make it impossible to test, and therefore prove, that hypnosis can be employed for antisocial purposes. The subjects in all such studies may have assumed that the situation was safe and no one would be hurt. As mentioned earlier, this explanation can even be used to explain the results obtained in naturalistic settings. In Orne and Evans' study, postexperimental inquiries did in fact reveal that "with few exceptions" the subjects felt "quite safe." The experimenters report "All subjects appeared to assume some form of safety precautions had been taken during the experiment" (Orne & Evans, 1965, p. 199).

However, how do we explain that individuals have committed criminal acts, even murder, after receiving hypnotic suggestions to engage in these acts (Estabrooks, 1943; Marcuse, 1959)? Another possible interpretation of Orne and Evans' (1965) findings is that hypnosis is not necessary in order to get at least certain people to engage in antisocial behavior. They will harm others in response to any orders (hypnotic or nonhypnotic) from anyone whom they perceive to be a legitimate authority figure. Certainly there are numerous examples from history, such as those of Nazi Germany, where subordinates obeyed the orders of authority figures to torture and kill helpless individuals. Hypnosis was not employed in these situations.

Milgram (1963) demonstrated that most people will comply with the instructions of an experimenter to engage in behavior that appears to be hurting another human being. He employed a "stooge" to pretend to be in great pain from the electric shock that the subject was instructed to deliver each time the "victim" (i.e., stooge) made a mistake on a learning task. Actually, the shock generator was a dummy, unbeknown to the subjects in the study. Every one of the 40 subjects went at least as far as delivering what was labeled as 300 volts, "Intense Shock," at which point the "victim" protested by kicking the walls of the room, where he was strapped to an electric chair, and finally became silent. Thirty-five of the 40 subjects continued to deliver progressively more intense shocks beyond the 300 volts point. Milgram reported that most of the subjects admitted during postexperimental inquiries that they were convinced that they were harming the stooge. Furthermore, behavioral observations indicated that the subjects were truly in a state of conflict. In Milgram's words: "Subjects were observed to sweat, tremble, stutter, bite their lips, groan and dig their fingernails into their flesh. These were characteristic rather than exceptional responses to the experiment. One sign of tension was the regular occurrence of nervous laughing fits. Fourteen of the 40 subjects showed definite signs of nervous laughter and smiling. The laughter seemed entirely out of place, even bizarre. Full-blown uncontrollable seizures were observed for three subjects. On one occasion we observed a seizure so violently convulsive that it was necessary to call a halt to the experiment" (1963, p. 375). Milgram concluded that obedience is a "deeply ingrained behavior tendency" that may be a "prepotent impulse overriding training in ethics, sympathy, and moral conduct" (1963, p. 371).

On the basis of Milgram's findings, as well as those of Orne and Evans (1965) and Levitt et al. (1975), it seems that, although hypnosis could be used to induce someone to behave in an antisocial manner, such an individual could probably be persuaded to engage in the same behavior *without* the aid of hypnosis. Then, we must question whether real-life criminal cases where hypnosis was used prove that hypnosis was responsible for the criminal act. The outcome may have been a function of the behavioral tendencies of the individual rather than the result of hypnosis. In fact, some courts have ruled that both the subject and the hypnotist are responsible for any criminal acts that are allegedly the result of hypnosis. In one of the murder cases cited earlier, which took place in Denmark, Nielson, the amateur hypnotist, was given a life sentence and Hardrup, the hypnotic subject who committed the murder, received a guilty verdict and a two-year prison sentence.

My opinion is that, even if hypnosis can be employed as a means of inducing an individual to commit a criminal act, it is very important to hold both the hypnotized subject and the hypnotist responsible for the act. It would be unwise for the courts to absolve individuals from responsibility for criminal acts on the basis of their having been hypnotized. Such a decision might be construed as giving individuals permission to engage in criminal acts under conditions where they could blame their behavior on hypnosis.

Let me now address myself to the concerns of the clinician about employing a method that may be used to induce people to engage in antisocial behavior. Just because a clinical tool can be used for criminal purposes does not mean that responsible professionals should refrain from using it. A tool is only dangerous if it is used improperly. Refraining from employing hypnosis for clinical purposes just because an unscrupulous person could abuse it is as absurd as surgeons' not performing surgery because scalpels can be used as murder weapons.

However, a legitimate cause for concern is whether experiencing clinical hypnosis increases a patient's susceptibility to unethical hypnotists. Watkins (1951) has reported that some subjects cannot resist hypnotic induction, especially if they have been previously hypnotized. On the other hand, Young (1927) has found that subjects trained in self-hypnosis are able to resist hypnotic suggestions. If obedience is a deeply ingrained behavioral tendency, as Milgram has claimed, then perhaps training in self-hypnosis provides the individual with a method for exercising control over negative behavioral tendencies. Araoz (1982) has discussed how training in positive self-hypnosis can be applied in overcoming one's negative self-hypnosis, i.e., the uncritical acceptance of negative suggestions. Patients are taught to recognize their own negative self-suggestions and to replace them with more positive ones, similar to what is done in cognitive-behavior therapy. I would predict that self-control approaches to hypnosis, such as the one employed by Araoz or myself (Golden, 1983; Golden & Friedberg, in press) would be particularly effective in helping individuals resist negative suggestions, regardless of whether the suggestions are hypnotic or nonhypnotic, or self-suggestions or commands from an authority figure.

References

Araoz, D. (1982). *Hypnosis and sex therapy.* New York: Brunner/Mazel.

Erickson, M. H. (1939). An experimental investigation of the possible antisocial uses of hypnosis. *Psychiatry, 2,* 391–414.

Estabrooks, G. H. (1943). *Hypnotism.* New York: Dutton.

Golden, W. L. (1983). Rational-emotive hypnotherapy: Principles and techniques. *British Journal of Cognitive Psychotherapy, 1,* 1, 47–56.

Golden, W. L. & Friedberg, F. (in press). Cognitive-behavioral hypnotherapy. In W. Dryden & W. L. Golden (Eds.). *Cognitive-behavioral approaches to psychotherapy.* London: Harper & Row.

Le Cron, L. M. (1964). *Self-hypnotism.* New York: Signet.

Levitt, E. E., Aronoff, G., Morgan, C. D., Overly, T. M. & Parish, M. J. (1975). Testing the coercive power of hypnosis: Committing objectionable acts. *International Journal of Clinical and Experimental Hypnosis, 23,* 1, 59–67.

Marcuse, F. L. (1959). *Hypnosis: Fact and fiction.* Baltimore: Penguin Books.

Milgram, S. (1963). Behavioral study of obedience. *Journal of Abnormal and Social Psychology, 67,* 371–378.

Orne, M. T., & Evans, F. J. (1965). Social control in the psychological experiment: Antisocial behavior and hypnosis. *Journal of Personality and Social Psychology, 1,* 3, 189–200.

Rowland, L. W. (1939). Will hypnotized persons try to harm themselves or others? *Journal of Abnormal and Social Psychology, 34*, 114–117.

Schneck, J. M. (1947). A military offense induced by hypnosis. *Journal of Nervous and Mental Disorders, 106*, 186–189.

Watkins, J. G. (1947). Anti-social compulsions induced under hypnotic trance. *Journal of Abnormal and Social Psychology, 42*, 256–259.

Watkins, J. G. (1951). A case of hypnotic trance induced in a resistant subject in spite of active opposition. *British Journal of Medical Hypnosis, 2*, 26–31.

Weitzenhoffer, A. M. (1953). *Hypnotism: An objective study in suggestibility.* New York: Wiley.

Wells, W. R. (1941). Experiments in the hypnotic production of crimes. *Journal of Psychology, 11*, 63–102.

Young, P. C. (1927). Is rapport an essential characteristic of hypnosis? *Journal of Abnormal and Social Psychology, 22*, 130–139.

Young, P. C. (1952). Antisocial uses of hypnosis. In L. M. Le Cron (Ed.). *Experimental hypnosis.* New York: Macmillan.

$\underset{A}{\overset{Q}{\mathcal{E}_3}}84$ Concern About
Practicing on Patients

Question:

> How can more skill and confidence in doing hypnosis be acquired without practicing on one's patients? I feel very uneasy about using patients as guinea pigs.

Discussion by MICHAEL FINEGOLD, M.D., &
M. GERALD EDELSTIEN, M.D.

It is not uncommon for beginning hypnotherapists to ask this question. Unfortunately, neither is it uncommon for them to respond to their own uncertainties by shying away from the use of hypnosis altogether, feeling that they should not practice on patients until their skills are sharply honed. Sadly, this is like not wanting to enter the water until one has learned to swim.

The importance of this question was made clear recently when a survey was done at a meeting of the San Francisco Academy of Hypnosis. Of all the members present at that meeting, almost 50% were not using hypnosis to any significant degree in their practices—despite the fact that all had had at least one formal course, many had had more than one course, and some had been attending academy meetings for several years.

Insecurity about using hypnosis occurs in two areas: the induction of the trance and the application of hypnotic techniques once the trance has been induced. The *source* of the insecurity may lie in any of several areas, and perhaps the lack of practice is the least important of these; we suspect that intrapersonal concerns are really much more significant.

The concern about practicing on patients is a noble one, but it can hardly represent the true reason for not working with patients. As professionals, every therapeutic technique we have ever used has been practiced on patients. Every technique we will use in the future will be practiced on patients. Why this sudden concern when we talk about hypnosis?

We have personally queried a number of beginning therapists about their reticence to use hypnosis, and it was interesting to observe the many reasons they gave for being uncomfortable with it. Although they were intellectually aware of the irrational nature of their concerns, their feelings were more powerful than that awareness. We would therefore say that the first step in becoming more comfortable in using hypnosis would be doing a self-inventory and seeing which, if any, of these factors might be present.

1) *Fear of failure.* For reasons we do not fully comprehend, practitioners, who have surely had failures in other aspects of their practices, seem to have an inordinate fear of failing in the use of hypnosis. Perhaps this is partly due to the fact that any failure is so rapidly apparent that that "shame" of failing is immediate rather than delayed. A poorly done gold inlay may not fall out for a year or more; a hernia repair may not break down for a number of months; or traditional psychotherapy may go on for several years before it is recognized as not working. When hypnotic techniques are not accomplishing their goals, this can be recognized rather quickly.

We like to believe that any conscientious practitioner would appreciate this aspect, for if it's seen that one mode of therapy is not working, then another form of treatment can be instituted without prolonged delay. After all, if hypnosis doesn't work, what's been lost? If the practitioner knows his specialty well and has used a modicum of common sense, there's remarkably little chance of serious harm being done. A little time has been lost, but at least the patient was given the opportunity of trying a method that might have saved him an enormous amount of time, money, or suffering. Perhaps it's a more grievous error to deny the patient that opportunity than to try hypnosis, even if it doesn't work.

2) *The fear of power.* Some beginners have said that they feel uncomfortable having so much control over their patients. This, of course, is an illusion. If hypnosis were as powerful as they imagine, then there would be no failures; each patient could merely be told, "Get well," and treatment would end successfully. Unfortunately, that's not the way it works.

3) *The misconception that others have better induction techniques or obtain deeper trances.* If speed of induction is the criterion for saying one is better than another, then, yes, some inductions are better than others. We know of no other indicators of relative superiority. It's possible that some patients may respond better to one induction and others to a different induction, but one of us uses one method almost exclusively and that one

method seldom fails. (We will not describe it here, in accordance with our belief that it's no better than any other.)

As far as depth of trance is concerned, this is a highly overrated concept, for there seems to be little correlation between the depth of trance and the effectiveness of the therapy.

4) *Fear of the unexpected.* Some beginners are frightened by the prospect that the hypnotized patient will give responses that had not been anticipated, and that then they will not know what to do. They fear that this could cause serious harm to the patient or, at the very least, severe embarrassment to the therapist. The unexpected responses do occur, as they do in all other forms of treatment, but as long as the practitioner is working within his own field of expertise, the chance of disaster is probably less than with almost any other form of therapy. Many of us find that the unexpected adds to the enjoyment of our work, and that by remaining calm and curious about what is happening, we usually can think of some way to deal with the problem.

If unexpected emotions burst forth, one can say, "Good, let those feelings come out now, and then we can discuss them," or, conversely, "Those feelings seem too disturbing for you to handle now, so just let them go back to where they came from, and we'll deal with them again later." Under other circumstances it is perfectly legitimate to say, "I really don't understand what's happening now, so I'll bring you out of hypnosis, and after I've had time to think about it, we'll get back to this issue again." There have been no major problems using these simple tactics.

5) *Fear of colleagues' disapproval.* Although hypnotherapy is continuing to gain broader acceptance in our professional communities, many of our colleagues still regard it with skepticism, if not disdain. Certainly, many of our professors talked disparagingly of it. Fear of censure by those we respect may unwittingly cause us to rationalize our hesitancy to use this treatment modality.

There are other subconscious reasons that cause therapists to embark reluctantly, if at all, into the use of hypnosis, but most of these can be relieved fairly easily once the therapist becomes aware of them. A careful self-inventory, using the above as reference points, is therefore highly recommended.

Assuming these subconscious fears are not present or have been resolved, how, then, is confidence achieved? We believe that confidence arises from two sources: delusions about one's competence, or prior success. We will not give advice on acquiring the former.

Prior success need not have been in the exact area as the new activity, but the closer to it, the greater the carryover. For example, a good tennis player may well be confident that he can become a good badminton player, but he would not necessarily feel confident that he could become a good bridge player. Using this simple principle, then, confidence in doing hypnotic inductions could be built up in a stepwise fashion.

First, one could write and rewrite a script until there was confidence in the words to be used. Those words could then be said out loud, in front of a mirror, or into a tape recorder, until there was confidence in the *sound* of those words. They could then be practiced on friends or relatives, a good percentage of whom would find themselves "hypnotized." By then, there should be enough confidence to try the induction on patients. Interestingly, we believe all of these steps could be bypassed by merely *pretending* to be confident, and the rapidly ensuing successes would make it no longer necessary to pretend.

Once there is comfort with the induction process, confidence in using specific therapeutic techniques can be acquired gradually. A list of those techniques deemed most useful could be extracted from courses taken or books read. They could be arranged according to relative difficulty, and attempted one by one, beginning with the easiest and progressing no faster than comfort permits. The more impulsive beginner could commence with the most difficult and feel that anything must be easy after that.

These methods have dealt primarily with what the student can do on his own. Outside help is also available and should be utilized. Included here would be the taking of further courses, reading of texts, joining professional organizations or informal study groups, and getting consultation from more experienced practitioners. Much later, it's surprising to find how greatly confidence can be increased by *teaching* courses or writing a book, but now we're getting into the area of how to achieve delusions of competency.

Index

abortions, spontaneous, 330–36
Abrams, S., 289, 293n
ACE test, 96
acupuncture, 6–7
acute pain, 287
adolescents, acting-out, 399–409
affect bridge, 146, 157, 281
age regression, 53–56, 145–46, 155–59
   contraindicated, 277
   and depth of trance, 129
   in Ericksonian technique, 227
   and stress management, 322
agoraphobia, 307–12
   and inductions, 105
   symptom recurrence, 63–64
Ahsen, A., 337, 342n
alcohol abuse, 272
Alman, B. M., 181–86, 233, 236n,
   287, 326, 329n
alpha waves, 9
Ambrose, G., 399, 409n
American Association for Marriage and
   Family Therapy (AAMFT), 232
American Journal of Clinical Hypnosis,
   96
American Medical Association, 46
American Society of Clinical Analysis, 233
American Society of Clinical Hypnosis, 442
amnesia:
   and communication mode, 194–95
   and depth of trance, 129, 130
   in Ericksonian technique, 230
   and forensic hypnosis, 40–44
   and interspersal technique, 256
   posthypnotic, 79, 171
   role of, 173–79
   source, 58–59, 174
   specific, 177
   spontaneous, 37–38, 39

analgesia, hypnotic suggestion of, 6–7
analgesics, 347–48
anecdote:
   see metaphor
anesthesia, 26, 258, 282–87
anemia, aplastic, 386–87
animal magnetism, 59
antidepressant medications, 347
antipsychotic medications, 347
antisocial behaviors, 470–75
applications, of hypnosis, 269, 271–73
   see also specific applications
Araoz, D. L., 107–8, 205, 210n,
   433–38, 475
arm levitation, 119
arthritis, 283
Artistry of Milton Erickson, M.D. The
   (video), 245
as-if electroshock therapy ("As-If-ECT"),
   281
asthma, 272
atasia abasia, 275–76
athletic performance, enhancing, 337–43
August, R. V., 14, 15n
authority, skepticism of, 88
autogenic relaxation, 449
automatic behavior, 194, 195
automatic writing and drawing, 363
autonomy, fear of loss of, 93

Bailly, J. S., 440, 443n
Baker, E. L., 289–93, 443, 444n,
   451, 452n
Baker, R. A., 41, 44n
Baker, S. R., 54, 59n
Bandler, R., 8, 112, 115, 117n
Barber, J. 98, 99n, 148–49, 283,
   287n, 325, 326, 329n
Barber, T. X., 9, 11, 13, 15n, 22–27,